# YOWAMUSHI PEDAL

WATARU WATANABE

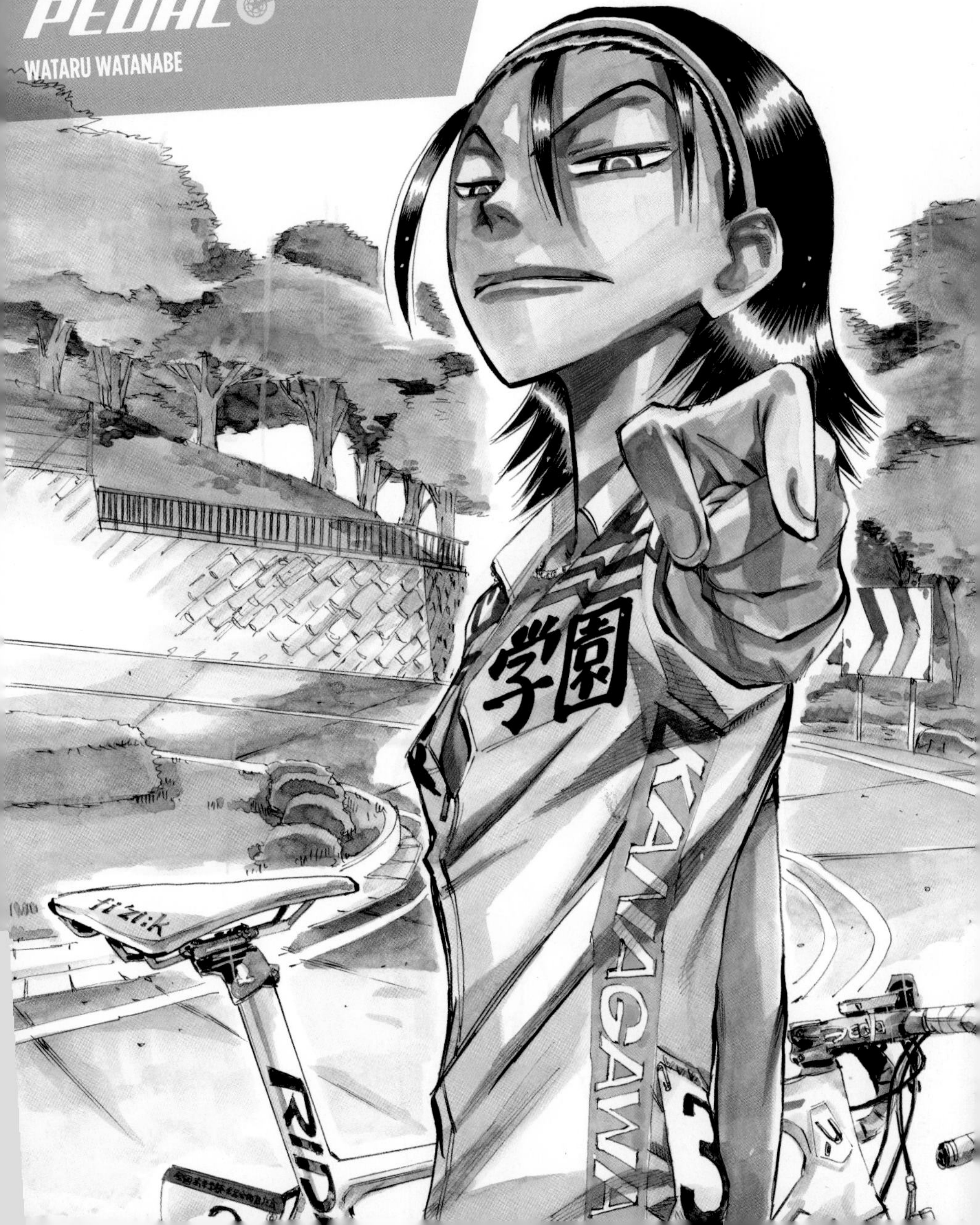
学園
KANAGAWA
fi'zi:k

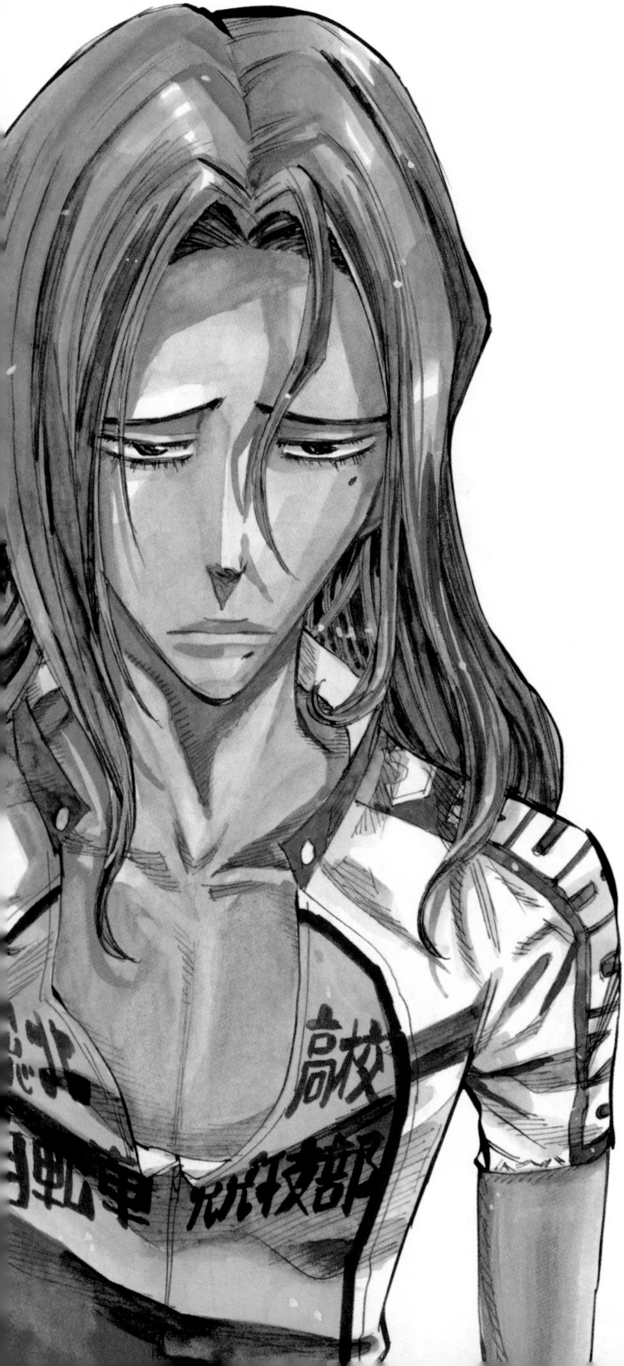
高校

# YOWAMUSHI PEDAL

## WATARU WATANABE

## 6

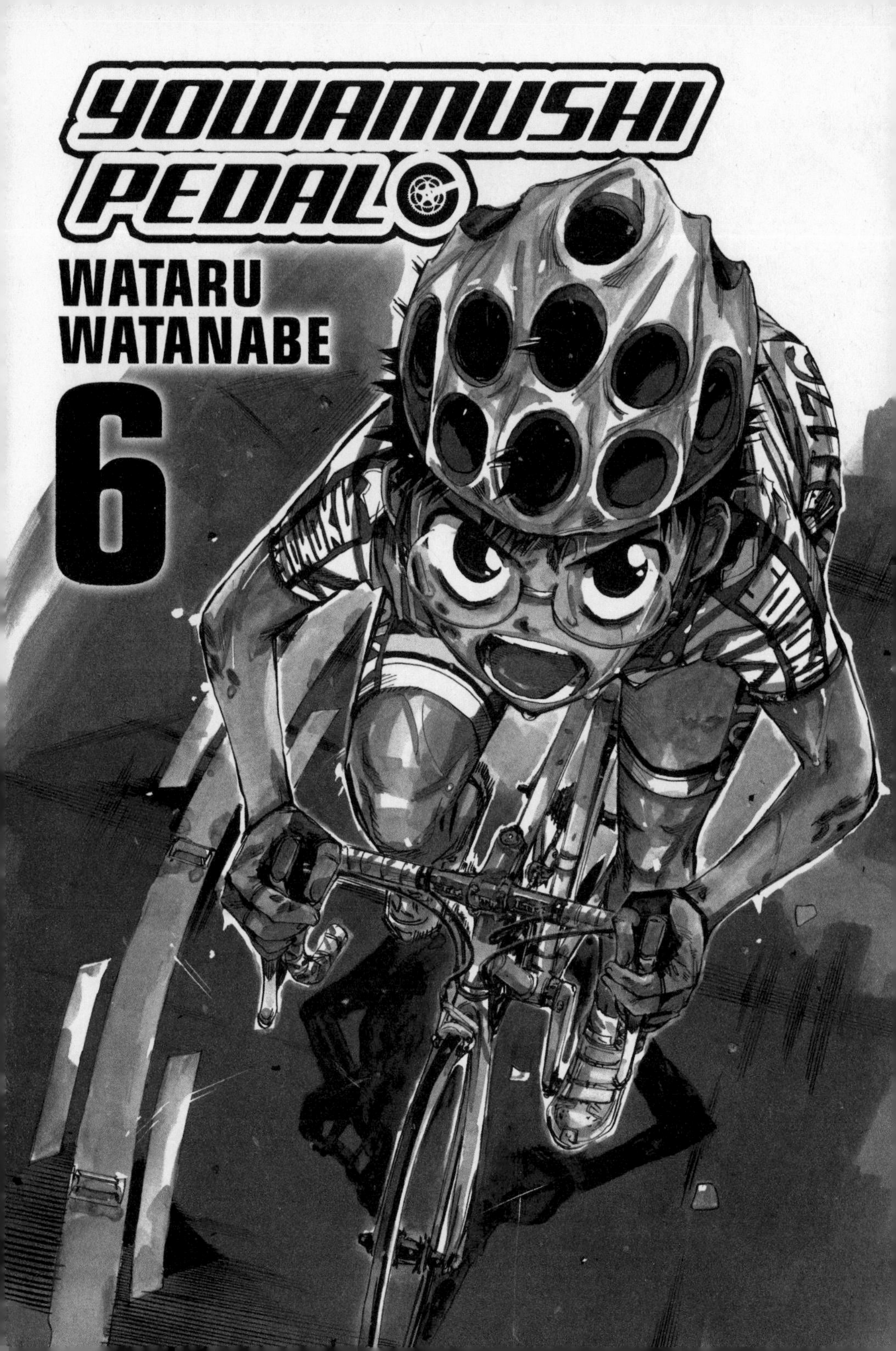

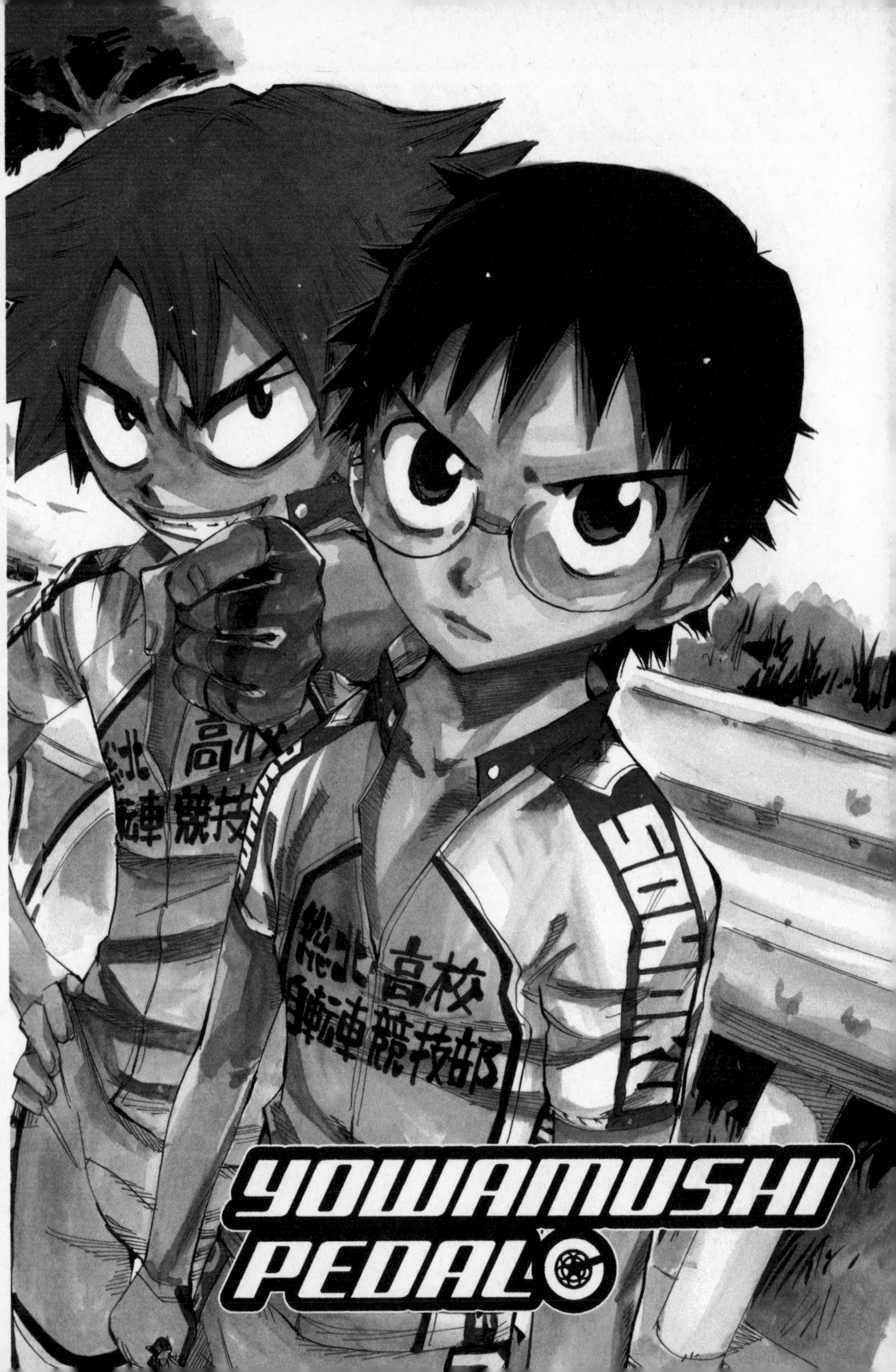
総北高校
自転車競技部
SOHOKU
YOWAMUSHI
PEDAL

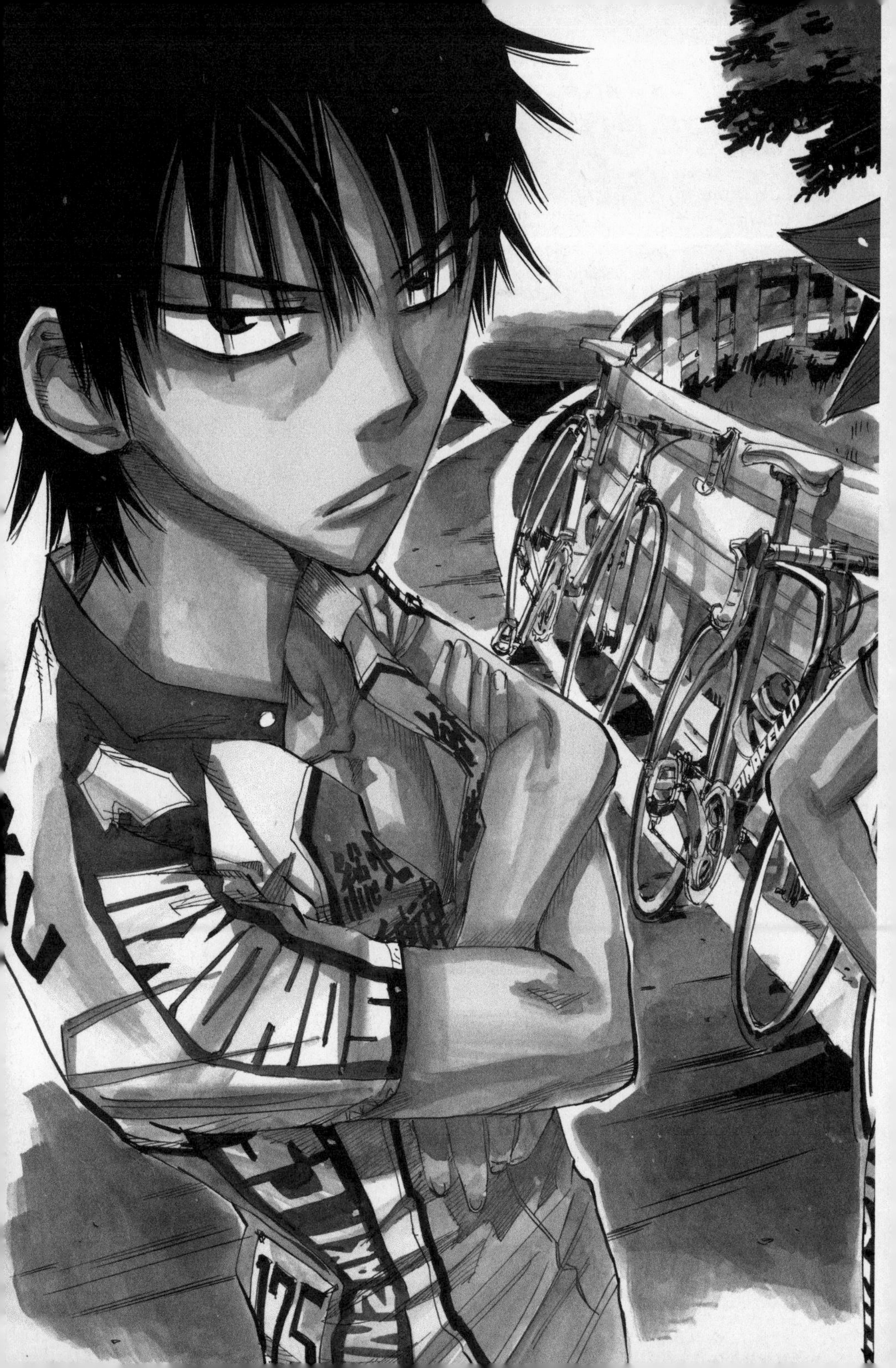

YOWAMUSHI PEDAL

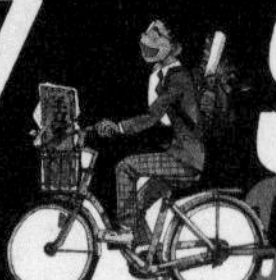

# STORY & CHARACTER INTRODUCTION

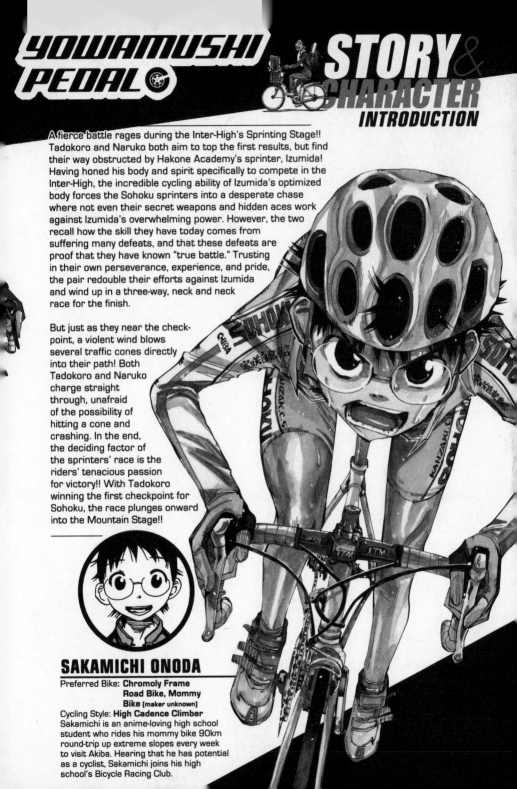

A fierce battle rages during the Inter-High's Sprinting Stage!! Tadokoro and Naruko both aim to top the first results, but find their way obstructed by Hakone Academy's sprinter, Izumida! Having honed his body and spirit specifically to compete in the Inter-High, the incredible cycling ability of Izumida's optimized body forces the Sohoku sprinters into a desperate chase where not even their secret weapons and hidden aces work against Izumida's overwhelming power. However, the two recall how the skill they have today comes from suffering many defeats, and that these defeats are proof that they have known "true battle." Trusting in their own perseverance, experience, and pride, the pair redouble their efforts against Izumida and wind up in a three-way, neck and neck race for the finish.

But just as they near the checkpoint, a violent wind blows several traffic cones directly into their path! Both Tadokoro and Naruko charge straight through, unafraid of the possibility of hitting a cone and crashing. In the end, the deciding factor of the sprinters' race is the riders' tenacious passion for victory!! With Tadokoro winning the first checkpoint for Sohoku, the race plunges onward into the Mountain Stage!!

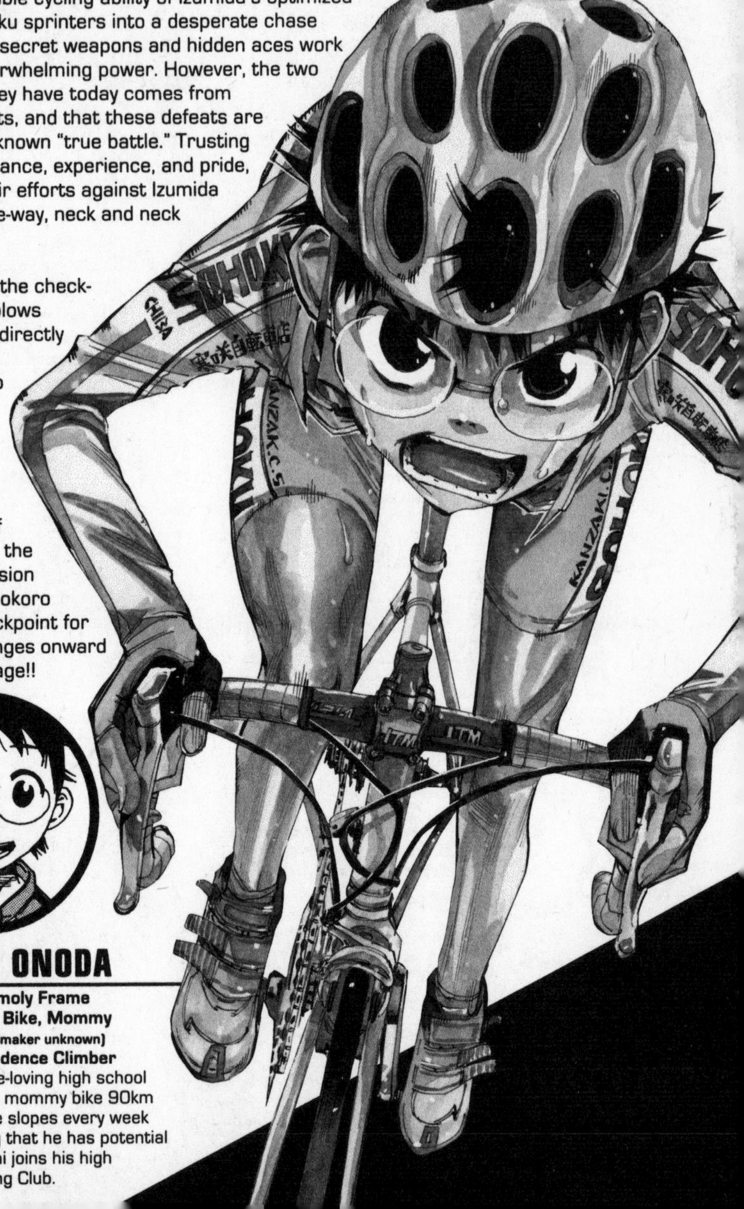
SOHOKU
CHIBA
KANZAKI C.S
SOHOKU
ITM

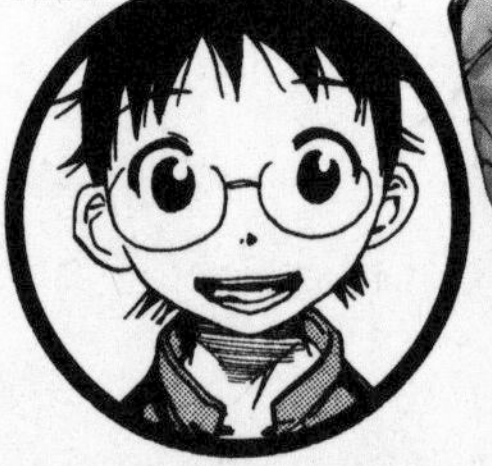

## SAKAMICHI ONODA

Preferred Bike: **Chromoly Frame Road Bike, Mommy Bike** (maker unknown)

Cycling Style: **High Cadence Climber**

Sakamichi is an anime-loving high school student who rides his mommy bike 90km round-trip up extreme slopes every week to visit Akiba. Hearing that he has potential as a cyclist, Sakamichi joins his high school's Bicycle Racing Club.

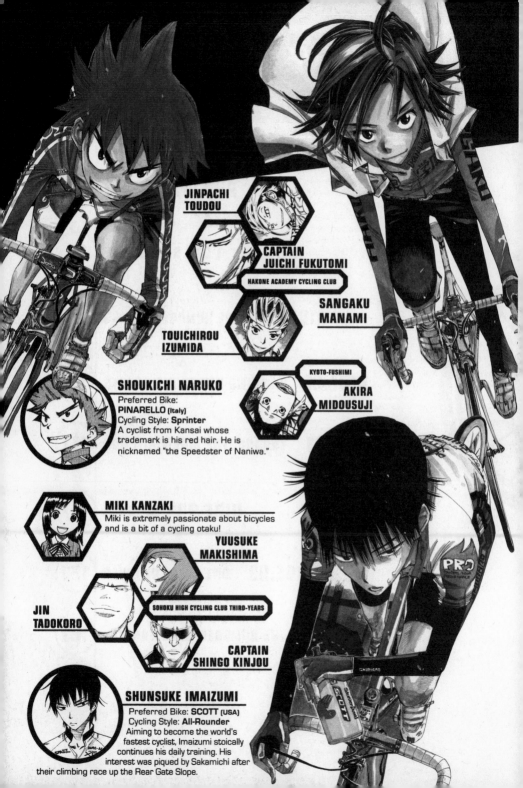

**JINPACHI TOUDOU**

**CAPTAIN JUICHI FUKUTOMI**

**HAKONE ACADEMY CYCLING CLUB**

**SANGAKU MANAMI**

**TOUICHIROU IZUMIDA**

**KYOTO-FUSHIMI**

**AKIRA MIDOUSUJI**

**SHOUKICHI NARUKO**
Preferred Bike:
**PINARELLO** (Italy)
Cycling Style: **Sprinter**
A cyclist from Kansai whose trademark is his red hair. He is nicknamed "the Speedster of Naniwa."

**MIKI KANZAKI**
Miki is extremely passionate about bicycles and is a bit of a cycling otaku!

**YUUSUKE MAKISHIMA**

**SOHOKU HIGH CYCLING CLUB THIRD-YEARS**

**JIN TADOKORO**

**CAPTAIN SHINGO KINJOU**

**SHUNSUKE IMAIZUMI**
Preferred Bike: **SCOTT** (USA)
Cycling Style: **All-Rounder**
Aiming to become the world's fastest cyclist, Imaizumi stoically continues his daily training. His interest was piqued by Sakamichi after their climbing race up the Rear Gate Slope.

# VOL.6

## YOWAMUSHI PEDAL CONTENTS

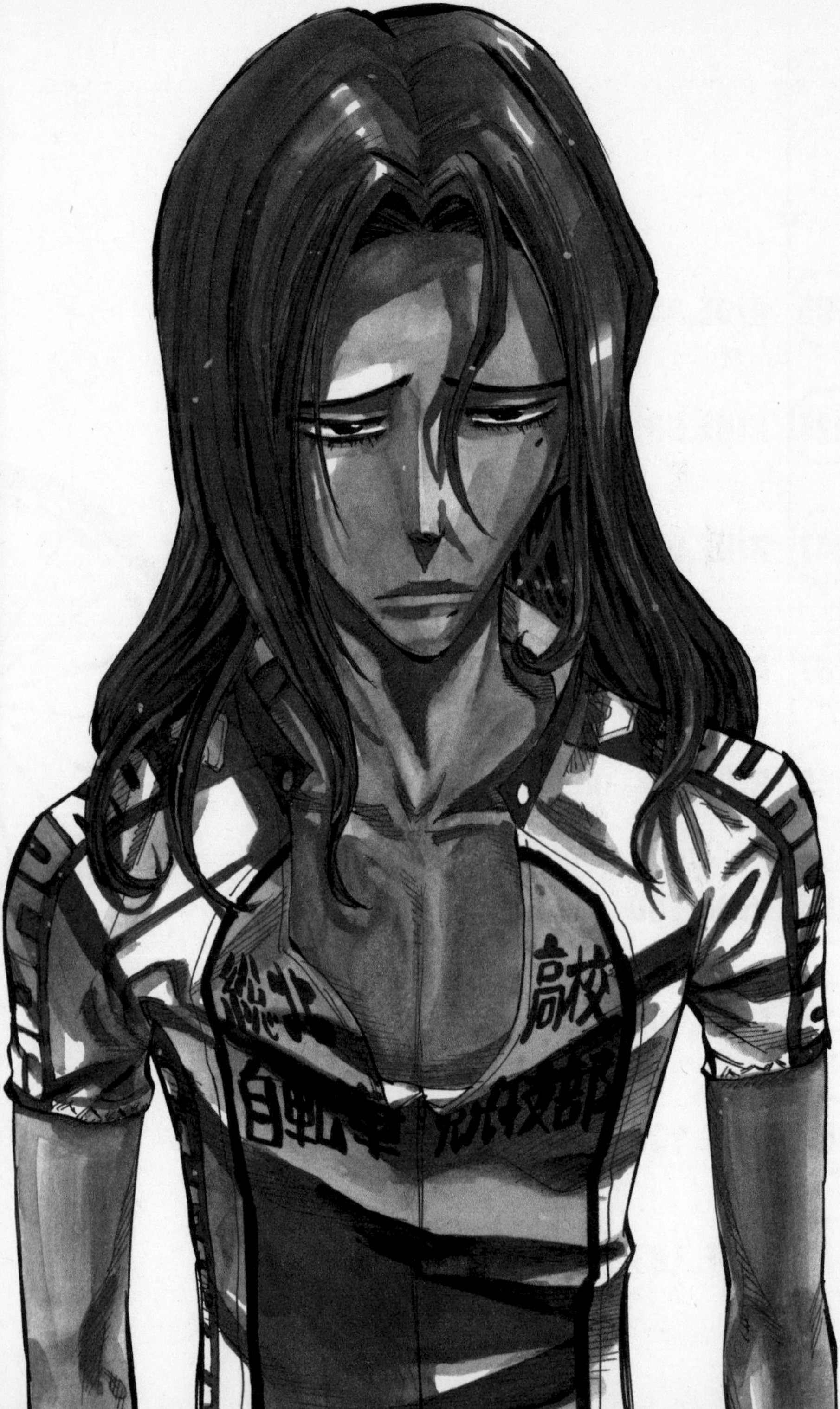
高校

# RIDE.87 HAKONE

ONODA.

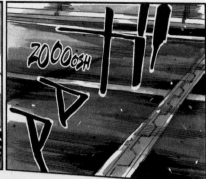

ZOOOOSH

LOOK, IT'S COMING INTO VIEW.

THUMP

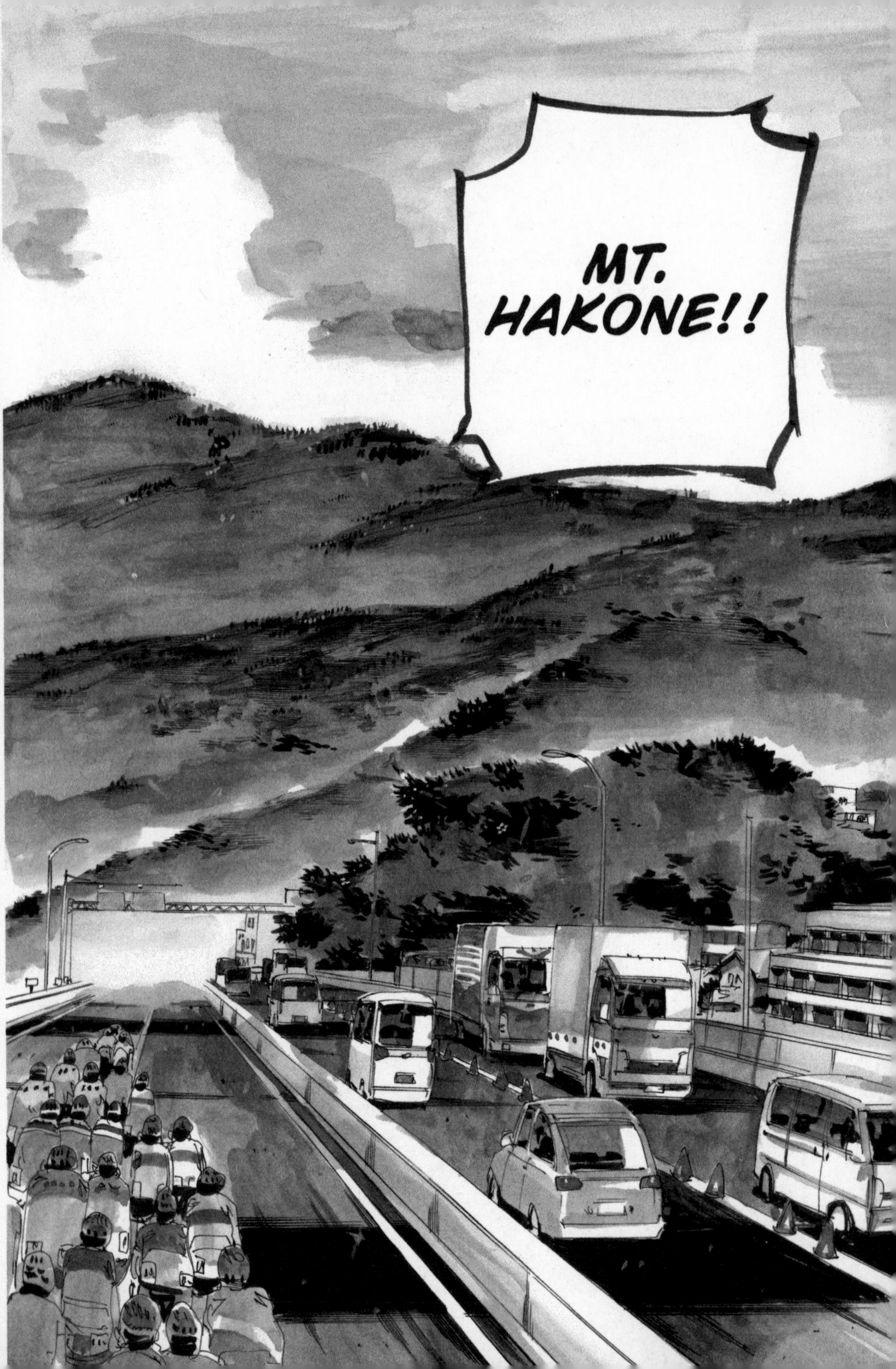
MT. HAKONE!!

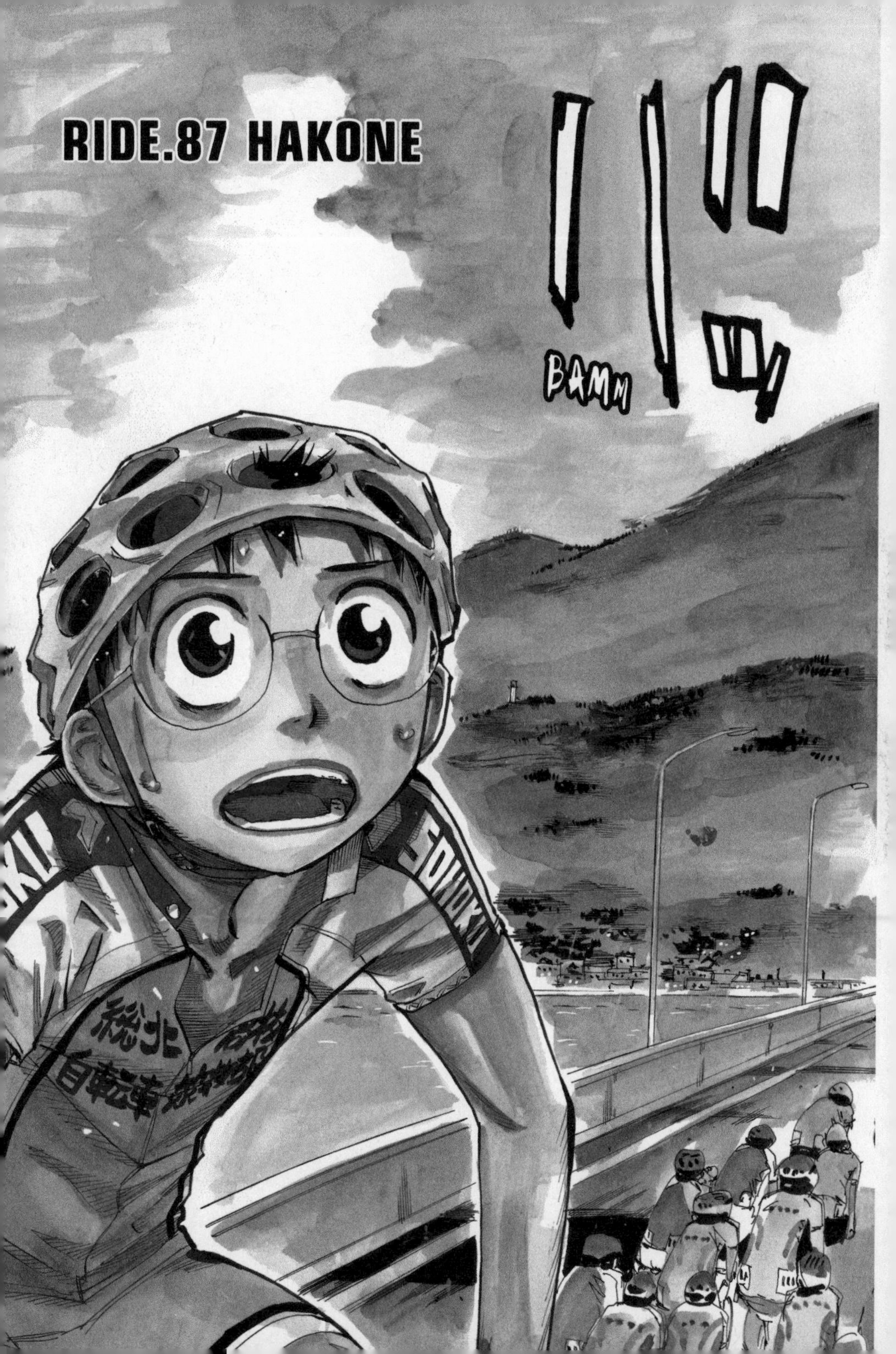
RIDE.87 HAKONE
BAMM

SAKAMICHI

YOWAMUSHI PEDAL

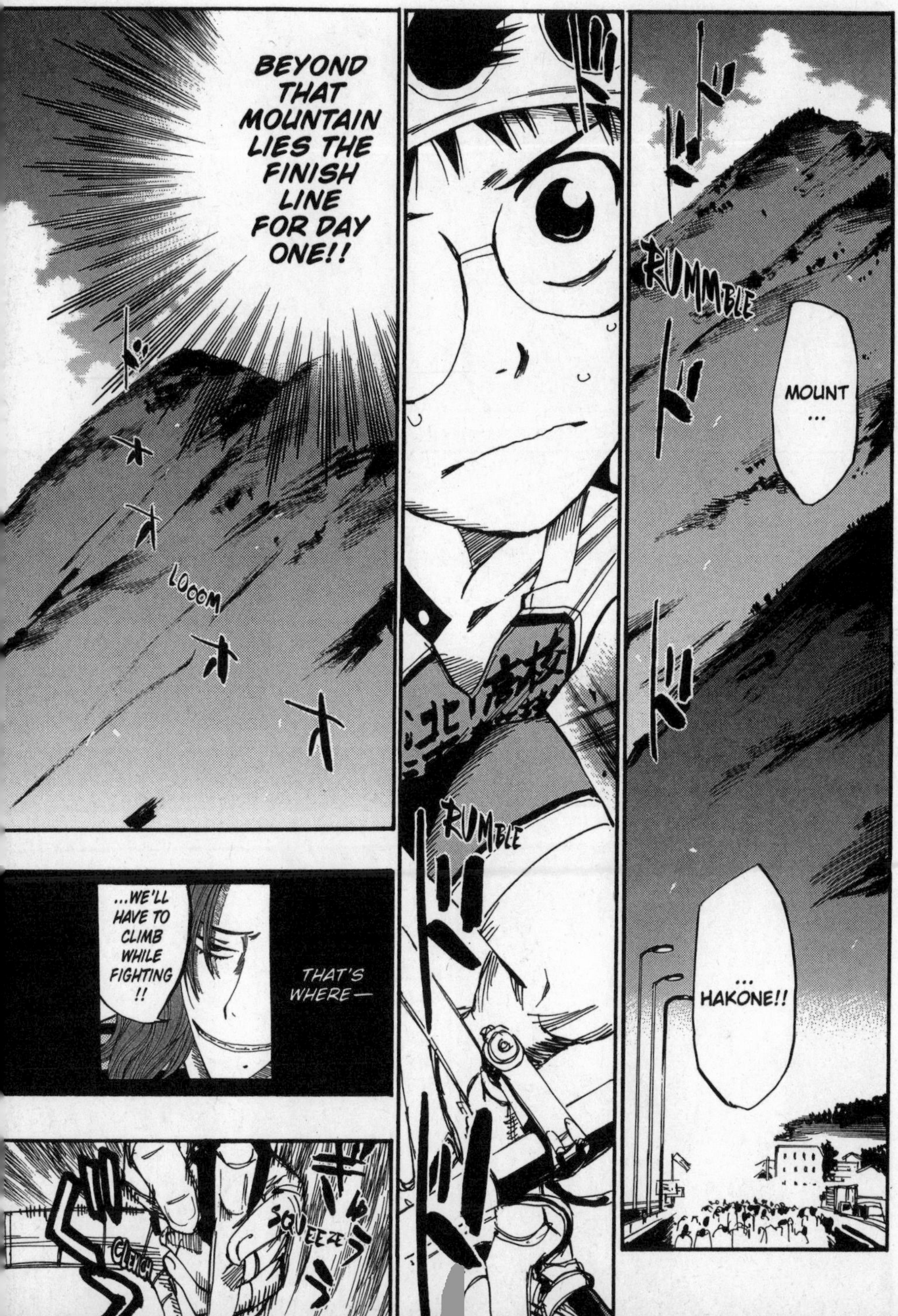
RUMMMBLE
MOUNT...
...HAKONE!!
RUMBLE
BEYOND THAT MOUNTAIN LIES THE FINISH LINE FOR DAY ONE!!
LOOOM
THAT'S WHERE—
...WE'LL HAVE TO CLIMB WHILE FIGHTING!!
SQUEEZE
CLENCH

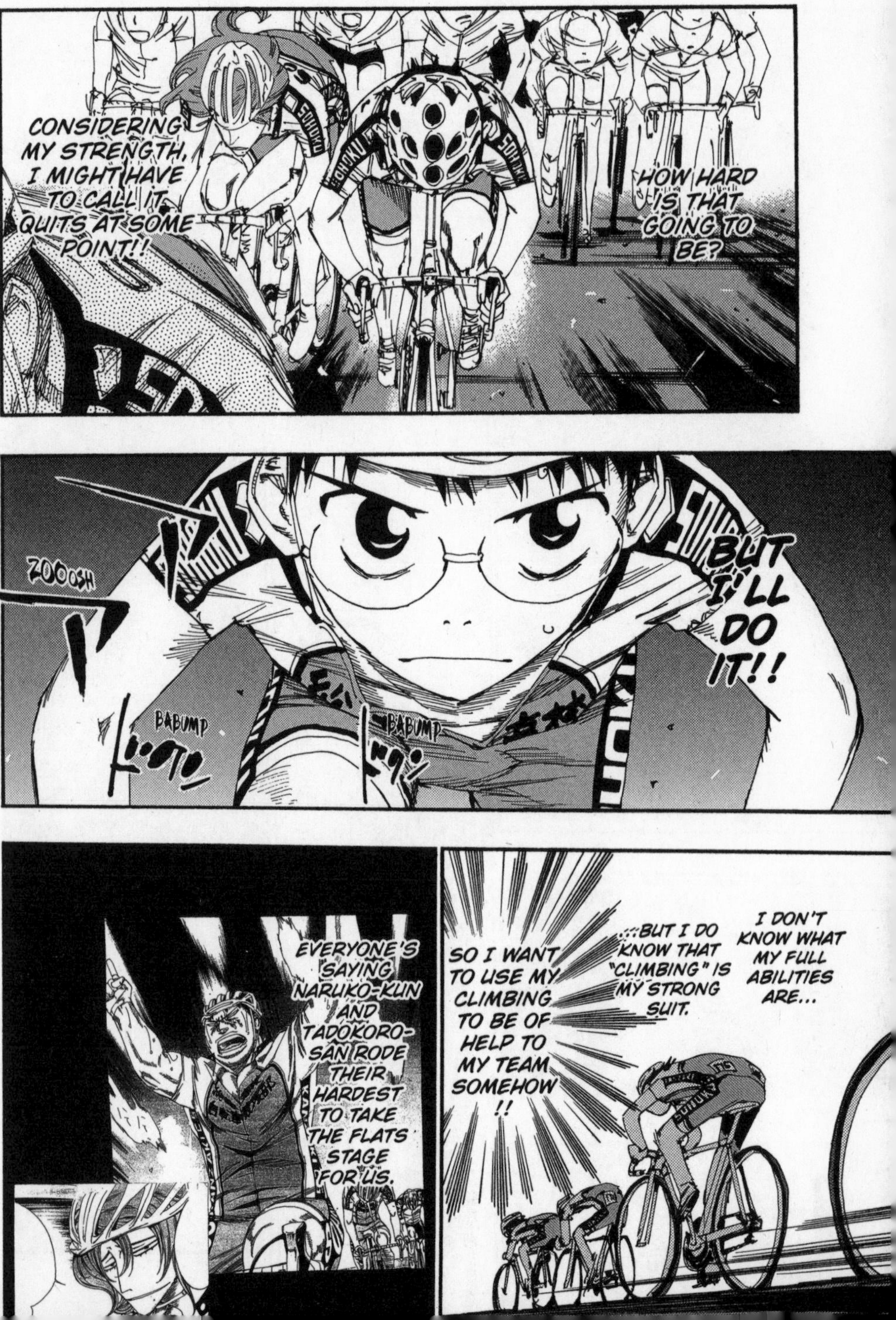
HOW HARD IS THAT GOING TO BE?
CONSIDERING MY STRENGTH, I MIGHT HAVE TO CALL IT QUITS AT SOME POINT!!
BUT I'LL DO IT!!
ZOOOSH
BABUMP
BABUMP
I DON'T KNOW WHAT MY FULL ABILITIES ARE...
...BUT I DO KNOW THAT "CLIMBING" IS MY STRONG SUIT.
SO I WANT TO USE MY CLIMBING TO BE OF HELP TO MY TEAM SOMEHOW!!
EVERYONE'S SAYING NARUKO-KUN AND TADOKORO-SAN RODE THEIR HARDEST TO TAKE THE FLATS STAGE FOR US.

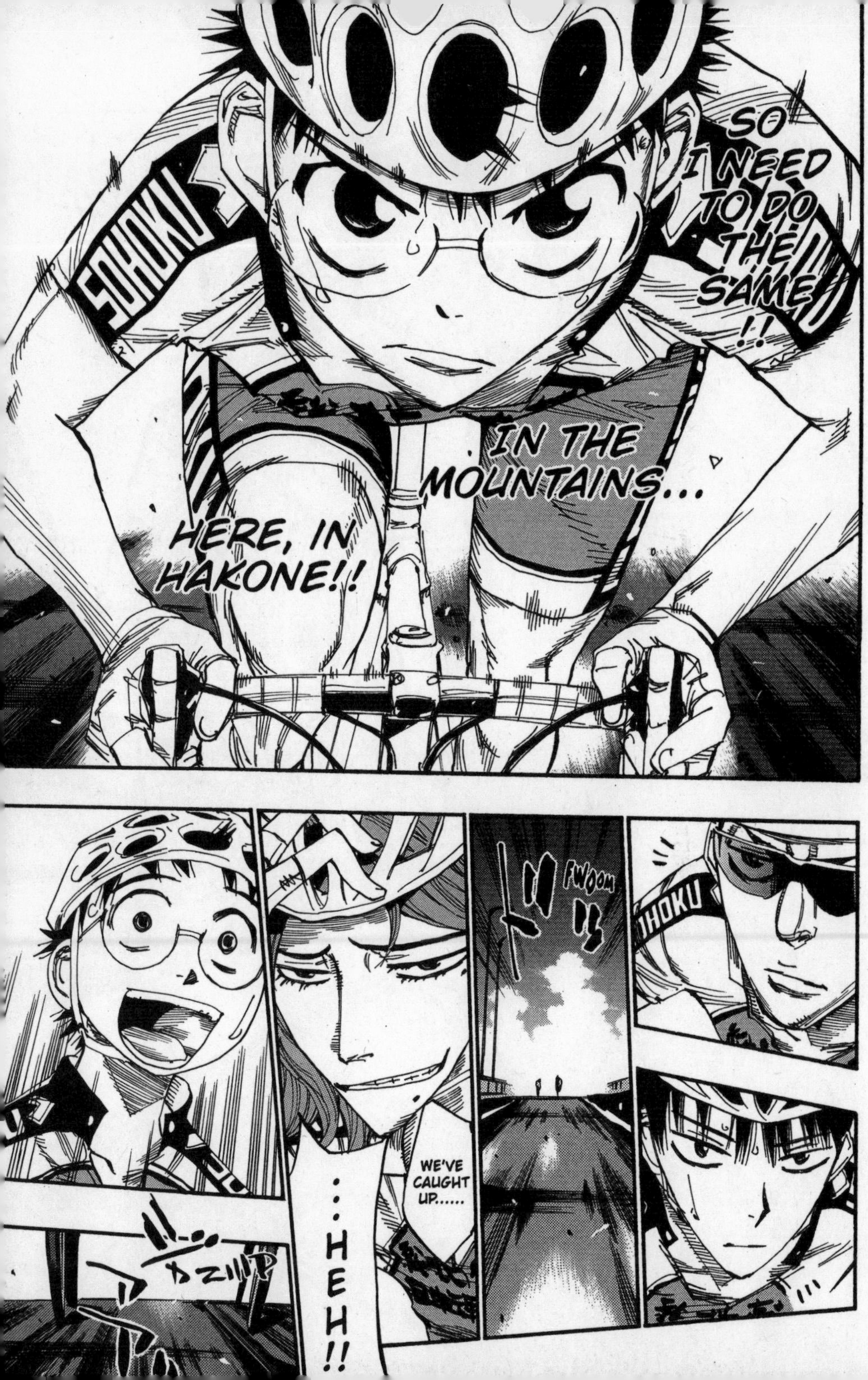
SO I NEED TO DO THE SAME!!
IN THE MOUNTAINS...
HERE, IN HAKONE!!
FWOOM
WE'VE CAUGHT UP......
...HEH!!
ZIIP

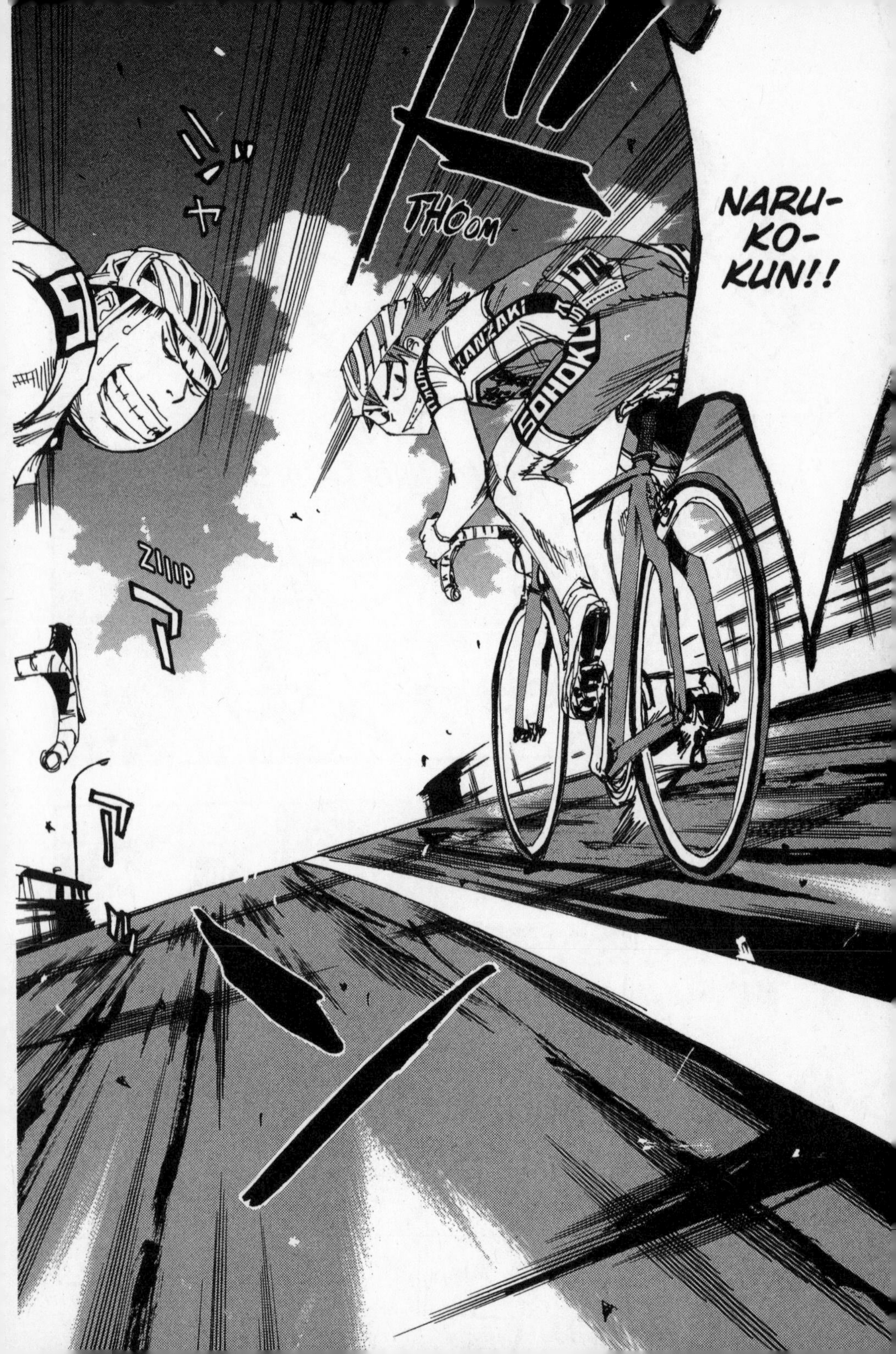
NARU-
KO-
KUN!!
THOOM
ZIIIP

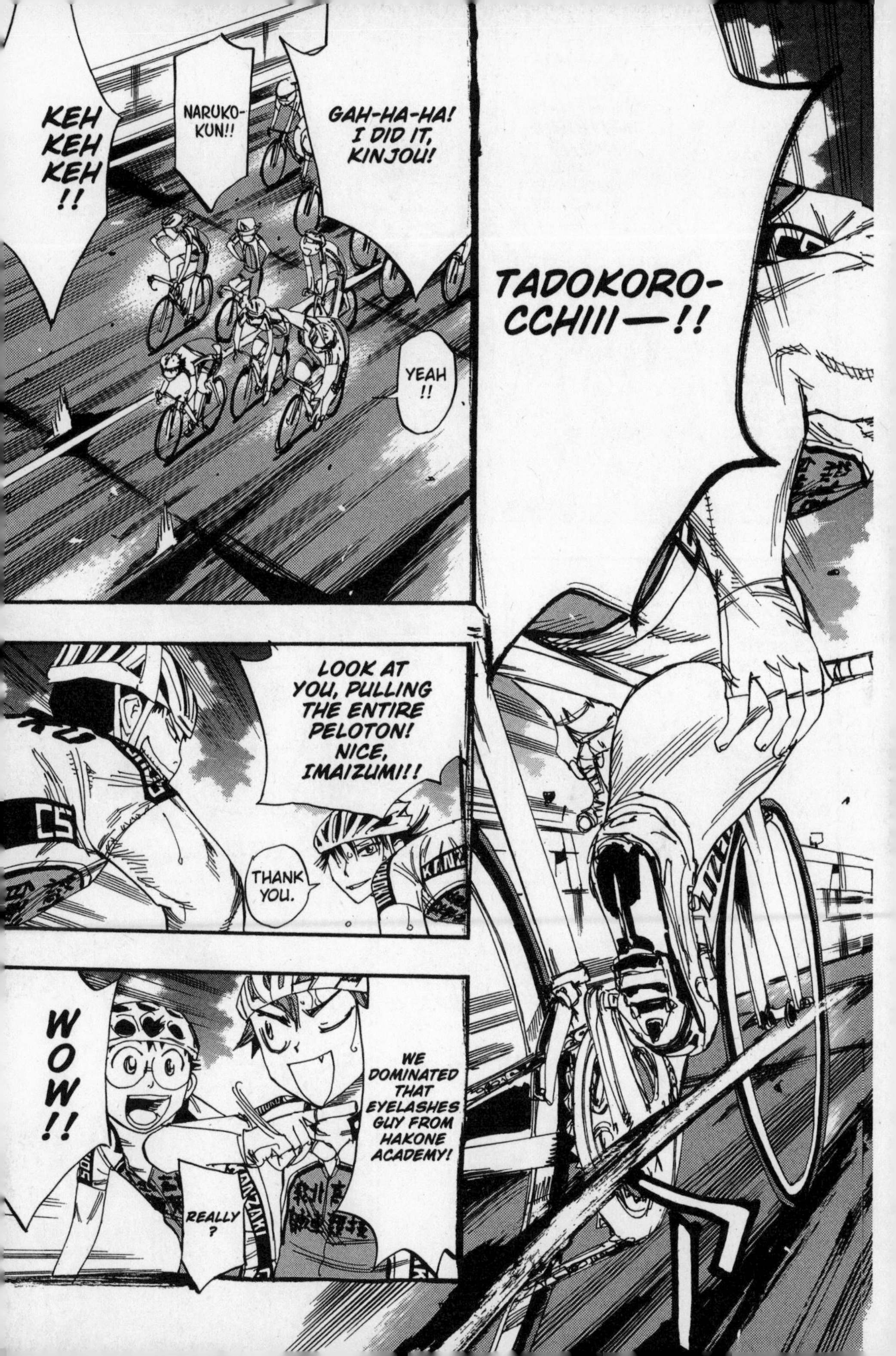
TADOKORO-CCHIIII—!!
GAH-HA-HA! I DID IT, KINJOU!
NARUKO-KUN!!
KEH KEH KEH!!
YEAH!!
LOOK AT YOU, PULLING THE ENTIRE PELOTON! NICE, IMAIZUMI!!
THANK YOU.
WE DOMINATED THAT EYELASHES GUY FROM HAKONE ACADEMY!
WOW!!
REALLY?

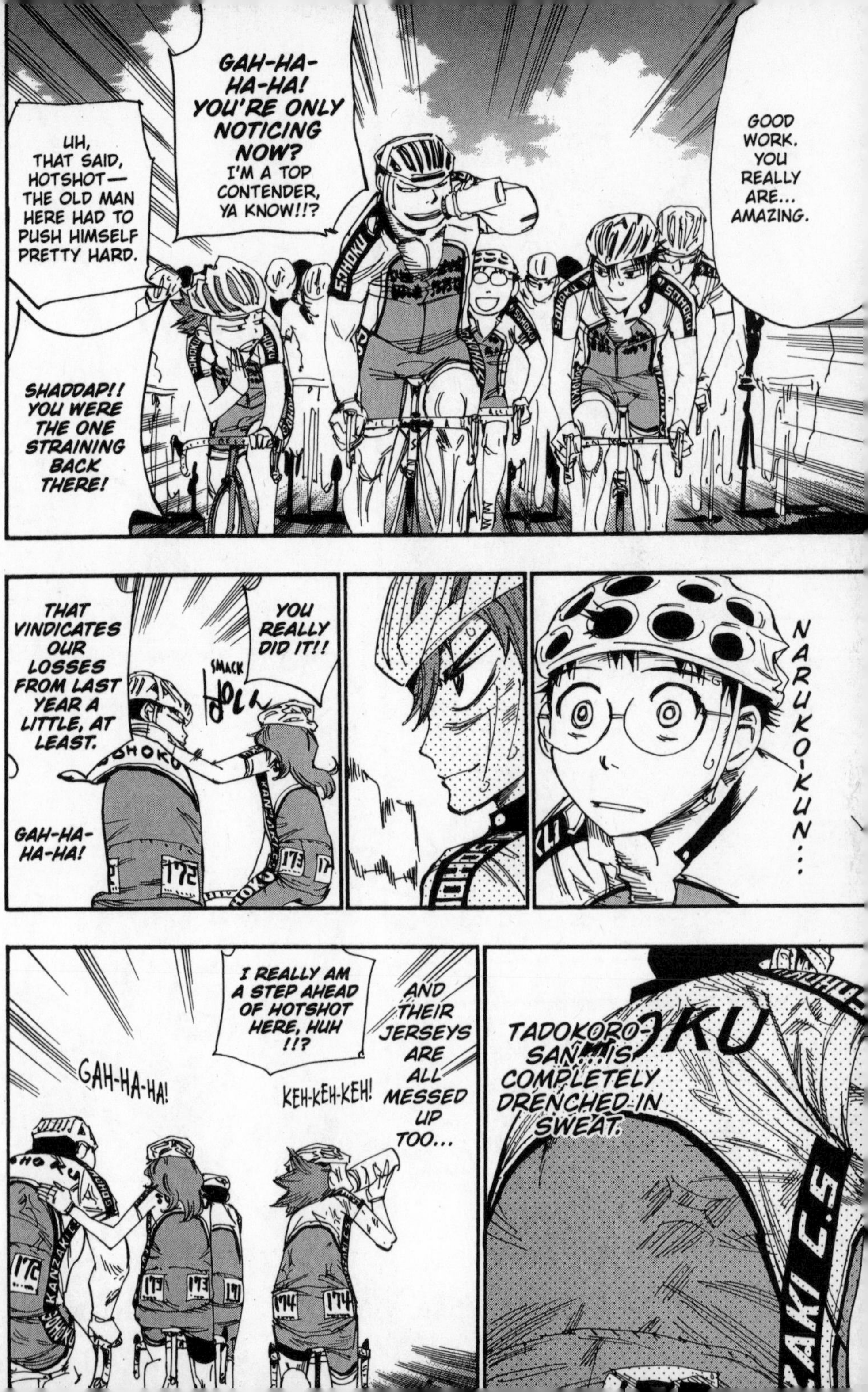
GOOD WORK. YOU REALLY ARE... AMAZING.
GAH-HA-HA-HA! YOU'RE ONLY NOTICING NOW? I'M A TOP CONTENDER, YA KNOW!!?
UH, THAT SAID, HOTSHOT— THE OLD MAN HERE HAD TO PUSH HIMSELF PRETTY HARD.
SHADDAP!! YOU WERE THE ONE STRAINING BACK THERE!
NARUKO-KUN...
YOU REALLY DID IT!!
SMACK
THAT VINDICATES OUR LOSSES FROM LAST YEAR A LITTLE, AT LEAST.
GAH-HA-HA-HA!
TADOKORO-SAN...IS COMPLETELY DRENCHED IN SWEAT.
AND THEIR JERSEYS ARE ALL MESSED UP TOO...
I REALLY AM A STEP AHEAD OF HOTSHOT HERE, HUH!!?
KEH-KEH-KEH!
GAH-HA-HA!

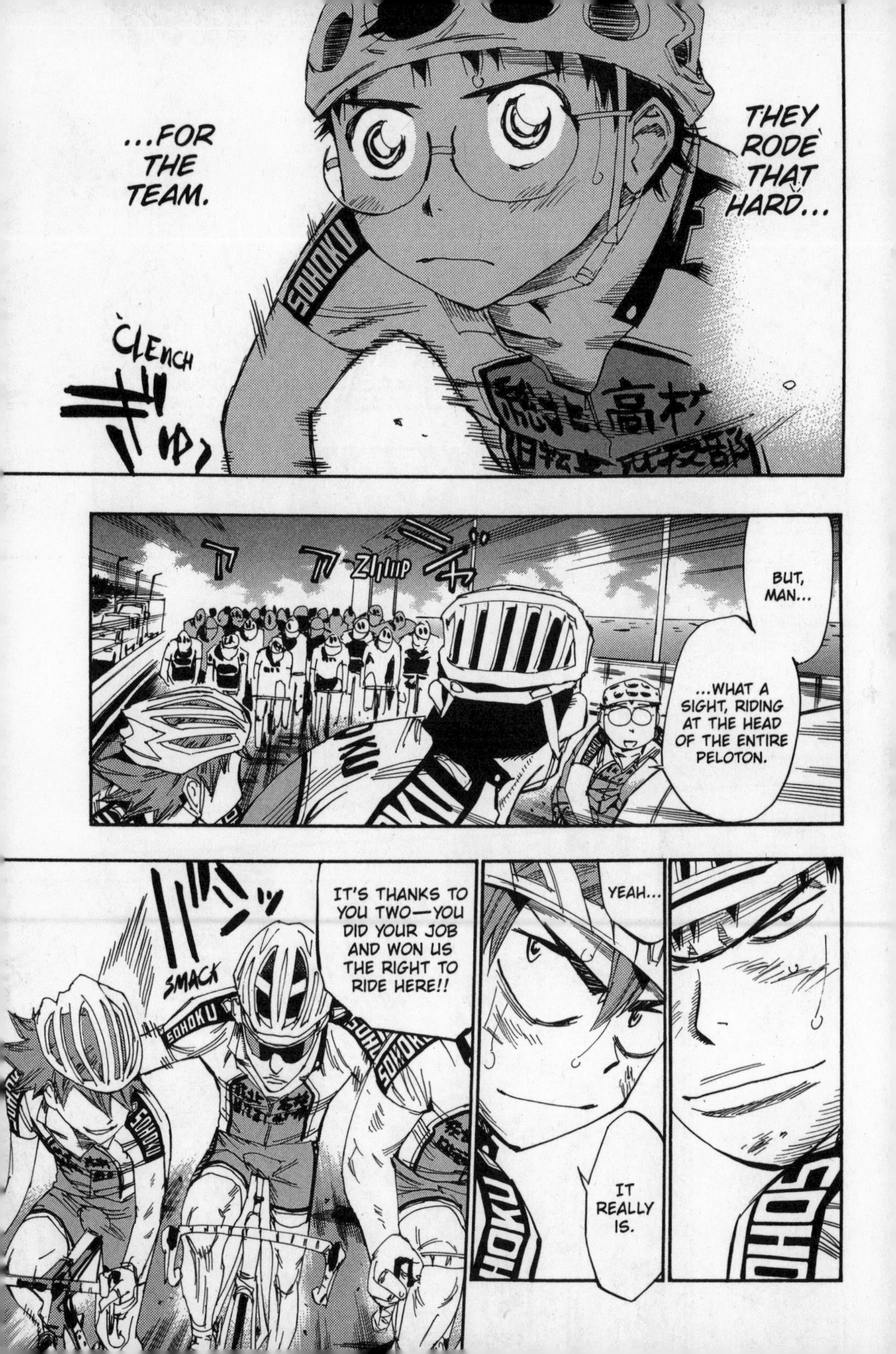
THEY RODE THAT HARD...
...FOR THE TEAM.
CLENCH
BUT, MAN...
...WHAT A SIGHT, RIDING AT THE HEAD OF THE ENTIRE PELOTON.
ZIIIIP
YEAH...
IT REALLY IS.
IT'S THANKS TO YOU TWO—YOU DID YOUR JOB AND WON US THE RIGHT TO RIDE HERE!!
SMACK

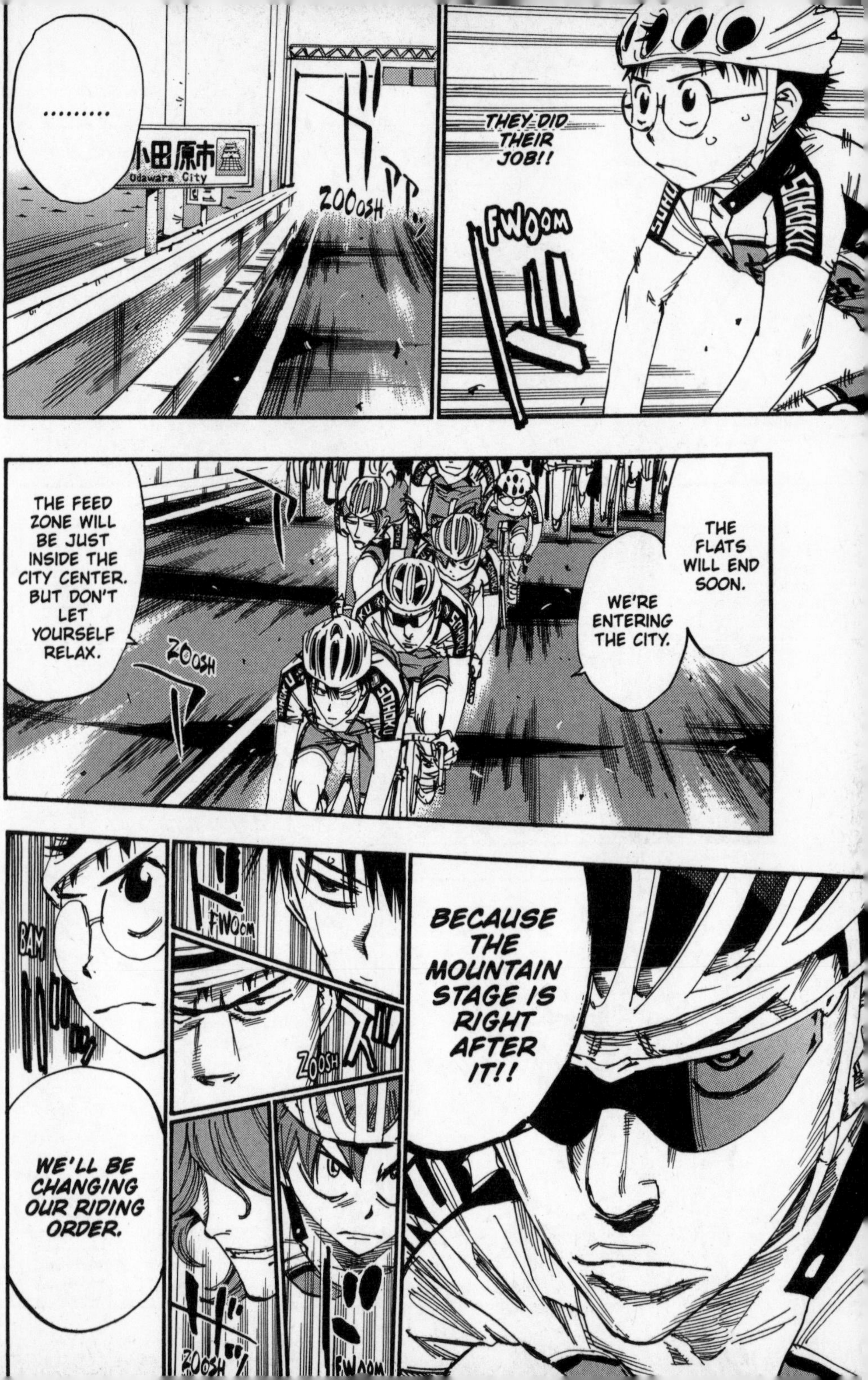THEY DID THEIR JOB!!
FWOOM
..........
小田原市
Odawara City
ZOOOSH
THE FLATS WILL END SOON.
WE'RE ENTERING THE CITY.
THE FEED ZONE WILL BE JUST INSIDE THE CITY CENTER. BUT DON'T LET YOURSELF RELAX.
ZOOSH
BECAUSE THE MOUNTAIN STAGE IS RIGHT AFTER IT!!
FWOOM
ZOOSH
ZOOSH
FWOOM
BAM
WE'LL BE CHANGING OUR RIDING ORDER.

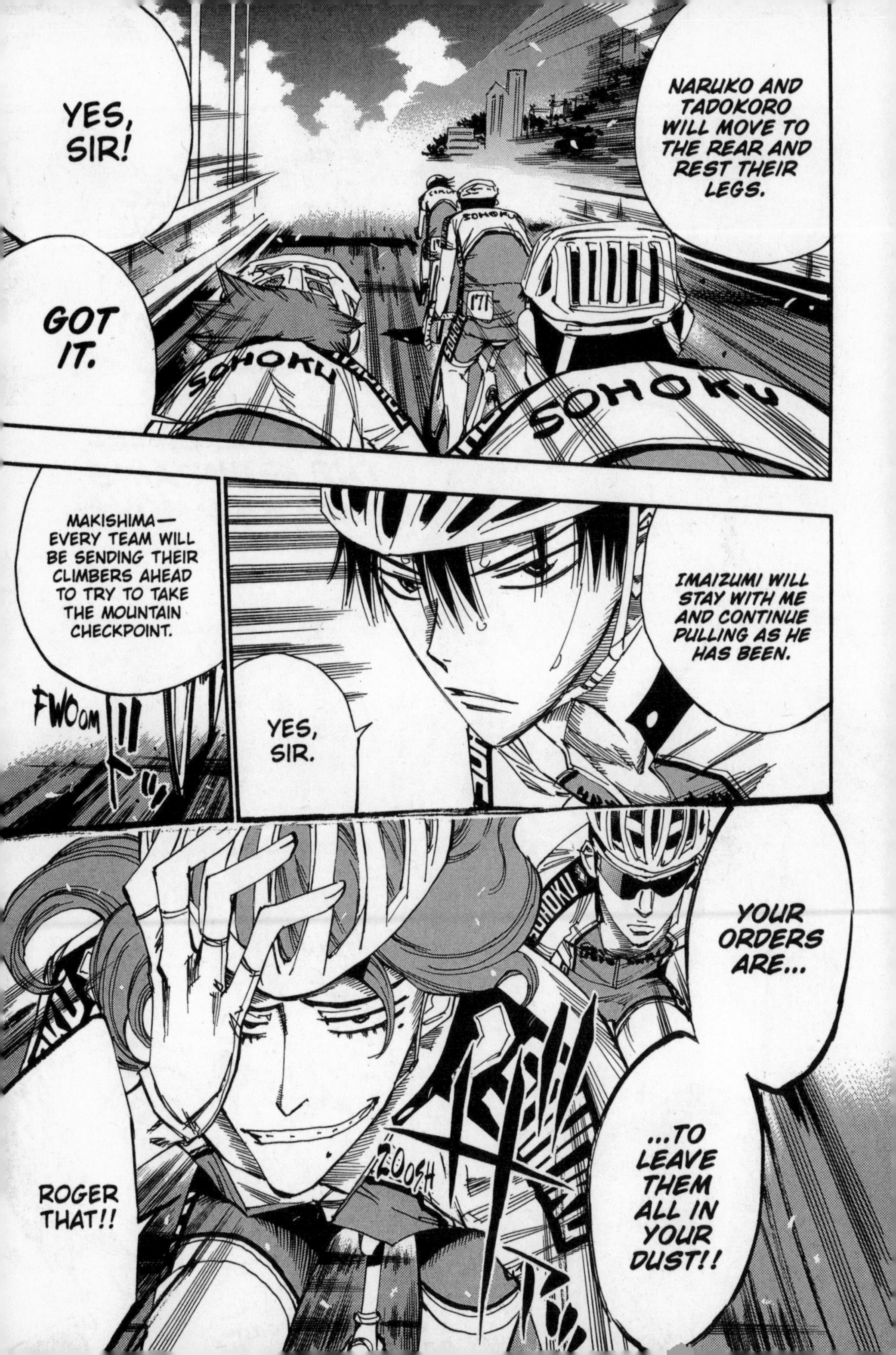

NARUKO AND TADOKORO WILL MOVE TO THE REAR AND REST THEIR LEGS.
YES, SIR!
GOT IT.
IMAIZUMI WILL STAY WITH ME AND CONTINUE PULLING AS HE HAS BEEN.
YES, SIR.
MAKISHIMA—EVERY TEAM WILL BE SENDING THEIR CLIMBERS AHEAD TO TRY TO TAKE THE MOUNTAIN CHECKPOINT.
FWOOM
YOUR ORDERS ARE...
...TO LEAVE THEM ALL IN YOUR DUST!!
ZOOSH
ROGER THAT!!

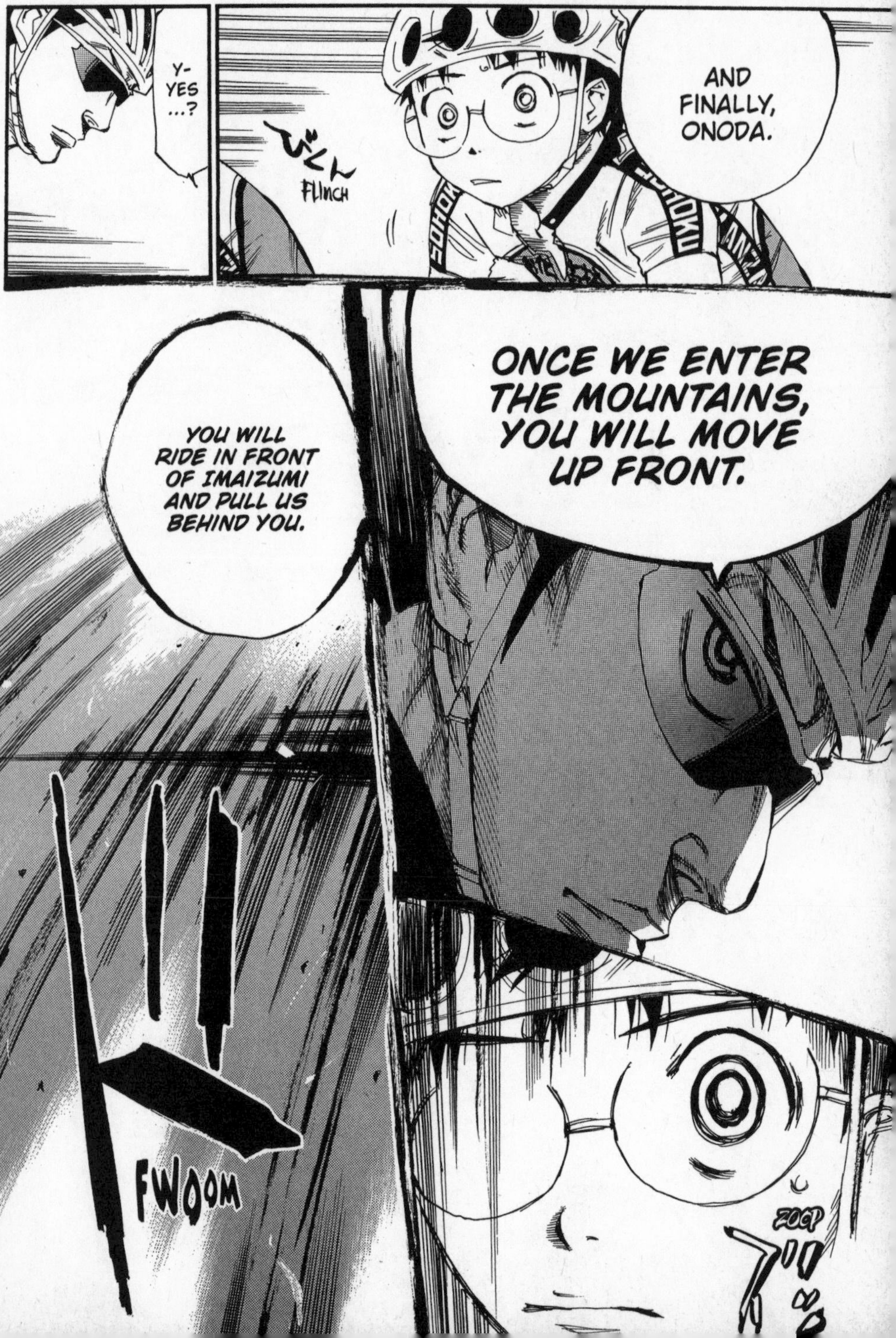
AND FINALLY, ONODA.
びくん
FLINCH
Y-YES...?
ONCE WE ENTER THE MOUNTAINS, YOU WILL MOVE UP FRONT.
YOU WILL RIDE IN FRONT OF IMAIZUMI AND PULL US BEHIND YOU.
ZOOP
FWOOM

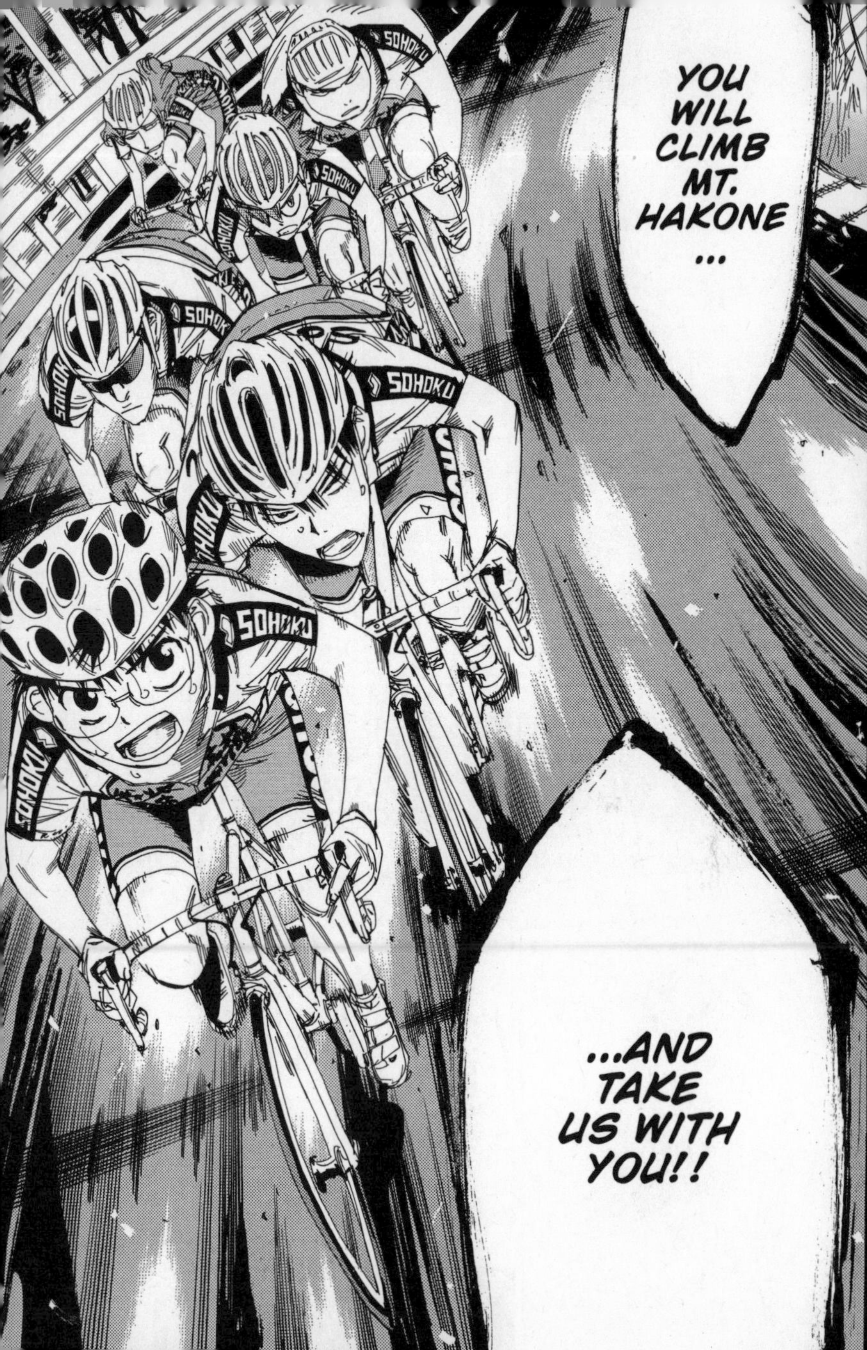
YOU WILL CLIMB MT. HAKONE ...
...AND TAKE US WITH YOU!!

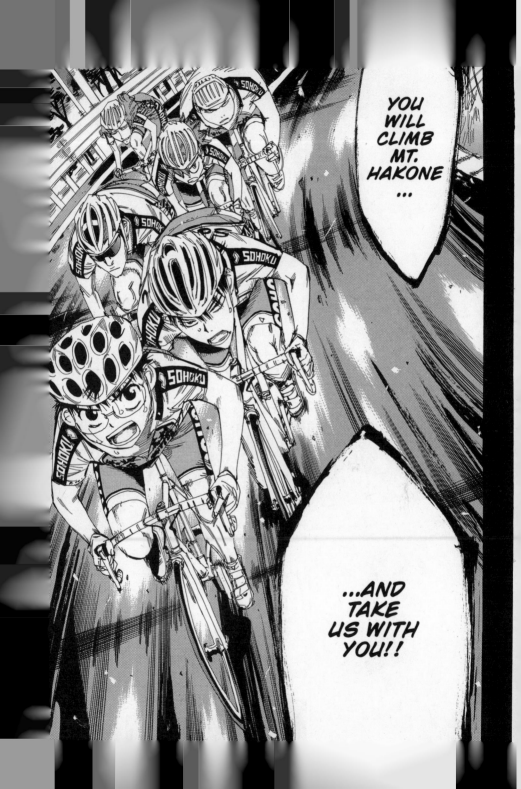

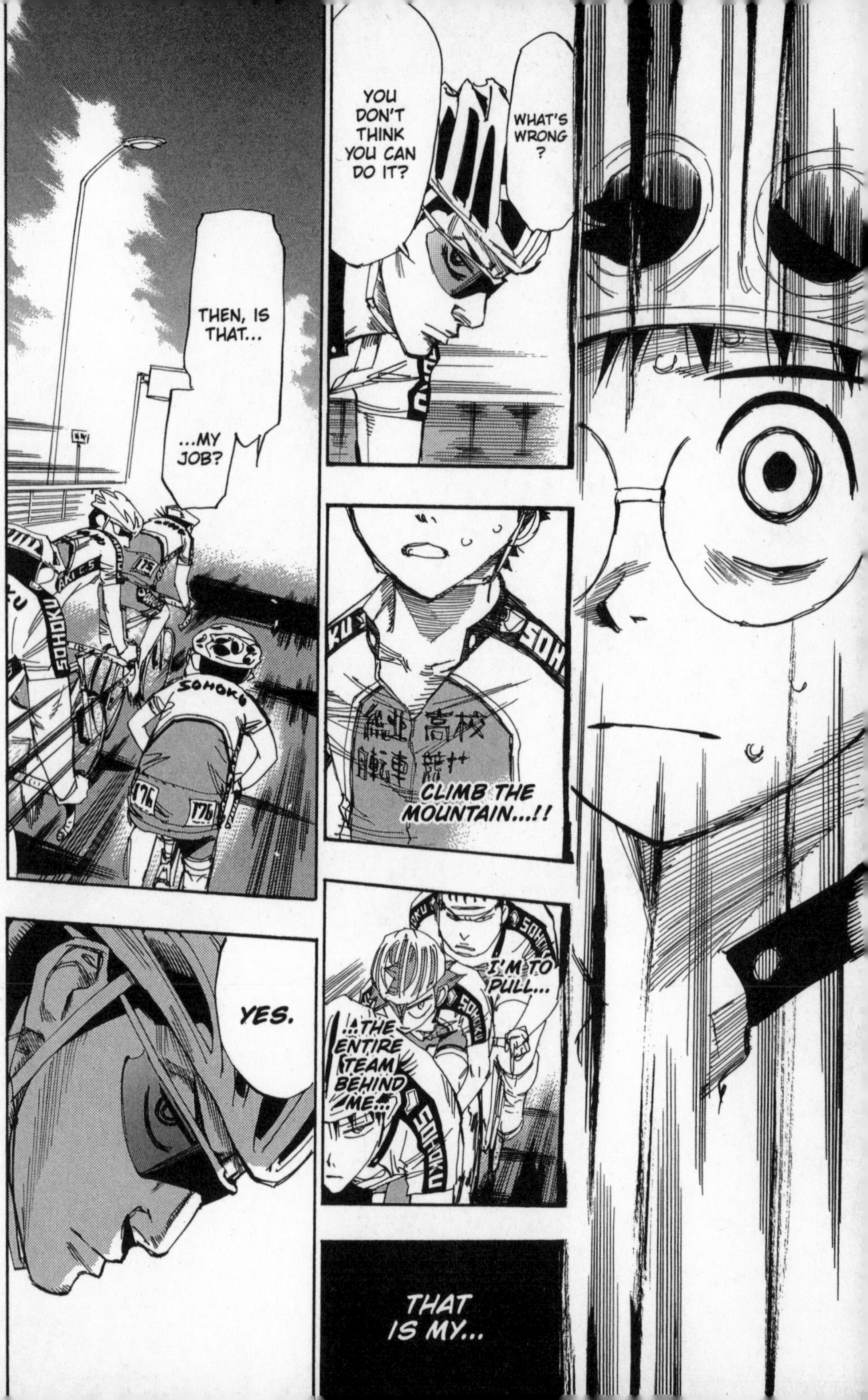
WHAT'S WRONG?
YOU DON'T THINK YOU CAN DO IT?
CLIMB THE MOUNTAIN...!!
I'M TO PULL...
...THE ENTIRE TEAM BEHIND ME...!
THAT IS MY...
THEN, IS THAT...
...MY JOB?
YES.

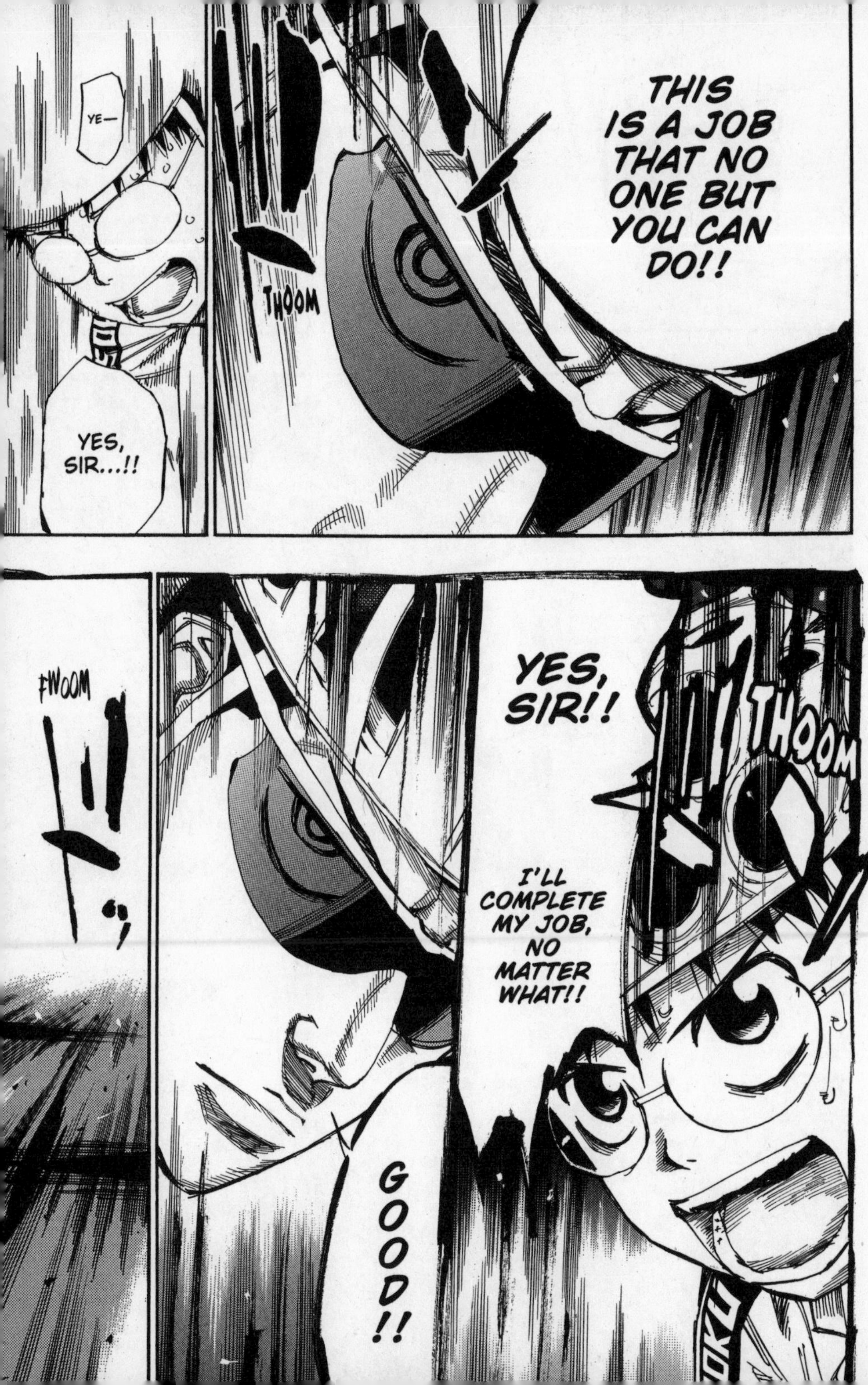
THIS IS A JOB THAT NO ONE BUT YOU CAN DO!!
THOOM
YE—
YES, SIR...!!
YES, SIR!!
THOOM
I'LL COMPLETE MY JOB, NO MATTER WHAT!!
GOOD!!
FWOOM

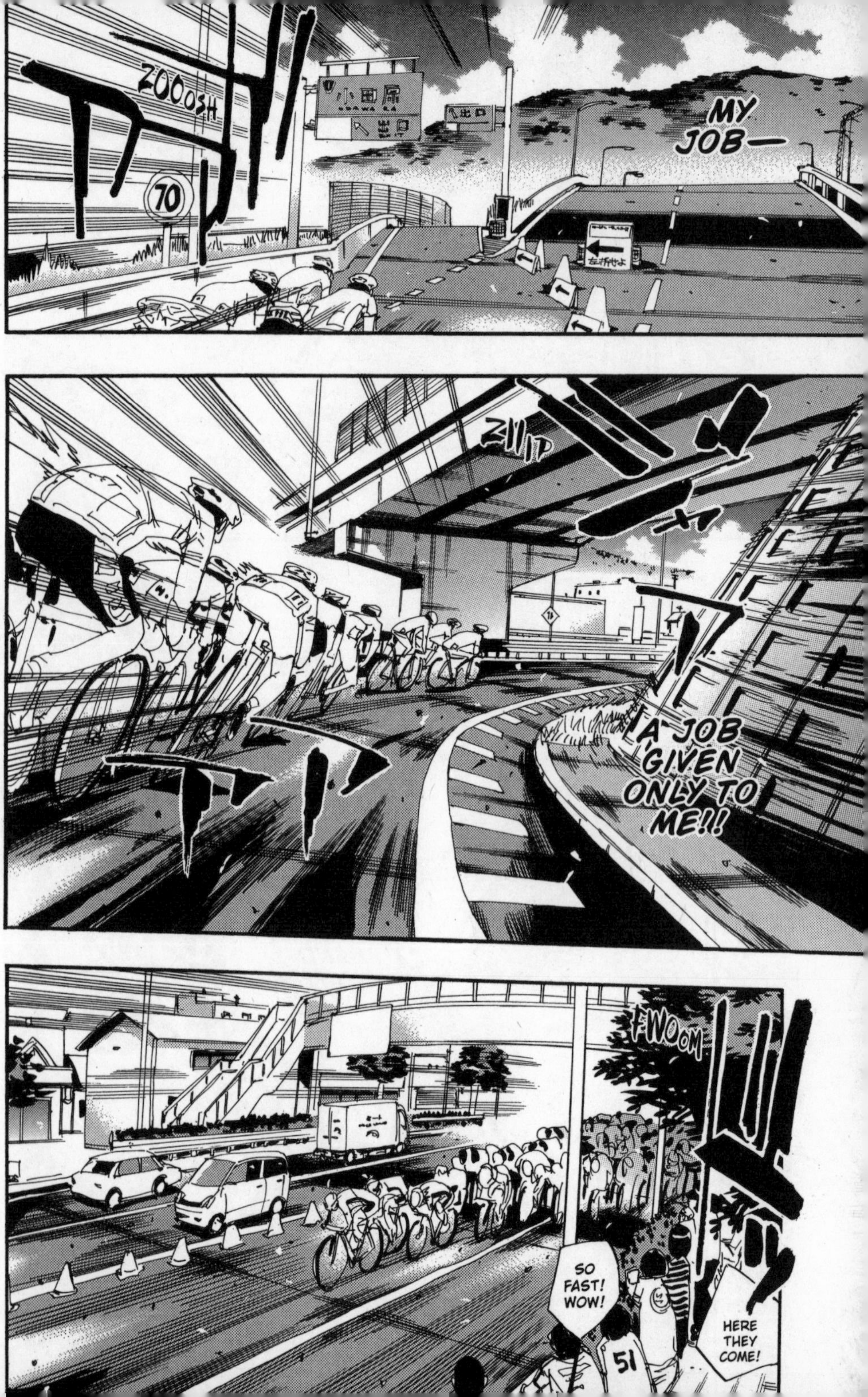
MY JOB—
小田原
ZOOOSH
ZIIIP
A JOB GIVEN ONLY TO ME!!
FWOOM
HERE THEY COME!
SO FAST! WOW!

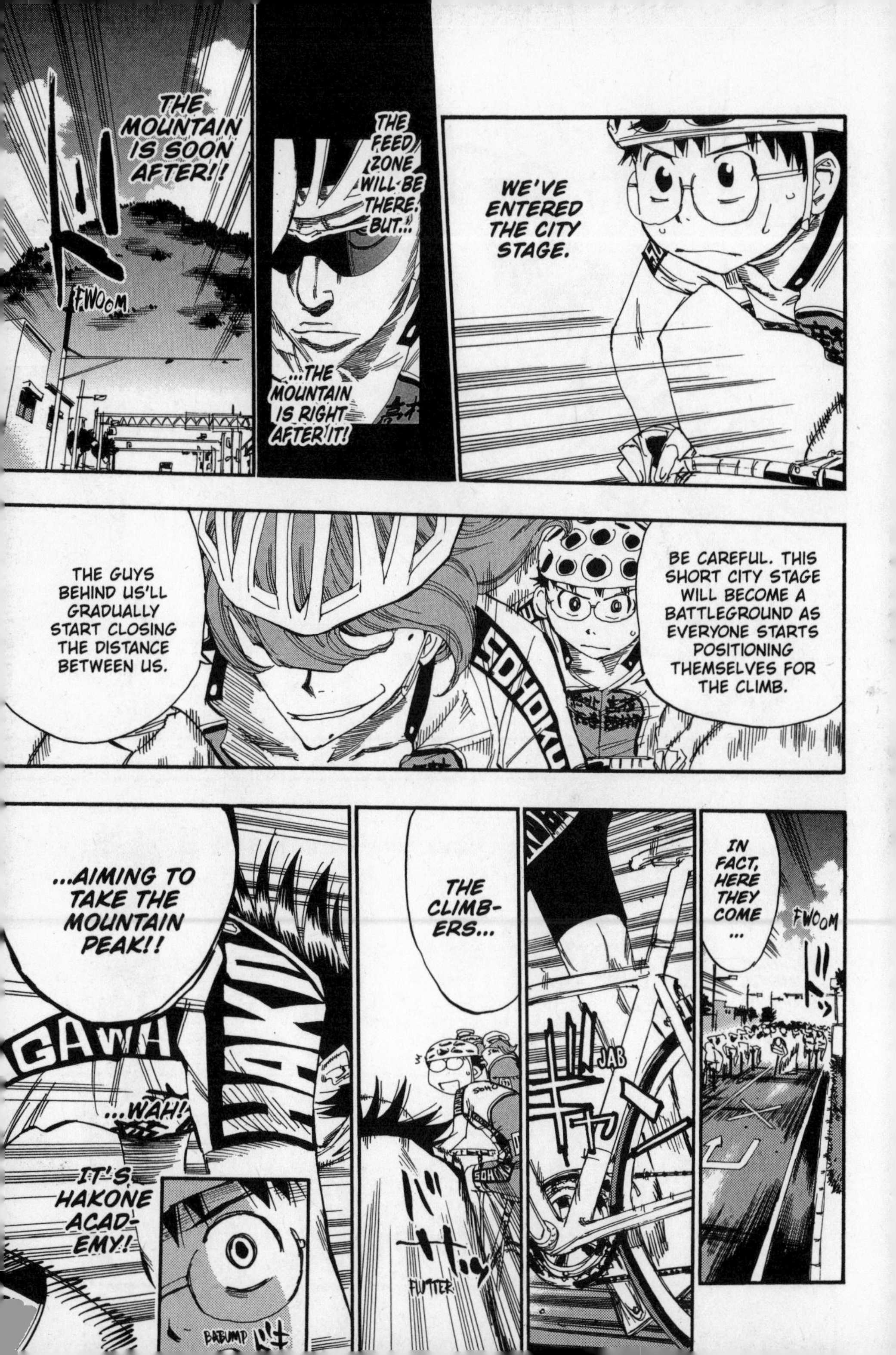
WE'VE ENTERED THE CITY STAGE.
THE FEED ZONE WILL BE THERE, BUT...
...THE MOUNTAIN IS RIGHT AFTER IT!
THE MOUNTAIN IS SOON AFTER!!
FWOOM
BE CAREFUL. THIS SHORT CITY STAGE WILL BECOME A BATTLEGROUND AS EVERYONE STARTS POSITIONING THEMSELVES FOR THE CLIMB.
THE GUYS BEHIND US'LL GRADUALLY START CLOSING THE DISTANCE BETWEEN US.
IN FACT, HERE THEY COME...
FWOOM
JAB
THE CLIMBERS...
FLUTTER
...AIMING TO TAKE THE MOUNTAIN PEAK!!
GAWH
...WAH!!
IT'S HAKONE ACADEMY!!
BABUMP

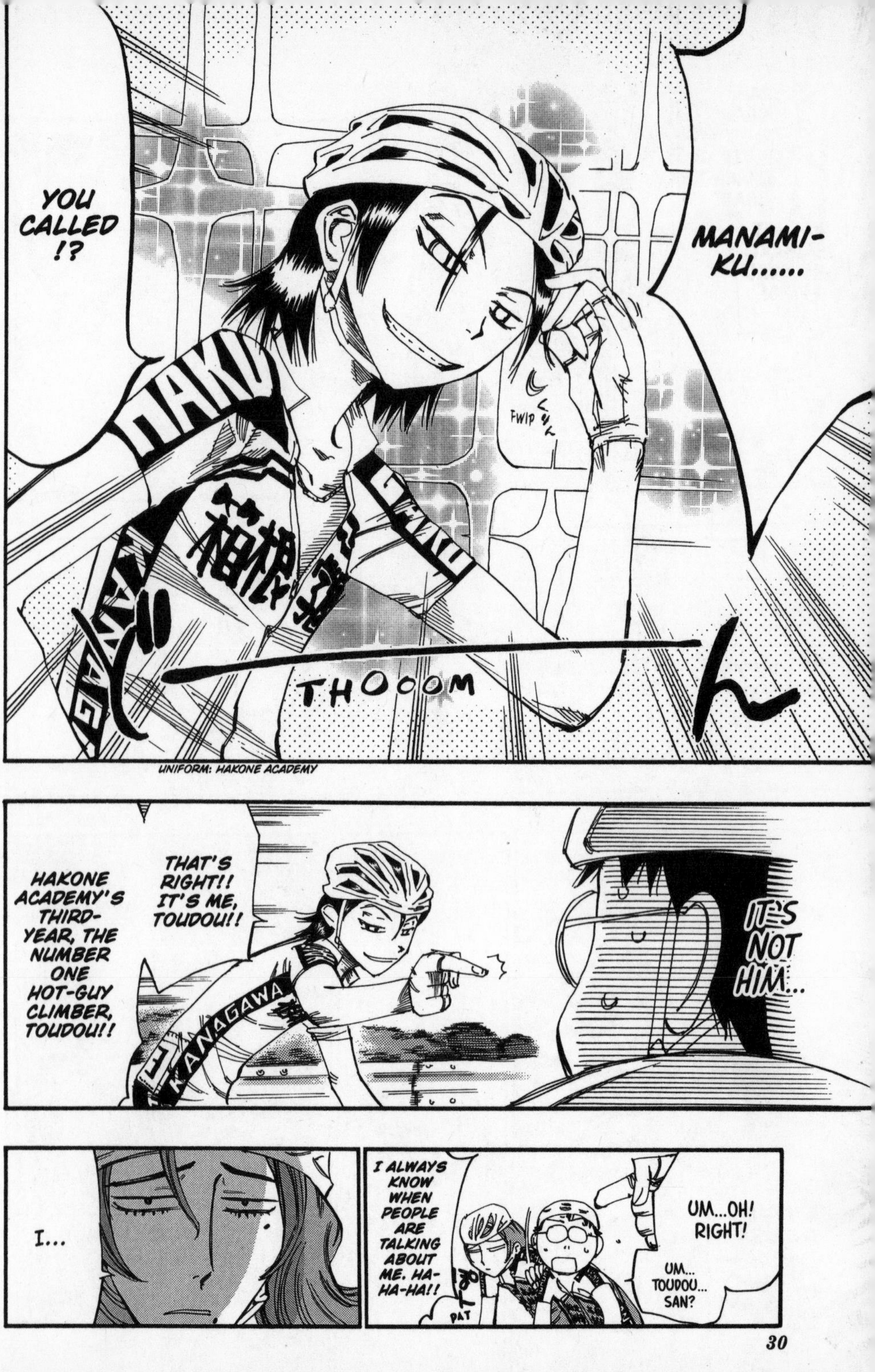
MANAMI-KU......
YOU CALLED!?
FWIP
THOOOM
UNIFORM: HAKONE ACADEMY
IT'S NOT HIM...
THAT'S RIGHT!! IT'S ME, TOUDOU!!
HAKONE ACADEMY'S THIRD-YEAR, THE NUMBER ONE HOT-GUY CLIMBER, TOUDOU!!
UM...OH! RIGHT!
UM... TOUDOU... SAN?
I ALWAYS KNOW WHEN PEOPLE ARE TALKING ABOUT ME. HA-HA-HA!!
PAT
I...

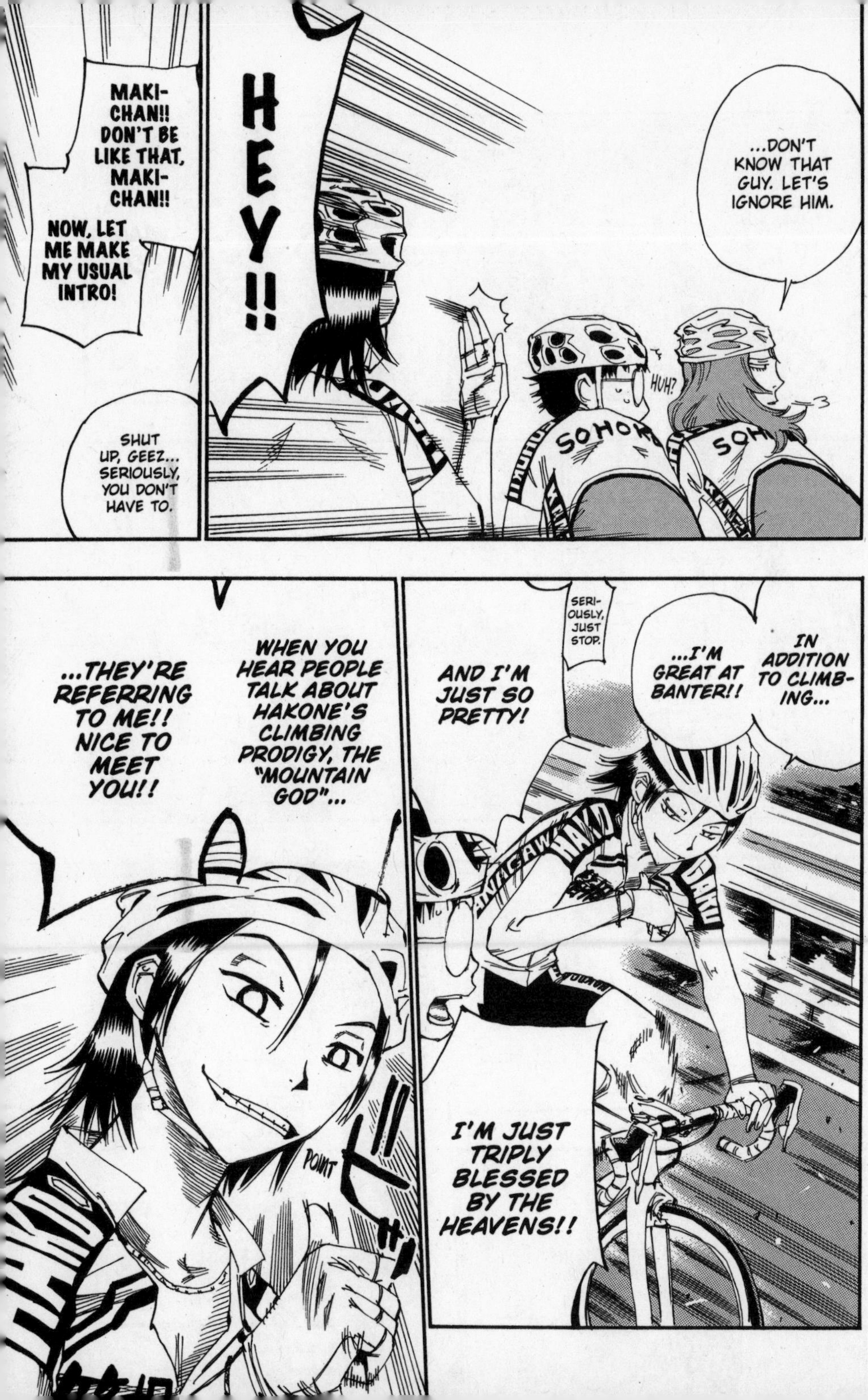
...DON'T KNOW THAT GUY. LET'S IGNORE HIM.
HUH?
HEY!!
MAKI-CHAN!! DON'T BE LIKE THAT, MAKI-CHAN!!
NOW, LET ME MAKE MY USUAL INTRO!
SHUT UP, GEEZ... SERIOUSLY, YOU DON'T HAVE TO.
IN ADDITION TO CLIMBING...
...I'M GREAT AT BANTER!!
SERIOUSLY, JUST STOP.
AND I'M JUST SO PRETTY!
I'M JUST TRIPLY BLESSED BY THE HEAVENS!!
WHEN YOU HEAR PEOPLE TALK ABOUT HAKONE'S CLIMBING PRODIGY, THE "MOUNTAIN GOD"...
...THEY'RE REFERRING TO ME!! NICE TO MEET YOU!!
POINT

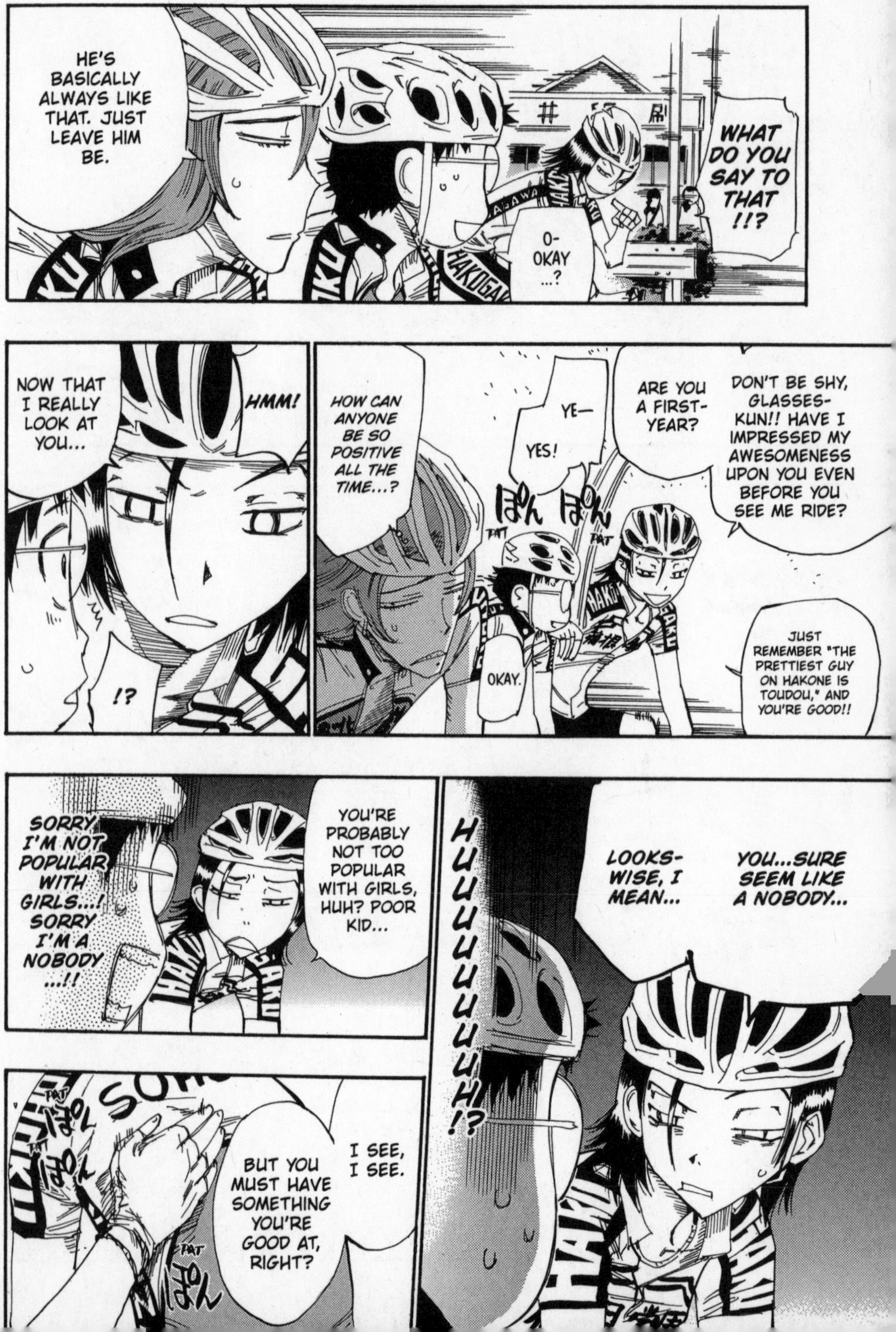
WHAT DO YOU SAY TO THAT!!?
O-OKAY...?
HE'S BASICALLY ALWAYS LIKE THAT. JUST LEAVE HIM BE.
DON'T BE SHY, GLASSES-KUN!! HAVE I IMPRESSED MY AWESOMENESS UPON YOU EVEN BEFORE YOU SEE ME RIDE?
ARE YOU A FIRST-YEAR?
YE—
YES!
ぱん PAT ぱん PAT
JUST REMEMBER "THE PRETTIEST GUY ON HAKONE IS TOUDOU," AND YOU'RE GOOD!!
OKAY.
HOW CAN ANYONE BE SO POSITIVE ALL THE TIME...?
HMM!
NOW THAT I REALLY LOOK AT YOU...
!?
YOU...SURE SEEM LIKE A NOBODY...
LOOKS-WISE, I MEAN...
HUUUUUUUUUH!?
YOU'RE PROBABLY NOT TOO POPULAR WITH GIRLS, HUH? POOR KID...
SORRY I'M NOT POPULAR WITH GIRLS...! SORRY I'M A NOBODY...!!
I SEE, I SEE.
BUT YOU MUST HAVE SOMETHING YOU'RE GOOD AT, RIGHT?
PAT ぱん PAT ぱん PAT ぱん

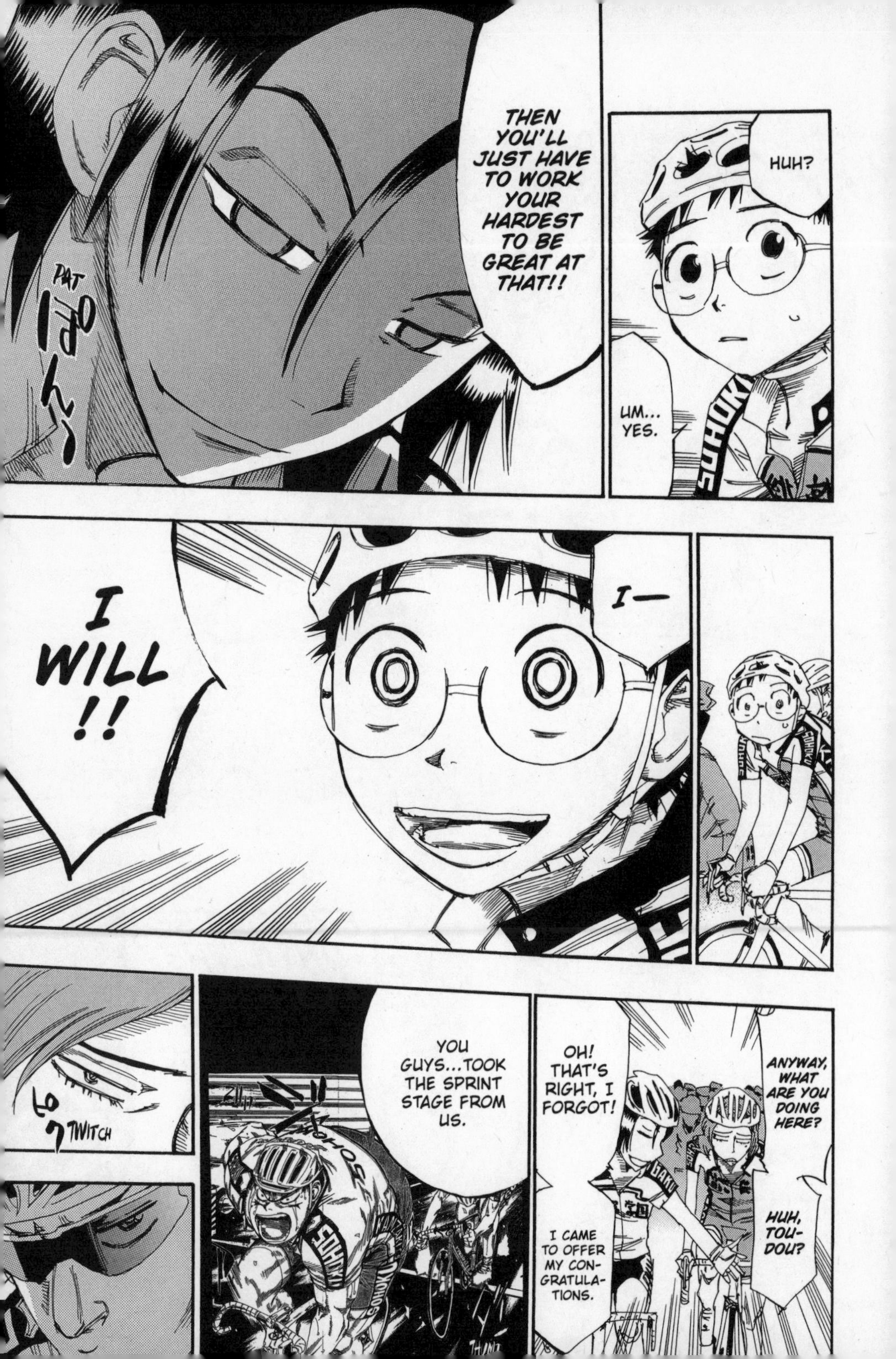
HUH?
UM... YES.
THEN YOU'LL JUST HAVE TO WORK YOUR HARDEST TO BE GREAT AT THAT!!
PAT
ぽん
I—
I WILL!!
ANYWAY, WHAT ARE YOU DOING HERE?
HUH, TOU-DOU?
OH! THAT'S RIGHT, I FORGOT!
I CAME TO OFFER MY CON-GRATULA-TIONS.
YOU GUYS...TOOK THE SPRINT STAGE FROM US.
ピク
TWITCH

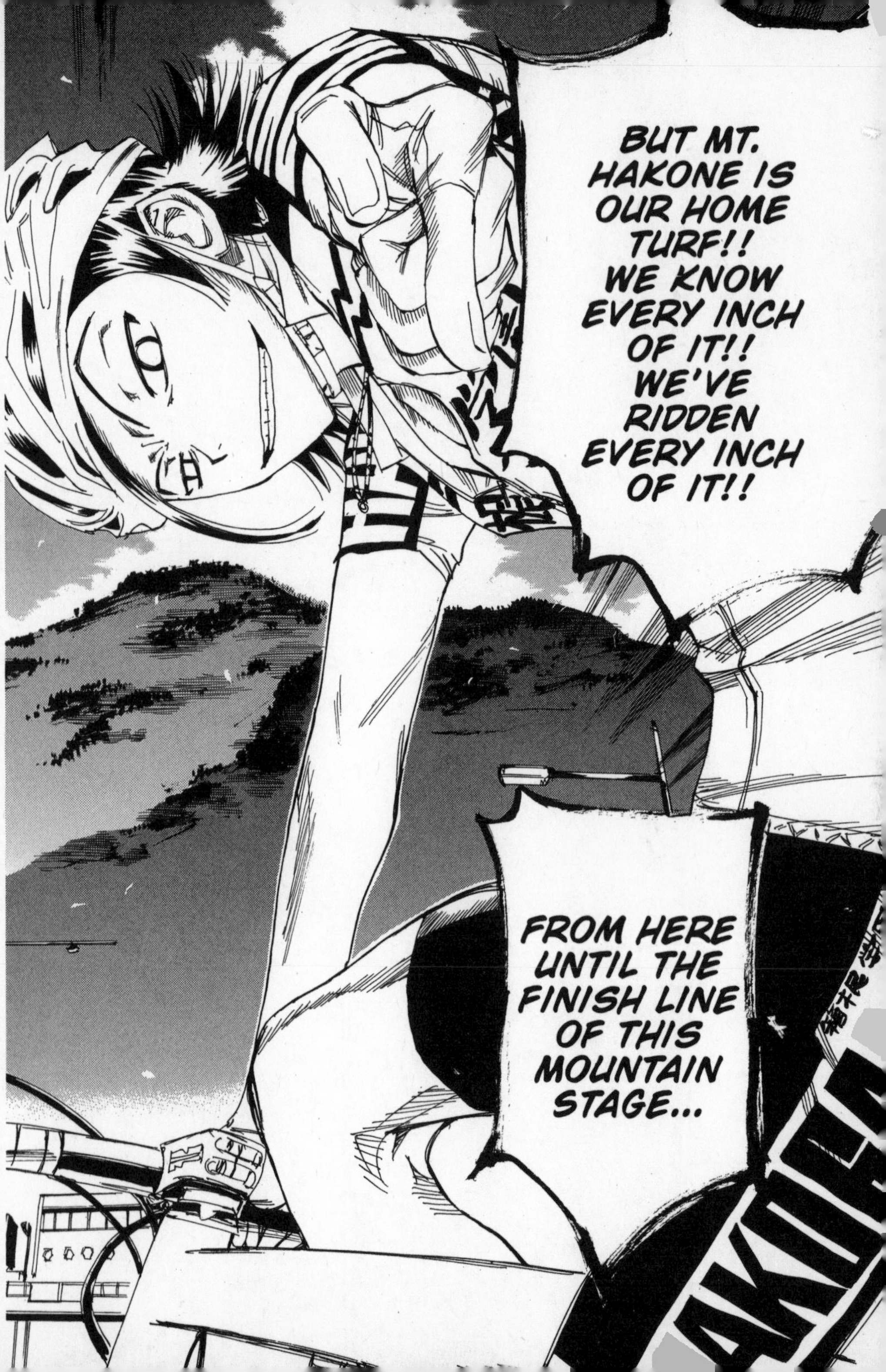
BUT MT. HAKONE IS OUR HOME TURF!! WE KNOW EVERY INCH OF IT!! WE'VE RIDDEN EVERY INCH OF IT!!
FROM HERE UNTIL THE FINISH LINE OF THIS MOUNTAIN STAGE...

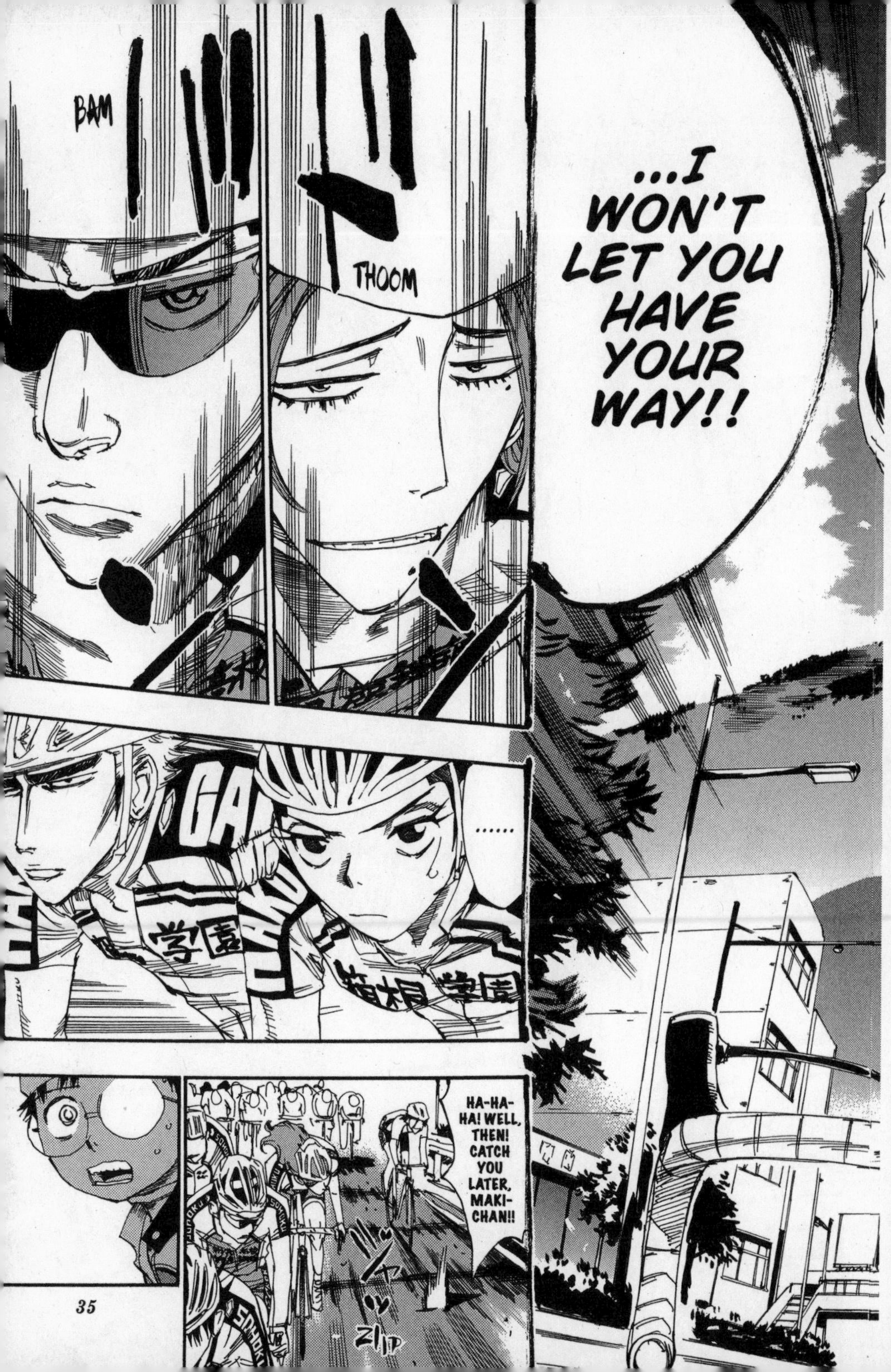
...I WON'T LET YOU HAVE YOUR WAY!!
THOOM
BAM
......
HA-HA! WELL, THEN! CATCH YOU LATER, MAKI-CHAN!!
ZIP

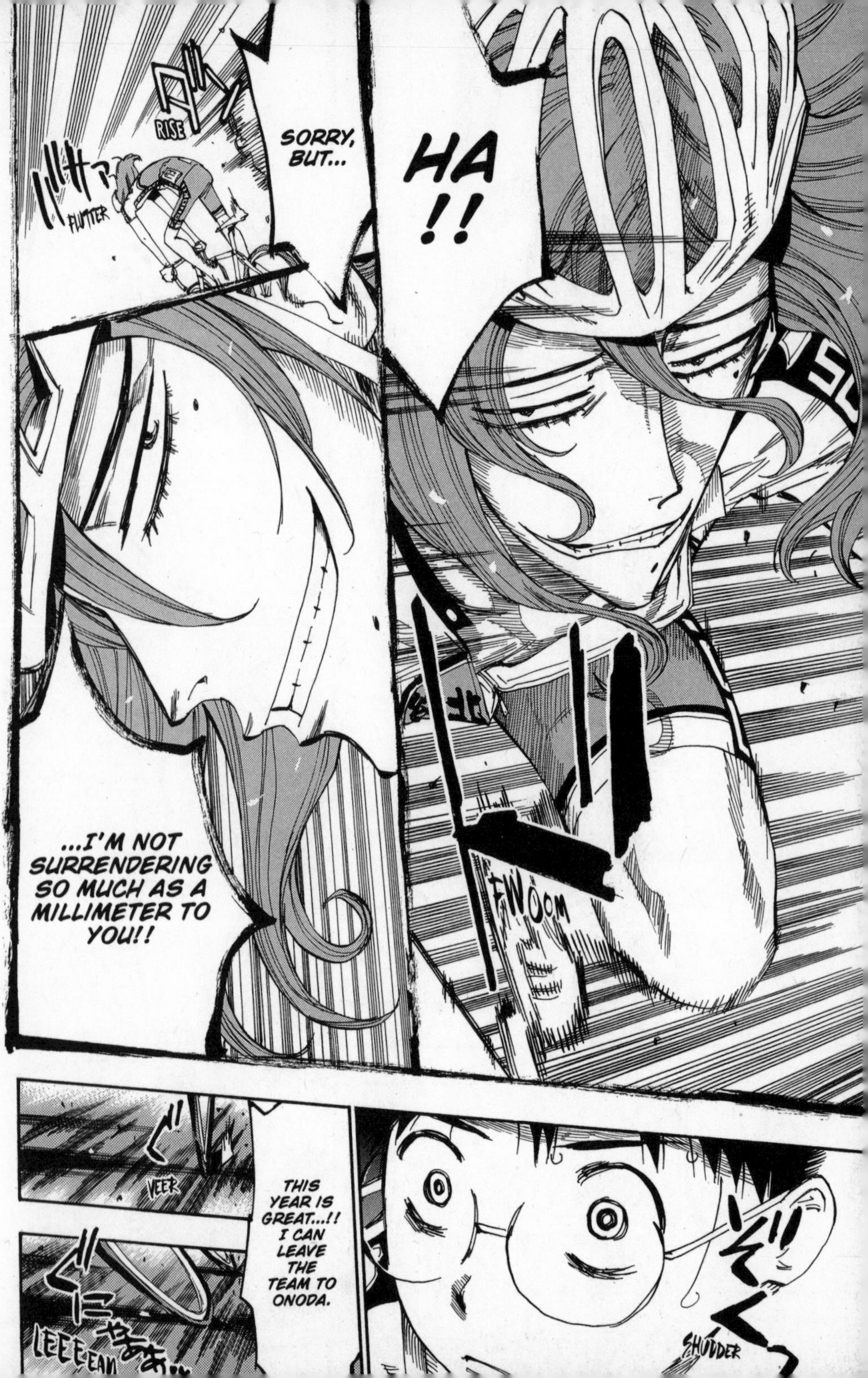
HA!!
FWOOM
RISE
FLUTTER
SORRY, BUT...
...I'M NOT SURRENDERING SO MUCH AS A MILLIMETER TO YOU!!
SHUDDER
VEER
THIS YEAR IS GREAT...!! I CAN LEAVE THE TEAM TO ONODA.
LEEEEAN

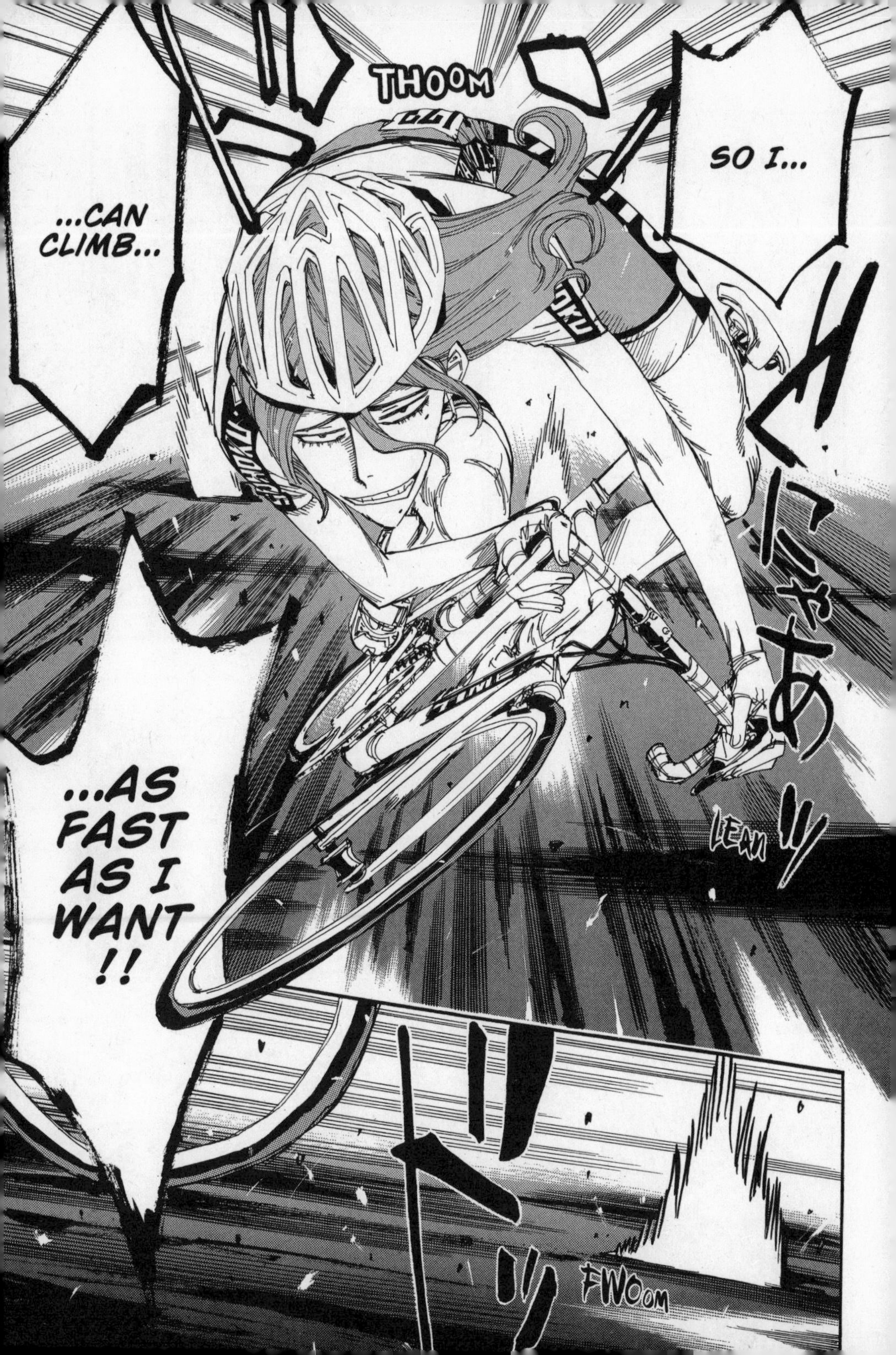
SO I...
THOOM
...CAN CLIMB...
にゃあ
LEAN
...AS FAST AS I WANT!!
FWOOM

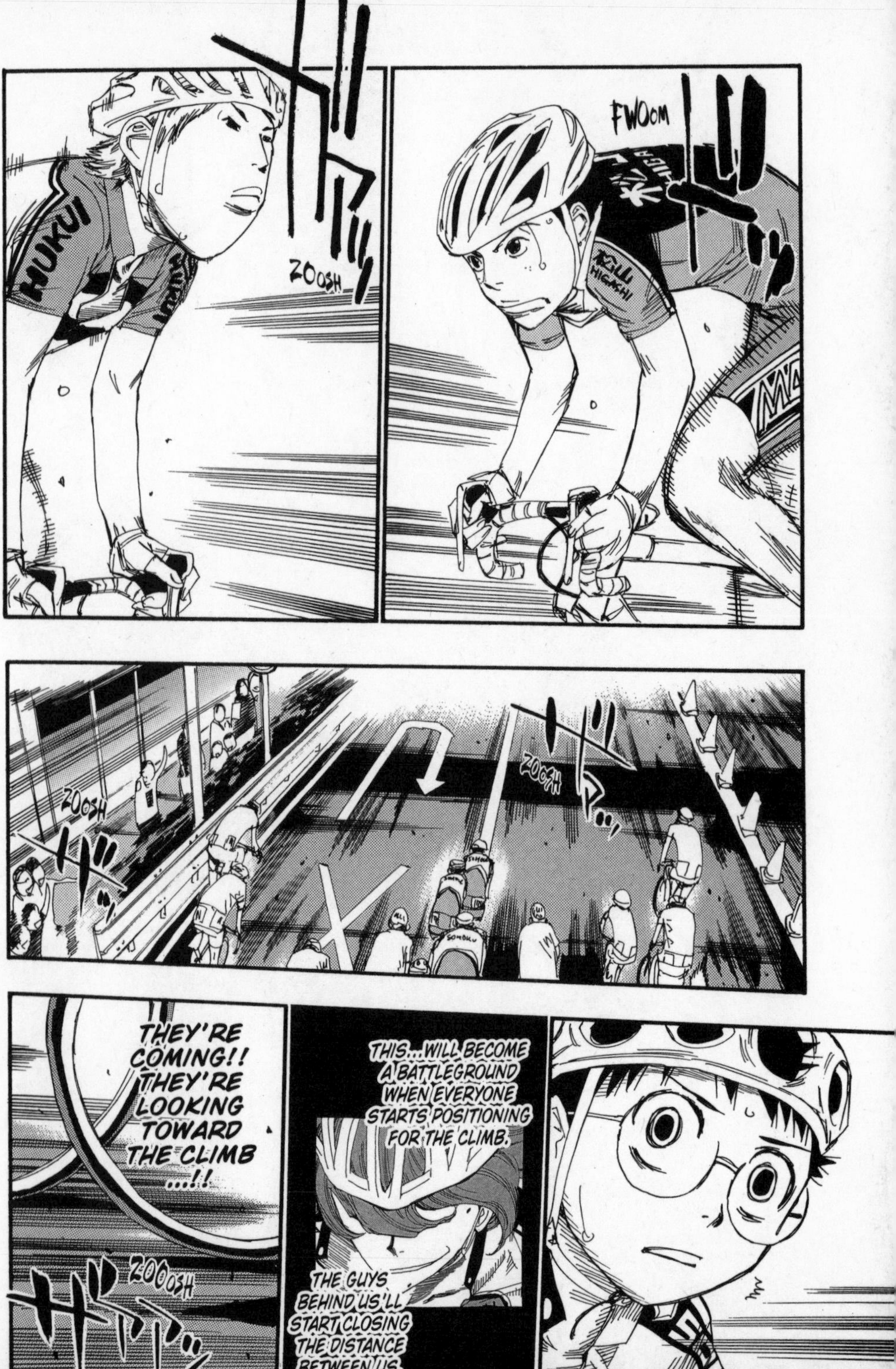
FWOOM
ZOOSH
ZOOSH
ZOOSH
THIS...WILL BECOME A BATTLEGROUND WHEN EVERYONE STARTS POSITIONING FOR THE CLIMB.
THE GUYS BEHIND US'LL START CLOSING THE DISTANCE BETWEEN US.
THEY'RE COMING!! THEY'RE LOOKING TOWARD THE CLIMB ...!!
ZOOOSH

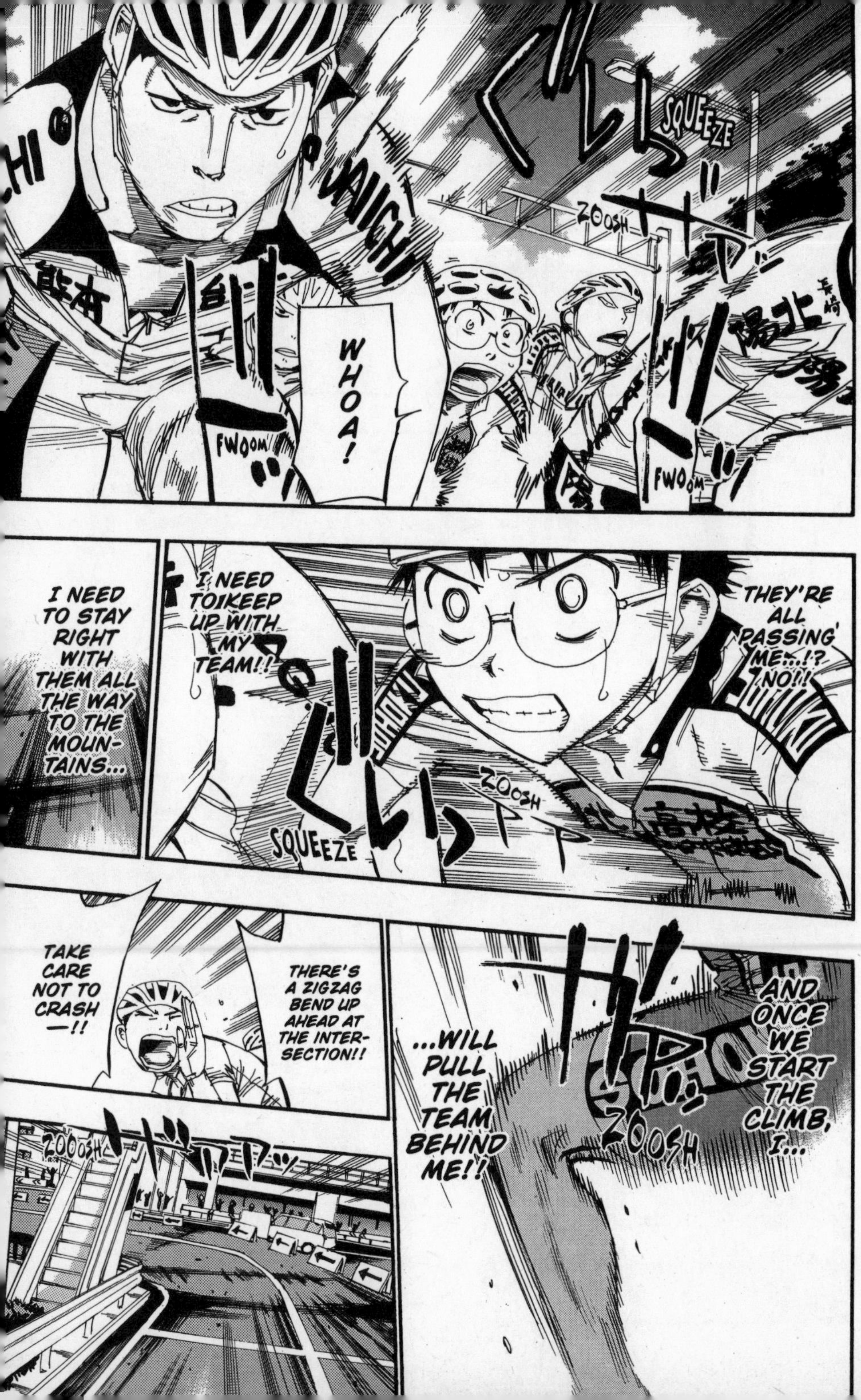
SQUEEZE
ZOOSH
FWOOM
WHOA!
FWOOM
THEY'RE ALL PASSING ME...!? NO!!
ZOOSH
I NEED TO KEEP UP WITH MY TEAM!!
SQUEEZE
I NEED TO STAY RIGHT WITH THEM ALL THE WAY TO THE MOUN-TAINS...
AND ONCE WE START THE CLIMB, I...
ZOOSH
...WILL PULL THE TEAM BEHIND ME!!
THERE'S A ZIGZAG BEND UP AHEAD AT THE INTER-SECTION!!
TAKE CARE NOT TO CRASH—!!
ZOOOSH

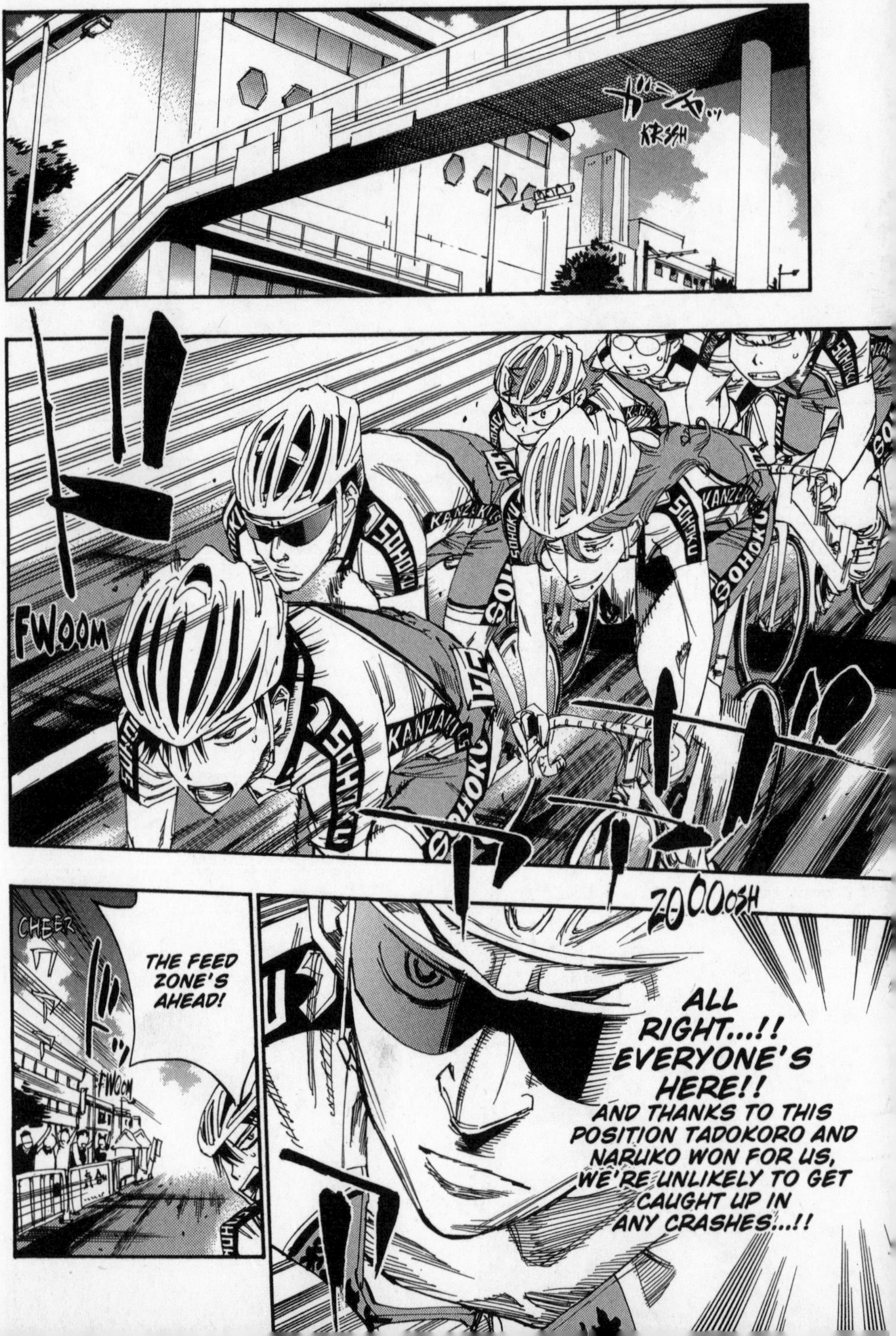
KR-SSH
FWOOM
ZOOOOSH
ALL RIGHT...!! EVERYONE'S HERE!!
AND THANKS TO THIS POSITION TADOKORO AND NARUKO WON FOR US, WE'RE UNLIKELY TO GET CAUGHT UP IN ANY CRASHES...!!
CHEER
THE FEED ZONE'S AHEAD!
FWOOM

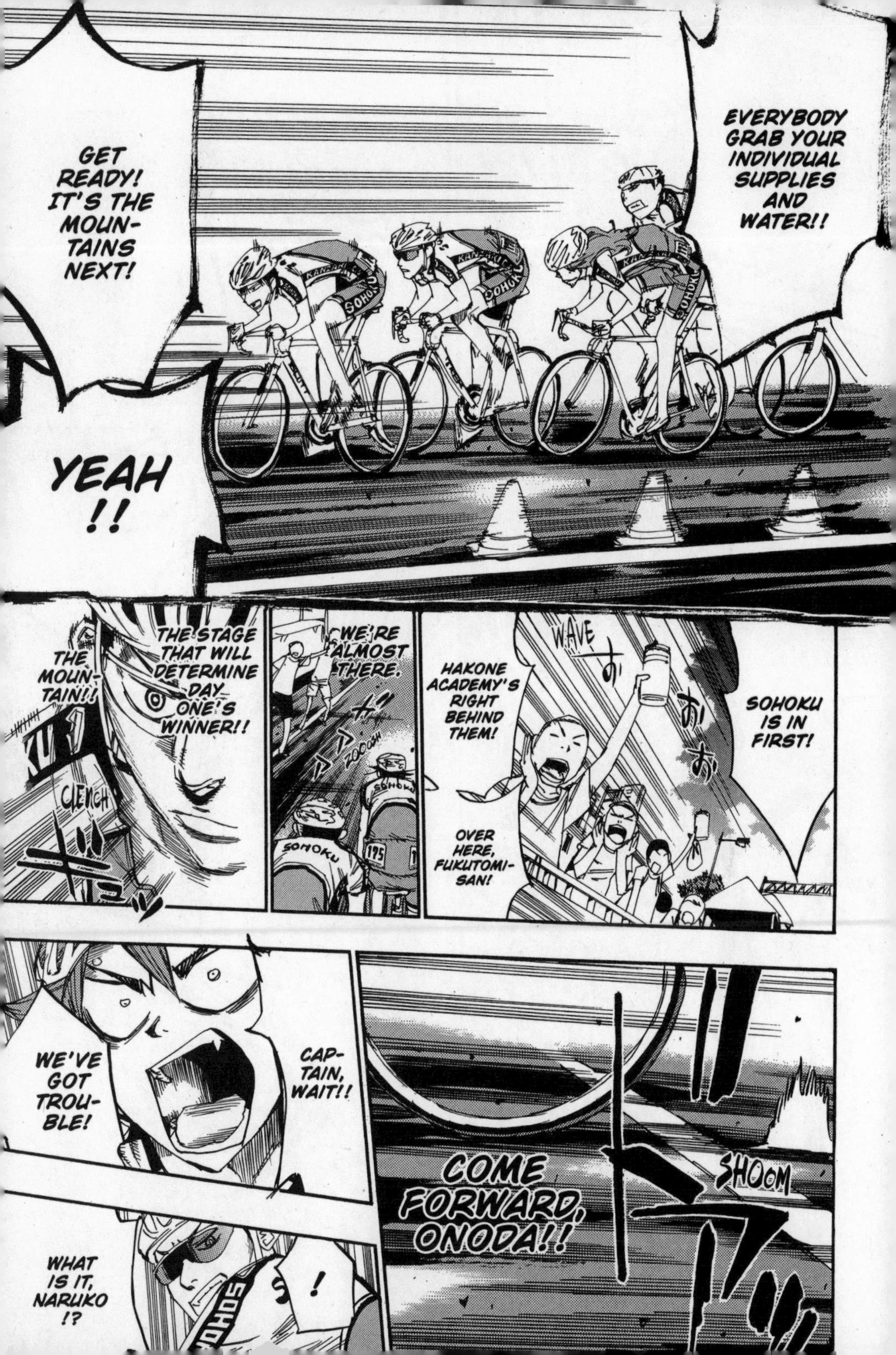
EVERYBODY GRAB YOUR INDIVIDUAL SUPPLIES AND WATER!!
GET READY! IT'S THE MOUN-TAINS NEXT!
YEAH!!
SOHOKU IS IN FIRST!
WAVE
HAKONE ACADEMY'S RIGHT BEHIND THEM!
OVER HERE, FUKUTOMI-SAN!
WE'RE ALMOST THERE.
THE STAGE THAT WILL DETERMINE DAY ONE'S WINNER!!
THE MOUN-TAIN!!
CLENCH
SHOOM
COME FORWARD, ONODA!!
CAP-TAIN, WAIT!!
WE'VE GOT TROU-BLE!
!
WHAT IS IT, NARUKO!?

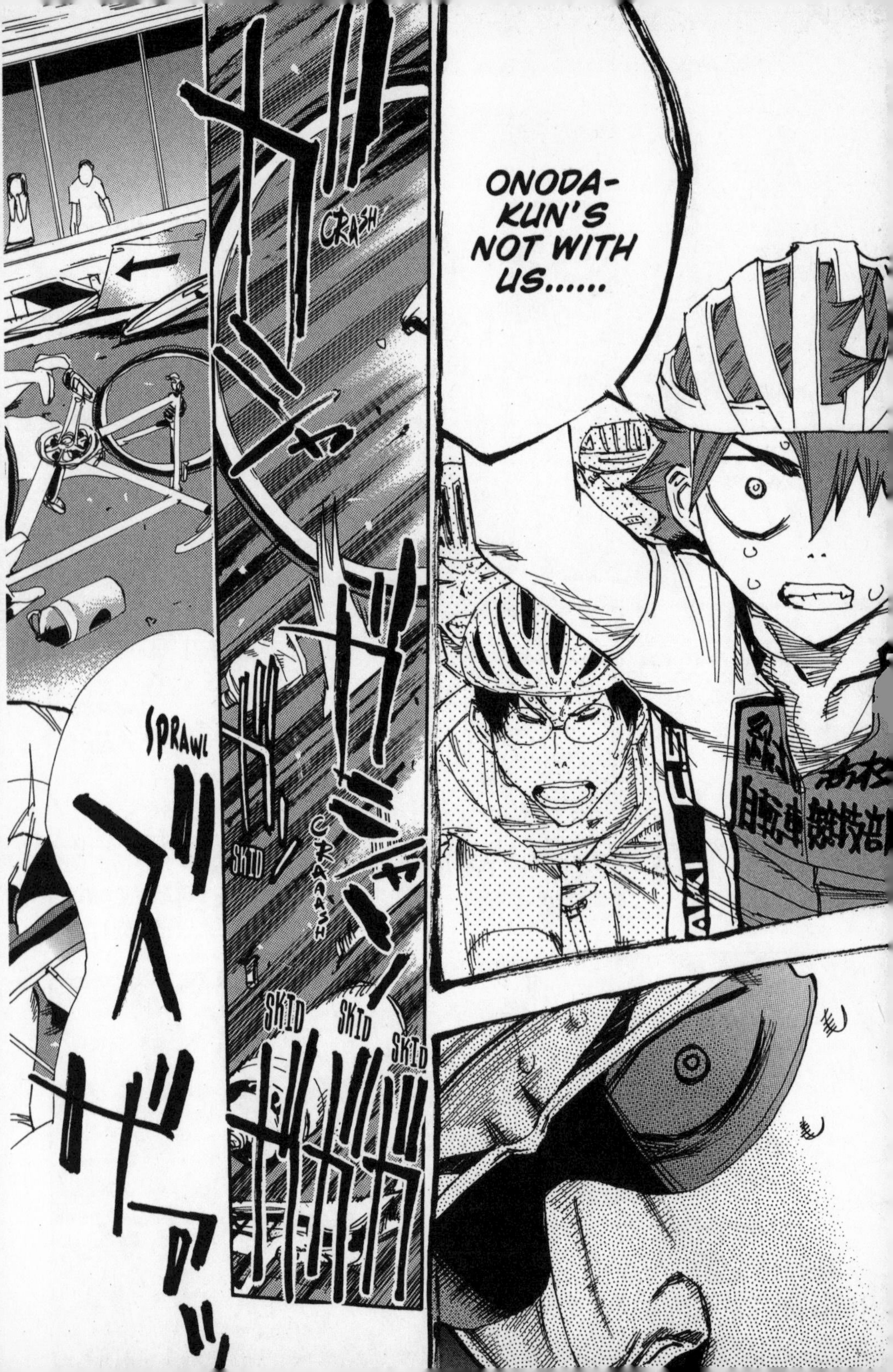
ONODA-KUN'S NOT WITH US......
CRASH
CRAAASH
SKID
SKID
SKID
SKID
SPRAWL

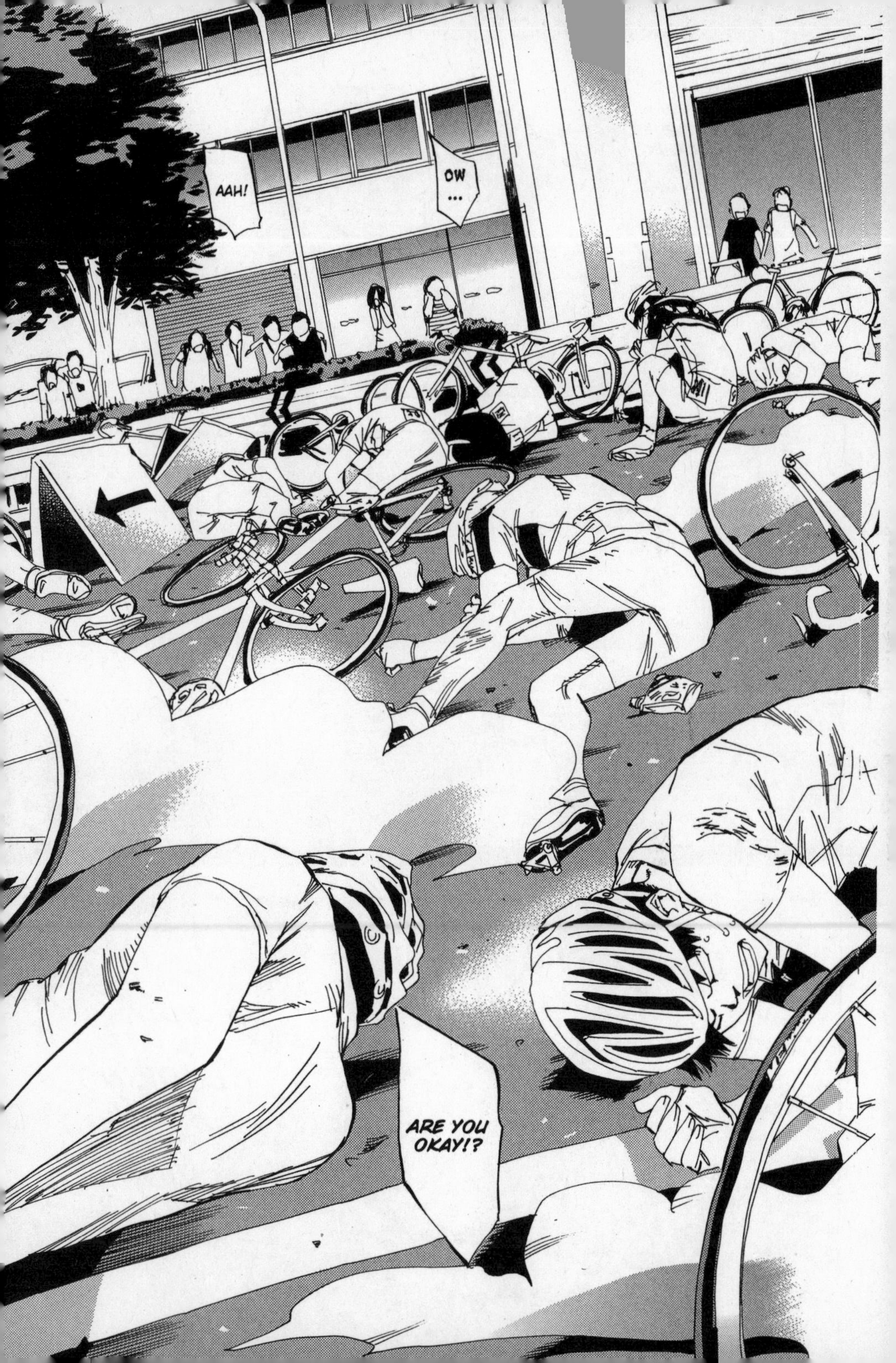
OW ...
AAH!
ARE YOU OKAY!?

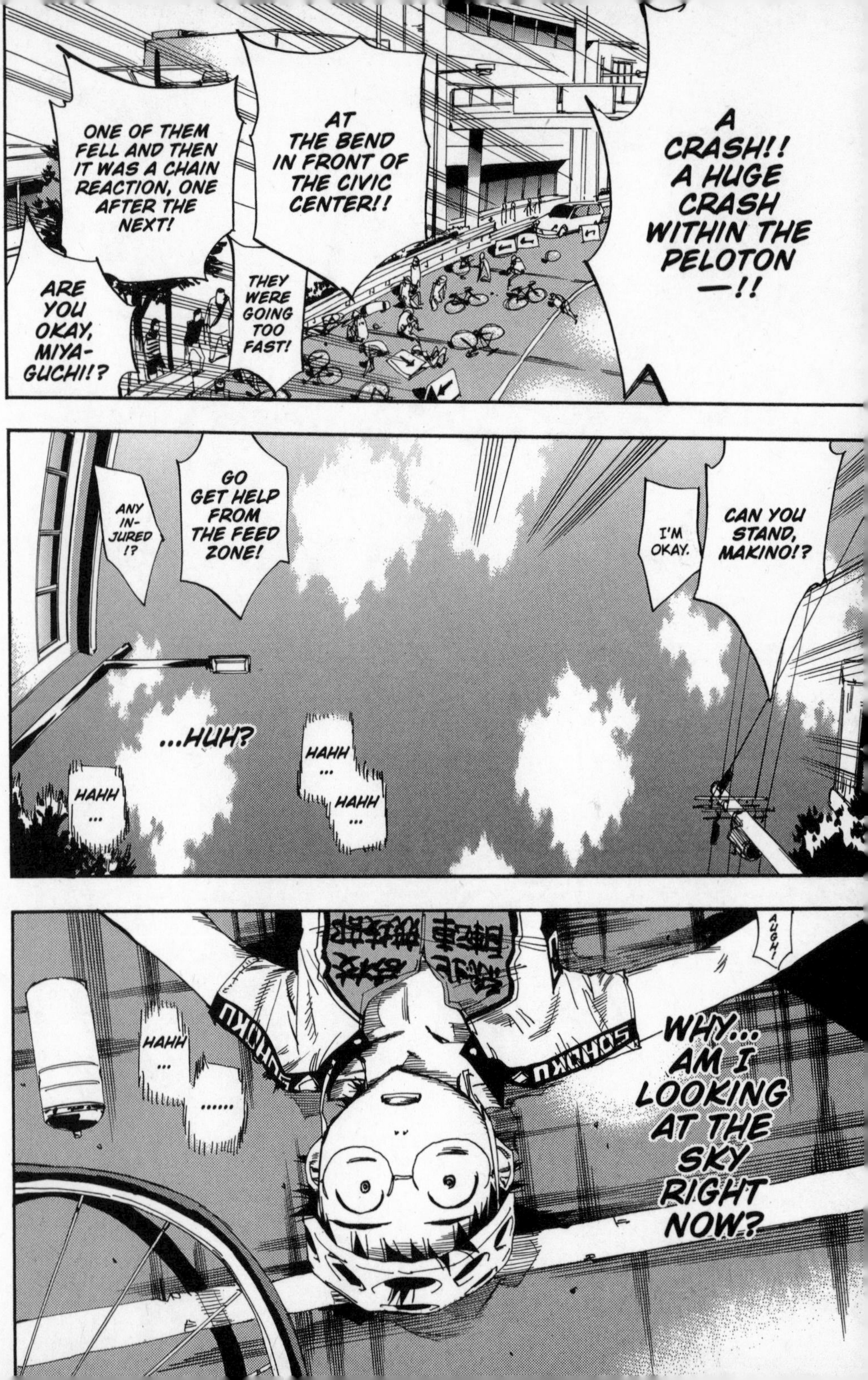
A CRASH!! A HUGE CRASH WITHIN THE PELOTON—!!
AT THE BEND IN FRONT OF THE CIVIC CENTER!!
ONE OF THEM FELL AND THEN IT WAS A CHAIN REACTION, ONE AFTER THE NEXT!
THEY WERE GOING TOO FAST!
ARE YOU OKAY, MIYAGUCHI!?
CAN YOU STAND, MAKINO!?
I'M OKAY.
GO GET HELP FROM THE FEED ZONE!
ANY INJURED!?
HAHH... HAHH...
...HUH?
HAHH...
AUGH!
WHY... AM I LOOKING AT THE SKY RIGHT NOW?
HAHH...
......

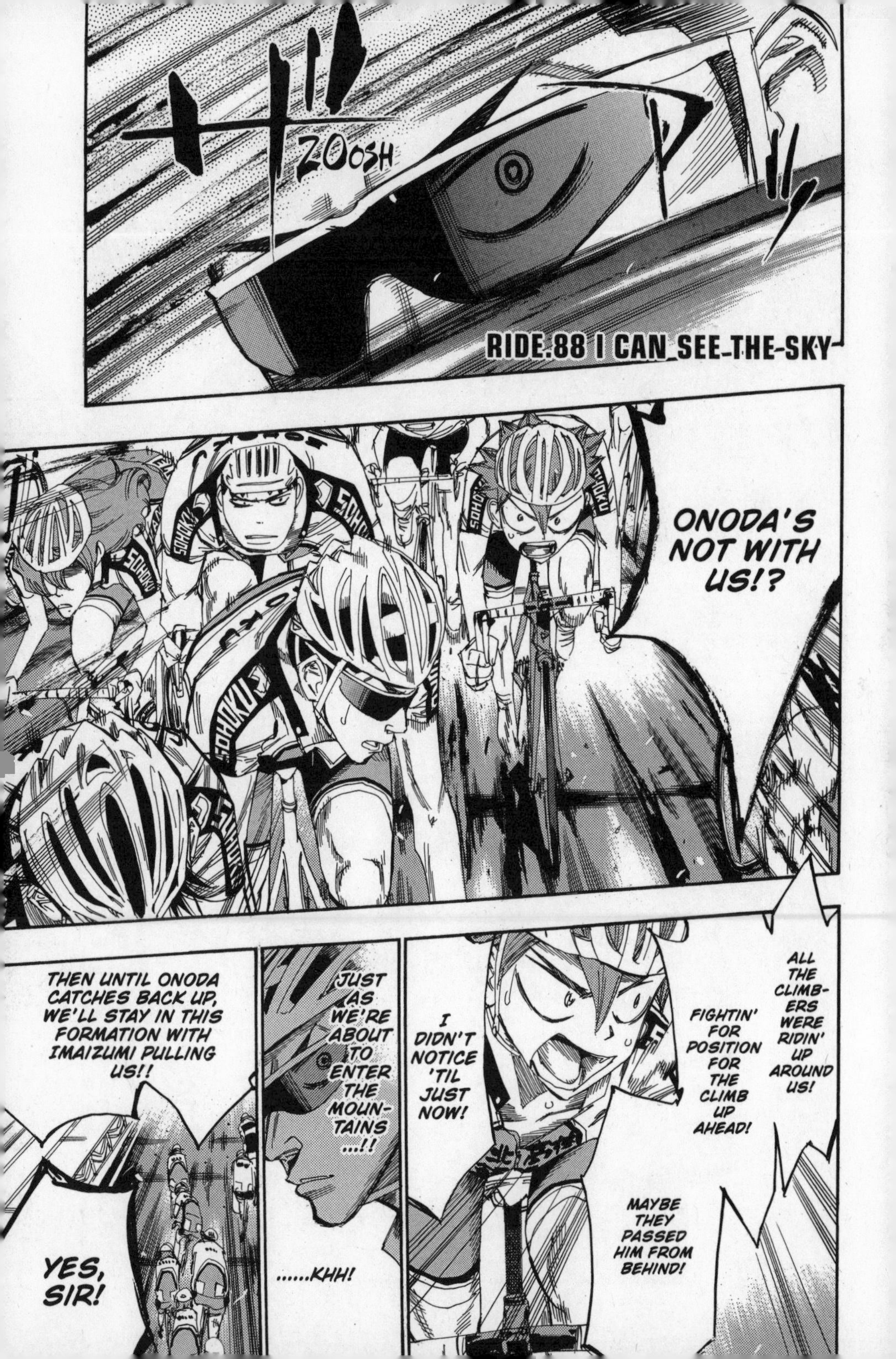
ZOOSH
RIDE.88 I CAN SEE THE SKY
ONODA'S NOT WITH US!?
ALL THE CLIMBERS WERE RIDIN' UP AROUND US!
FIGHTIN' FOR POSITION FOR THE CLIMB UP AHEAD!
MAYBE THEY PASSED HIM FROM BEHIND!
I DIDN'T NOTICE 'TIL JUST NOW!
JUST AS WE'RE ABOUT TO ENTER THE MOUNTAINS ...!!
......KHH!
THEN UNTIL ONODA CATCHES BACK UP, WE'LL STAY IN THIS FORMATION WITH IMAIZUMI PULLING US!!
YES, SIR!

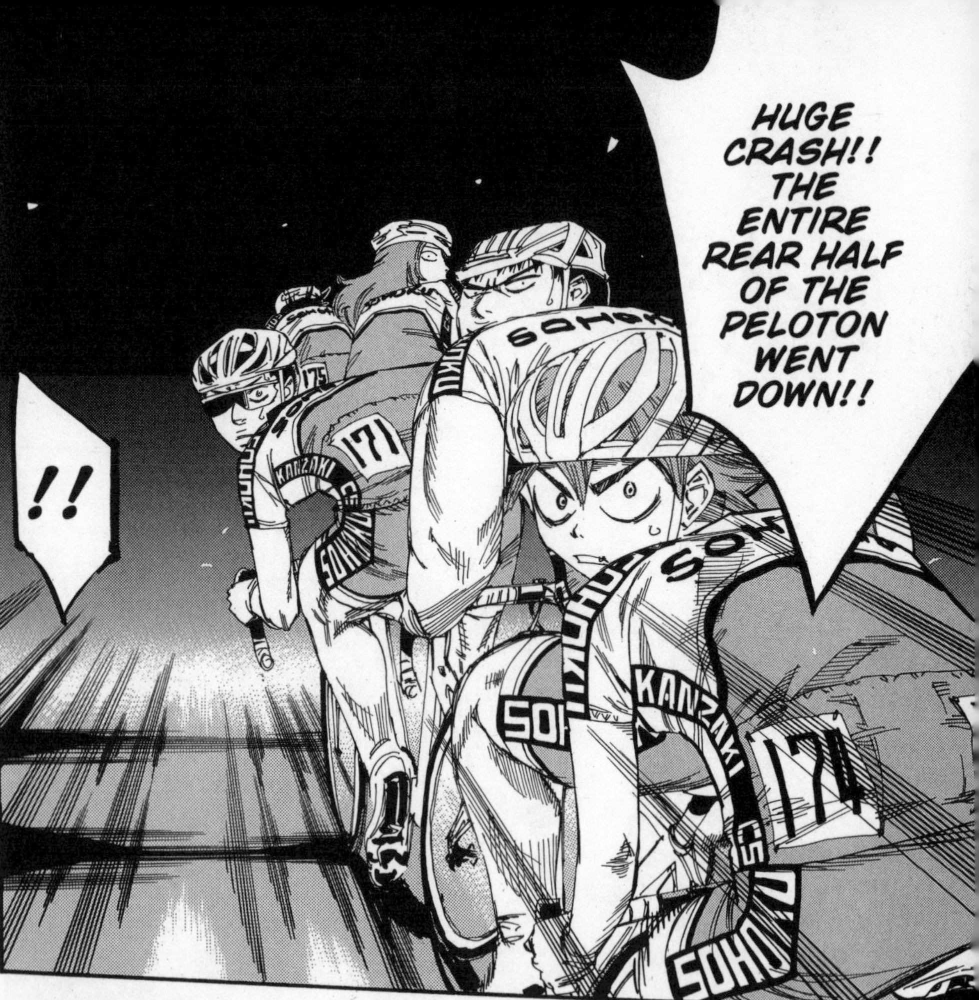
HUGE CRASH!! THE ENTIRE REAR HALF OF THE PELOTON WENT DOWN!!
!!

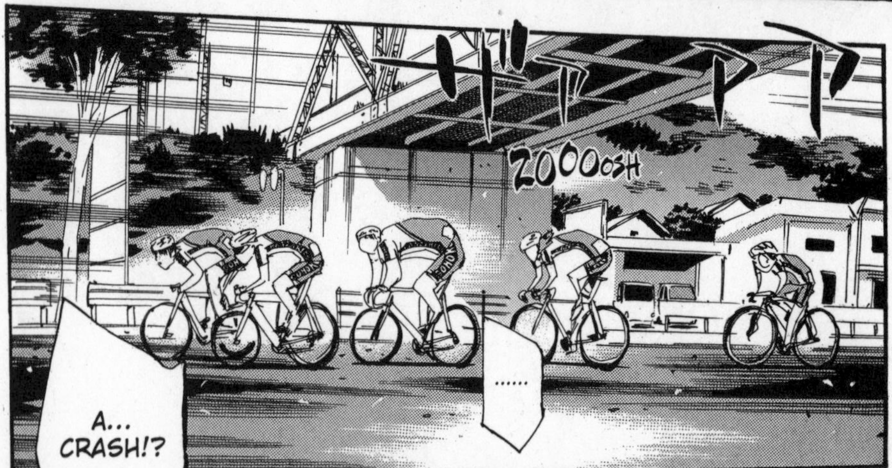
ZOOOOSH
......
A... CRASH!?

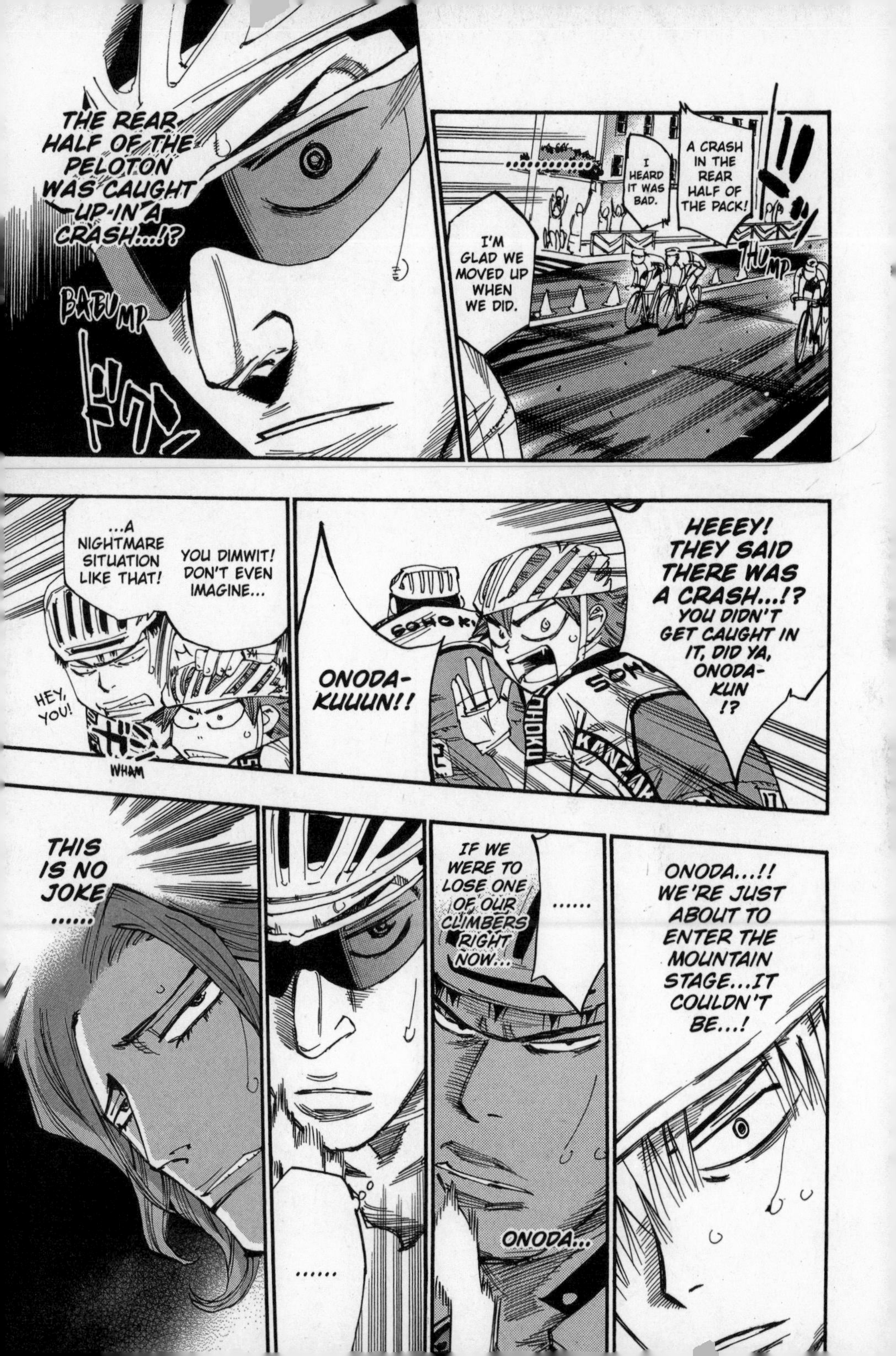
A CRASH IN THE REAR HALF OF THE PACK!
I HEARD IT WAS BAD.
I'M GLAD WE MOVED UP WHEN WE DID.
THUMP
THE REAR HALF OF THE PELOTON WAS CAUGHT UP IN A CRASH...!?
BABUMP
HEEEY! THEY SAID THERE WAS A CRASH...!? YOU DIDN'T GET CAUGHT IN IT, DID YA, ONODA-KUN!?
ONODA-KUUUN!!
YOU DIMWIT! DON'T EVEN IMAGINE...
...A NIGHTMARE SITUATION LIKE THAT!
HEY, YOU!
WHAM
ONODA...!! WE'RE JUST ABOUT TO ENTER THE MOUNTAIN STAGE...IT COULDN'T BE...!
......
IF WE WERE TO LOSE ONE OF OUR CLIMBERS RIGHT NOW...
ONODA...
......
THIS IS NO JOKE......

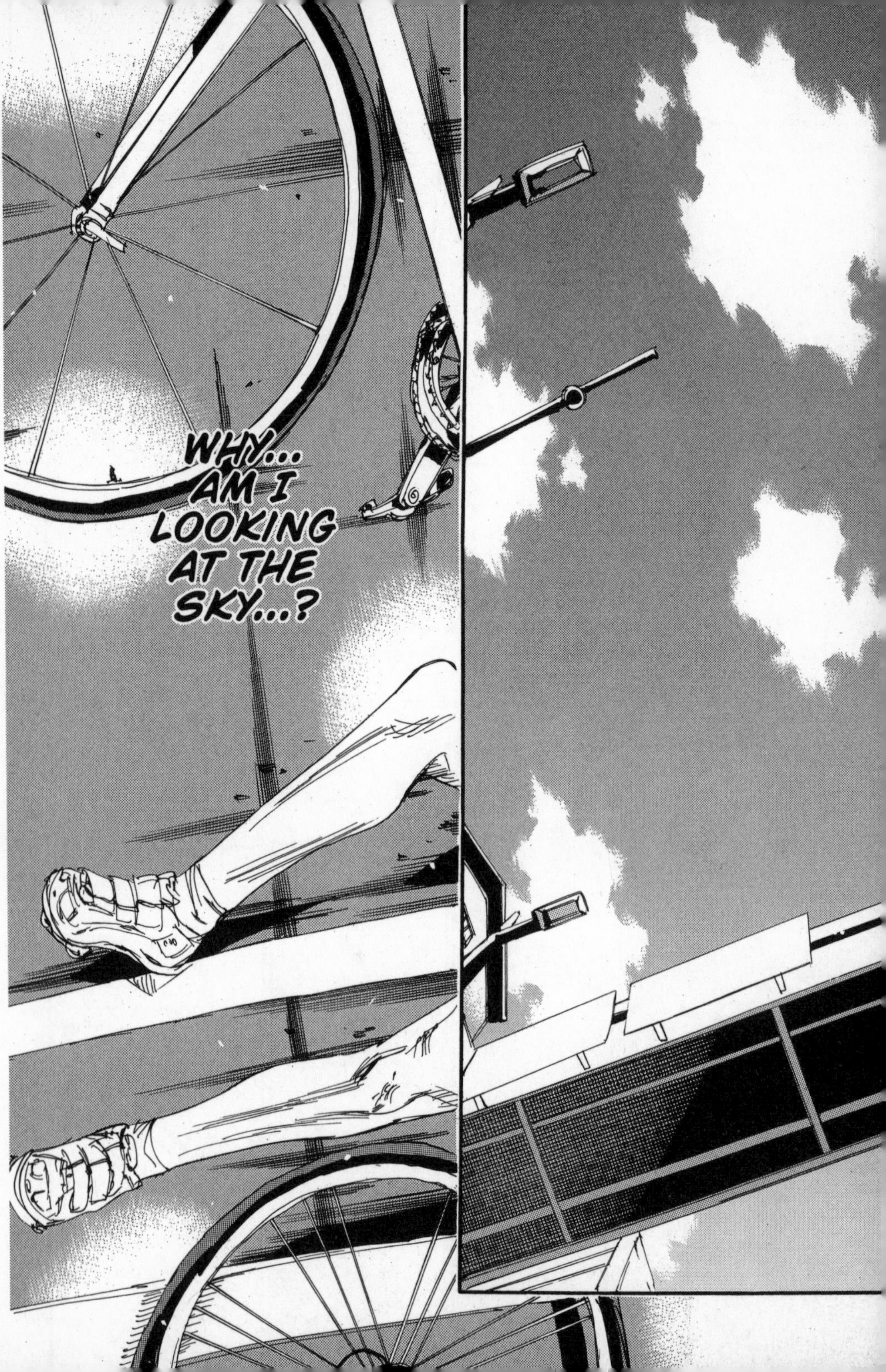
WHY... AM I LOOKING AT THE SKY...?

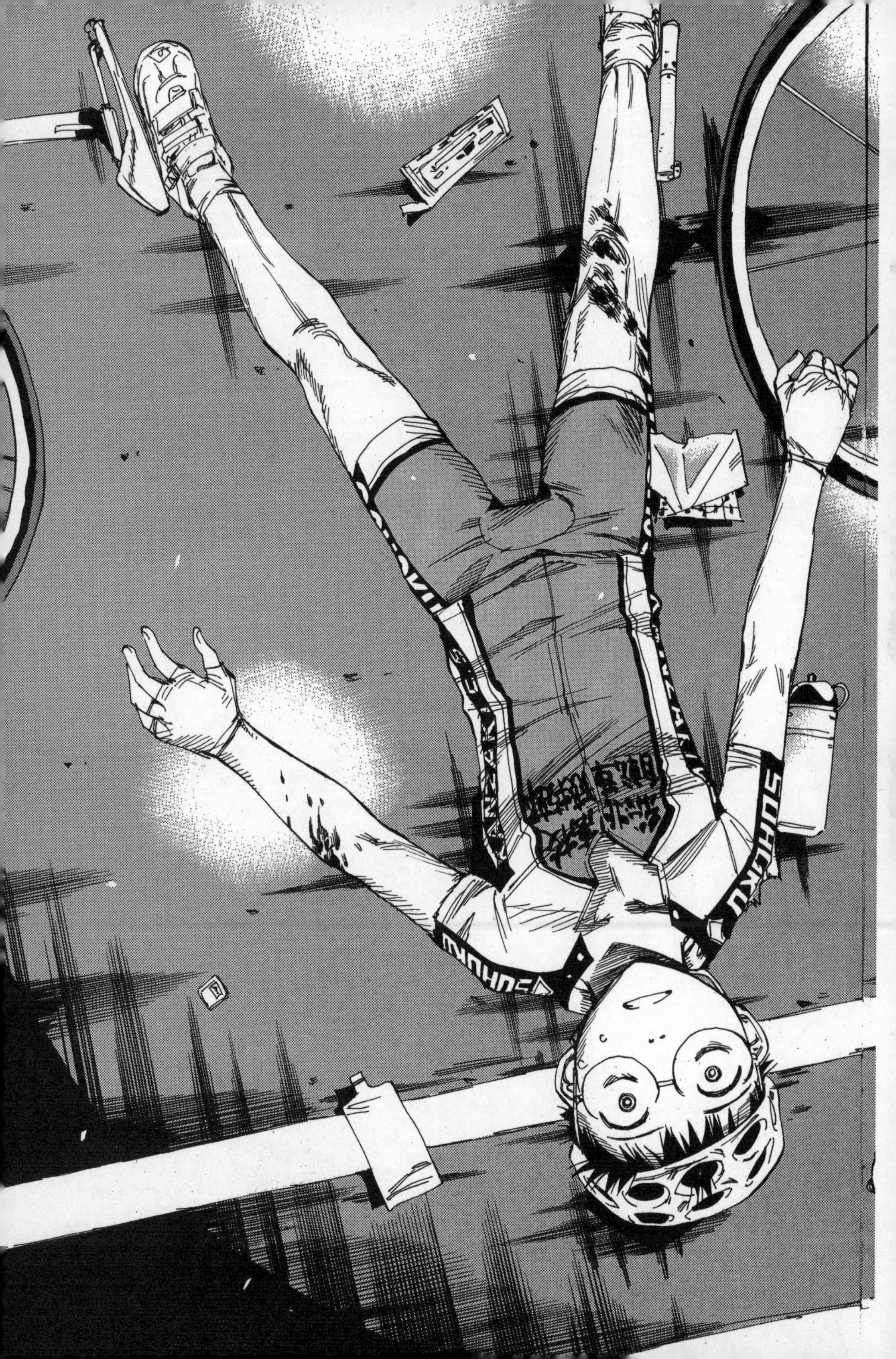

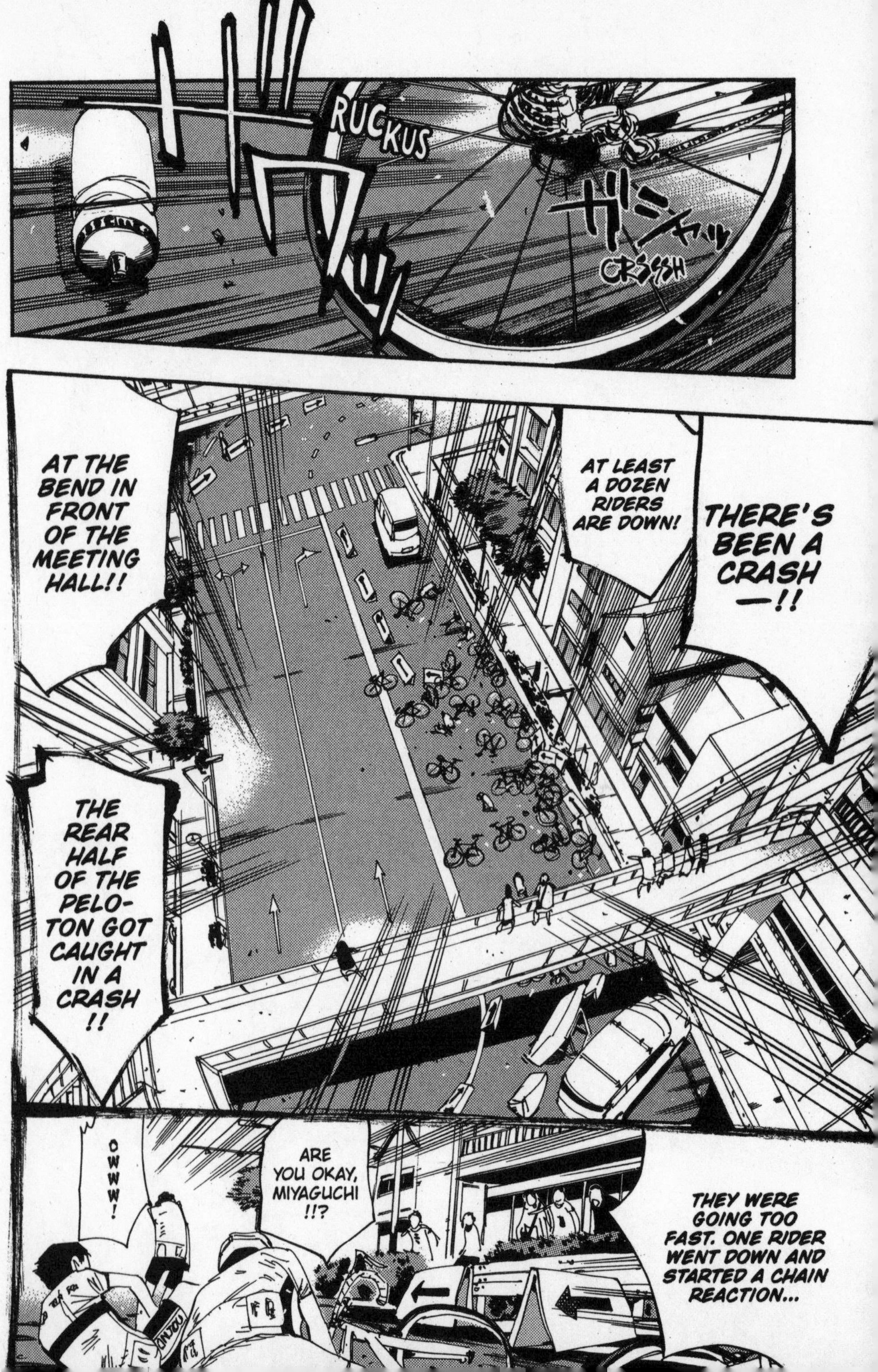
RUCKUS
ガシャッ
CRSSH
THERE'S BEEN A CRASH—!!
AT LEAST A DOZEN RIDERS ARE DOWN!
AT THE BEND IN FRONT OF THE MEETING HALL!!
THE REAR HALF OF THE PELOTON GOT CAUGHT IN A CRASH!!
THEY WERE GOING TOO FAST. ONE RIDER WENT DOWN AND STARTED A CHAIN REACTION...
ARE YOU OKAY, MIYAGUCHI!!?
OWWW!

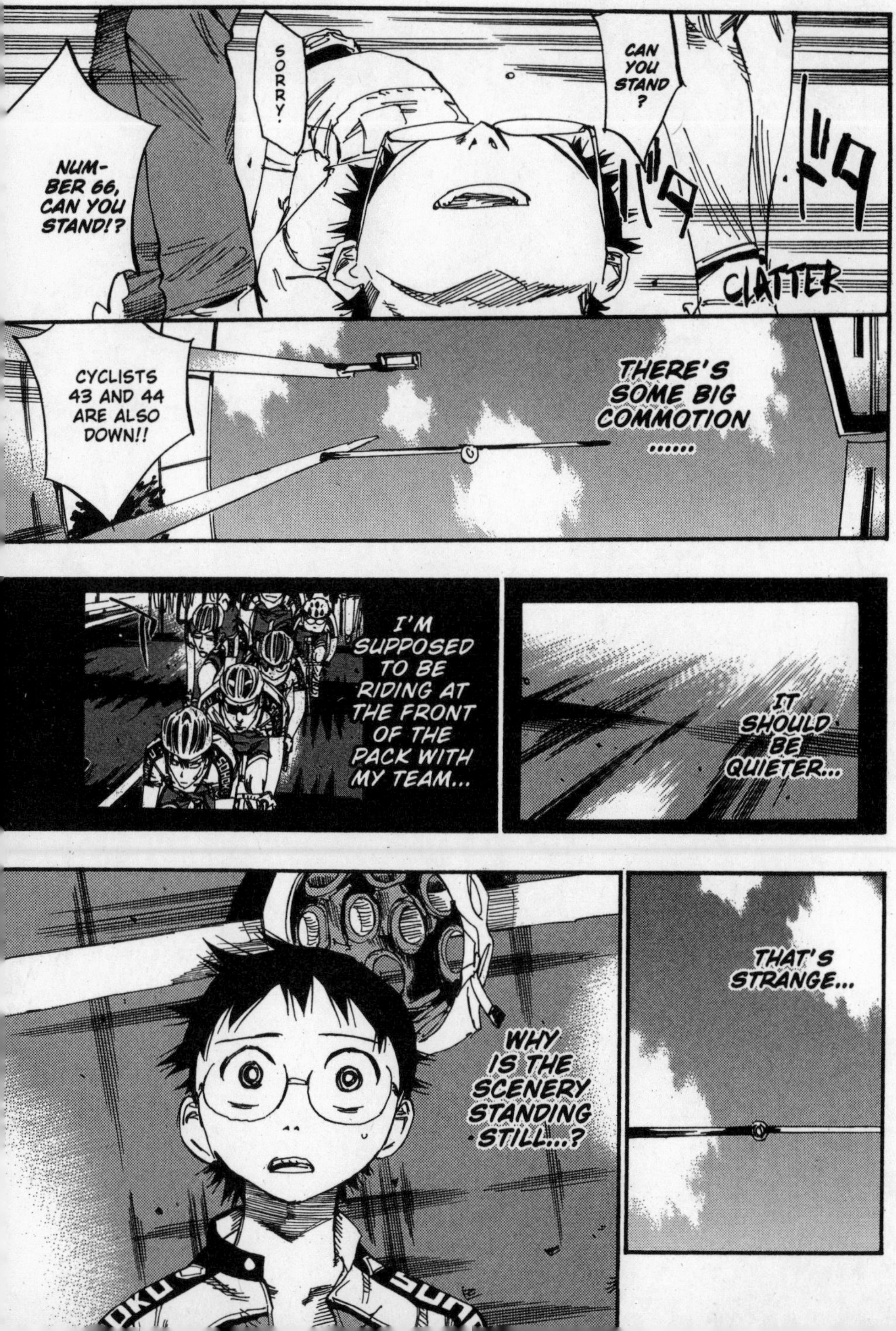
CAN YOU STAND?
SORRY.
NUMBER 66, CAN YOU STAND!?
CLATTER
THERE'S SOME BIG COMMOTION ......
CYCLISTS 43 AND 44 ARE ALSO DOWN!!
IT SHOULD BE QUIETER...
I'M SUPPOSED TO BE RIDING AT THE FRONT OF THE PACK WITH MY TEAM...
THAT'S STRANGE...
WHY IS THE SCENERY STANDING STILL...?

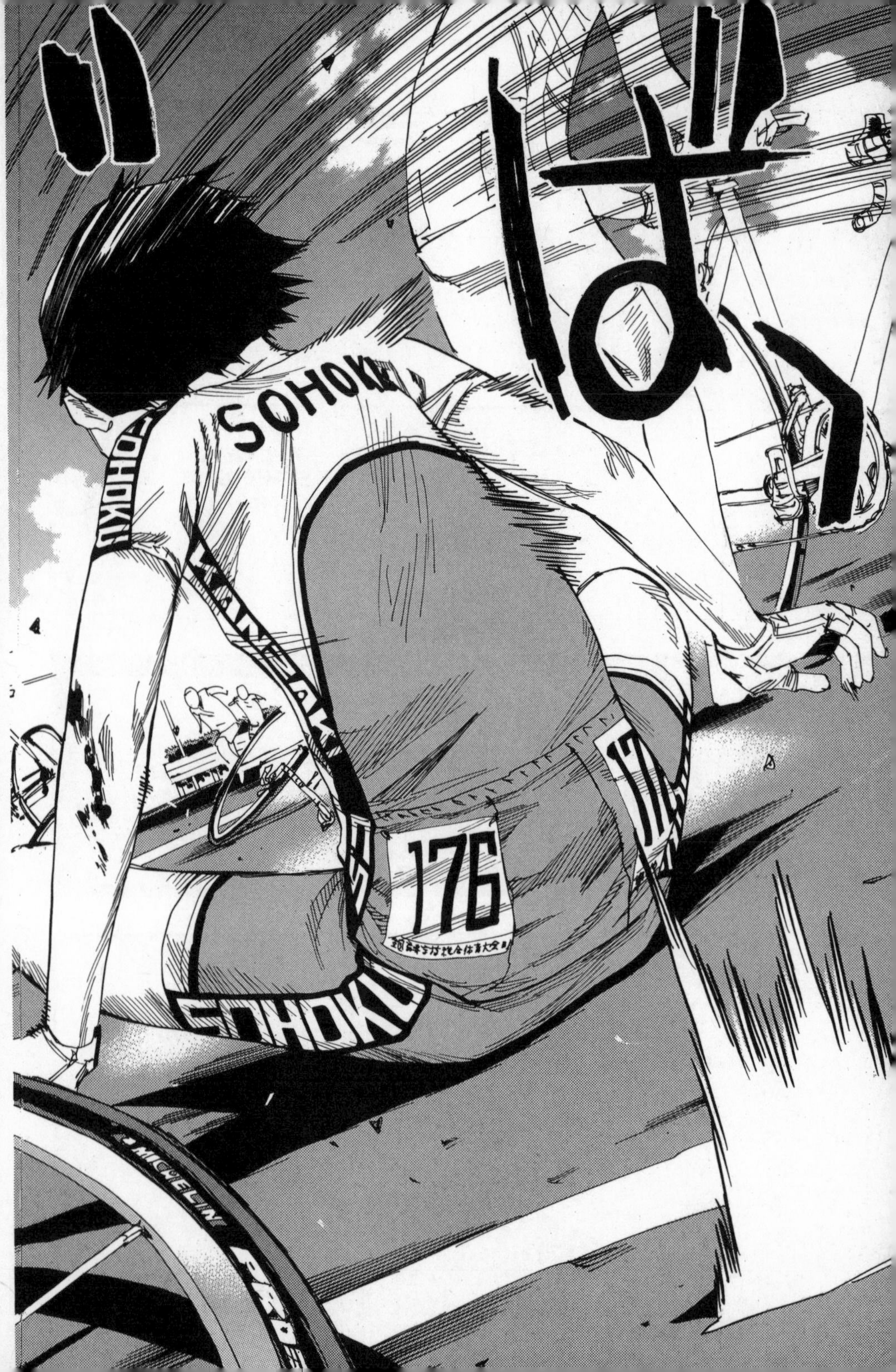
ば
SOHOKU
SOHOKU
176
SOHOKU

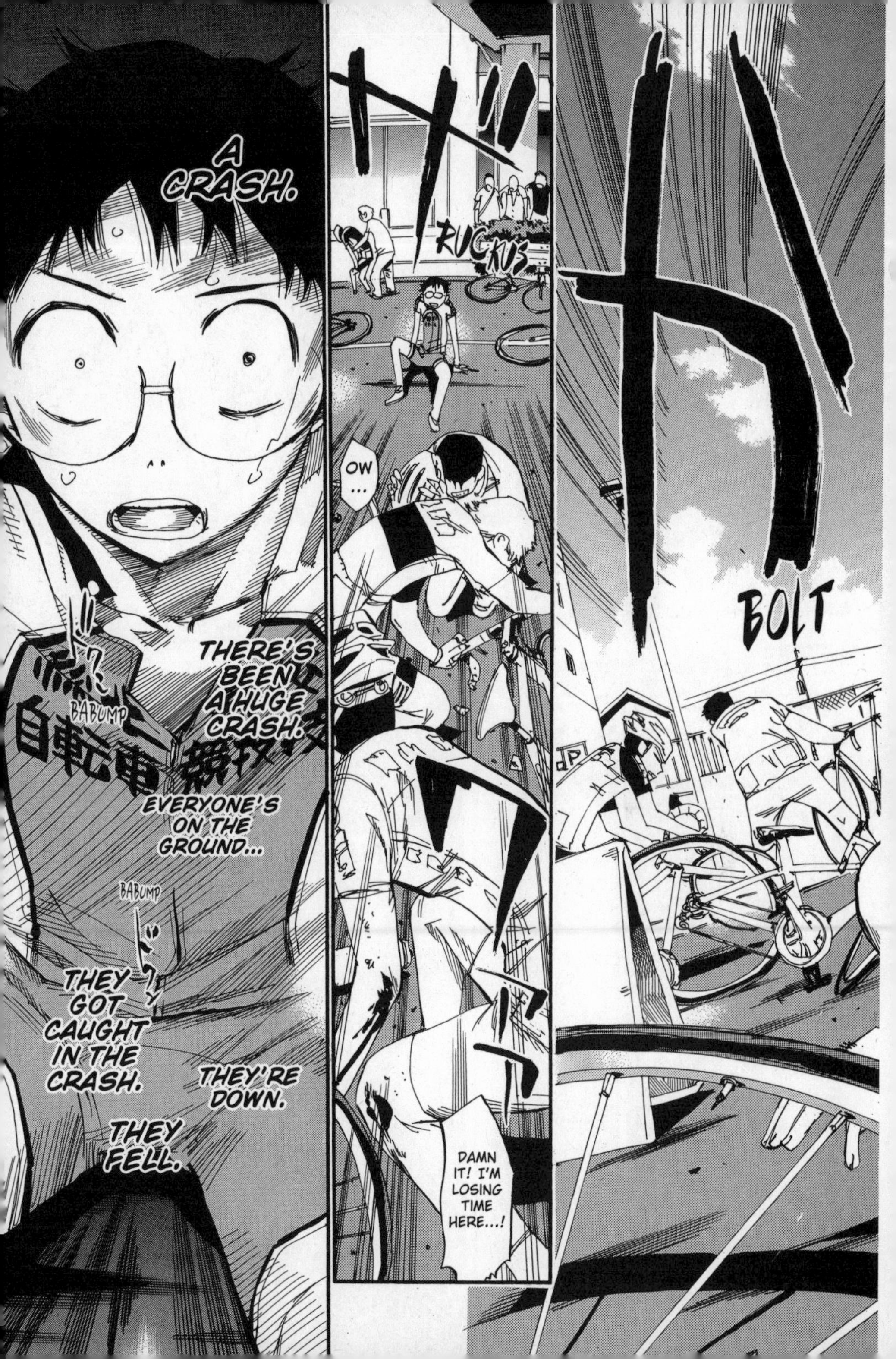
BOLT
RUCKUS
OW ...
DAMN IT! I'M LOSING TIME HERE...!
A CRASH.
THERE'S BEEN A HUGE CRASH.
BABUMP
EVERYONE'S ON THE GROUND...
BABUMP
THEY'RE DOWN.
THEY GOT CAUGHT IN THE CRASH.
THEY FELL.

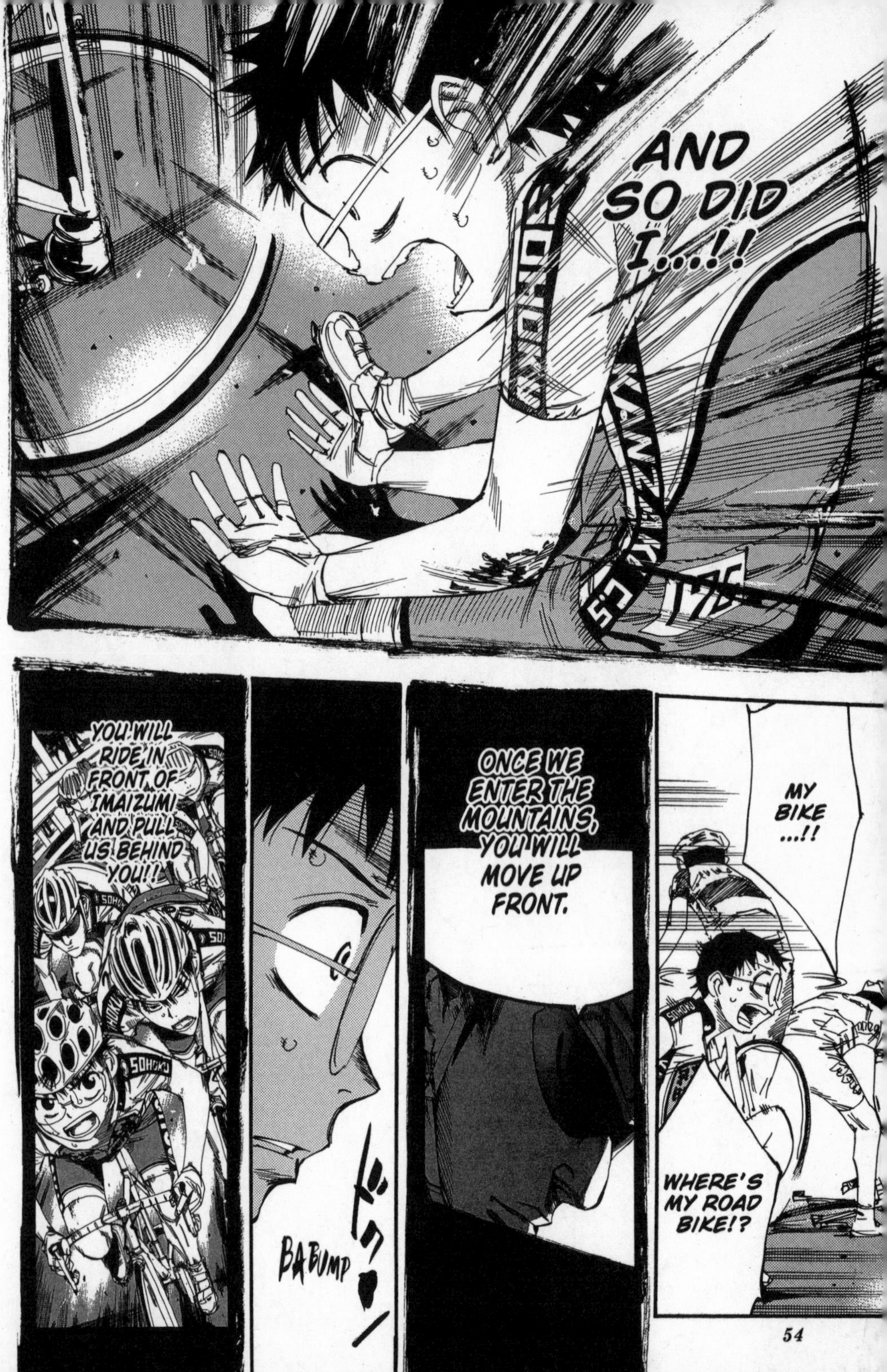
AND SO DID I...!!
MY BIKE ...!!
WHERE'S MY ROAD BIKE!?
ONCE WE ENTER THE MOUNTAINS, YOU WILL MOVE UP FRONT.
BABUMP
YOU WILL RIDE IN FRONT OF IMAIZUMI AND PULL US BEHIND YOU!!

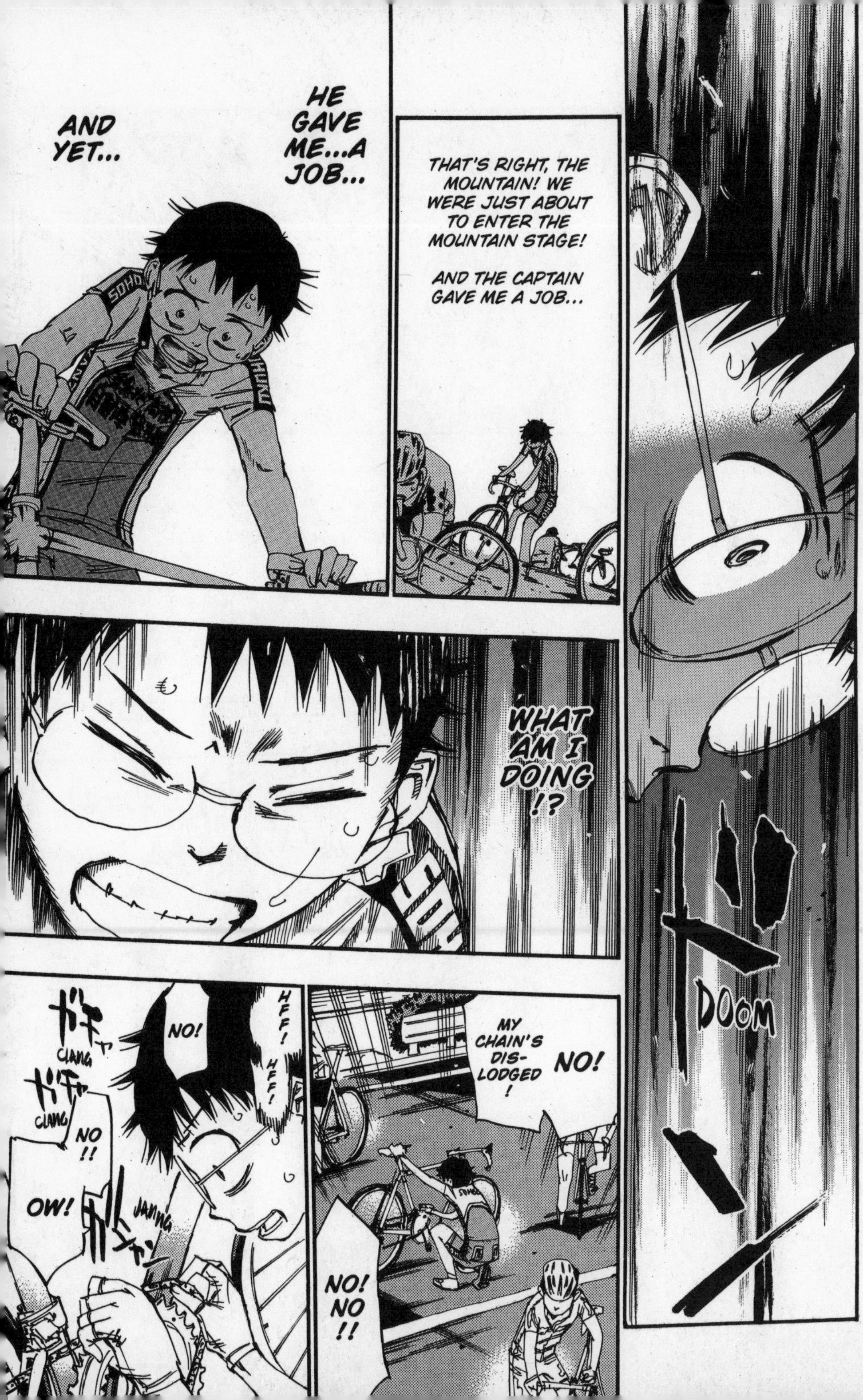
DOOM
THAT'S RIGHT, THE MOUNTAIN! WE WERE JUST ABOUT TO ENTER THE MOUNTAIN STAGE!
AND THE CAPTAIN GAVE ME A JOB...
HE GAVE ME...A JOB...
AND YET...
WHAT AM I DOING!?
NO!
MY CHAIN'S DIS-LODGED!
NO! NO!!
HFF! HFF!
NO!
CLANG
CLANG
NO!!
OW!
JANNG

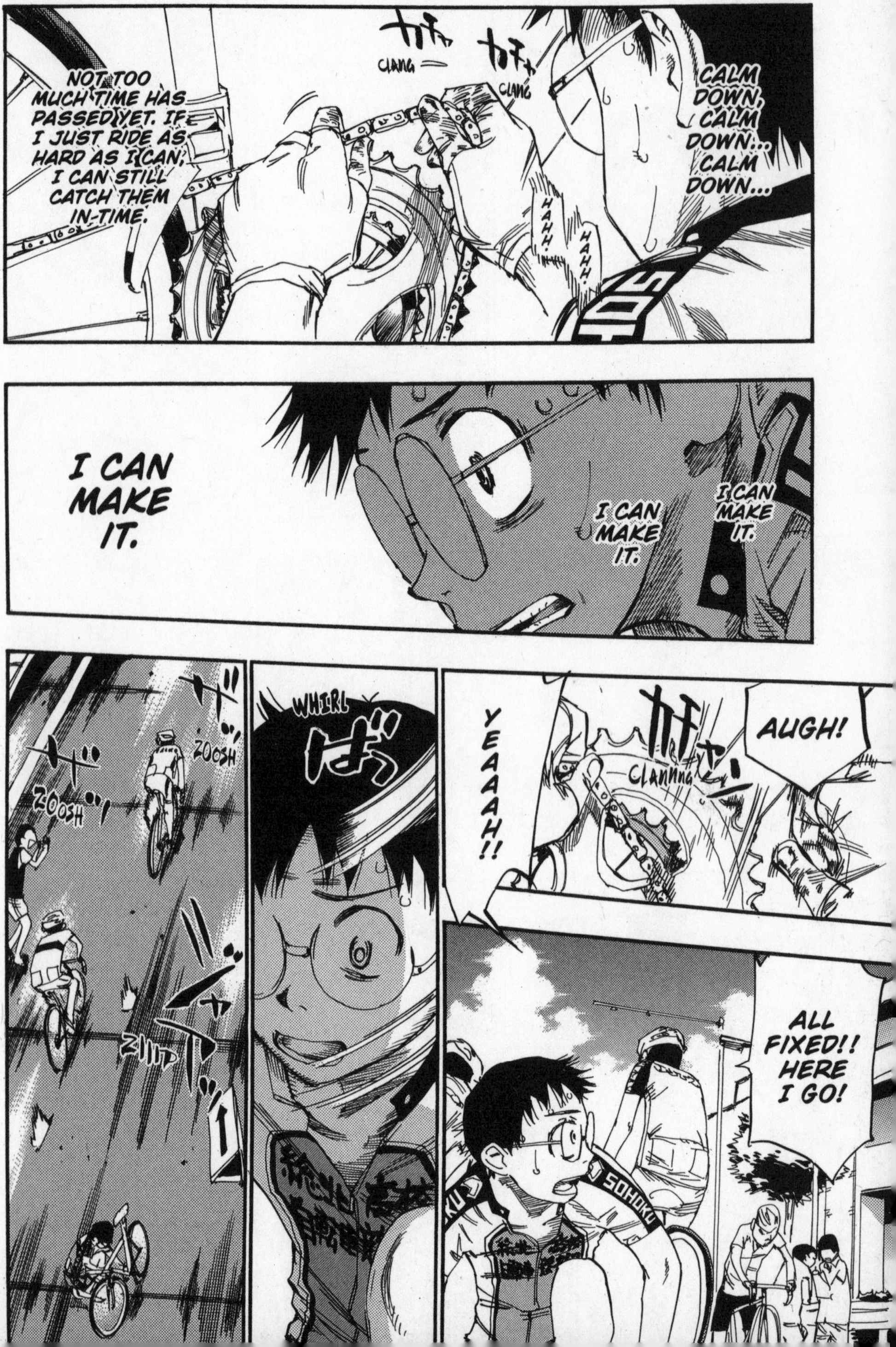
CALM DOWN, CALM DOWN... CALM DOWN...
カチャ
CLANG
カチャ
CLANG
HAHH!
HAHH!
NOT TOO MUCH TIME HAS PASSED YET. IF I JUST RIDE AS HARD AS I CAN, I CAN STILL CATCH THEM IN TIME.
I CAN MAKE IT.
I CAN MAKE IT.
I CAN MAKE IT.
AUGH!
カチャッ
CLANNNG
YEAAAAH!!
ALL FIXED!! HERE I GO!
WHIRL
ばっ
ZOOSH
ZOOSH
ZIIIP

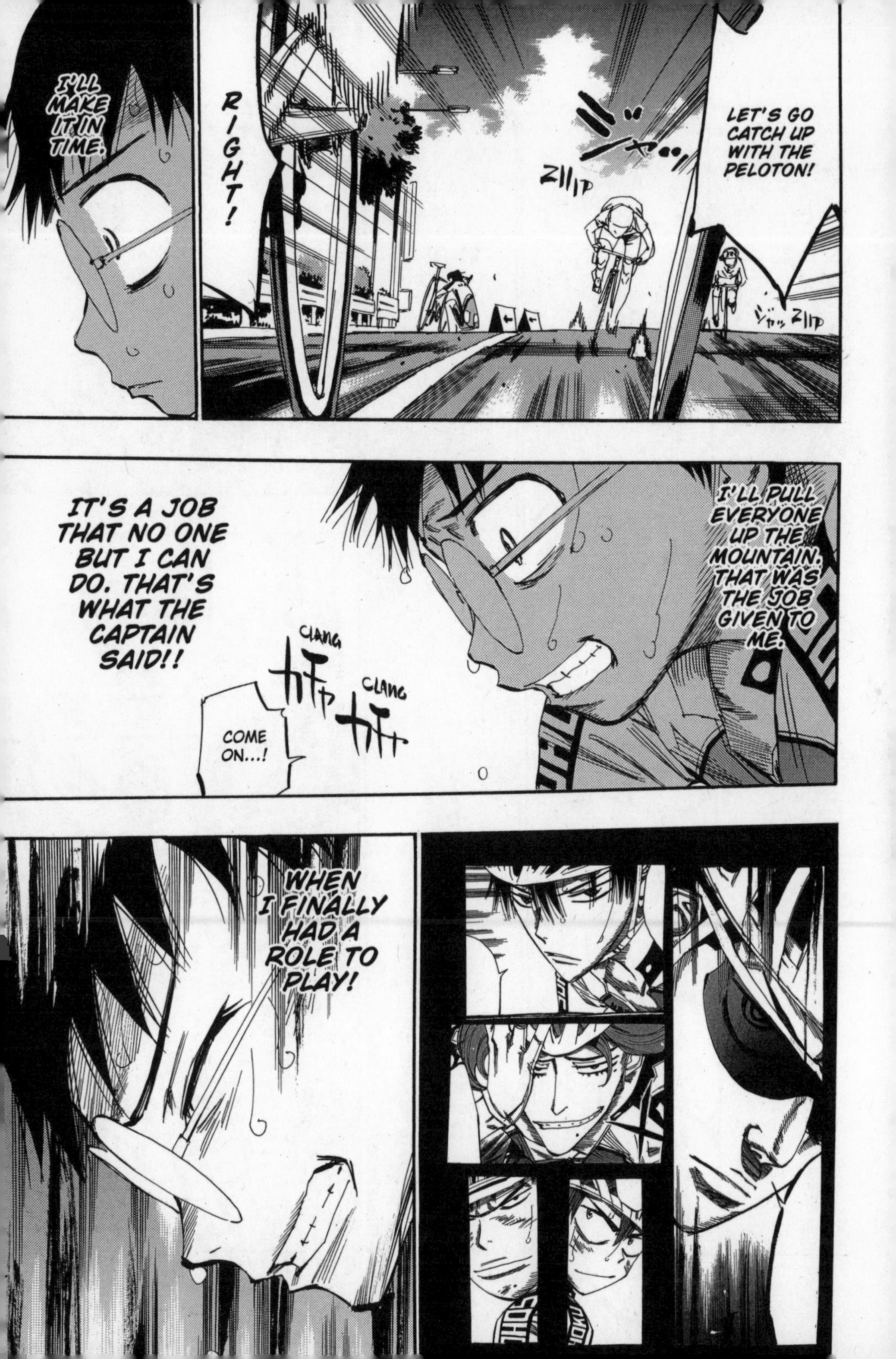
LET'S GO CATCH UP WITH THE PELOTON!
ZIIIP
RIGHT!
ZIIIP
I'LL MAKE IT IN TIME.
I'LL PULL EVERYONE UP THE MOUNTAIN. THAT WAS THE JOB GIVEN TO ME.
IT'S A JOB THAT NO ONE BUT I CAN DO. THAT'S WHAT THE CAPTAIN SAID!!
CLANG
CLANG
COME ON...!
WHEN I FINALLY HAD A ROLE TO PLAY!

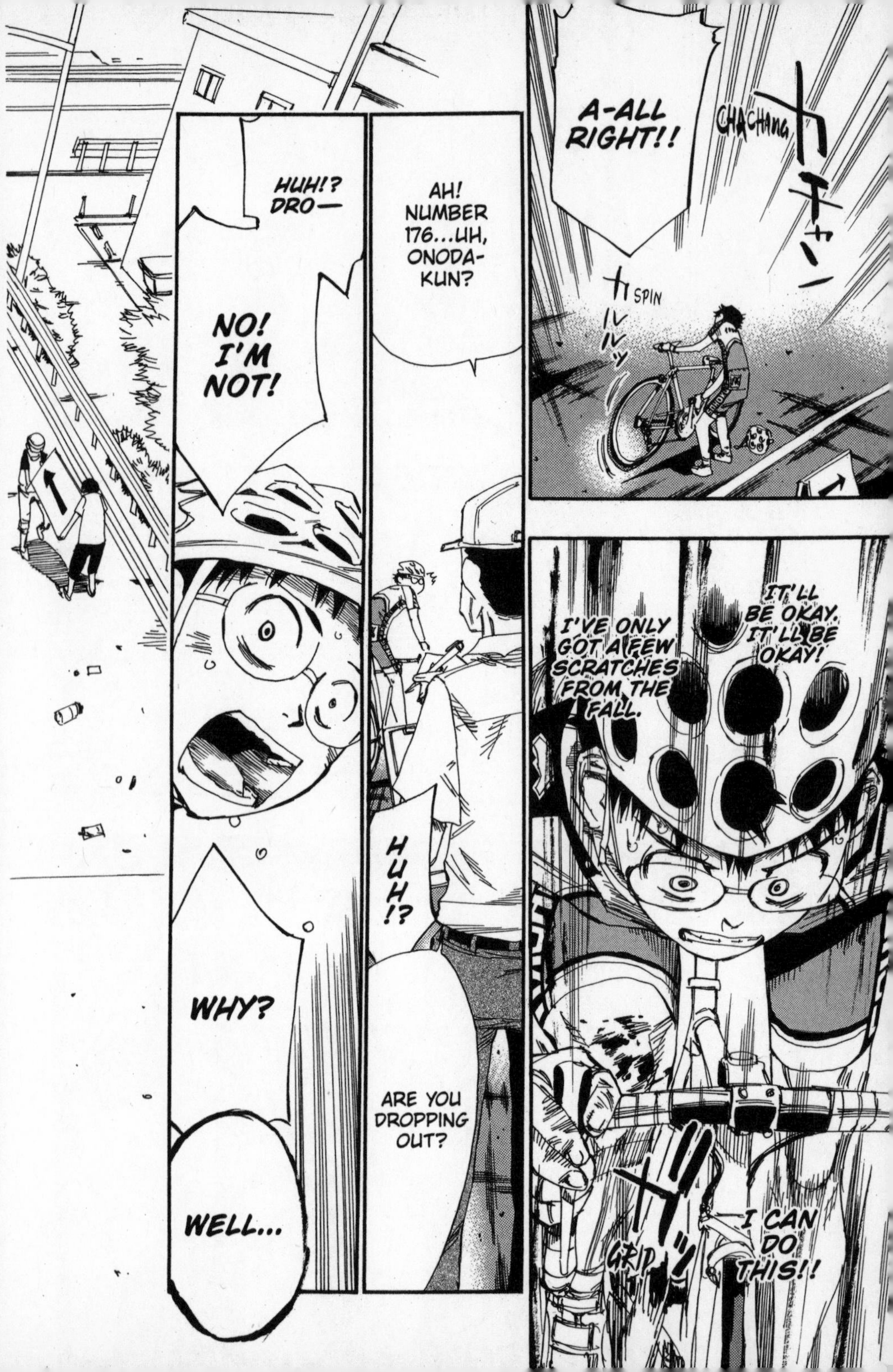
A-ALL RIGHT!!
CHACHANG
SPIN
I'VE ONLY GOT A FEW SCRATCHES FROM THE FALL.
IT'LL BE OKAY. IT'LL BE OKAY!
I CAN DO THIS!!
GRIP
AH! NUMBER 176...UH, ONODA-KUN?
HUH!?
ARE YOU DROPPING OUT?
HUH!? DRO—
NO! I'M NOT!
WHY?
WELL...

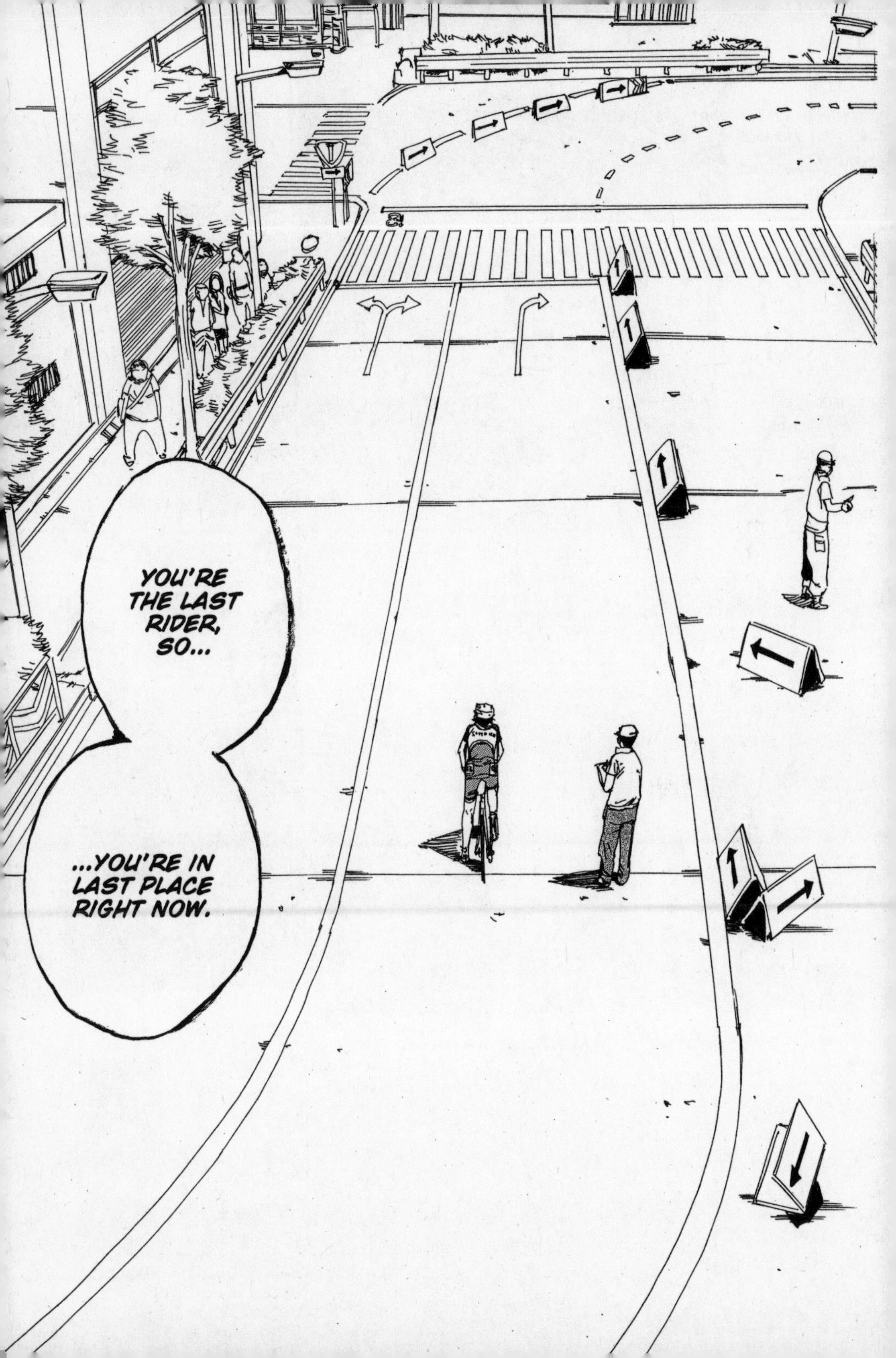
YOU'RE THE LAST RIDER, SO...
...YOU'RE IN LAST PLACE RIGHT NOW.

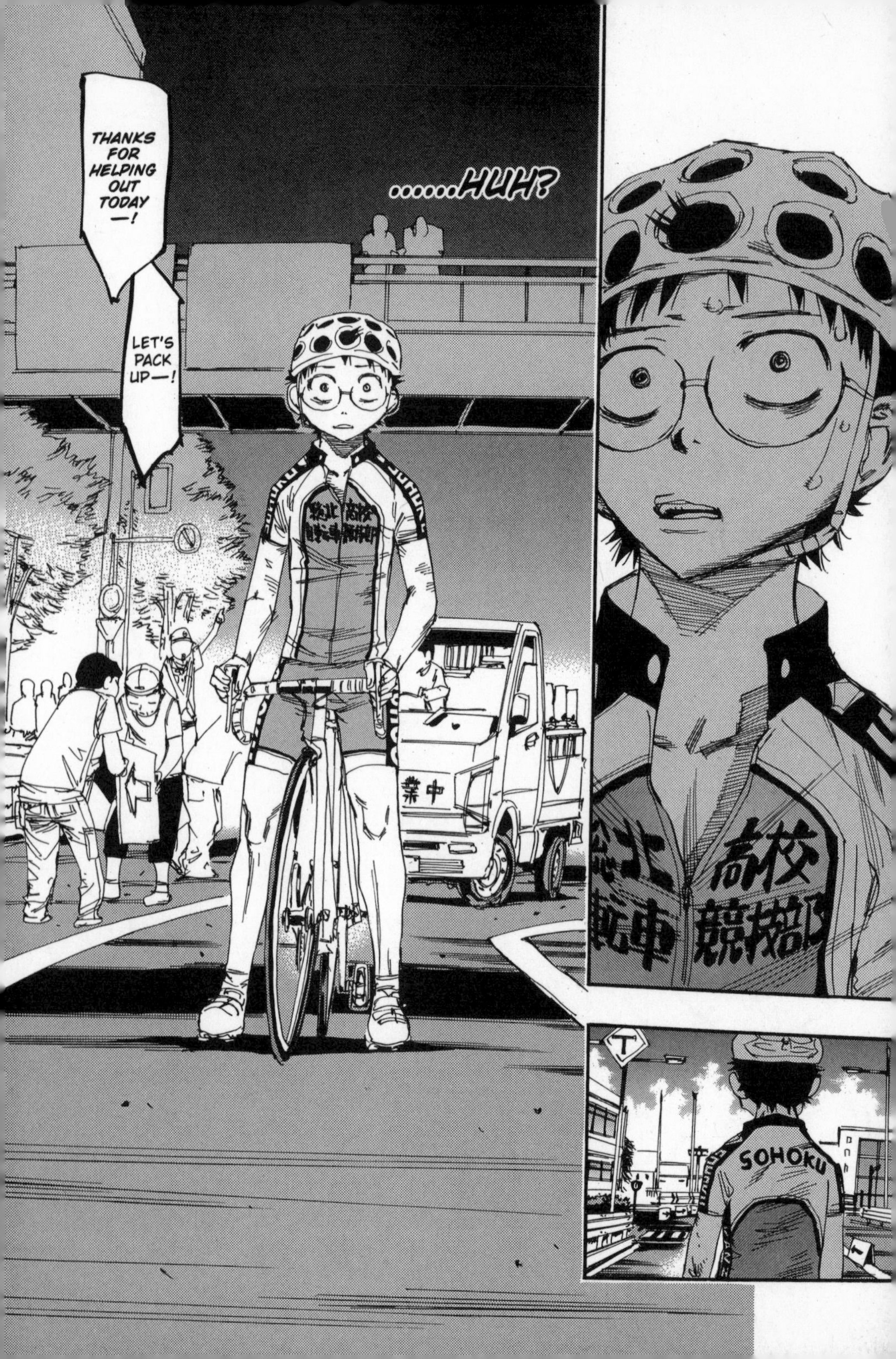
高校
競技部
SOHOKU
THANKS FOR HELPING OUT TODAY—!
LET'S PACK UP—!
......HUH?

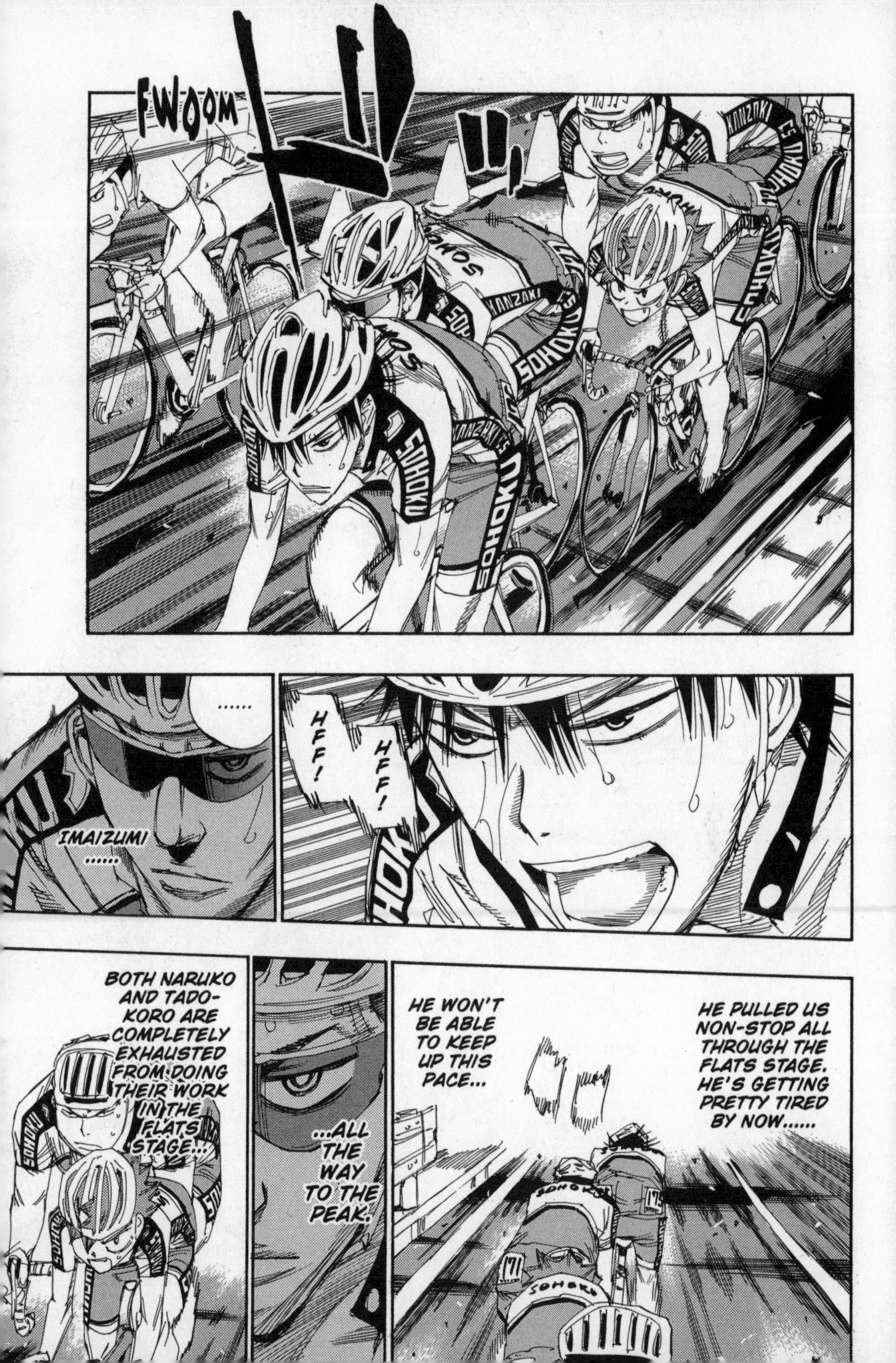
FWOOM
HFF! HFF!
......
IMAIZUMI ......
HE PULLED US NON-STOP ALL THROUGH THE FLATS STAGE. HE'S GETTING PRETTY TIRED BY NOW......
HE WON'T BE ABLE TO KEEP UP THIS PACE...
...ALL THE WAY TO THE PEAK.
BOTH NARUKO AND TADO-KORO ARE COMPLETELY EXHAUSTED FROM DOING THEIR WORK IN THE FLATS STAGE...

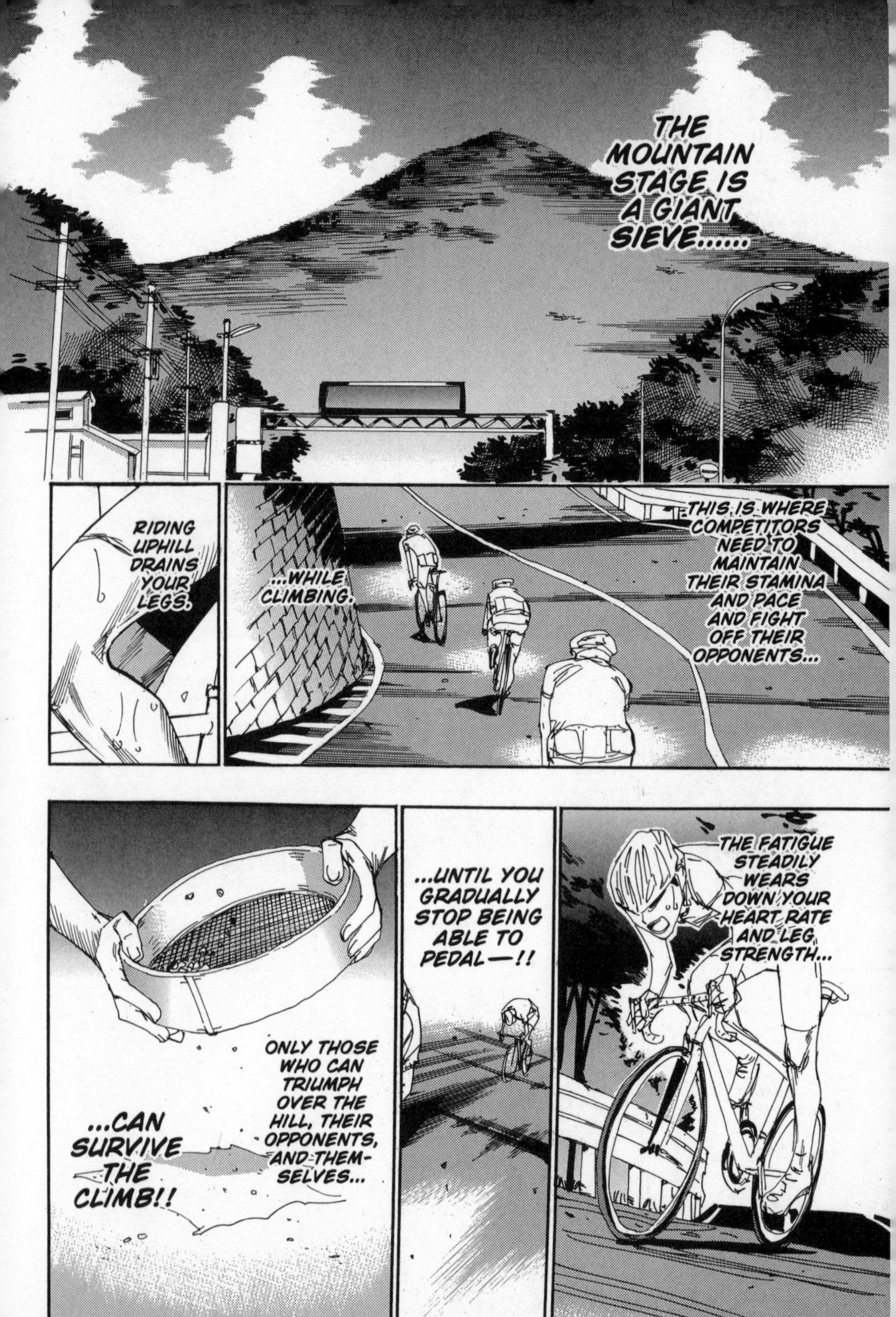
THE MOUNTAIN STAGE IS A GIANT SIEVE......
THIS IS WHERE COMPETITORS NEED TO MAINTAIN THEIR STAMINA AND PACE AND FIGHT OFF THEIR OPPONENTS...
...WHILE CLIMBING.
RIDING UPHILL DRAINS YOUR LEGS.
THE FATIGUE STEADILY WEARS DOWN YOUR HEART RATE AND LEG STRENGTH...
...UNTIL YOU GRADUALLY STOP BEING ABLE TO PEDAL—!!
ONLY THOSE WHO CAN TRIUMPH OVER THE HILL, THEIR OPPONENTS, AND THEM-SELVES...
...CAN SURVIVE THE CLIMB!!

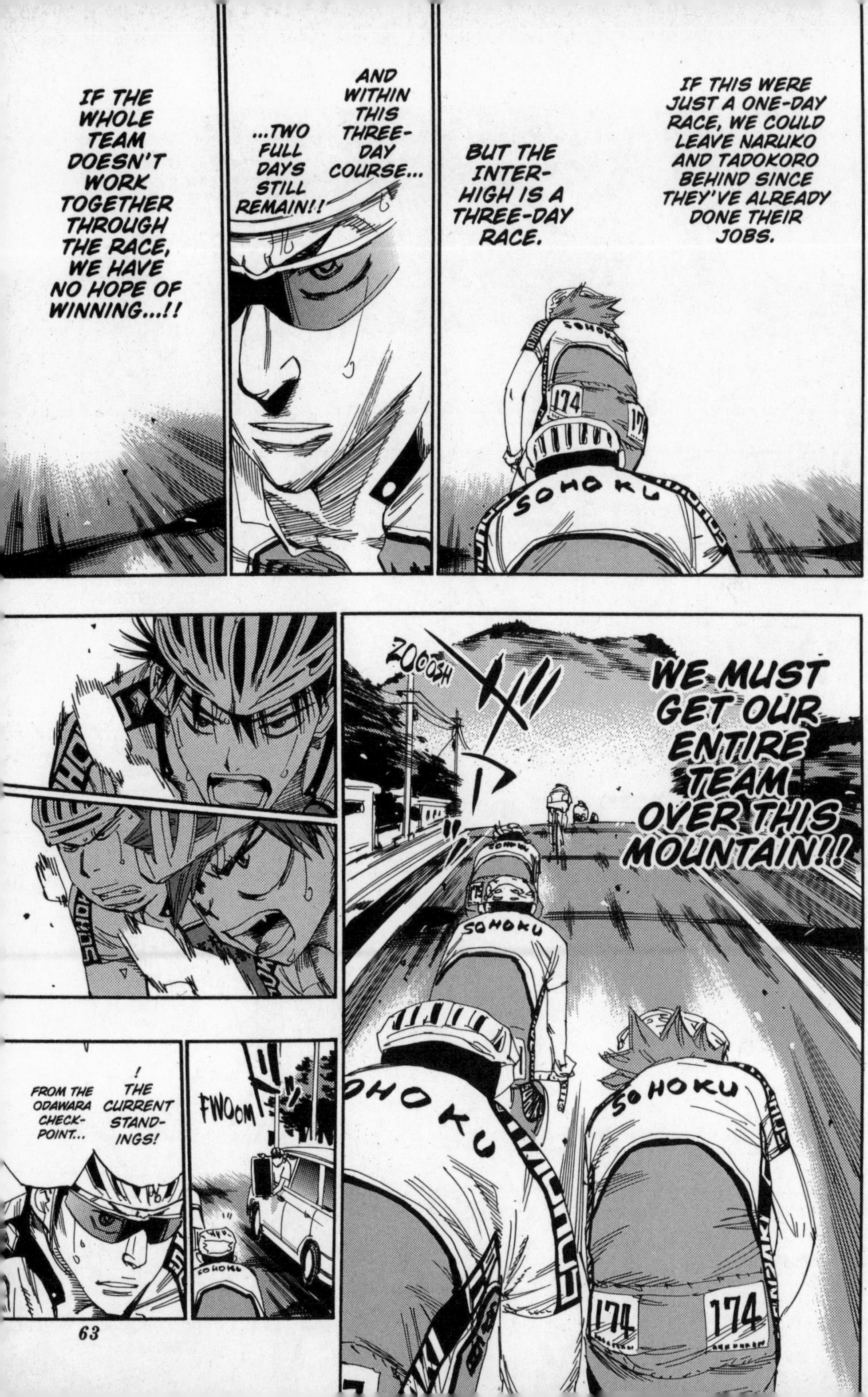
IF THIS WERE JUST A ONE-DAY RACE, WE COULD LEAVE NARUKO AND TADOKORO BEHIND SINCE THEY'VE ALREADY DONE THEIR JOBS.
BUT THE INTER-HIGH IS A THREE-DAY RACE.
AND WITHIN THIS THREE-DAY COURSE...
...TWO FULL DAYS STILL REMAIN!!
IF THE WHOLE TEAM DOESN'T WORK TOGETHER THROUGH THE RACE, WE HAVE NO HOPE OF WINNING...!!
ZOOOSH
WE MUST GET OUR ENTIRE TEAM OVER THIS MOUNTAIN!!
FWOOM
! THE CURRENT STANDINGS!
FROM THE ODAWARA CHECK-POINT...

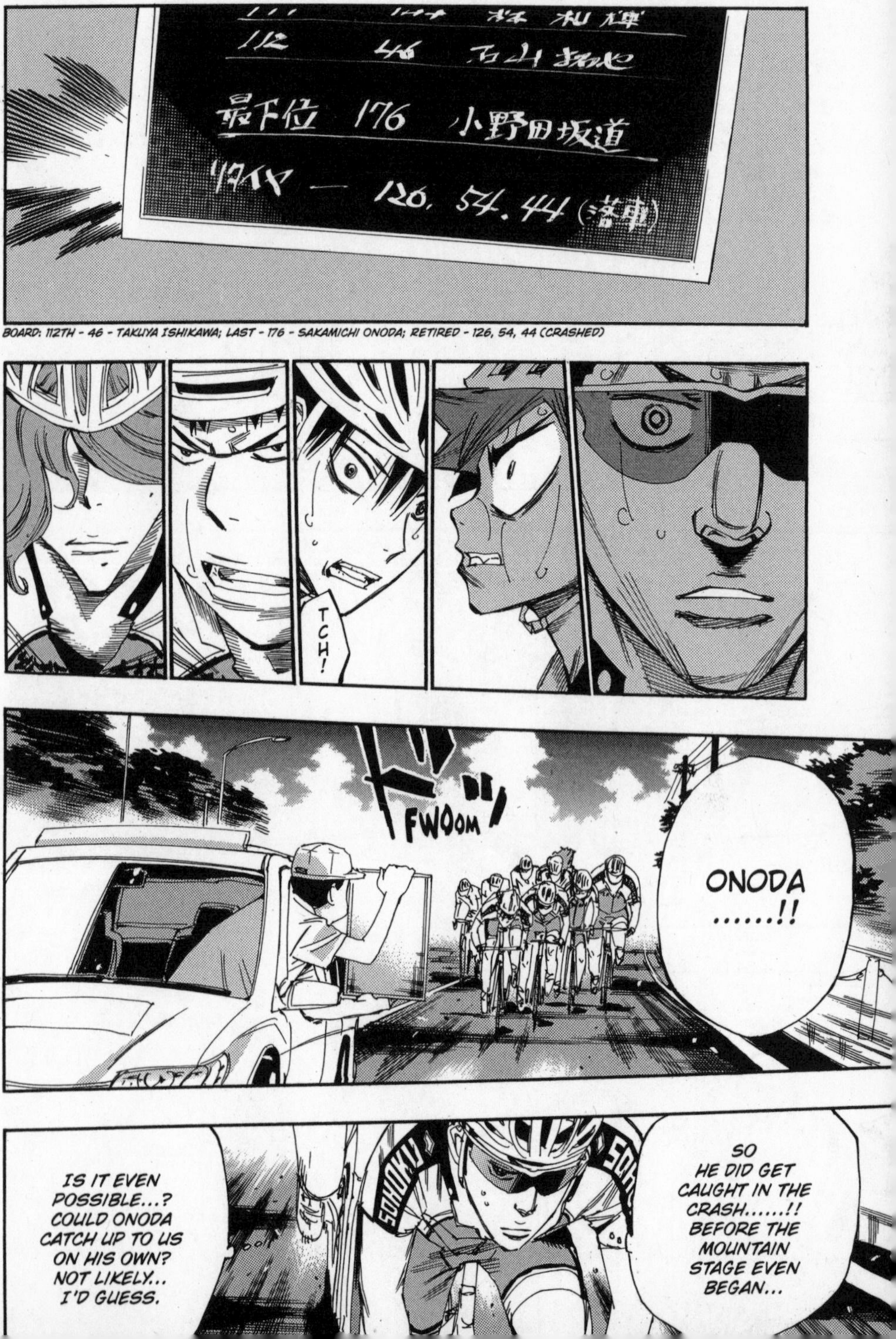
最下位 176 小野田坂道
リタイア ー 126, 54, 44 (落車)
BOARD: 112TH - 46 - TAKUYA ISHIKAWA; LAST - 176 - SAKAMICHI ONODA; RETIRED - 126, 54, 44 (CRASHED)
TCH!
FWOOM
ONODA ......!!
SO HE DID GET CAUGHT IN THE CRASH......!! BEFORE THE MOUNTAIN STAGE EVEN BEGAN...
IS IT EVEN POSSIBLE...? COULD ONODA CATCH UP TO US ON HIS OWN? NOT LIKELY... I'D GUESS.

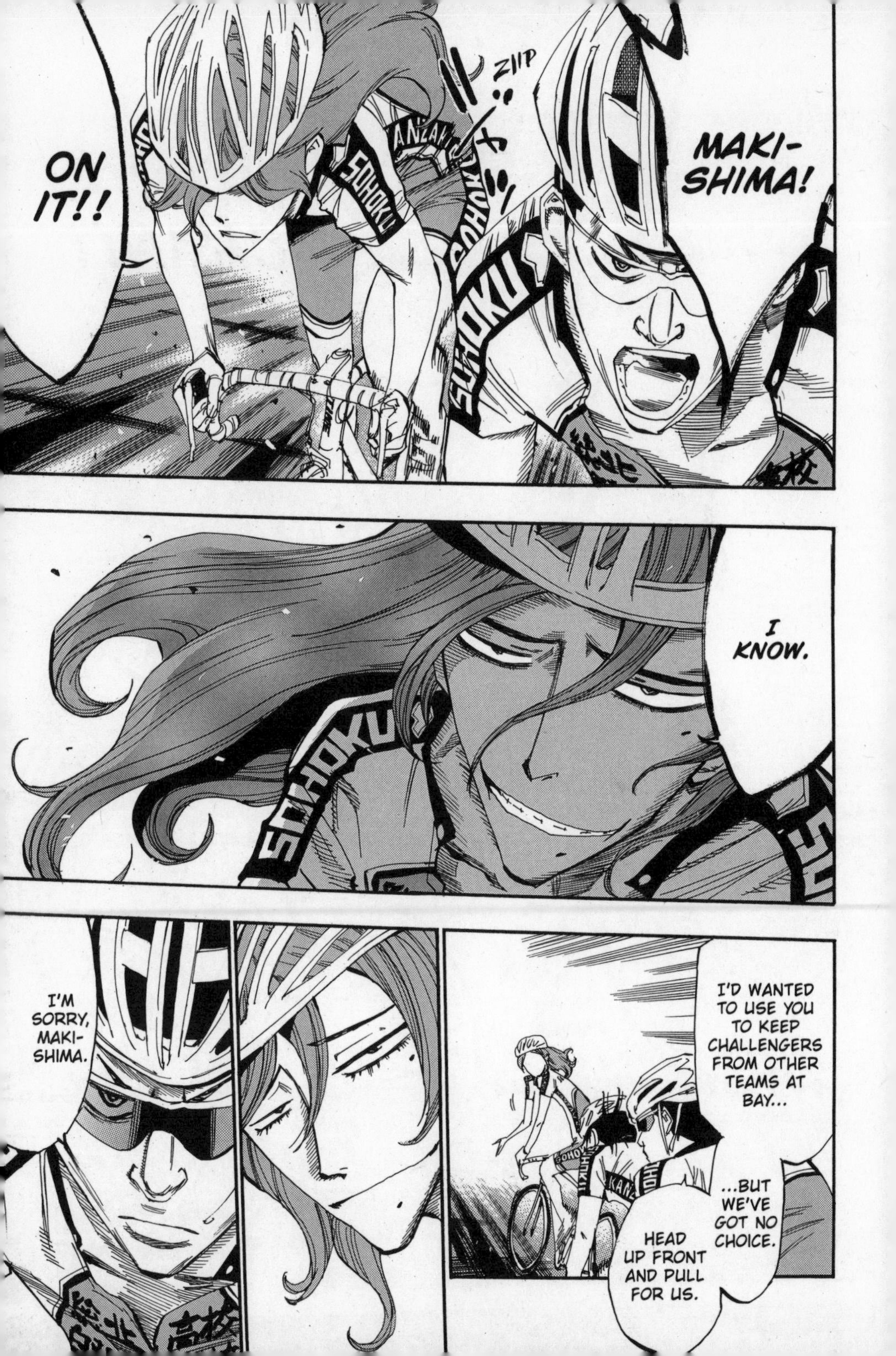
MAKI-SHIMA!
ZIIP
ON IT!!
I KNOW.
I'D WANTED TO USE YOU TO KEEP CHALLENGERS FROM OTHER TEAMS AT BAY...
...BUT WE'VE GOT NO CHOICE.
HEAD UP FRONT AND PULL FOR US.
I'M SORRY, MAKI-SHIMA.

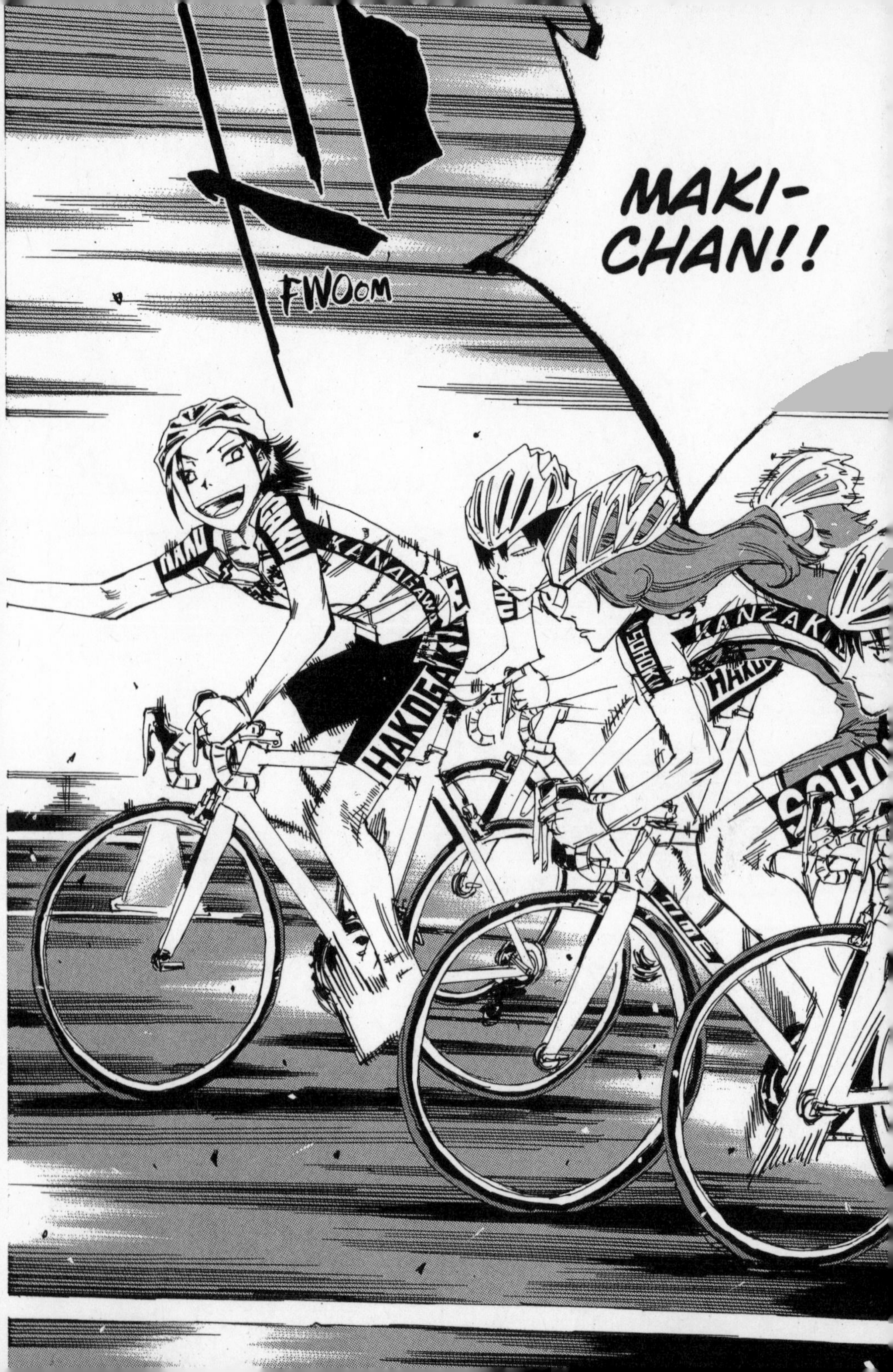
MAKI-
CHAN!!
FWOOM

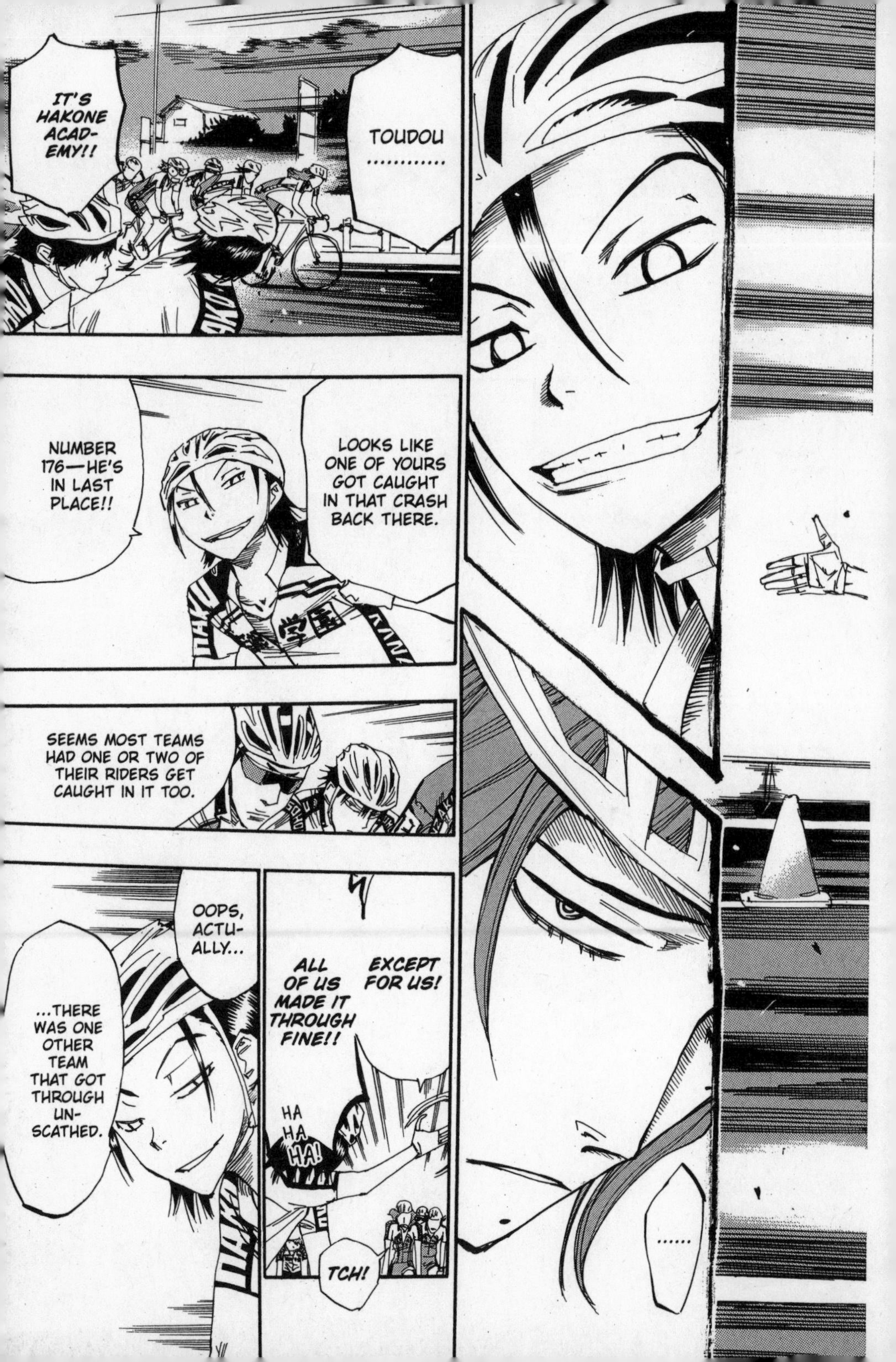
......
TOUDOU ......
IT'S HAKONE ACADEMY!!
LOOKS LIKE ONE OF YOURS GOT CAUGHT IN THAT CRASH BACK THERE.
NUMBER 176—HE'S IN LAST PLACE!!
SEEMS MOST TEAMS HAD ONE OR TWO OF THEIR RIDERS GET CAUGHT IN IT TOO.
EXCEPT FOR US!
ALL OF US MADE IT THROUGH FINE!!
HA HA HA!
TCH!
OOPS, ACTUALLY...
...THERE WAS ONE OTHER TEAM THAT GOT THROUGH UNSCATHED.

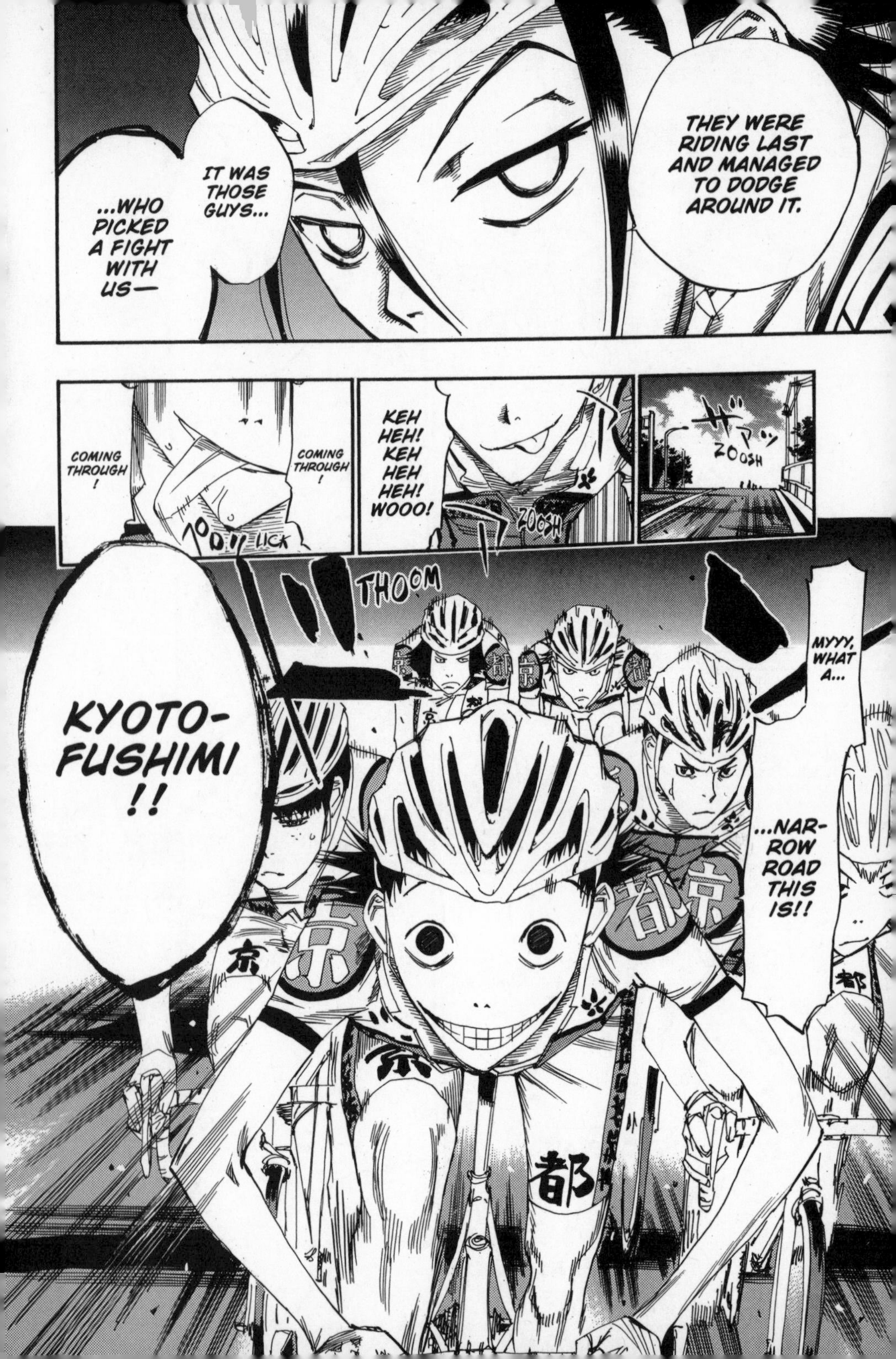
THEY WERE RIDING LAST AND MANAGED TO DODGE AROUND IT.
IT WAS THOSE GUYS...
...WHO PICKED A FIGHT WITH US—
ザァッ
ZOOSH
KEH HEH! KEH HEH HEH! WOOO!
ZOOSH
COMING THROUGH!
COMING THROUGH!
LICK
THOOM
MYYY, WHAT A...
...NARROW ROAD THIS IS!!
KYOTO-FUSHIMI!!

# RIDE.89 ONE HUNDRED RIDERS

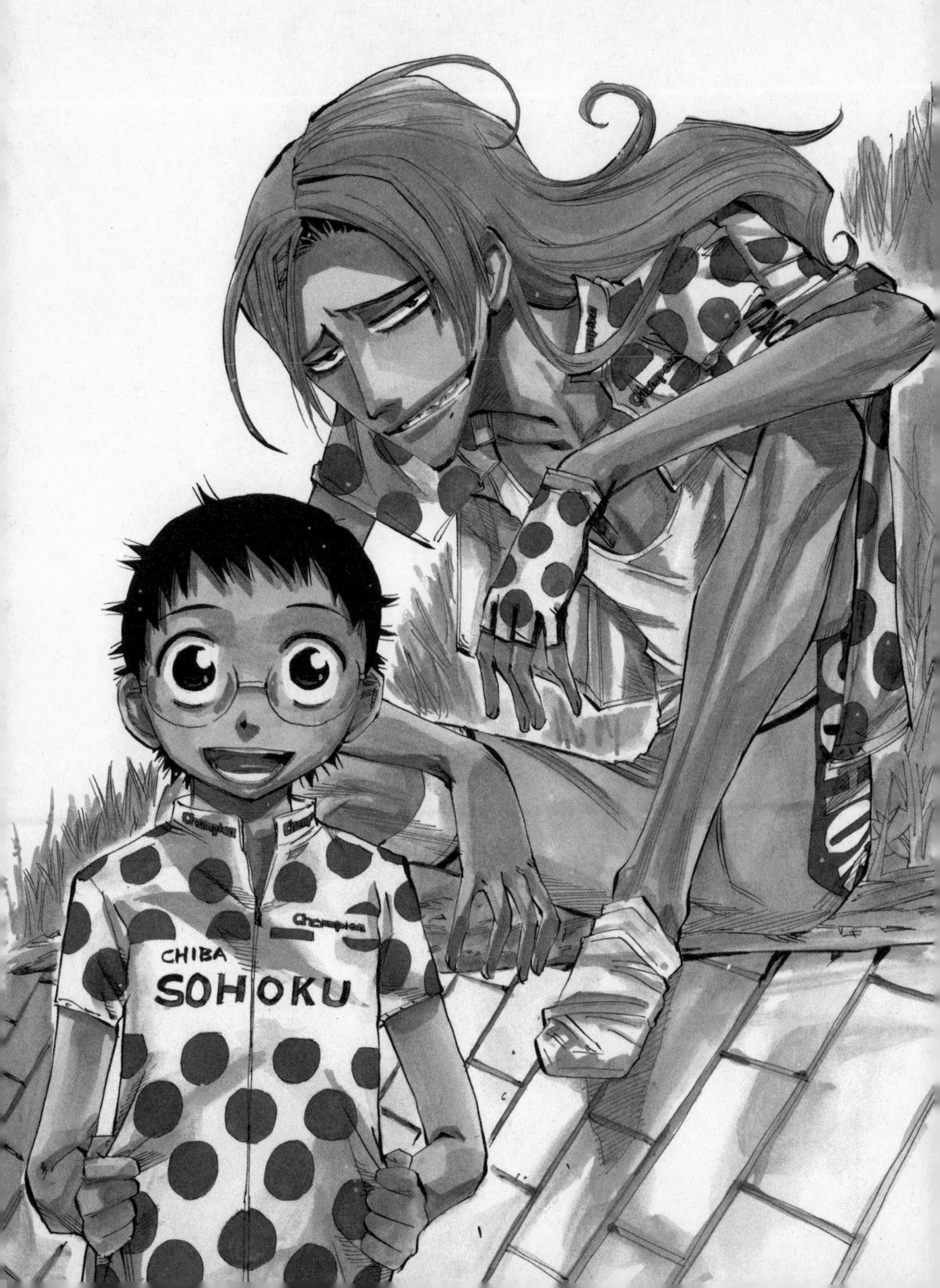
CHIBA
SOHOKU

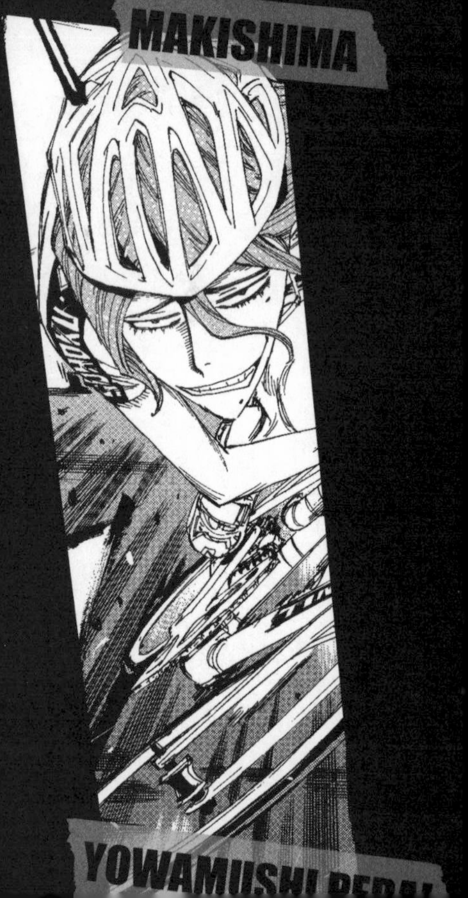
MAKISHIMA
YOWAMUSHI

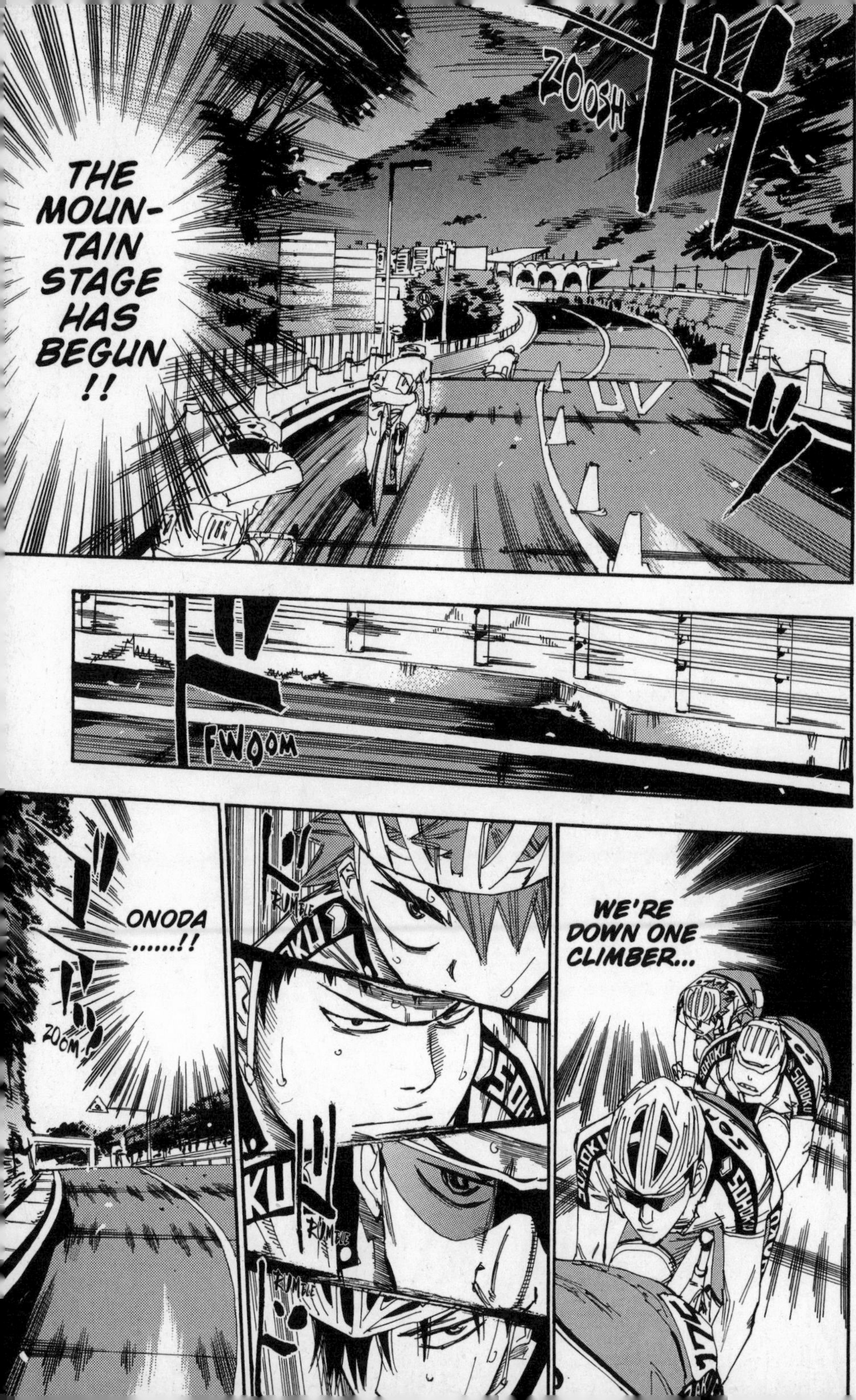
ZOOSH
THE MOUN-TAIN STAGE HAS BEGUN!!
FWOOM
WE'RE DOWN ONE CLIMBER...
RUMBLE
RUMBLE
RUMBLE
ONODA ......!!
ZOOM

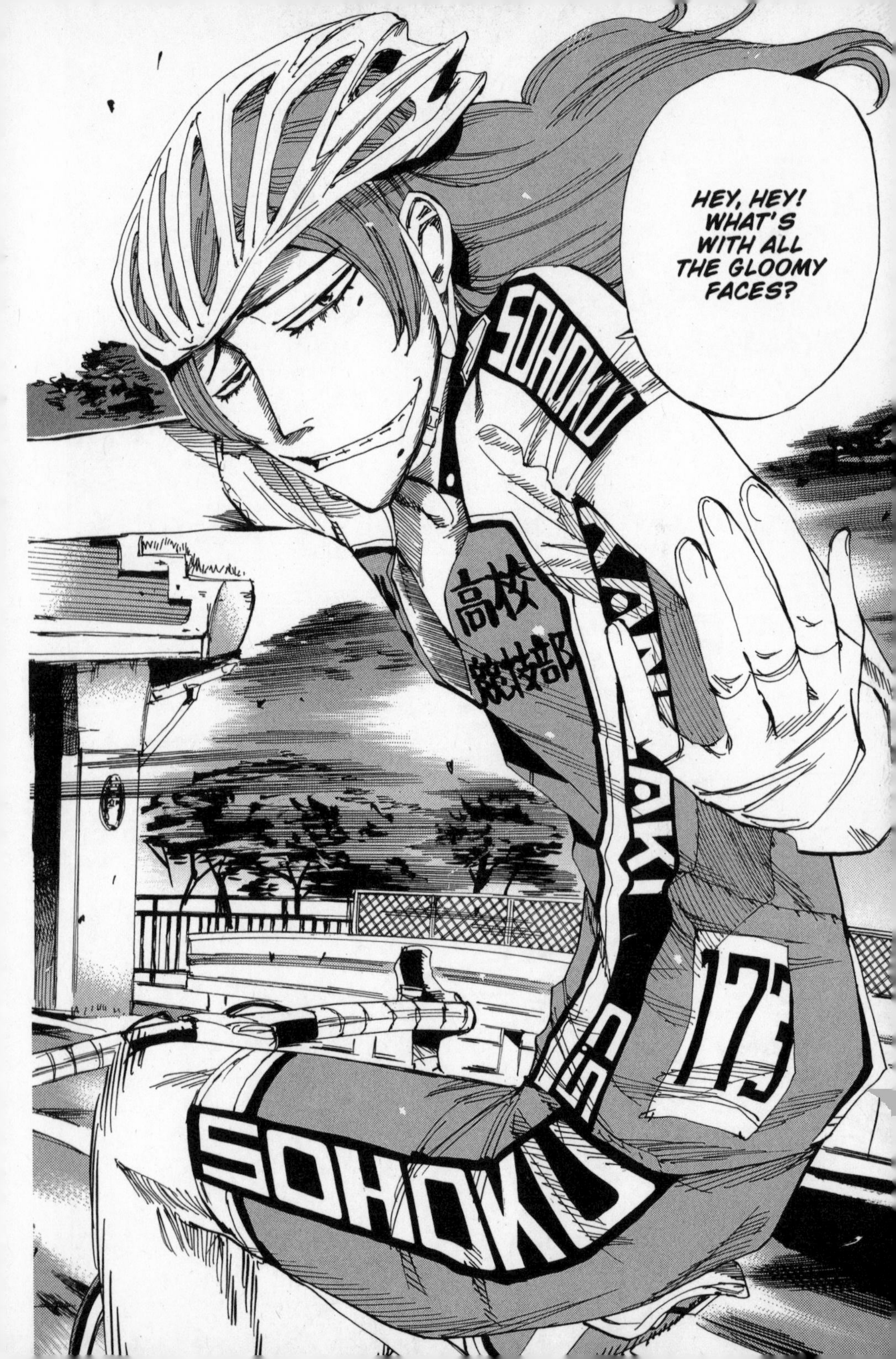
HEY, HEY! WHAT'S WITH ALL THE GLOOMY FACES?
SOHOKU
高校
競技部
173
SOHOKU

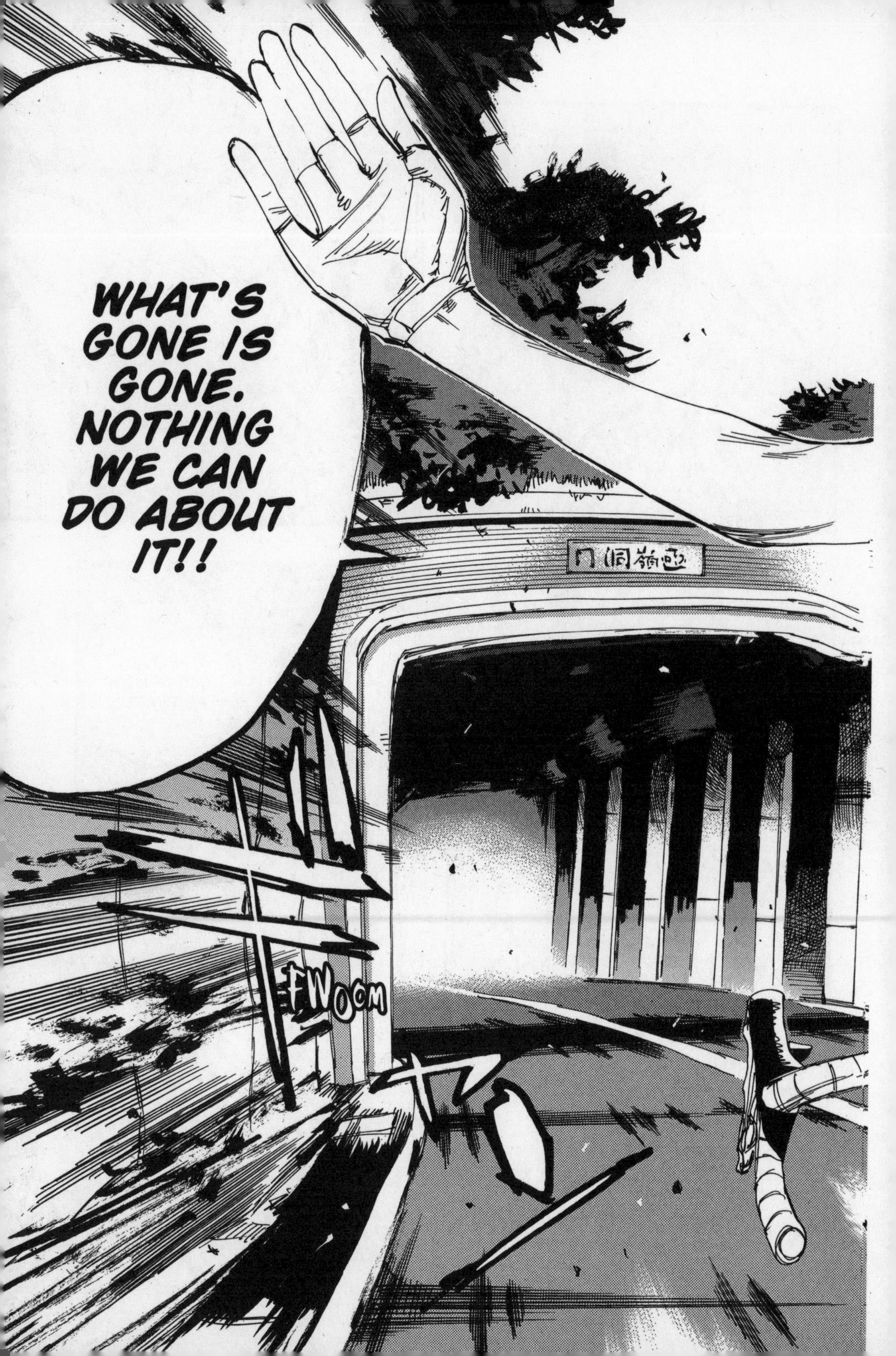
WHAT'S GONE IS GONE. NOTHING WE CAN DO ABOUT IT!!
FWOOM

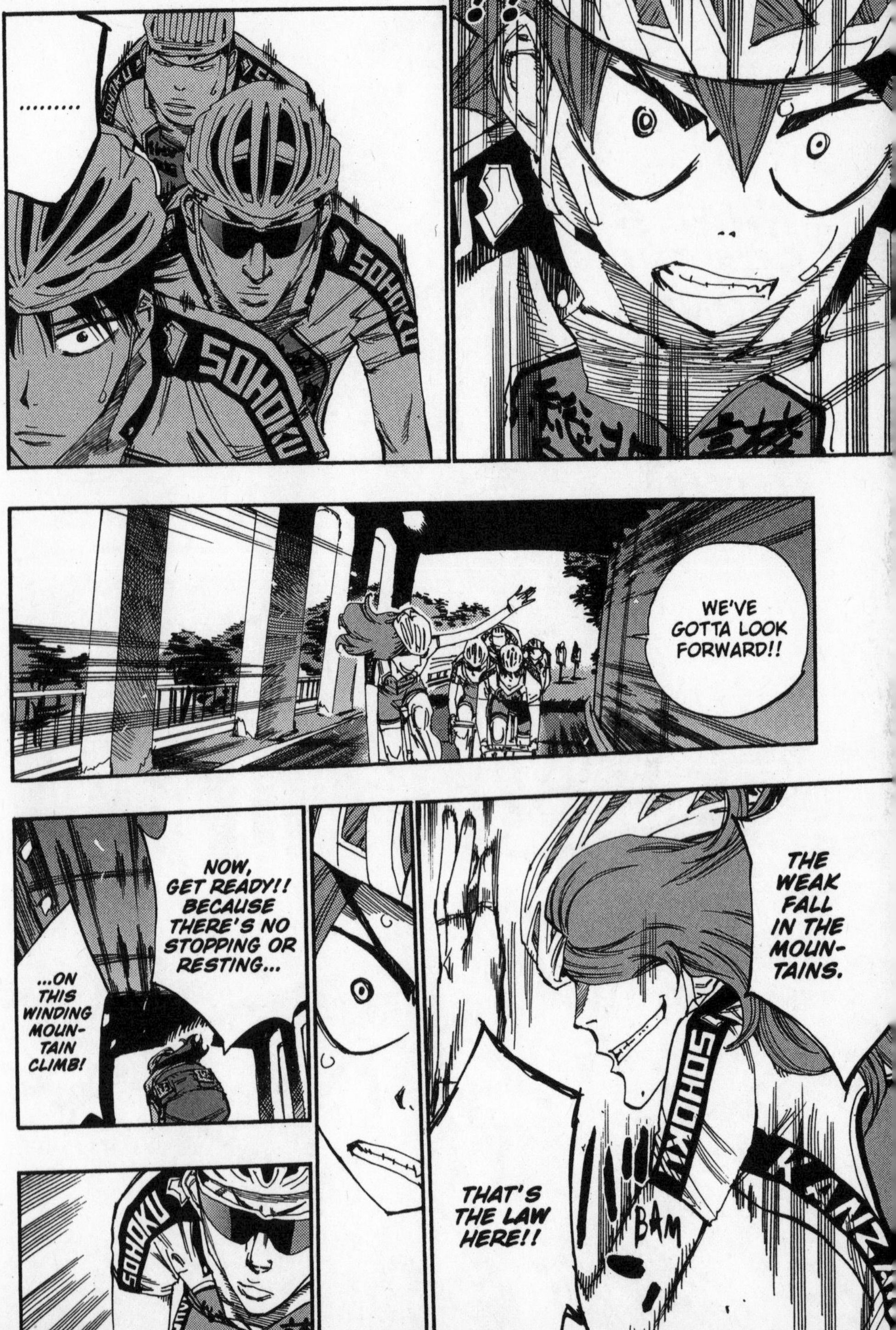
!!
.........
WE'VE GOTTA LOOK FORWARD!!
THE WEAK FALL IN THE MOUNTAINS.
THAT'S THE LAW HERE!!
BAM
NOW, GET READY!! BECAUSE THERE'S NO STOPPING OR RESTING...
...ON THIS WINDING MOUNTAIN CLIMB!

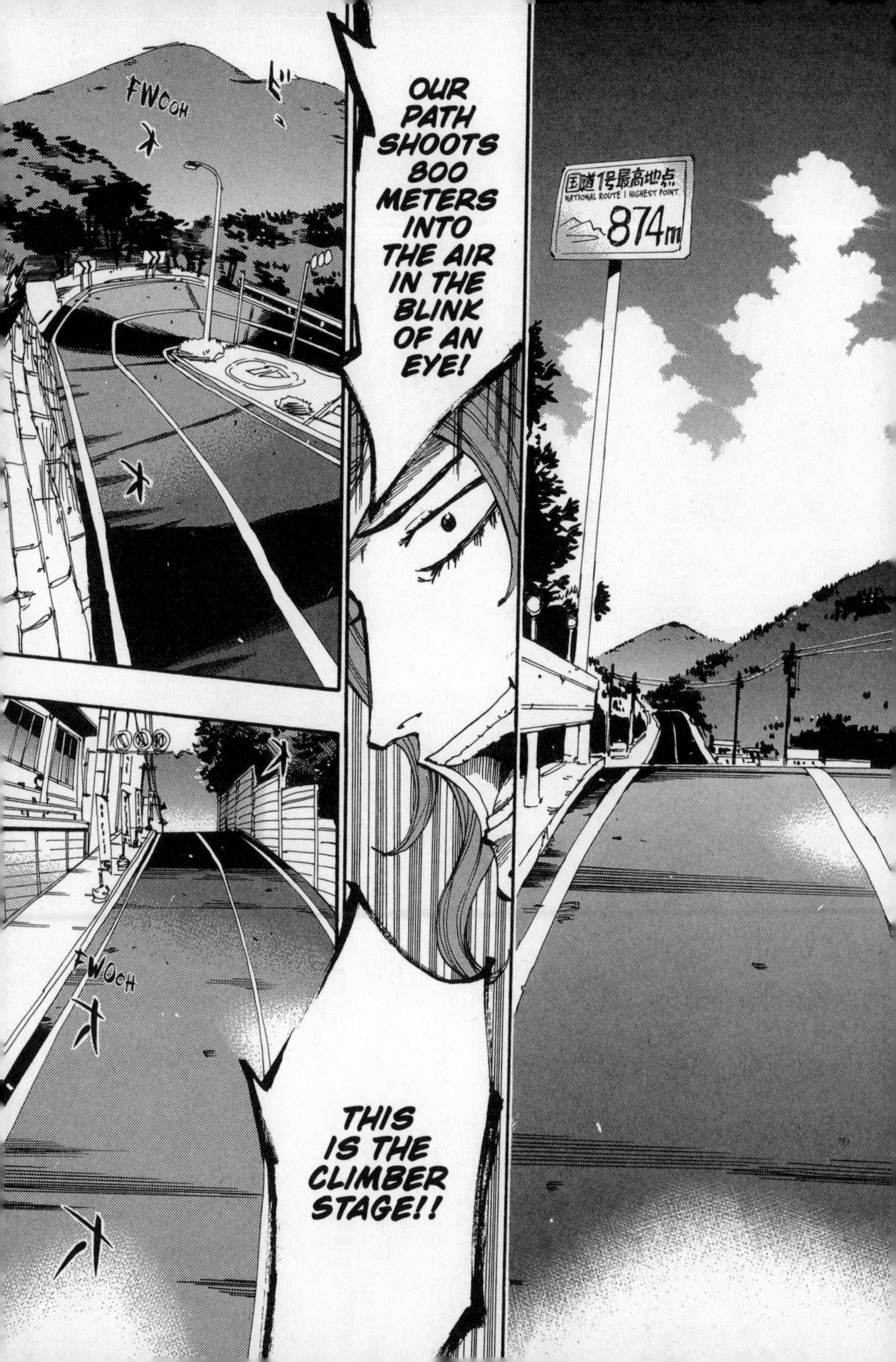
国道1号最高地点
NATIONAL ROUTE 1 HIGHEST POINT
874m
OUR PATH SHOOTS 800 METERS INTO THE AIR IN THE BLINK OF AN EYE!
FWOOH
FWOOH
THIS IS THE CLIMBER STAGE!!

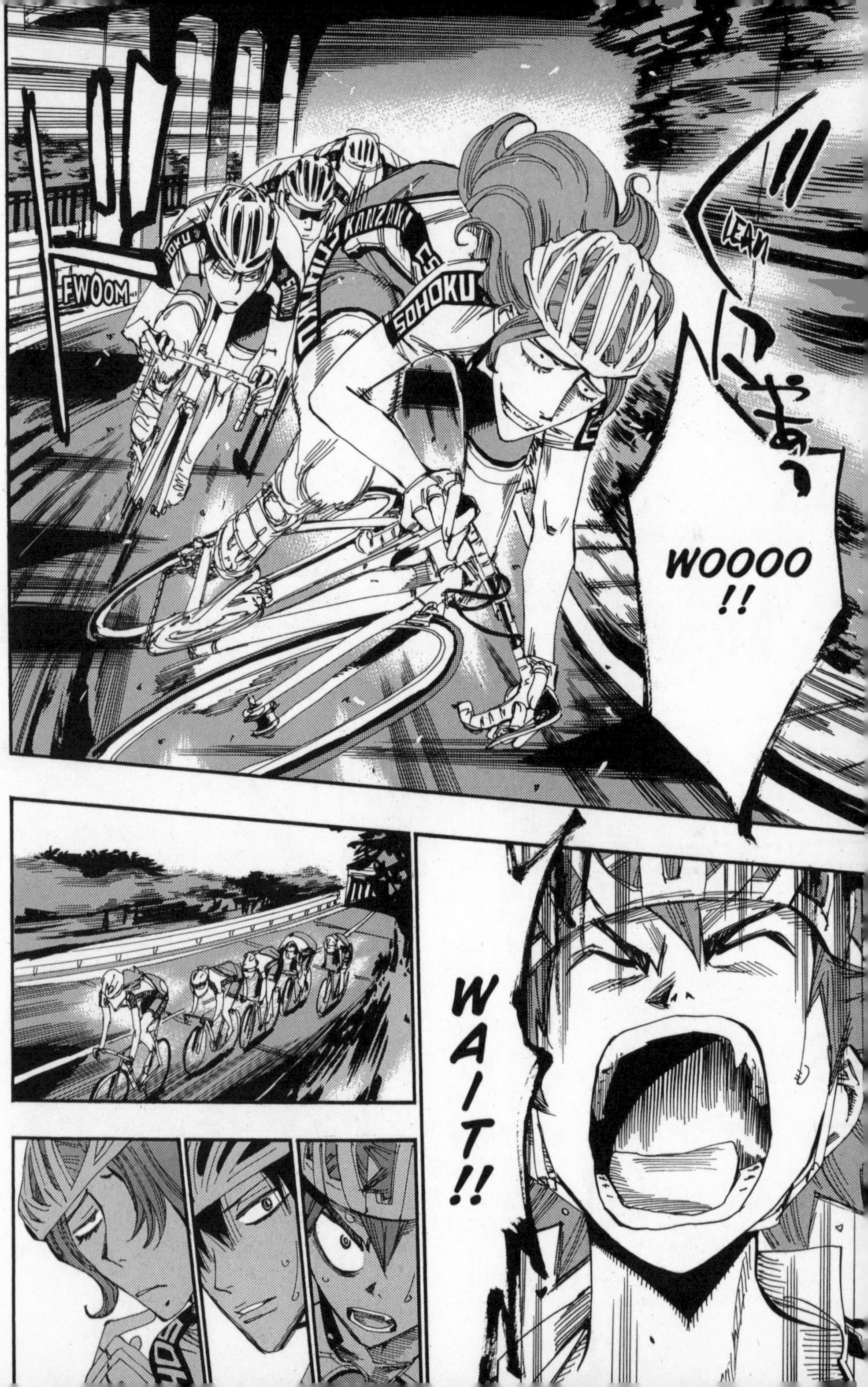

LEAN
WOOOO!!
FWOOM...
WAIT!!

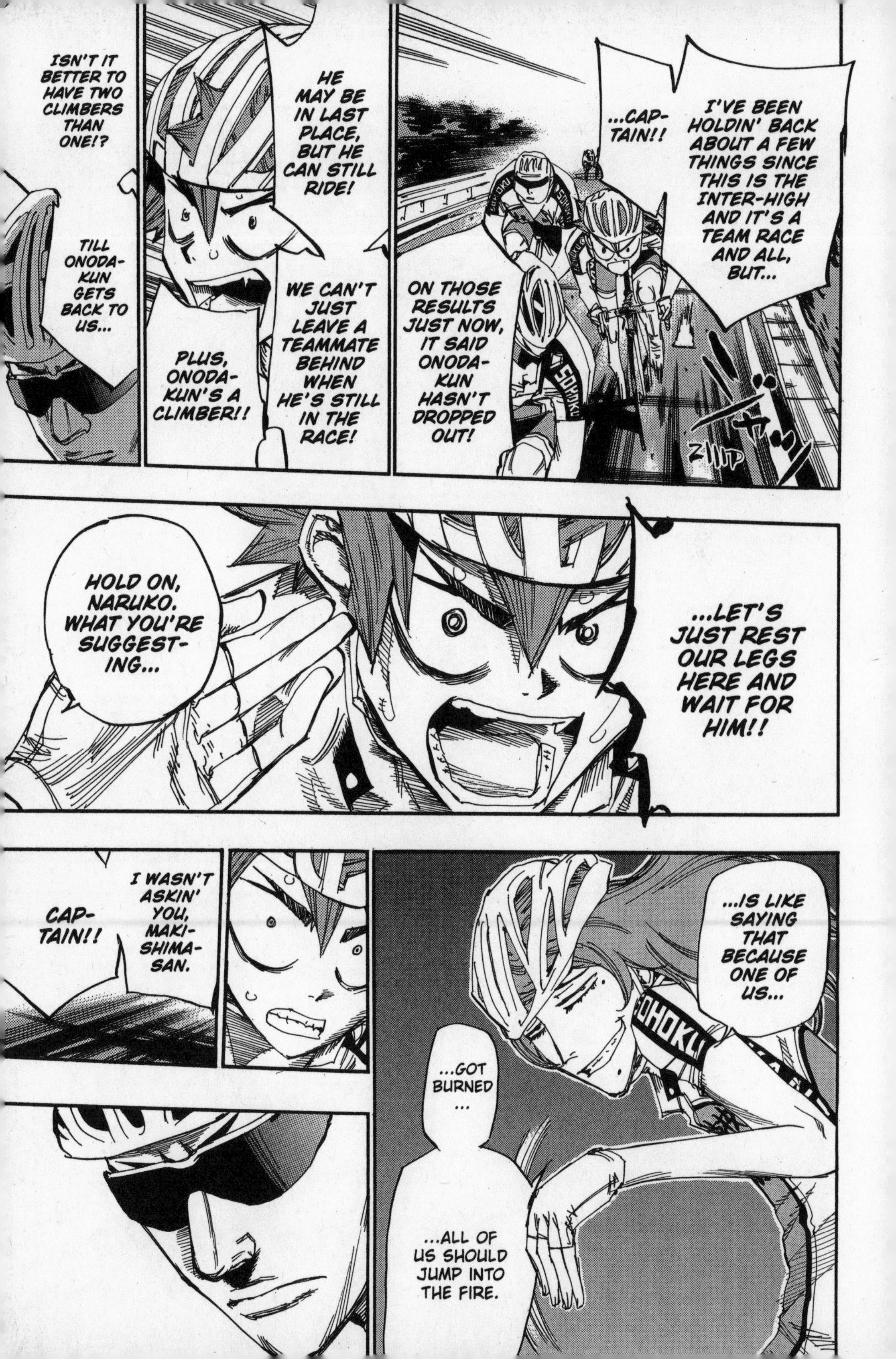
I'VE BEEN HOLDIN' BACK ABOUT A FEW THINGS SINCE THIS IS THE INTER-HIGH AND IT'S A TEAM RACE AND ALL, BUT...
...CAP-TAIN!!
ON THOSE RESULTS JUST NOW, IT SAID ONODA-KUN HASN'T DROPPED OUT!
ZIIIP
HE MAY BE IN LAST PLACE, BUT HE CAN STILL RIDE!
WE CAN'T JUST LEAVE A TEAMMATE BEHIND WHEN HE'S STILL IN THE RACE!
PLUS, ONODA-KUN'S A CLIMBER!!
ISN'T IT BETTER TO HAVE TWO CLIMBERS THAN ONE!?
TILL ONODA-KUN GETS BACK TO US...
...LET'S JUST REST OUR LEGS HERE AND WAIT FOR HIM!!
HOLD ON, NARUKO. WHAT YOU'RE SUGGEST-ING...
...IS LIKE SAYING THAT BECAUSE ONE OF US...
...GOT BURNED...
...ALL OF US SHOULD JUMP INTO THE FIRE.
I WASN'T ASKIN' YOU, MAKI-SHIMA-SAN.
CAP-TAIN!!

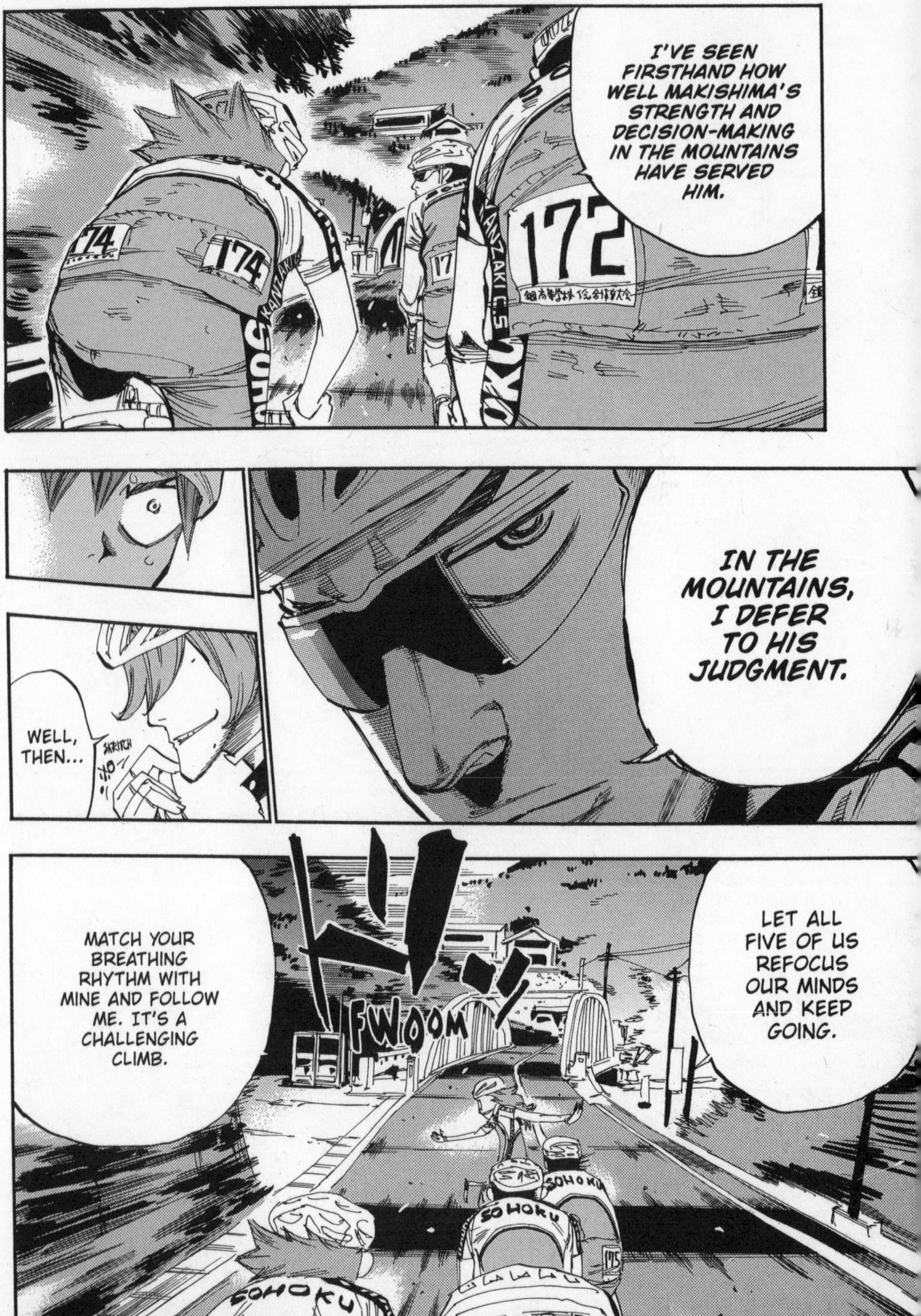
I'VE SEEN FIRSTHAND HOW WELL MAKISHIMA'S STRENGTH AND DECISION-MAKING IN THE MOUNTAINS HAVE SERVED HIM.
IN THE MOUNTAINS, I DEFER TO HIS JUDGMENT.
WELL, THEN...
SKRITCH
LET ALL FIVE OF US REFOCUS OUR MINDS AND KEEP GOING.
FWOOM
MATCH YOUR BREATHING RHYTHM WITH MINE AND FOLLOW ME. IT'S A CHALLENGING CLIMB.

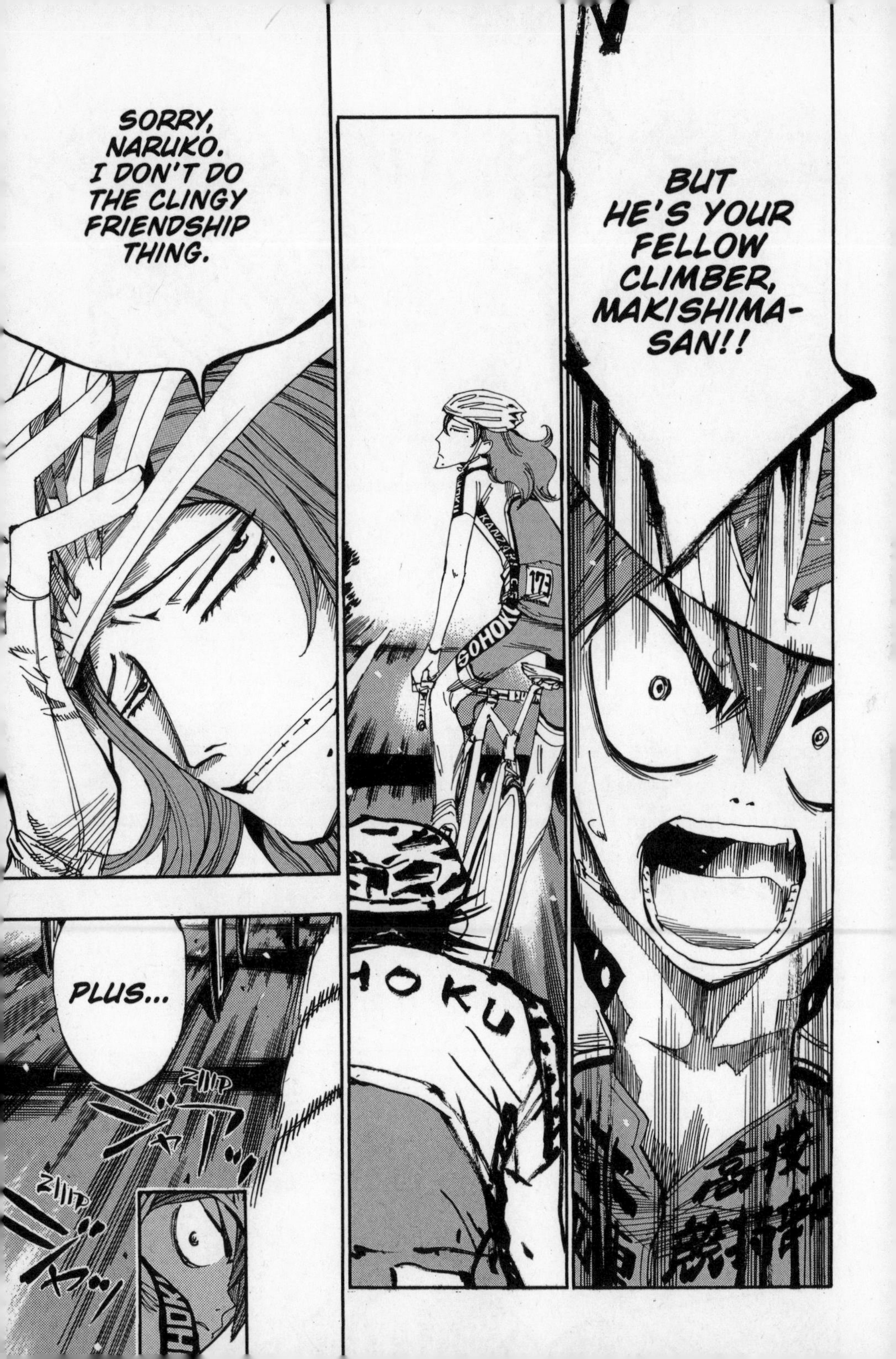
BUT HE'S YOUR FELLOW CLIMBER, MAKISHIMA-SAN!!
SORRY, NARUKO. I DON'T DO THE CLINGY FRIENDSHIP THING.
PLUS...
ZIIIP
ZIIIP

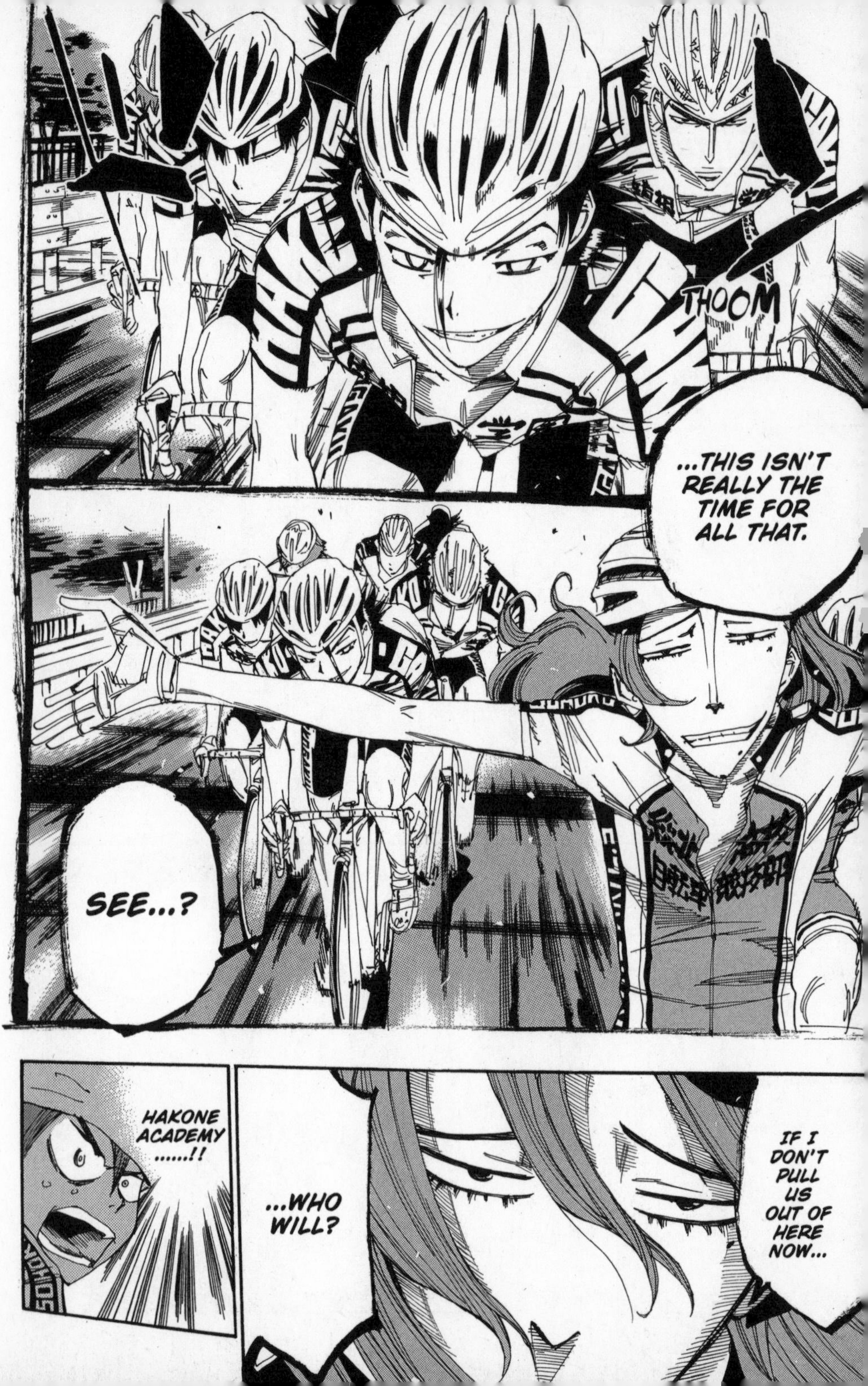
THOOM
...THIS ISN'T REALLY THE TIME FOR ALL THAT.
SEE...?
IF I DON'T PULL US OUT OF HERE NOW...
...WHO WILL?
HAKONE ACADEMY ......!!

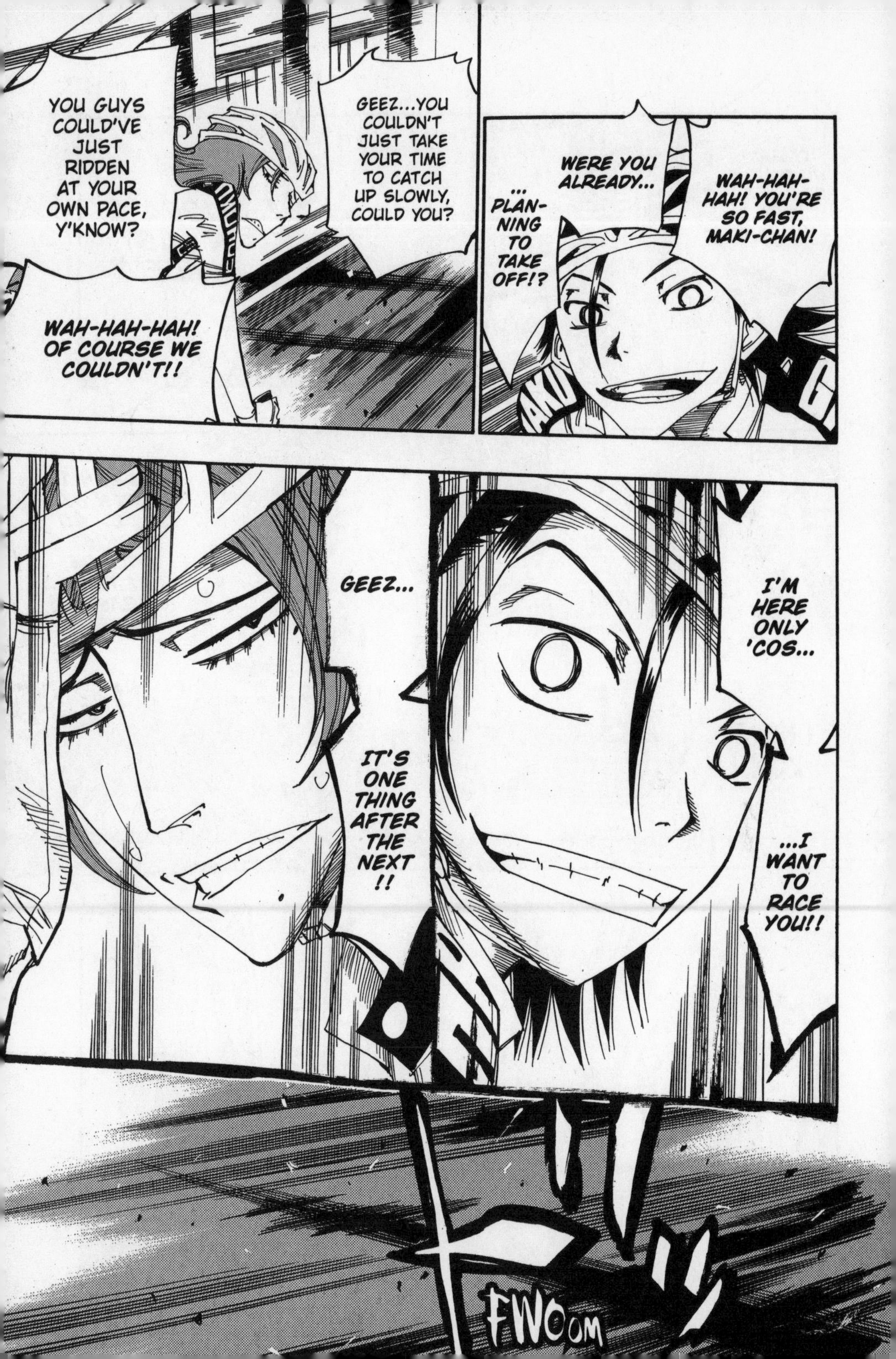
WAH-HAH-HAH! YOU'RE SO FAST, MAKI-CHAN!
WERE YOU ALREADY...
...PLANNING TO TAKE OFF!?
GEEZ...YOU COULDN'T JUST TAKE YOUR TIME TO CATCH UP SLOWLY, COULD YOU?
YOU GUYS COULD'VE JUST RIDDEN AT YOUR OWN PACE, Y'KNOW?
WAH-HAH-HAH! OF COURSE WE COULDN'T!!
I'M HERE ONLY 'COS...
...I WANT TO RACE YOU!!
GEEZ...
IT'S ONE THING AFTER THE NEXT!!
FWOOM

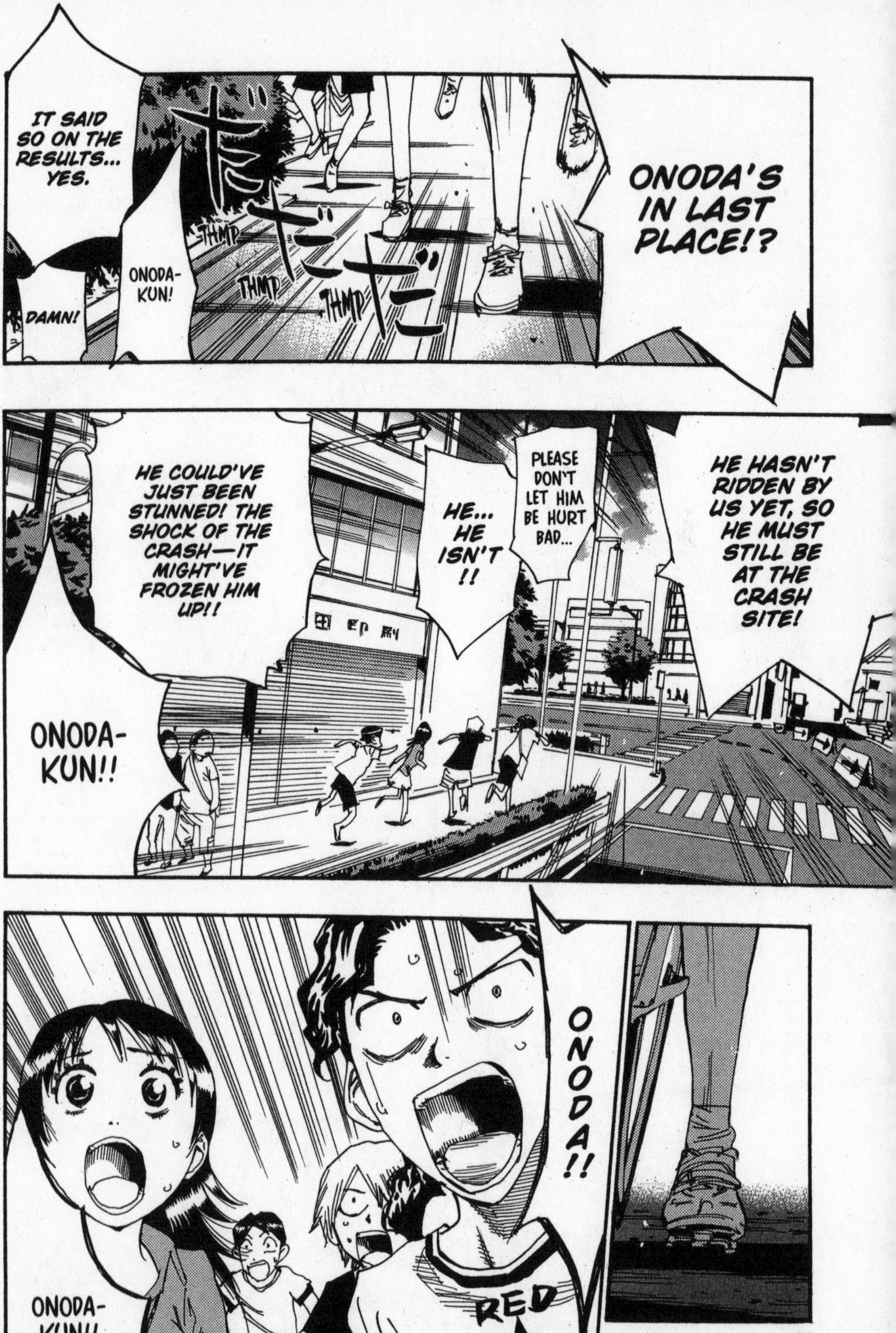

ONODA'S IN LAST PLACE!?
IT SAID SO ON THE RESULTS... YES.
THMP
THMP
THMP
ONODA-KUN!
DAMN!
HE HASN'T RIDDEN BY US YET, SO HE MUST STILL BE AT THE CRASH SITE!
PLEASE DON'T LET HIM BE HURT BAD...
HE... HE ISN'T!!
HE COULD'VE JUST BEEN STUNNED! THE SHOCK OF THE CRASH—IT MIGHT'VE FROZEN HIM UP!!
ONODA-KUN!!
ONODA!!
RED
ONODA-KUN!!

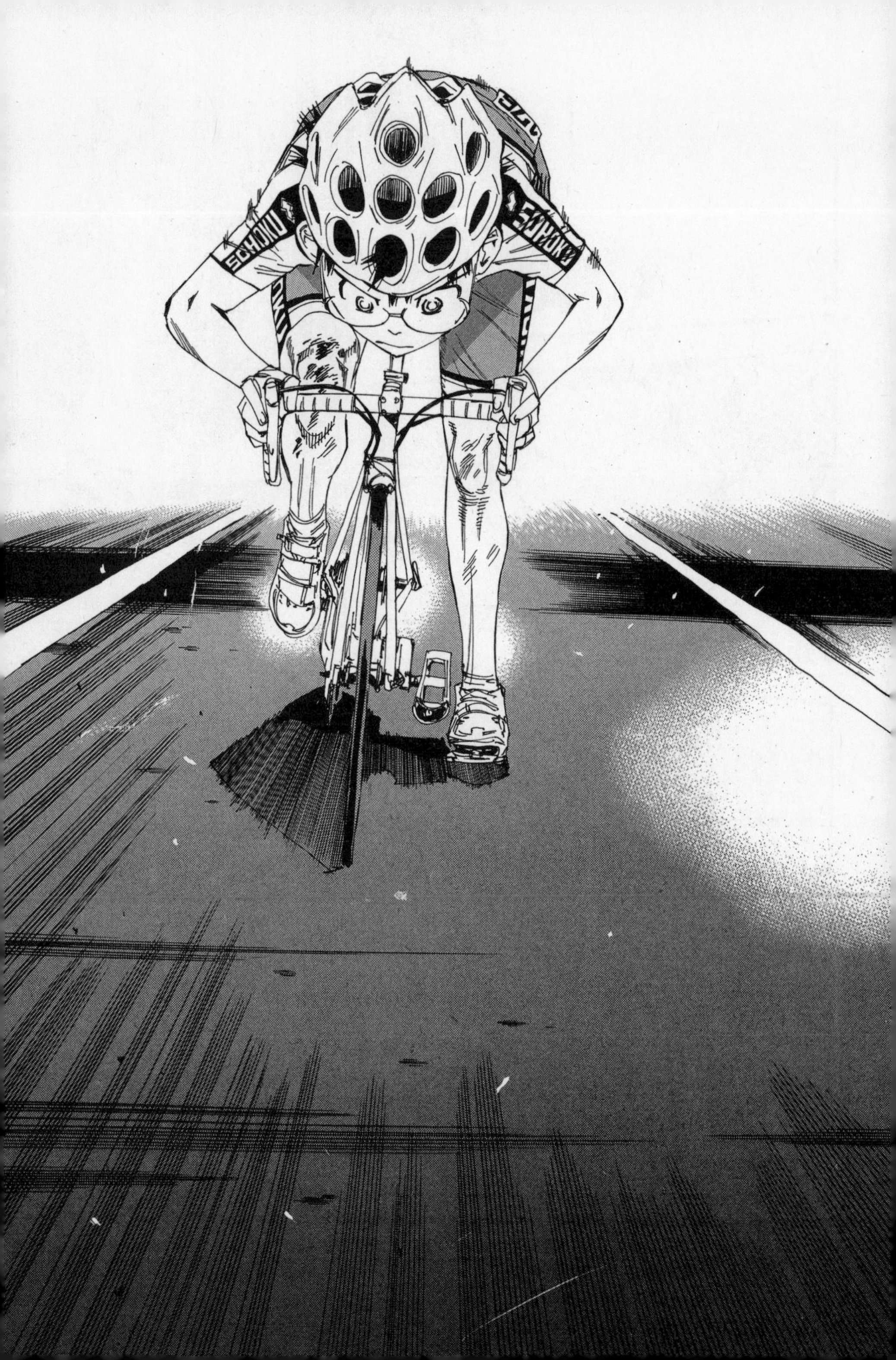
SOHOKU
SOHOKU

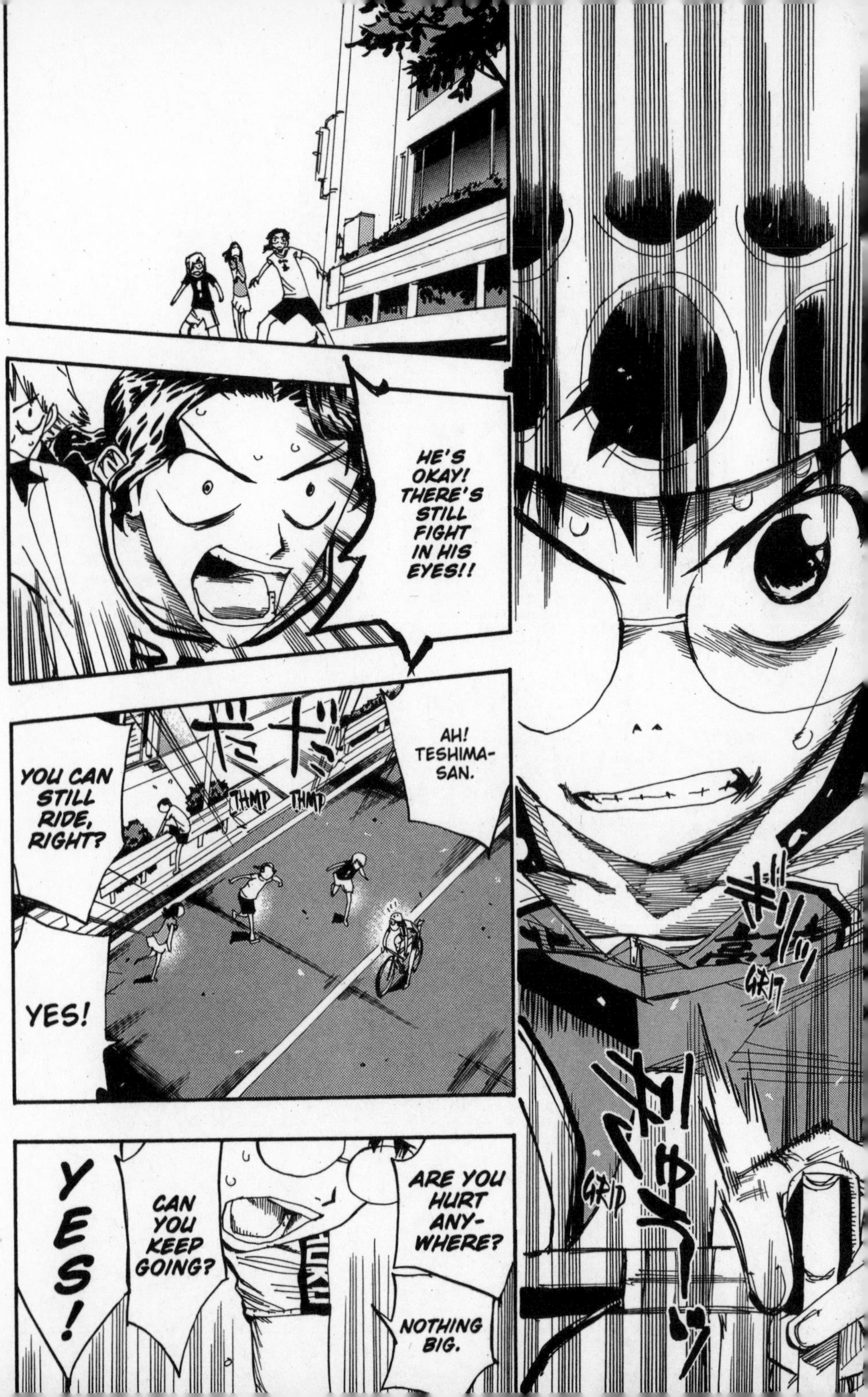
GRIT
GRIP
HE'S OKAY! THERE'S STILL FIGHT IN HIS EYES!!
AH! TESHIMA-SAN.
THMP THMP
YOU CAN STILL RIDE, RIGHT?
YES!
ARE YOU HURT ANY-WHERE?
NOTHING BIG.
CAN YOU KEEP GOING?
YES!

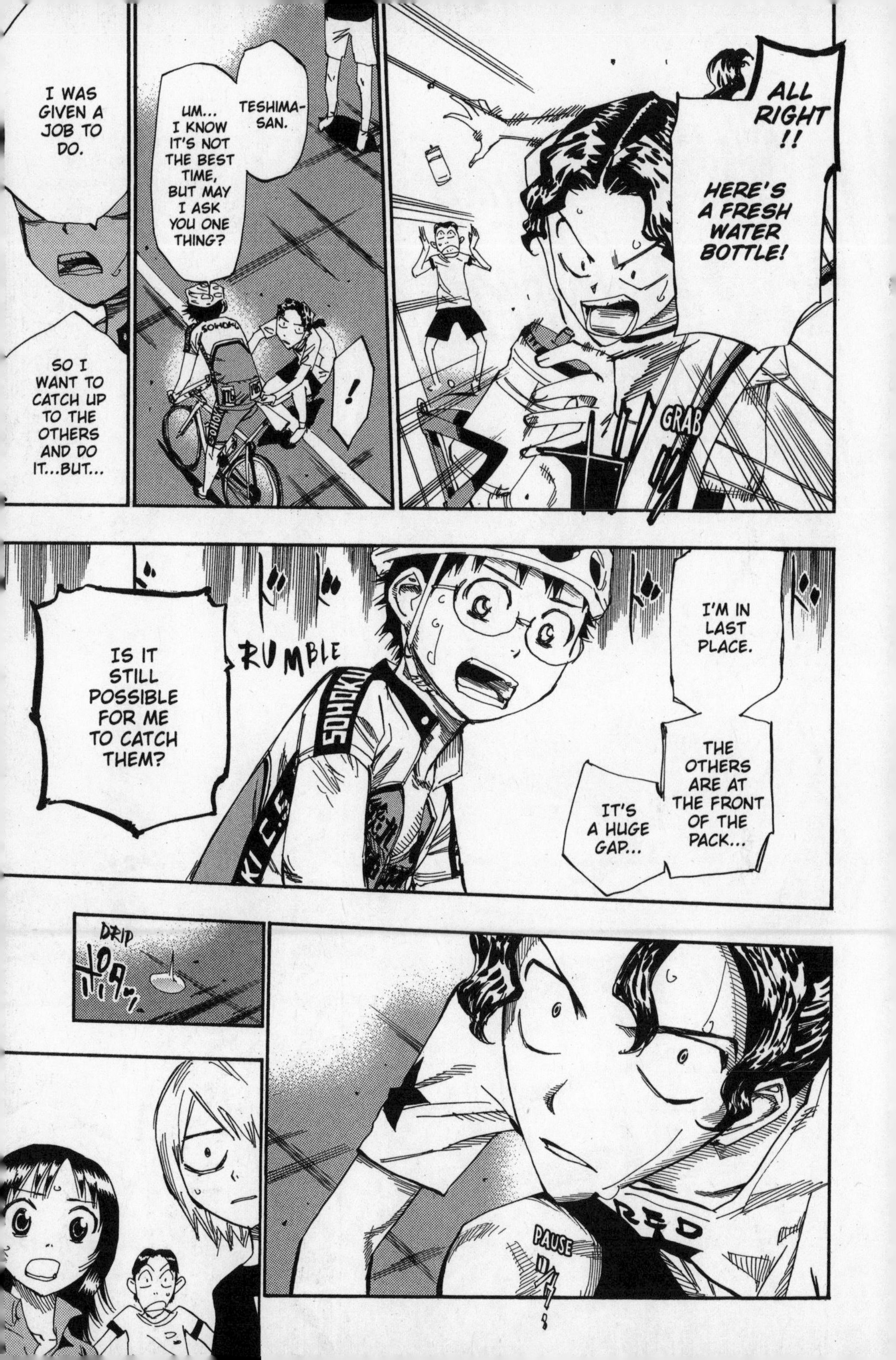
ALL RIGHT!!
HERE'S A FRESH WATER BOTTLE!
GRAB
TESHIMA-SAN.
UM... I KNOW IT'S NOT THE BEST TIME, BUT MAY I ASK YOU ONE THING?
!
I WAS GIVEN A JOB TO DO.
SO I WANT TO CATCH UP TO THE OTHERS AND DO IT...BUT...
I'M IN LAST PLACE.
THE OTHERS ARE AT THE FRONT OF THE PACK...
IT'S A HUGE GAP...
RUMBLE
IS IT STILL POSSIBLE FOR ME TO CATCH THEM?
PAUSE
DRIP

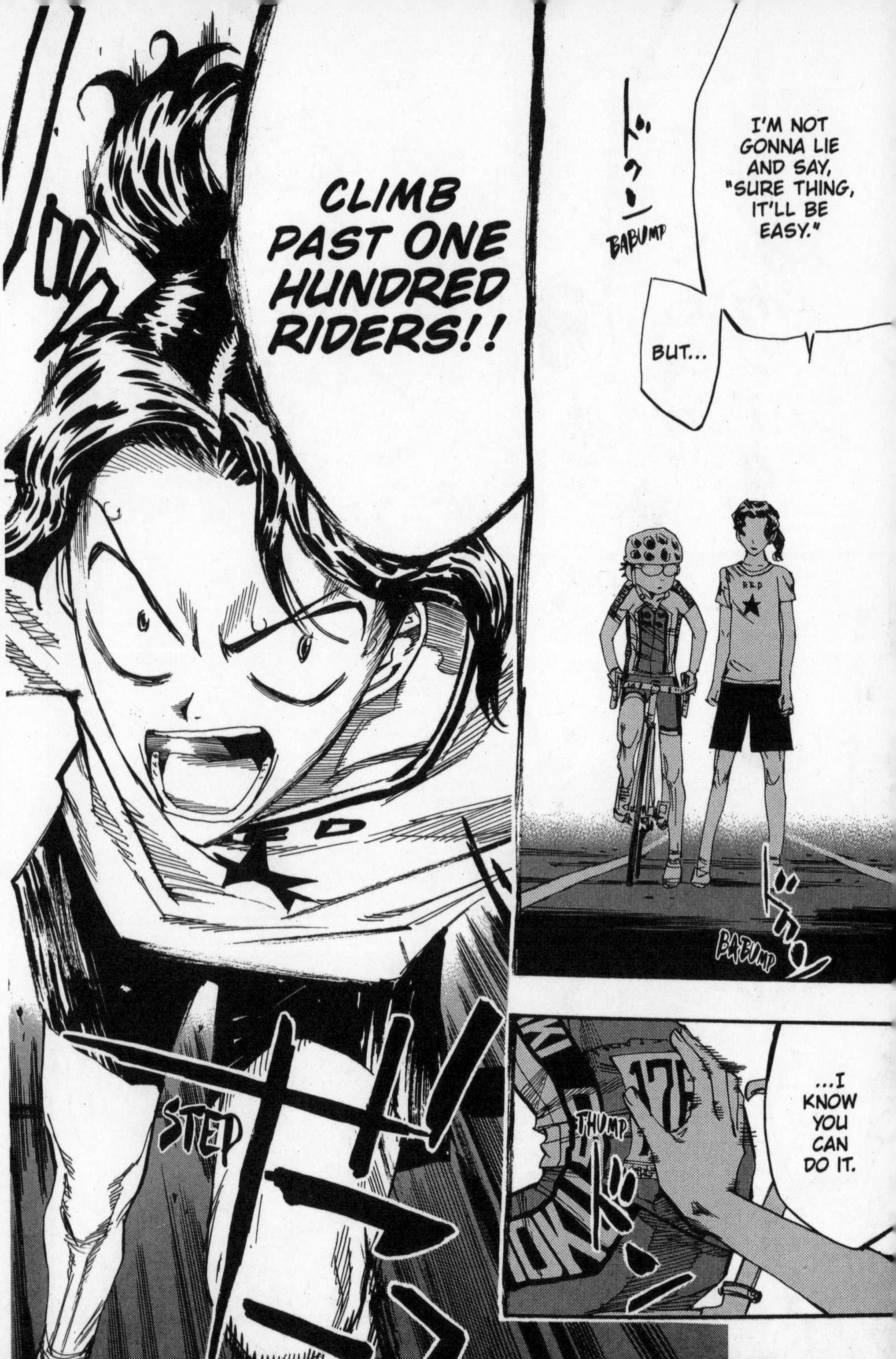
I'M NOT GONNA LIE AND SAY, "SURE THING, IT'LL BE EASY."
BABUMP
BUT...
BABUMP
...I KNOW YOU CAN DO IT.
THUMP
CLIMB PAST ONE HUNDRED RIDERS!!
STEP

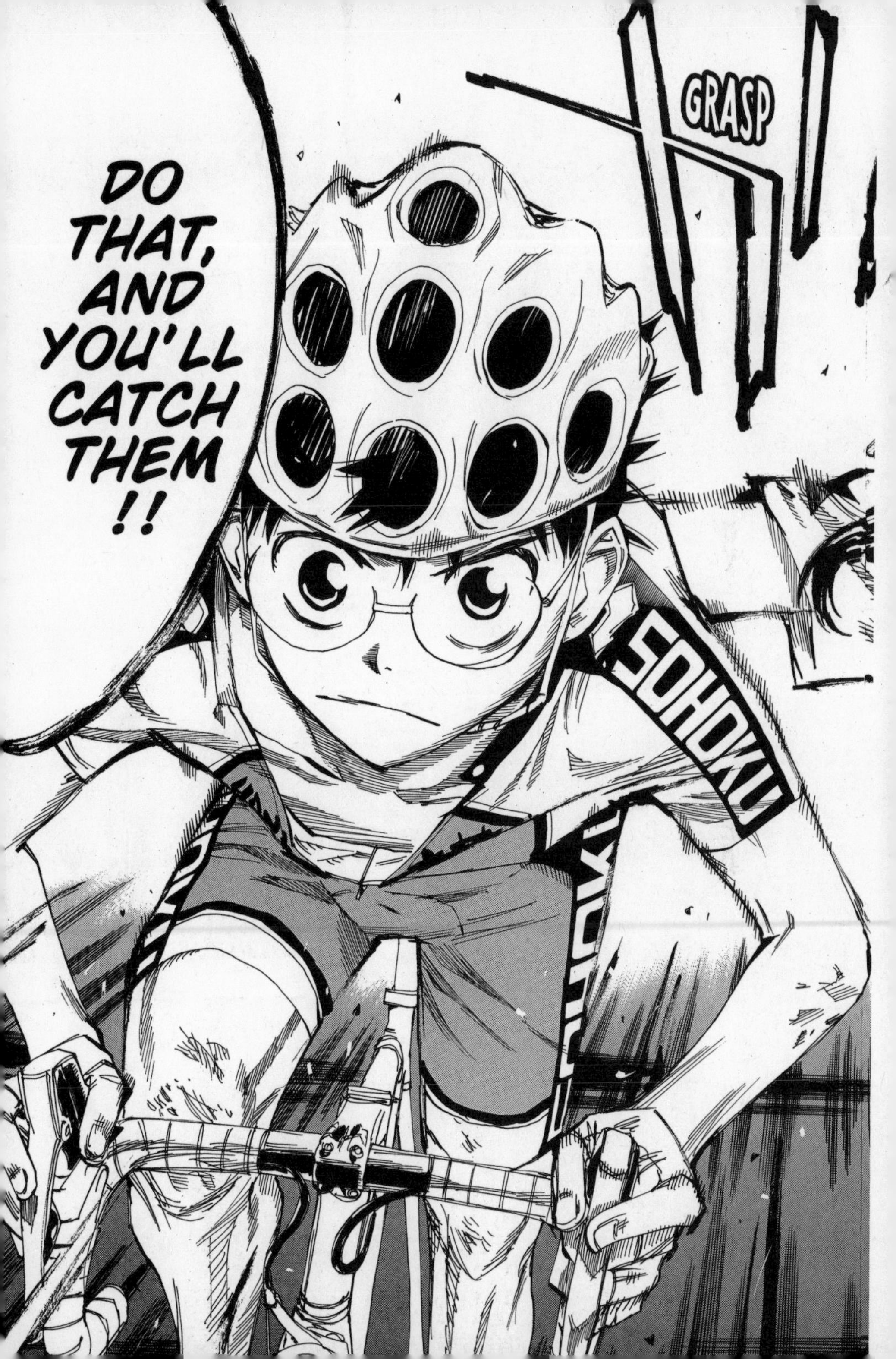
GRASP
DO THAT, AND YOU'LL CATCH THEM!!
SOHOKU

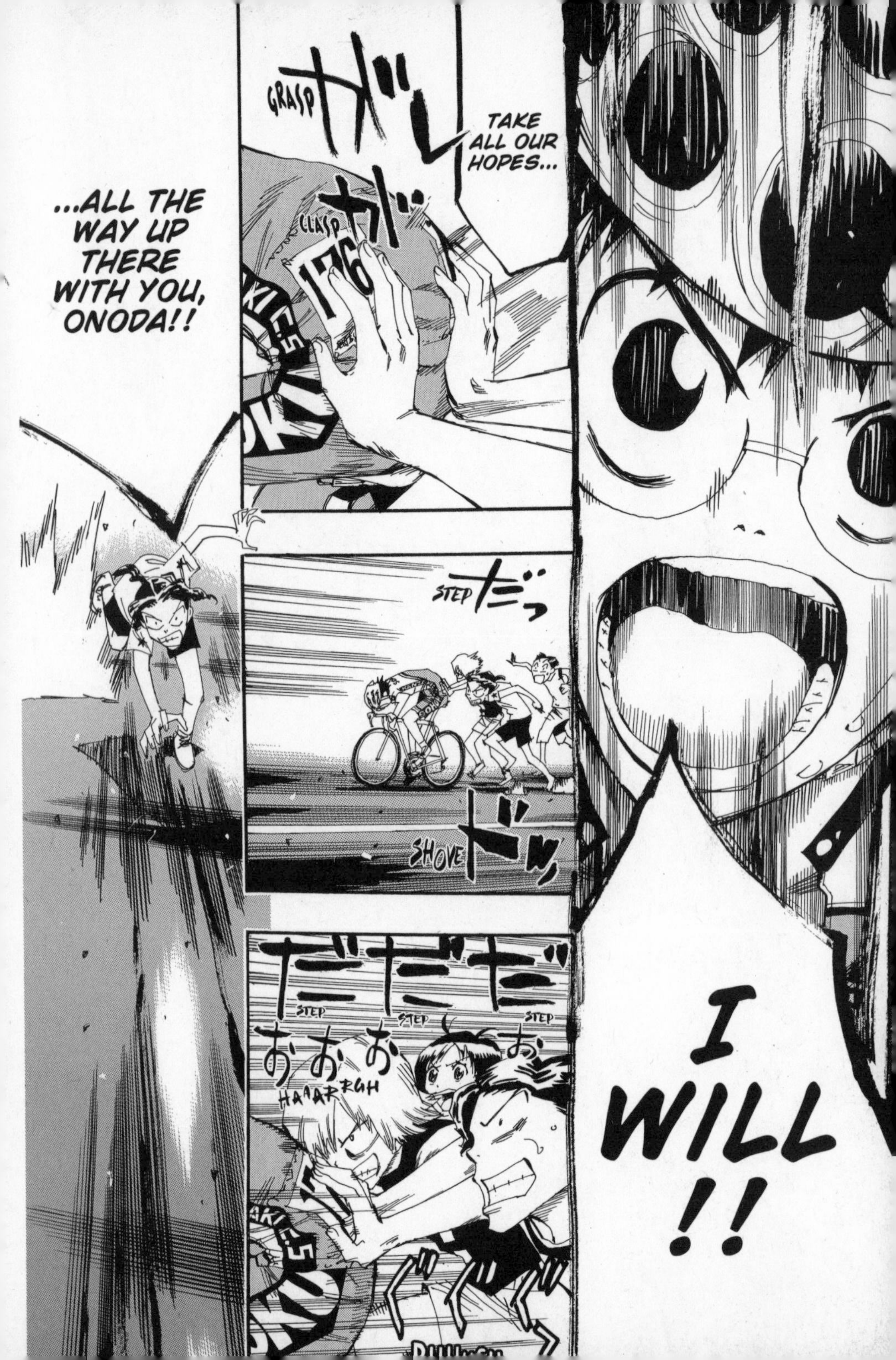

I WILL!!
GRASP
TAKE ALL OUR HOPES...
CLASP
STEP
SHOVE
STEP
STEP
STEP
HAAARRGH
...ALL THE WAY UP THERE WITH YOU, ONODA!!

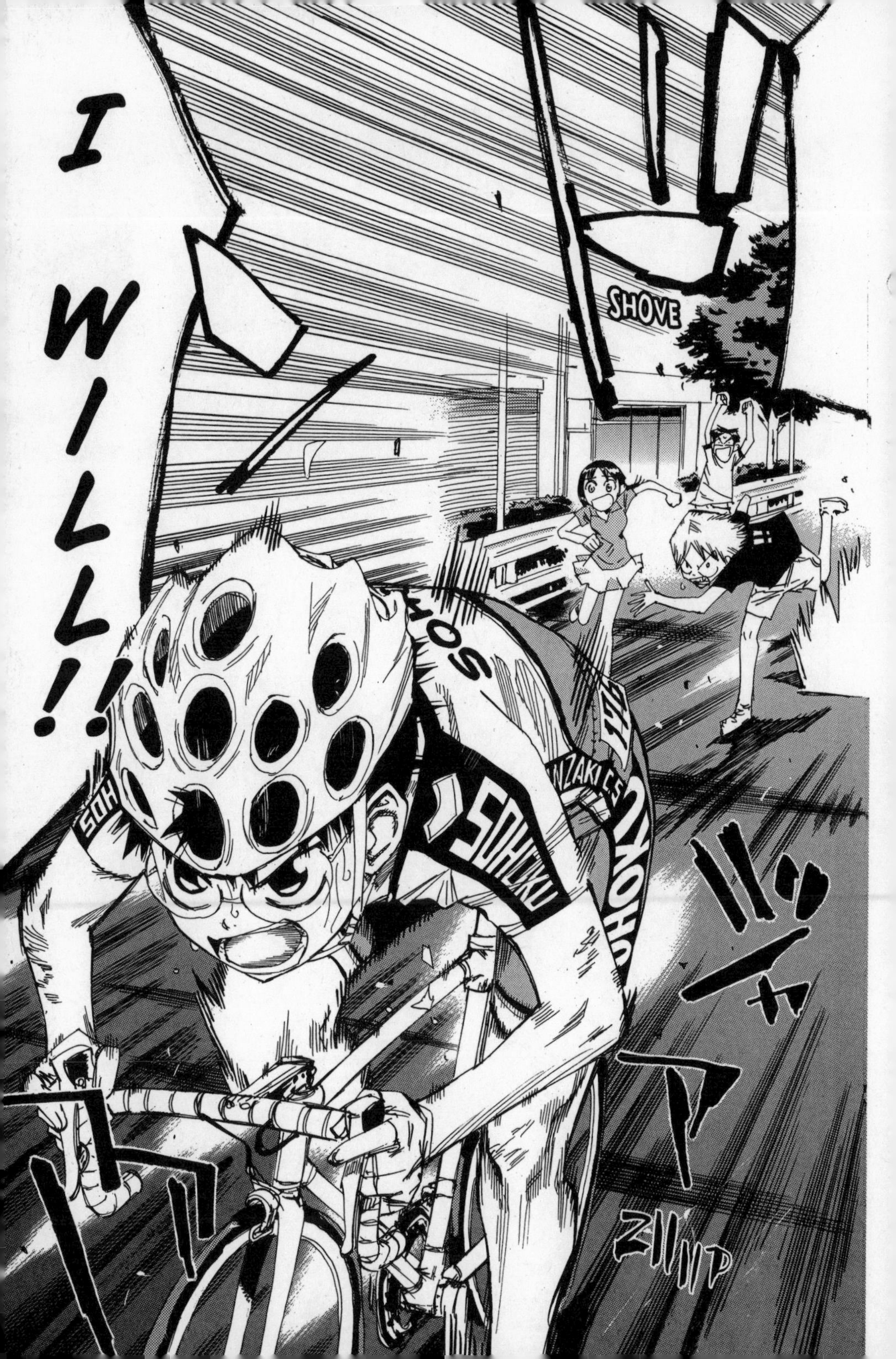
SHOVE
I WILL!!
ZIIIP

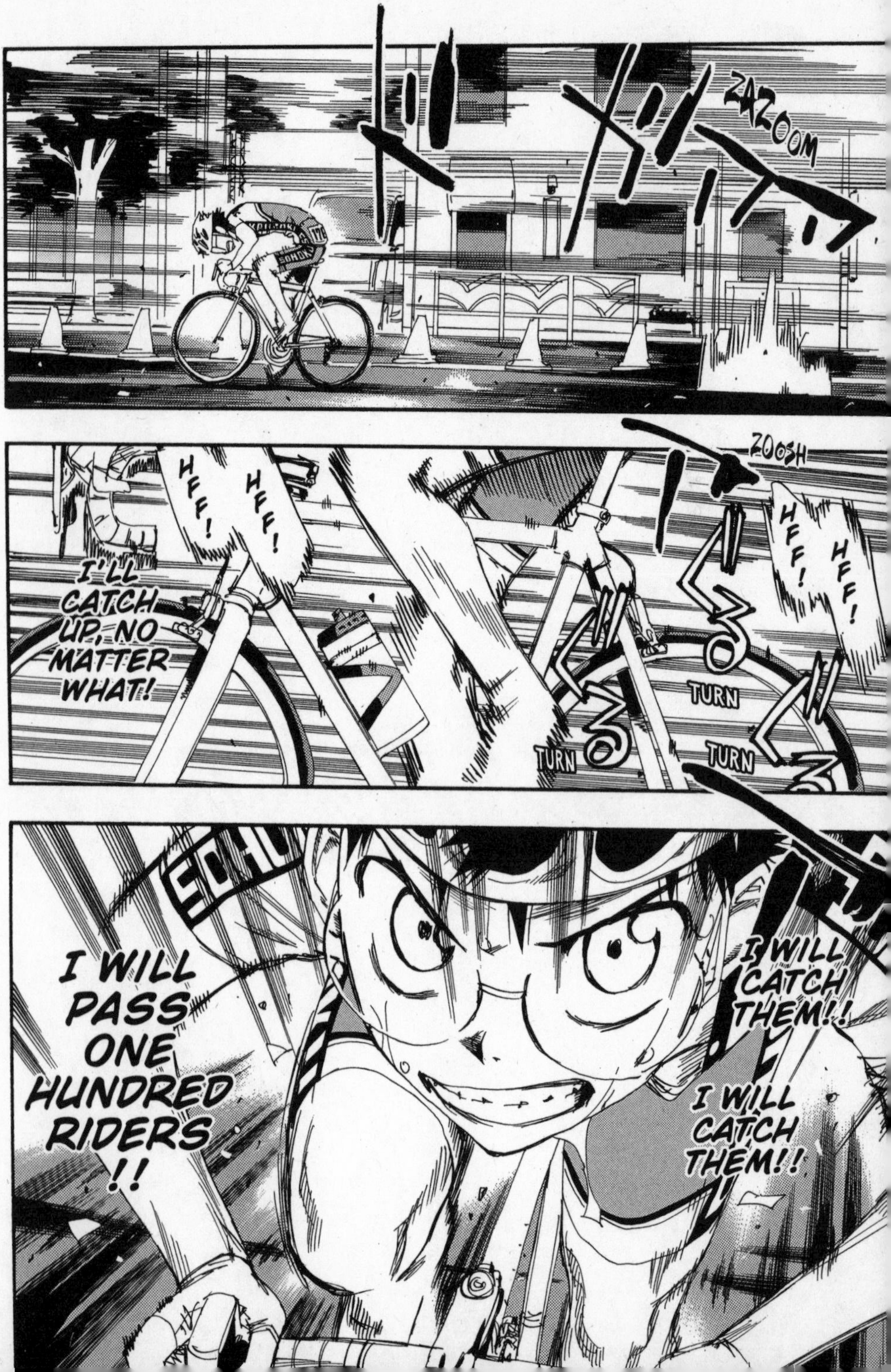
ZAZOOM
ZOOSH
HFF! HFF!
TURN
TURN
TURN
HFF! HFF!
I'LL CATCH UP, NO MATTER WHAT!
I WILL CATCH THEM!!
I WILL CATCH THEM!!
I WILL PASS ONE HUNDRED RIDERS!!

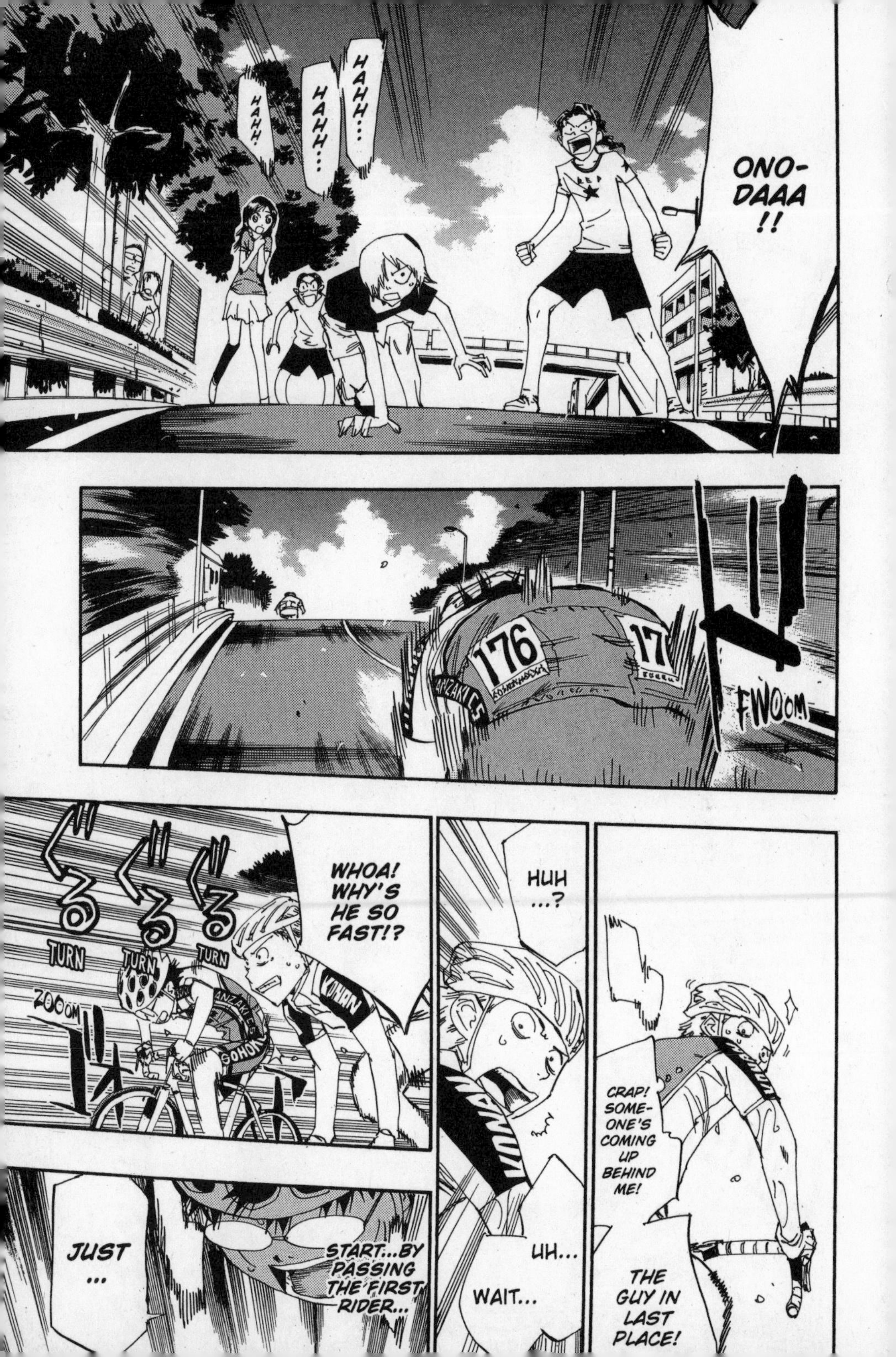
ONO-DAAA!!
HAHH... HAHH...
HAHH... HAHH...
HAHH!
FWOOM
176
17
CRAP! SOME-ONE'S COMING UP BEHIND ME!
THE GUY IN LAST PLACE!
HUH ...?
UH...
WAIT...
WHOA! WHY'S HE SO FAST!?
TURN
TURN
TURN
ZOOOM
JUST ...
START...BY PASSING THE FIRST RIDER...

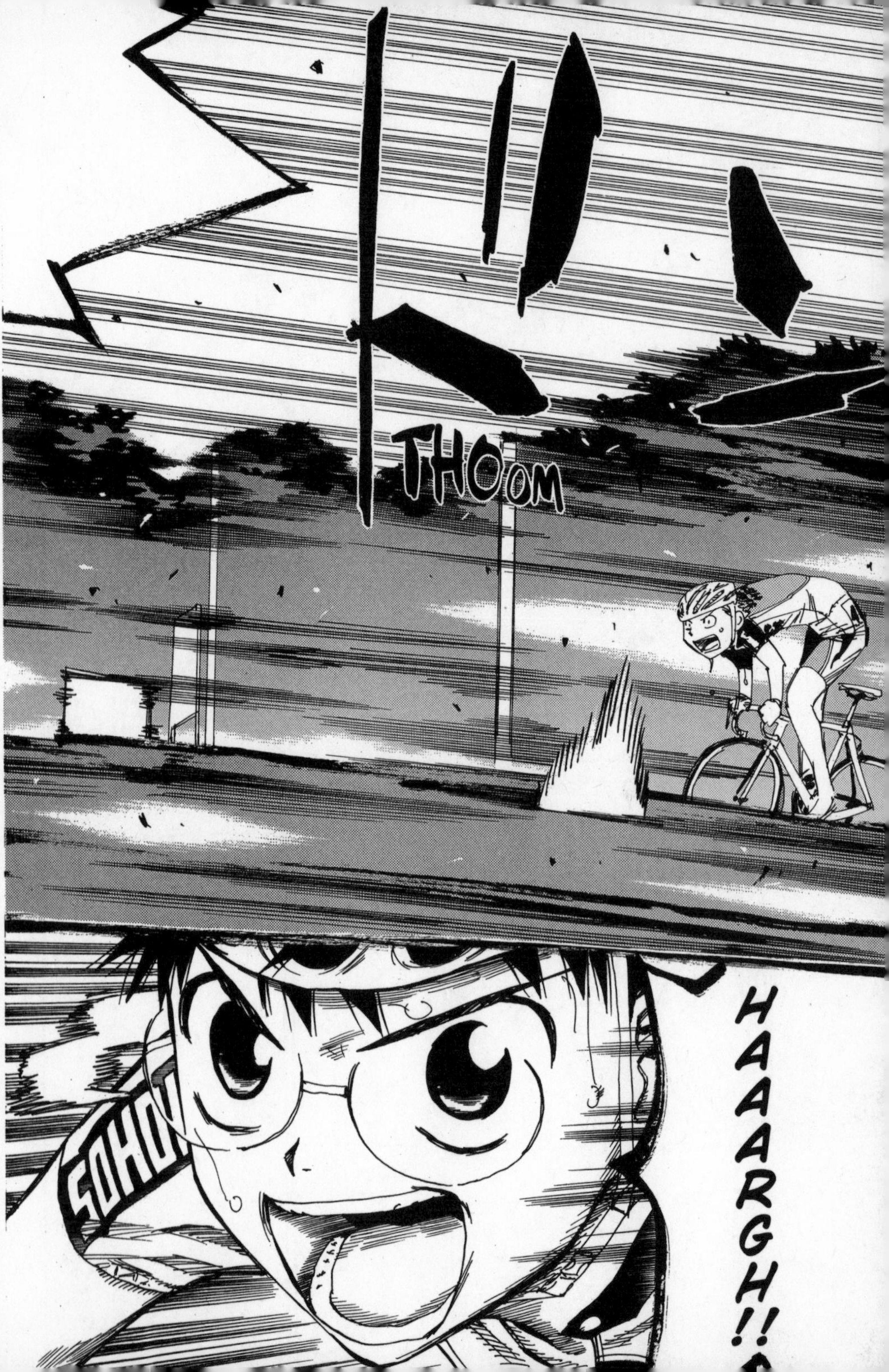
THOOM
HAAAARGH!!

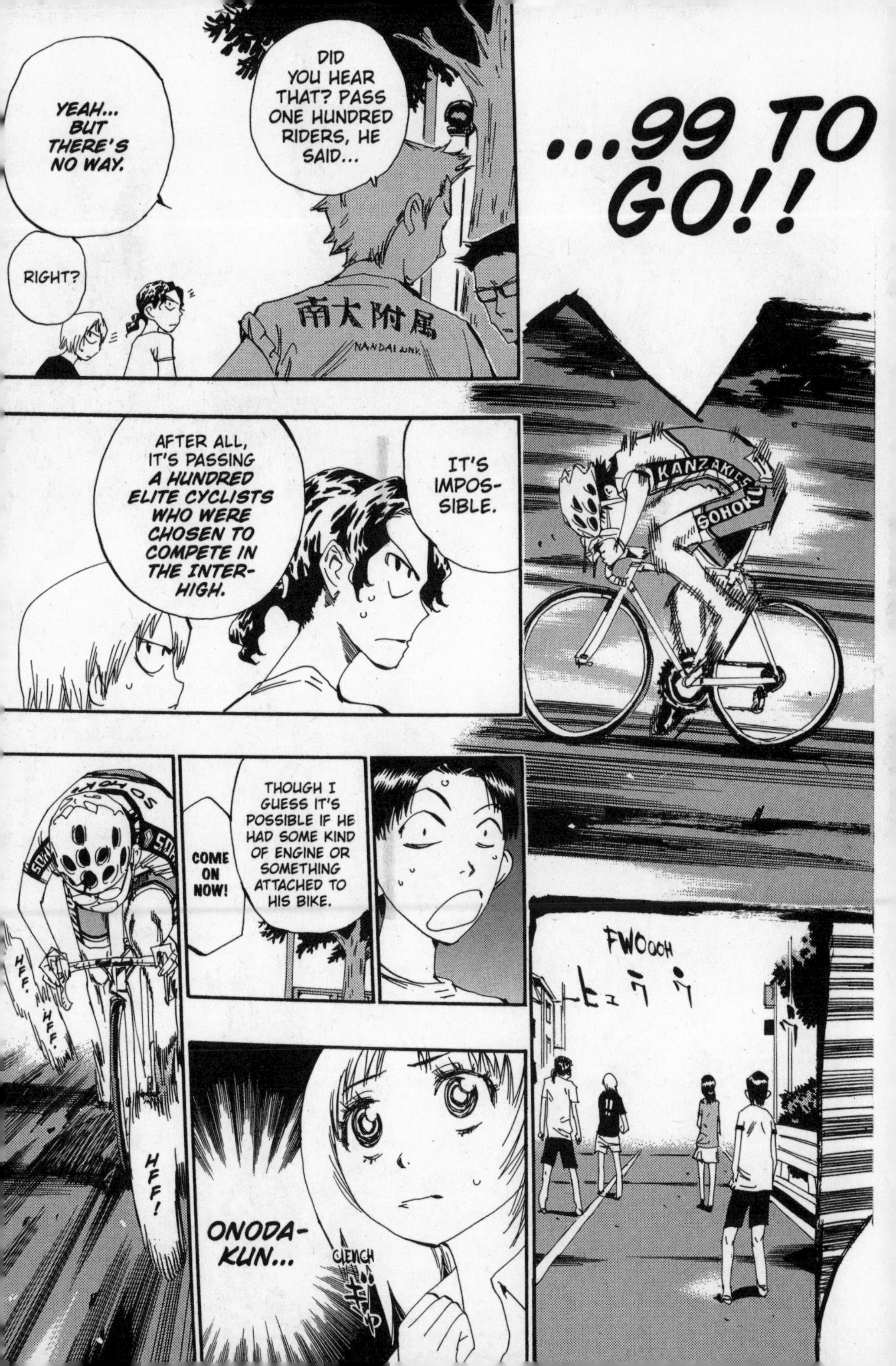
...99 TO GO!!
DID YOU HEAR THAT? PASS ONE HUNDRED RIDERS, HE SAID...
YEAH... BUT THERE'S NO WAY.
RIGHT?
南大附属
IT'S IMPOSSIBLE.
AFTER ALL, IT'S PASSING A HUNDRED ELITE CYCLISTS WHO WERE CHOSEN TO COMPETE IN THE INTER-HIGH.
SOHOKU
FWOOOH
THOUGH I GUESS IT'S POSSIBLE IF HE HAD SOME KIND OF ENGINE OR SOMETHING ATTACHED TO HIS BIKE.
COME ON NOW!
HFF. HFF. HFF!
ONODA-KUN...
CLENCH

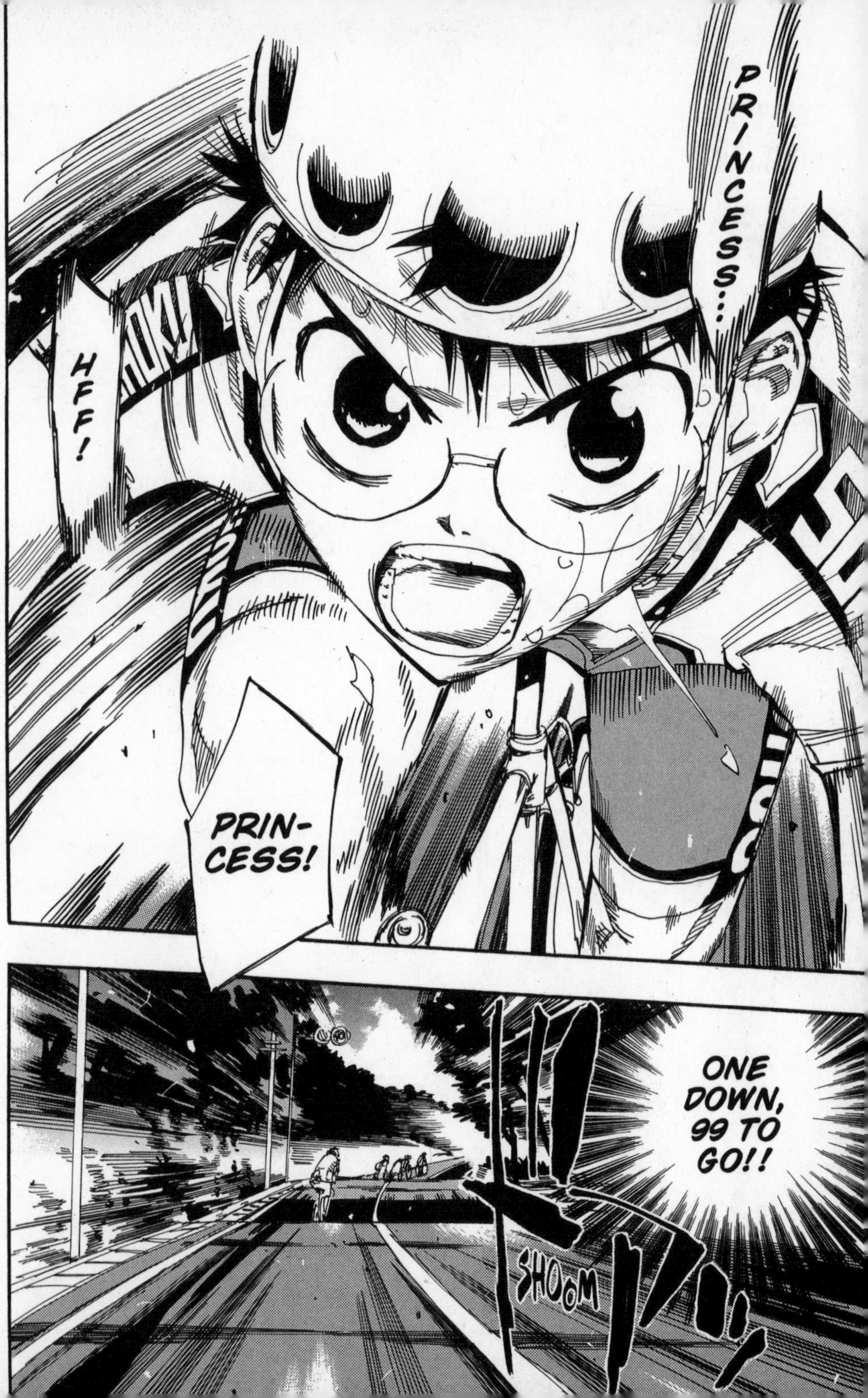
PRINCESS...
HFF!
PRIN-
CESS!
ONE DOWN, 99 TO GO!!
SHOOM

# RIDE.90 SINGING UNDER HIS BREATH

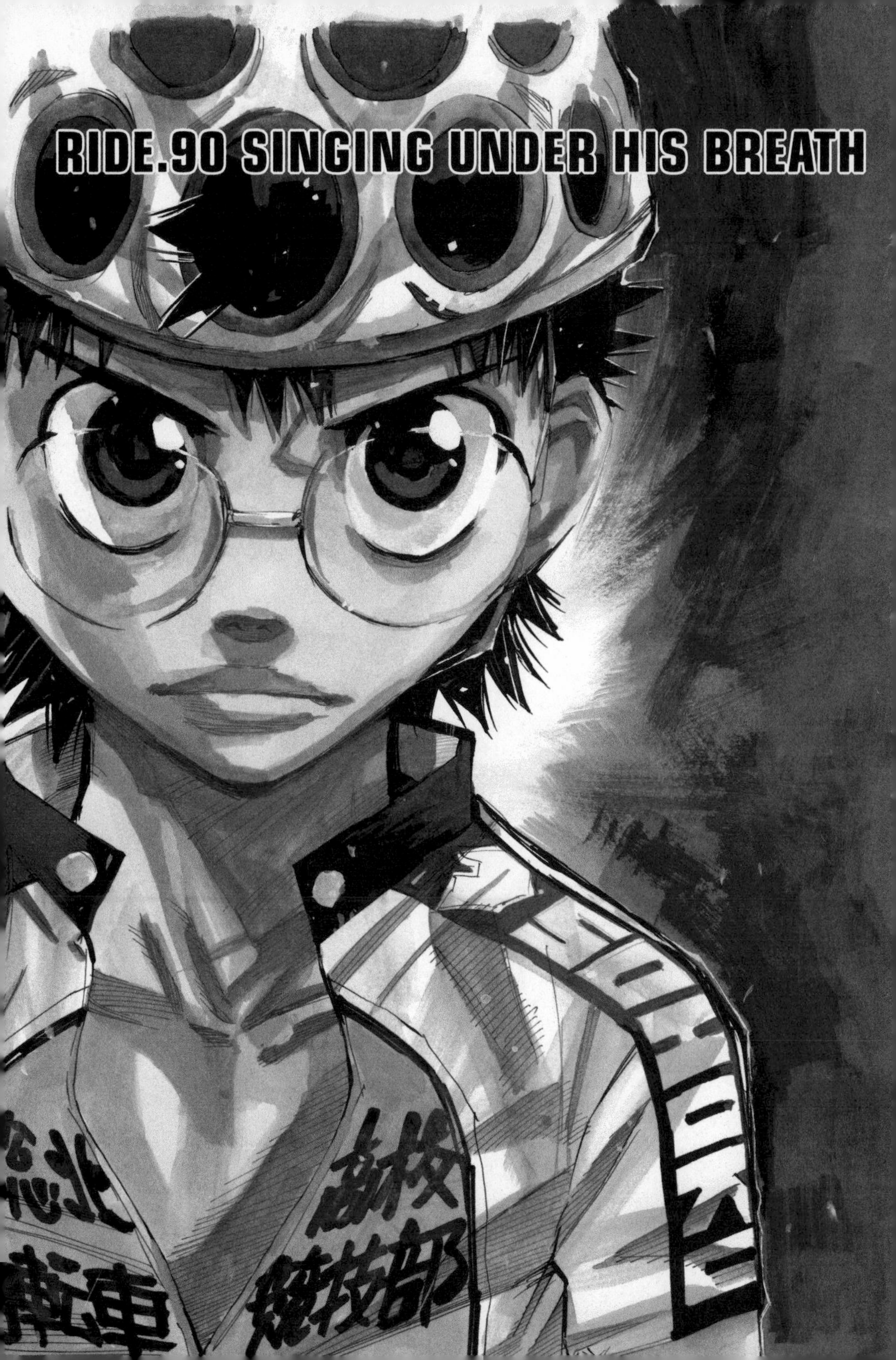

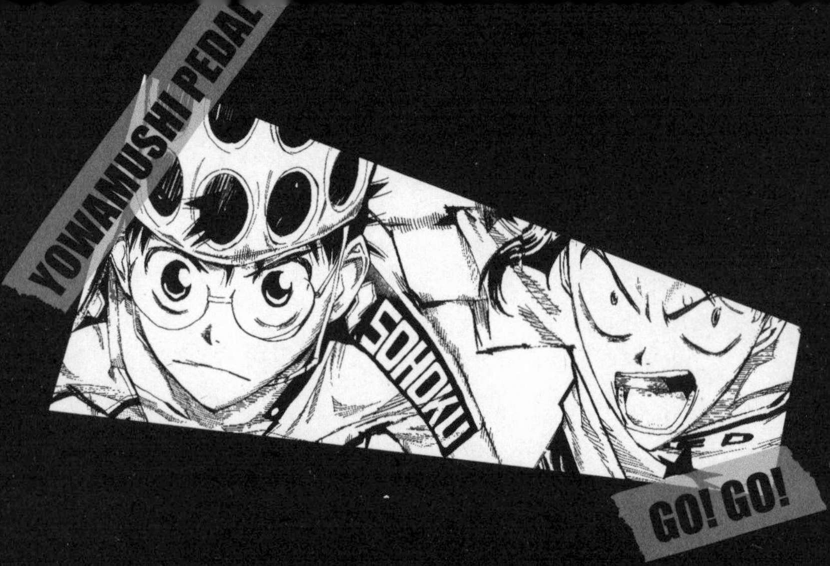
YOWAMUSHI PEDAL
SOHOKU
GO! GO!

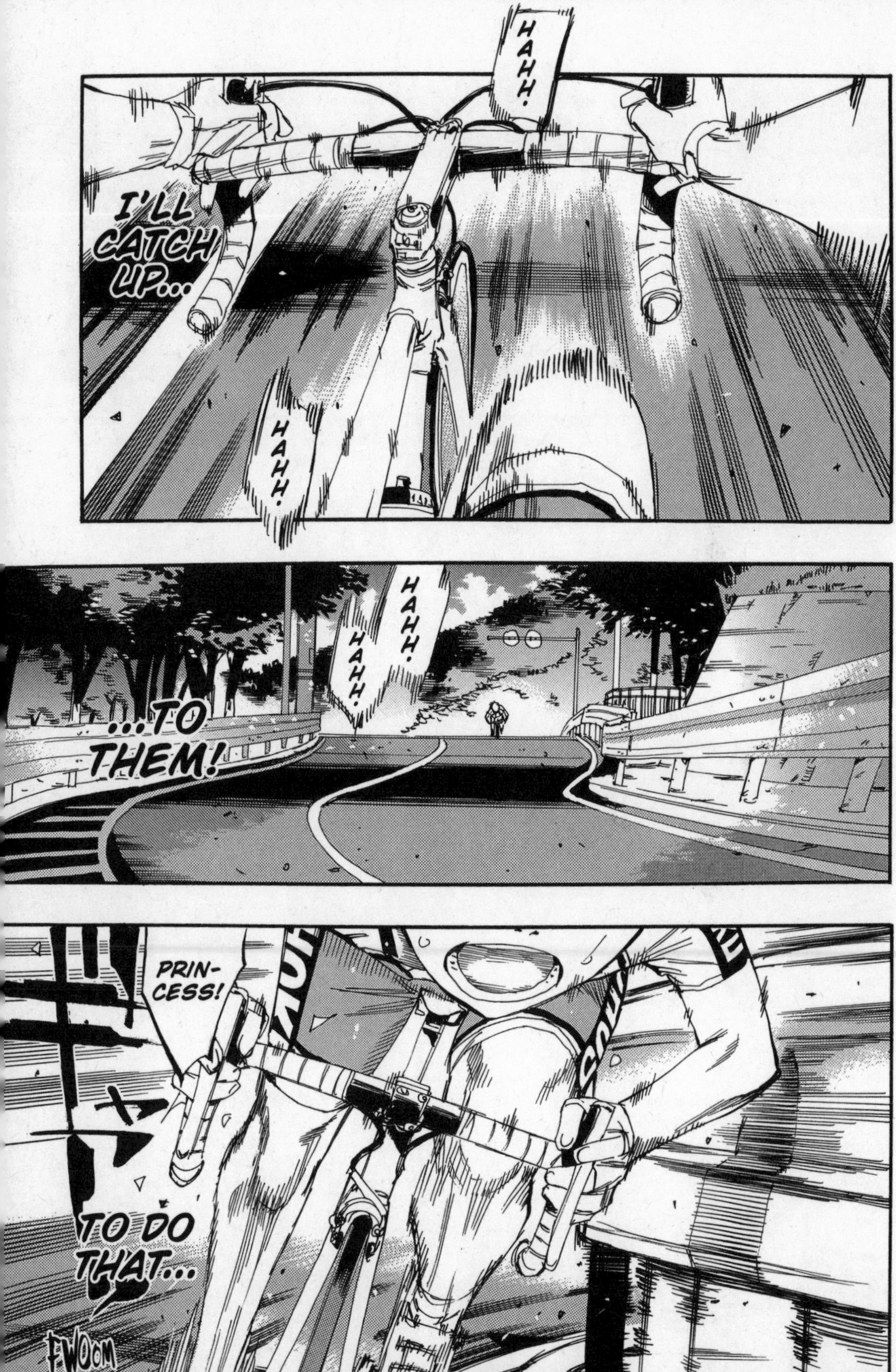
HAHH.
I'LL CATCH UP...
HAHH.
HAHH.
HAHH.
...TO THEM!
PRIN-CESS!
TO DO THAT...
FWOOM

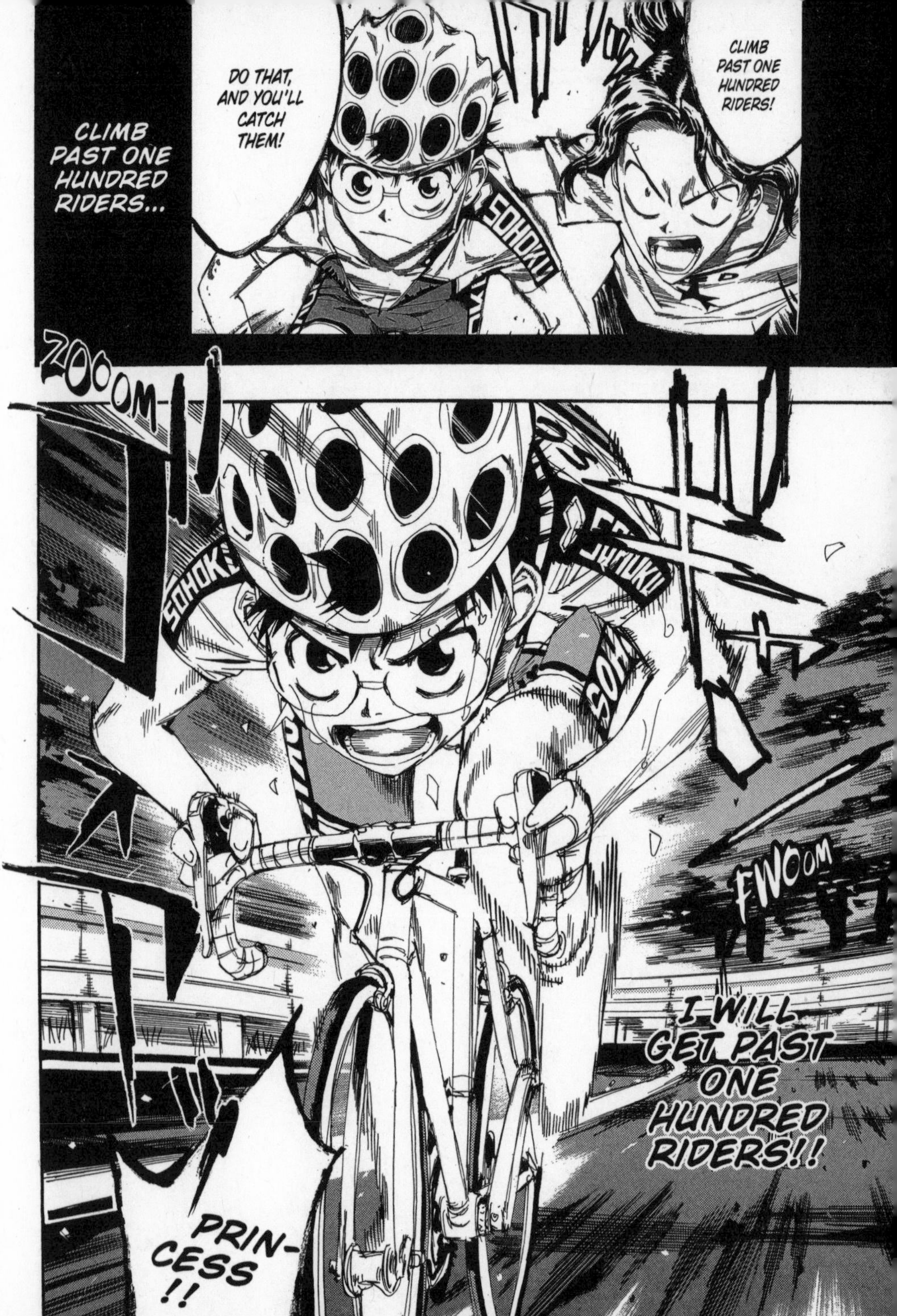
CLIMB PAST ONE HUNDRED RIDERS!
DO THAT, AND YOU'LL CATCH THEM!
CLIMB PAST ONE HUNDRED RIDERS...
ZOOOM
FWOOM
I WILL GET PAST ONE HUNDRED RIDERS!!
PRIN-CESS!!

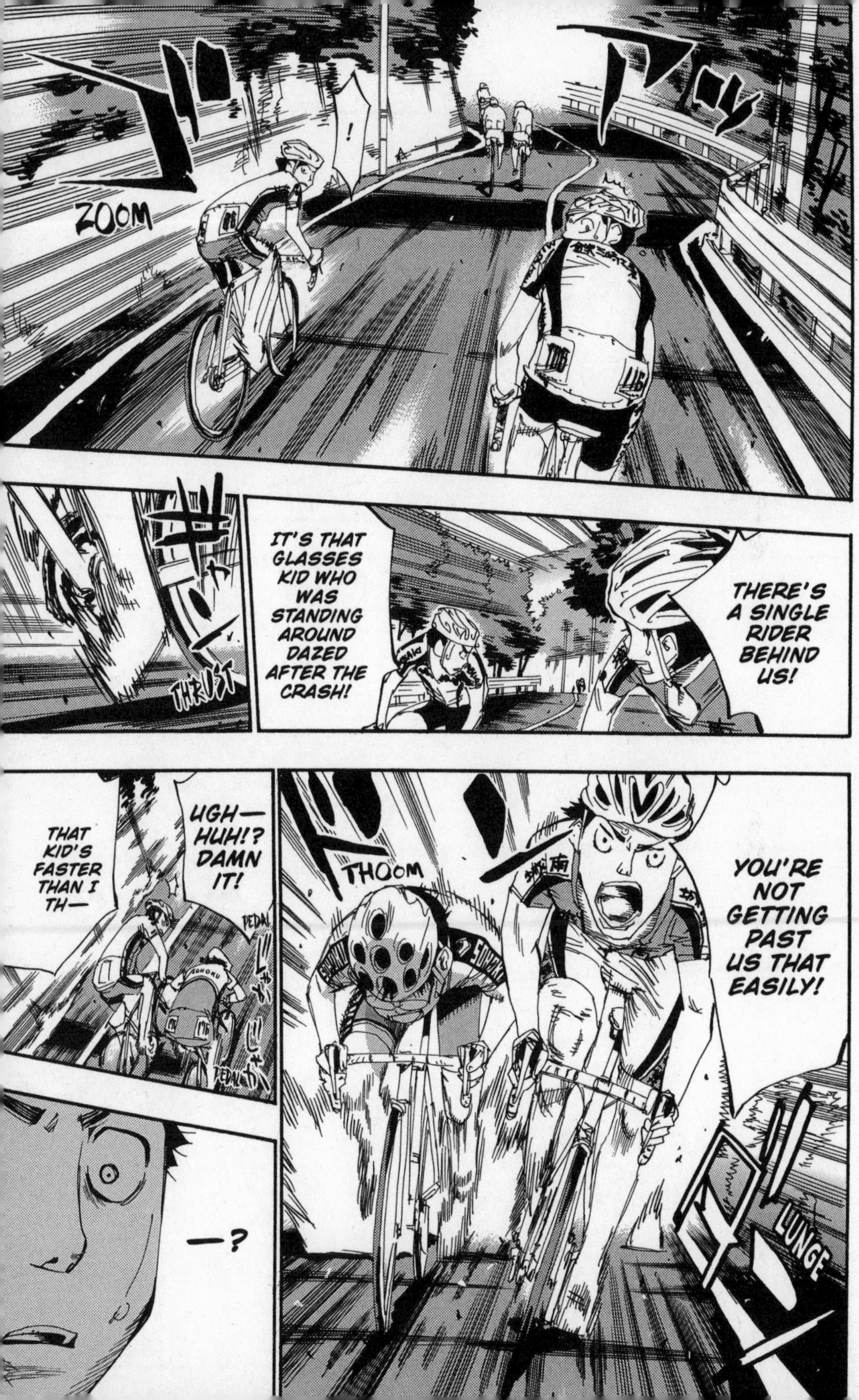
!
ZOOM
THERE'S A SINGLE RIDER BEHIND US!
IT'S THAT GLASSES KID WHO WAS STANDING AROUND DAZED AFTER THE CRASH!
THRUST
YOU'RE NOT GETTING PAST US THAT EASILY!
THOOM
LUNGE
UGH—HUH!? DAMN IT!
THAT KID'S FASTER THAN I TH—
PEDAL
PEDAL
—?

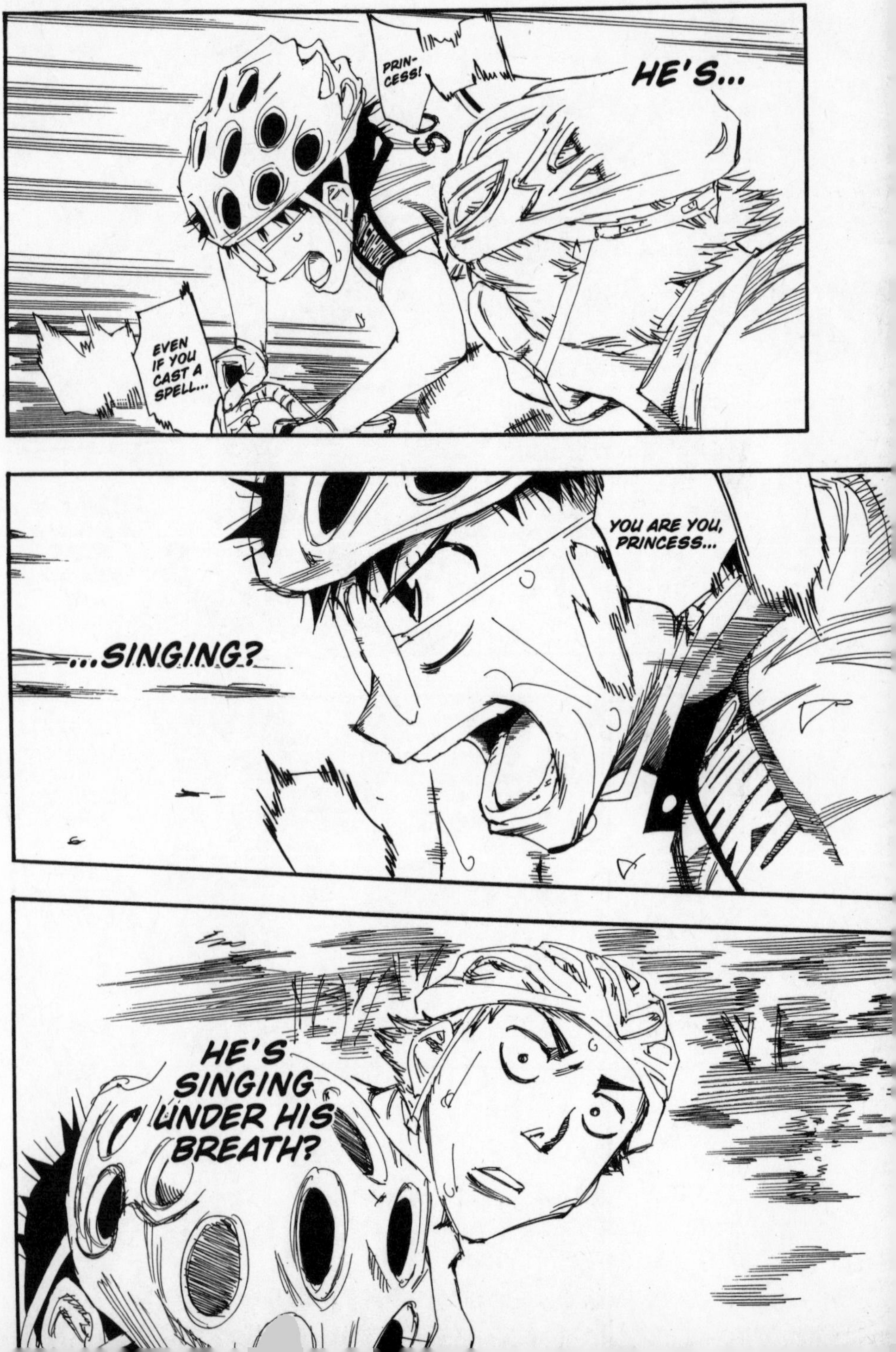
HE'S...
PRIN-CESS!
EVEN IF YOU CAST A SPELL...
YOU ARE YOU, PRINCESS...
...SINGING?
HE'S SINGING UNDER HIS BREATH?

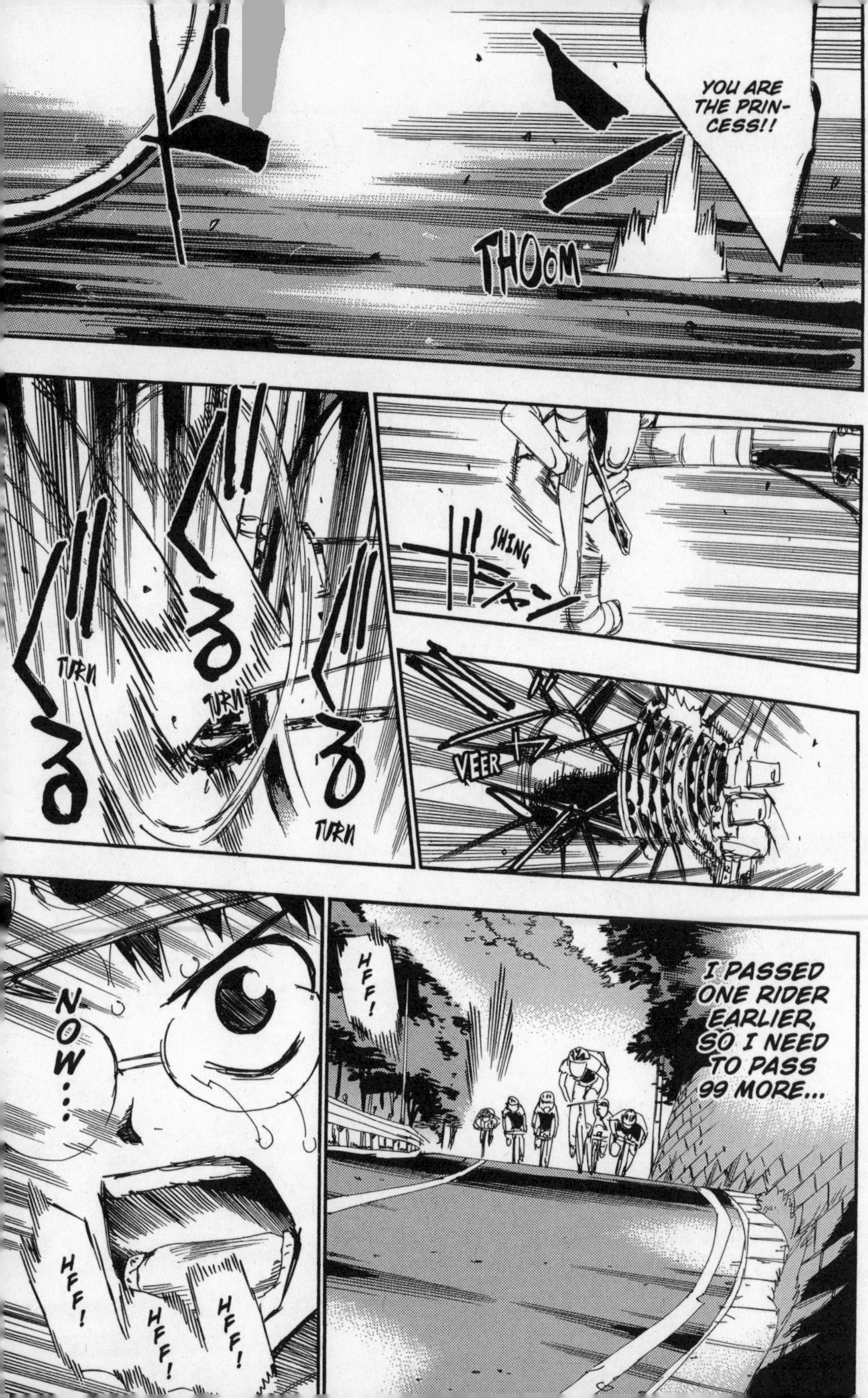
YOU ARE THE PRIN-CESS!!
THOOM
SHING
ガシャン
VEER
くるくる
TURN
TURN
TURN
I PASSED ONE RIDER EARLIER, SO I NEED TO PASS 99 MORE...
HFF!
NOW...
HFF!
HFF!
HFF!

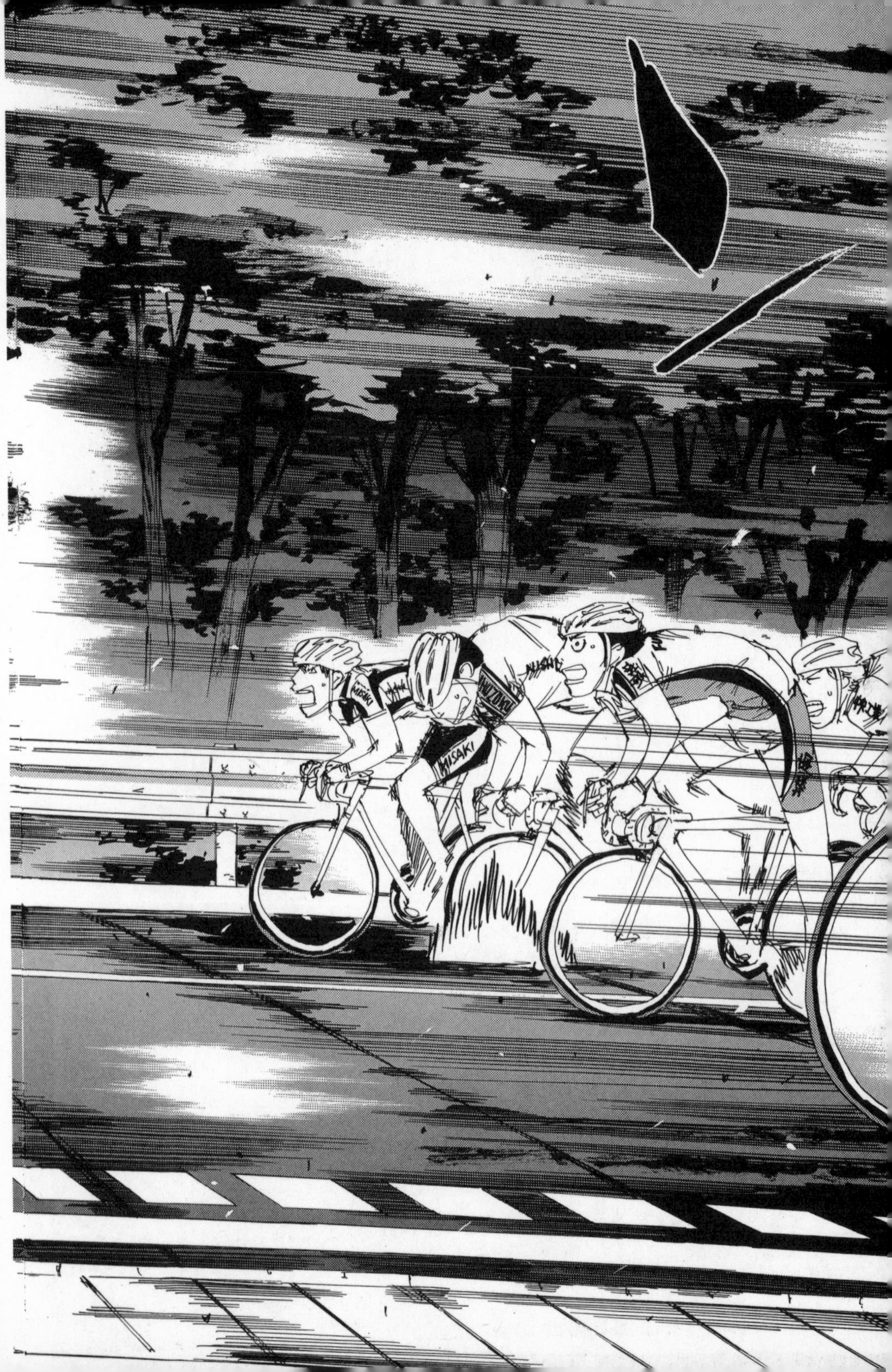

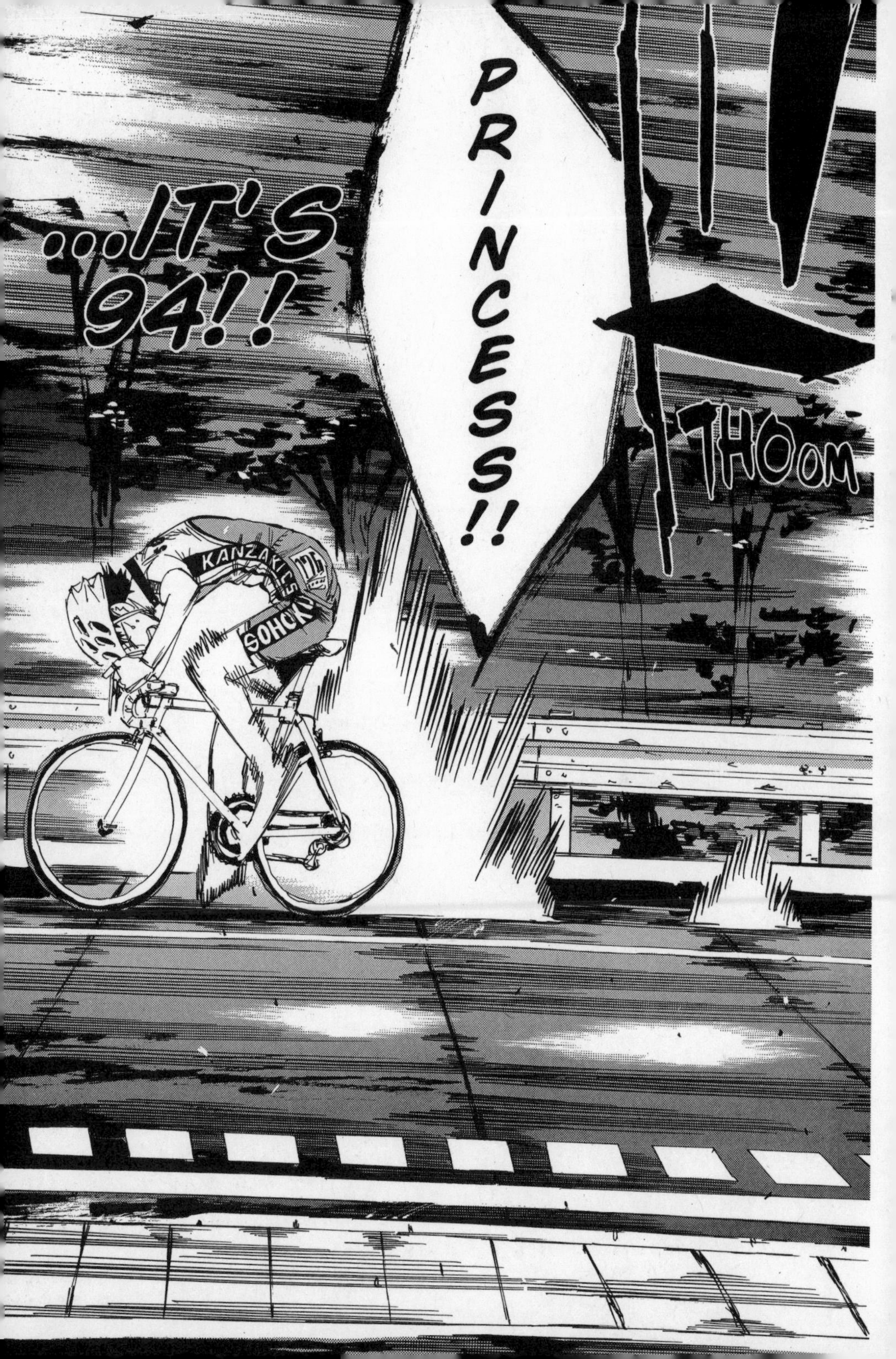
PRINCESS!!
THOOM
...IT'S 94!!

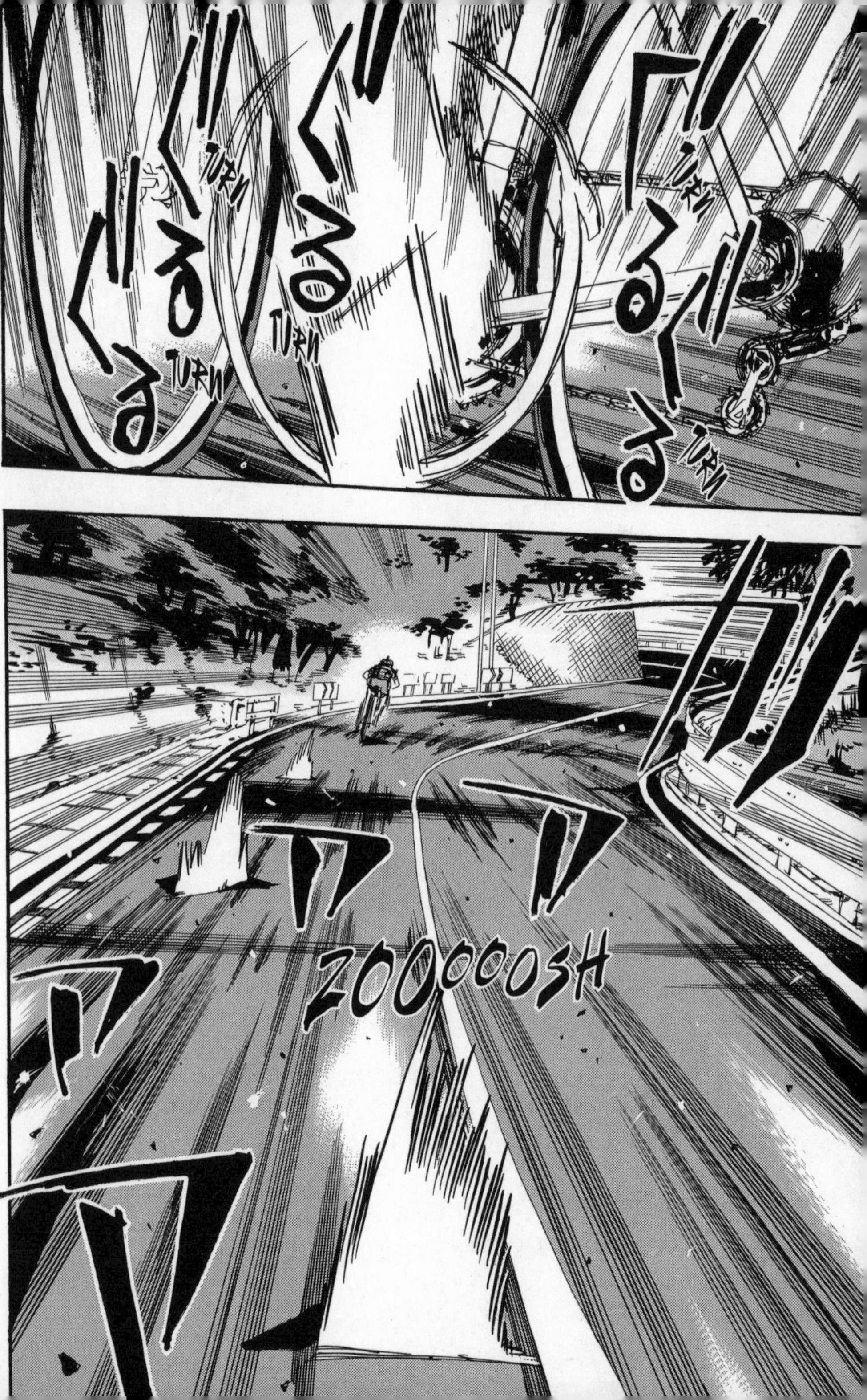
ぐるぐる
TURN
TURN
ぐる
TURN
ぐるぐる
TURN
TURN
ZOOOOOSH

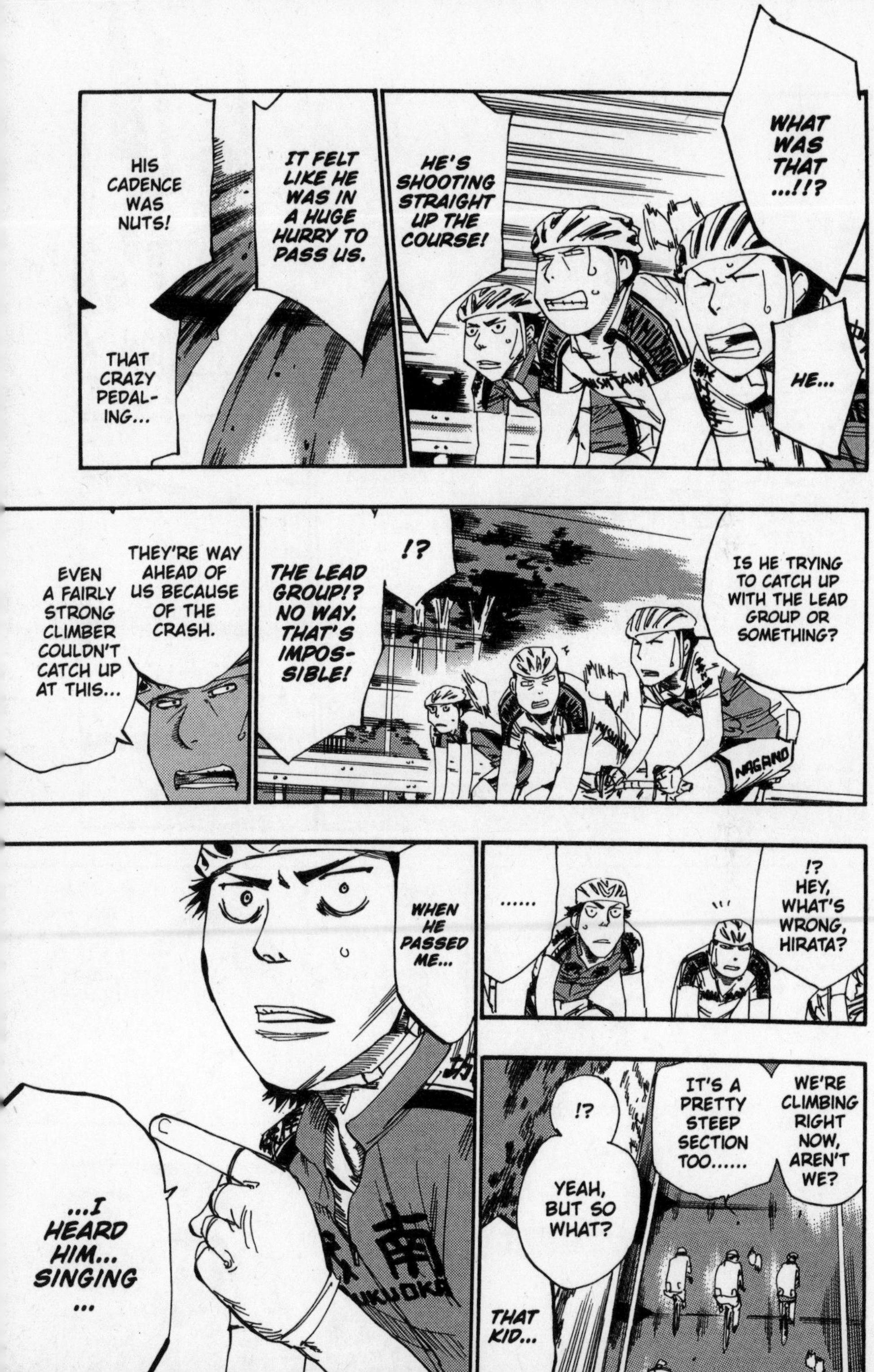
WHAT WAS THAT ...!!?
HE...
HE'S SHOOTING STRAIGHT UP THE COURSE!
IT FELT LIKE HE WAS IN A HUGE HURRY TO PASS US.
HIS CADENCE WAS NUTS!
THAT CRAZY PEDAL-ING...
IS HE TRYING TO CATCH UP WITH THE LEAD GROUP OR SOMETHING?
!?
THE LEAD GROUP!? NO WAY. THAT'S IMPOS-SIBLE!
THEY'RE WAY AHEAD OF US BECAUSE OF THE CRASH.
EVEN A FAIRLY STRONG CLIMBER COULDN'T CATCH UP AT THIS...
!? HEY, WHAT'S WRONG, HIRATA?
......
WE'RE CLIMBING RIGHT NOW, AREN'T WE?
IT'S A PRETTY STEEP SECTION TOO......
!?
YEAH, BUT SO WHAT?
THAT KID...
WHEN HE PASSED ME...
...I HEARD HIM... SINGING ...

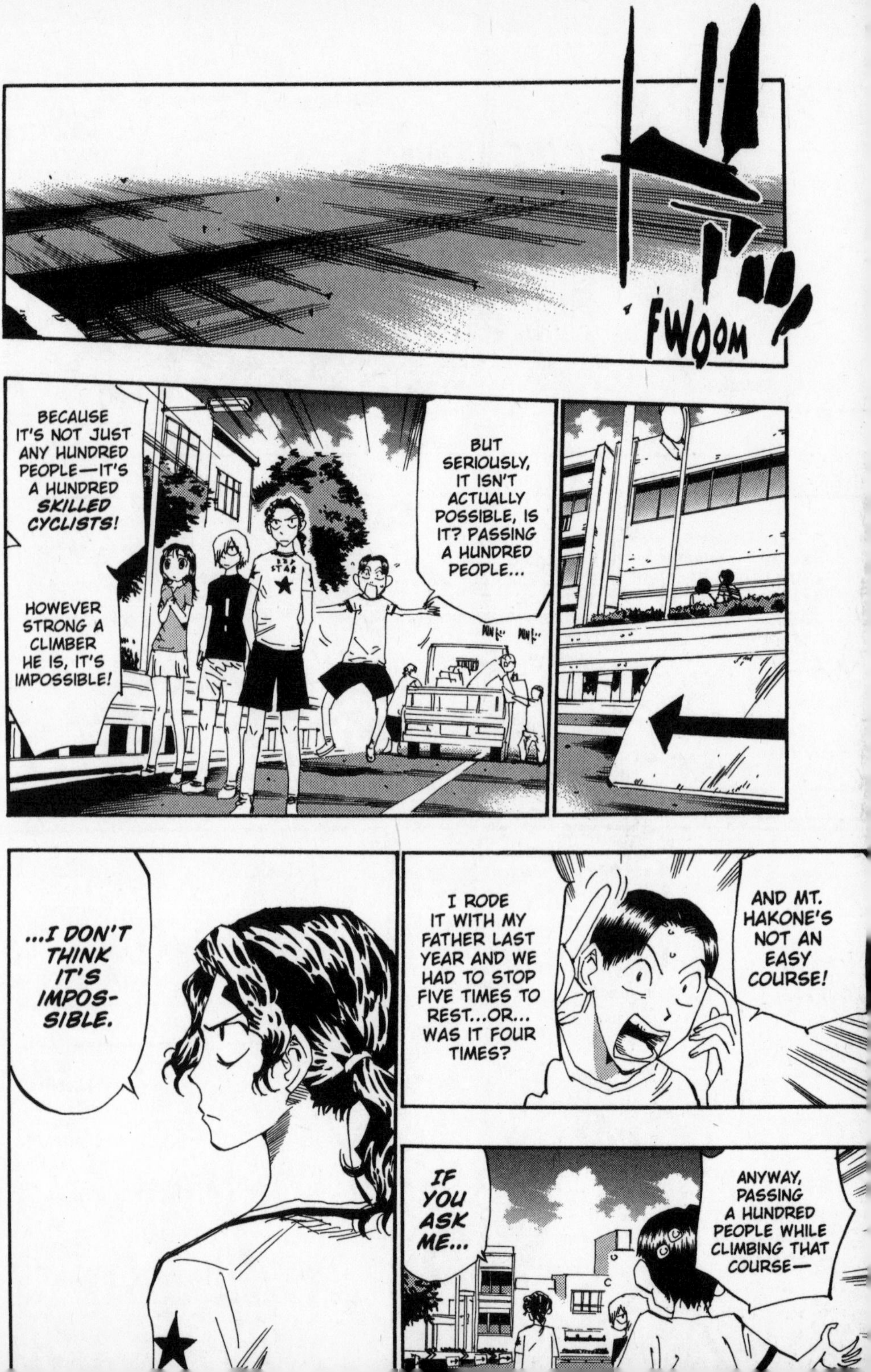
FWOOM
BUT SERIOUSLY, IT ISN'T ACTUALLY POSSIBLE, IS IT? PASSING A HUNDRED PEOPLE...
BECAUSE IT'S NOT JUST ANY HUNDRED PEOPLE—IT'S A HUNDRED *SKILLED CYCLISTS*!
HOWEVER STRONG A CLIMBER HE IS, IT'S IMPOSSIBLE!
AND MT. HAKONE'S NOT AN EASY COURSE!
I RODE IT WITH MY FATHER LAST YEAR AND WE HAD TO STOP FIVE TIMES TO REST...OR... WAS IT FOUR TIMES?
ANYWAY, PASSING A HUNDRED PEOPLE WHILE CLIMBING THAT COURSE—
*IF YOU ASK ME...*
*...I DON'T THINK IT'S IMPOS-SIBLE.*

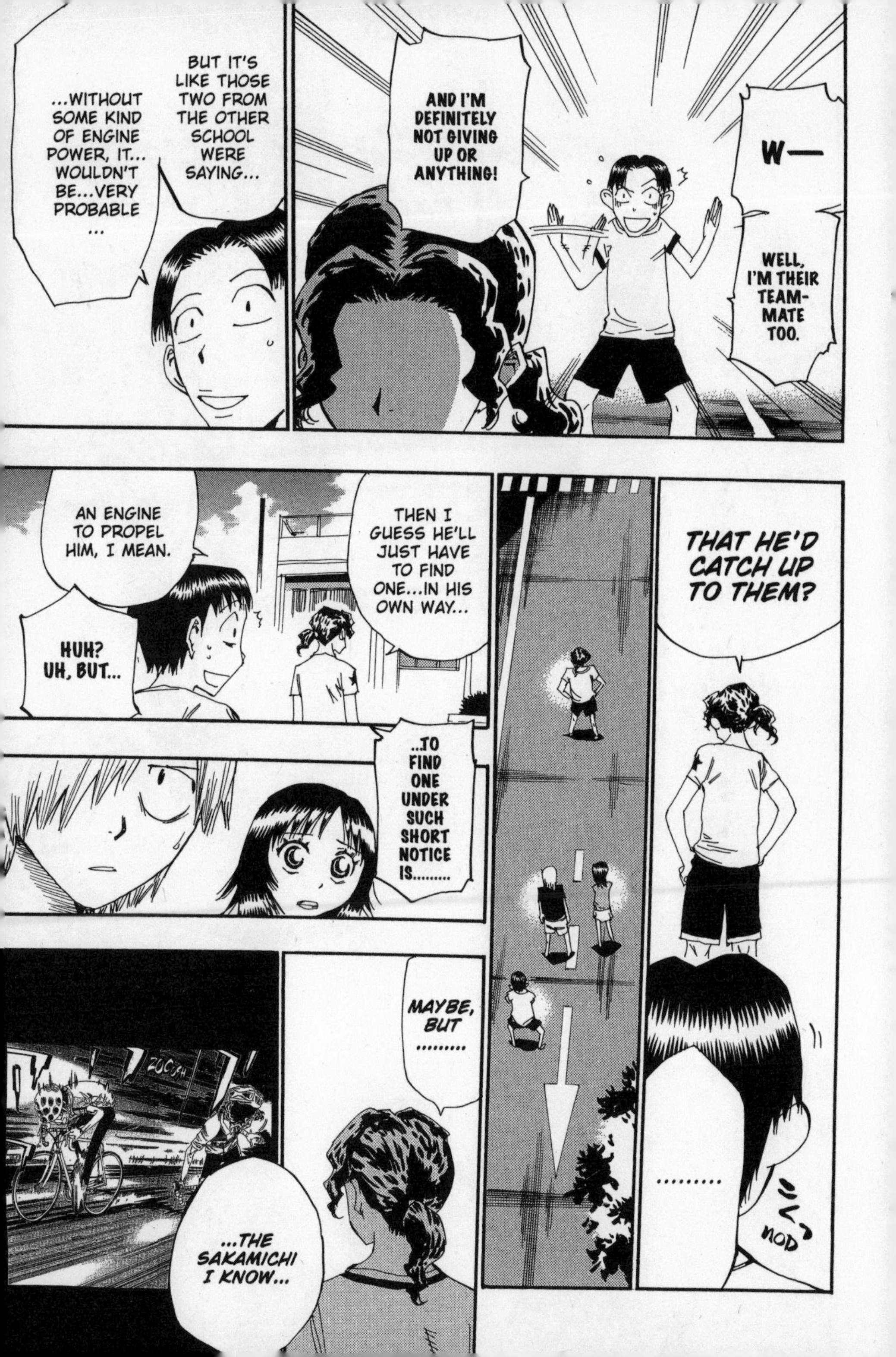

W—
WELL, I'M THEIR TEAM-MATE TOO.
AND I'M DEFINITELY NOT GIVING UP OR ANYTHING!
BUT IT'S LIKE THOSE TWO FROM THE OTHER SCHOOL WERE SAYING...
...WITHOUT SOME KIND OF ENGINE POWER, IT... WOULDN'T BE...VERY PROBABLE...
THAT HE'D CATCH UP TO THEM?
..........
NOD
THEN I GUESS HE'LL JUST HAVE TO FIND ONE...IN HIS OWN WAY...
AN ENGINE TO PROPEL HIM, I MEAN.
HUH? UH, BUT...
...TO FIND ONE UNDER SUCH SHORT NOTICE IS.........
MAYBE, BUT ..........
...THE SAKAMICHI I KNOW...
ZOOSH

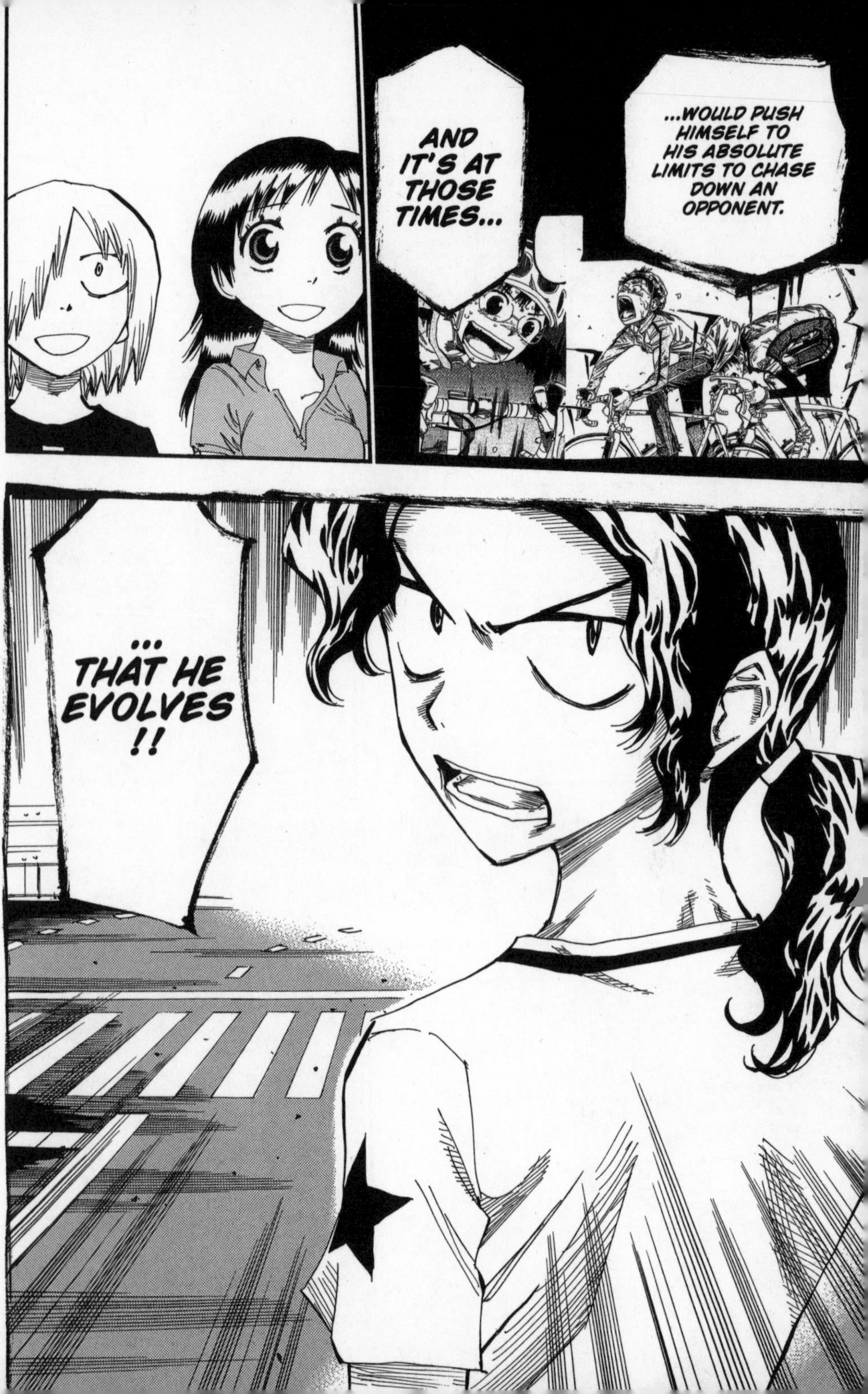
...WOULD PUSH HIMSELF TO HIS ABSOLUTE LIMITS TO CHASE DOWN AN OPPONENT.
AND IT'S AT THOSE TIMES...
...THAT HE EVOLVES!!

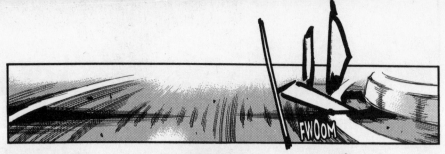

FWOOM

SOHOKU

TADOKORO-SAN...

NARUKO-KUN... IMAIZUMI-KUN... CAPTAIN...

HAHH
HAHH
HAHH

ZOOM

HEF!

40

THOOM

MAKISHIMA-SAN!!

JUST WAIT! I'LL CATCH UP TO YOU, NO MATTER WHAT!!

PRIN-CESS!

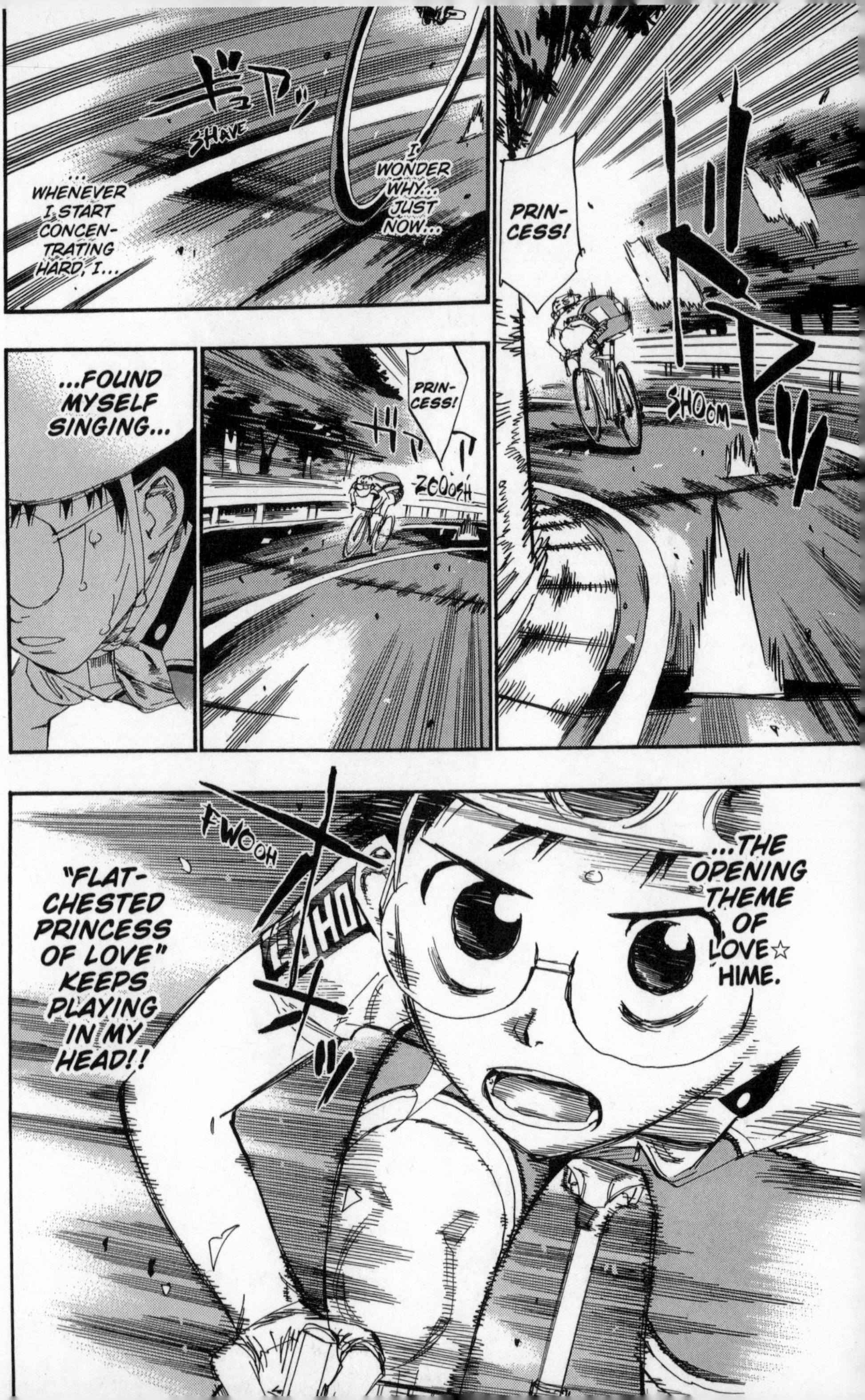
PRIN-CESS!
SHOOM
SHAVE
I WONDER WHY... JUST NOW...
...WHENEVER I START CONCEN-TRATING HARD, I...
PRIN-CESS!
ZOOOSH
...FOUND MYSELF SINGING...
...THE OPENING THEME OF LOVE☆HIME.
FWOOH
"FLAT-CHESTED PRINCESS OF LOVE" KEEPS PLAYING IN MY HEAD!!

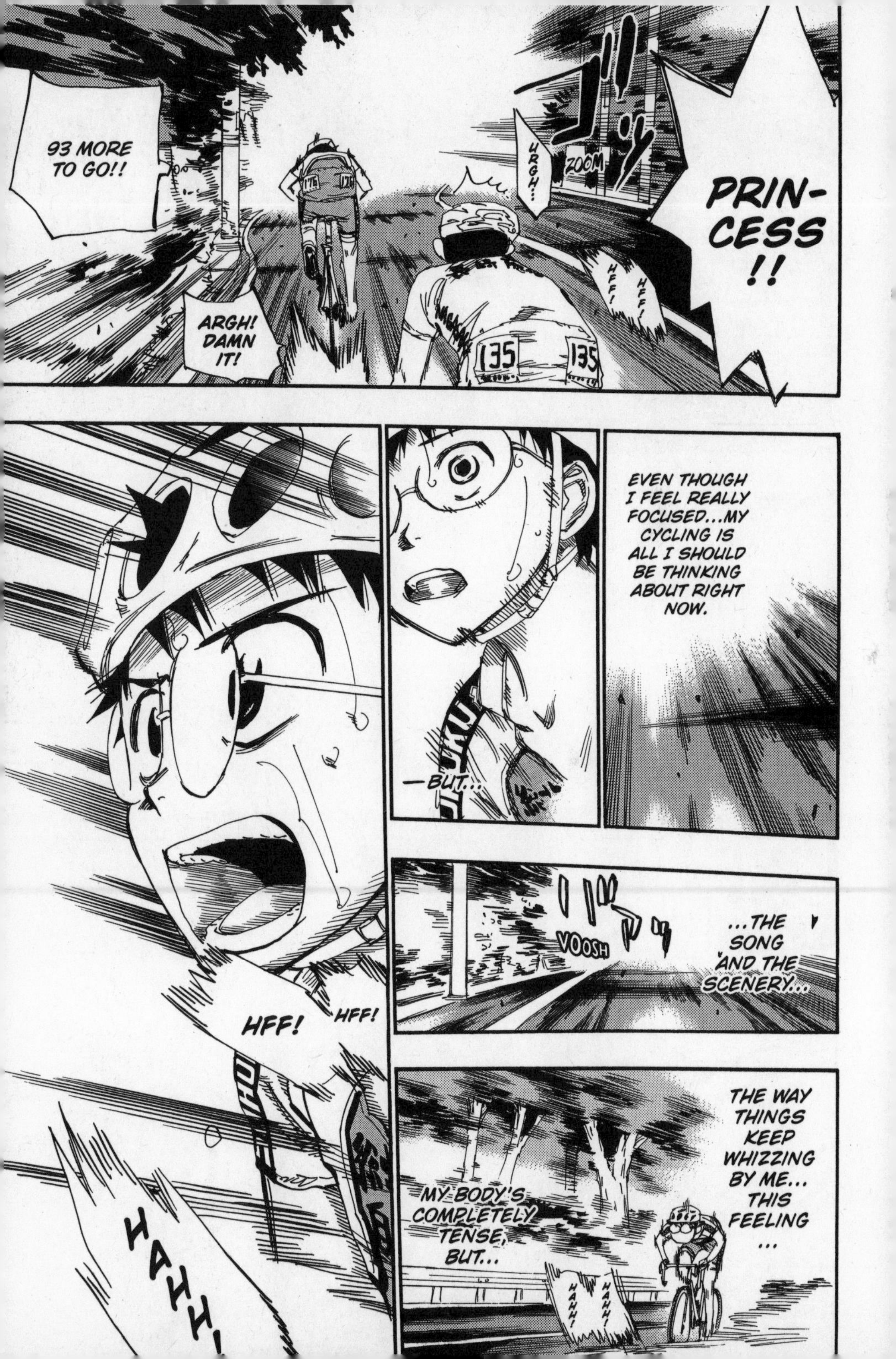
PRIN-CESS!!
URGH..
ZOOM
HFF! HFF!
93 MORE TO GO!!
ARGH! DAMN IT!
EVEN THOUGH I FEEL REALLY FOCUSED...MY CYCLING IS ALL I SHOULD BE THINKING ABOUT RIGHT NOW.
—BUT...
...THE SONG AND THE SCENERY...
VOOSH
THE WAY THINGS KEEP WHIZZING BY ME... THIS FEELING...
MY BODY'S COMPLETELY TENSE, BUT...
HAHH HAHH
HFF! HFF!
HAHH!

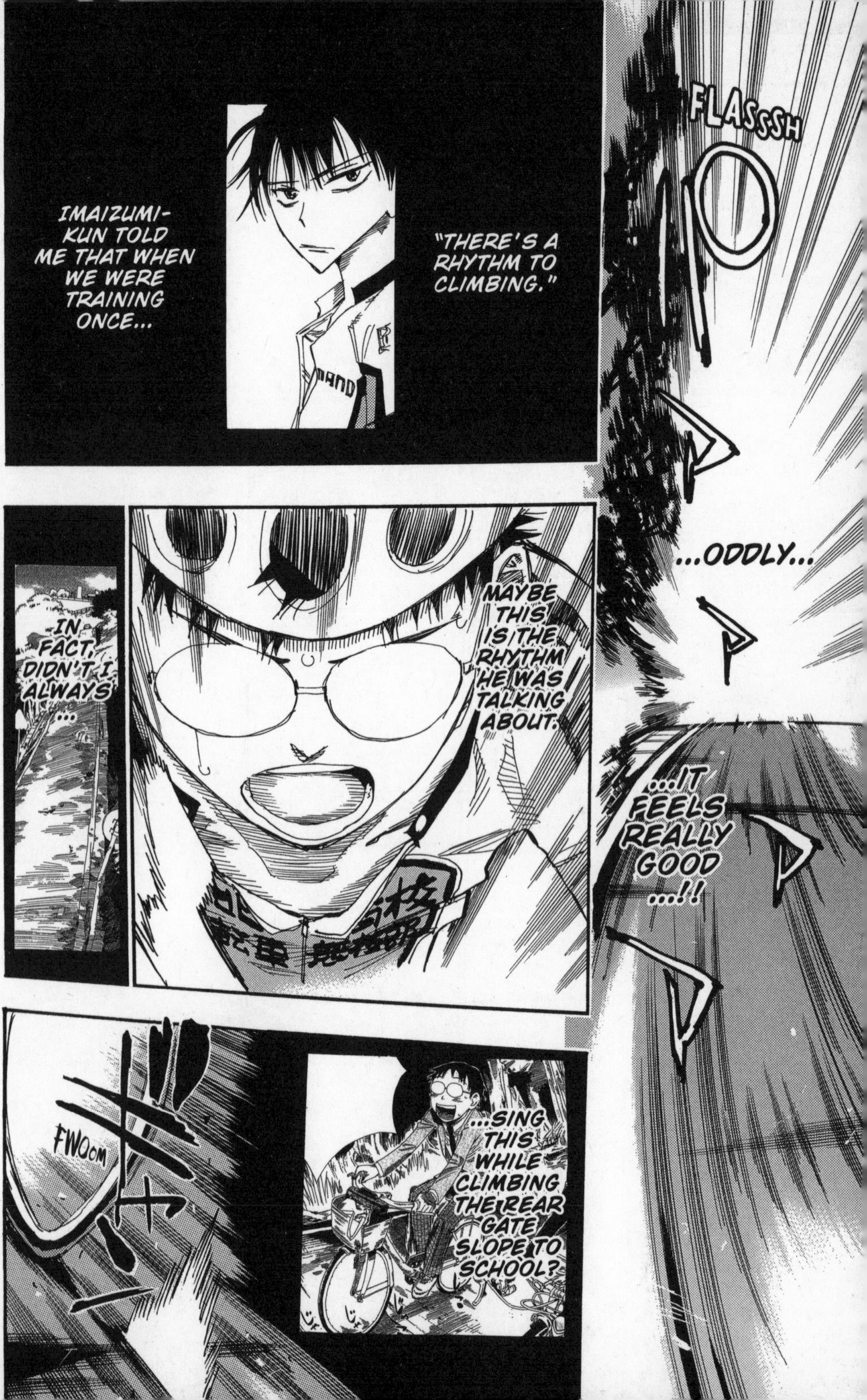
FLASSSH
...ODDLY...
...IT FEELS REALLY GOOD ...!!
IMAIZUMI-KUN TOLD ME THAT WHEN WE WERE TRAINING ONCE...
"THERE'S A RHYTHM TO CLIMBING."
MAYBE THIS IS THE RHYTHM HE WAS TALKING ABOUT.
IN FACT, DIDN'T I ALWAYS ...
...SING THIS WHILE CLIMBING THE REAR GATE SLOPE TO SCHOOL?
FWOOM

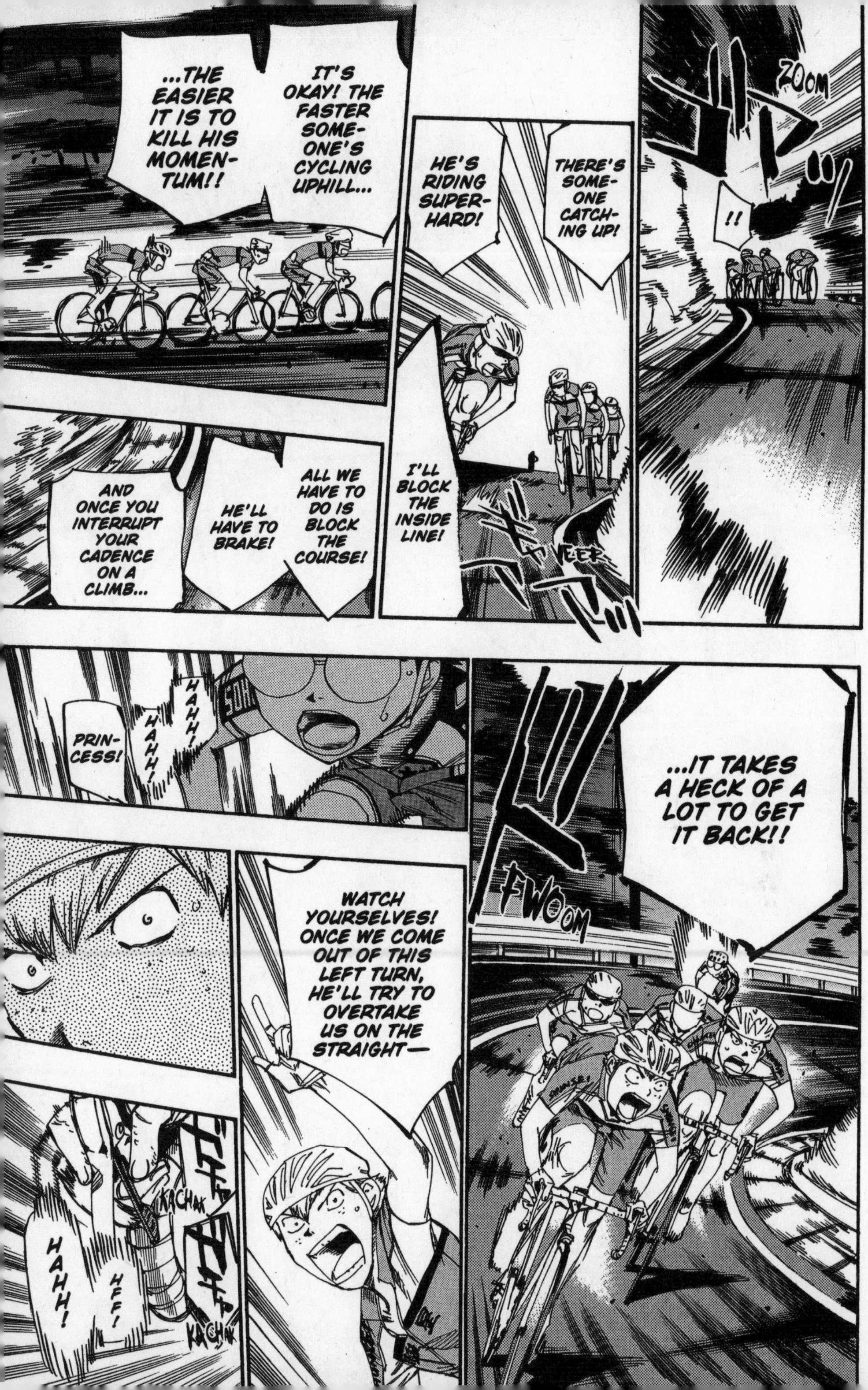
ZOOM
!!
THERE'S SOMEONE CATCHING UP!
HE'S RIDING SUPERHARD!
I'LL BLOCK THE INSIDE LINE!
VEER
IT'S OKAY! THE FASTER SOMEONE'S CYCLING UPHILL...
...THE EASIER IT IS TO KILL HIS MOMENTUM!!
ALL WE HAVE TO DO IS BLOCK THE COURSE!
HE'LL HAVE TO BRAKE!
AND ONCE YOU INTERRUPT YOUR CADENCE ON A CLIMB...
...IT TAKES A HECK OF A LOT TO GET IT BACK!!
FWOOM
HAHH! HAHH!
PRINCESS!
WATCH YOURSELVES! ONCE WE COME OUT OF THIS LEFT TURN, HE'LL TRY TO OVERTAKE US ON THE STRAIGHT—
KACHAK
HEF!
HAHH!
KACHAK

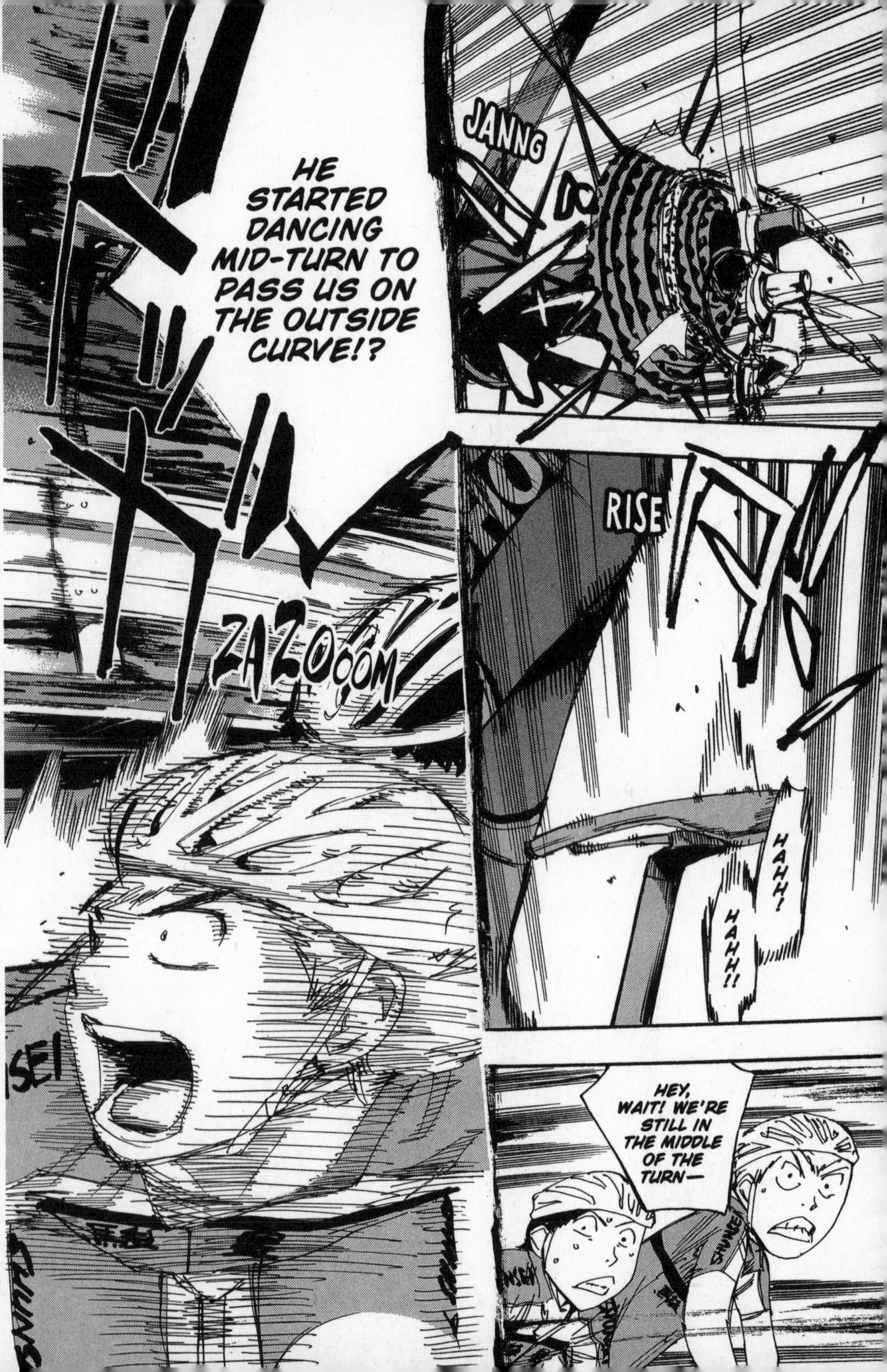
JANNG
RISE
HAHH!
HAHH!!
HEY, WAIT! WE'RE STILL IN THE MIDDLE OF THE TURN—
HE STARTED DANCING MID-TURN TO PASS US ON THE OUTSIDE CURVE!?
ZAZOOOM

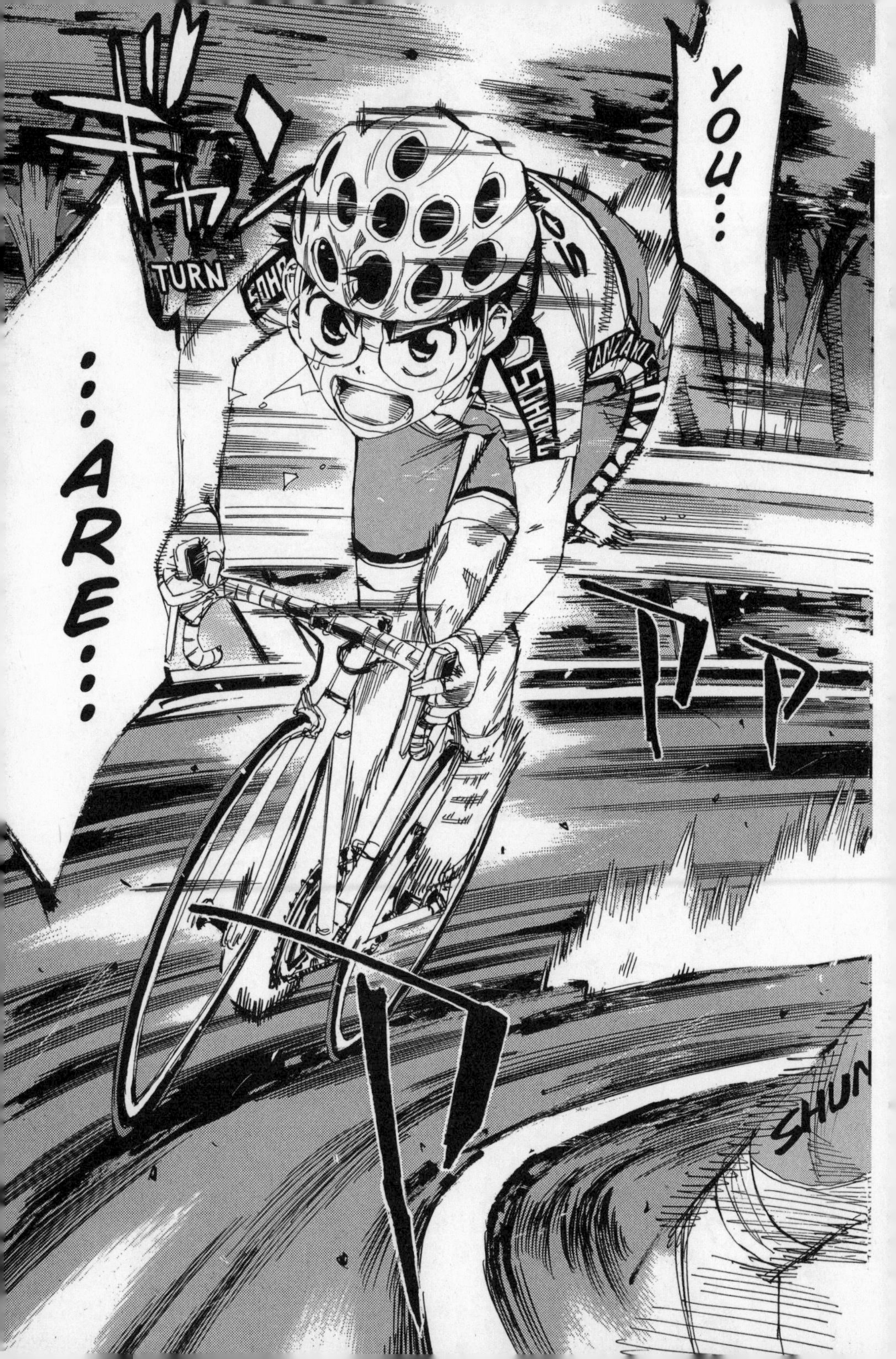
YOU...
TURN
...ARE...
SHUN

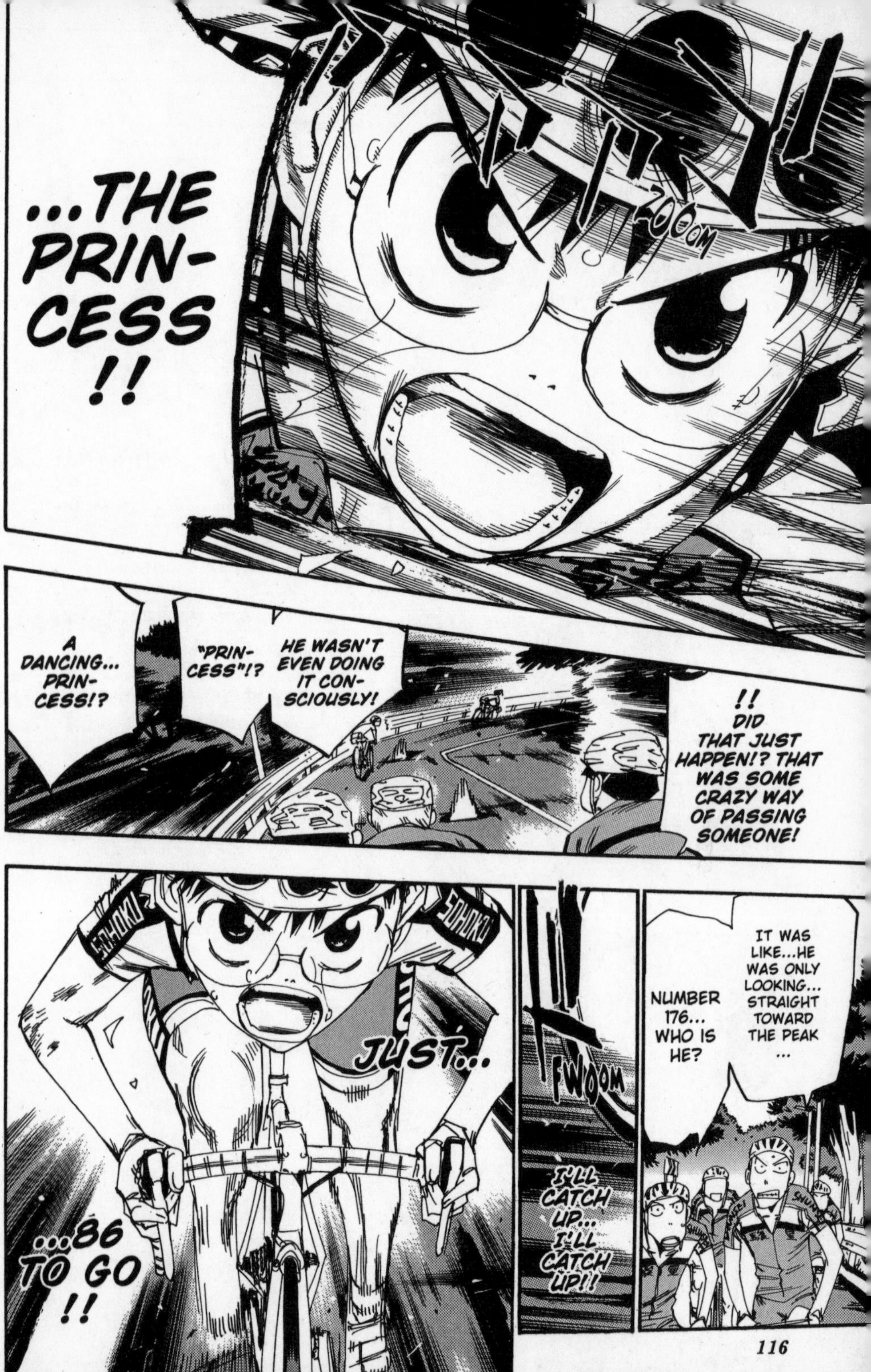
ZOOM
...THE PRIN-CESS !!
!! DID THAT JUST HAPPEN!? THAT WAS SOME CRAZY WAY OF PASSING SOMEONE!
HE WASN'T EVEN DOING IT CON-SCIOUSLY!
"PRIN-CESS"!?
A DANCING... PRIN-CESS!?
IT WAS LIKE...HE WAS ONLY LOOKING... STRAIGHT TOWARD THE PEAK ...
NUMBER 176... WHO IS HE?
FWOOM
I'LL CATCH UP... I'LL CATCH UP!!
JUST...
...86 TO GO !!

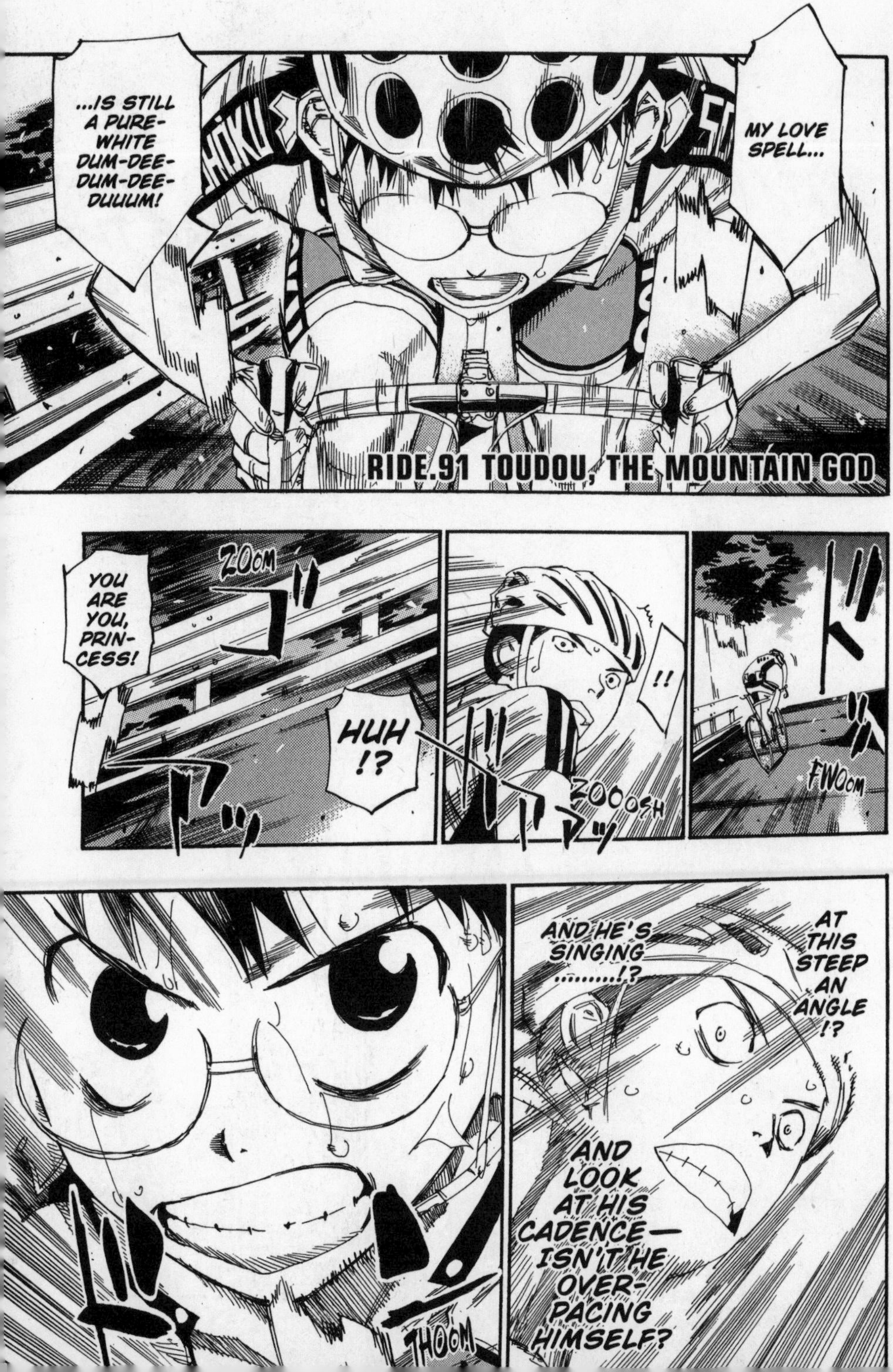
MY LOVE SPELL...
...IS STILL A PURE-WHITE DUM-DEE-DUM-DEE-DUUUM!
RIDE.91 TOUDOU, THE MOUNTAIN GOD
FWOOM
!!
ZOOOSH
YOU ARE YOU, PRINCESS!
HUH !?
ZOOM
AT THIS STEEP AN ANGLE !?
AND HE'S SINGING .........!?
AND LOOK AT HIS CADENCE—ISN'T HE OVER-PACING HIMSELF?
THOOM

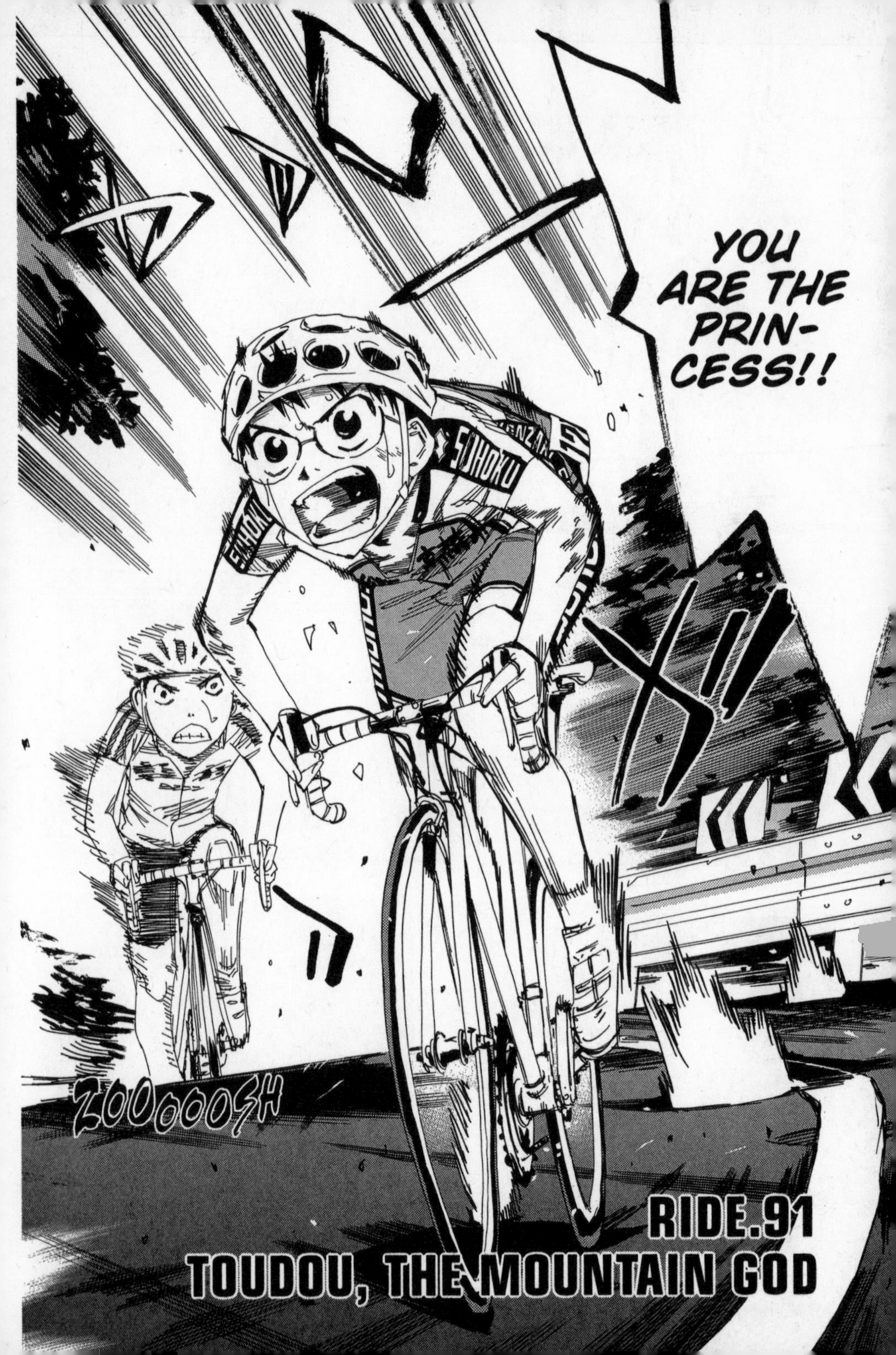
YOU ARE THE PRIN-CESS!!
ZOOOOOOSH

RIDE.91
TOUDOU, THE MOUNTAIN GOD

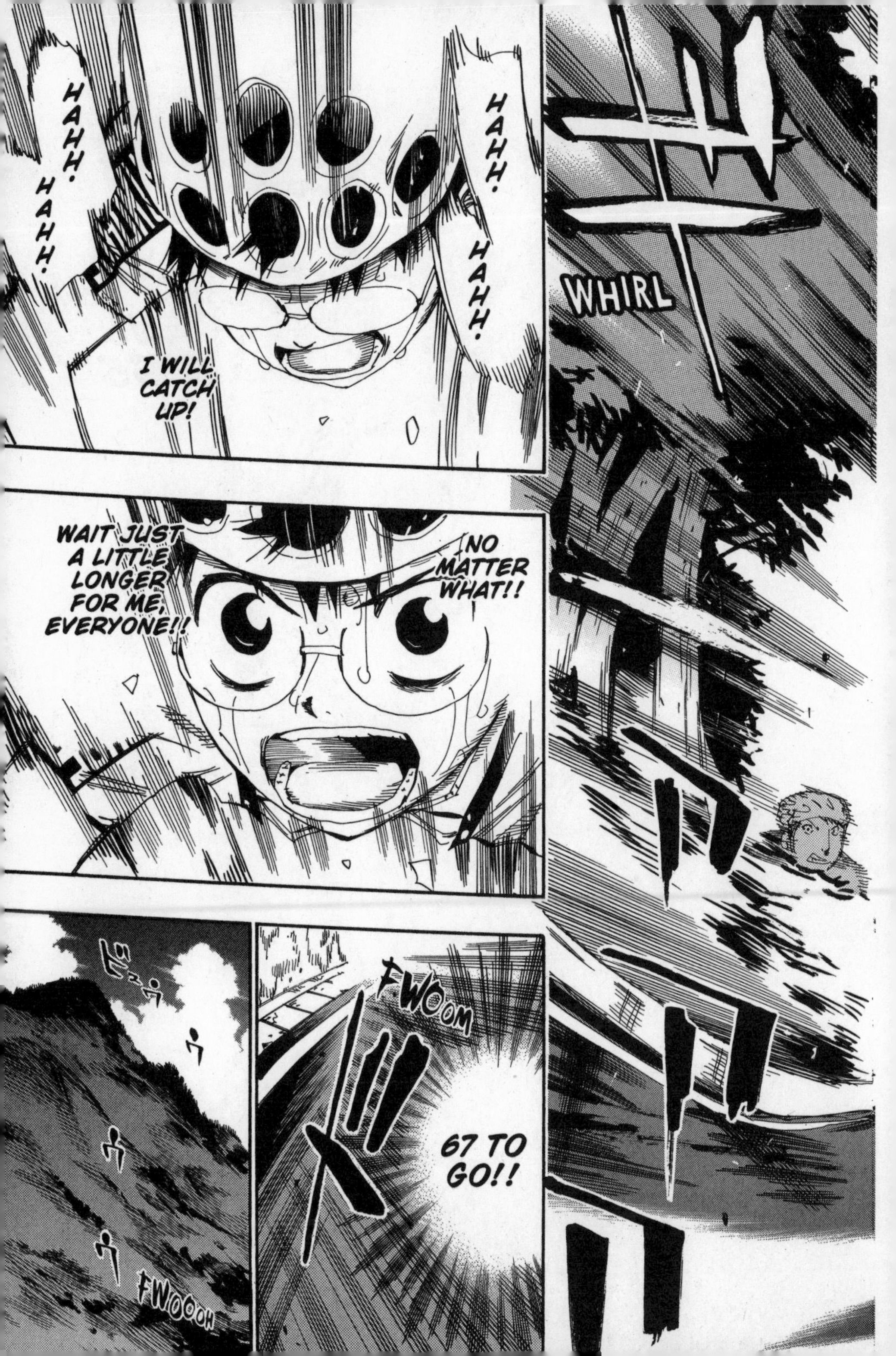
WHIRL
HAHH. HAHH.
HAHH. HAHH.
I WILL CATCH UP!
NO MATTER WHAT!!
WAIT JUST A LITTLE LONGER FOR ME, EVERYONE!!
FWOOM
67 TO GO!!
FWOOOH

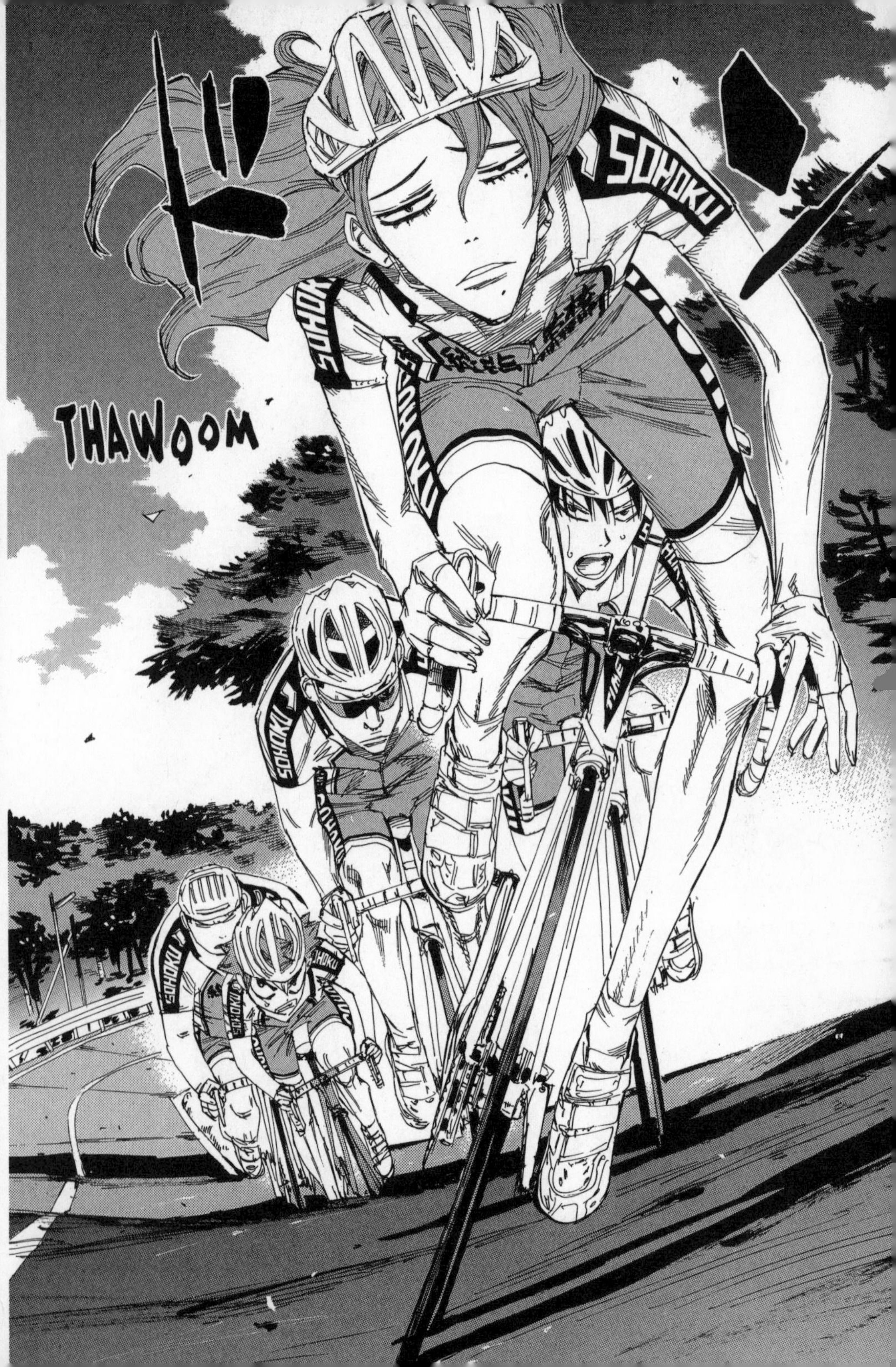
THAWOOM

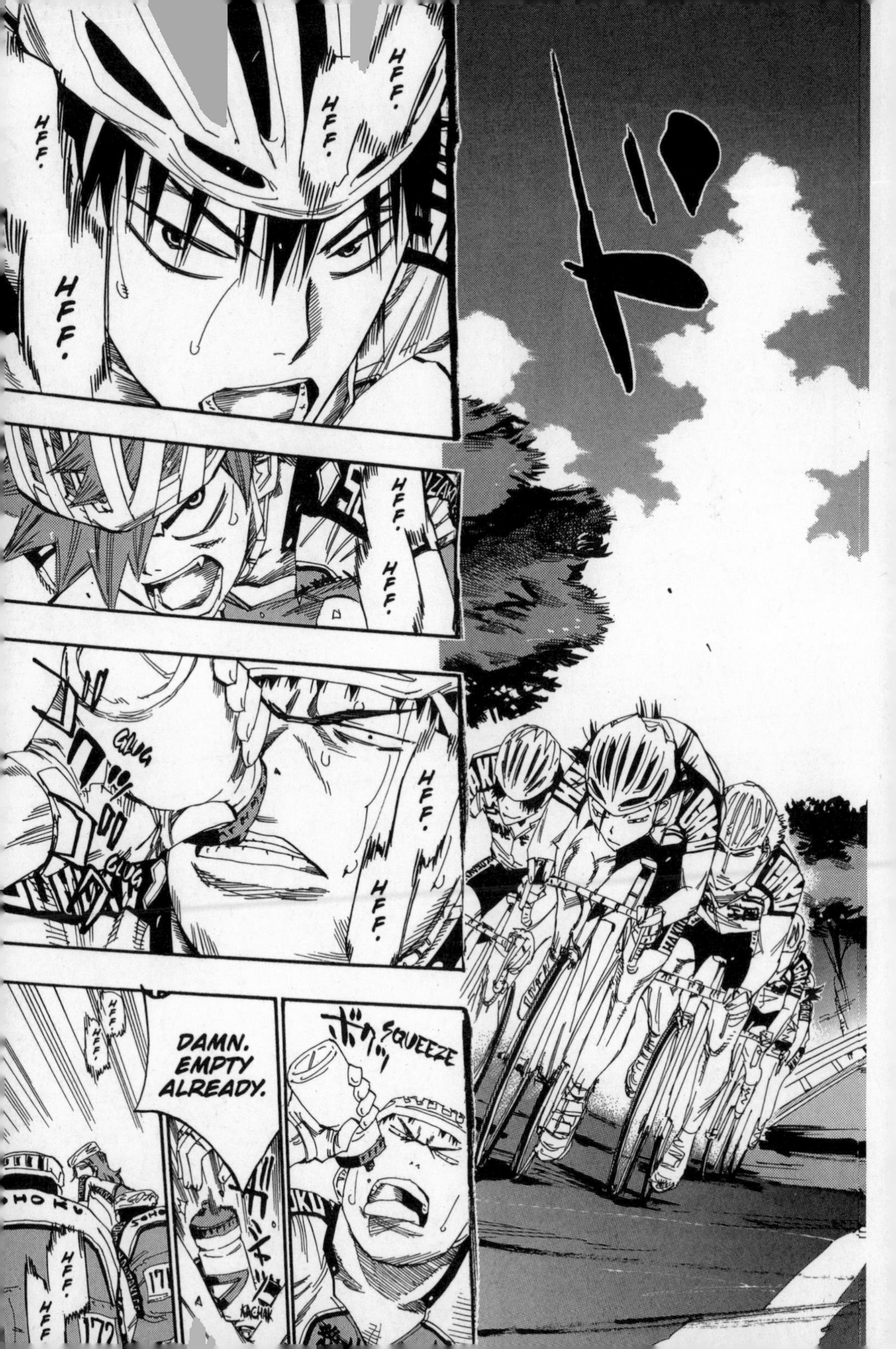
HFF.
HFF.
HFF.
HFF.
HFF.
HFF.
HFF.
GLUG
GLUG
HFF.
HFF.
SQUEEZE
KACHAK
DAMN. EMPTY ALREADY.
HFF.
HFF.
HFF.
HFF

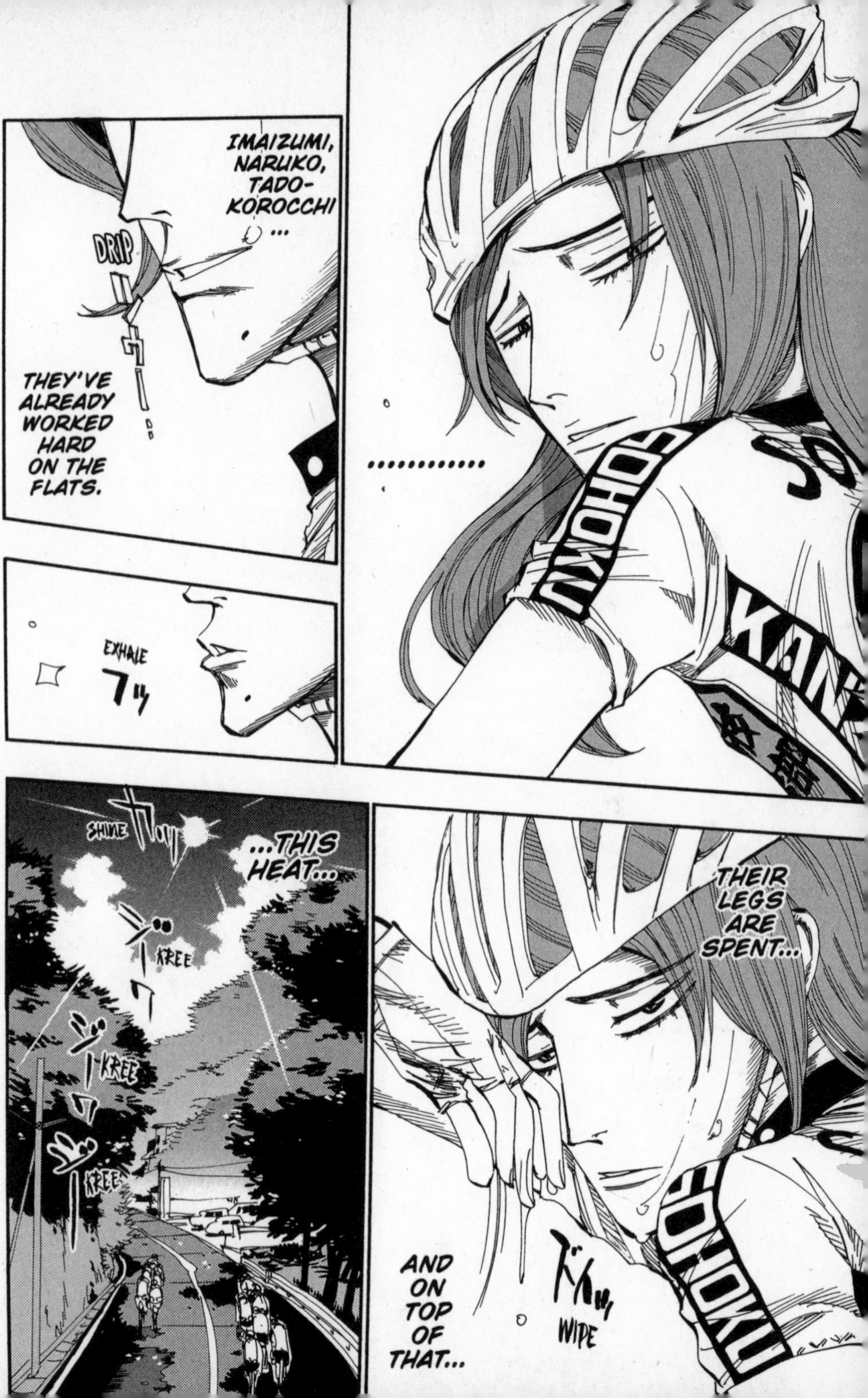

..............
IMAIZUMI, NARUKO, TADO-KOROCCHI ...
DRIP
THEY'VE ALREADY WORKED HARD ON THE FLATS.
EXHALE
THEIR LEGS ARE SPENT...
WIPE
AND ON TOP OF THAT...
SHINE
...THIS HEAT...
KREE
KREE
KREE

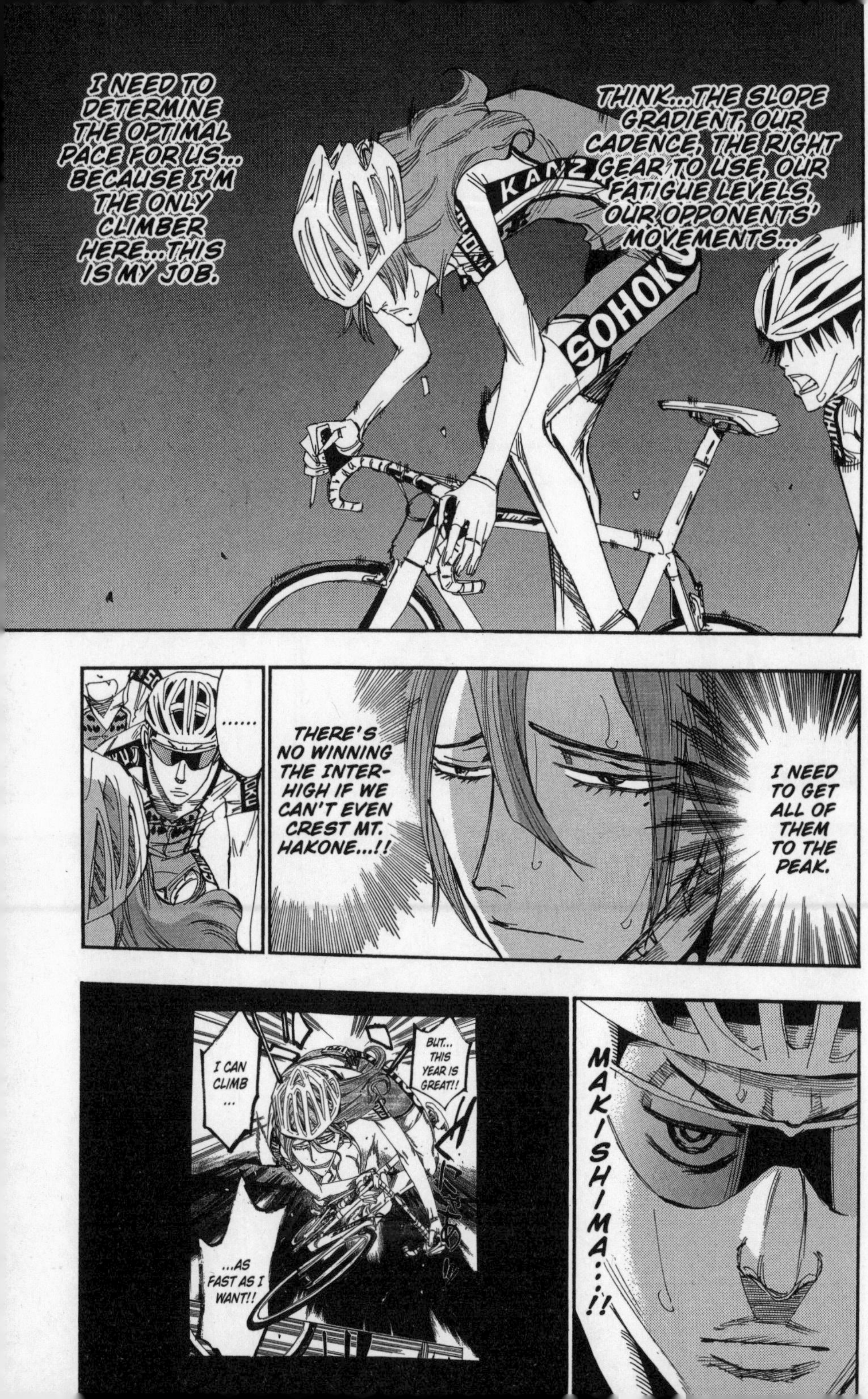
THINK...THE SLOPE GRADIENT, OUR CADENCE, THE RIGHT GEAR TO USE, OUR FATIGUE LEVELS, OUR OPPONENTS' MOVEMENTS...
I NEED TO DETERMINE THE OPTIMAL PACE FOR US... BECAUSE I'M THE ONLY CLIMBER HERE...THIS IS MY JOB.
I NEED TO GET ALL OF THEM TO THE PEAK.
THERE'S NO WINNING THE INTER-HIGH IF WE CAN'T EVEN CREST MT. HAKONE...!!
......
MAKISHIMA...!!
BUT... THIS YEAR IS GREAT!!
I CAN CLIMB ...
...AS FAST AS I WANT!!

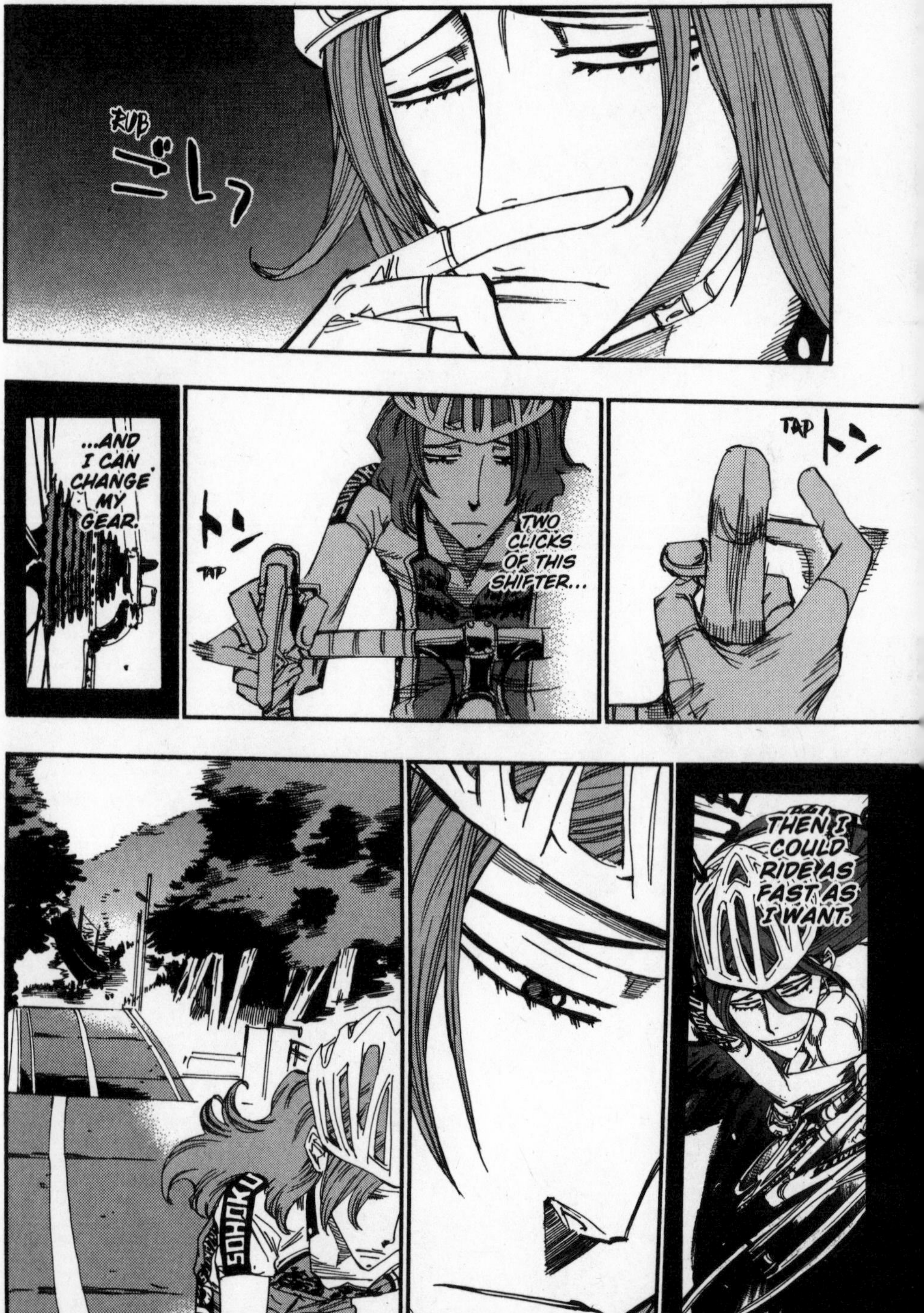
RUB
TAP
トン
TWO CLICKS OF THIS SHIFTER...
トン
TAP
...AND I CAN CHANGE MY GEAR.
THEN I COULD RIDE AS FAST AS I WANT.

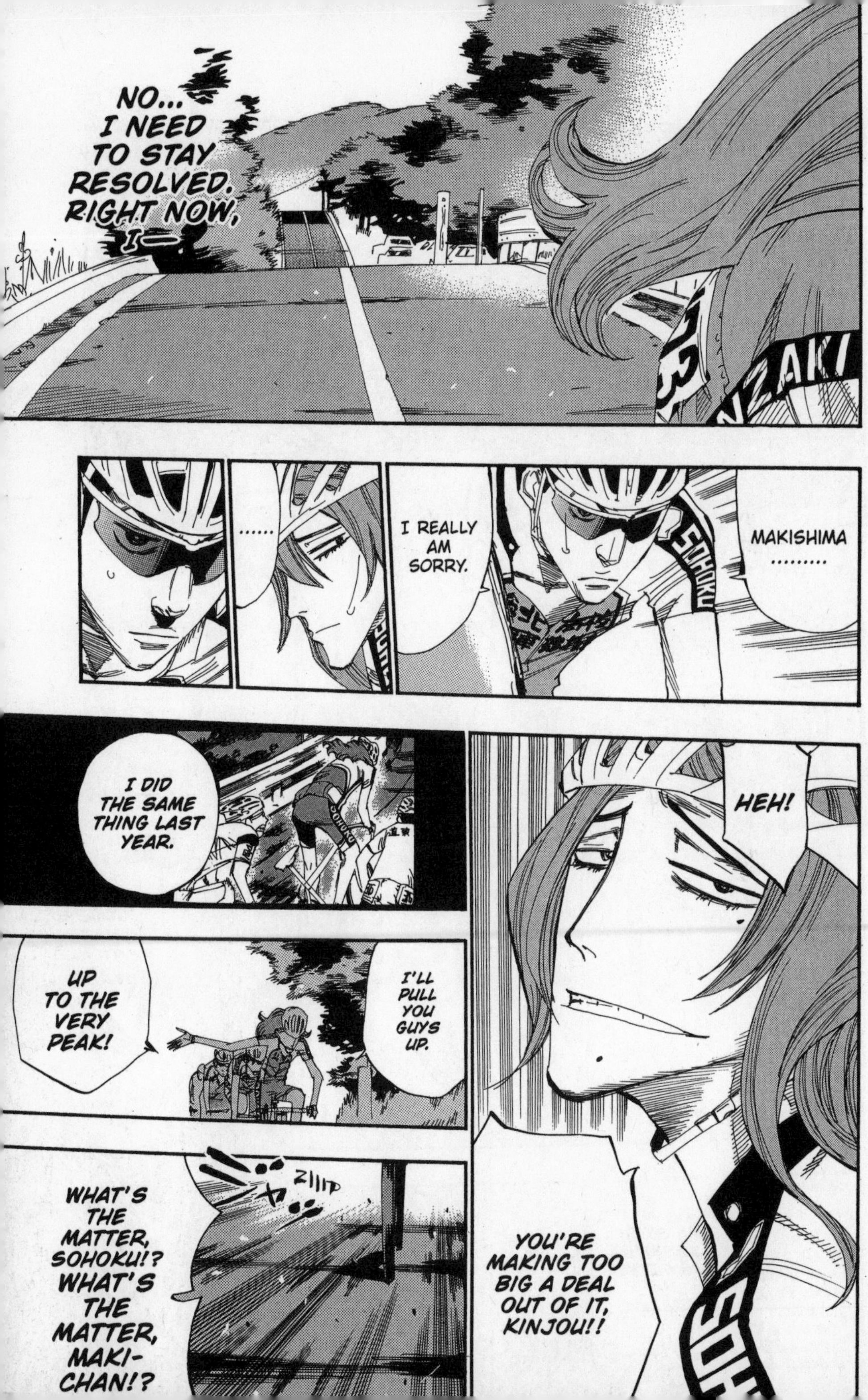
NO... I NEED TO STAY RESOLVED. RIGHT NOW, I—
MAKISHIMA .........
I REALLY AM SORRY.
......
HEH!
YOU'RE MAKING TOO BIG A DEAL OUT OF IT, KINJOU!!
I DID THE SAME THING LAST YEAR.
I'LL PULL YOU GUYS UP.
UP TO THE VERY PEAK!
ZIIIP
WHAT'S THE MATTER, SOHOKU!? WHAT'S THE MATTER, MAKI-CHAN!?

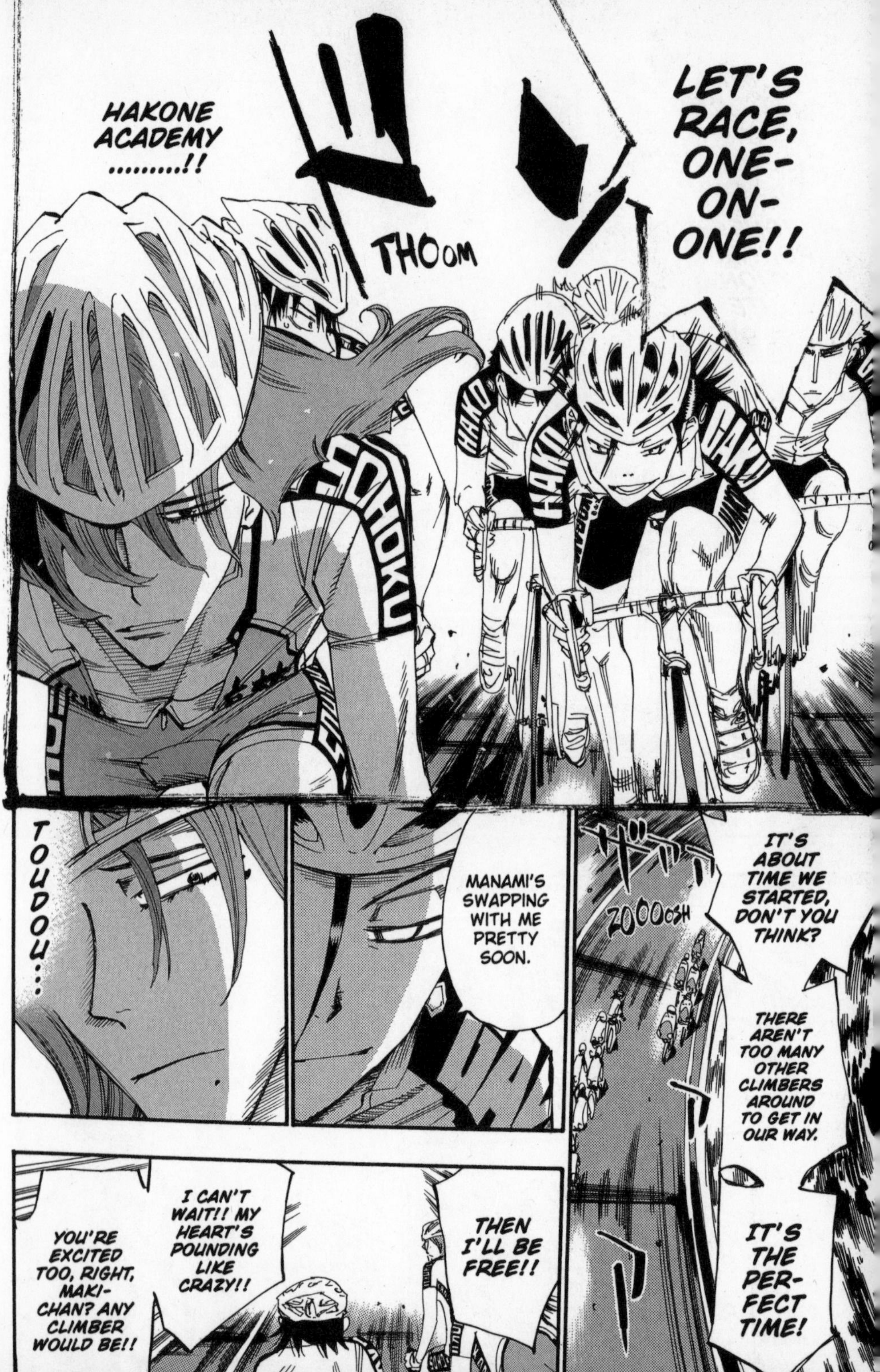
LET'S RACE, ONE-ON-ONE!!
THOOM
HAKONE ACADEMY ..........!!
IT'S ABOUT TIME WE STARTED, DON'T YOU THINK?
ZOOOOSH
THERE AREN'T TOO MANY OTHER CLIMBERS AROUND TO GET IN OUR WAY.
IT'S THE PERFECT TIME!
MANAMI'S SWAPPING WITH ME PRETTY SOON.
TOUDOU...
THEN I'LL BE FREE!!
I CAN'T WAIT!! MY HEART'S POUNDING LIKE CRAZY!!
YOU'RE EXCITED TOO, RIGHT, MAKI-CHAN? ANY CLIMBER WOULD BE!!

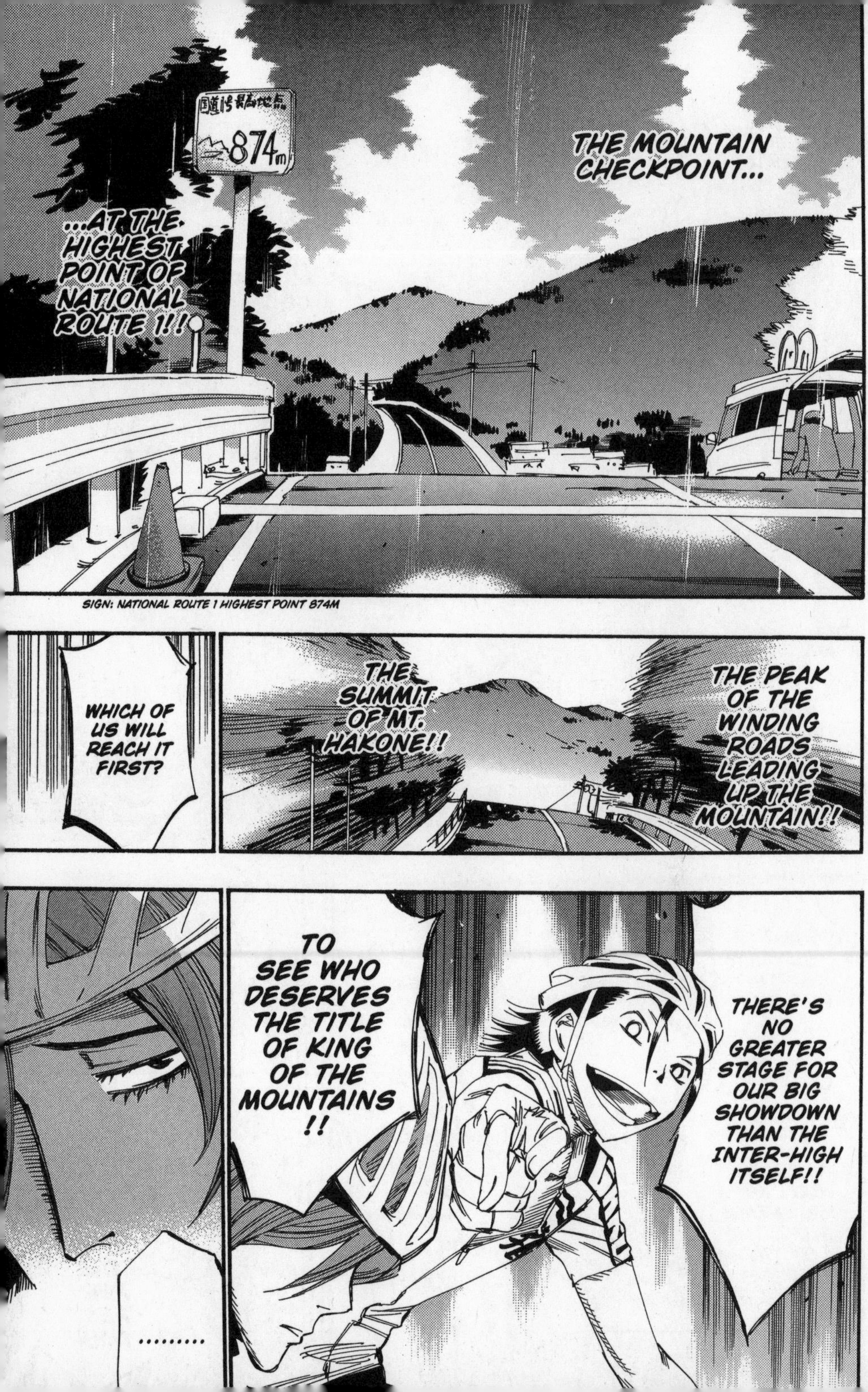
THE MOUNTAIN CHECKPOINT...
...AT THE HIGHEST POINT OF NATIONAL ROUTE 1!!
874m
SIGN: NATIONAL ROUTE 1 HIGHEST POINT 874M
THE PEAK OF THE WINDING ROADS LEADING UP THE MOUNTAIN!!
THE SUMMIT OF MT. HAKONE!!
WHICH OF US WILL REACH IT FIRST?
THERE'S NO GREATER STAGE FOR OUR BIG SHOWDOWN THAN THE INTER-HIGH ITSELF!!
TO SEE WHO DESERVES THE TITLE OF KING OF THE MOUNTAINS!!
.........

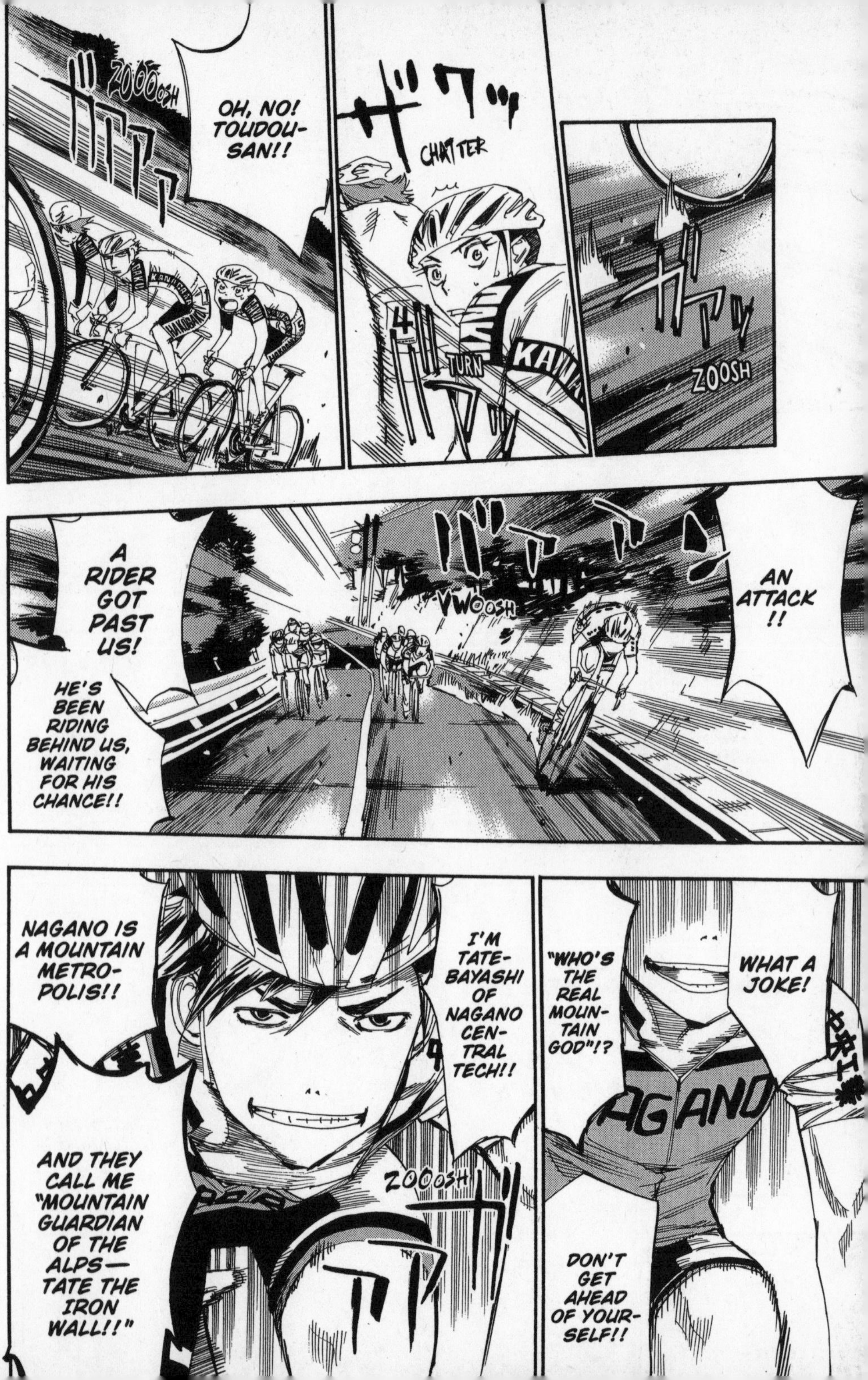
ZOOSH
CHATTER
TURN
OH, NO! TOUDOU-SAN!!
ZOOOOSH
AN ATTACK!!
VWOOSH
A RIDER GOT PAST US!
HE'S BEEN RIDING BEHIND US, WAITING FOR HIS CHANCE!!
WHAT A JOKE!
"WHO'S THE REAL MOUNTAIN GOD"!?
DON'T GET AHEAD OF YOURSELF!!
I'M TATEBAYASHI OF NAGANO CENTRAL TECH!!
NAGANO IS A MOUNTAIN METROPOLIS!!
AND THEY CALL ME "MOUNTAIN GUARDIAN OF THE ALPS—TATE THE IRON WALL!!"
ZOOOSH

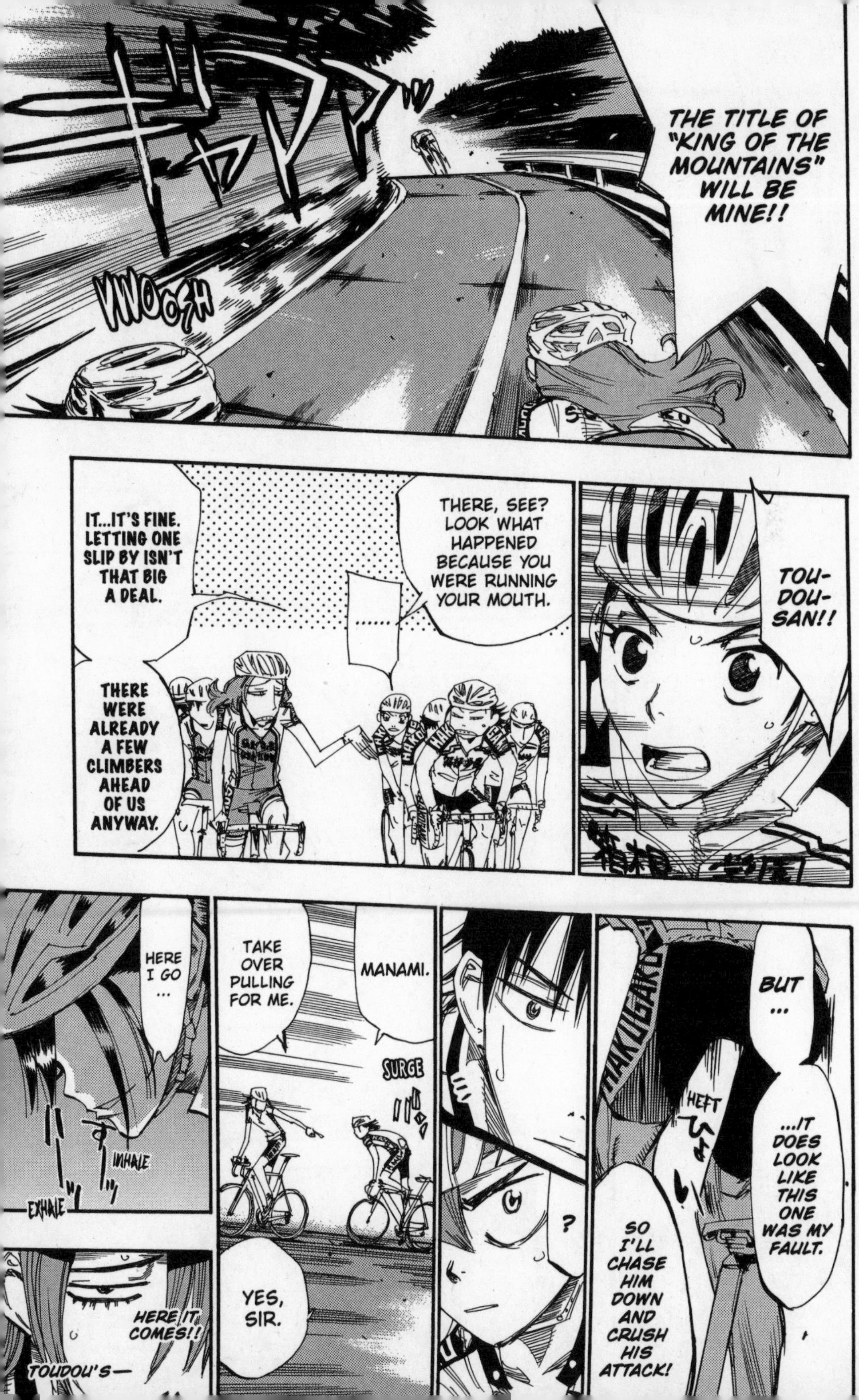
THE TITLE OF "KING OF THE MOUNTAINS" WILL BE MINE!!
VWOOSH
TOU-DOU-SAN!!
THERE, SEE? LOOK WHAT HAPPENED BECAUSE YOU WERE RUNNING YOUR MOUTH.
......
IT...IT'S FINE. LETTING ONE SLIP BY ISN'T THAT BIG A DEAL.
THERE WERE ALREADY A FEW CLIMBERS AHEAD OF US ANYWAY.
BUT ...
HEFT
...IT DOES LOOK LIKE THIS ONE WAS MY FAULT.
SO I'LL CHASE HIM DOWN AND CRUSH HIS ATTACK!
?
MANAMI.
TAKE OVER PULLING FOR ME.
SURGE
YES, SIR.
HERE I GO ...
INHALE
EXHALE
HERE IT COMES!!
TOUDOU'S—

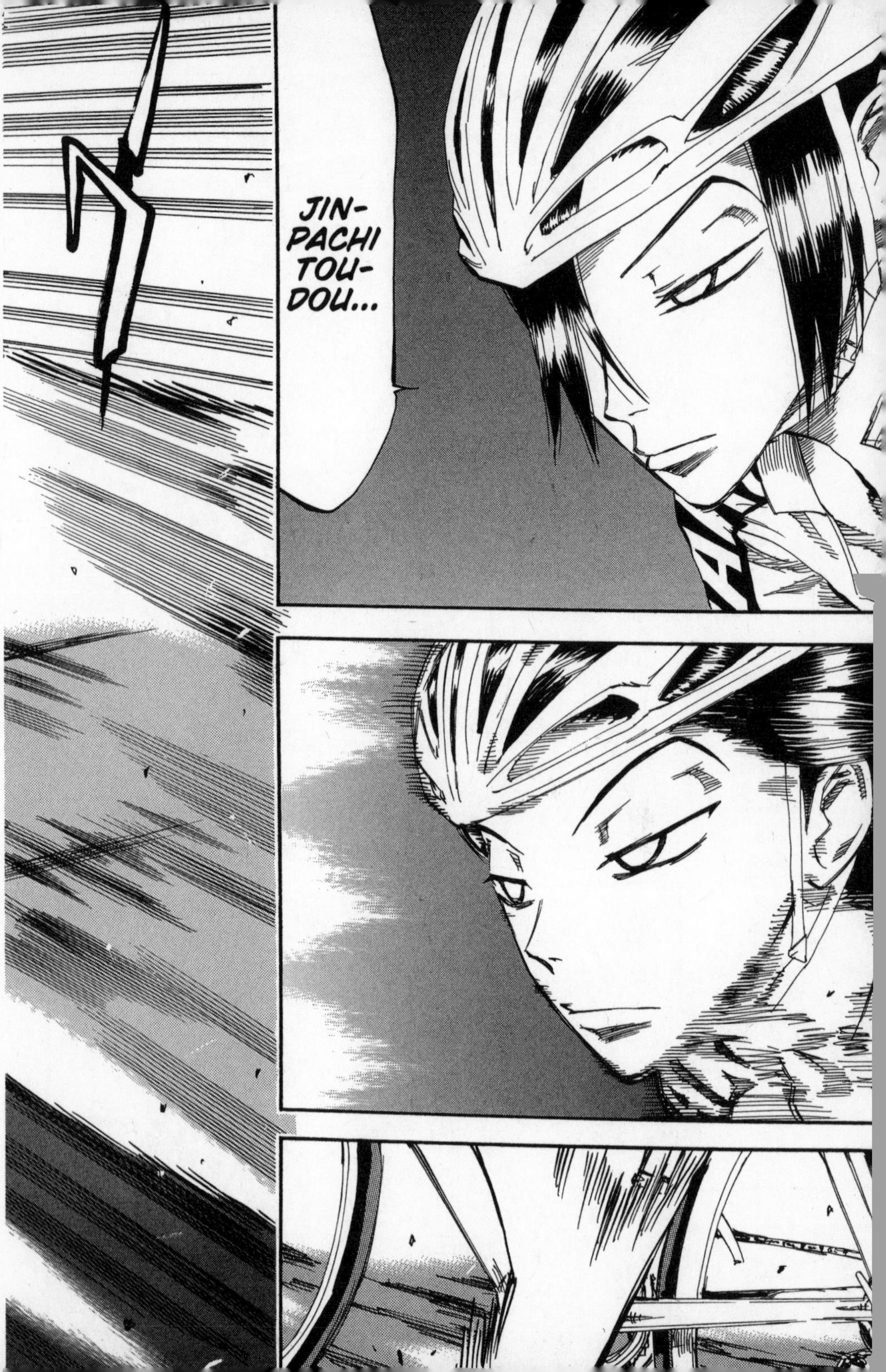
JIN-PACHI TOU-DOU...

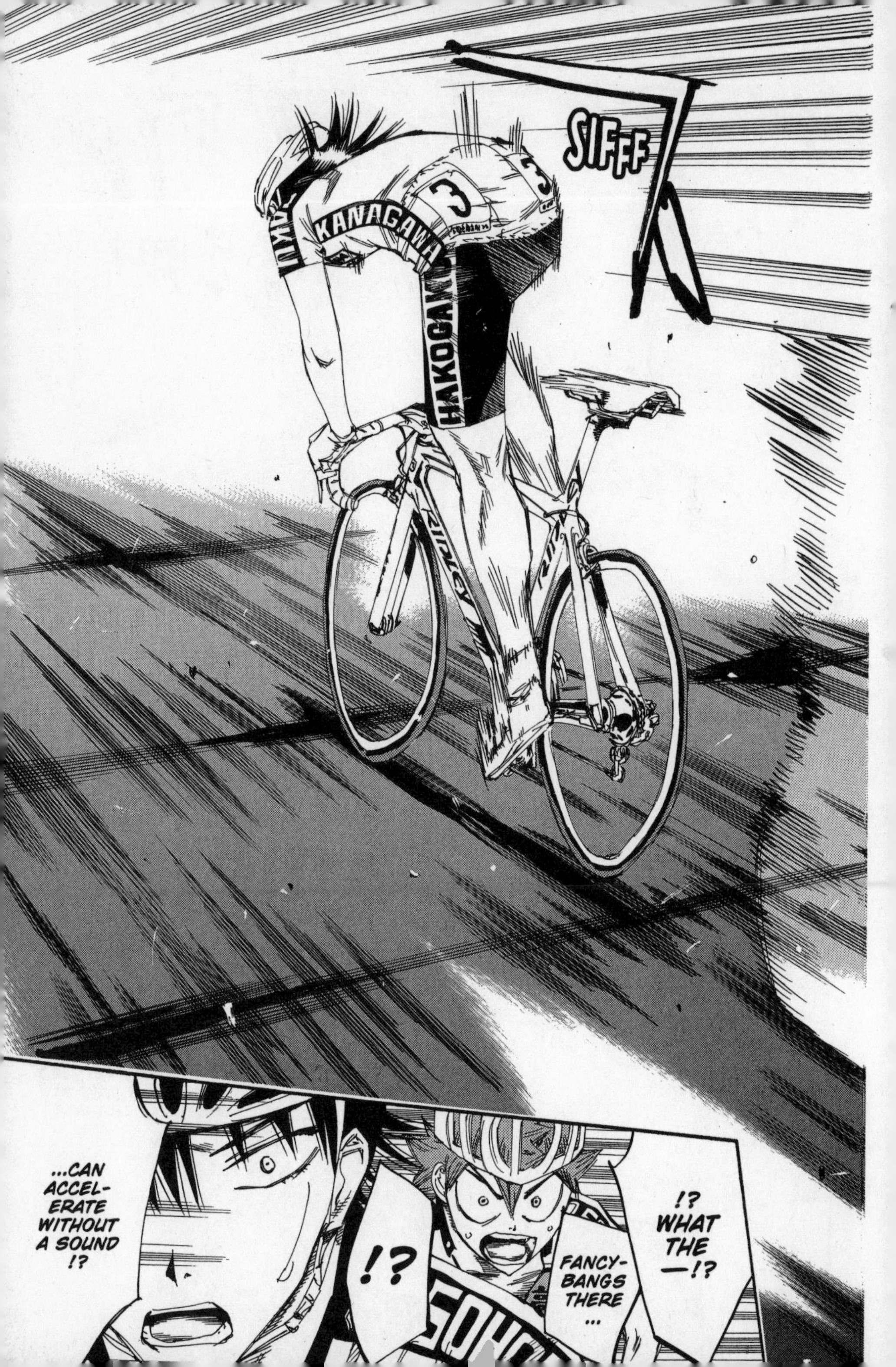

SIFFF
!? WHAT THE—!?
FANCY-BANGS THERE ...
!?
...CAN ACCEL-ERATE WITHOUT A SOUND !?

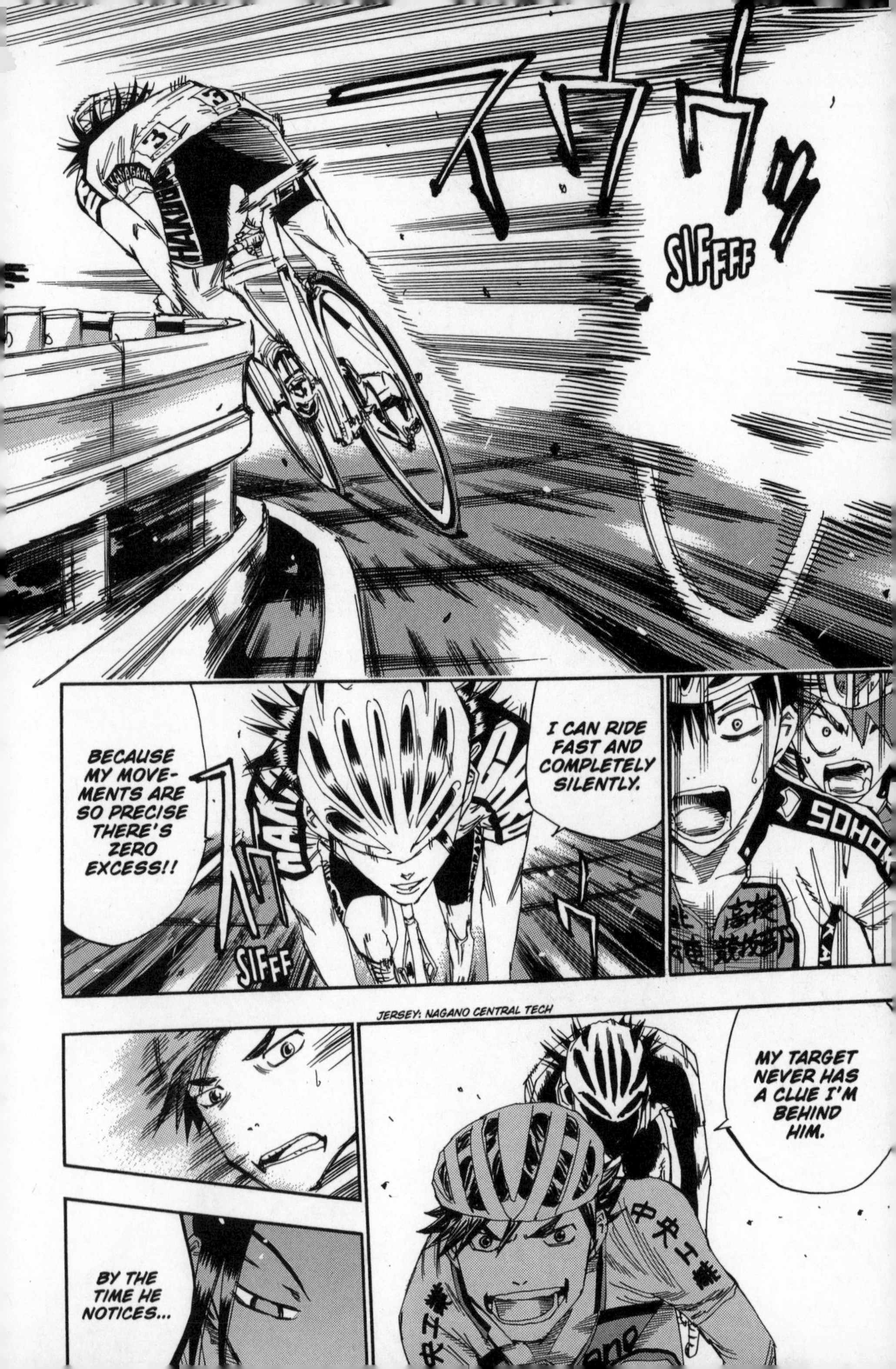
スウウッ
SIFFFF
I CAN RIDE FAST AND COMPLETELY SILENTLY.
BECAUSE MY MOVEMENTS ARE SO PRECISE THERE'S ZERO EXCESS!!
SIFFF
JERSEY: NAGANO CENTRAL TECH
MY TARGET NEVER HAS A CLUE I'M BEHIND HIM.
BY THE TIME HE NOTICES...

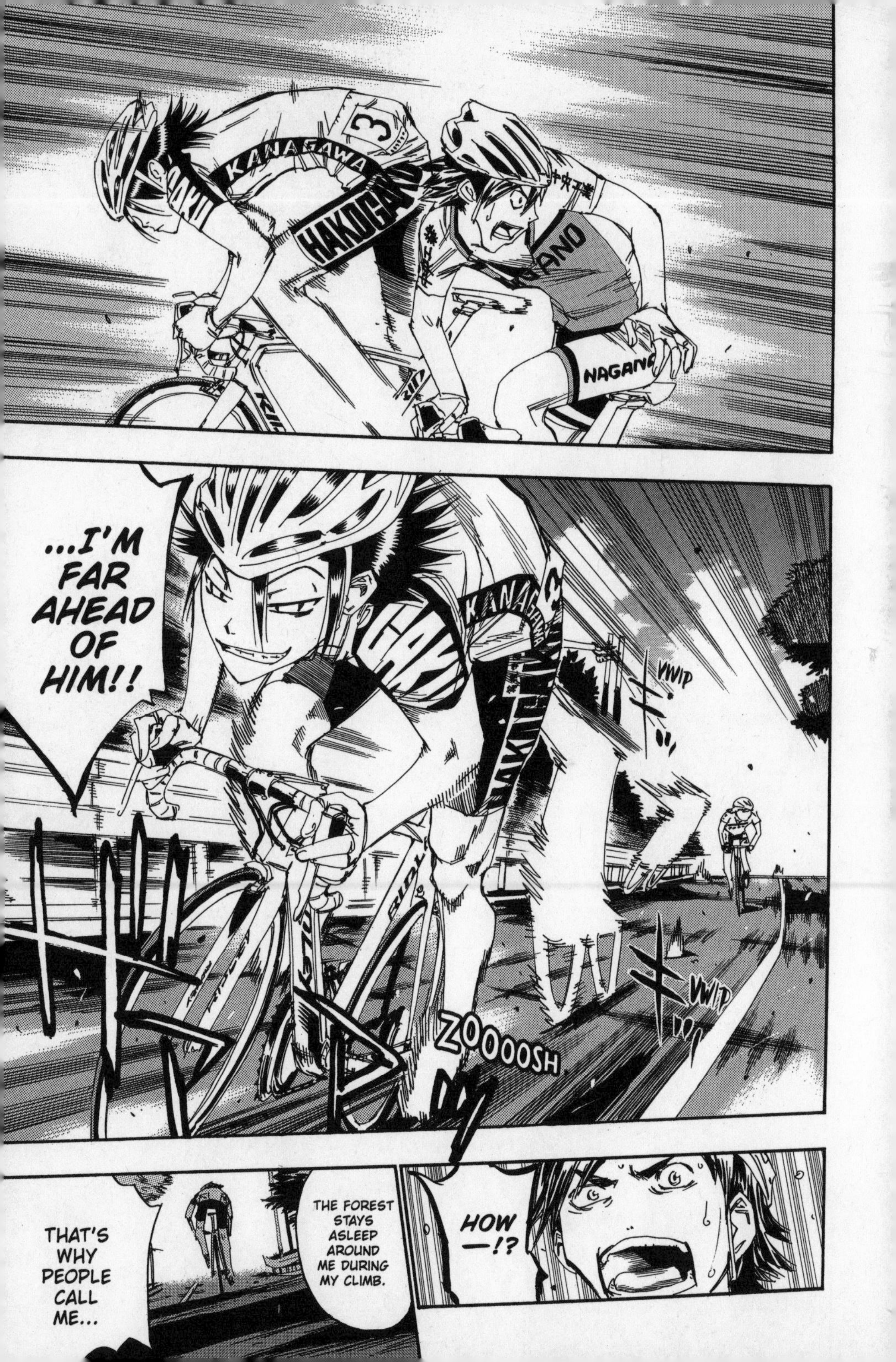
...I'M FAR AHEAD OF HIM!!
VWIP
ZOOOOSH
VWIP
HOW—!?
THE FOREST STAYS ASLEEP AROUND ME DURING MY CLIMB.
THAT'S WHY PEOPLE CALL ME...

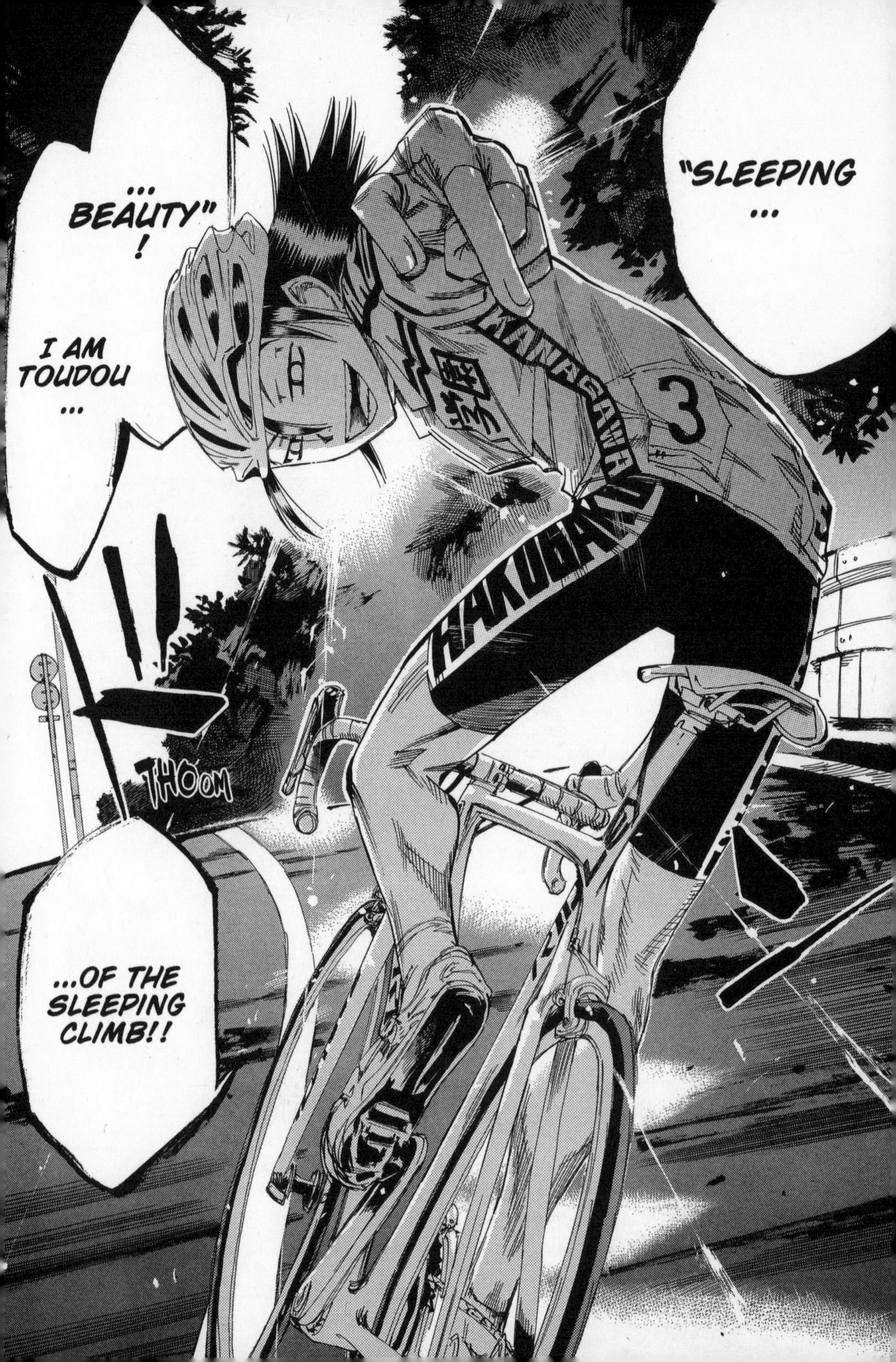
"SLEEPING
...
... BEAUTY"
!
I AM TOUDOU
...
THOOM
...OF THE SLEEPING CLIMB!!

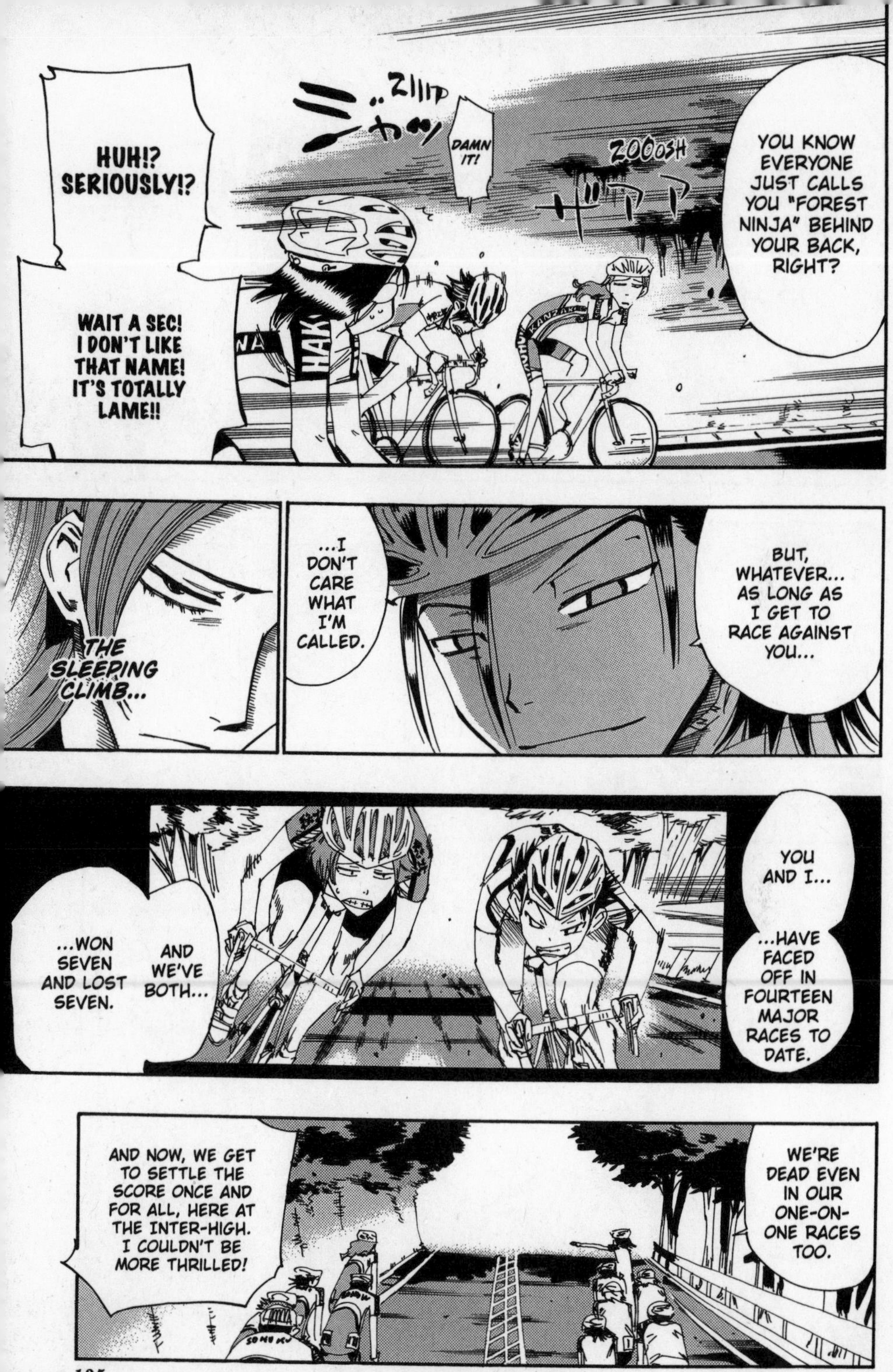

YOU KNOW EVERYONE JUST CALLS YOU "FOREST NINJA" BEHIND YOUR BACK, RIGHT?
ZOOOSH
ZIIIP
DAMN IT!
HUH!? SERIOUSLY!?
WAIT A SEC! I DON'T LIKE THAT NAME! IT'S TOTALLY LAME!!
BUT, WHATEVER... AS LONG AS I GET TO RACE AGAINST YOU...
...I DON'T CARE WHAT I'M CALLED.
THE SLEEPING CLIMB...
YOU AND I...
...HAVE FACED OFF IN FOURTEEN MAJOR RACES TO DATE.
AND WE'VE BOTH...
...WON SEVEN AND LOST SEVEN.
WE'RE DEAD EVEN IN OUR ONE-ON-ONE RACES TOO.
AND NOW, WE GET TO SETTLE THE SCORE ONCE AND FOR ALL, HERE AT THE INTER-HIGH. I COULDN'T BE MORE THRILLED!

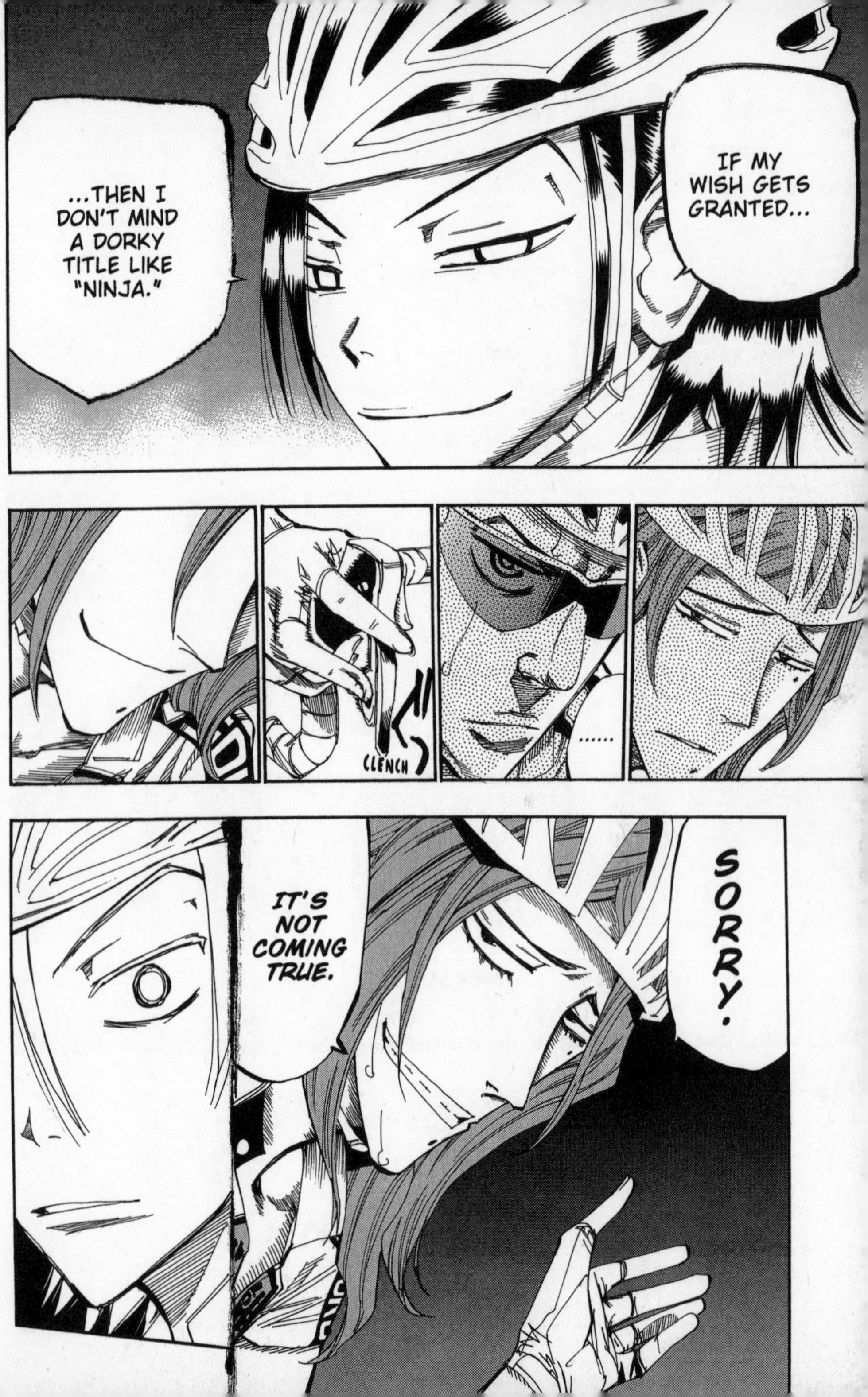
IF MY WISH GETS GRANTED...
...THEN I DON'T MIND A DORKY TITLE LIKE "NINJA."
......
CLENCH
SORRY.
IT'S NOT COMING TRUE.

# RIDE.92 CLIMBER

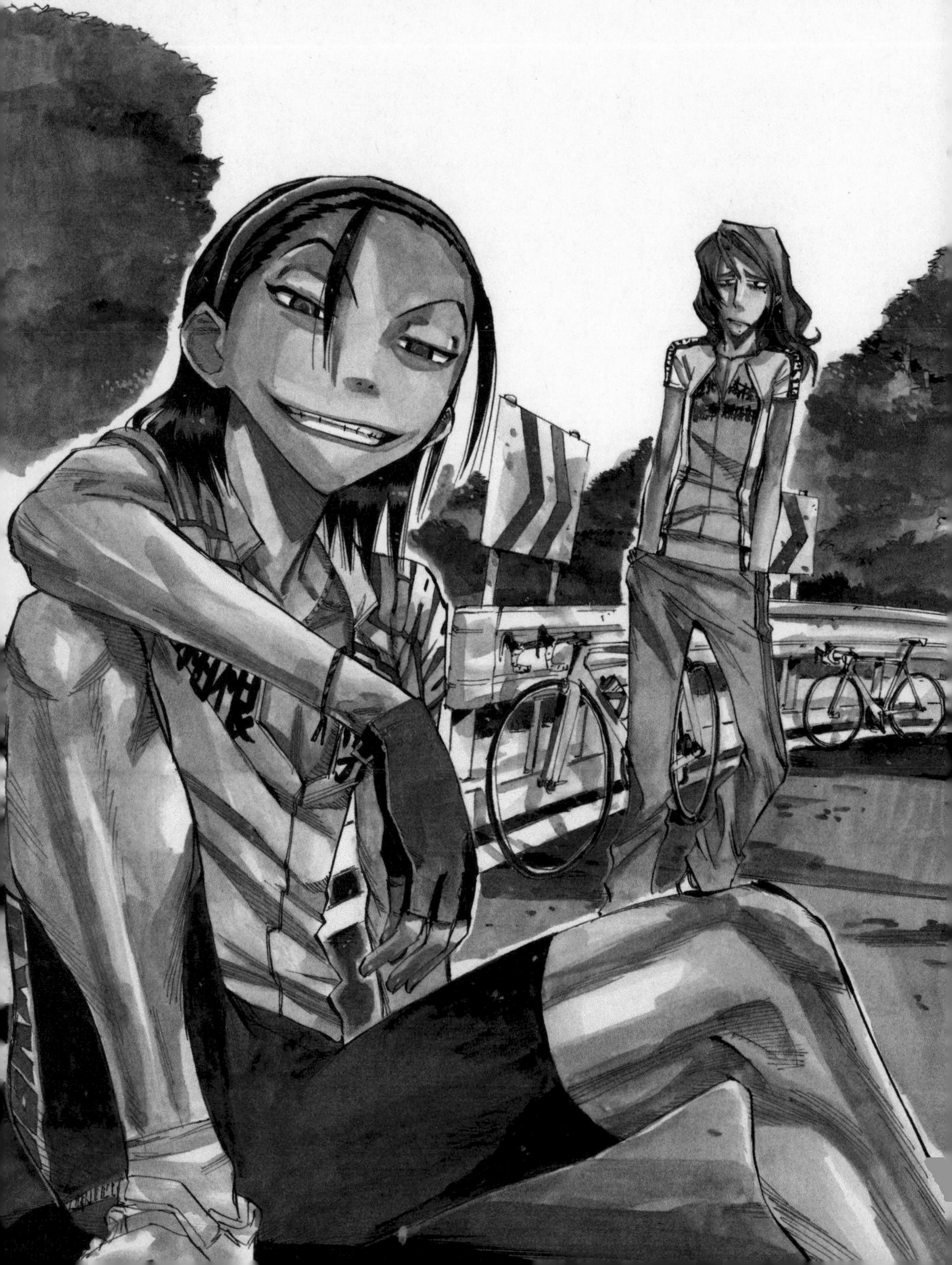

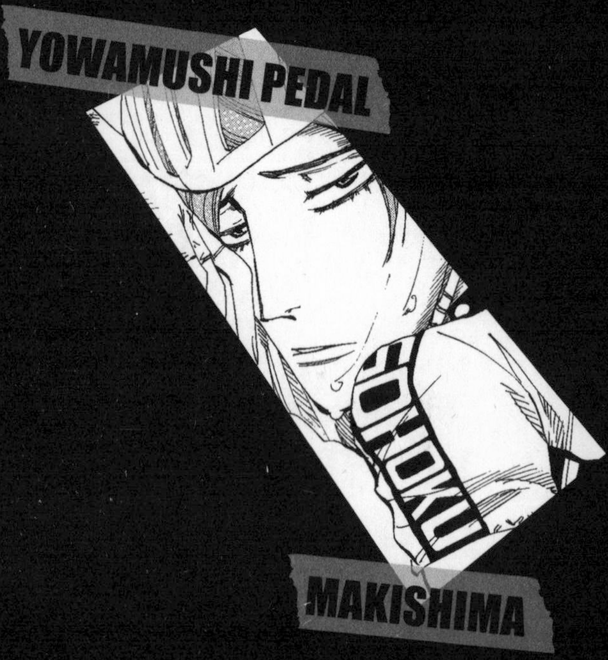
YOWAMUSHI PEDAL
SOHOKU
MAKISHIMA

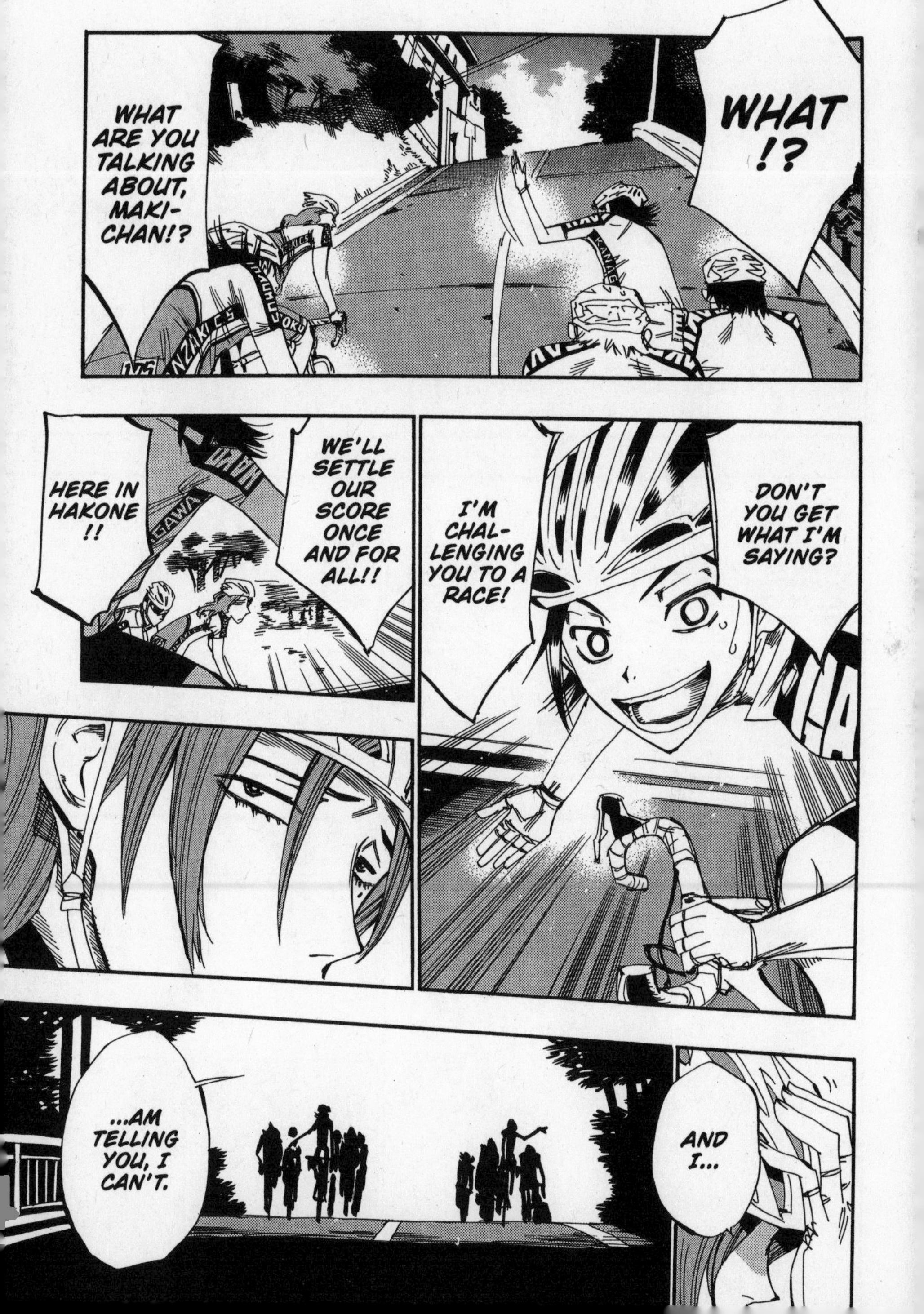
WHAT !?
WHAT ARE YOU TALKING ABOUT, MAKI-CHAN!?
DON'T YOU GET WHAT I'M SAYING?
I'M CHAL-LENGING YOU TO A RACE!
WE'LL SETTLE OUR SCORE ONCE AND FOR ALL!!
HERE IN HAKONE !!
AND I...
...AM TELLING YOU, I CAN'T.

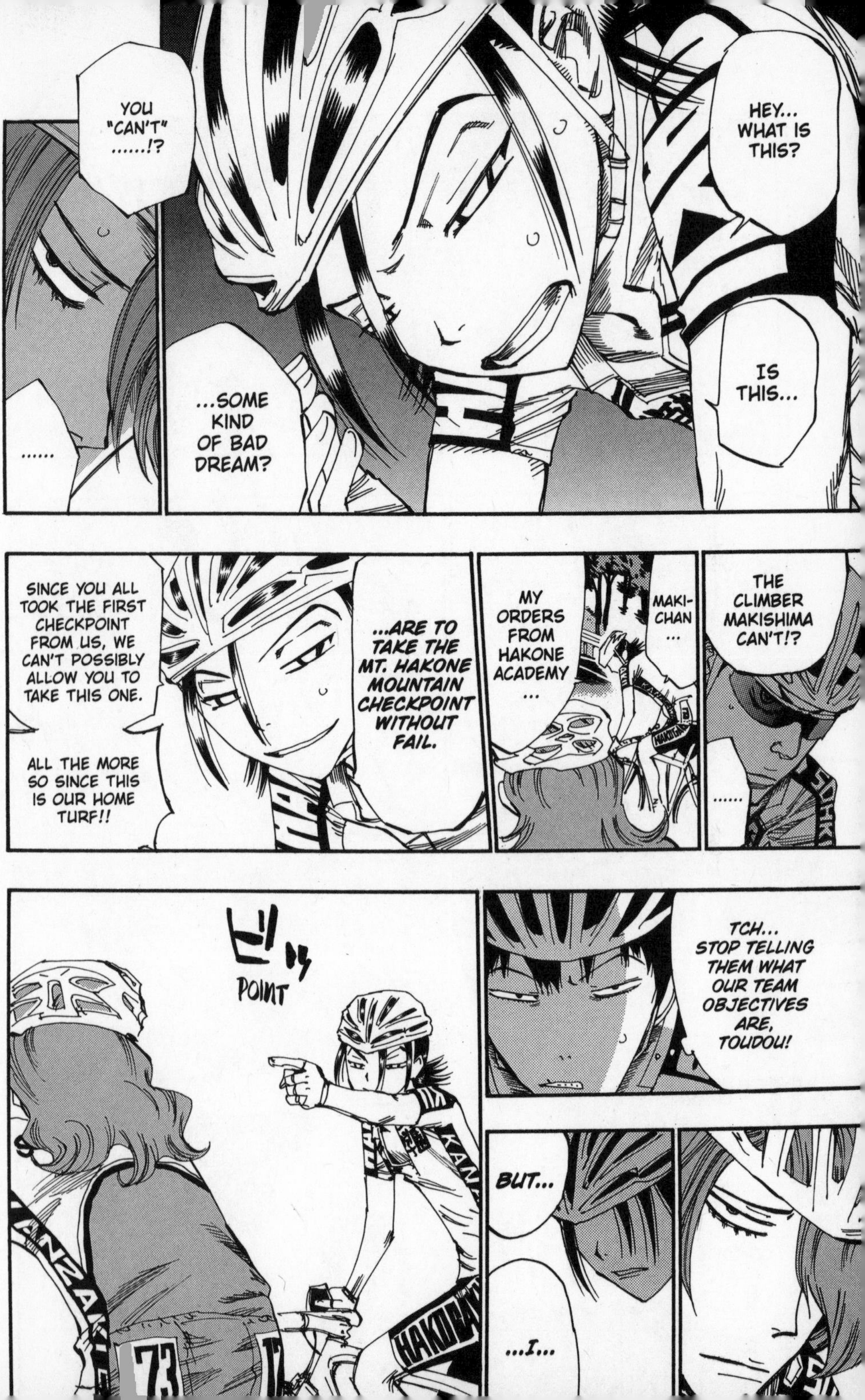

HEY... WHAT IS THIS?
IS THIS...
...SOME KIND OF BAD DREAM?
YOU "CAN'T" ......!?
......
THE CLIMBER MAKISHIMA CAN'T!?
......
MAKI-CHAN...
MY ORDERS FROM HAKONE ACADEMY...
...ARE TO TAKE THE MT. HAKONE MOUNTAIN CHECKPOINT WITHOUT FAIL.
SINCE YOU ALL TOOK THE FIRST CHECKPOINT FROM US, WE CAN'T POSSIBLY ALLOW YOU TO TAKE THIS ONE.
ALL THE MORE SO SINCE THIS IS OUR HOME TURF!!
TCH... STOP TELLING THEM WHAT OUR TEAM OBJECTIVES ARE, TOUDOU!
BUT...
...I...
POINT

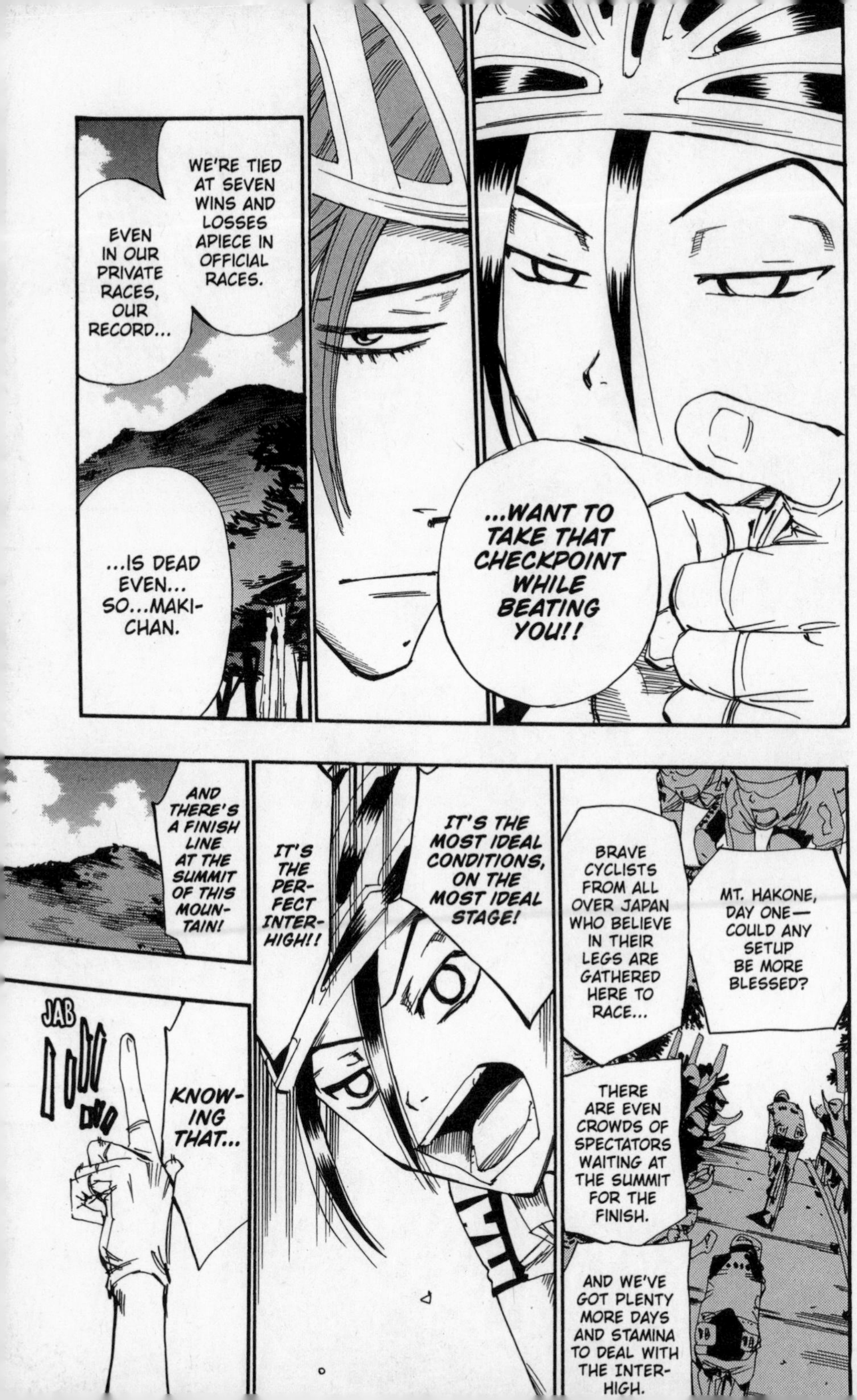
...WANT TO TAKE THAT CHECKPOINT WHILE BEATING YOU!!
WE'RE TIED AT SEVEN WINS AND LOSSES APIECE IN OFFICIAL RACES.
EVEN IN OUR PRIVATE RACES, OUR RECORD...
...IS DEAD EVEN... SO...MAKI-CHAN.
MT. HAKONE, DAY ONE—COULD ANY SETUP BE MORE BLESSED?
BRAVE CYCLISTS FROM ALL OVER JAPAN WHO BELIEVE IN THEIR LEGS ARE GATHERED HERE TO RACE...
THERE ARE EVEN CROWDS OF SPECTATORS WAITING AT THE SUMMIT FOR THE FINISH.
AND WE'VE GOT PLENTY MORE DAYS AND STAMINA TO DEAL WITH THE INTER-HIGH.
IT'S THE MOST IDEAL CONDITIONS, ON THE MOST IDEAL STAGE!
IT'S THE PERFECT INTER-HIGH!!
AND THERE'S A FINISH LINE AT THE SUMMIT OF THIS MOUNTAIN!
KNOWING THAT...
JAB

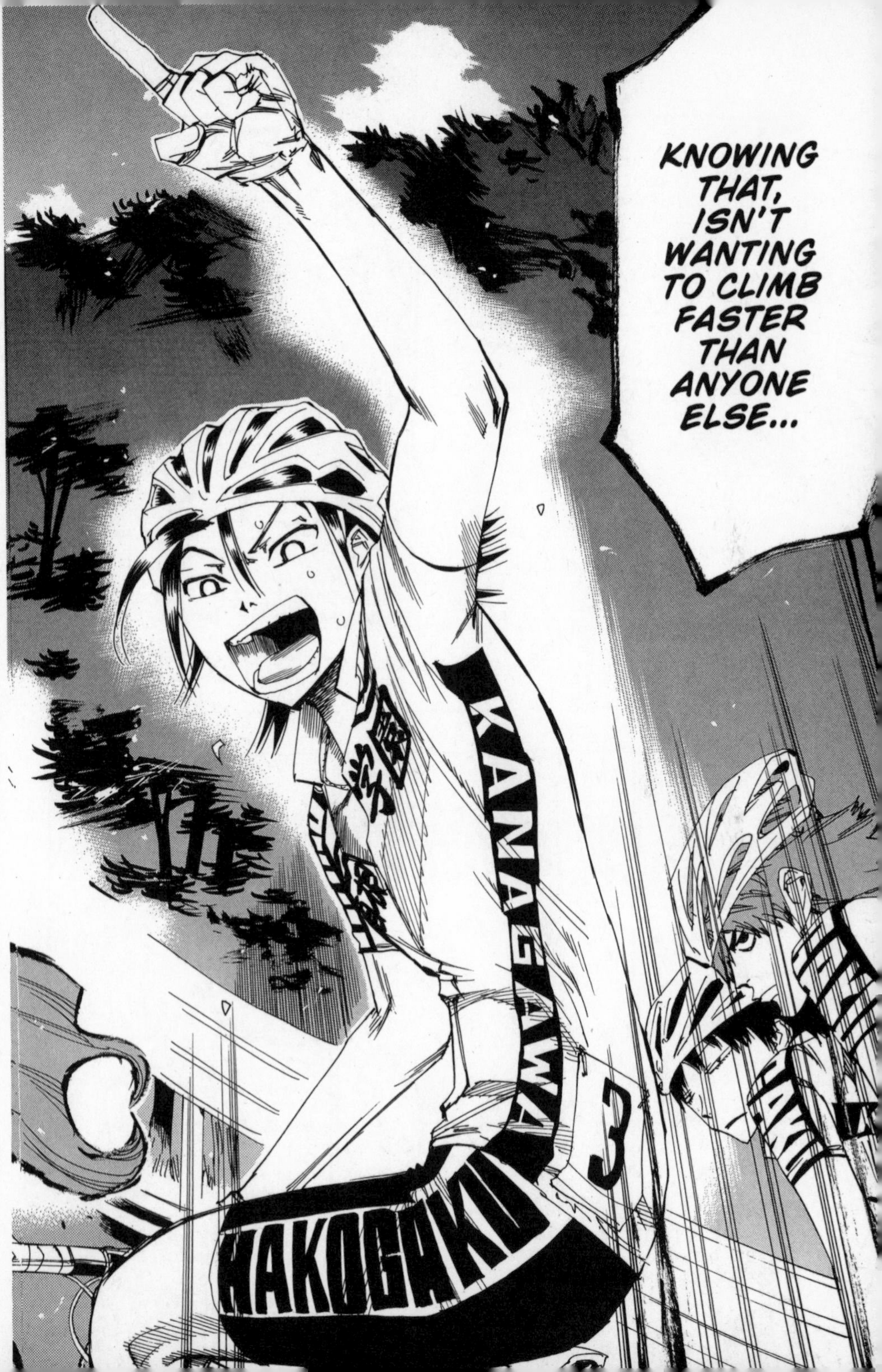
KNOWING THAT, ISN'T WANTING TO CLIMB FASTER THAN ANYONE ELSE...
KANAGAWA
HAKOGAKU

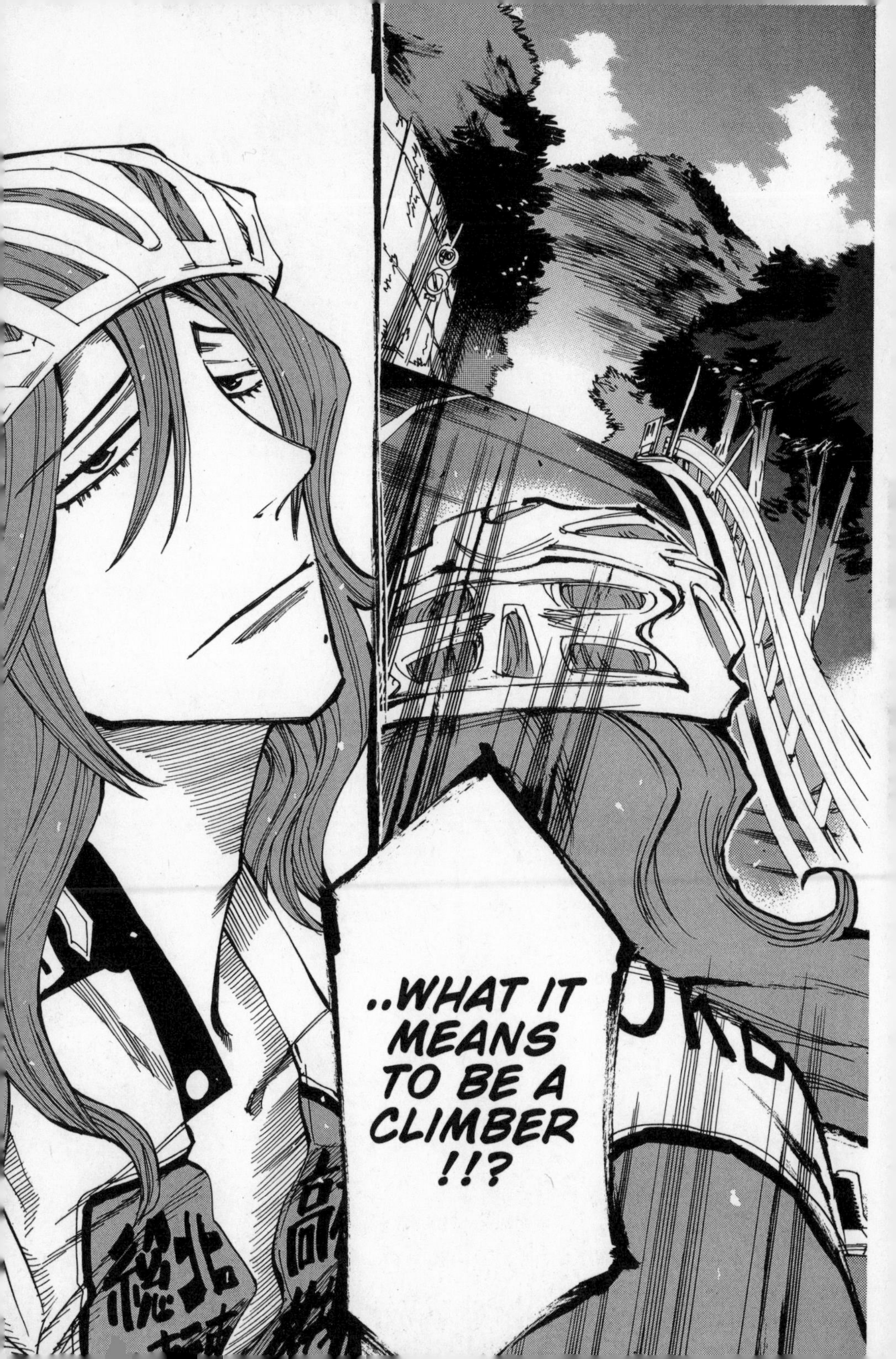
..WHAT IT MEANS TO BE A CLIMBER !!?

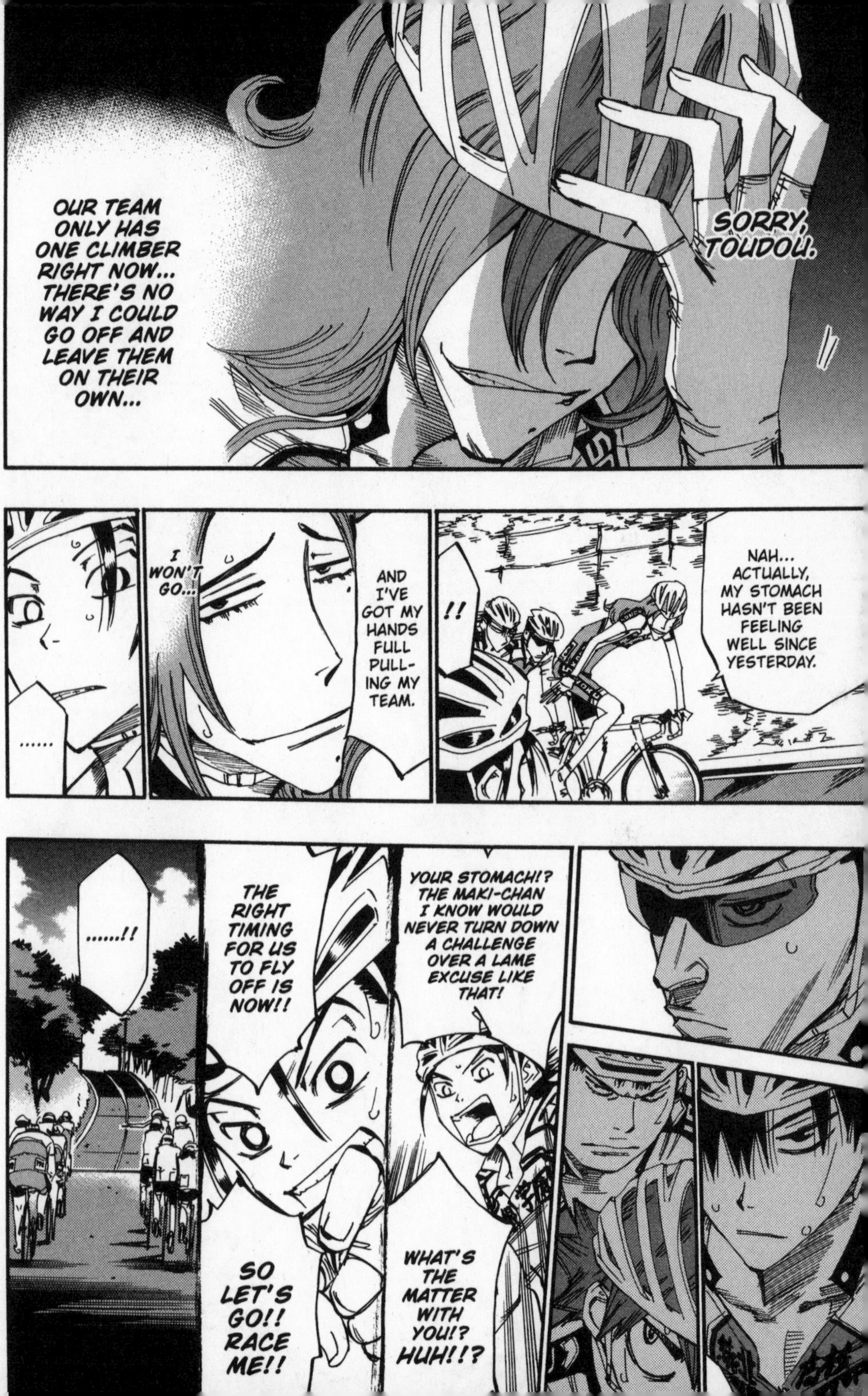
SORRY, TOUDOU.
OUR TEAM ONLY HAS ONE CLIMBER RIGHT NOW... THERE'S NO WAY I COULD GO OFF AND LEAVE THEM ON THEIR OWN...
NAH... ACTUALLY, MY STOMACH HASN'T BEEN FEELING WELL SINCE YESTERDAY.
!!
AND I'VE GOT MY HANDS FULL PULL-ING MY TEAM.
I WON'T GO...
......
YOUR STOMACH!? THE MAKI-CHAN I KNOW WOULD NEVER TURN DOWN A CHALLENGE OVER A LAME EXCUSE LIKE THAT!
WHAT'S THE MATTER WITH YOU!? HUH!!?
THE RIGHT TIMING FOR US TO FLY OFF IS NOW!!
SO LET'S GO!! RACE ME!!
......!!

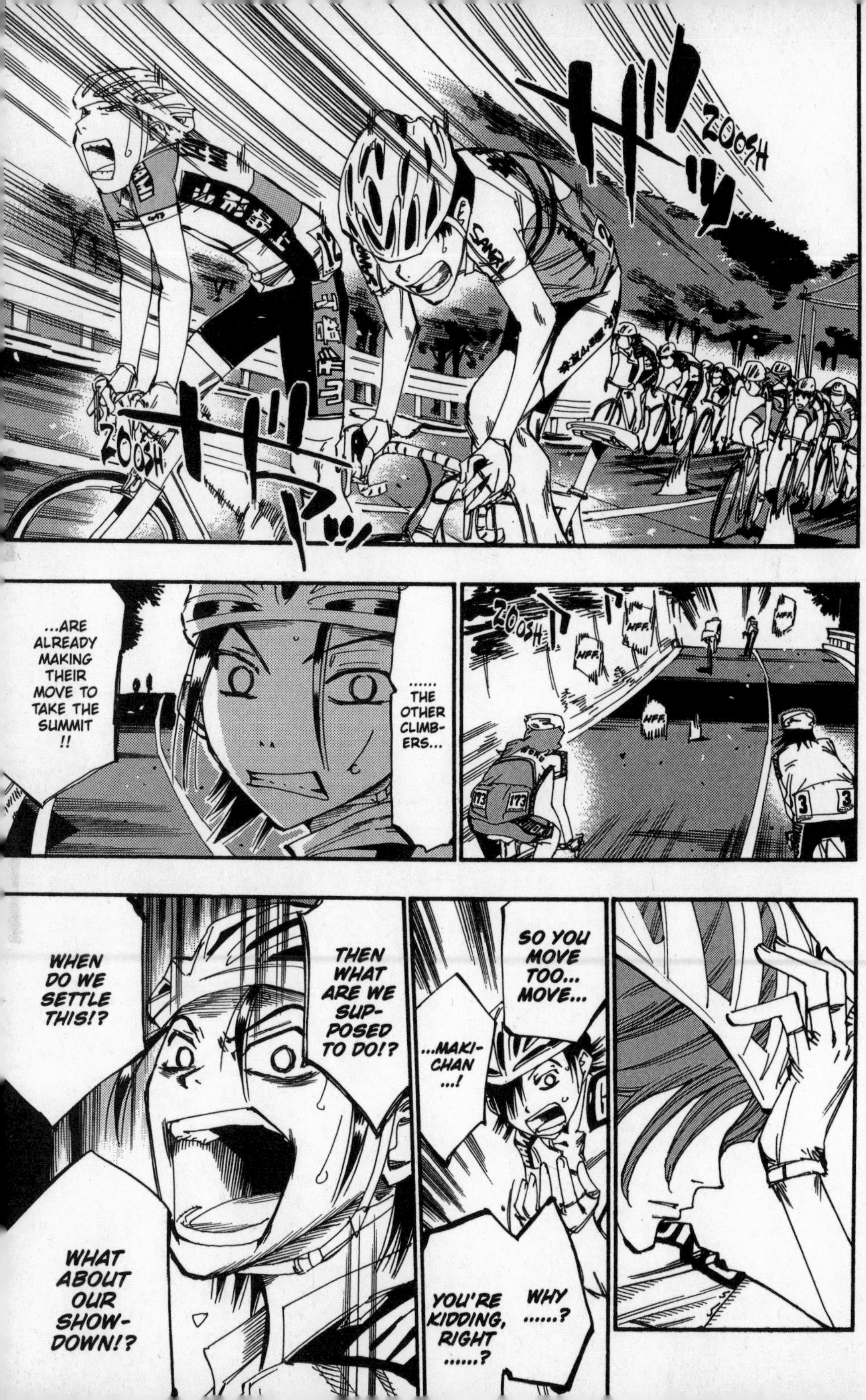
ZOOSH
ZOOSH
ZOOSH
HFF
HFF
HFF
HFF
...... THE OTHER CLIMB-ERS...
...ARE ALREADY MAKING THEIR MOVE TO TAKE THE SUMMIT !!
SO YOU MOVE TOO... MOVE...
...MAKI-CHAN ...!
WHY ......?
YOU'RE KIDDING, RIGHT ......?
THEN WHAT ARE WE SUP-POSED TO DO!?
WHEN DO WE SETTLE THIS!?
WHAT ABOUT OUR SHOW-DOWN!?

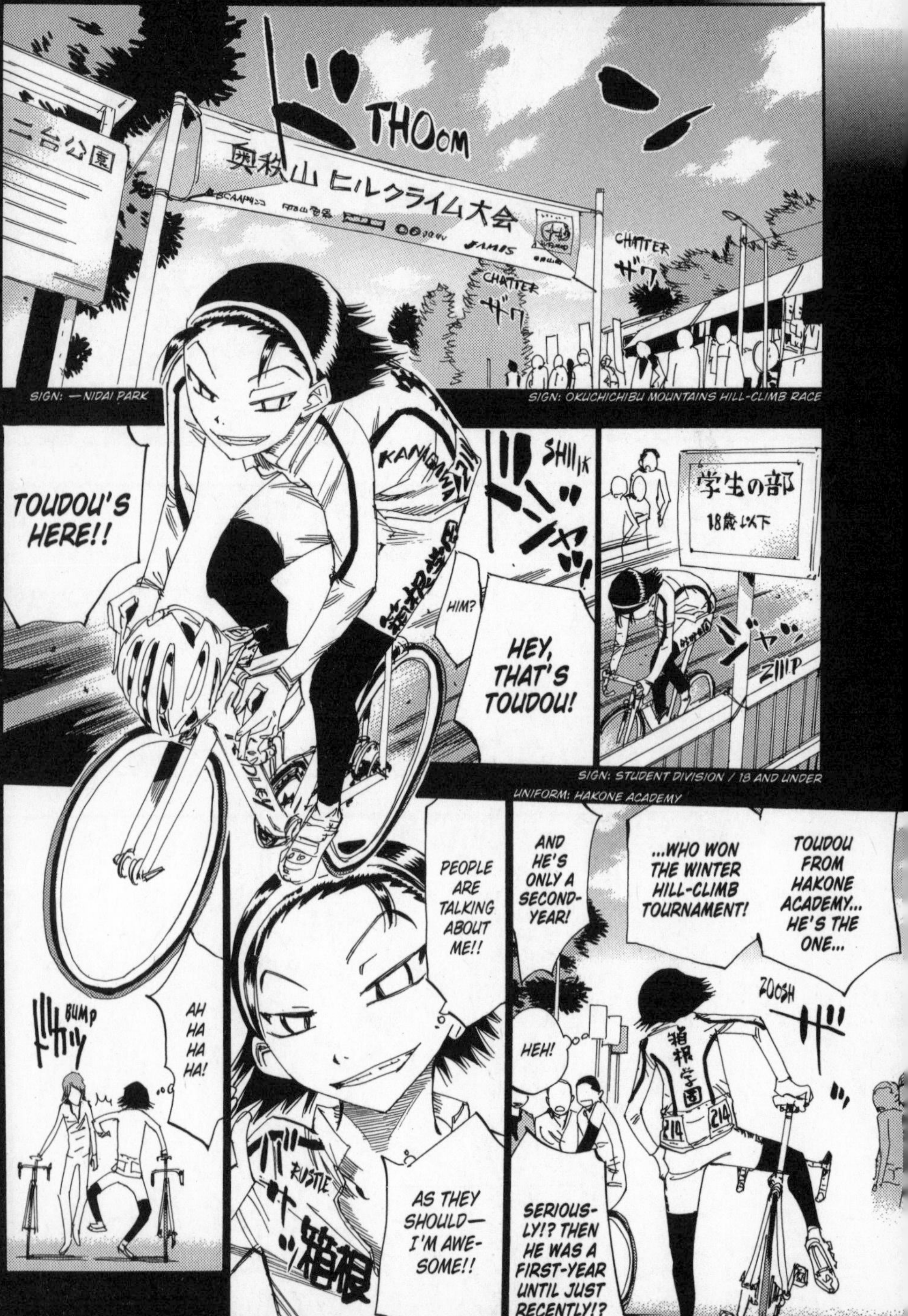
THOOM
CHATTER
CHATTER
SIGN: OKUCHICHIBU MOUNTAINS HILL-CLIMB RACE
SIGN: —NIDAI PARK
ZIIIP
SIGN: STUDENT DIVISION / 18 AND UNDER
SHIIIK
HEY, THAT'S TOUDOU!
HIM?
TOUDOU'S HERE!!
UNIFORM: HAKONE ACADEMY
TOUDOU FROM HAKONE ACADEMY... HE'S THE ONE...
...WHO WON THE WINTER HILL-CLIMB TOURNAMENT!
AND HE'S ONLY A SECOND-YEAR!
ZOOSH
HEH!
SERIOUSLY!? THEN HE WAS A FIRST-YEAR UNTIL JUST RECENTLY!?
PEOPLE ARE TALKING ABOUT ME!!
RUSTLE
AS THEY SHOULD—I'M AWESOME!!
AH HA HA HA!
BUMP

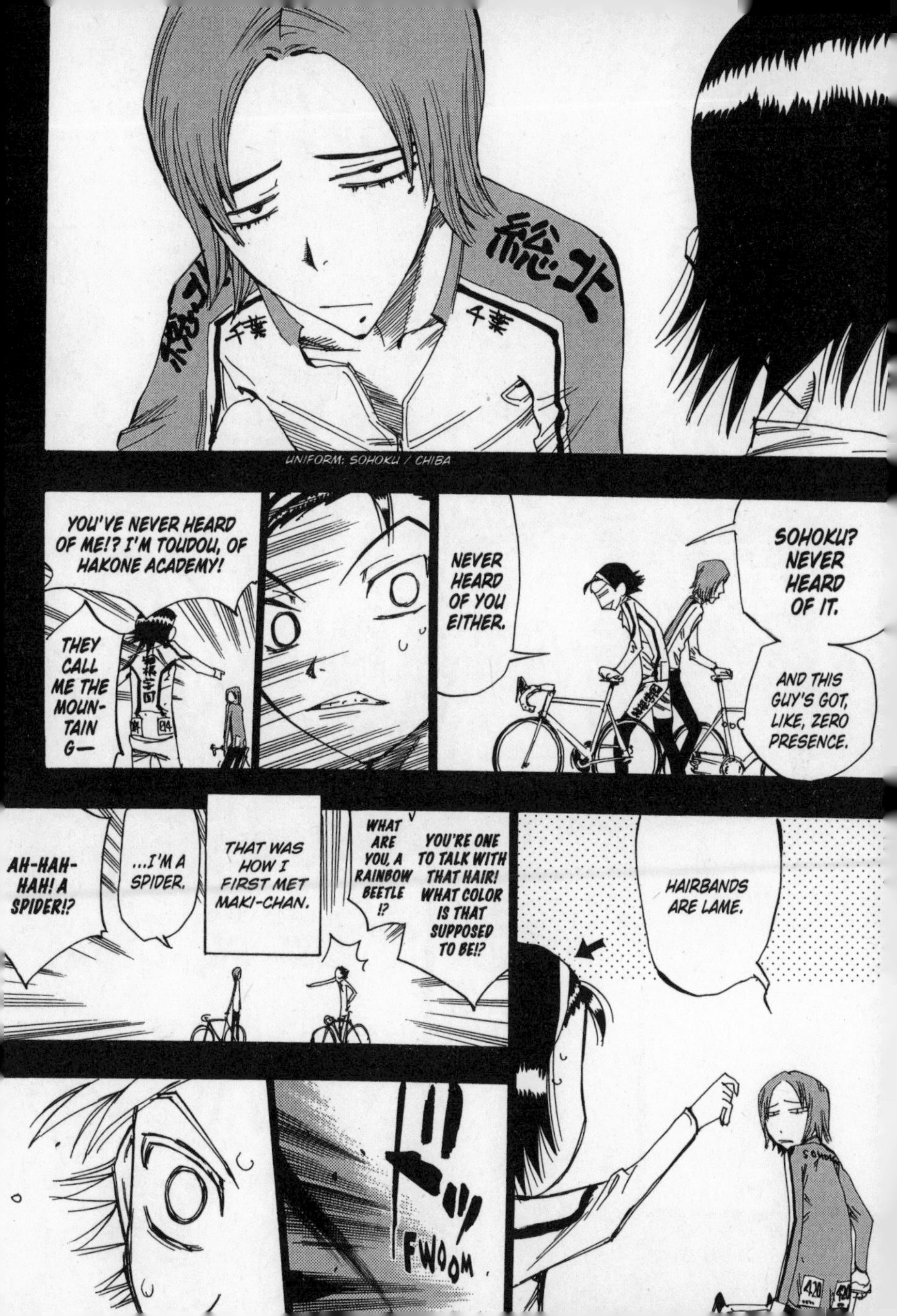
UNIFORM: SOHOKU / CHIBA
SOHOKU? NEVER HEARD OF IT.
AND THIS GUY'S GOT, LIKE, ZERO PRESENCE.
NEVER HEARD OF YOU EITHER.
YOU'VE NEVER HEARD OF ME!? I'M TOUDOU, OF HAKONE ACADEMY!
THEY CALL ME THE MOUN-TAIN G—
HAIRBANDS ARE LAME.
YOU'RE ONE TO TALK WITH THAT HAIR! WHAT COLOR IS THAT SUPPOSED TO BE!?
WHAT ARE YOU, A RAINBOW BEETLE!?
THAT WAS HOW I FIRST MET MAKI-CHAN.
...I'M A SPIDER.
AH-HAH-HAH! A SPIDER!?
FWOOM

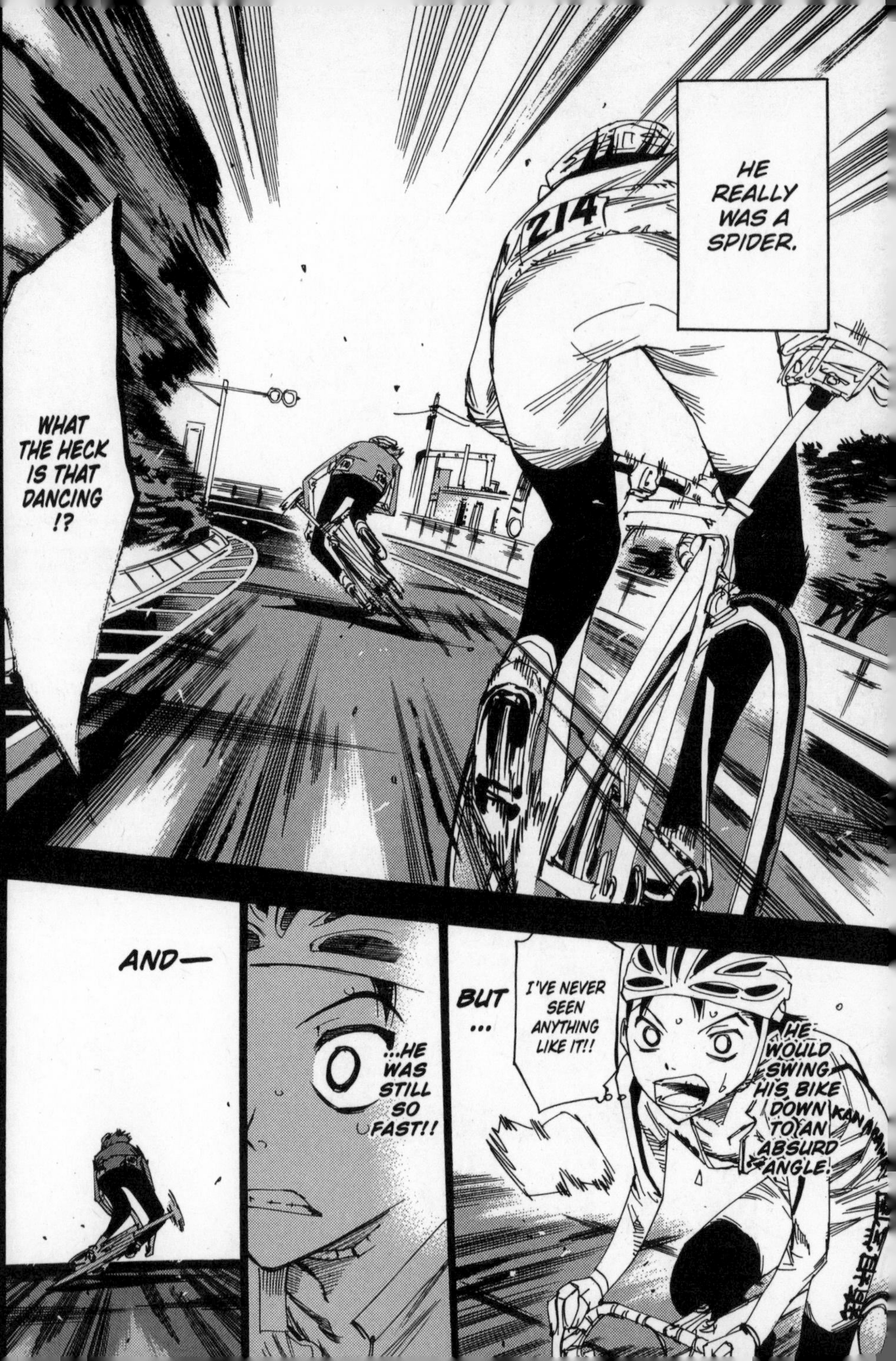
HE REALLY WAS A SPIDER.
WHAT THE HECK IS THAT DANCING!?
HE WOULD SWING HIS BIKE DOWN TO AN ABSURD ANGLE.
I'VE NEVER SEEN ANYTHING LIKE IT!!
BUT...
...HE WAS STILL SO FAST!!
AND—

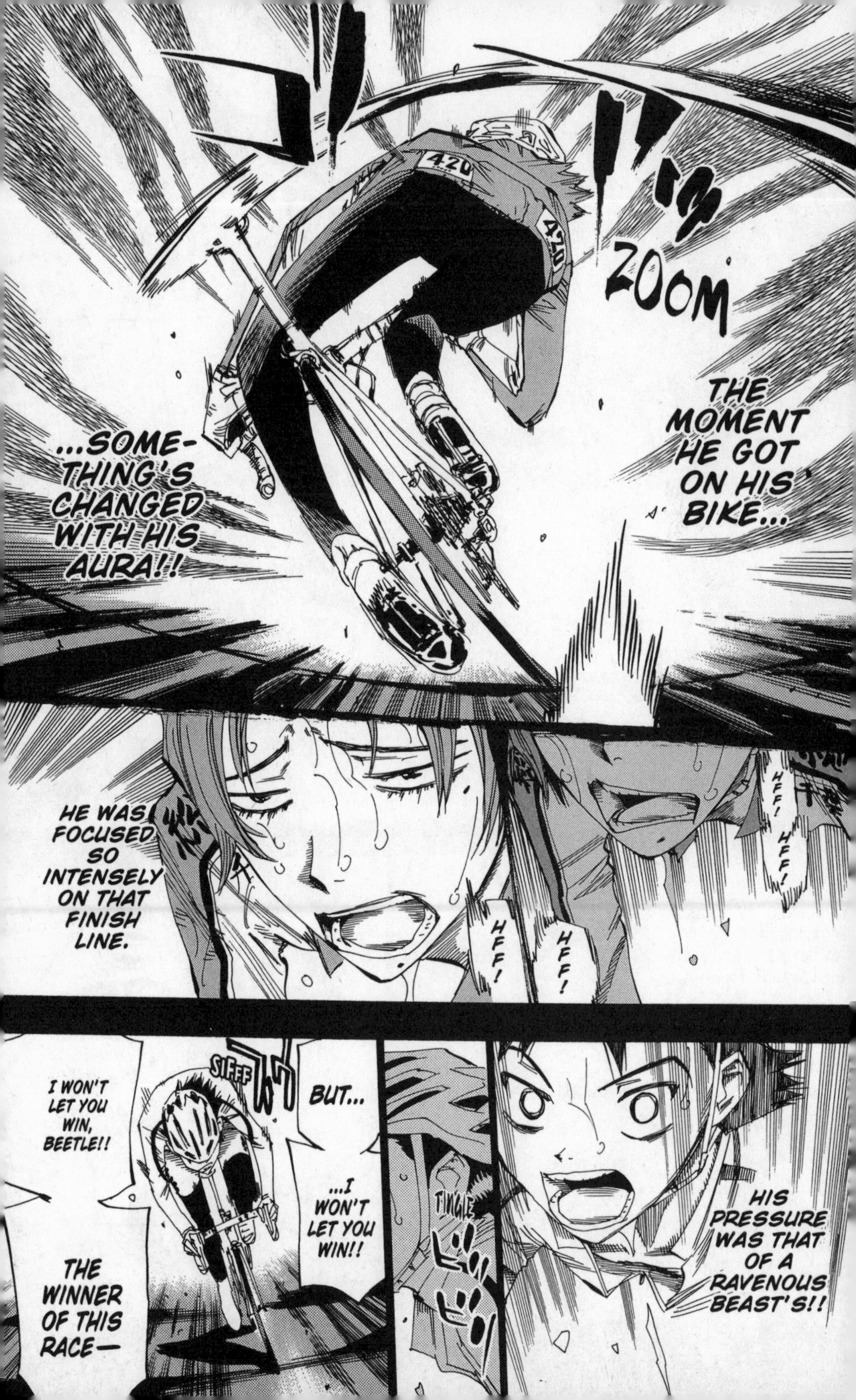
ZOOM
THE MOMENT HE GOT ON HIS BIKE...
...SOMETHING'S CHANGED WITH HIS AURA!!
HFF! HFF!
HFF! HFF!
HE WAS FOCUSED SO INTENSELY ON THAT FINISH LINE.
TINGLE
HIS PRESSURE WAS THAT OF A RAVENOUS BEAST'S!!
BUT...
...I WON'T LET YOU WIN!!
I WON'T LET YOU WIN, BEETLE!!
THE WINNER OF THIS RACE—

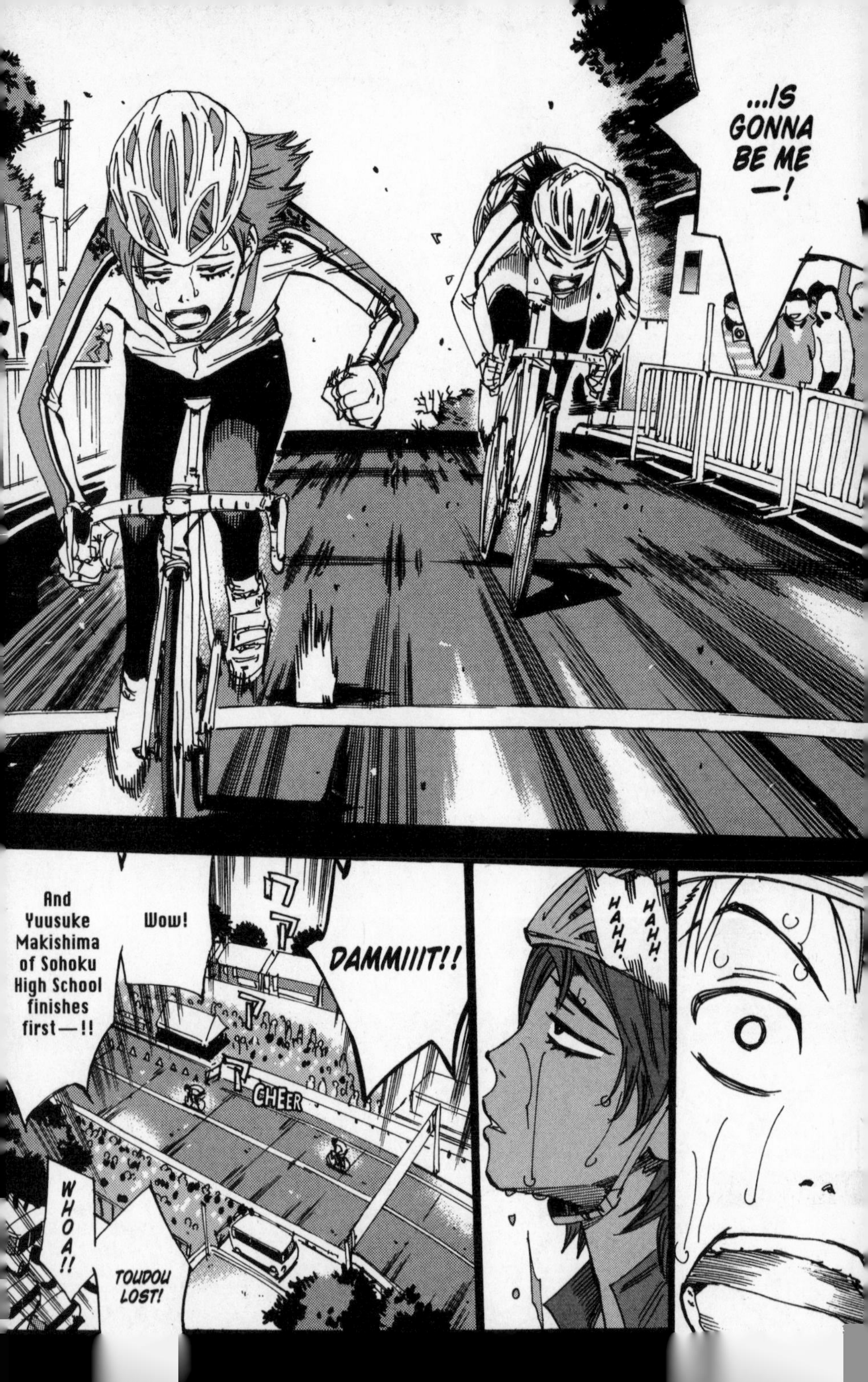
...IS GONNA BE ME —!
HAHH HAHH
DAMMIIIT!!
Wow!
And Yuusuke Makishima of Sohoku High School finishes first—!!
CHEER
TOUDOU LOST!
WHOA!!

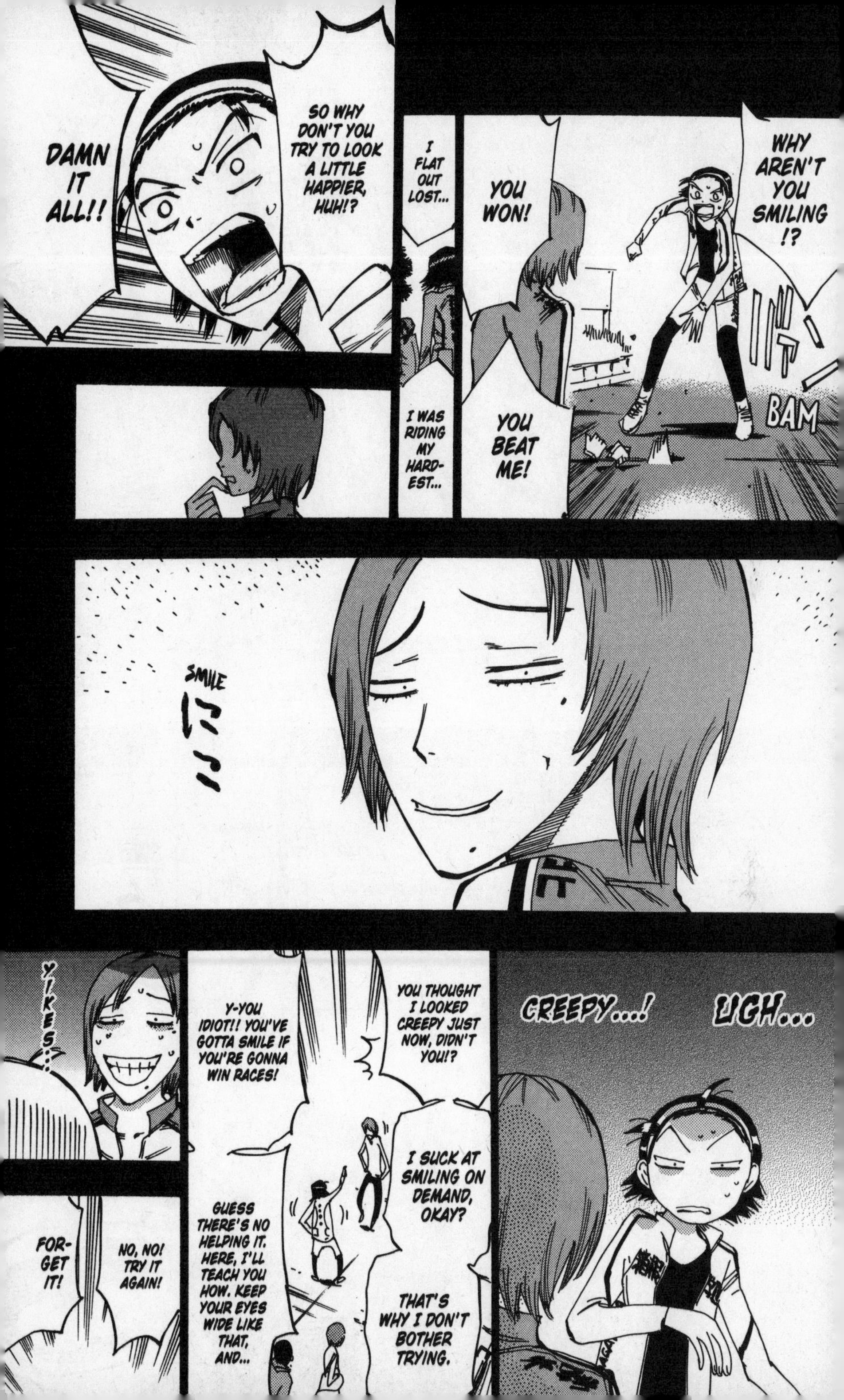
WHY AREN'T YOU SMILING!?
BAM
YOU WON!
YOU BEAT ME!
I FLAT OUT LOST...
I WAS RIDING MY HARDEST...
SO WHY DON'T YOU TRY TO LOOK A LITTLE HAPPIER, HUH!?
DAMN IT ALL!!
SMILE
にこ
UGH...
CREEPY...!
YOU THOUGHT I LOOKED CREEPY JUST NOW, DIDN'T YOU!?
I SUCK AT SMILING ON DEMAND, OKAY?
THAT'S WHY I DON'T BOTHER TRYING.
Y-YOU IDIOT!! YOU'VE GOTTA SMILE IF YOU'RE GONNA WIN RACES!
GUESS THERE'S NO HELPING IT. HERE, I'LL TEACH YOU HOW. KEEP YOUR EYES WIDE LIKE THAT, AND...
YIKES...
NO, NO! TRY IT AGAIN!
FOR-GET IT!

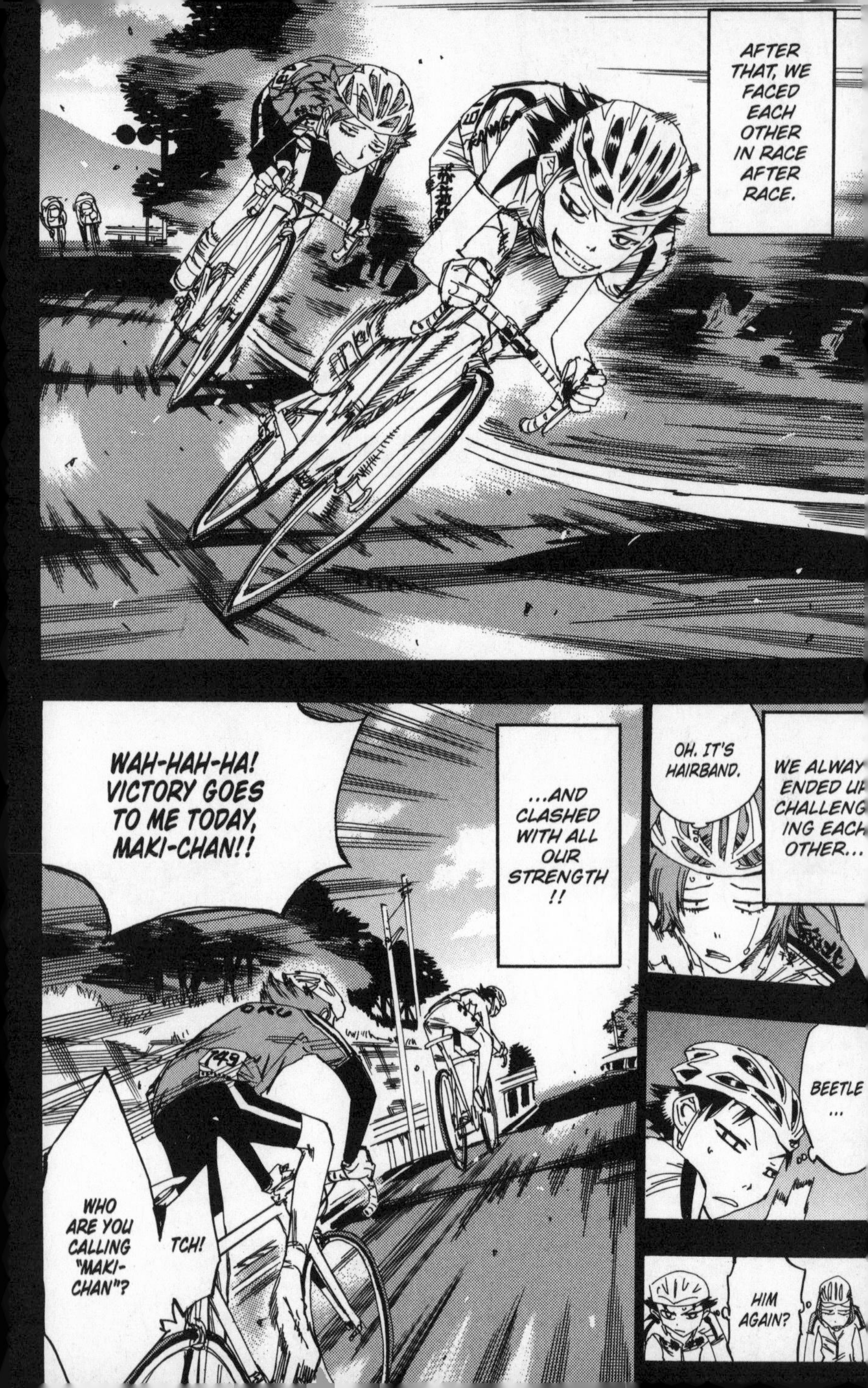
AFTER THAT, WE FACED EACH OTHER IN RACE AFTER RACE.
WE ALWAY ENDED UP CHALLENG-ING EACH OTHER...
OH. IT'S HAIRBAND.
BEETLE ...
HIM AGAIN?
...AND CLASHED WITH ALL OUR STRENGTH!!
WAH-HAH-HA! VICTORY GOES TO ME TODAY, MAKI-CHAN!!
TCH!
WHO ARE YOU CALLING "MAKI-CHAN"?

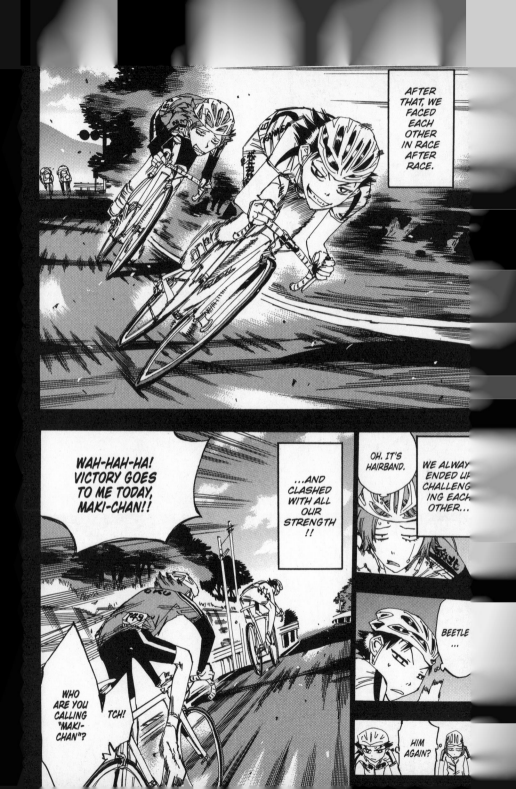

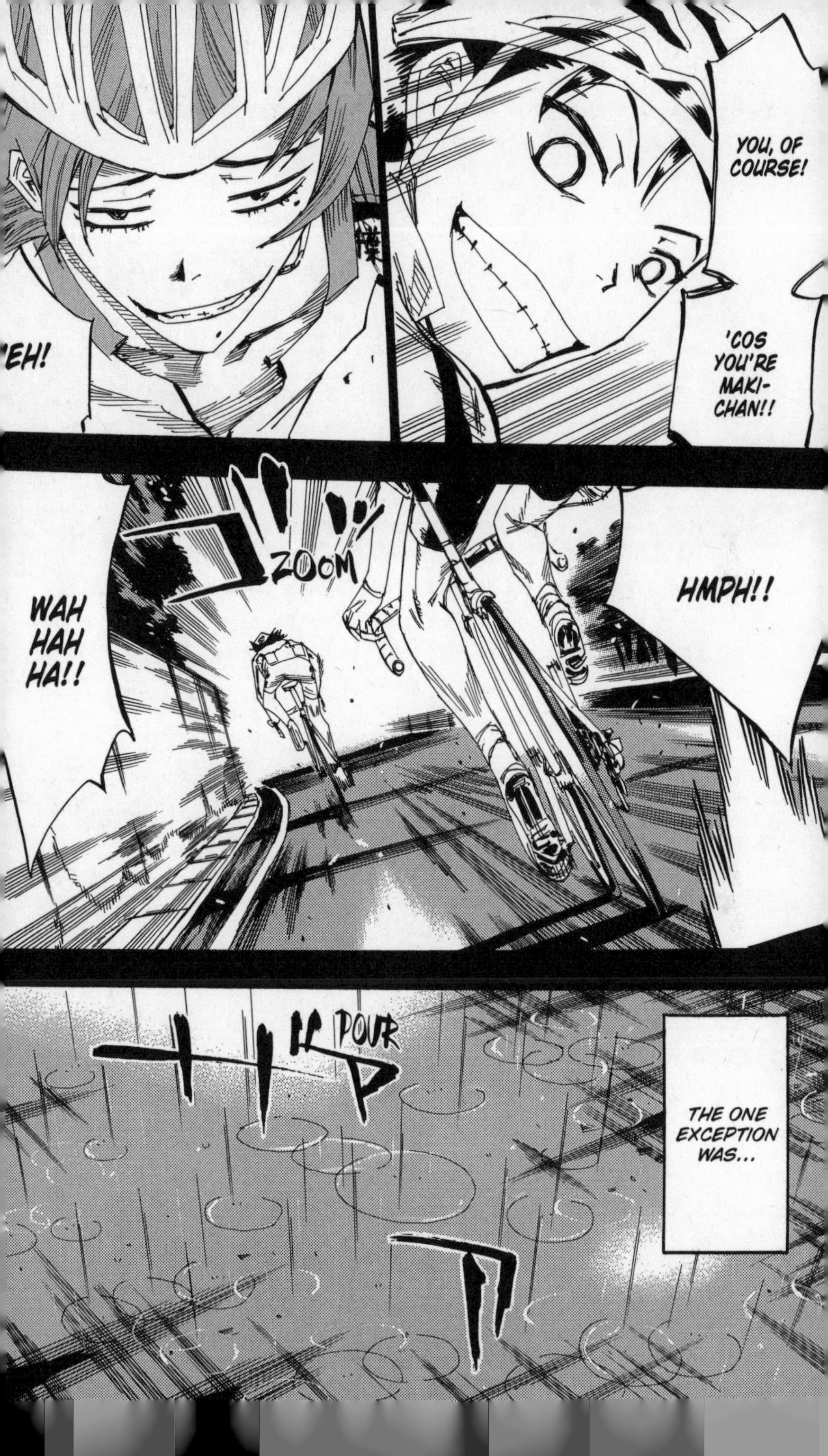
YOU, OF COURSE!
'COS YOU'RE MAKI-CHAN!!
EH!
HMPH!!
ZOOM
WAH HAH HA!!
THE ONE EXCEPTION WAS...
POUR

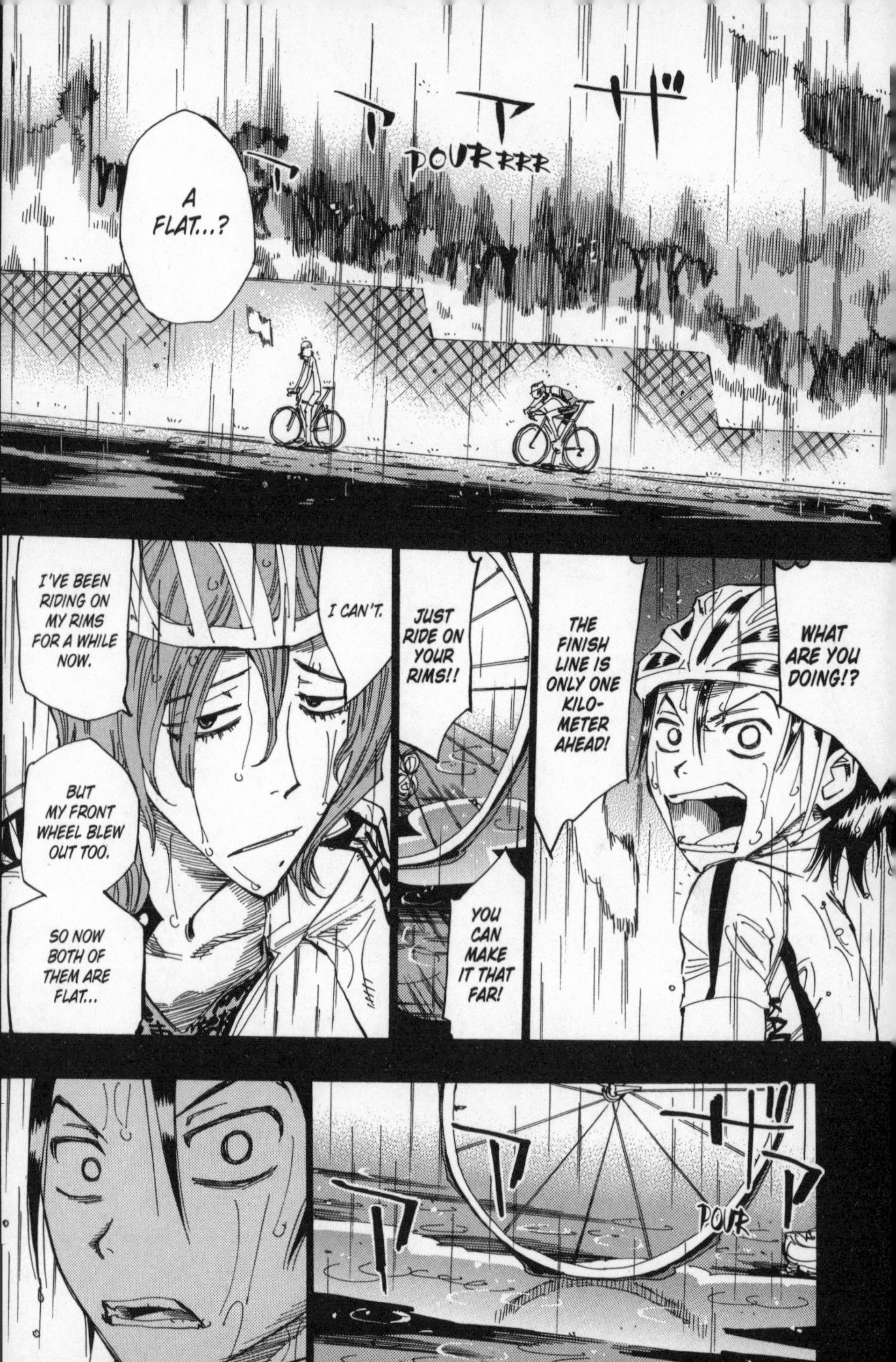
ザァァァ
DOURRRR
A FLAT...?
WHAT ARE YOU DOING!?
THE FINISH LINE IS ONLY ONE KILOMETER AHEAD!
JUST RIDE ON YOUR RIMS!!
YOU CAN MAKE IT THAT FAR!
I CAN'T.
I'VE BEEN RIDING ON MY RIMS FOR A WHILE NOW.
BUT MY FRONT WHEEL BLEW OUT TOO.
SO NOW BOTH OF THEM ARE FLAT...
ザァァァ
DOUR

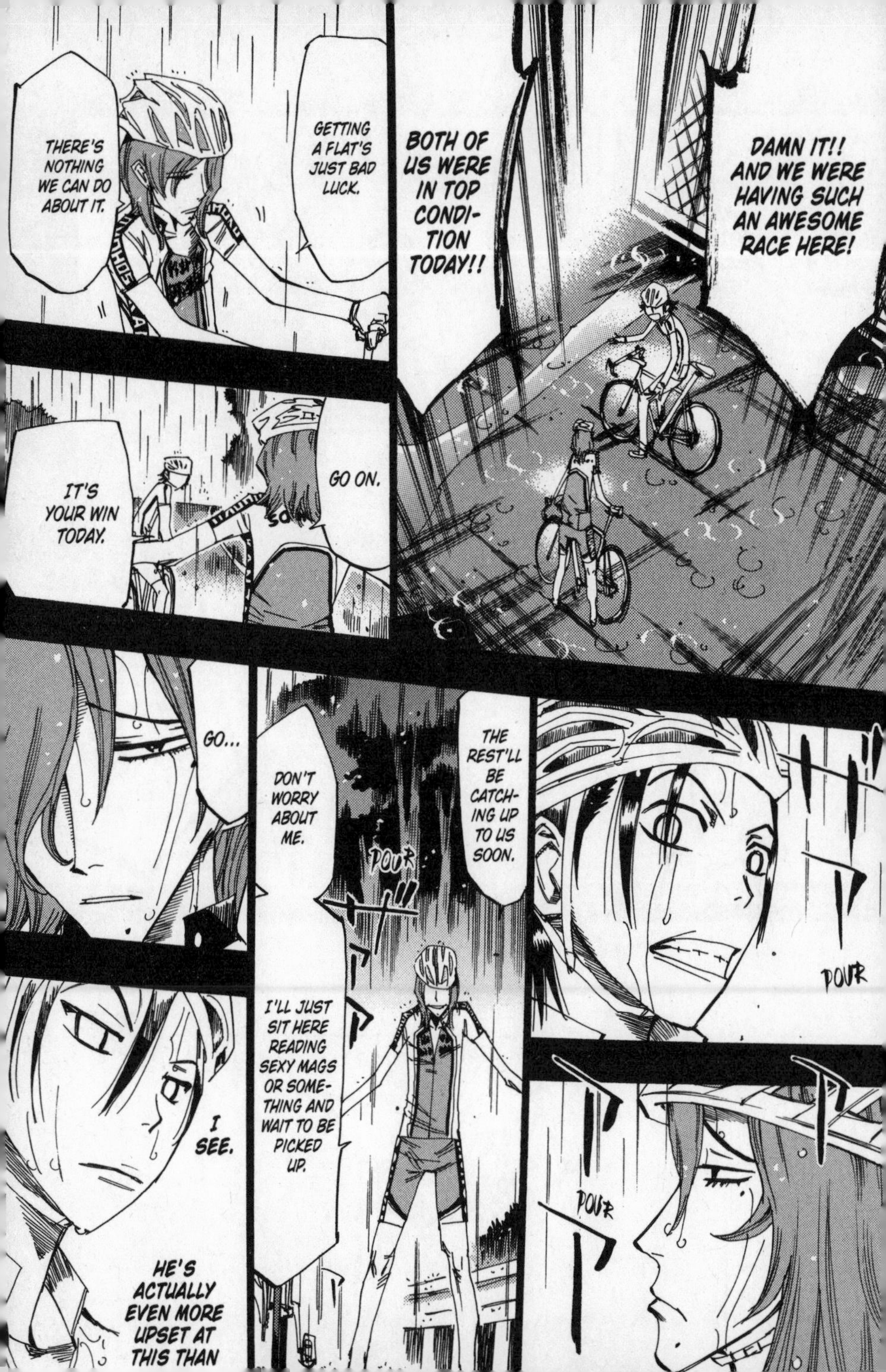
DAMN IT!! AND WE WERE HAVING SUCH AN AWESOME RACE HERE!
BOTH OF US WERE IN TOP CONDITION TODAY!!
GETTING A FLAT'S JUST BAD LUCK.
THERE'S NOTHING WE CAN DO ABOUT IT.
GO ON.
IT'S YOUR WIN TODAY.
POUR
POUR
THE REST'LL BE CATCHING UP TO US SOON.
DON'T WORRY ABOUT ME.
POUR
I'LL JUST SIT HERE READING SEXY MAGS OR SOMETHING AND WAIT TO BE PICKED UP.
GO...
I SEE.
HE'S ACTUALLY EVEN MORE UPSET AT THIS THAN

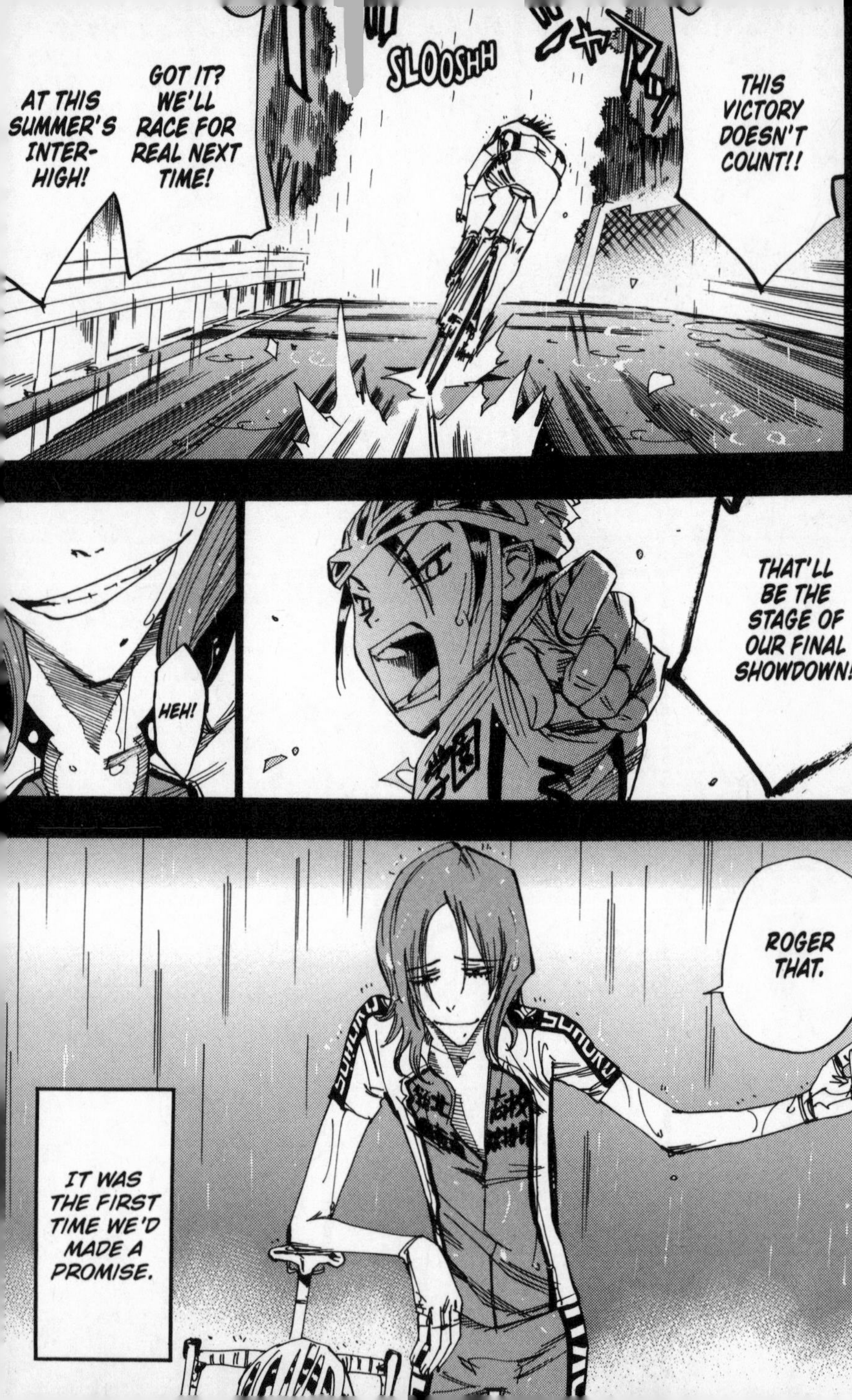
THIS VICTORY DOESN'T COUNT!!
SLOOSHH
GOT IT? WE'LL RACE FOR REAL NEXT TIME!
AT THIS SUMMER'S INTER-HIGH!
THAT'LL BE THE STAGE OF OUR FINAL SHOWDOWN!
HEH!
ROGER THAT.
IT WAS THE FIRST TIME WE'D MADE A PROMISE.

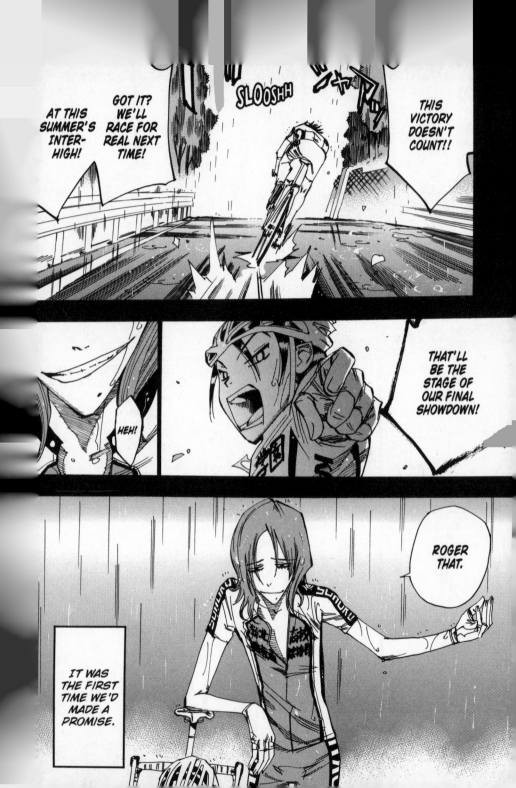

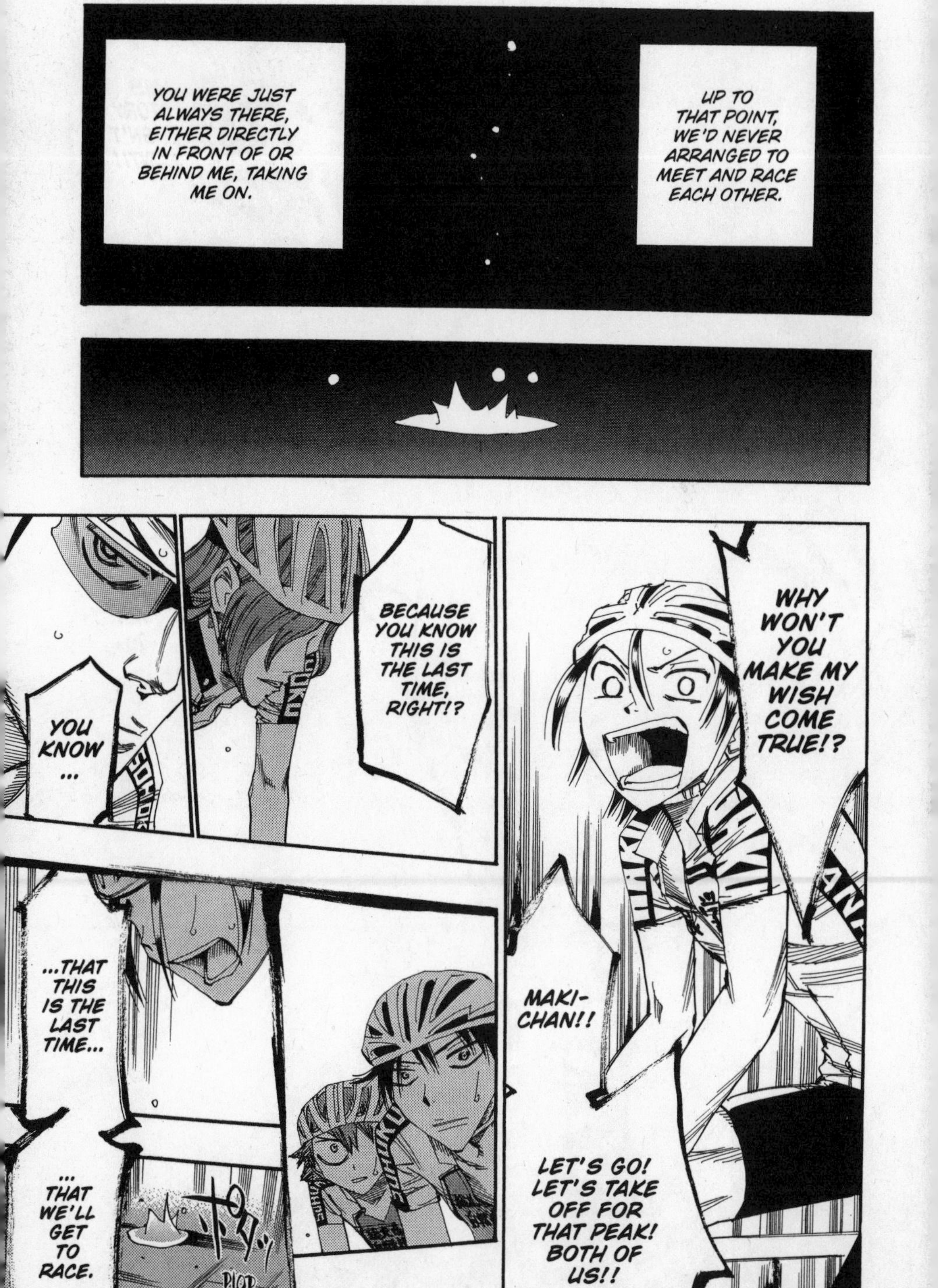
UP TO THAT POINT, WE'D NEVER ARRANGED TO MEET AND RACE EACH OTHER.
YOU WERE JUST ALWAYS THERE, EITHER DIRECTLY IN FRONT OF OR BEHIND ME, TAKING ME ON.
WHY WON'T YOU MAKE MY WISH COME TRUE!?
MAKI-CHAN!!
LET'S GO! LET'S TAKE OFF FOR THAT PEAK! BOTH OF US!!
BECAUSE YOU KNOW THIS IS THE LAST TIME, RIGHT!?
YOU KNOW ...
...THAT THIS IS THE LAST TIME...
... THAT WE'LL GET TO RACE.
PLOP

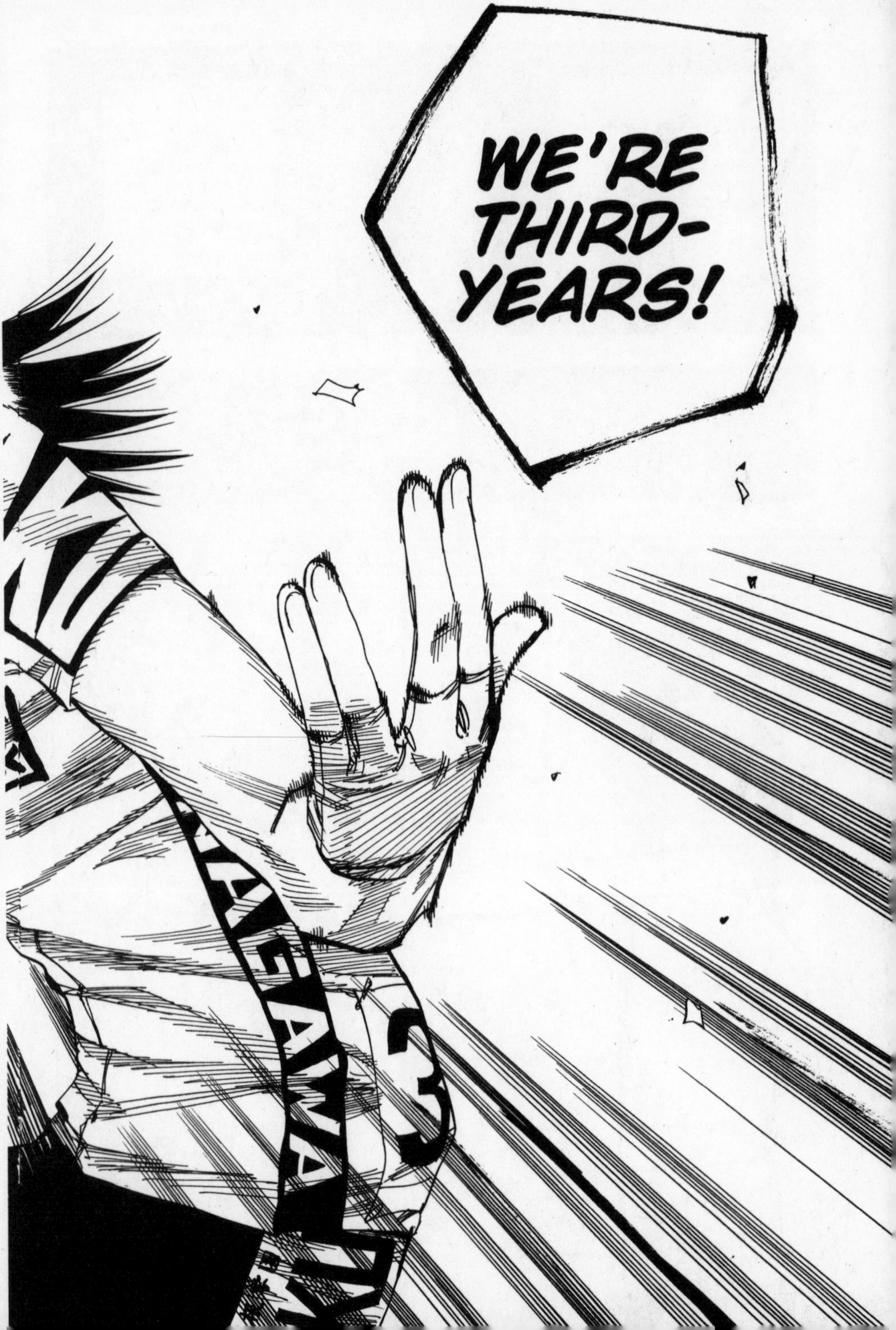
WE'RE THIRD-YEARS!

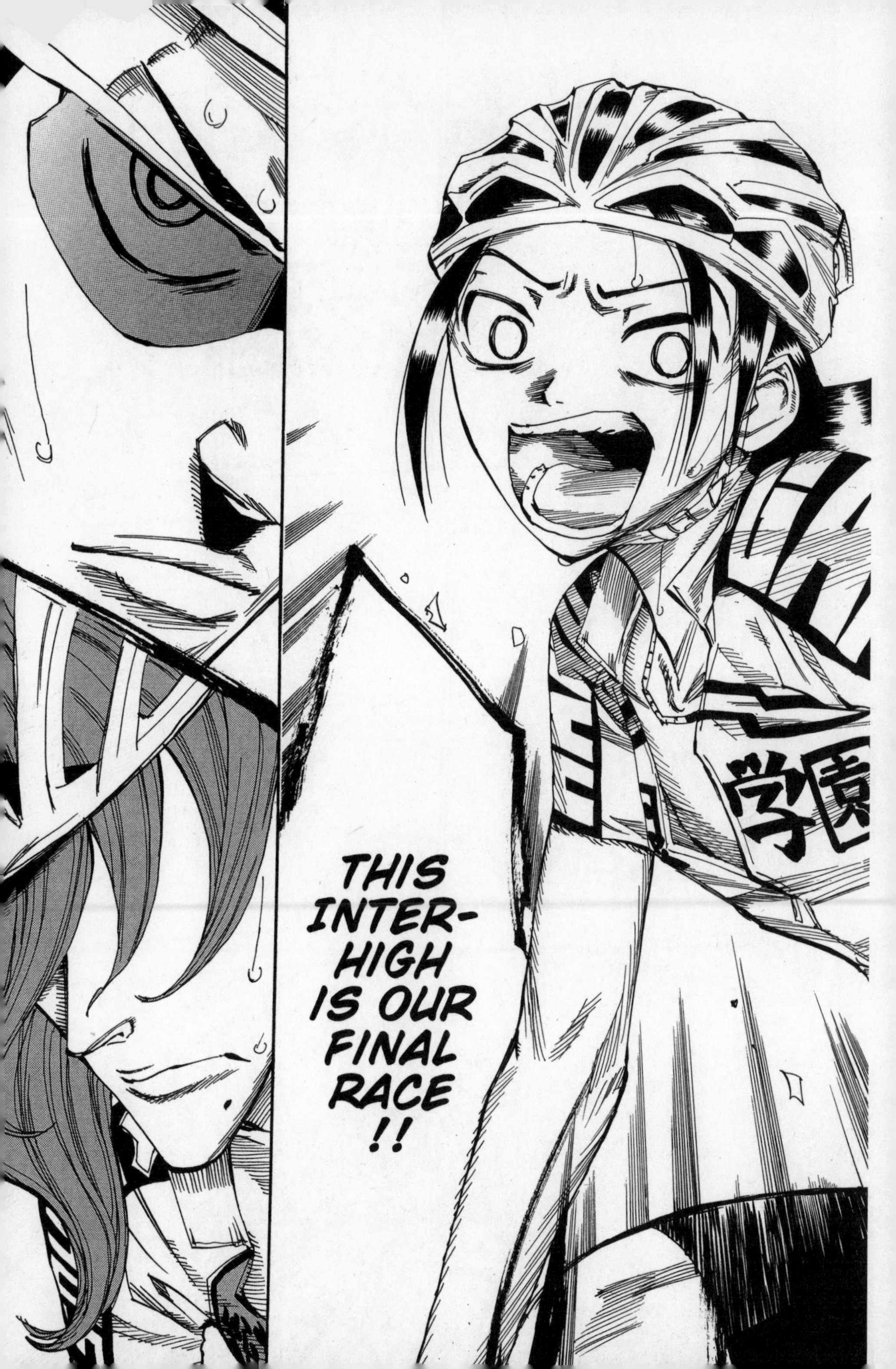
THIS INTER-HIGH IS OUR FINAL RACE !!
学園

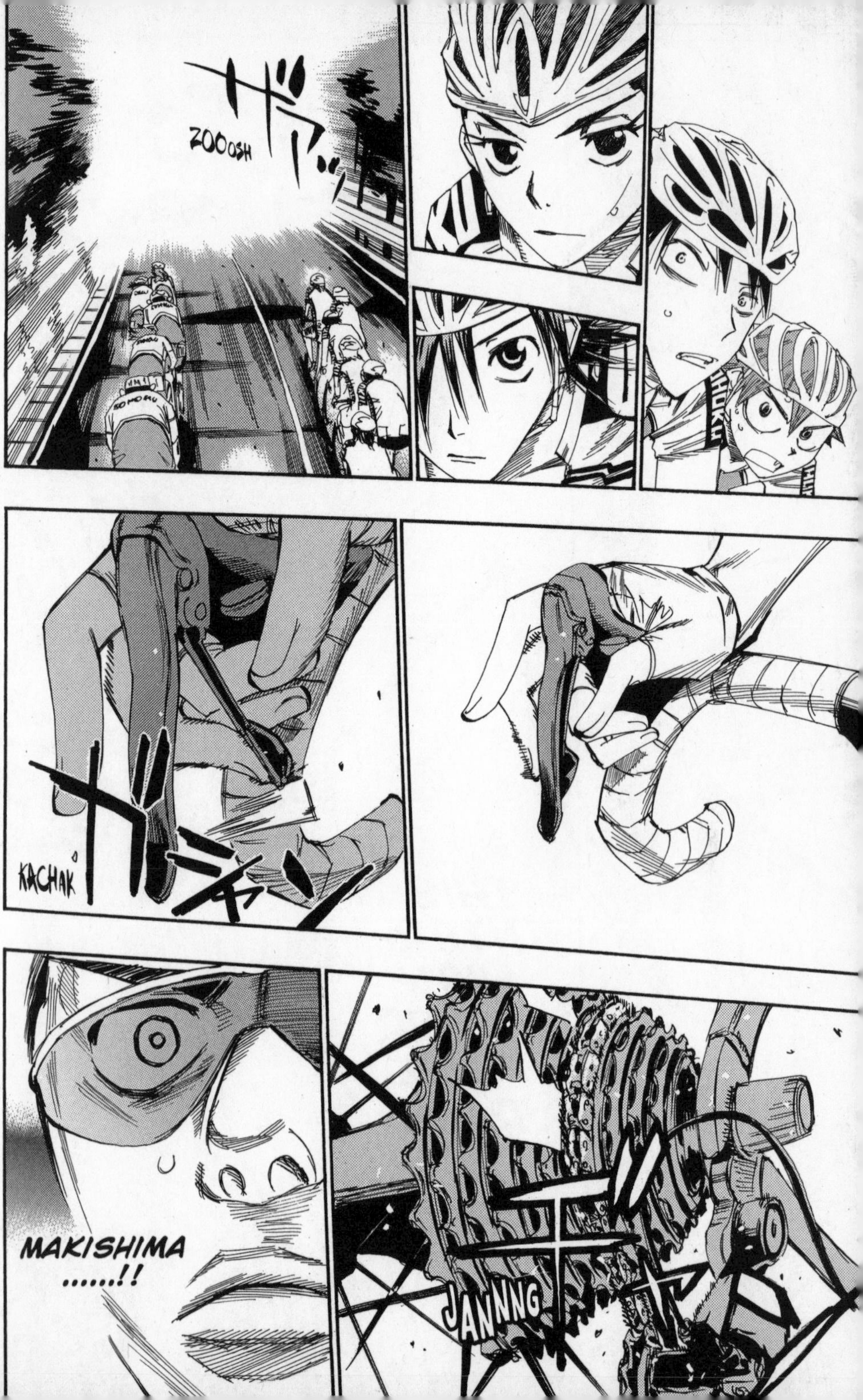
ZOOOSH
KACHAK
JANNNG
MAKISHIMA ......!!

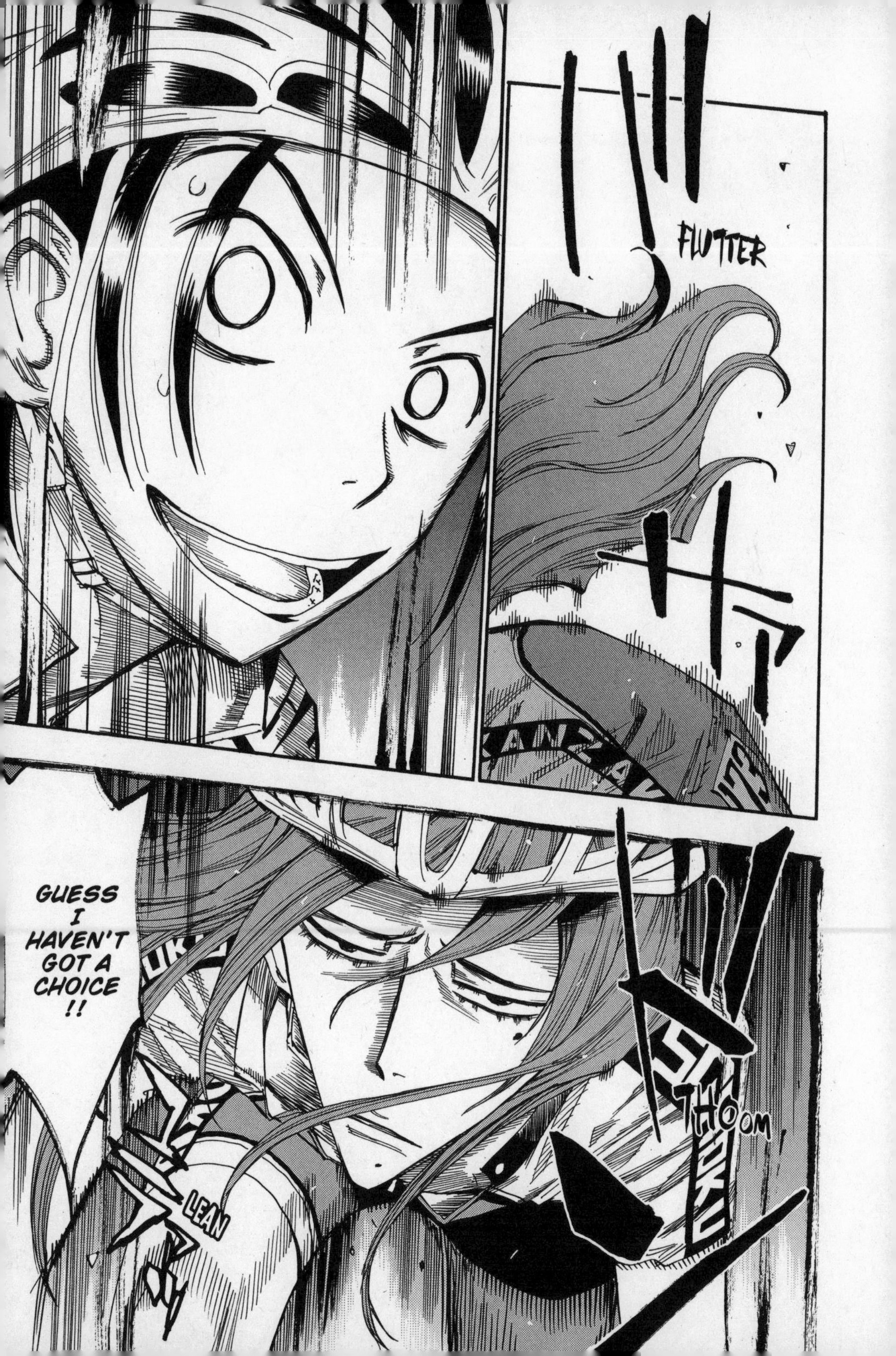
FLUTTER
THOOM
GUESS I HAVEN'T GOT A CHOICE!!
LEAN

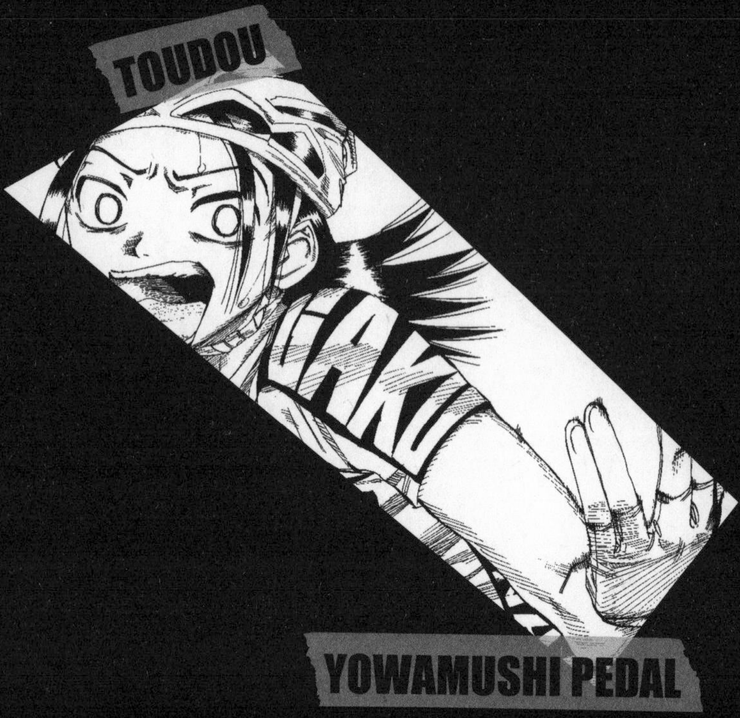
TOUDOU
YOWAMUSHI PEDAL

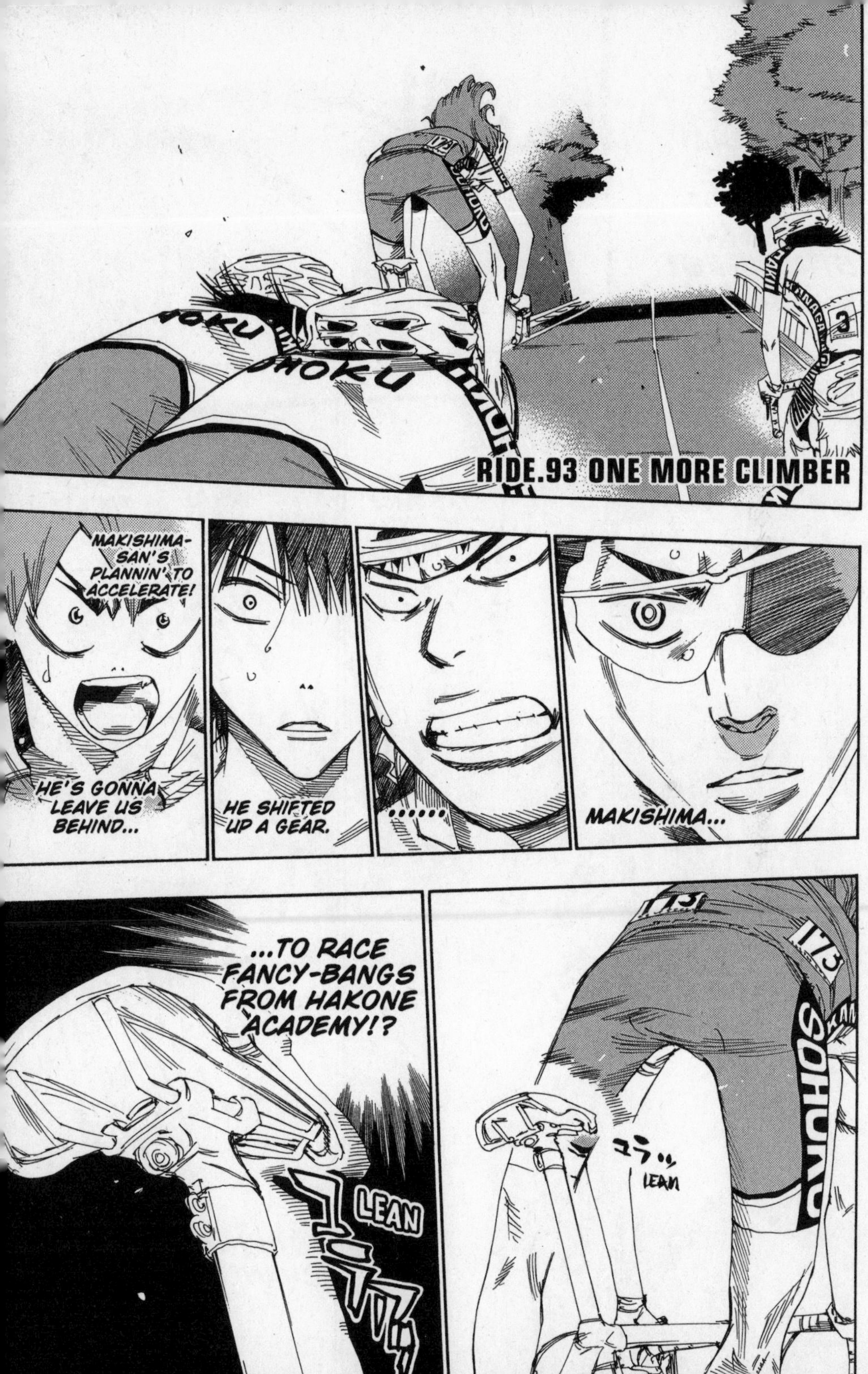
RIDE.93 ONE MORE CLIMBER
MAKISHIMA...
......
HE SHIFTED UP A GEAR.
MAKISHIMA-SAN'S PLANNIN' TO ACCELERATE!
HE'S GONNA LEAVE US BEHIND...
ユラッ
LEAN
...TO RACE FANCY-BANGS FROM HAKONE ACADEMY!?
LEAN
ユラッ

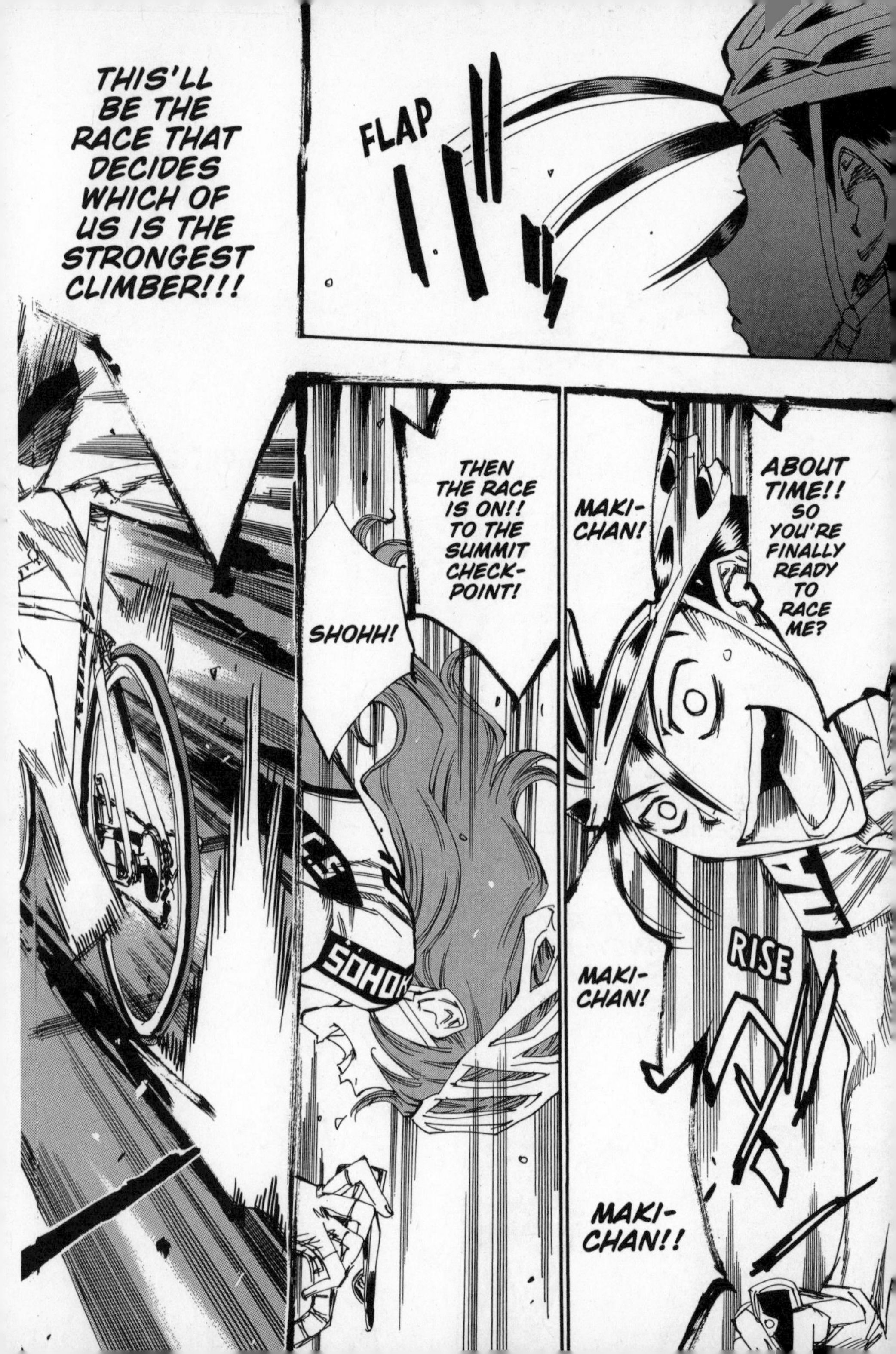
FLAP
ABOUT TIME!! SO YOU'RE FINALLY READY TO RACE ME?
MAKI-CHAN!
RISE
MAKI-CHAN!
MAKI-CHAN!!
THEN THE RACE IS ON!! TO THE SUMMIT CHECK-POINT!
SHOHH!
SOHOK
THIS'LL BE THE RACE THAT DECIDES WHICH OF US IS THE STRONGEST CLIMBER!!!

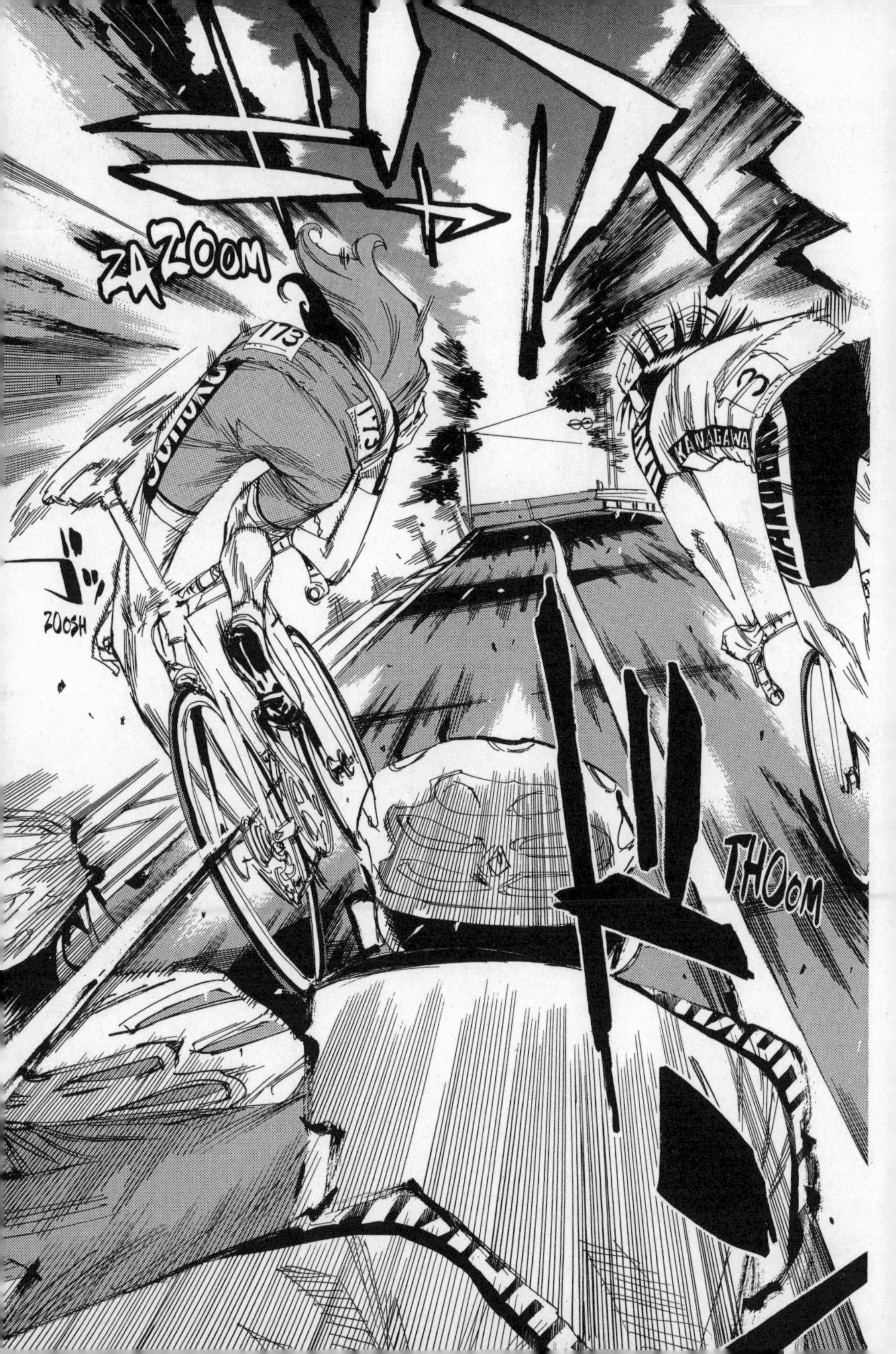
ZAZOOM
173
KANAGAWA
THOOM
ZOOSH

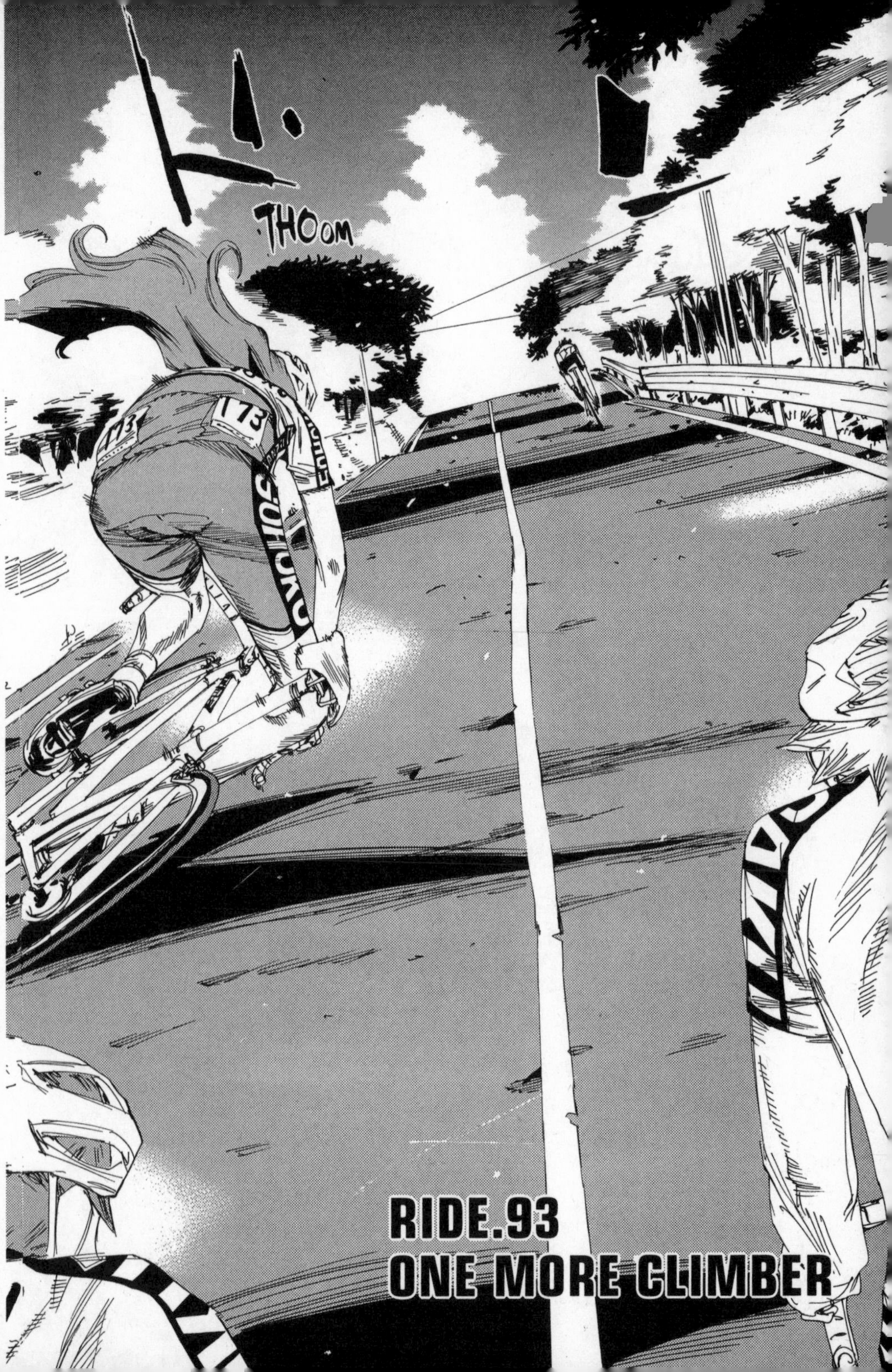
THOOM
173
SOHOKU
RIDE.93
ONE MORE CLIMBER

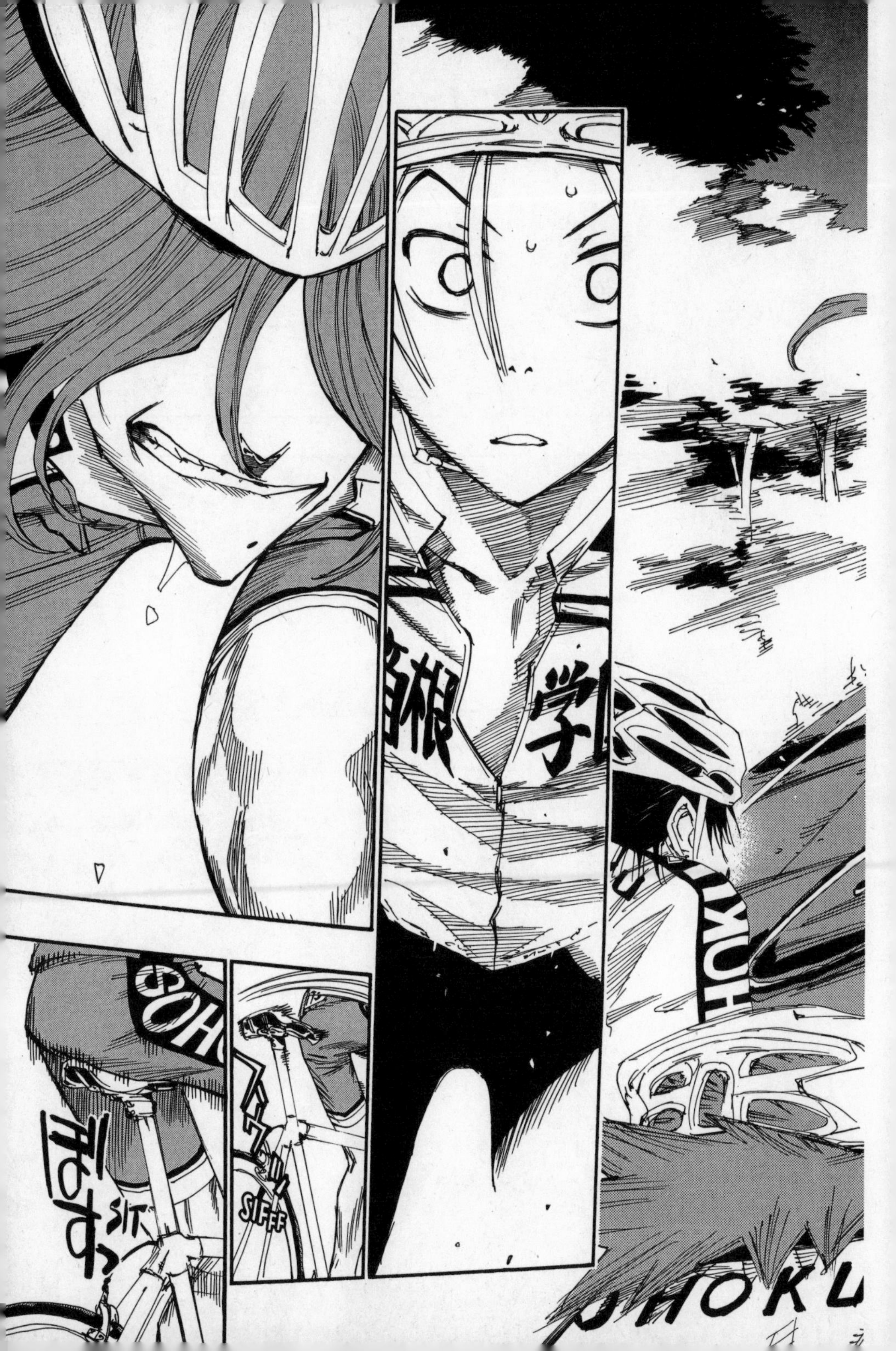
SIFFF
SIT

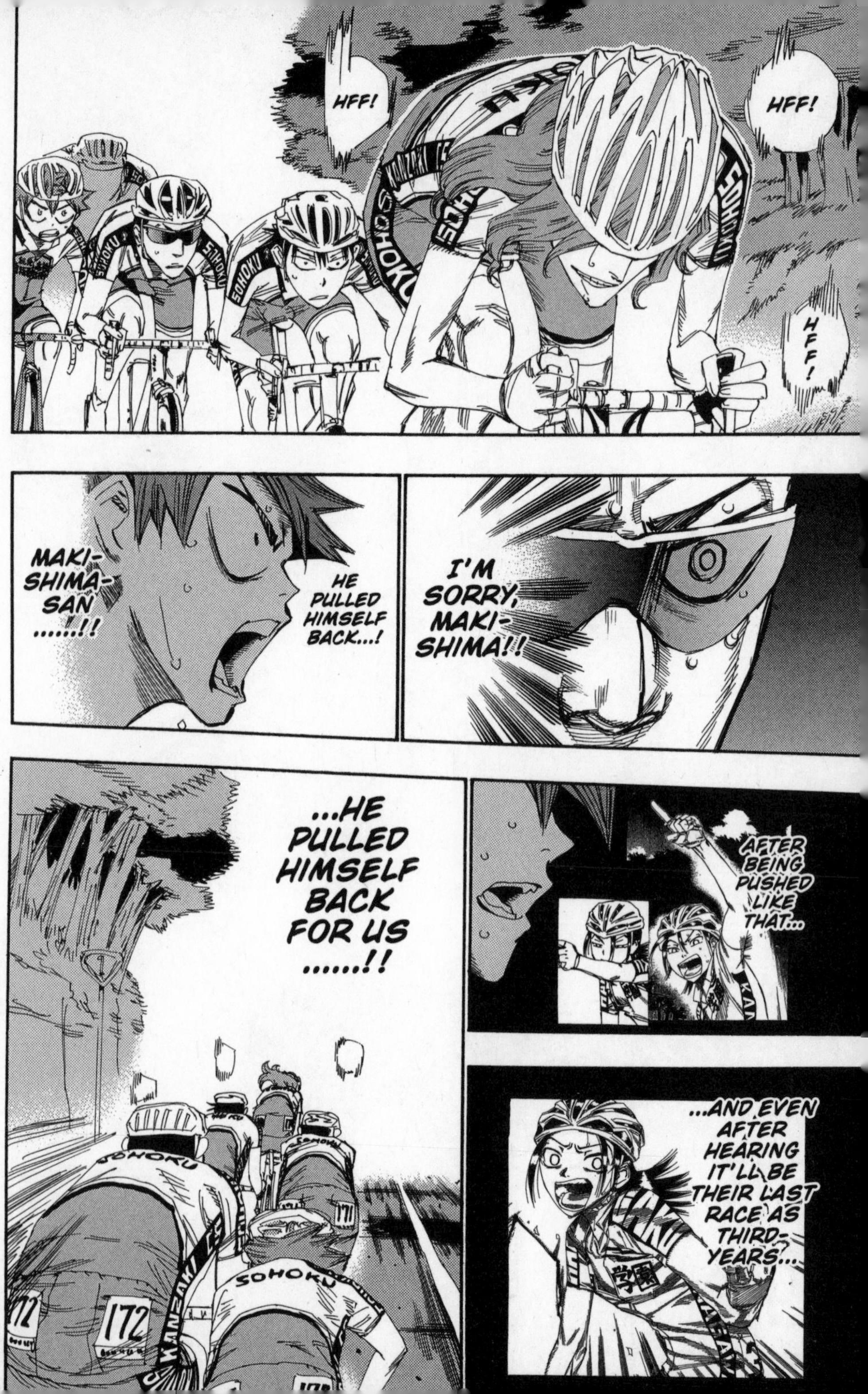
HFF!
HFF!
HFF!
I'M SORRY, MAKI-SHIMA!!
HE PULLED HIMSELF BACK...!
MAKI-SHIMA-SAN ......!!
AFTER BEING PUSHED LIKE THAT...
...AND EVEN AFTER HEARING IT'LL BE THEIR LAST RACE AS THIRD-YEARS...
...HE PULLED HIMSELF BACK FOR US ......!!

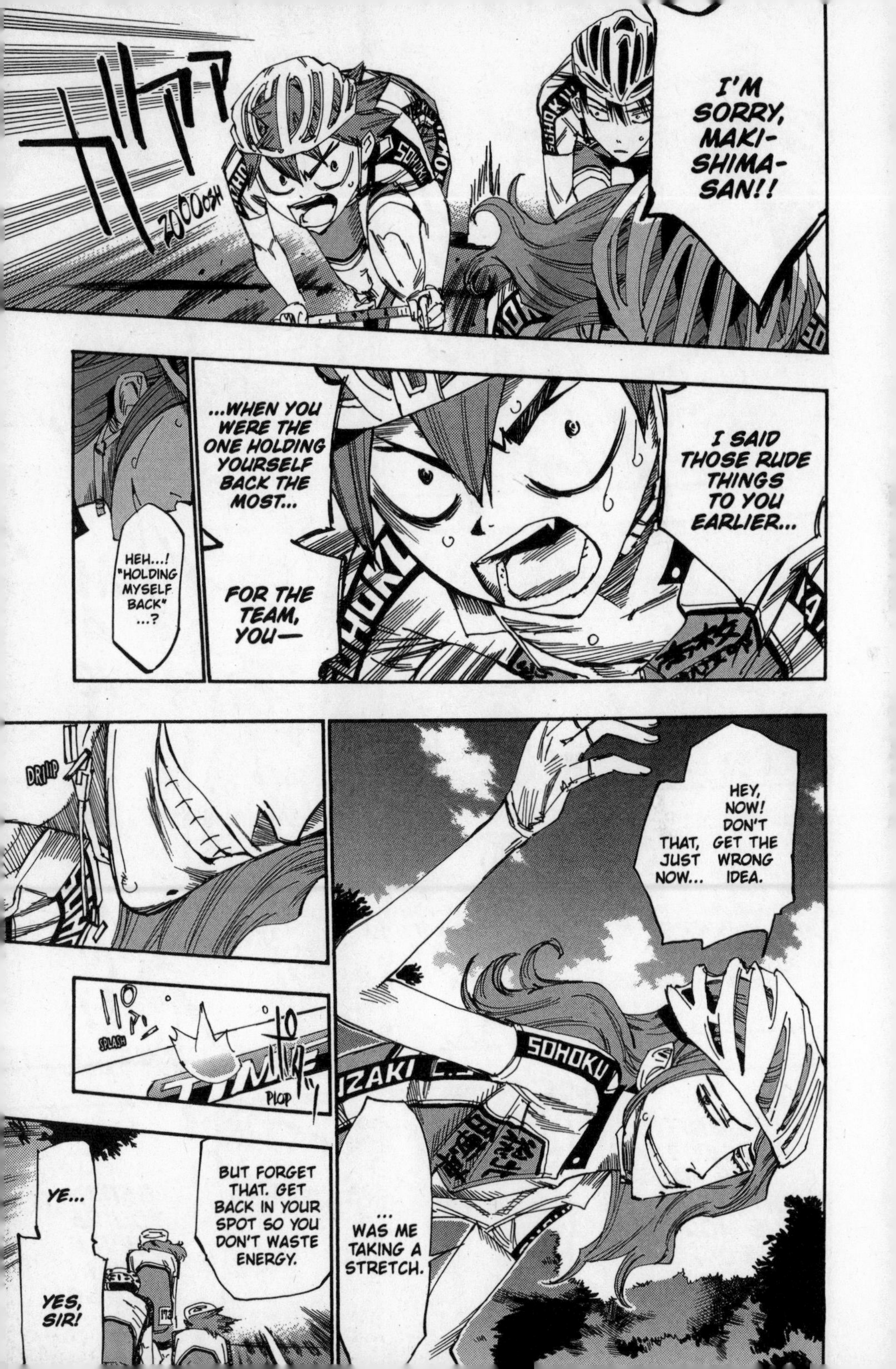
ZOOOOSH
I'M SORRY, MAKI-SHIMA-SAN!!
I SAID THOSE RUDE THINGS TO YOU EARLIER...
...WHEN YOU WERE THE ONE HOLDING YOURSELF BACK THE MOST...
FOR THE TEAM, YOU—
HEH...! "HOLDING MYSELF BACK" ...?
HEY, NOW! DON'T GET THE WRONG IDEA.
THAT, JUST NOW...
...WAS ME TAKING A STRETCH.
DRIIP
SPLASH
PLOP
BUT FORGET THAT. GET BACK IN YOUR SPOT SO YOU DON'T WASTE ENERGY.
YE...
YES, SIR!

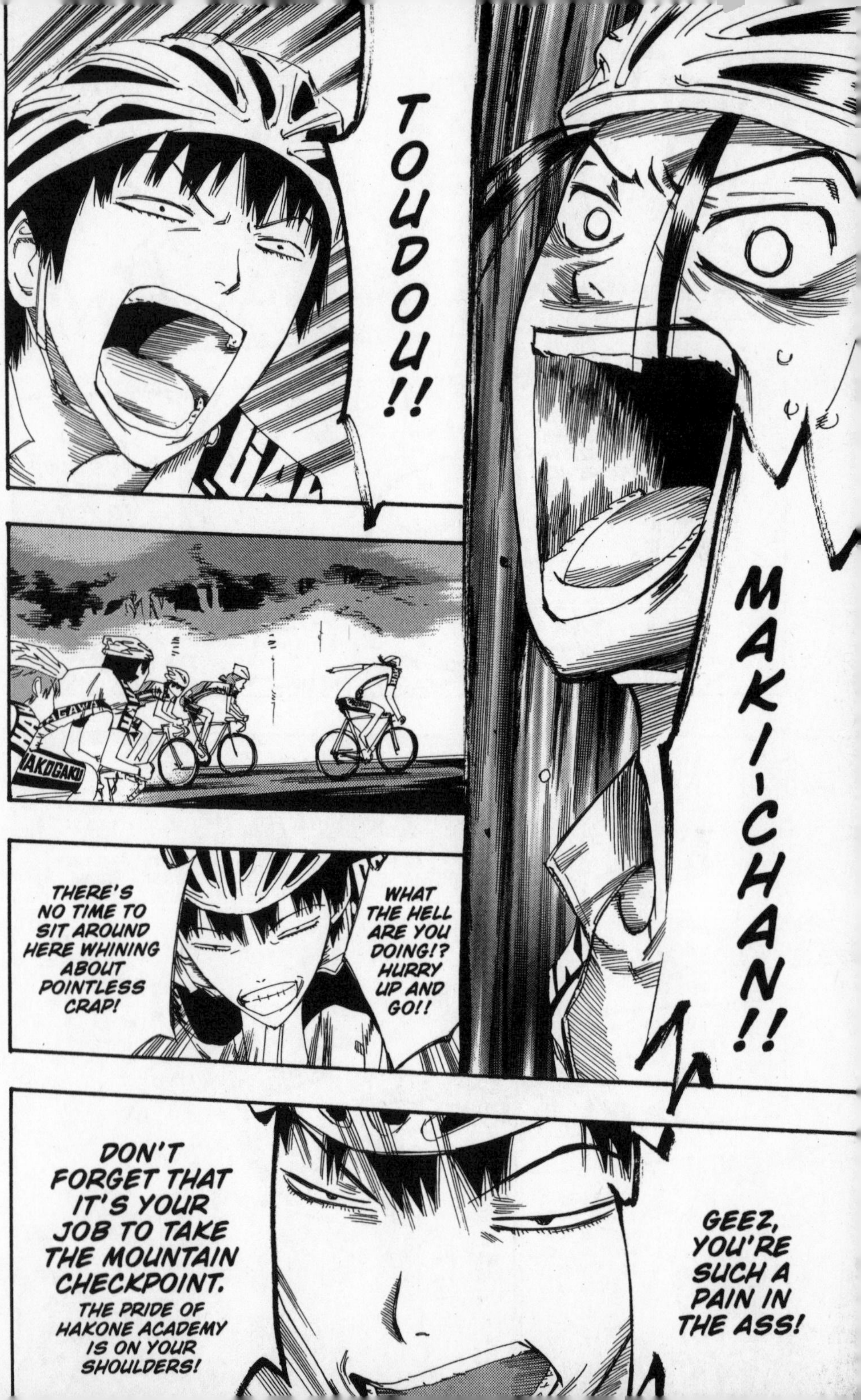
MAKI-CHAN!!
TOUDOU!!
WHAT THE HELL ARE YOU DOING!? HURRY UP AND GO!!
THERE'S NO TIME TO SIT AROUND HERE WHINING ABOUT POINTLESS CRAP!
GEEZ, YOU'RE SUCH A PAIN IN THE ASS!
DON'T FORGET THAT IT'S YOUR JOB TO TAKE THE MOUNTAIN CHECKPOINT.
THE PRIDE OF HAKONE ACADEMY IS ON YOUR SHOULDERS!

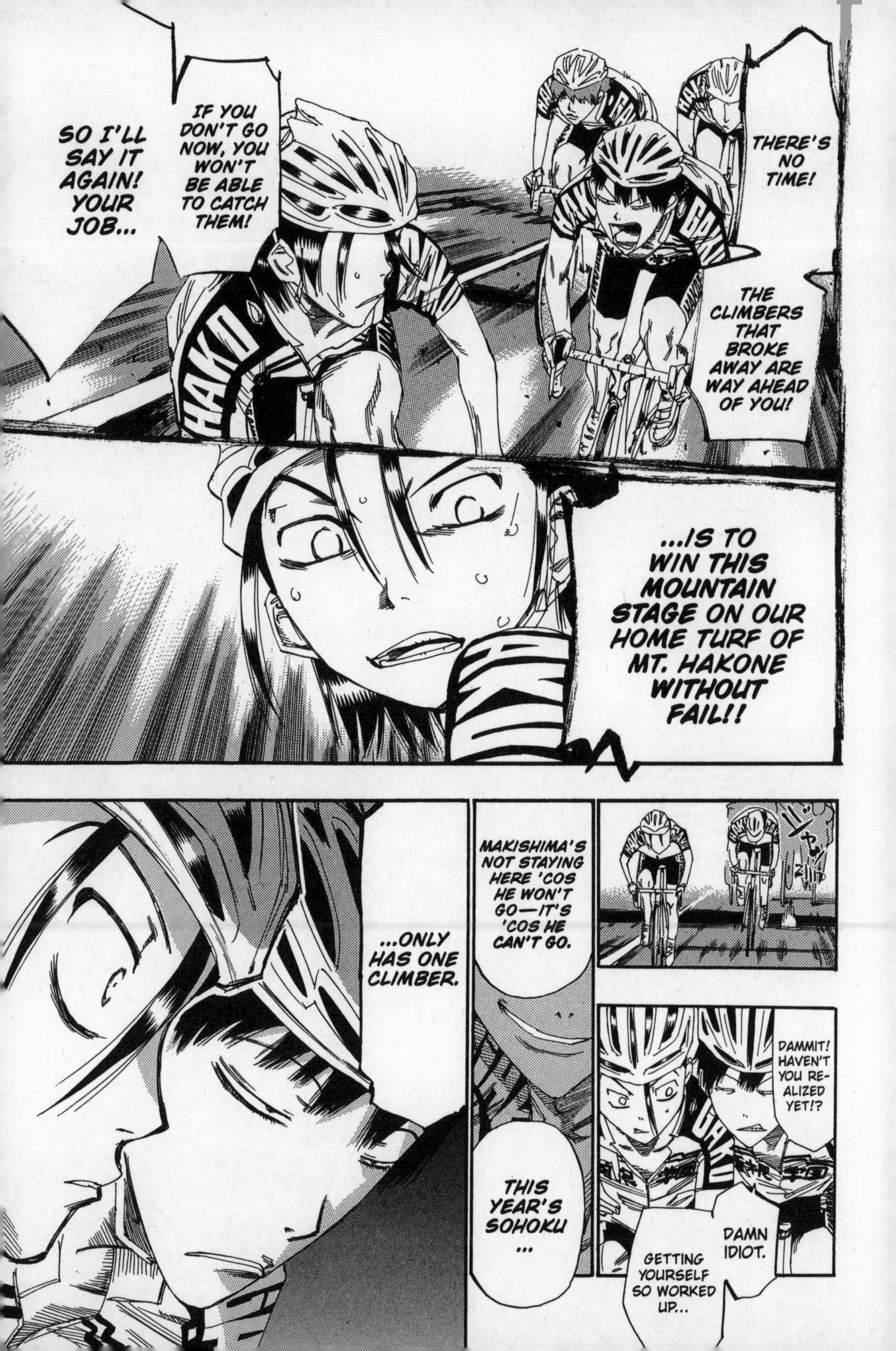
THERE'S NO TIME!
THE CLIMBERS THAT BROKE AWAY ARE WAY AHEAD OF YOU!
IF YOU DON'T GO NOW, YOU WON'T BE ABLE TO CATCH THEM!
SO I'LL SAY IT AGAIN! YOUR JOB...
...IS TO WIN THIS MOUNTAIN STAGE ON OUR HOME TURF OF MT. HAKONE WITHOUT FAIL!!
DAMMIT! HAVEN'T YOU REALIZED YET!?
DAMN IDIOT.
GETTING YOURSELF SO WORKED UP...
MAKISHIMA'S NOT STAYING HERE 'COS HE WON'T GO—IT'S 'COS HE CAN'T GO.
THIS YEAR'S SOHOKU ...
...ONLY HAS ONE CLIMBER.

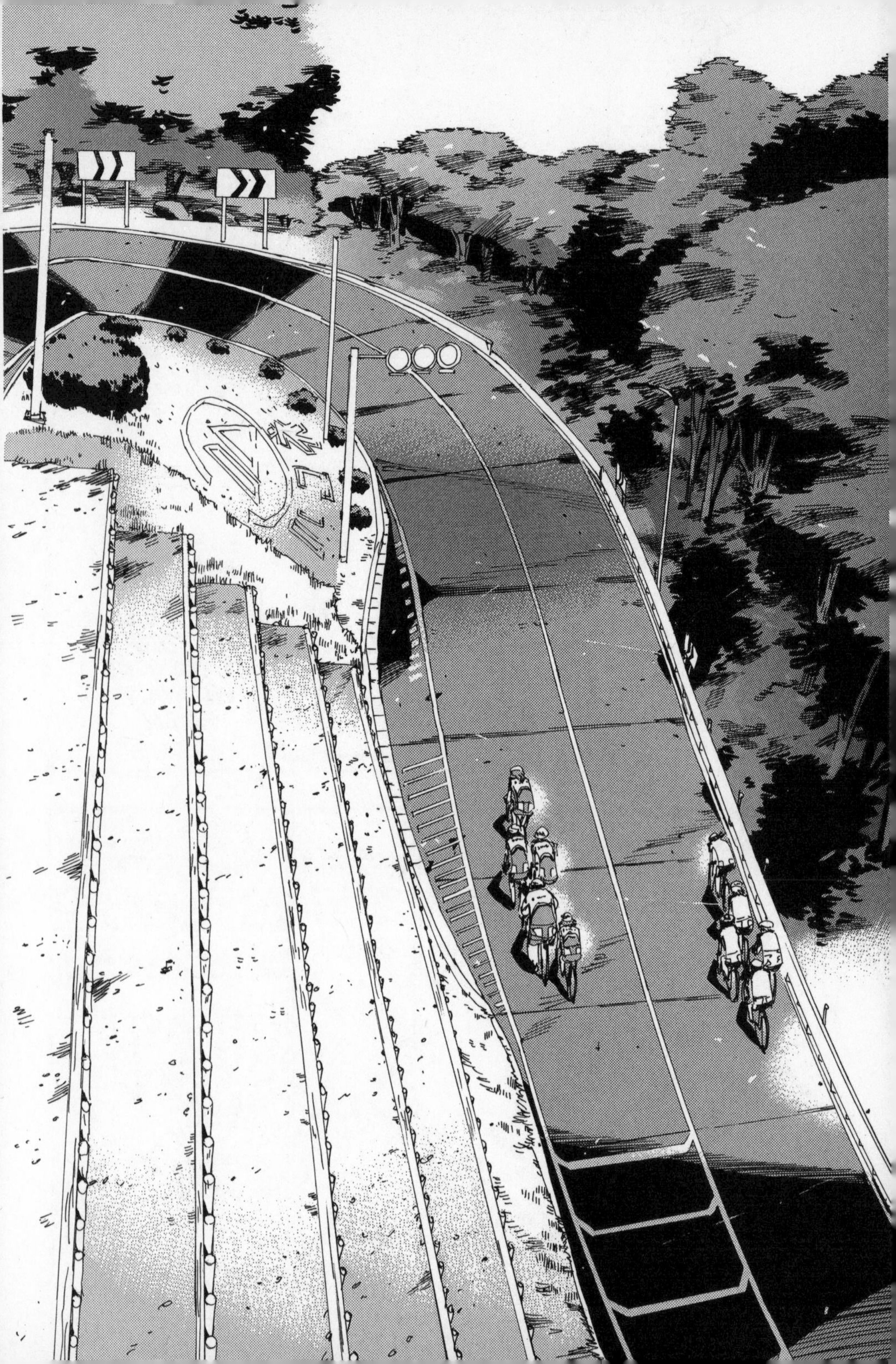

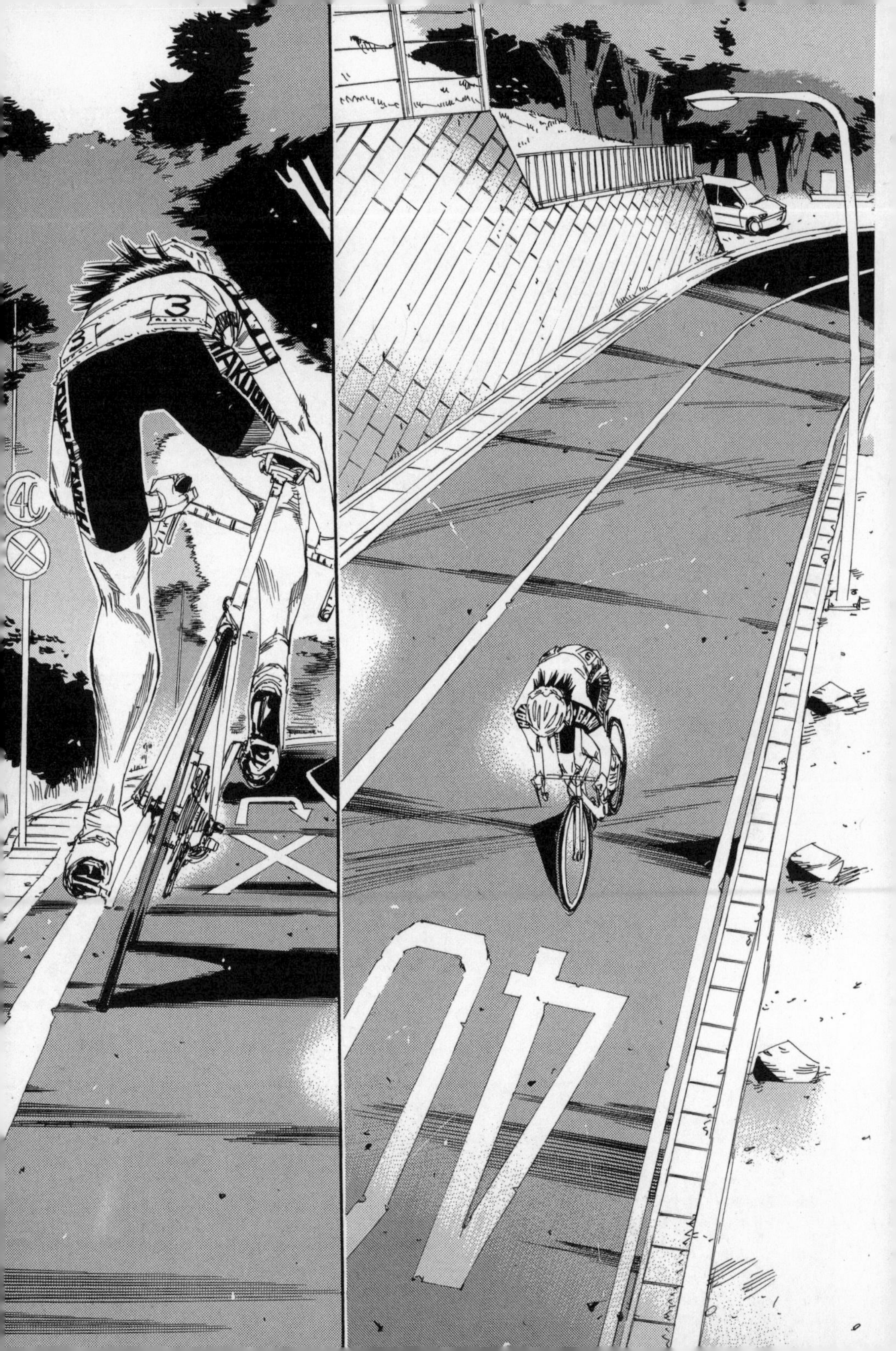

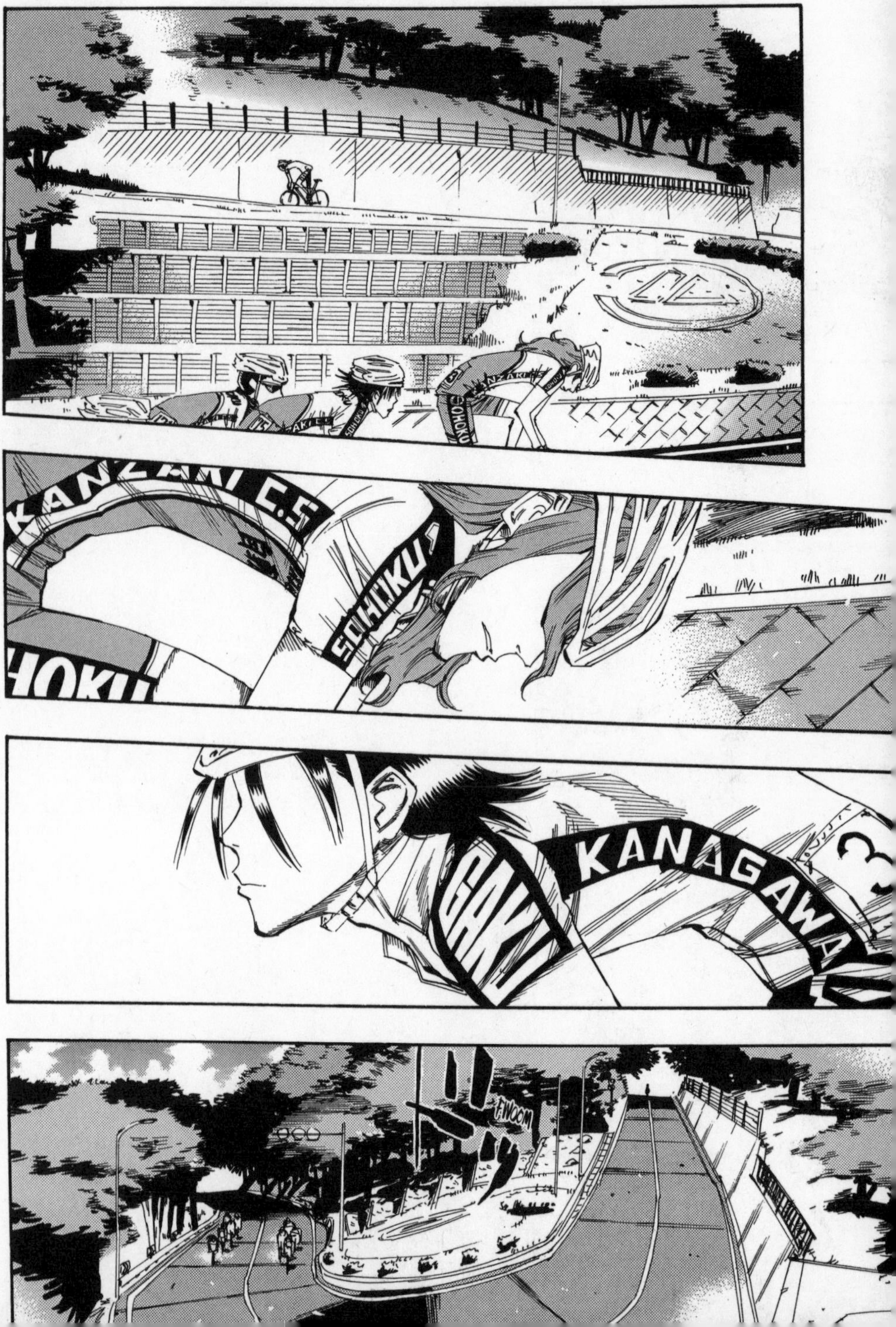
KANZAKI C.S
SOHOKU
KANAGAWA
FWOOM

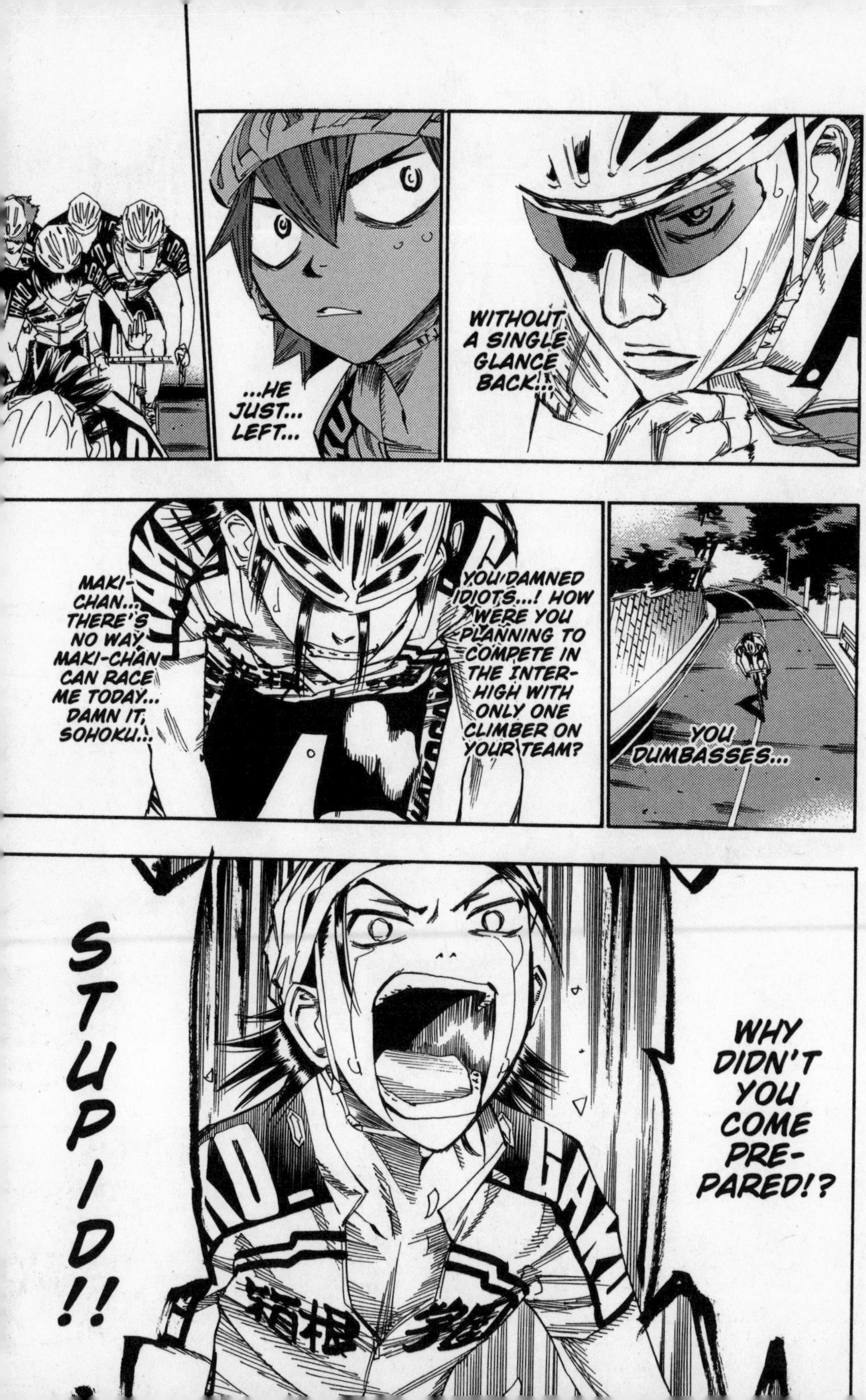
WITHOUT A SINGLE GLANCE BACK...
...HE JUST... LEFT...
YOU DUMBASSES...
YOU DAMNED IDIOTS...! HOW WERE YOU PLANNING TO COMPETE IN THE INTER-HIGH WITH ONLY ONE CLIMBER ON YOUR TEAM?
MAKI-CHAN... THERE'S NO WAY MAKI-CHAN CAN RACE ME TODAY... DAMN IT, SOHOKU...
WHY DIDN'T YOU COME PRE-PARED!?
STUPID!!

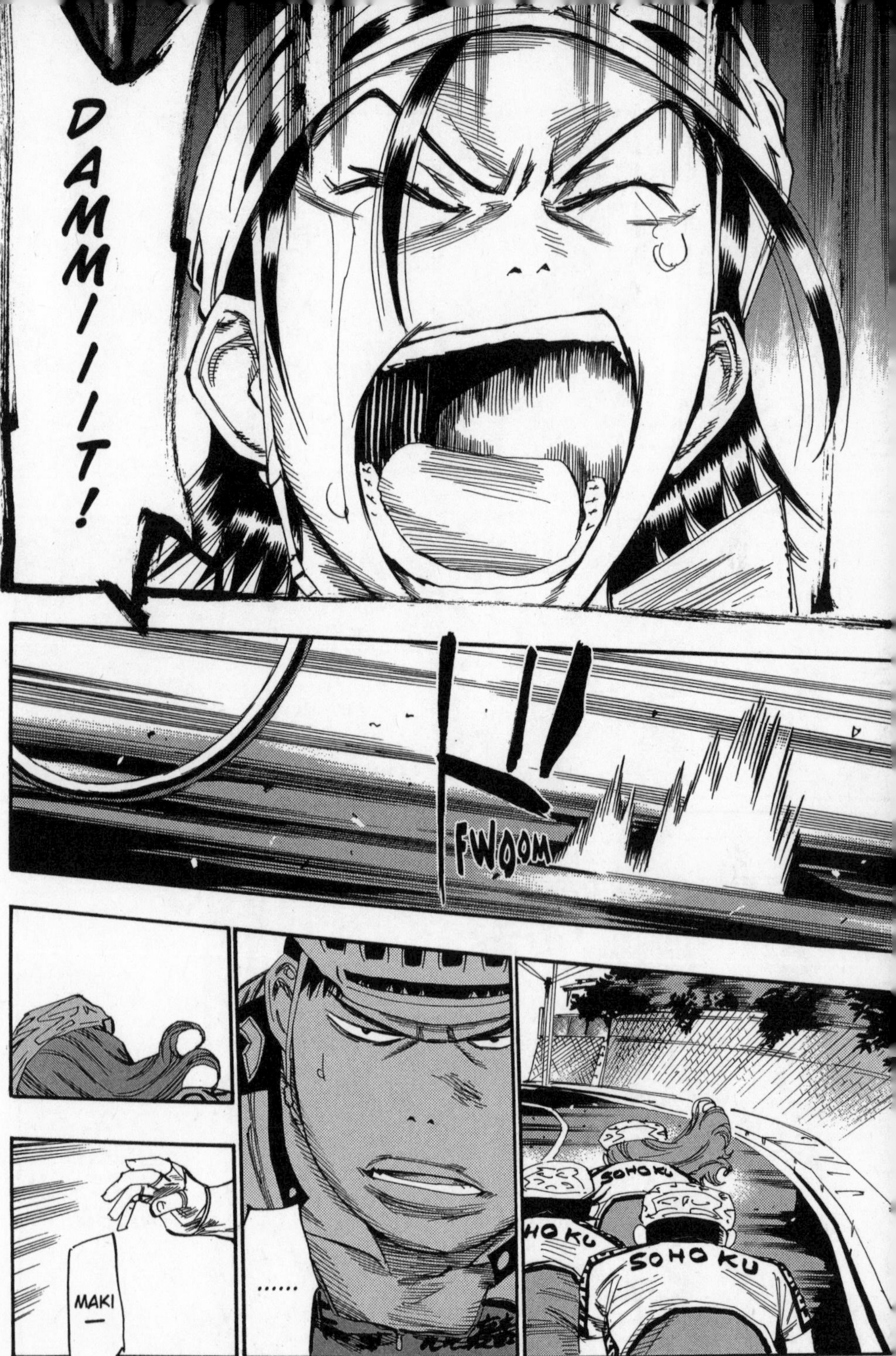
DAMMIIIIT!
FWOOM
SOHOKU
HOKU
SOHOKU
......
MAKI—

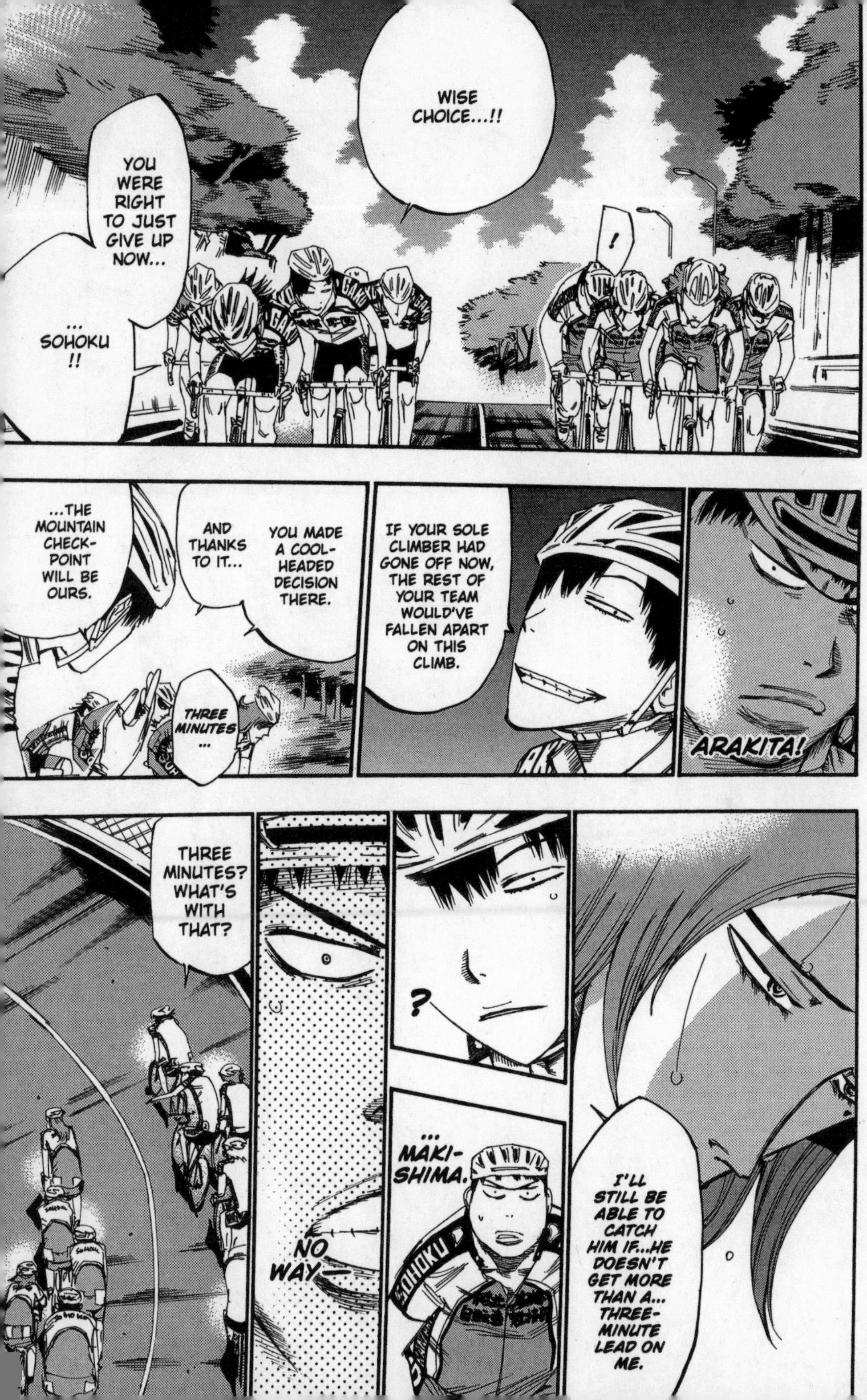
WISE CHOICE...!!
YOU WERE RIGHT TO JUST GIVE UP NOW...
...SOHOKU!!
!
ARAKITA!
IF YOUR SOLE CLIMBER HAD GONE OFF NOW, THE REST OF YOUR TEAM WOULD'VE FALLEN APART ON THIS CLIMB.
YOU MADE A COOL-HEADED DECISION THERE.
AND THANKS TO IT...
...THE MOUNTAIN CHECK-POINT WILL BE OURS.
THREE MINUTES...
I'LL STILL BE ABLE TO CATCH HIM IF...HE DOESN'T GET MORE THAN A... THREE-MINUTE LEAD ON ME.
?
...MAKISHIMA.
NO WAY—
THREE MINUTES? WHAT'S WITH THAT?

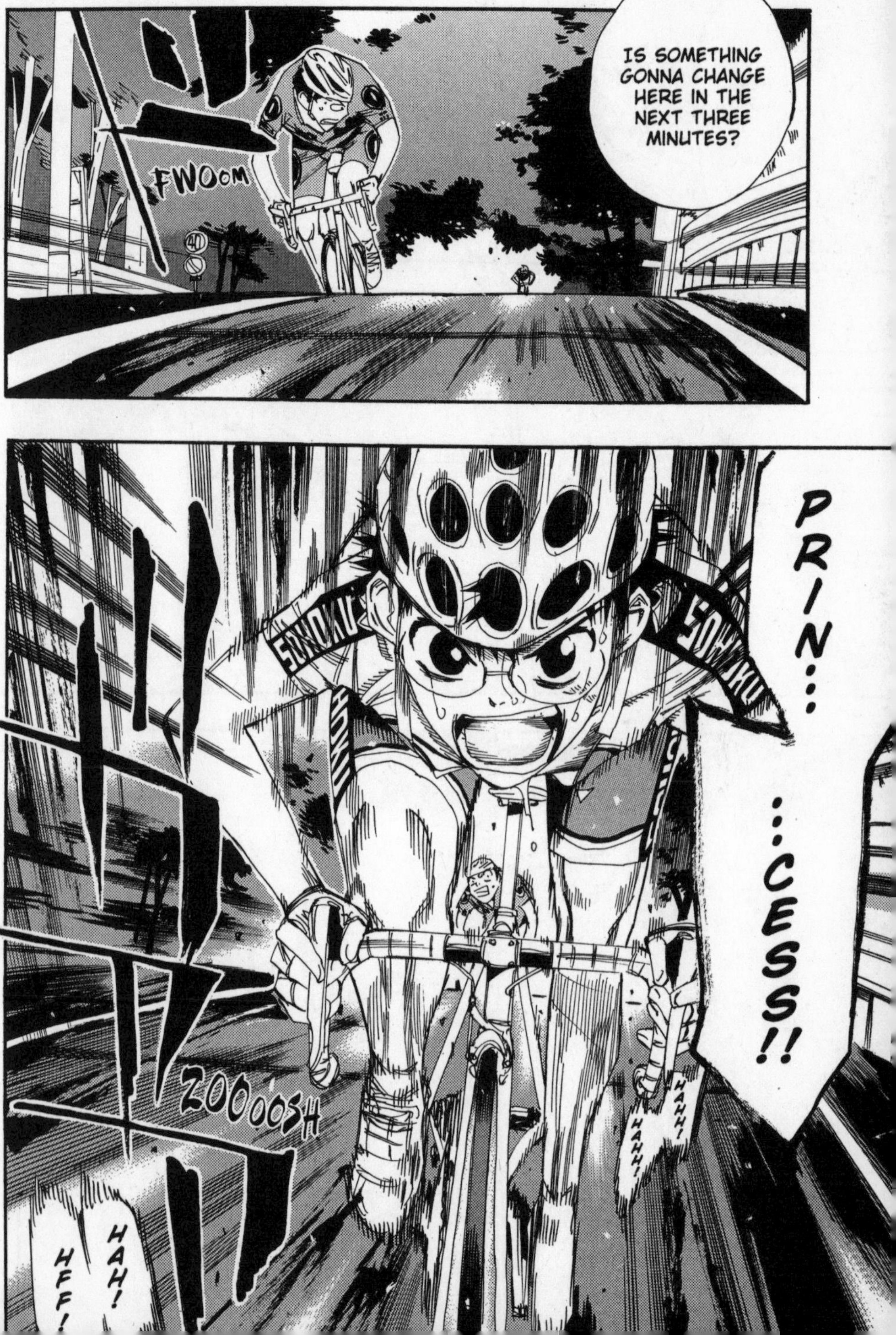
IS SOMETHING GONNA CHANGE HERE IN THE NEXT THREE MINUTES?
FWOOM
40
PRIN...
...CESS!!
HAHH! HAHH!
ZOOOOSH
HAH! HFF!

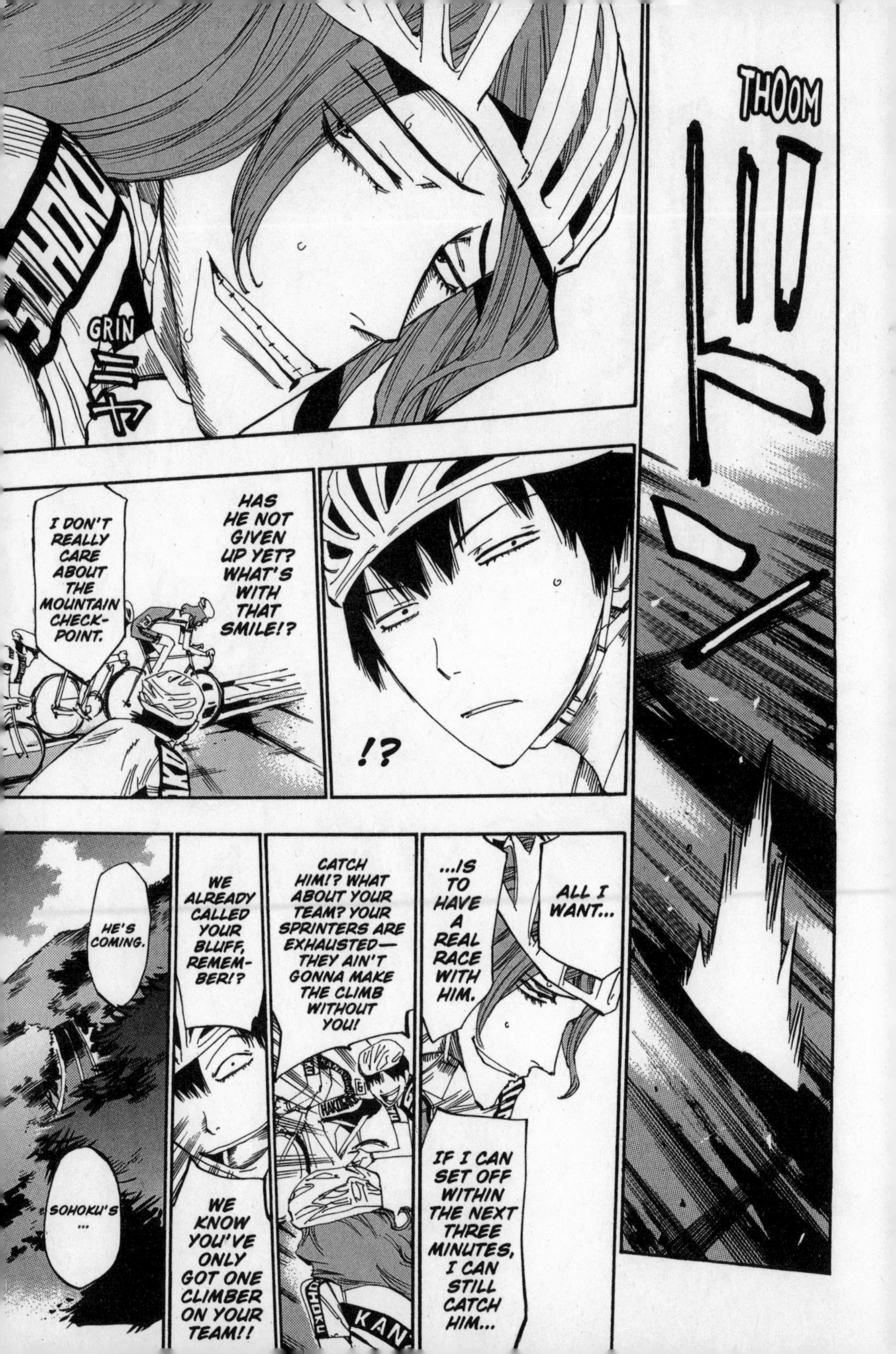
THOOM
GRIN
!?
HAS HE NOT GIVEN UP YET? WHAT'S WITH THAT SMILE!?
I DON'T REALLY CARE ABOUT THE MOUNTAIN CHECK-POINT.
ALL I WANT...
...IS TO HAVE A REAL RACE WITH HIM.
IF I CAN SET OFF WITHIN THE NEXT THREE MINUTES, I CAN STILL CATCH HIM...
CATCH HIM!? WHAT ABOUT YOUR TEAM? YOUR SPRINTERS ARE EXHAUSTED—THEY AIN'T GONNA MAKE THE CLIMB WITHOUT YOU!
WE ALREADY CALLED YOUR BLUFF, REMEMBER!?
WE KNOW YOU'VE ONLY GOT ONE CLIMBER ON YOUR TEAM!!
HE'S COMING.
SOHOKU'S...

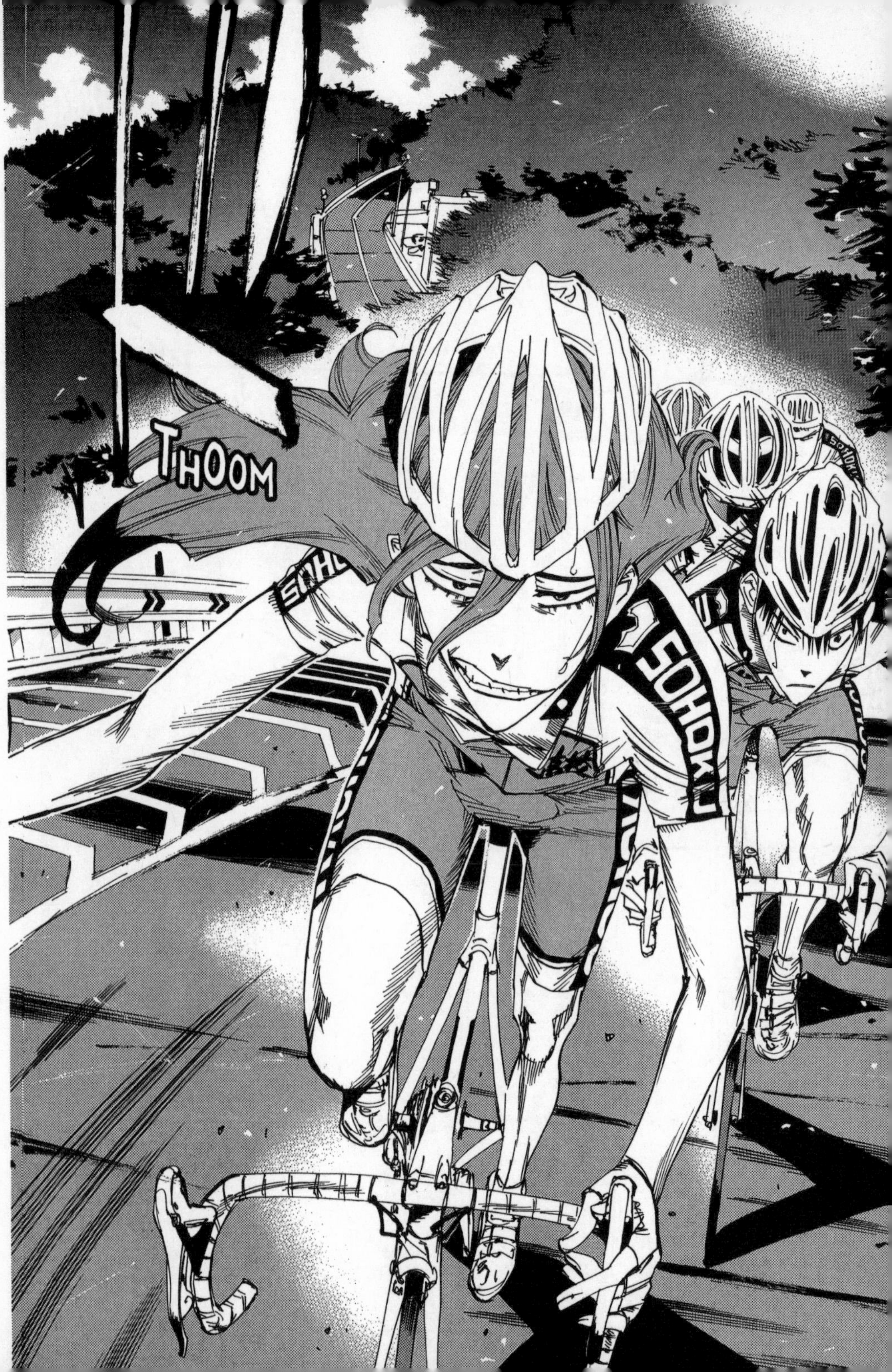
THOOM

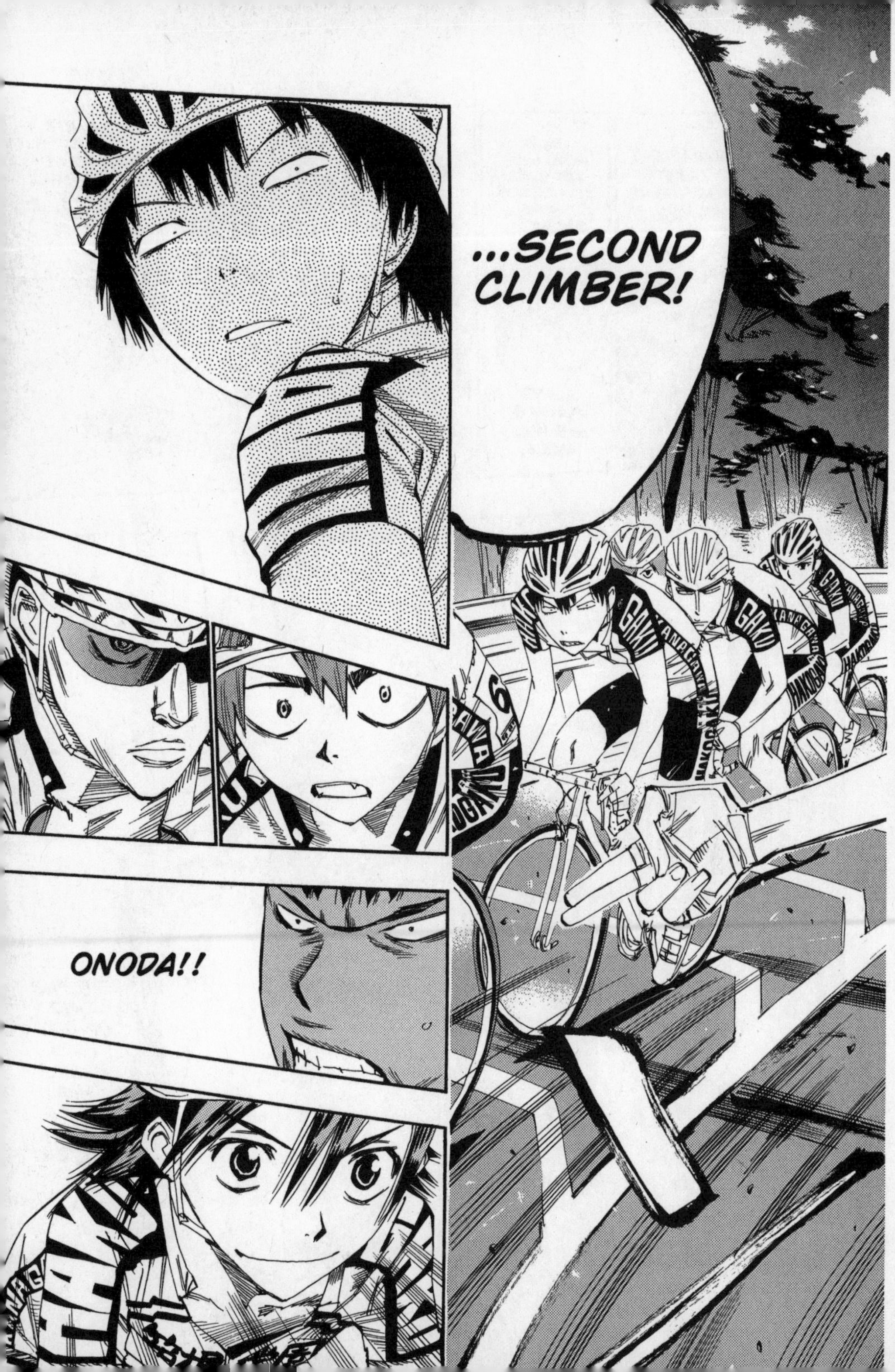
...SECOND CLIMBER!
ONODA!!

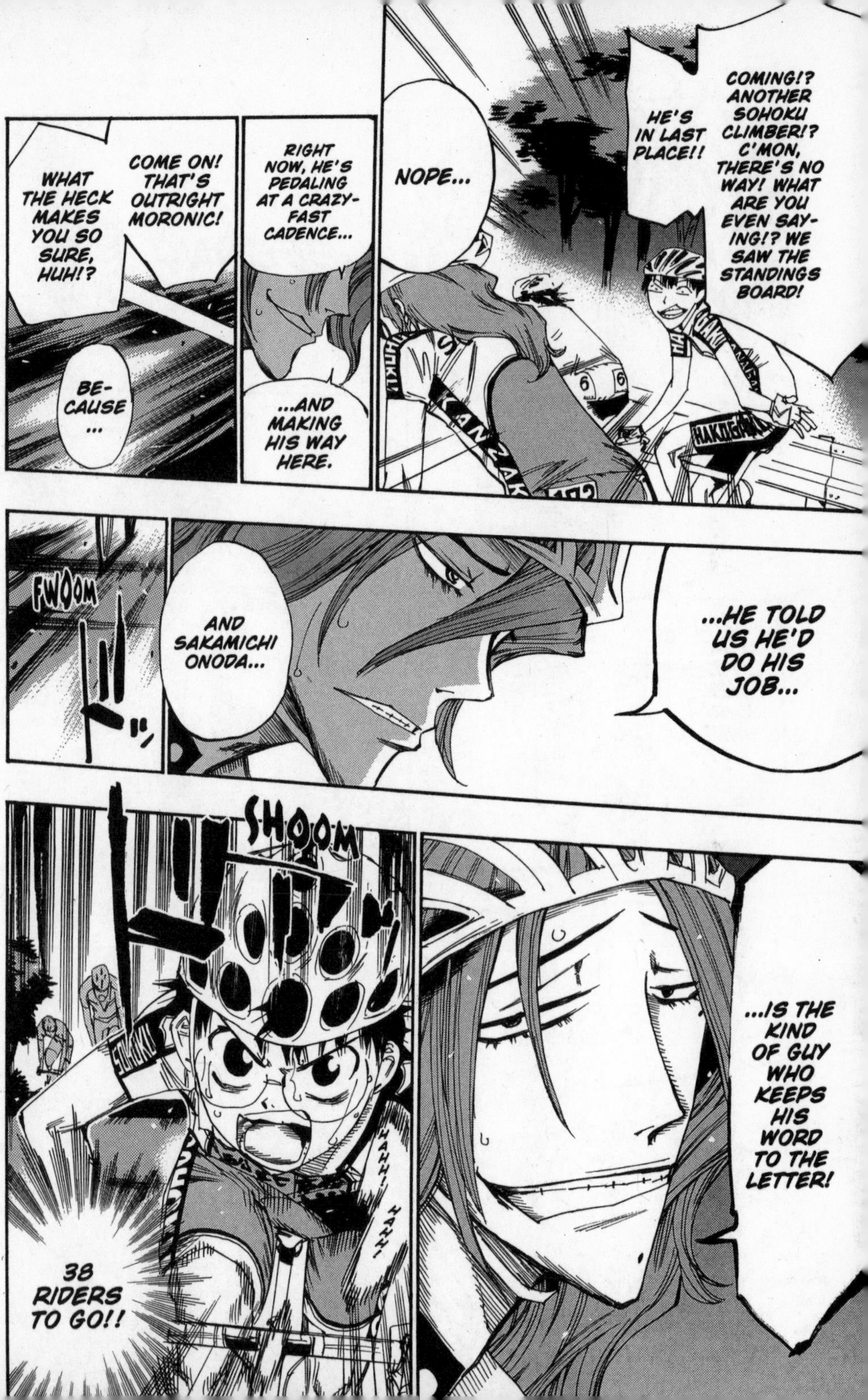
COMING!? ANOTHER SOHOKU CLIMBER!? C'MON, THERE'S NO WAY! WHAT ARE YOU EVEN SAYING!? WE SAW THE STANDINGS BOARD!
HE'S IN LAST PLACE!!
NOPE...
RIGHT NOW, HE'S PEDALING AT A CRAZY-FAST CADENCE...
...AND MAKING HIS WAY HERE.
COME ON! THAT'S OUTRIGHT MORONIC!
WHAT THE HECK MAKES YOU SO SURE, HUH!?
BE-CAUSE ...
...HE TOLD US HE'D DO HIS JOB...
AND SAKAMICHI ONODA...
FWOOM
...IS THE KIND OF GUY WHO KEEPS HIS WORD TO THE LETTER!
SHOOM
HAHH! HAHH!
38 RIDERS TO GO!!

# RIDE.94 THE HUNDRED-MAN BARRIER

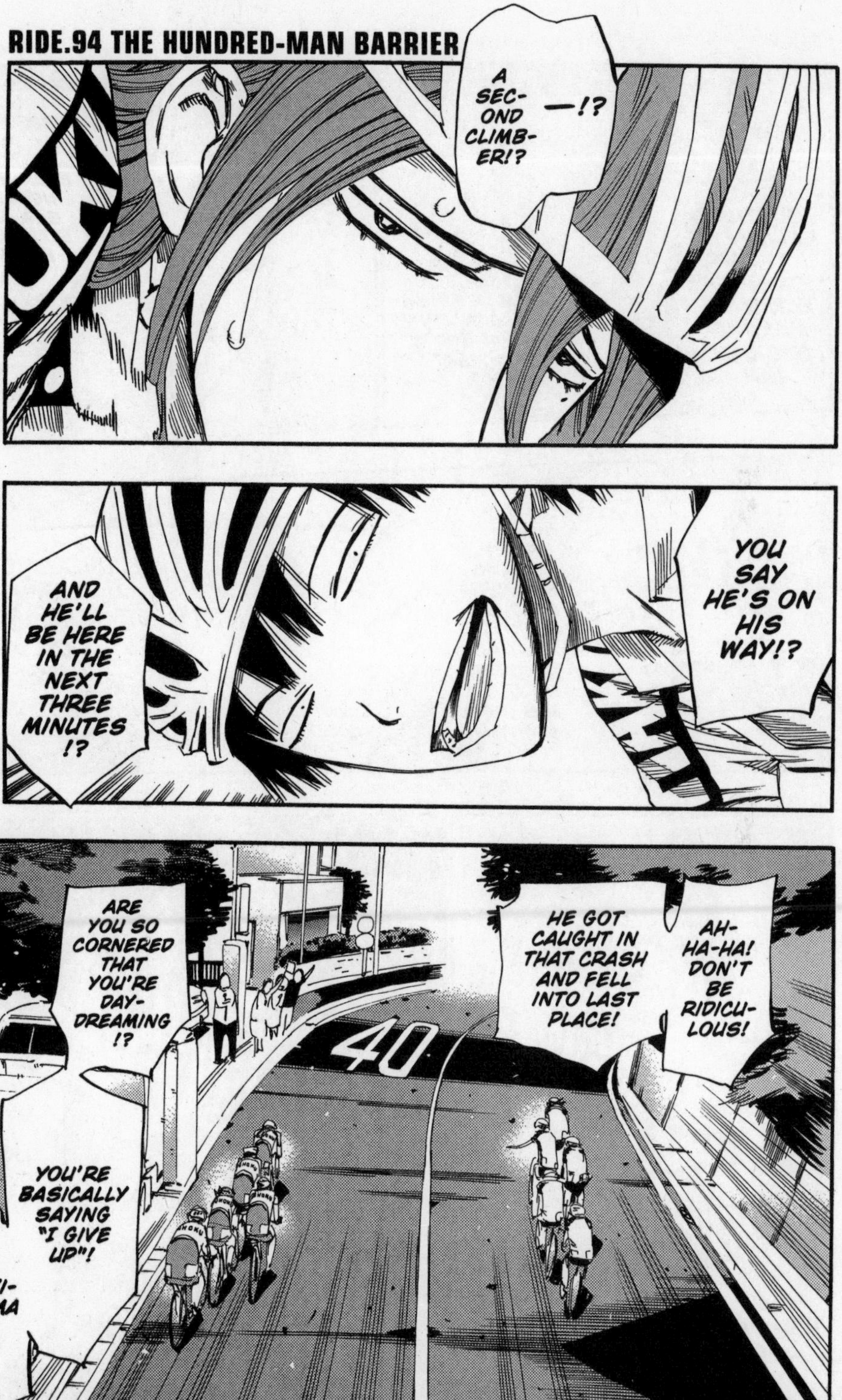
A SECOND CLIMBER!?
—!?
YOU SAY HE'S ON HIS WAY!?
AND HE'LL BE HERE IN THE NEXT THREE MINUTES!?
AH-HA-HA! DON'T BE RIDICULOUS!
HE GOT CAUGHT IN THAT CRASH AND FELL INTO LAST PLACE!
ARE YOU SO CORNERED THAT YOU'RE DAYDREAMING!?
40
YOU'RE BASICALLY SAYING "I GIVE UP"!
MAKISHIMA!!

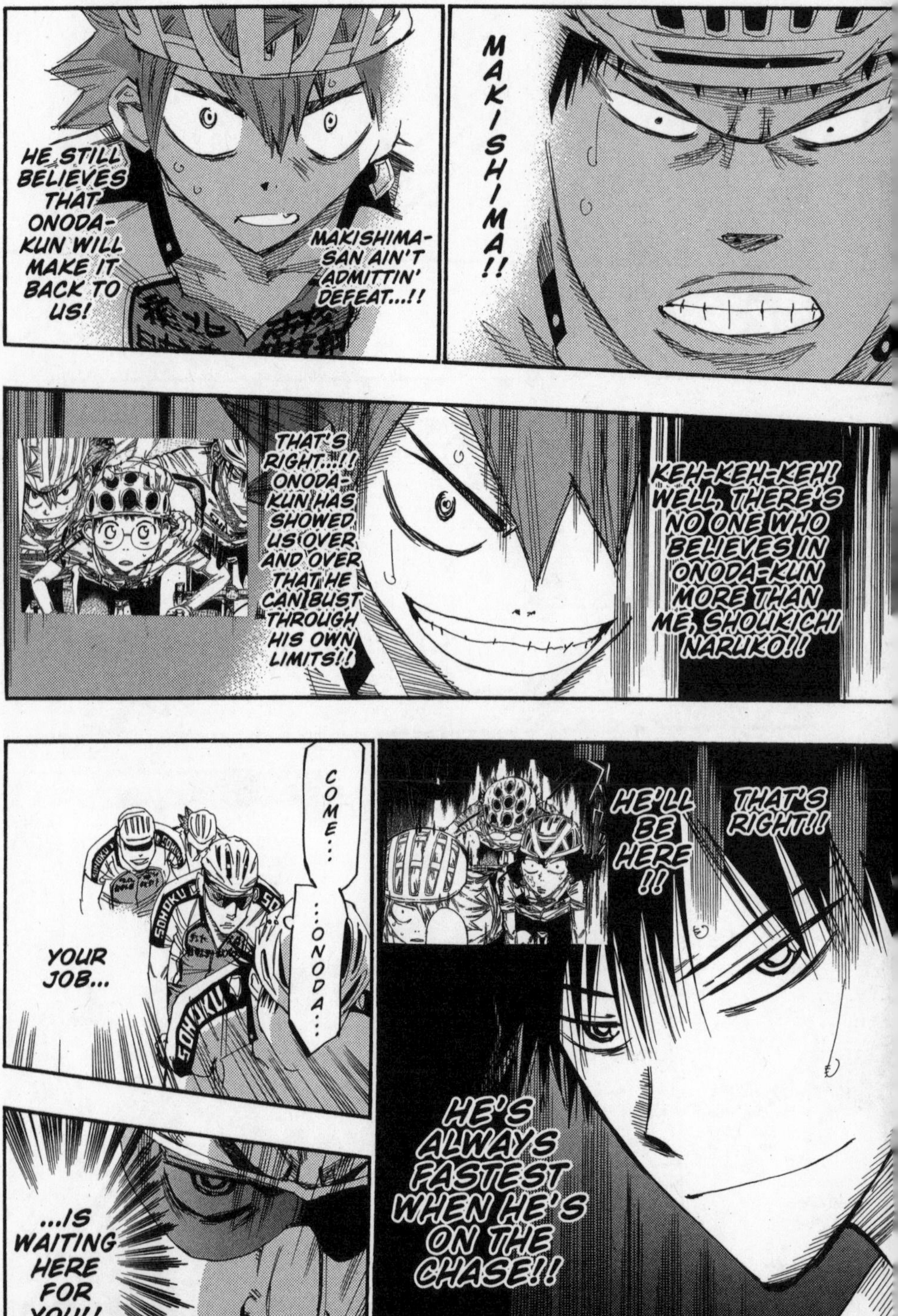
MAKISHIMA!!
MAKISHIMA-SAN AIN'T ADMITTIN' DEFEAT...!!
HE STILL BELIEVES THAT ONODA-KUN WILL MAKE IT BACK TO US!
KEH-KEH-KEH! WELL, THERE'S NO ONE WHO BELIEVES IN ONODA-KUN MORE THAN ME, SHOUKICHI NARUKO!!
THAT'S RIGHT...!! ONODA-KUN HAS SHOWED US OVER AND OVER THAT HE CAN BUST THROUGH HIS OWN LIMITS!!
THAT'S RIGHT!!
HE'LL BE HERE!!
HE'S ALWAYS FASTEST WHEN HE'S ON THE CHASE!!
COME... ...ONODA...
YOUR JOB...
...IS WAITING HERE FOR YOU!!

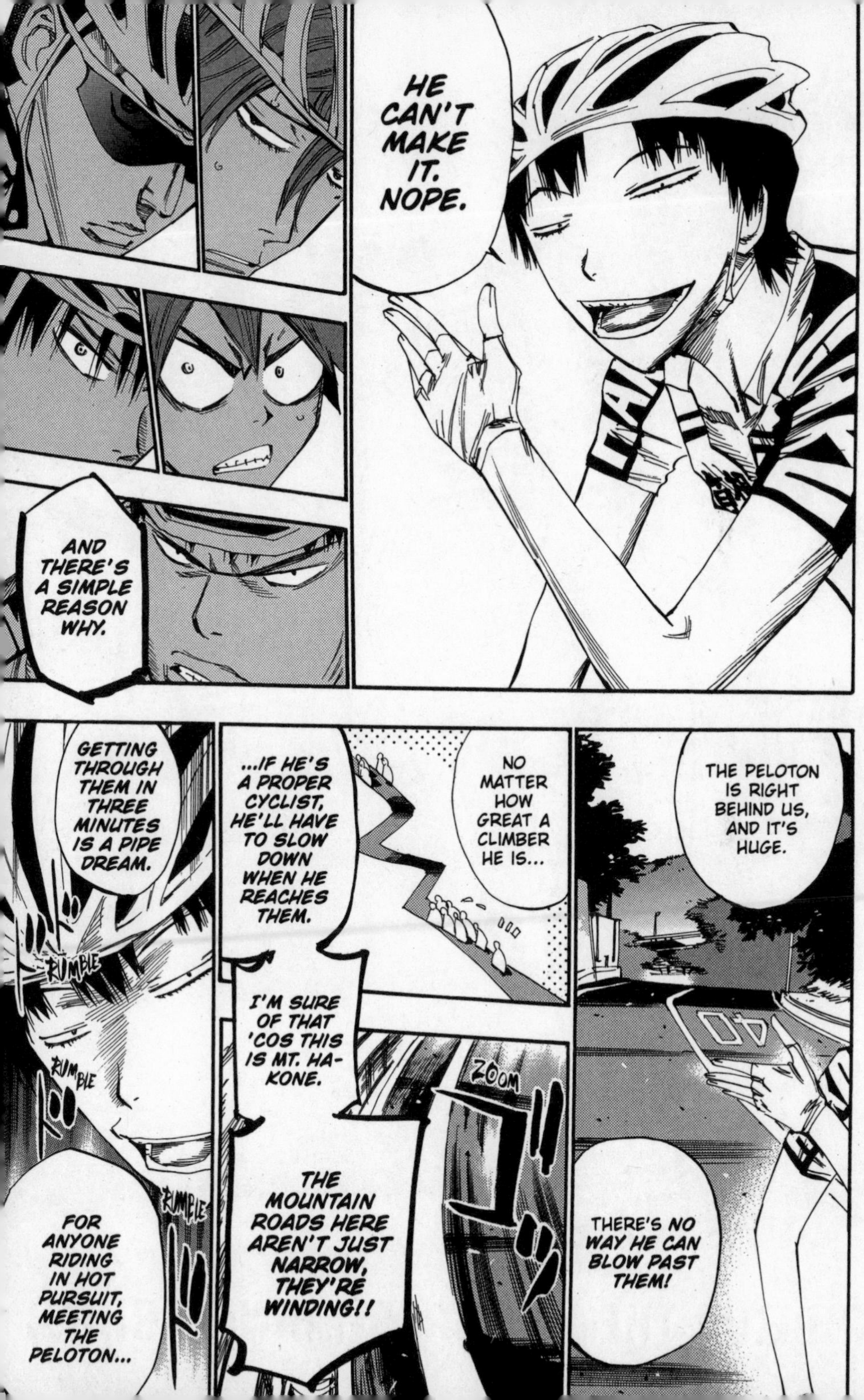
HE CAN'T MAKE IT. NOPE.
AND THERE'S A SIMPLE REASON WHY.
THE PELOTON IS RIGHT BEHIND US, AND IT'S HUGE.
THERE'S NO WAY HE CAN BLOW PAST THEM!
NO MATTER HOW GREAT A CLIMBER HE IS...
...IF HE'S A PROPER CYCLIST, HE'LL HAVE TO SLOW DOWN WHEN HE REACHES THEM.
I'M SURE OF THAT 'COS THIS IS MT. HAKONE.
ZOOM
THE MOUNTAIN ROADS HERE AREN'T JUST NARROW, THEY'RE WINDING!!
GETTING THROUGH THEM IN THREE MINUTES IS A PIPE DREAM.
RUMBLE
RUMBLE
RUMBLE
FOR ANYONE RIDING IN HOT PURSUIT, MEETING THE PELOTON...

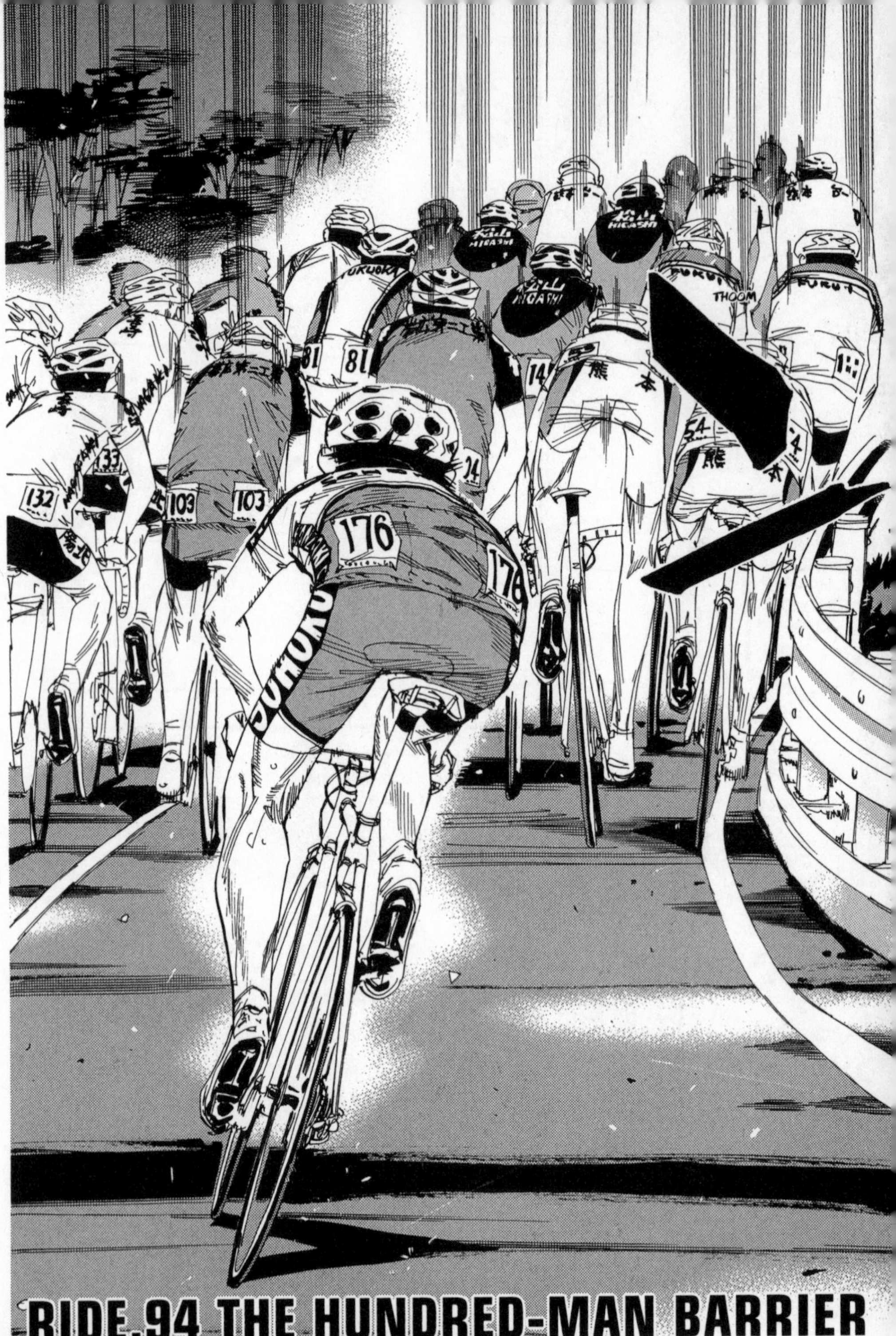
THOOM

# RIDE.94 THE HUNDRED-MAN BARRIER

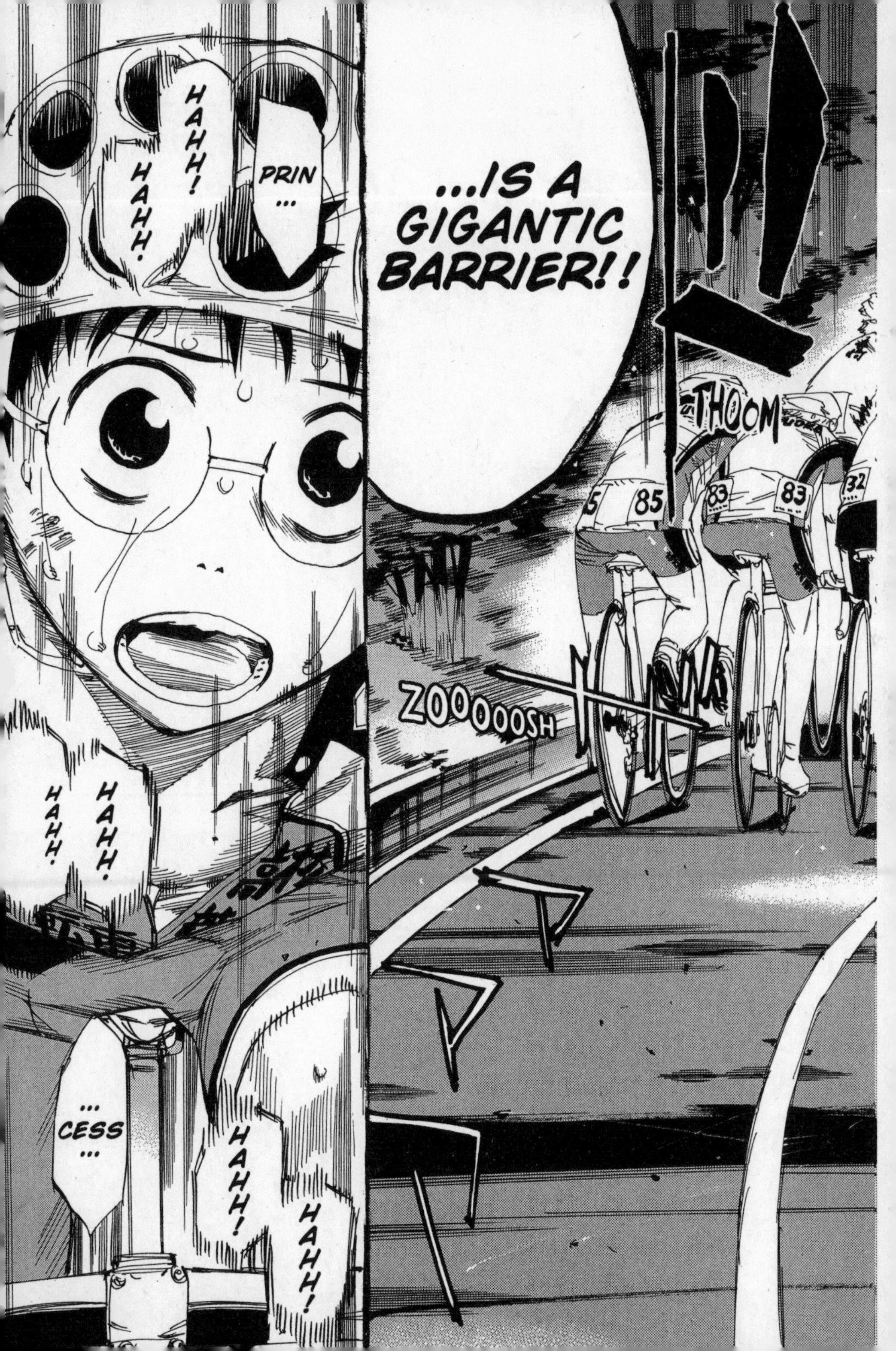

...IS A GIGANTIC BARRIER!!
THOOM
ZOOOOOSH
PRIN...
HAHH! HAHH!
HAHH! HAHH!
...CESS...
HAHH! HAHH!

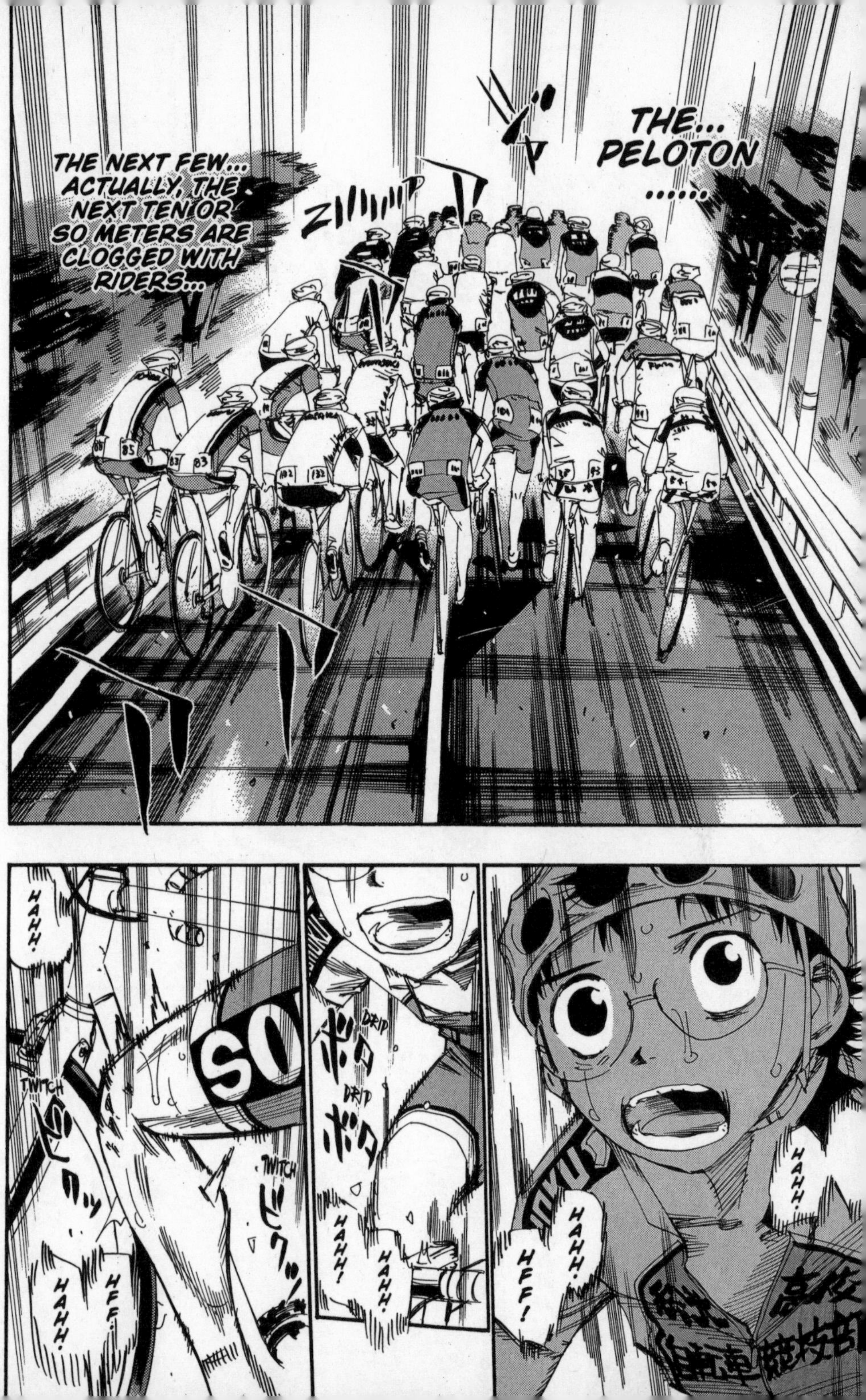
THE... PELOTON ......
ZIIIIIII
THE NEXT FEW... ACTUALLY, THE NEXT TEN OR SO METERS ARE CLOGGED WITH RIDERS...
HAHH!
HAHH!
HFF!
DRIP
DRIP
TWITCH
HAHH!
HAHH!
HAHH!
TWITCH
HFF!
HAHH

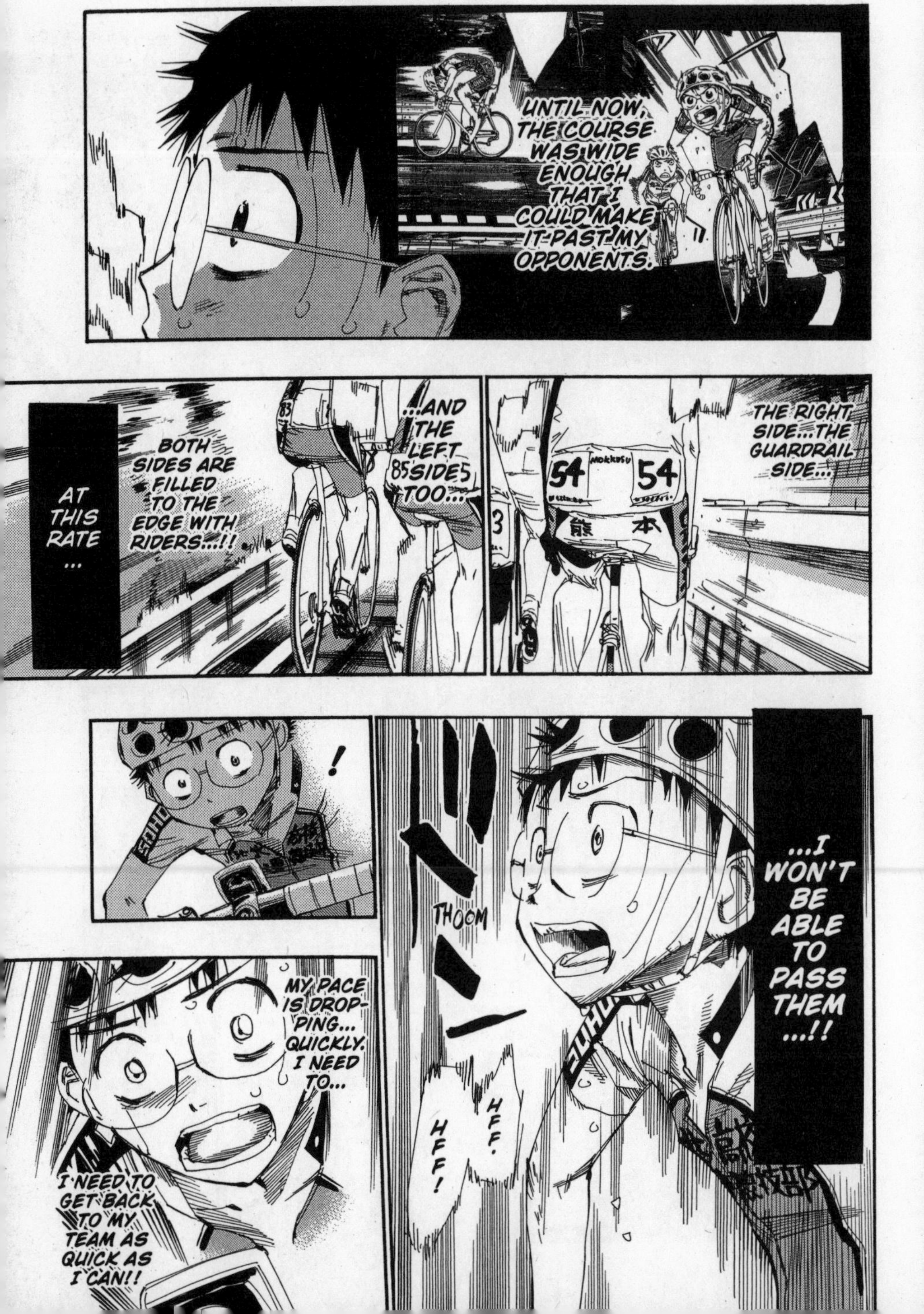
UNTIL NOW, THE COURSE WAS WIDE ENOUGH THAT I COULD MAKE IT PAST MY OPPONENTS.
THE RIGHT SIDE...THE GUARDRAIL SIDE...
54
54
...AND THE LEFT SIDE TOO...
BOTH SIDES ARE FILLED TO THE EDGE WITH RIDERS...!!
AT THIS RATE ...
...I WON'T BE ABLE TO PASS THEM ...!!
THOOM
HFF. HFF!
!
MY PACE IS DROPPING... QUICKLY. I NEED TO...
I NEED TO GET BACK TO MY TEAM AS QUICK AS I CAN!!

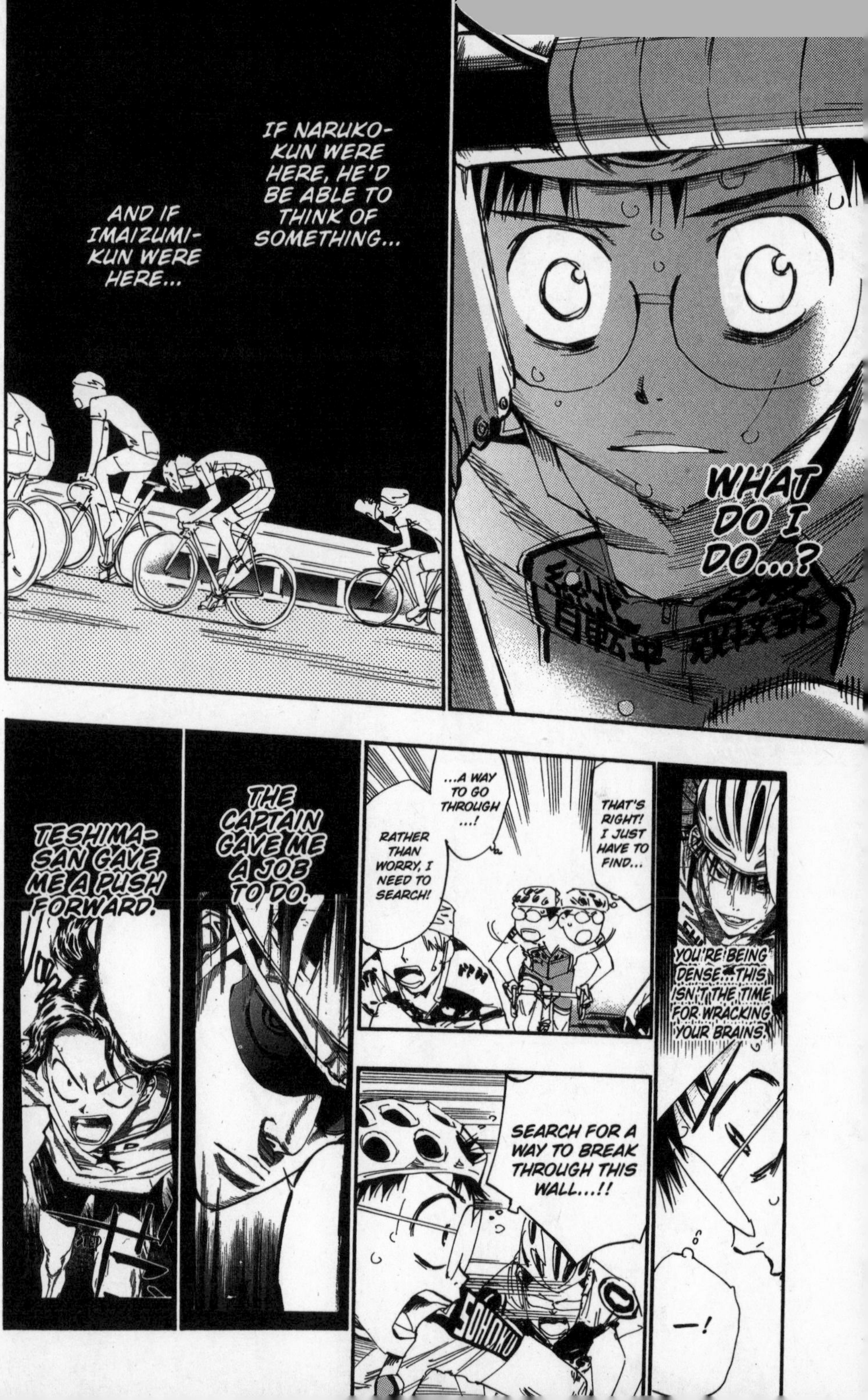
WHAT DO I DO...?
IF NARUKO-KUN WERE HERE, HE'D BE ABLE TO THINK OF SOMETHING...
AND IF IMAIZUMI-KUN WERE HERE...
YOU'RE BEING DENSE... THIS ISN'T THE TIME FOR WRACKING YOUR BRAINS.
THAT'S RIGHT! I JUST HAVE TO FIND...
...A WAY TO GO THROUGH...!
RATHER THAN WORRY, I NEED TO SEARCH!
SEARCH FOR A WAY TO BREAK THROUGH THIS WALL...!!
—!
THE CAPTAIN GAVE ME A JOB TO DO.
TESHIMA-SAN GAVE ME A PUSH FORWARD.

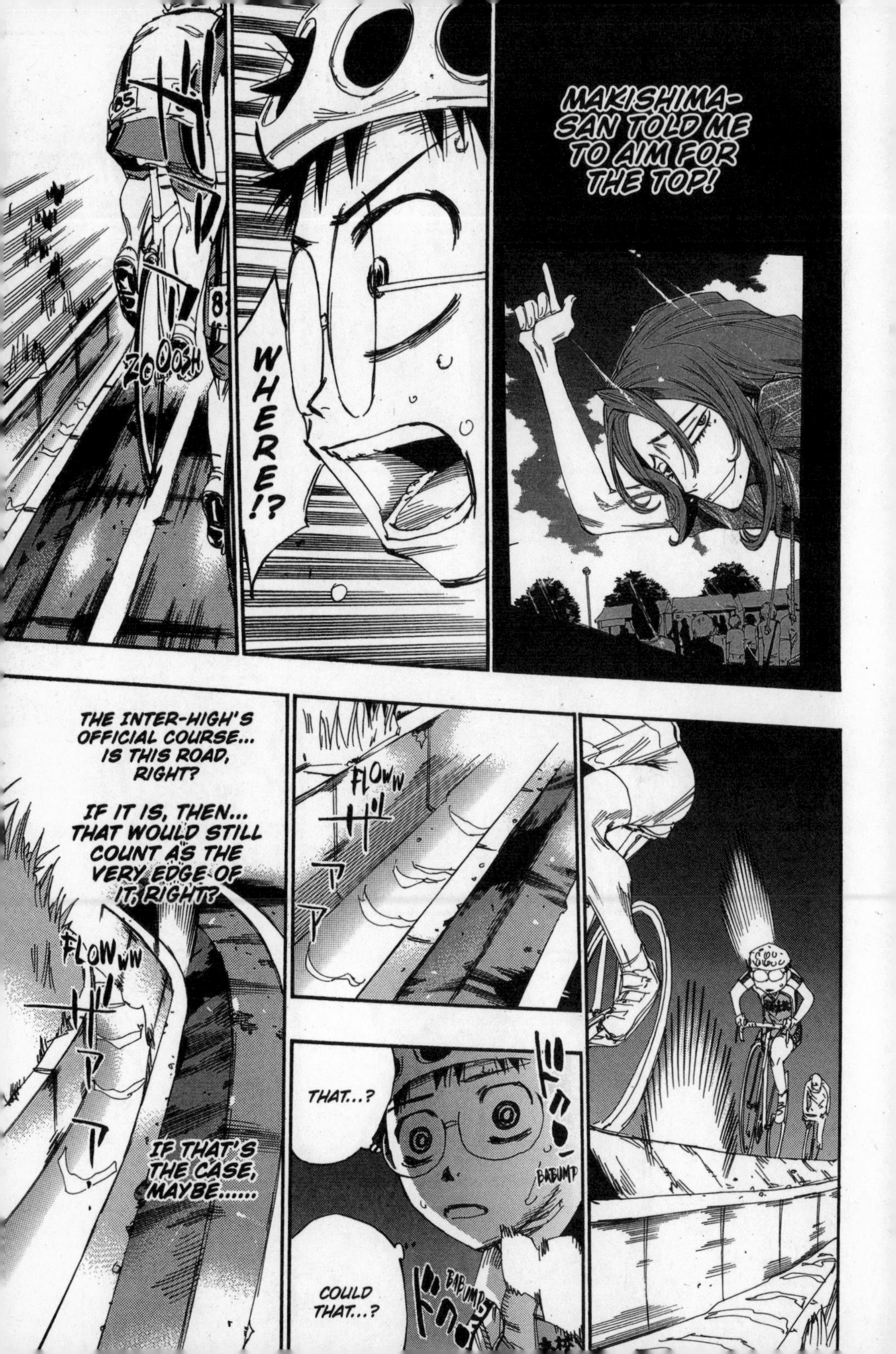

MAKISHIMA-SAN TOLD ME TO AIM FOR THE TOP!
WHERE!?
ZOOOSH
FLOWW
THAT...?
BABUMP
COULD THAT...?
BABUMP
THE INTER-HIGH'S OFFICIAL COURSE... IS THIS ROAD, RIGHT?
IF IT IS, THEN... THAT WOULD STILL COUNT AS THE VERY EDGE OF IT, RIGHT?
FLOWWW
IF THAT'S THE CASE, MAYBE......

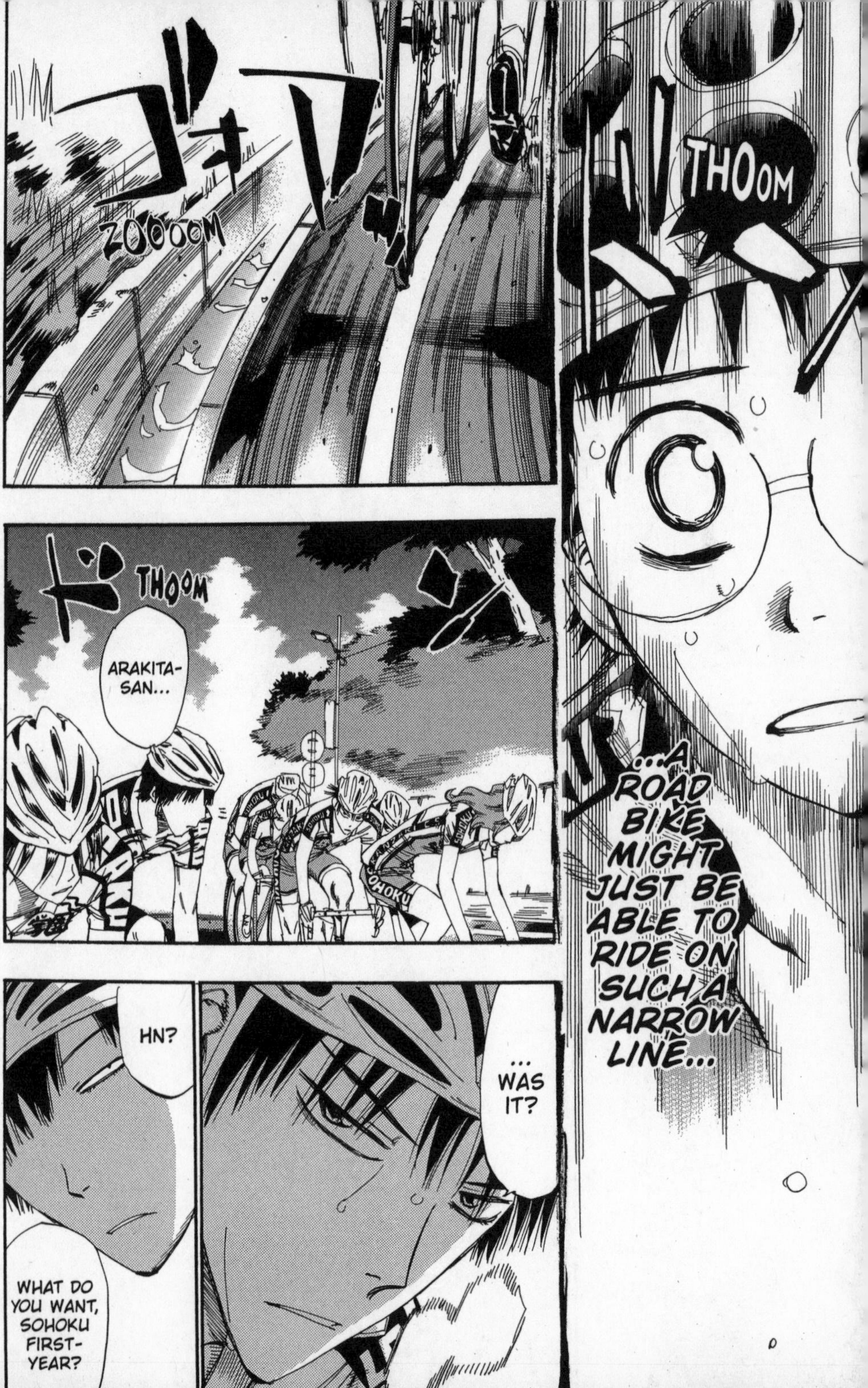
THOOM
...A ROAD BIKE MIGHT JUST BE ABLE TO RIDE ON SUCH A NARROW LINE...
ZOOOOM
THOOM
ARAKITA-SAN...
... WAS IT?
HN?
WHAT DO YOU WANT, SOHOKU FIRST-YEAR?

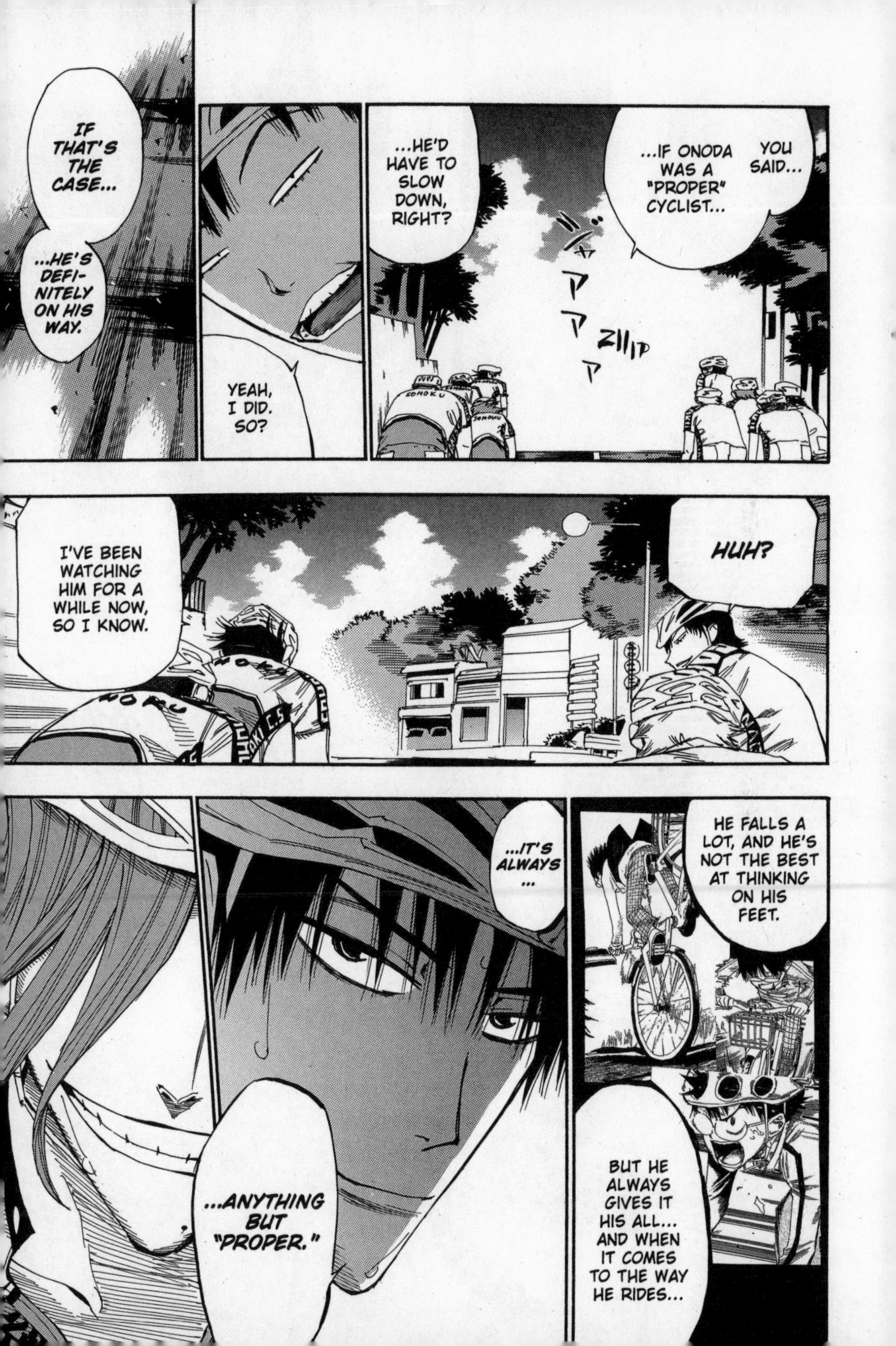
YOU SAID...
...IF ONODA WAS A "PROPER" CYCLIST...
...HE'D HAVE TO SLOW DOWN, RIGHT?
YEAH, I DID. SO?
IF THAT'S THE CASE...
...HE'S DEFI-NITELY ON HIS WAY.
HUH?
I'VE BEEN WATCHING HIM FOR A WHILE NOW, SO I KNOW.
HE FALLS A LOT, AND HE'S NOT THE BEST AT THINKING ON HIS FEET.
BUT HE ALWAYS GIVES IT HIS ALL... AND WHEN IT COMES TO THE WAY HE RIDES...
...IT'S ALWAYS ...
...ANYTHING BUT "PROPER."

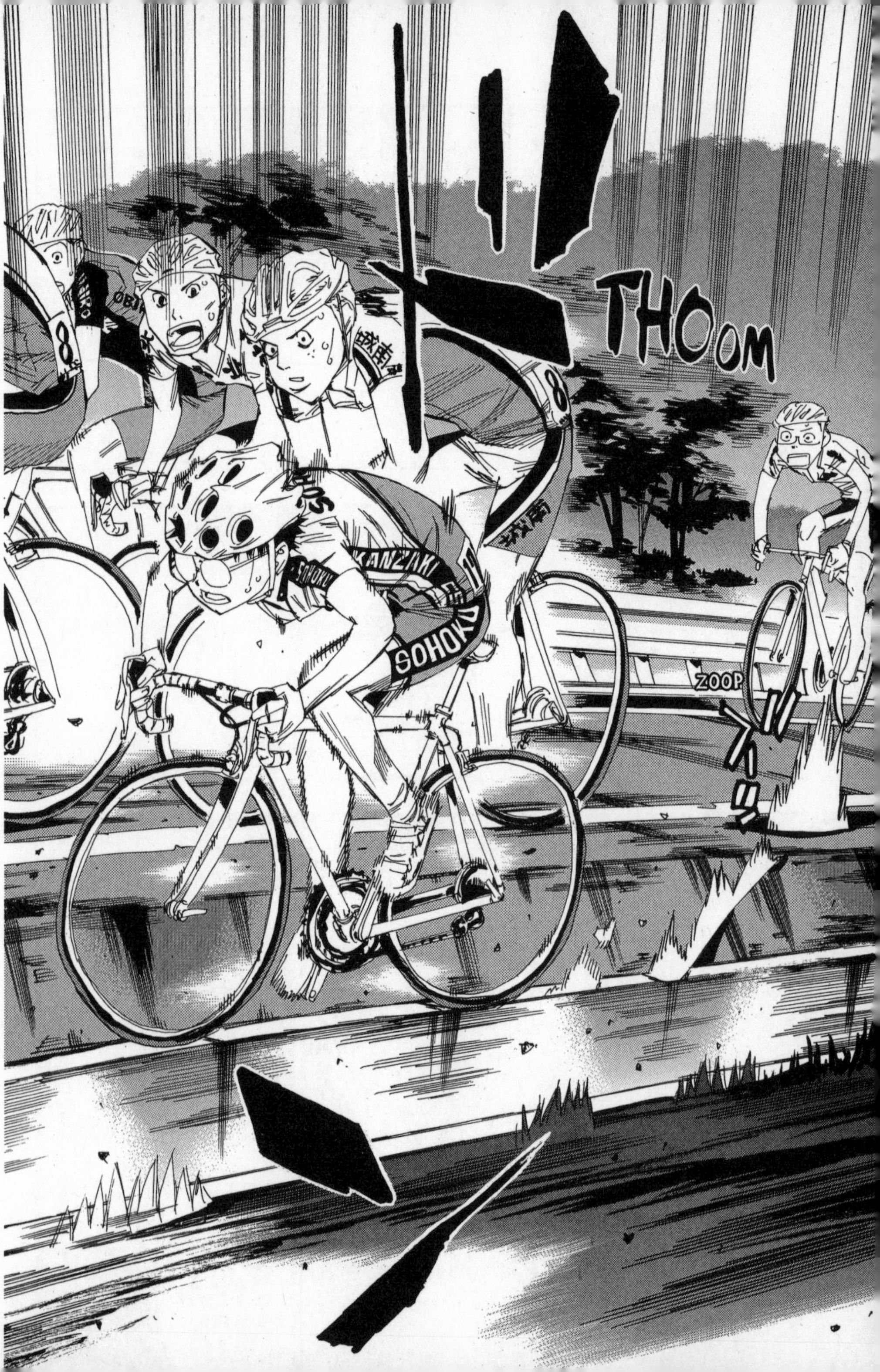
THOOM
ZOOP

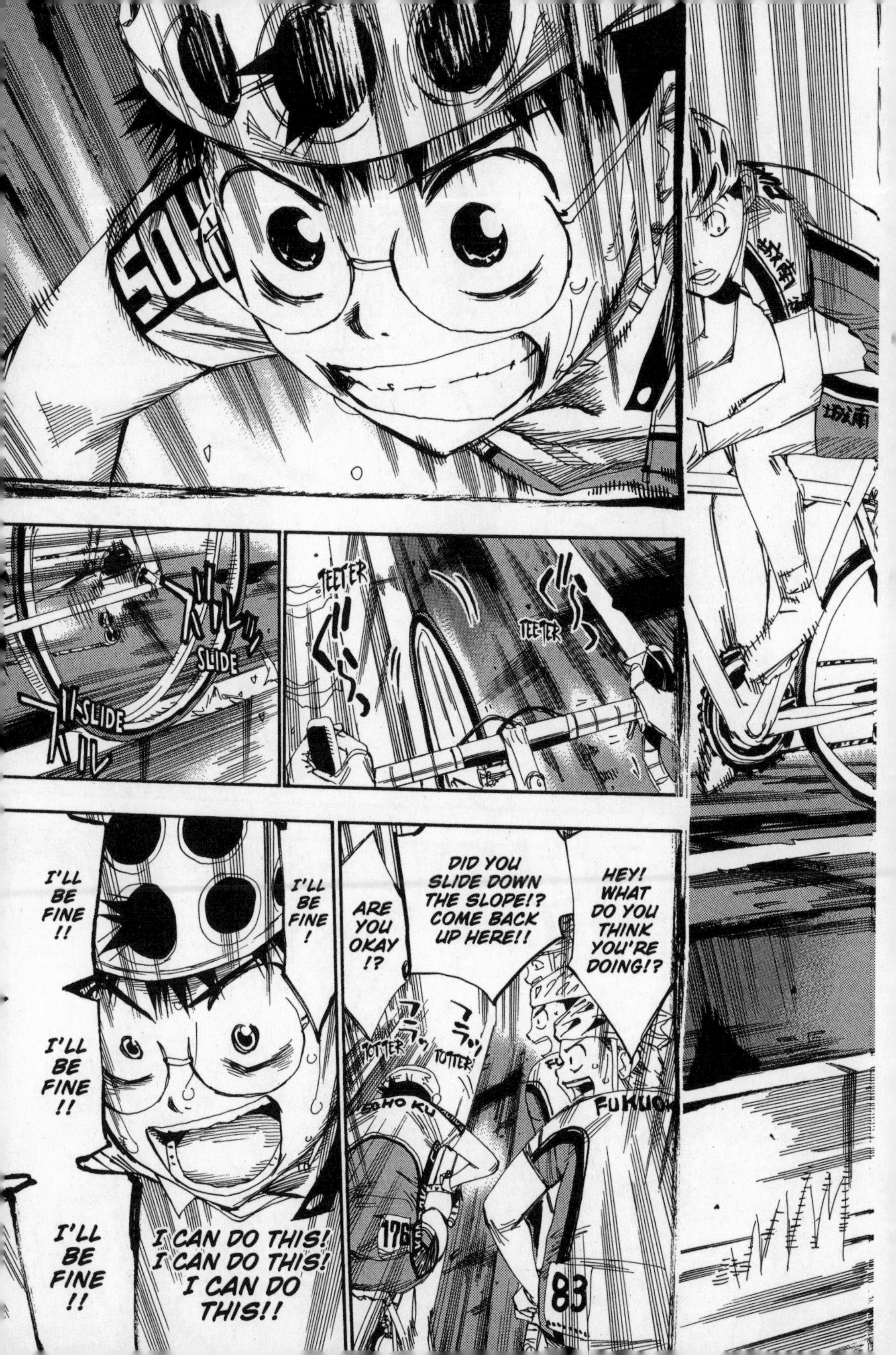
TEETER
TEETER
SLIDE
SLIDE
HEY! WHAT DO YOU THINK YOU'RE DOING!?
DID YOU SLIDE DOWN THE SLOPE!? COME BACK UP HERE!!
ARE YOU OKAY!?
I'LL BE FINE!
TOTTER
TOTTER
I'LL BE FINE!!
I'LL BE FINE!!
I'LL BE FINE!!
I CAN DO THIS! I CAN DO THIS! I CAN DO THIS!!

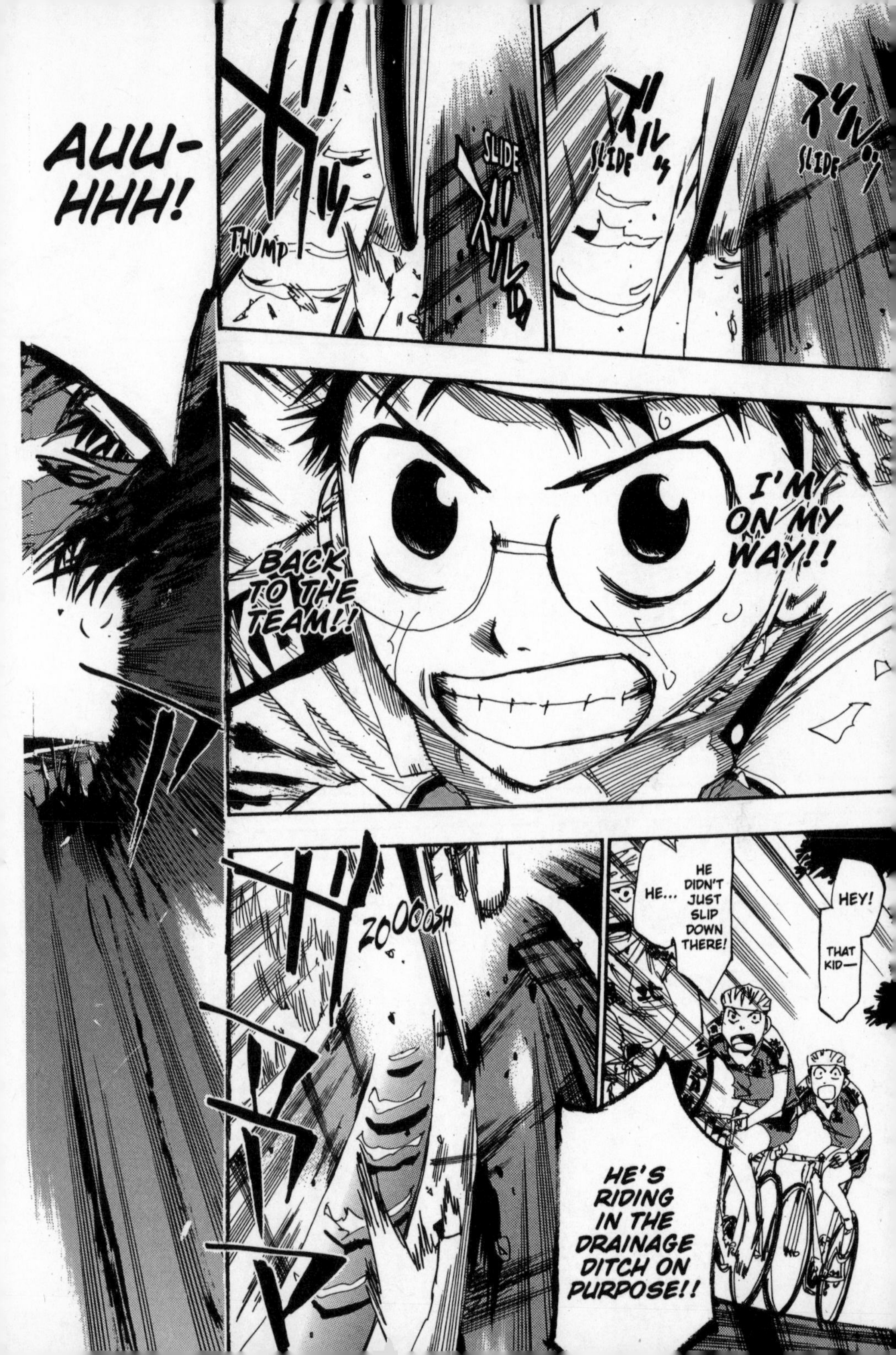
SLIDE
SLIDE
SLIDE
THUMP
I'M ON MY WAY!!
BACK TO THE TEAM!!
HEY!
THAT KID—
HE...
HE DIDN'T JUST SLIP DOWN THERE!
HE'S RIDING IN THE DRAINAGE DITCH ON PURPOSE!!
ZOOOOSH
AUU-HHH!

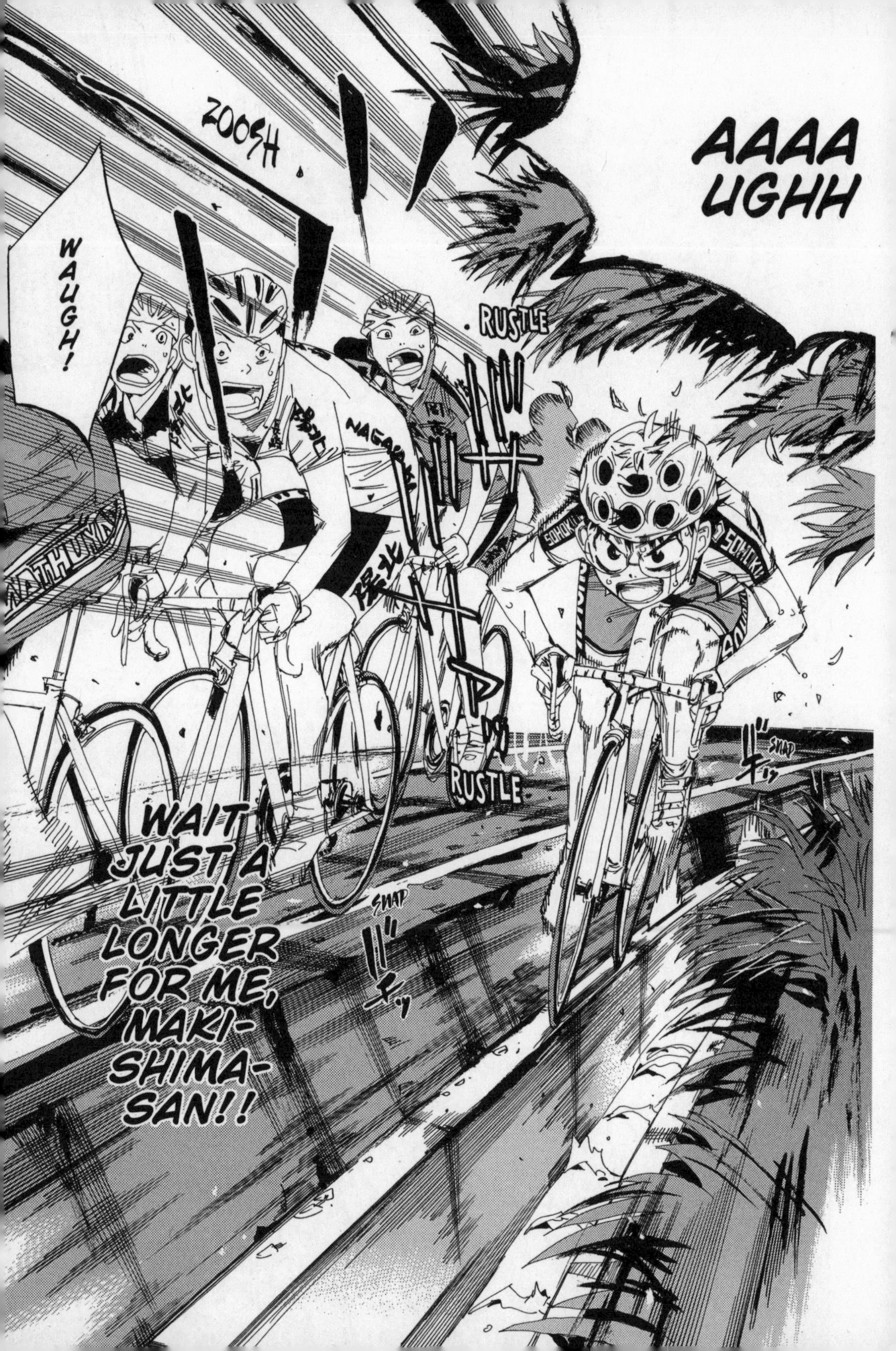
AAAA UGHH
RUSTLE
ZOOSH
WAUGH!
SNAP
RUSTLE
WAIT JUST A LITTLE LONGER FOR ME, MAKI-SHIMA-SAN!!
SNAP

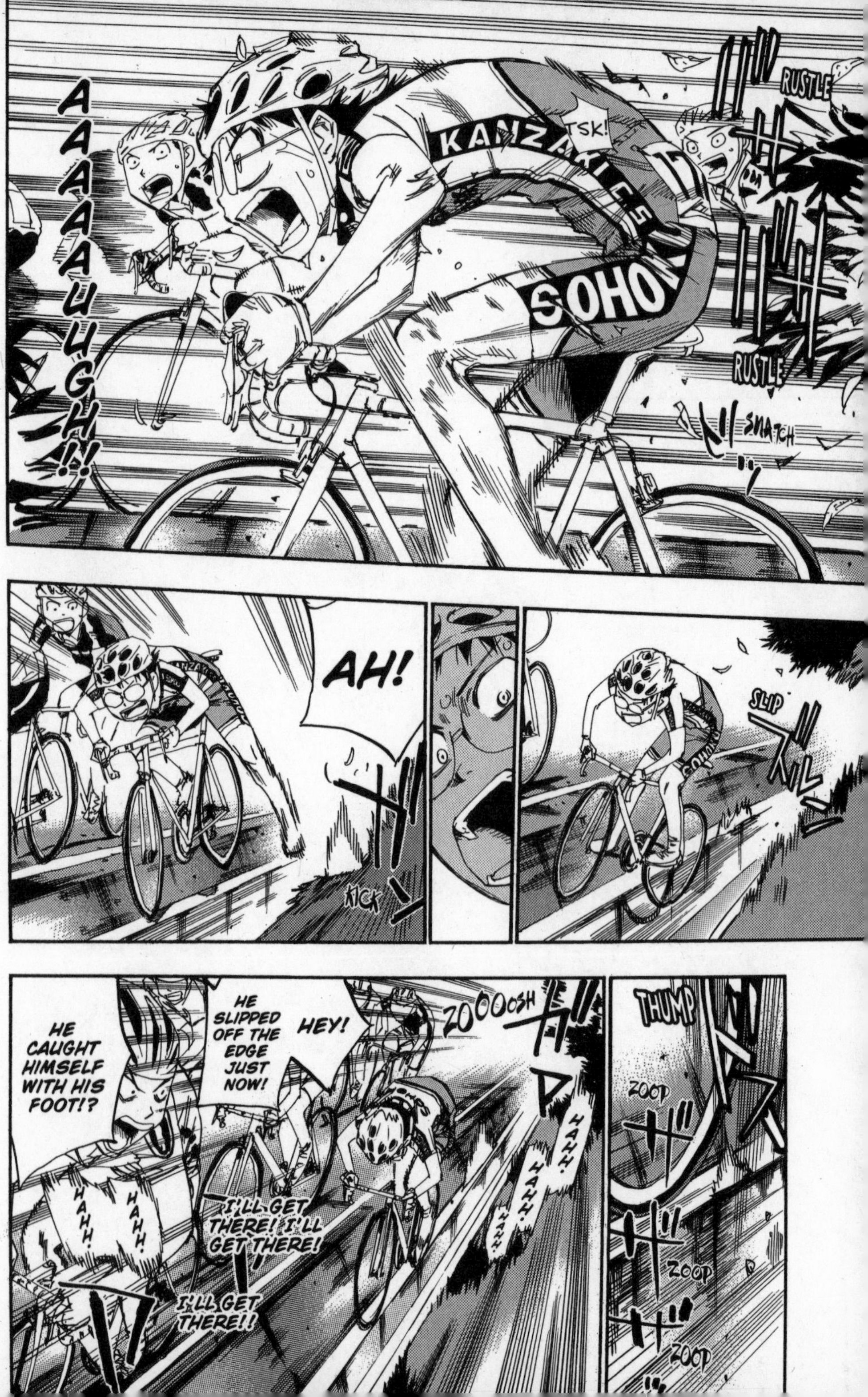
RUSTLE
TSK!
KANZAKI CS
SOHOKU
RUSTLE
SNATCH
AAAAAAUUGH!!
SLIP
AH!
KICK
THUMP
ZOOP
ZOOP
ZOOP
ZOOOOSH
HAHH.
HAHH.
HAHH.
HEY!
HE SLIPPED OFF THE EDGE JUST NOW!
I'LL GET THERE! I'LL GET THERE!
I'LL GET THERE!!
HE CAUGHT HIMSELF WITH HIS FOOT!?
HAHH.
HAHH.

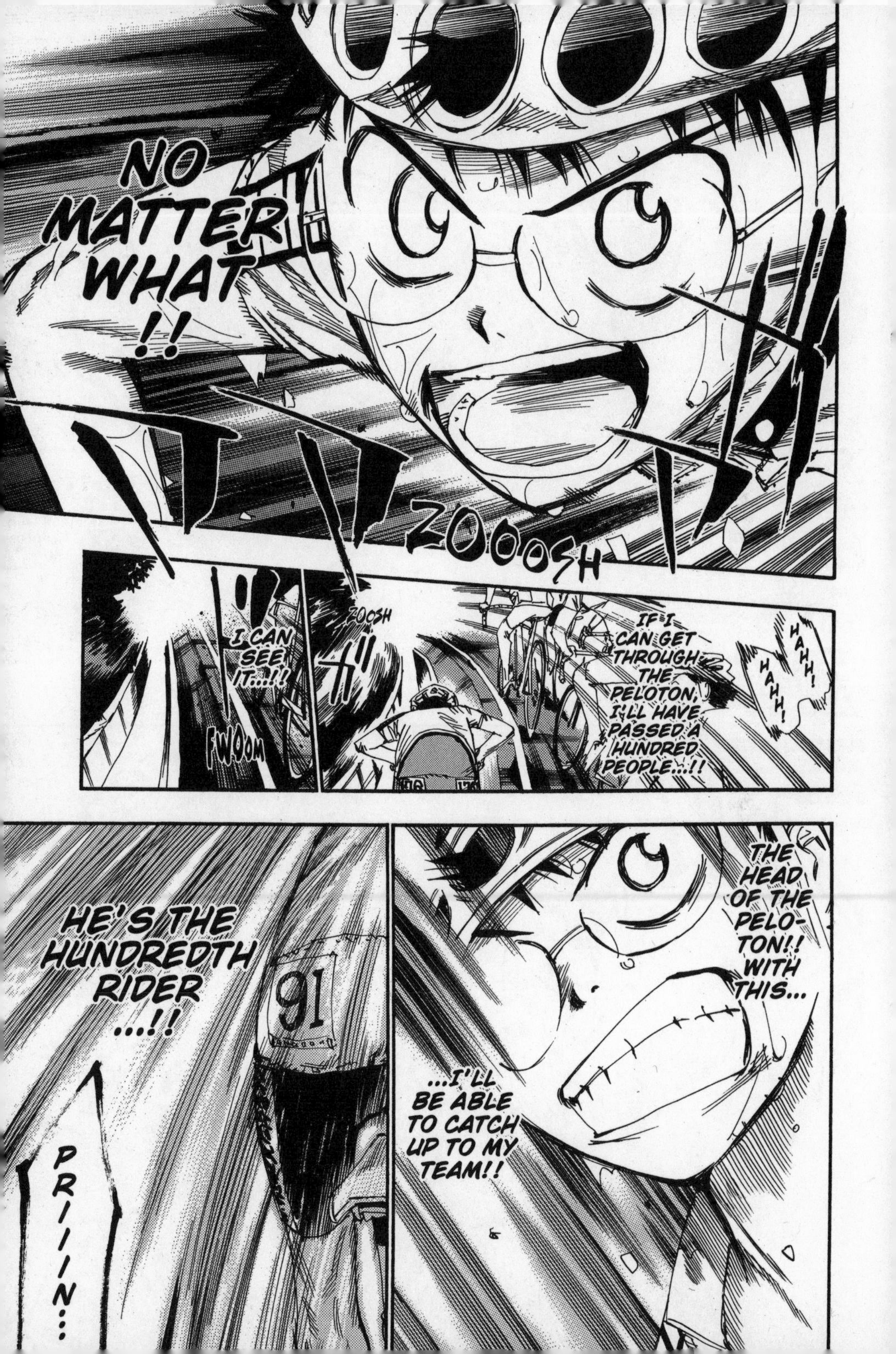
NO MATTER WHAT!!
ZOOOOSH
HAHH! HAHH!
IF I CAN GET THROUGH THE PELOTON, I'LL HAVE PASSED A HUNDRED PEOPLE...!!
ZOOSH
I CAN SEE IT...!!
FWOOM
THE HEAD OF THE PELOTON!! WITH THIS...
...I'LL BE ABLE TO CATCH UP TO MY TEAM!!
HE'S THE HUNDREDTH RIDER...!!
91
PRIIIN...

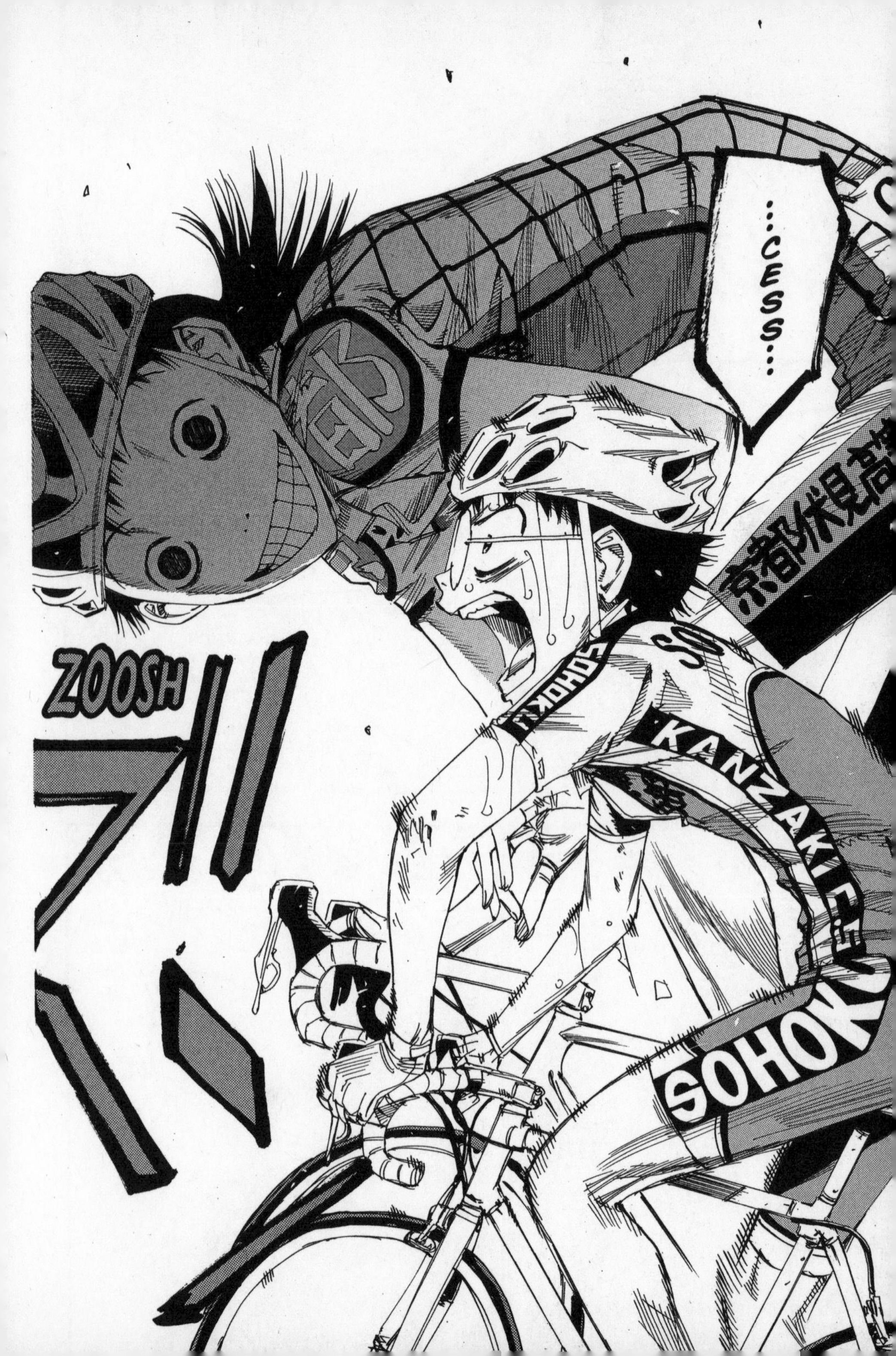
...CESS...
ZOOSH

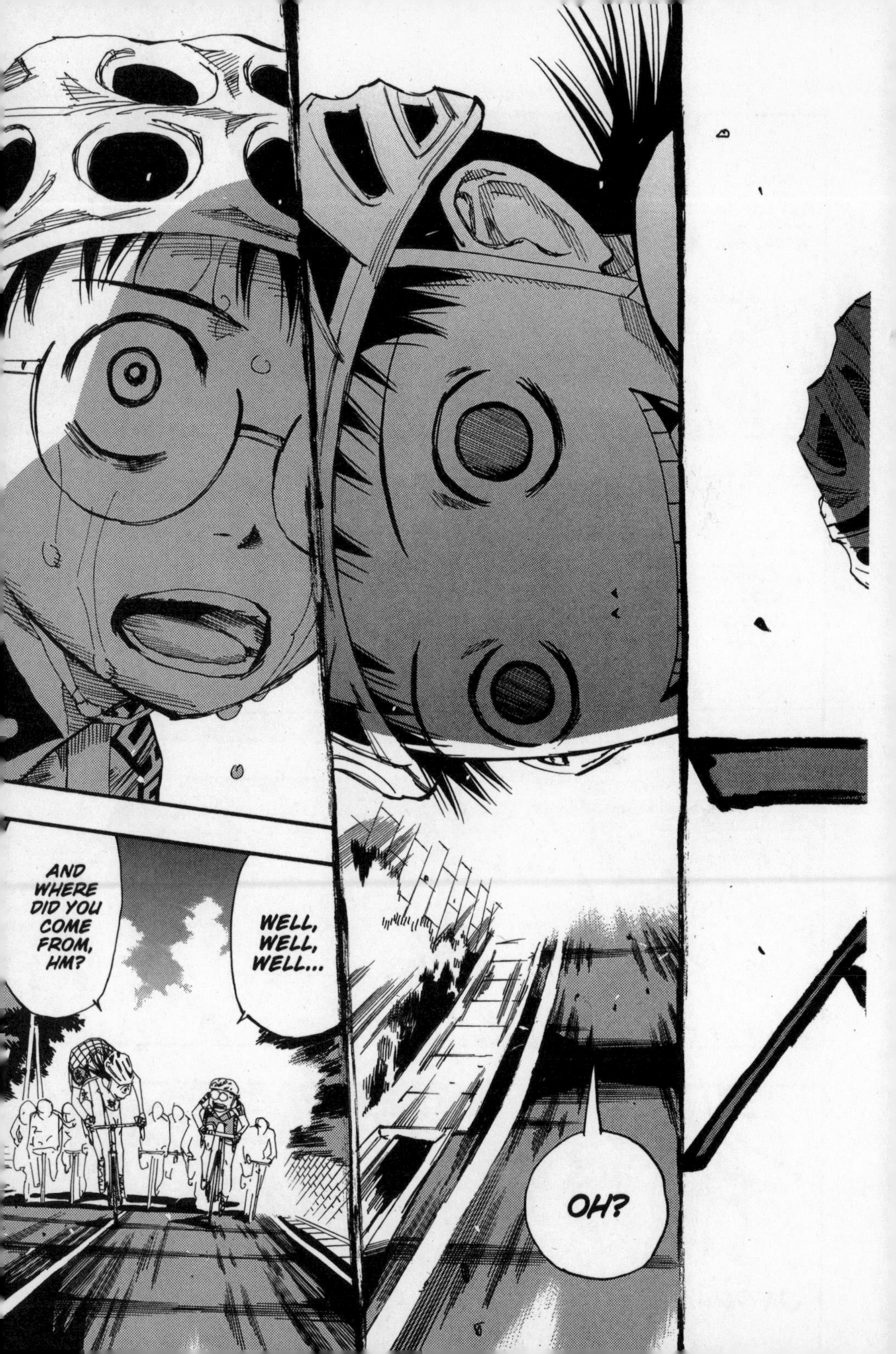
OH?
WELL, WELL, WELL...
AND WHERE DID YOU COME FROM, HM?

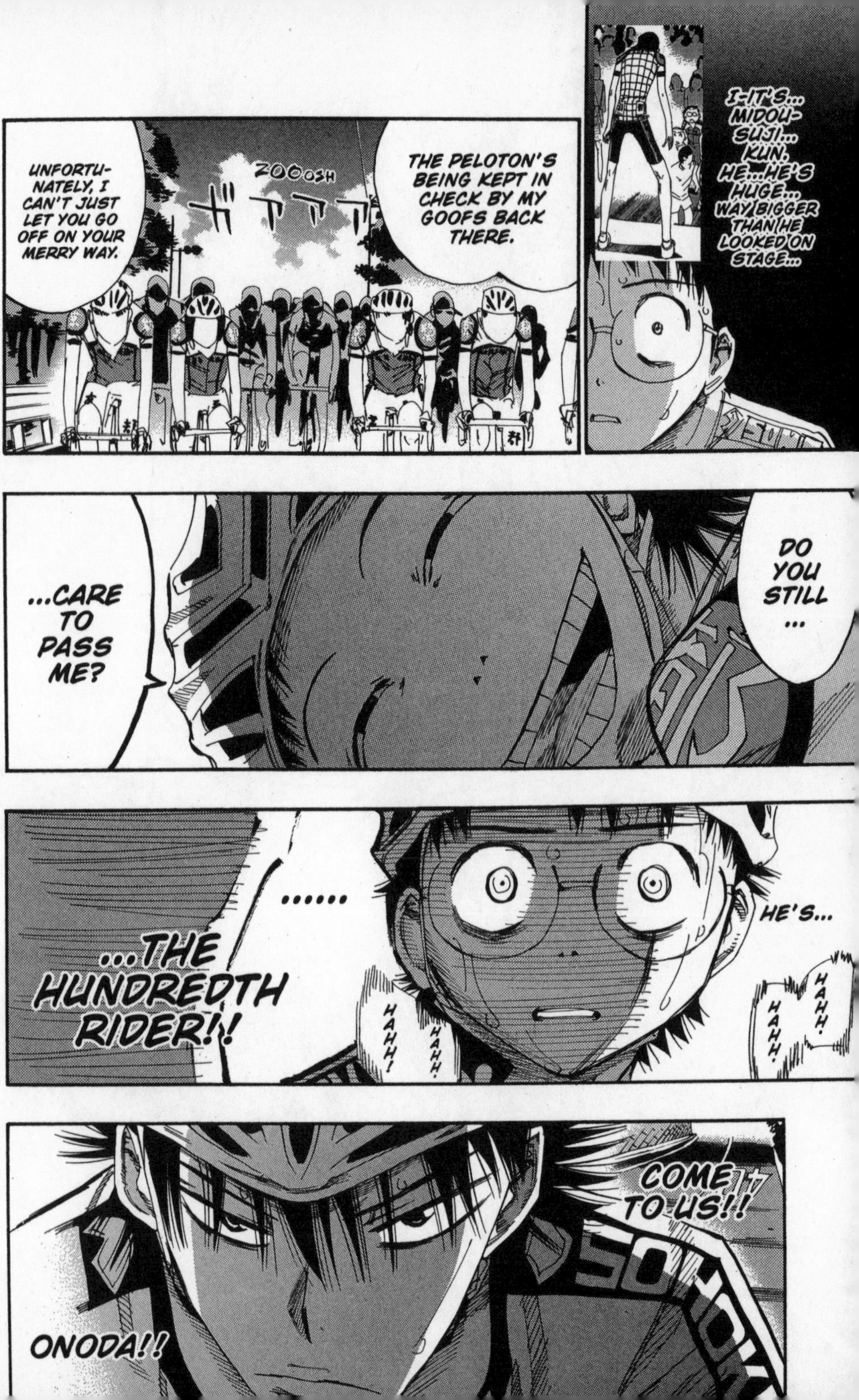
I-IT'S... MIDOU-SUJI... KUN. HE... HE'S HUGE... WAY BIGGER THAN HE LOOKED ON STAGE...
THE PELOTON'S BEING KEPT IN CHECK BY MY GOOFS BACK THERE.
ZOOOSH
ガァァァ
UNFORTUNATELY, I CAN'T JUST LET YOU GO OFF ON YOUR MERRY WAY.
DO YOU STILL ...
...CARE TO PASS ME?
HAHH. HAHH.
HE'S...
......
HAHH. HAHH!
...THE HUNDREDTH RIDER!!
COME TO US!!
ONODA!!

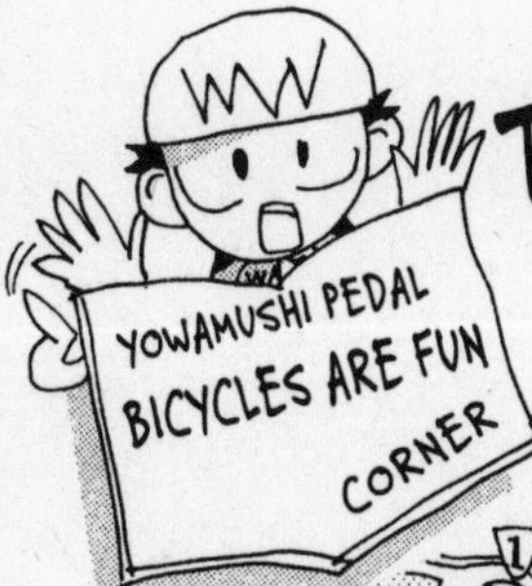
YOWAMUSHI PEDAL
BICYCLES ARE FUN
CORNER

# THE STAGE IS HAKONE

IN THIS VOLUME, THE SETTING IS PRIMARILY THE SEGMENT OF NATIONAL ROUTE 1 THAT GOES UP MT. HAKONE. I'VE MENTIONED THIS IN THE MANGA BEFORE, BUT OVER THE NEW YEAR'S HOLIDAY, THERE'S A TELEVISED COLLEGE FOOT RACE CALLED THE **"HAKONE EKIDEN"** THAT IS RUN ON THIS SAME STRETCH OF NATIONAL ROUTE 1. SO I'D LIKE TO TALK A BIT ABOUT THIS COURSE TODAY!

※ NATIONAL ROUTE 1 GOES ALL THE WAY FROM NIHONBASHI IN TOKYO TO THE CITY OF OSAKA. TANGENTIALLY, NATIONAL ROUTE 2 GOES FROM OSAKA TO SHIMONOSEKI, AND NATIONAL ROUTE 3 TRAVERSES THE ISLAND OF KYUSHU.

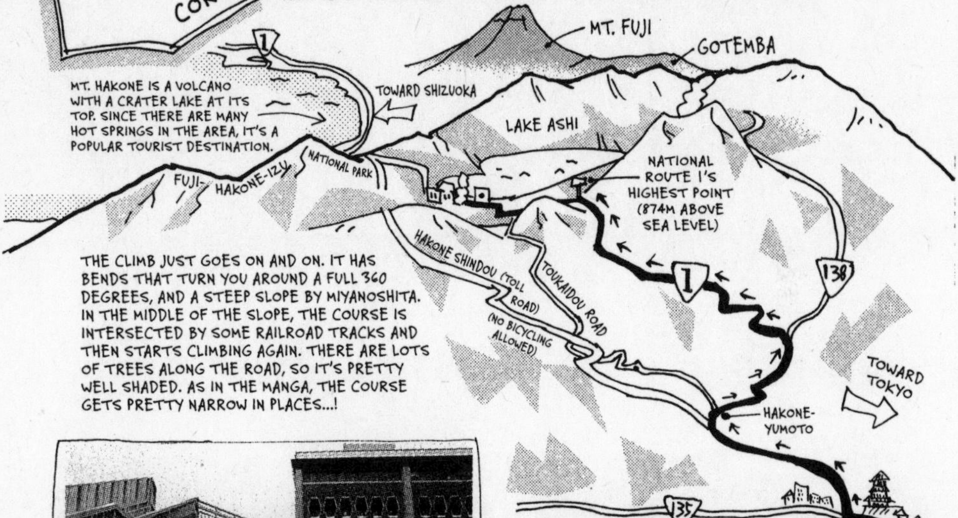
MT. FUJI
GOTEMBA
1
TOWARD SHIZUOKA
MT. HAKONE IS A VOLCANO WITH A CRATER LAKE AT ITS TOP. SINCE THERE ARE MANY HOT SPRINGS IN THE AREA, IT'S A POPULAR TOURIST DESTINATION.
LAKE ASHI
FUJI-HAKONE-IZU NATIONAL PARK
NATIONAL ROUTE 1'S HIGHEST POINT (874M ABOVE SEA LEVEL)
HAKONE SHINDOU (TOLL ROAD) (NO BICYCLING ALLOWED)
TOUKAIDOU ROAD
1
138
TOWARD TOKYO
HAKONE-YUMOTO
135
ODAWARA

THE CLIMB JUST GOES ON AND ON. IT HAS BENDS THAT TURN YOU AROUND A FULL 360 DEGREES, AND A STEEP SLOPE BY MIYANOSHITA. IN THE MIDDLE OF THE SLOPE, THE COURSE IS INTERSECTED BY SOME RAILROAD TRACKS AND THEN STARTS CLIMBING AGAIN. THERE ARE LOTS OF TREES ALONG THE ROAD, SO IT'S PRETTY WELL SHADED. AS IN THE MANGA, THE COURSE GETS PRETTY NARROW IN PLACES...!

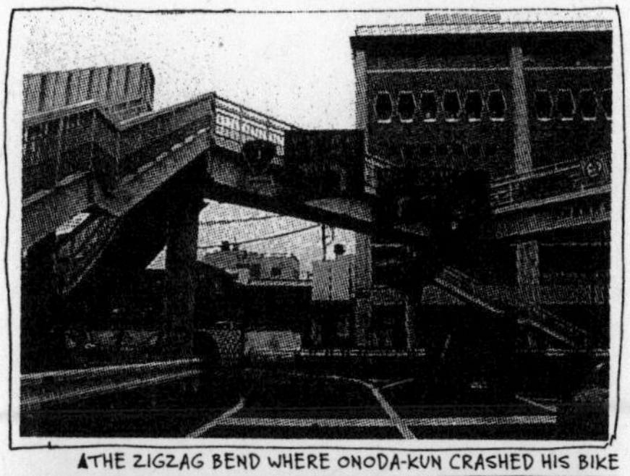

▲THE ZIGZAG BEND WHERE ONODA-KUN CRASHED HIS BIKE

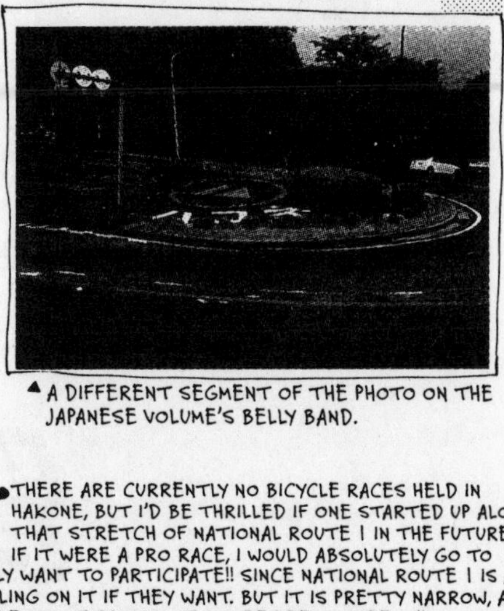

▲ A DIFFERENT SEGMENT OF THE PHOTO ON THE JAPANESE VOLUME'S BELLY BAND.

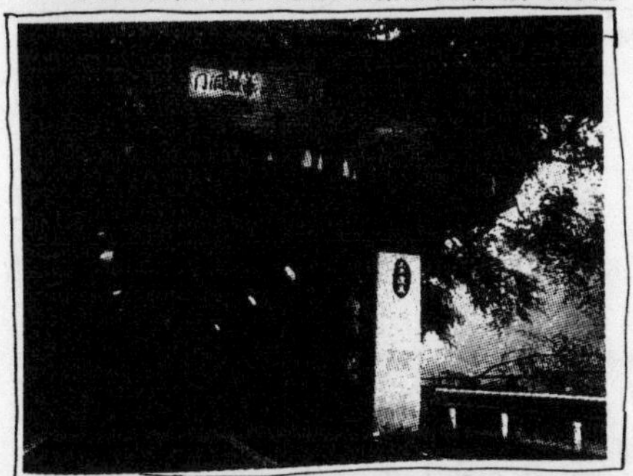

▲ KANREI DOUMON TUNNEL

● THERE ARE CURRENTLY NO BICYCLE RACES HELD IN HAKONE, BUT I'D BE THRILLED IF ONE STARTED UP ALONG THAT STRETCH OF NATIONAL ROUTE 1 IN THE FUTURE. IF IT WERE A PRO RACE, I WOULD ABSOLUTELY GO TO WATCH! BUT IF IT WERE AN AMATEUR RACE, I'D TOTALLY WANT TO PARTICIPATE!! SINCE NATIONAL ROUTE 1 IS A (REGULAR) HIGHWAY, PEOPLE CAN (OF COURSE) GO CYCLING ON IT IF THEY WANT. BUT IT IS PRETTY NARROW, AND IT GETS PLENTY OF VEHICULAR TRAFFIC, SO DO USE PLENTY OF CAUTION IF YOU DECIDE TO RIDE IT!!

YOWAMUSHI
PEDAL

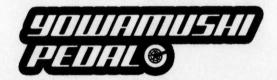

# RIDE.95 THE HUNDREDTH RIDER

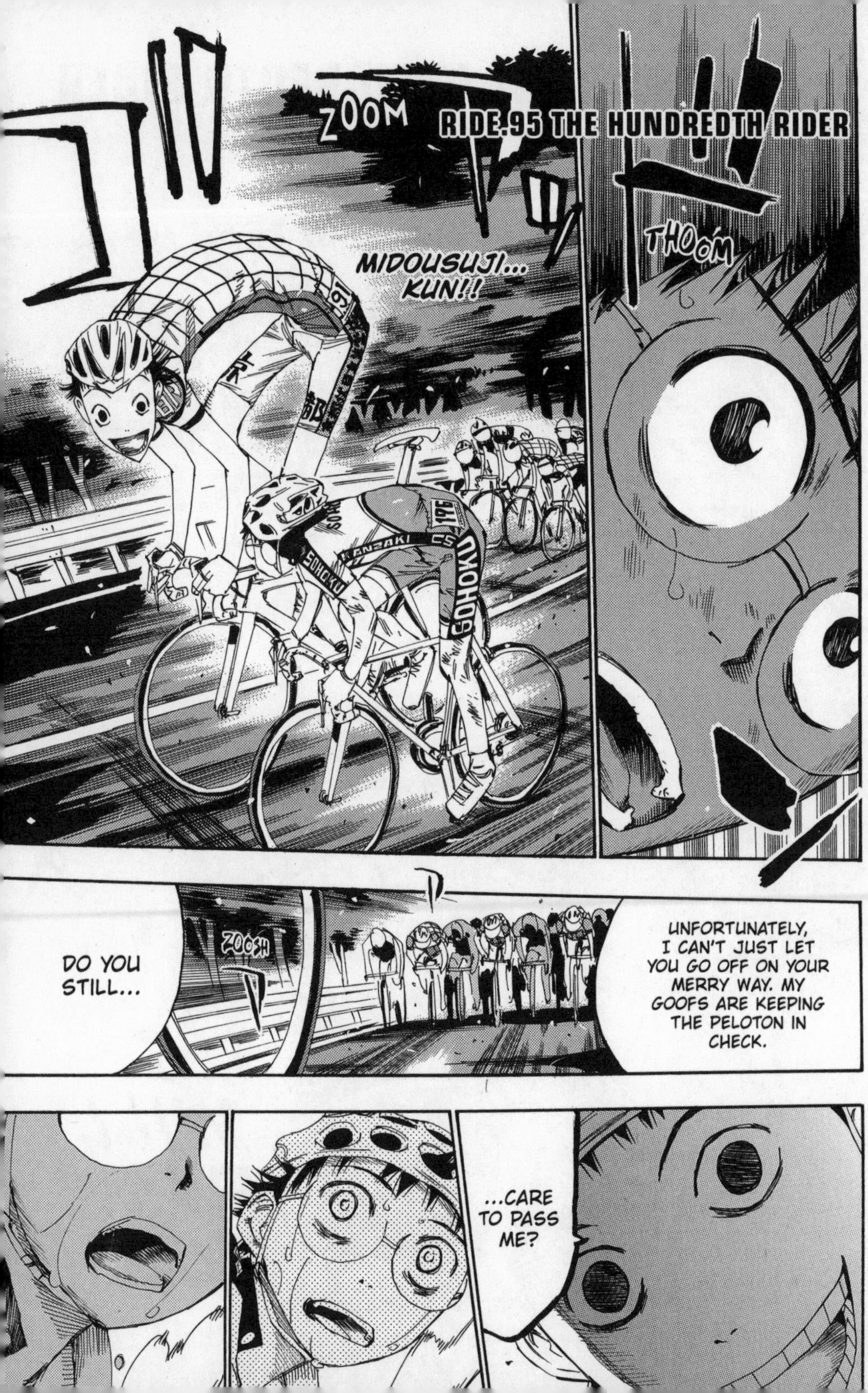
THOOM
ZOOM
MIDOUSUJI... KUN!!
UNFORTUNATELY, I CAN'T JUST LET YOU GO OFF ON YOUR MERRY WAY. MY GOOFS ARE KEEPING THE PELOTON IN CHECK.
ZOOSH
DO YOU STILL...
...CARE TO PASS ME?

# RIDE.95 THE HUNDREDTH RIDER

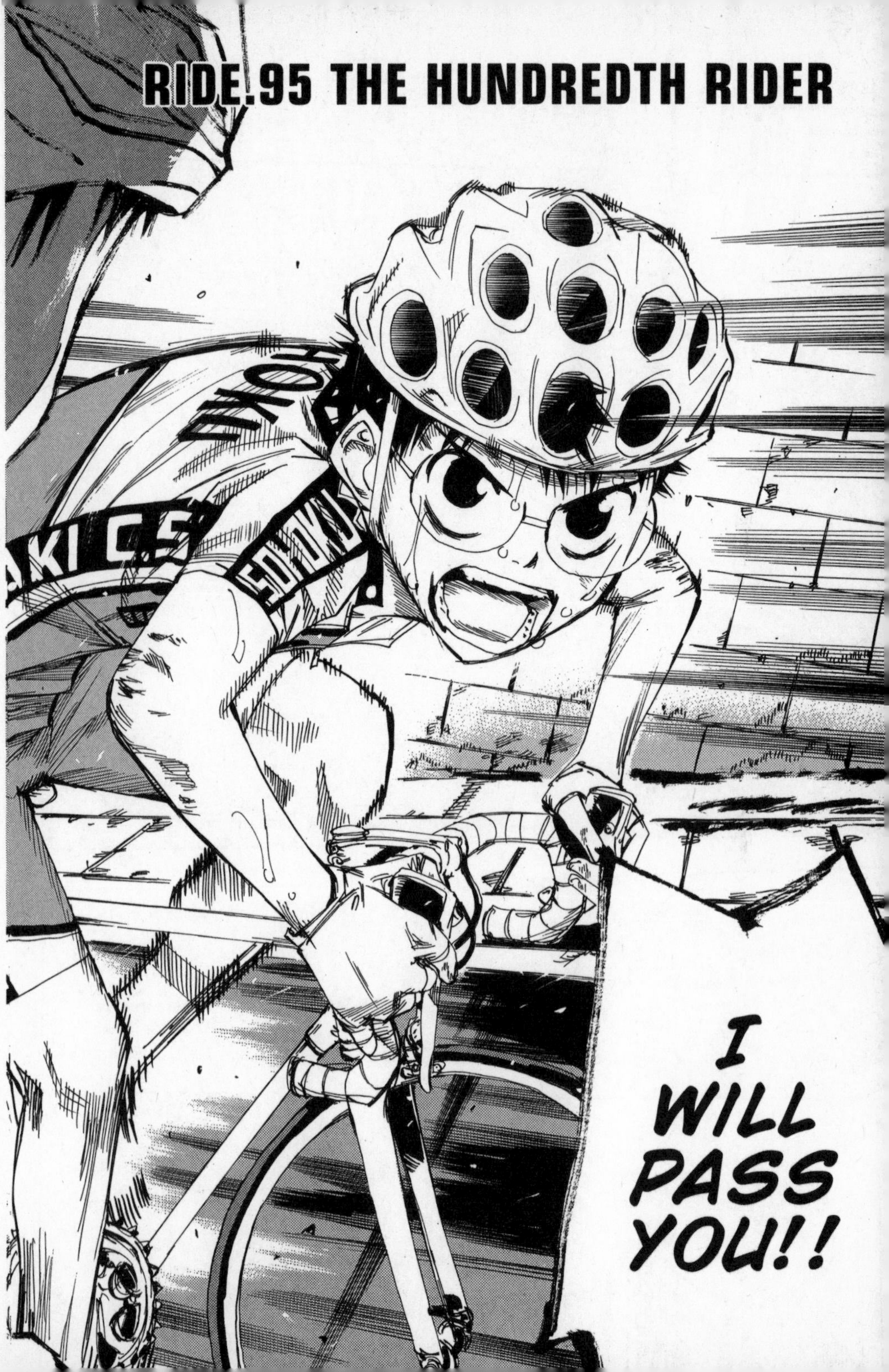
I WILL PASS YOU!!

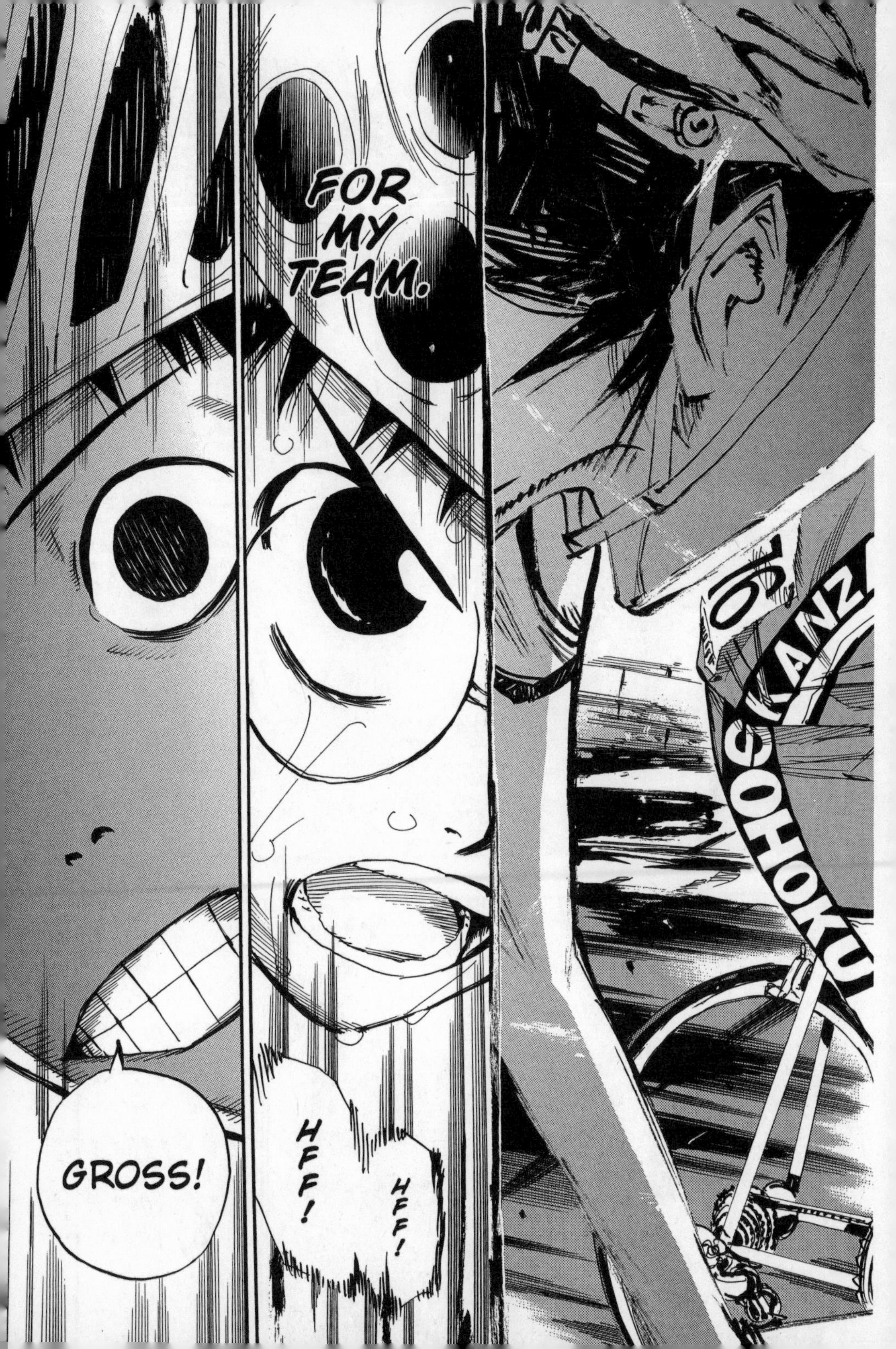
FOR MY TEAM.
HFF! HFF!
GROSS!

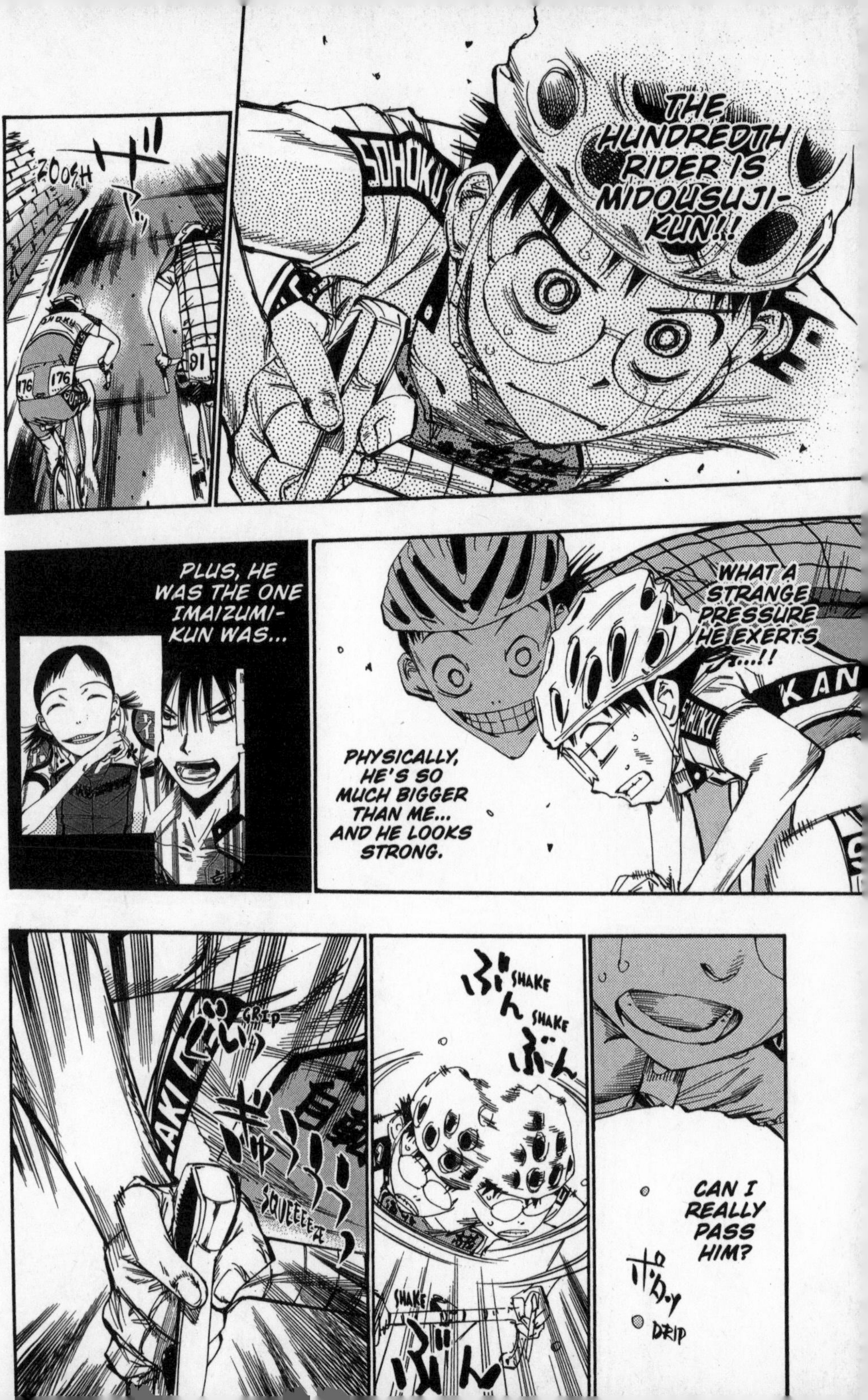
SOHOKU
THE HUNDREDTH RIDER IS MIDOUSUJI-KUN!!
ZOOSH
WHAT A STRANGE PRESSURE HE EXERTS...!!
PHYSICALLY, HE'S SO MUCH BIGGER THAN ME... AND HE LOOKS STRONG.
PLUS, HE WAS THE ONE IMAIZUMI-KUN WAS...
CAN I REALLY PASS HIM?
DRIP
SHAKE
SHAKE
SHAKE
GRIP
SQUEEEEE

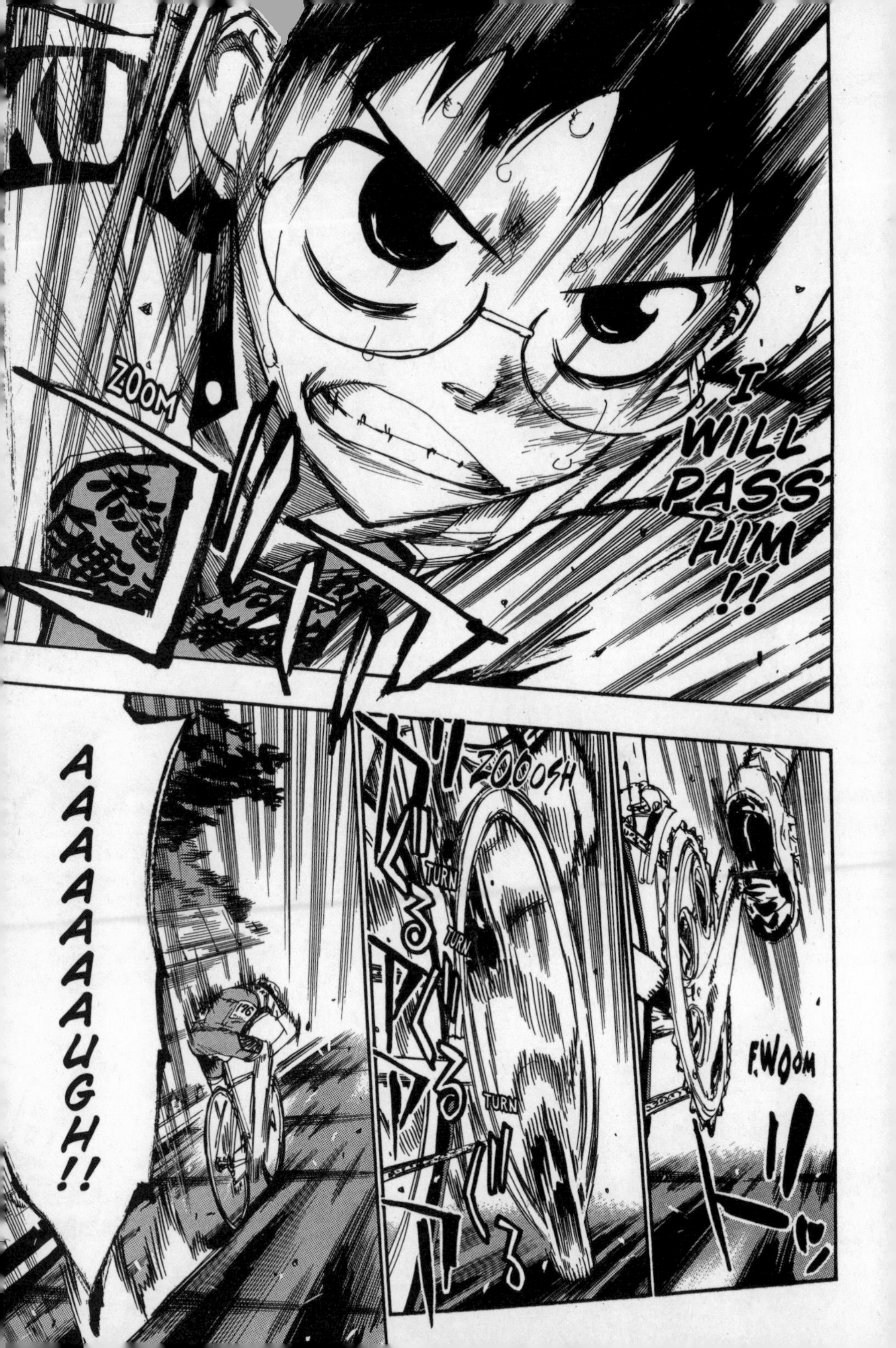
I WILL PASS HIM!!
ZOOM
F.WOOM
ZOOOSH
TURN
TURN
TURN
AAAAAAAUGH!!

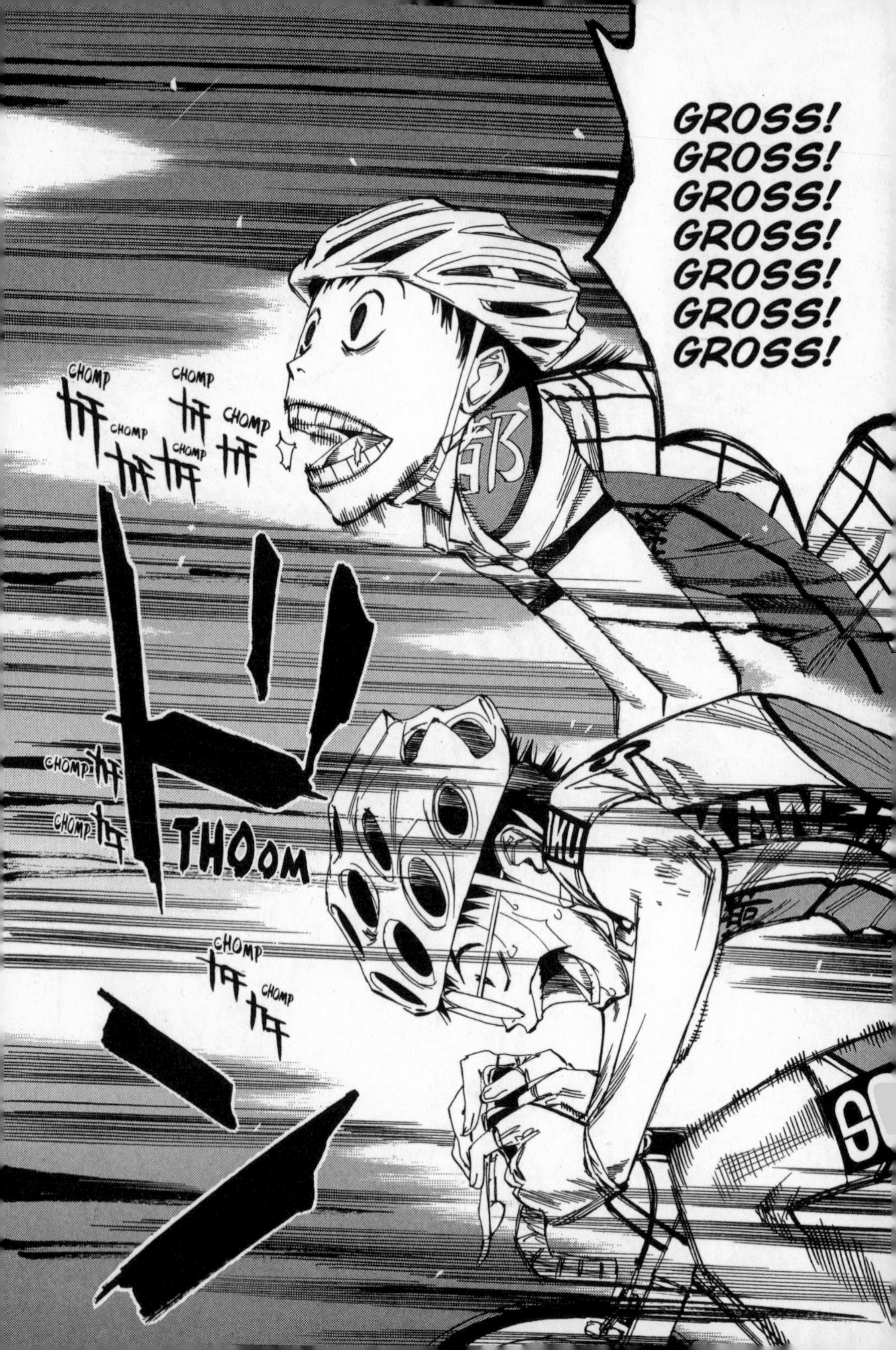
GROSS!
GROSS!
GROSS!
GROSS!
GROSS!
GROSS!
GROSS!
CHOMP
CHOMP
CHOMP
CHOMP
CHOMP
CHOMP
CHOMP
THOOM
CHOMP
CHOMP

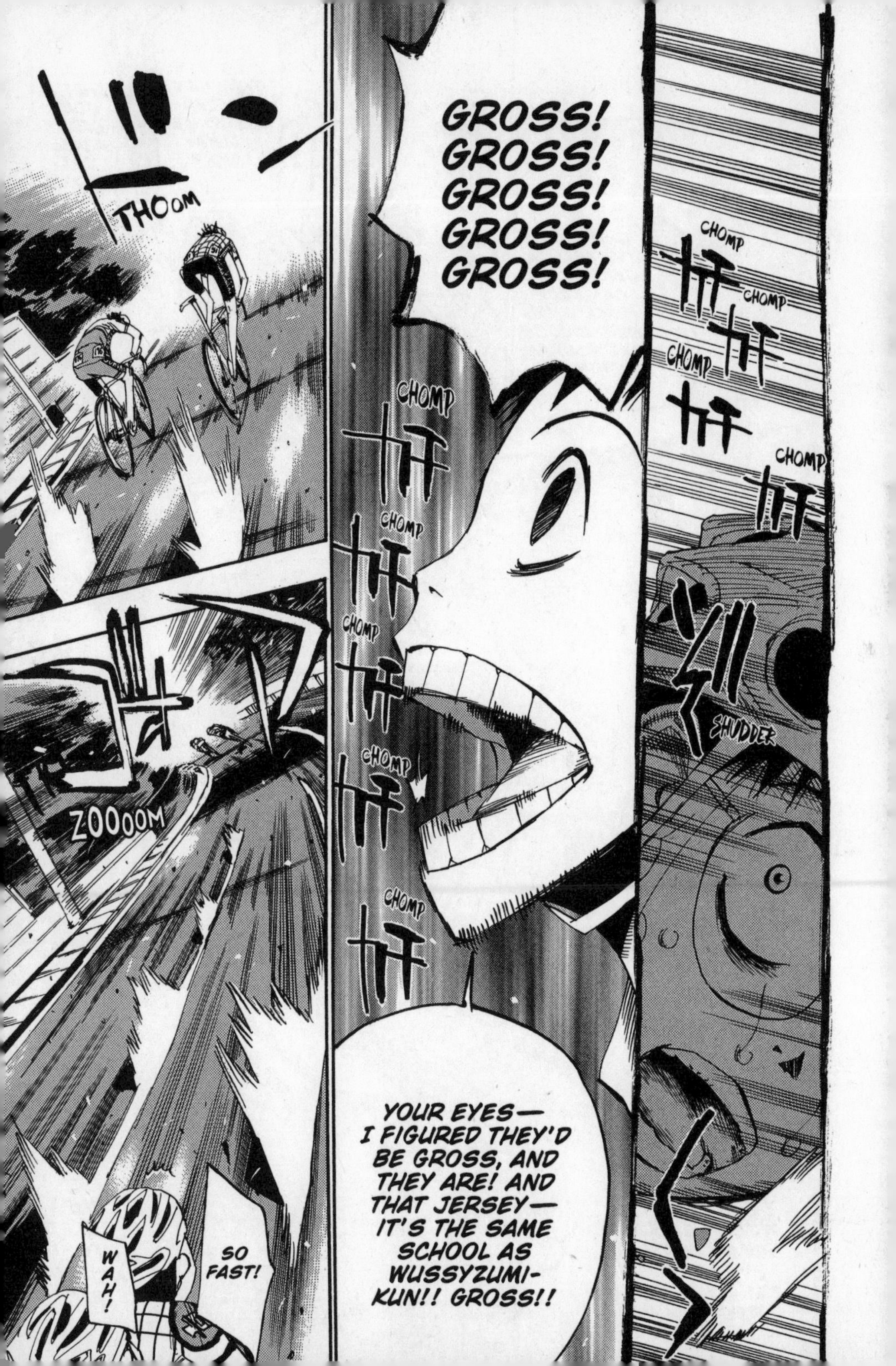
CHOMP
CHOMP
CHOMP
CHOMP
SHUDDER
GROSS! GROSS! GROSS! GROSS! GROSS!
CHOMP
CHOMP
CHOMP
CHOMP
CHOMP
YOUR EYES— I FIGURED THEY'D BE GROSS, AND THEY ARE! AND THAT JERSEY— IT'S THE SAME SCHOOL AS WUSSYZUMI-KUN!! GROSS!!
THOOM
ZOOOOM
SO FAST!
WAH!

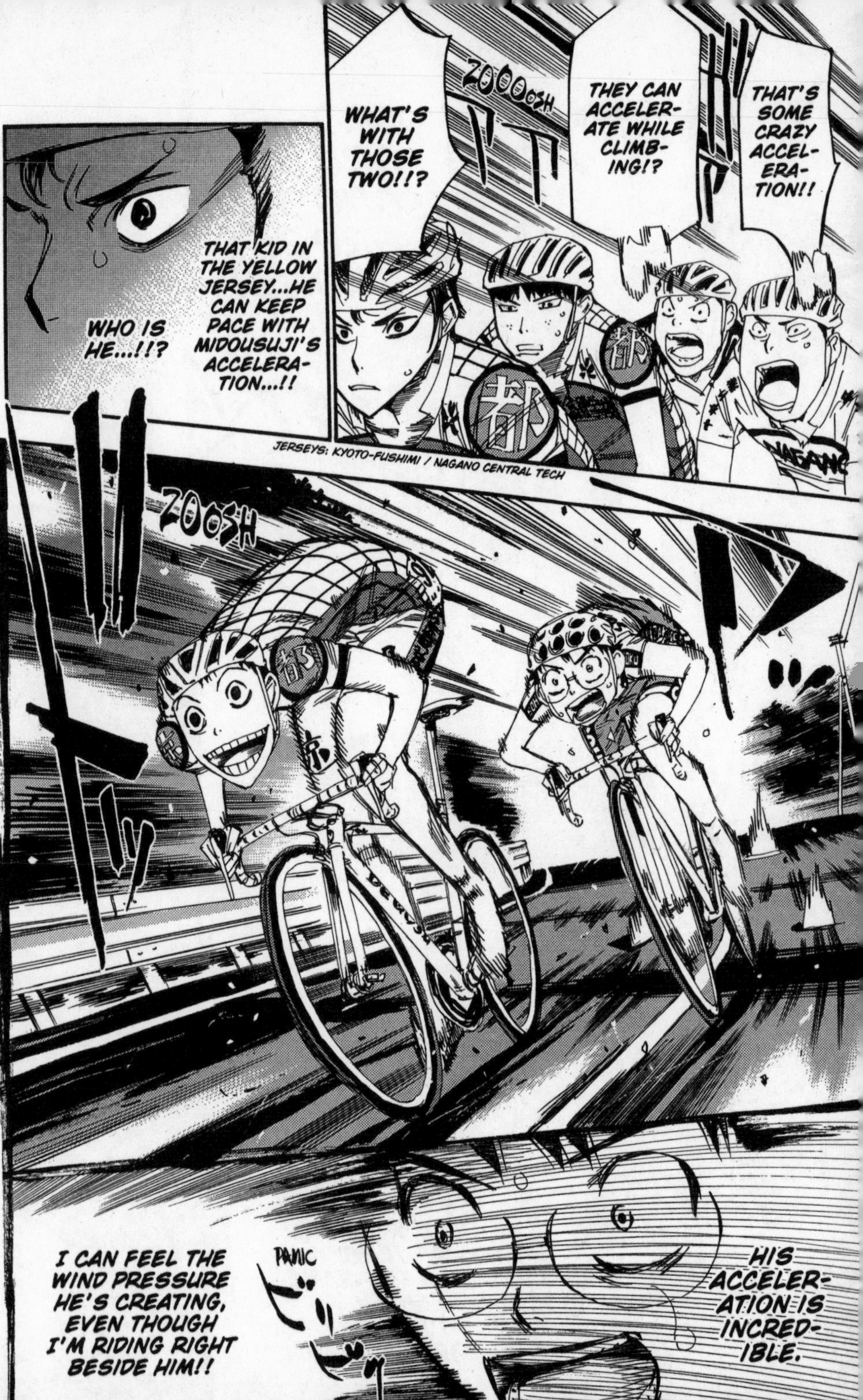

THAT'S SOME CRAZY ACCEL-ERA-TION!!
THEY CAN ACCELER-ATE WHILE CLIMB-ING!?
ZOOOOSH
WHAT'S WITH THOSE TWO!!?
JERSEYS: KYOTO-FUSHIMI / NAGANO CENTRAL TECH
THAT KID IN THE YELLOW JERSEY...HE CAN KEEP PACE WITH MIDOUSUJI'S ACCELERA-TION...!!
WHO IS HE...!!?
ZOOSH
HIS ACCELER-ATION IS INCRED-IBLE.
PANIC
I CAN FEEL THE WIND PRESSURE HE'S CREATING, EVEN THOUGH I'M RIDING RIGHT BESIDE HIM!!

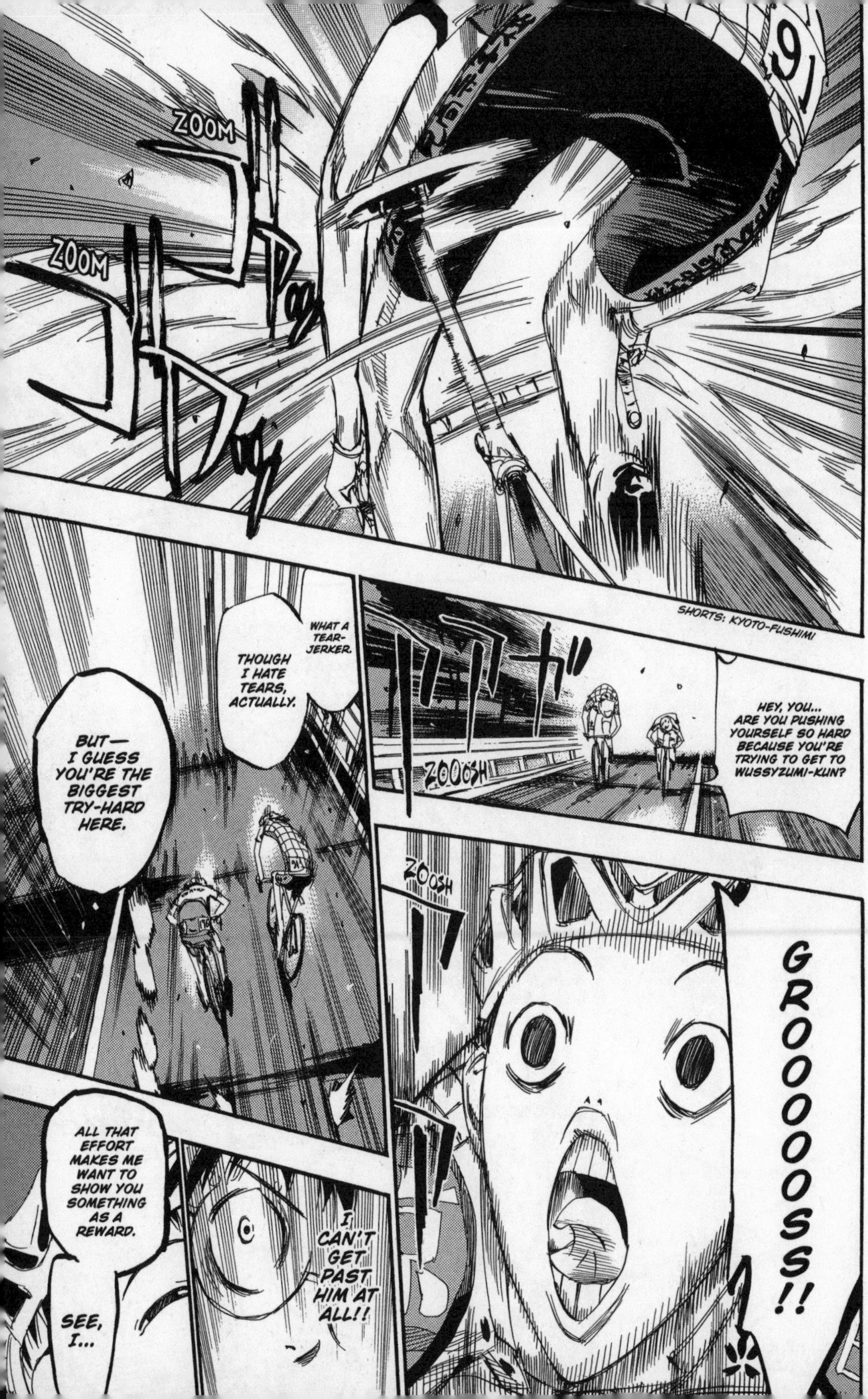
ZOOM
ZOOM
SHORTS: KYOTO-FUSHIMI
HEY, YOU... ARE YOU PUSHING YOURSELF SO HARD BECAUSE YOU'RE TRYING TO GET TO WUSSYZUMI-KUN?
ZOOOSH
WHAT A TEAR-JERKER.
THOUGH I HATE TEARS, ACTUALLY.
BUT— I GUESS YOU'RE THE BIGGEST TRY-HARD HERE.
GROOOOOOOSS!!
ZOOSH
I CAN'T GET PAST HIM AT ALL!!
ALL THAT EFFORT MAKES ME WANT TO SHOW YOU SOMETHING AS A REWARD.
SEE, I...

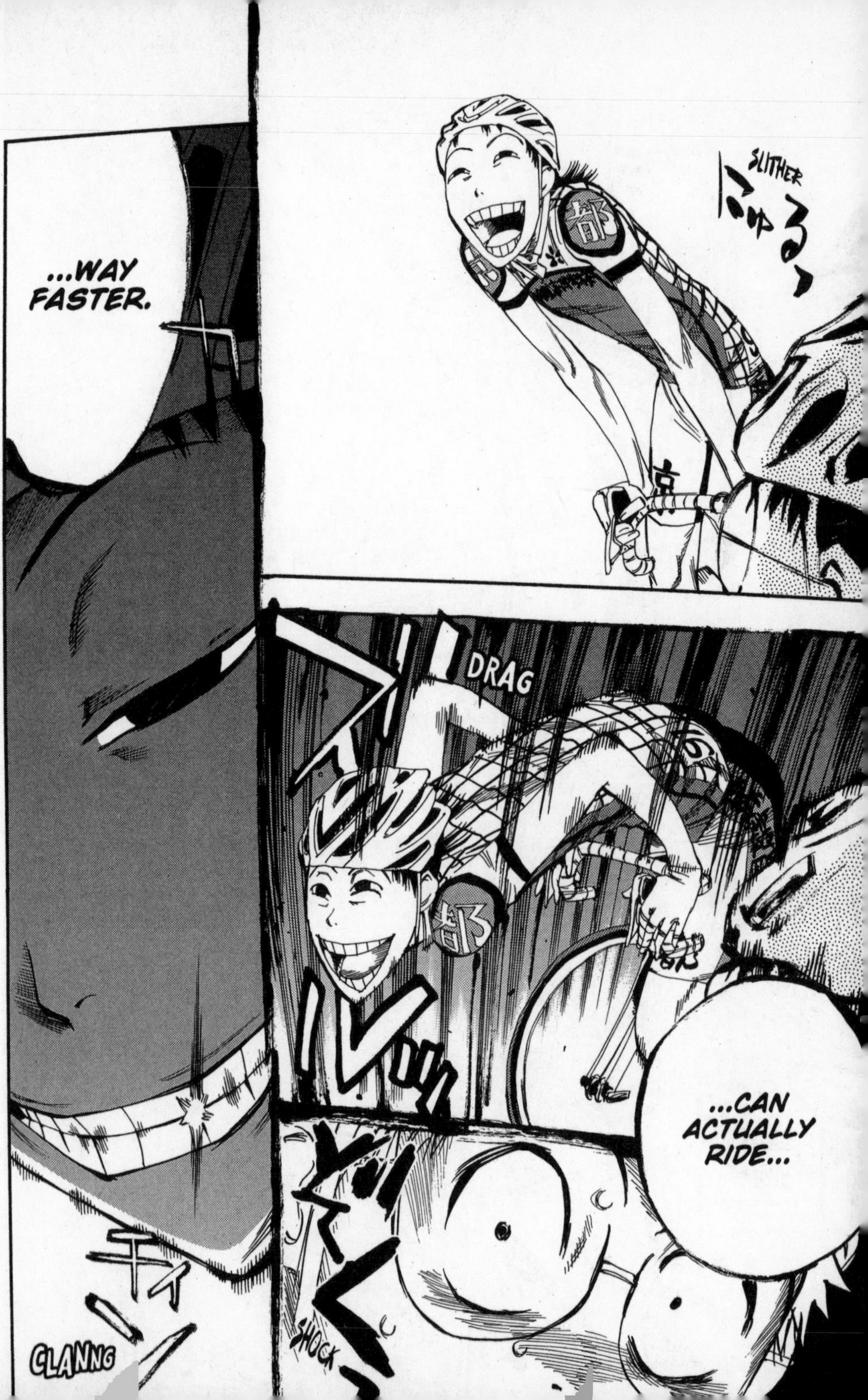
SLITHER
DRAG
...CAN ACTUALLY RIDE...
SHOCK
...WAY FASTER.
CLANNG

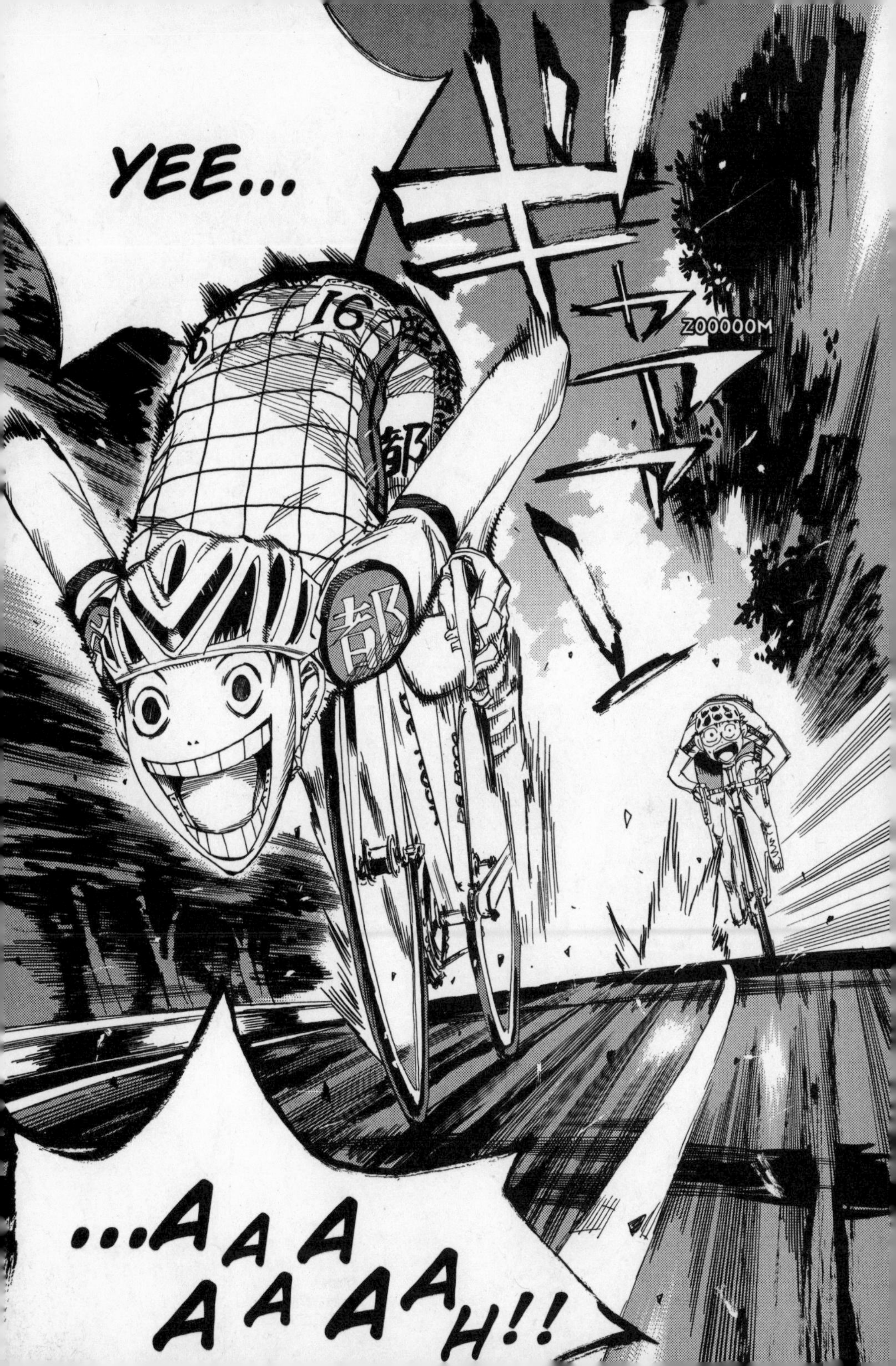
YEE...
ZOOOOOM
...AAAAAAAH!!

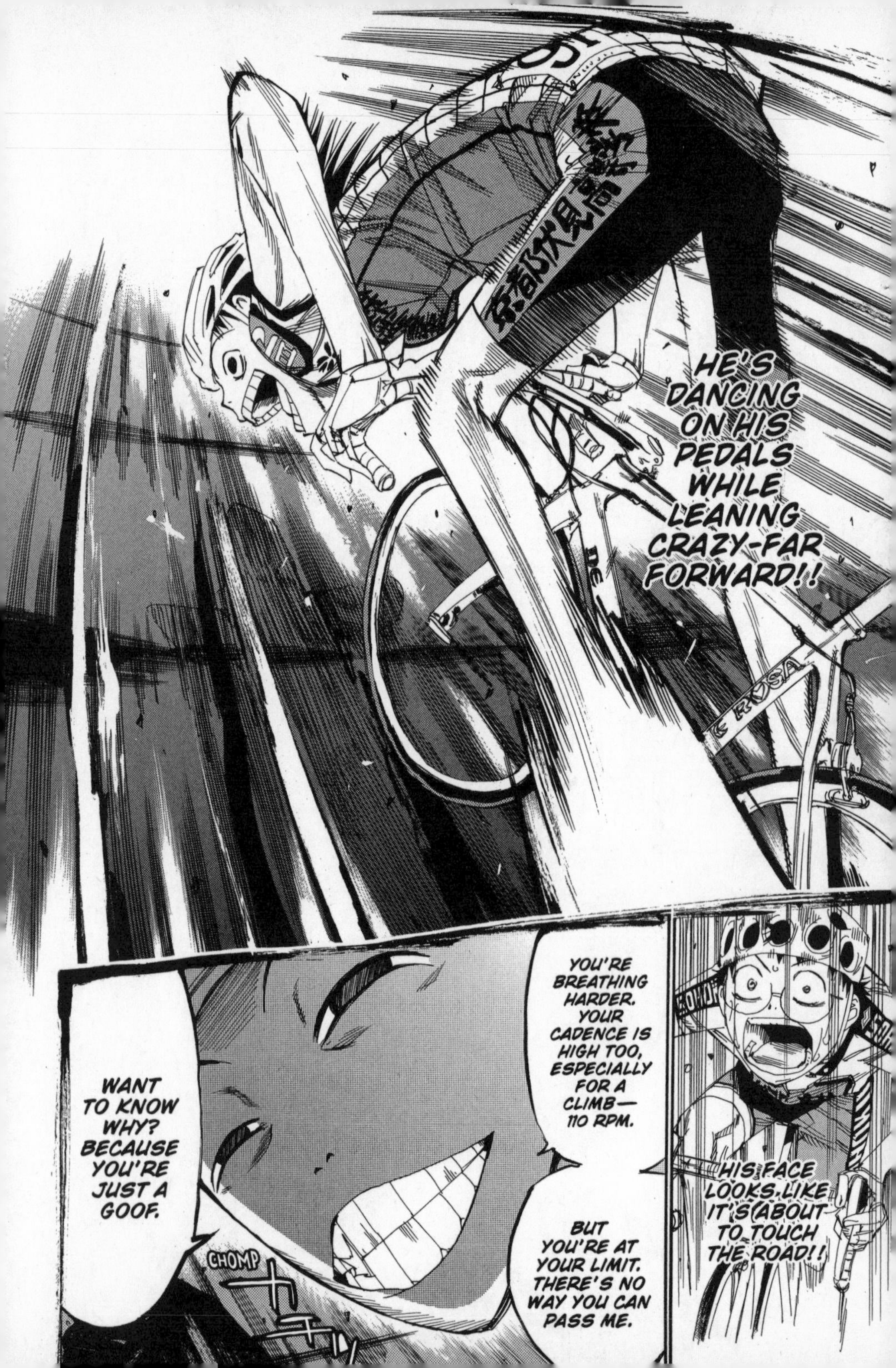
HE'S DANCING ON HIS PEDALS WHILE LEANING CRAZY-FAR FORWARD!!
HIS FACE LOOKS LIKE IT'S ABOUT TO TOUCH THE ROAD!!
YOU'RE BREATHING HARDER. YOUR CADENCE IS HIGH TOO, ESPECIALLY FOR A CLIMB— 110 RPM.
WANT TO KNOW WHY? BECAUSE YOU'RE JUST A GOOF.
BUT YOU'RE AT YOUR LIMIT. THERE'S NO WAY YOU CAN PASS ME.
CHOMP

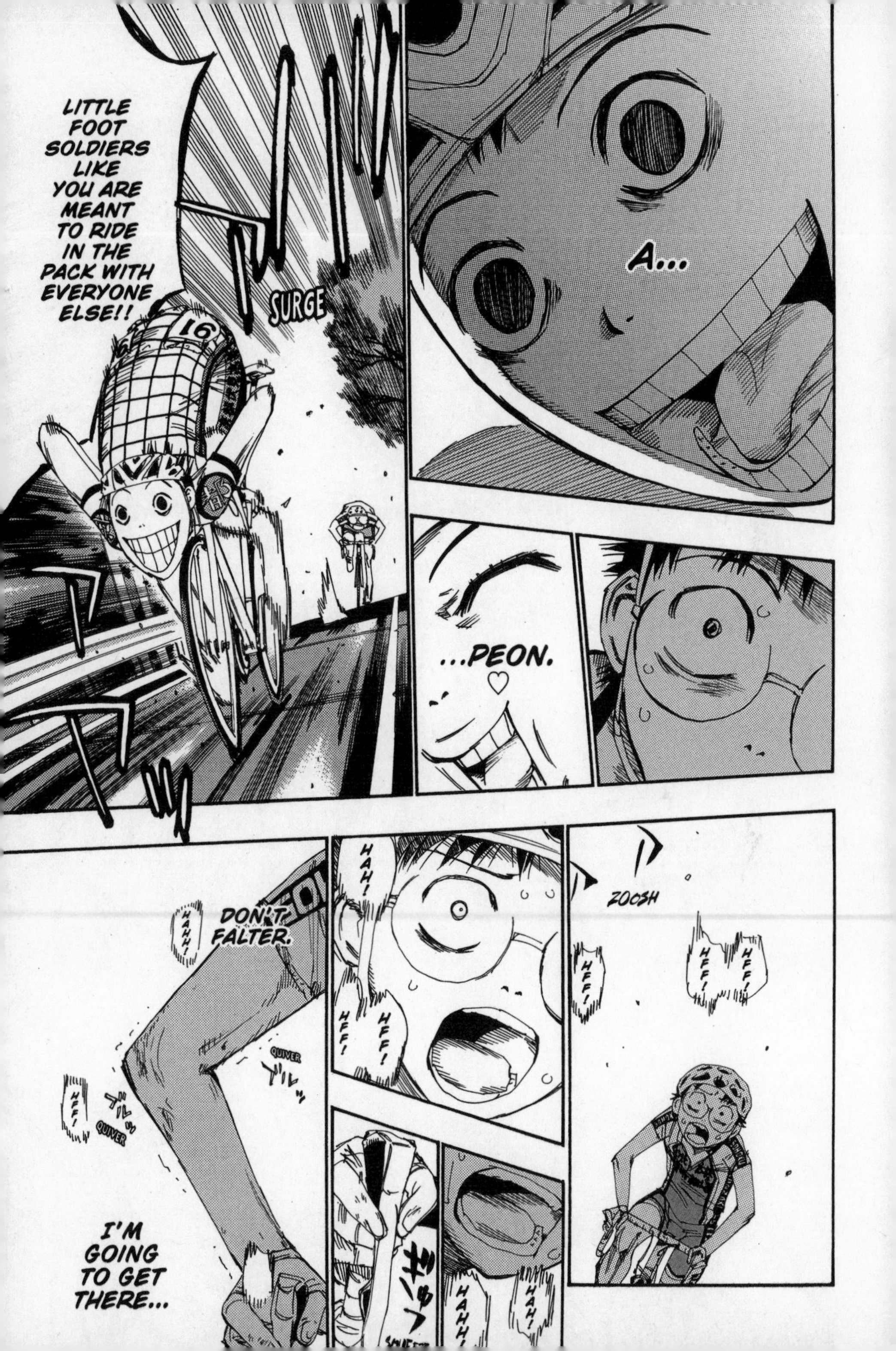
A...
...PEON. ♡
LITTLE FOOT SOLDIERS LIKE YOU ARE MEANT TO RIDE IN THE PACK WITH EVERYONE ELSE!!
SURGE
ZOOSH
HFF! HFF!
HAH!
HFF! HFF!
HAHH!
HAH!
DON'T FALTER.
HAHH!
QUIVER
QUIVER
HFF!
I'M GOING TO GET THERE...

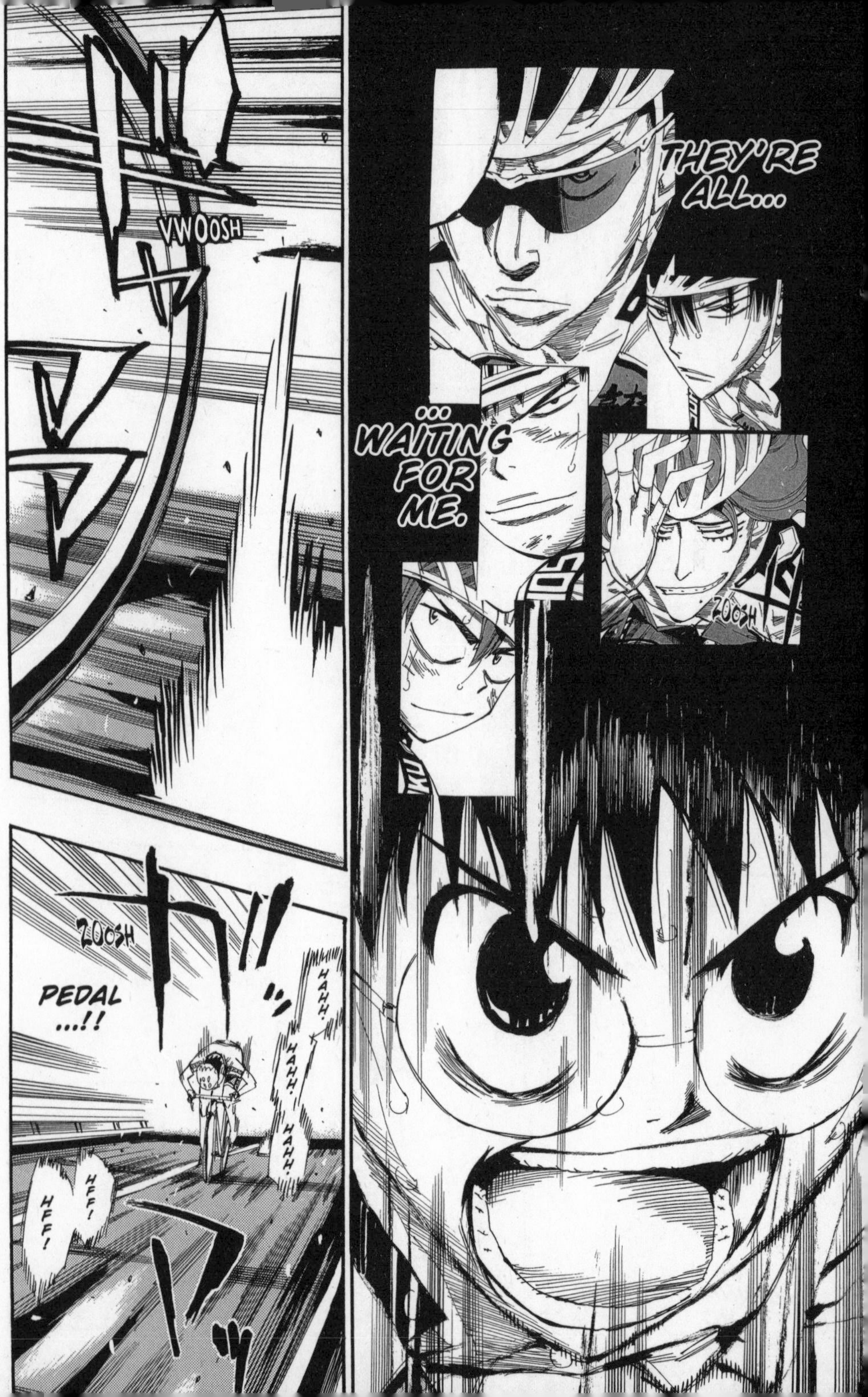
THEY'RE ALL...
...WAITING FOR ME.
ZOOSH
VWOOSH
ZOOSH
PEDAL ...!!
HAHH HAHH HAHH
HFF! HFF!

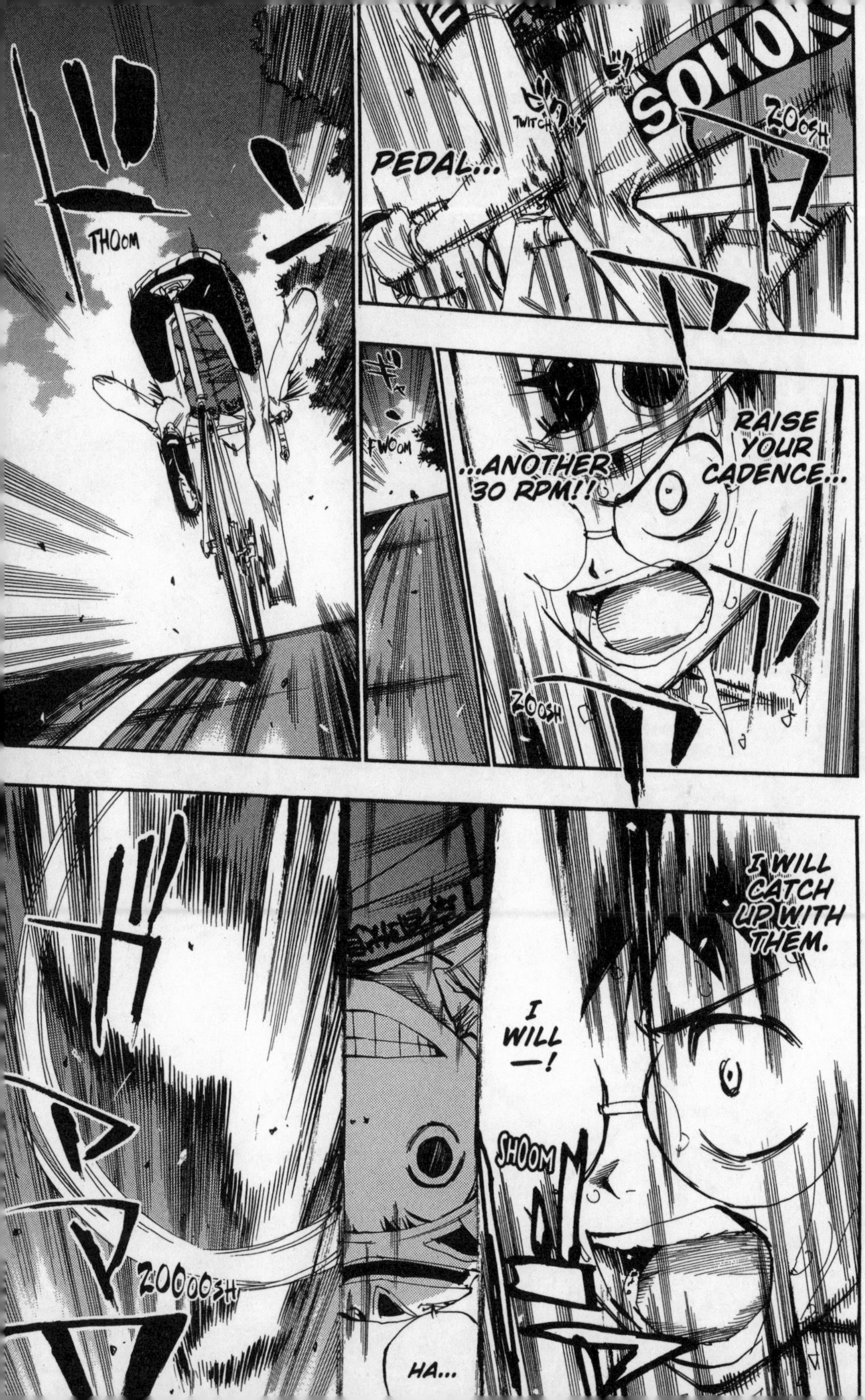
SOHOK
TWITCH
TWITCH
ZOOSH
PEDAL...
RAISE YOUR CADENCE...
...ANOTHER 30 RPM!!
FWOOM
ZOOSH
THOOM
I WILL CATCH UP WITH THEM.
I WILL—!
SHOOM
HA...
ZOOOOSH

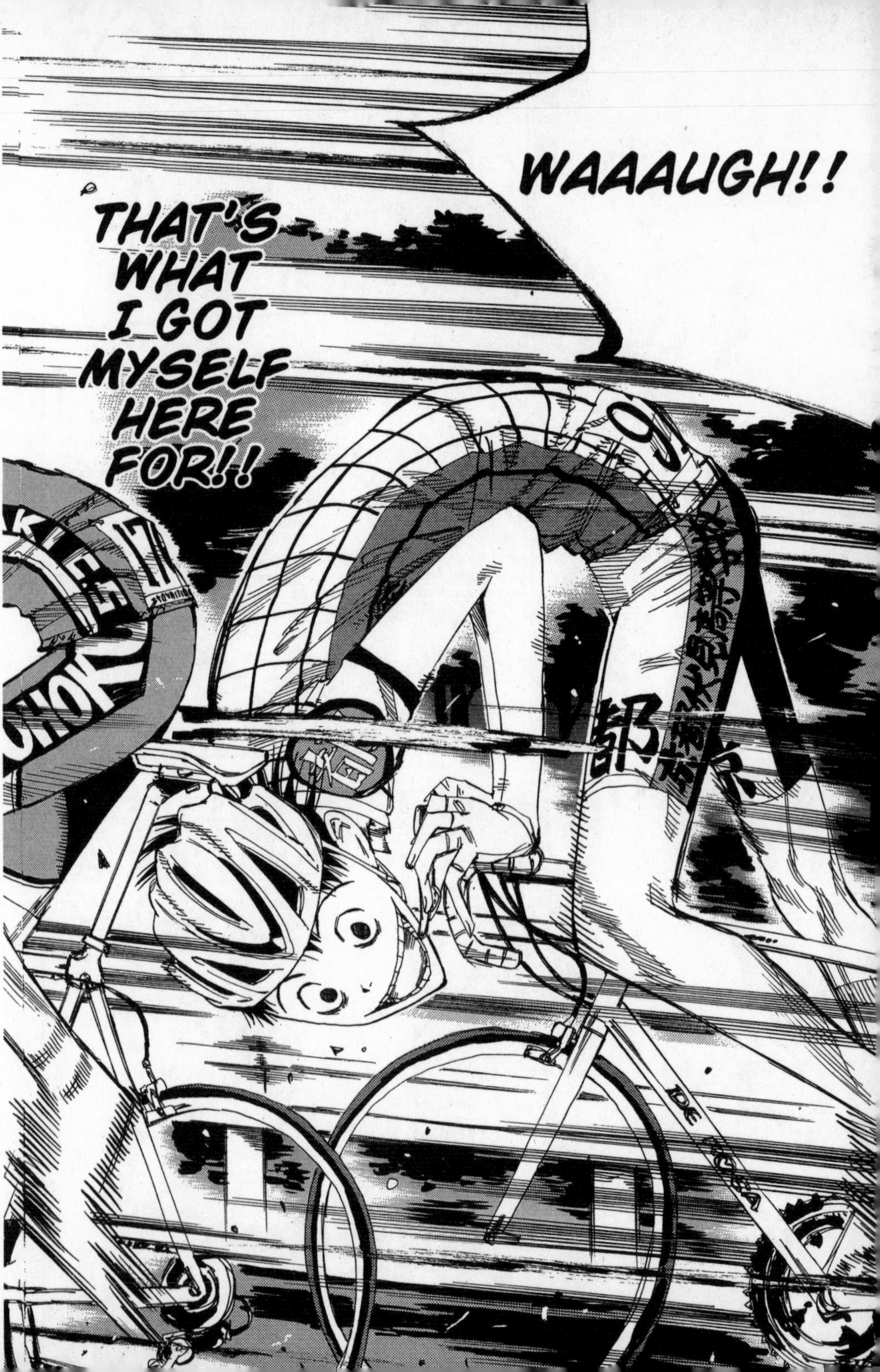
WAAAUGH!!
THAT'S WHAT I GOT MYSELF HERE FOR!!

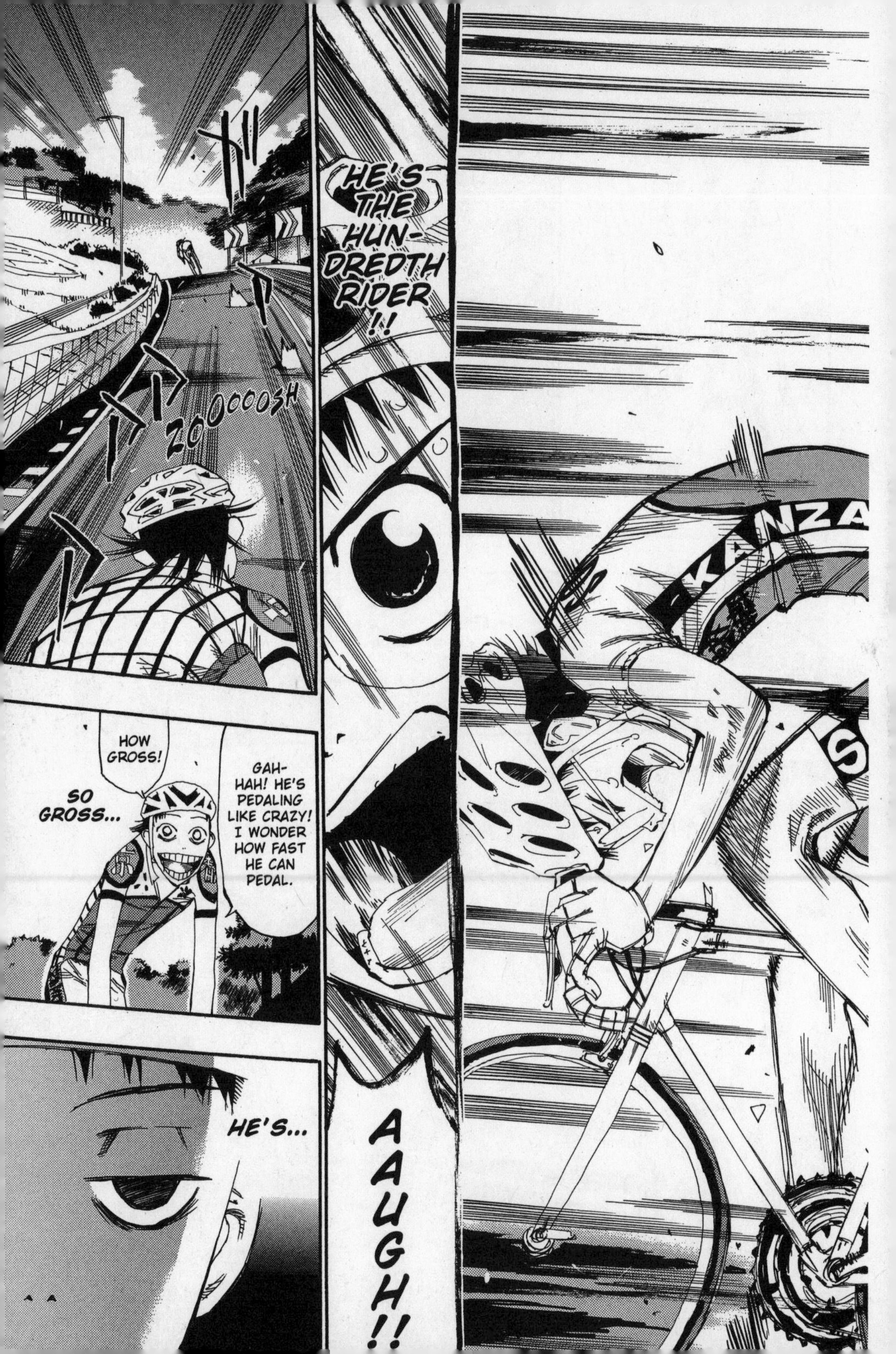

HE'S THE HUN-DREDTH RIDER!!
AAUGH!!
ZOOOOOOSH
GAH-HAH! HE'S PEDALING LIKE CRAZY! I WONDER HOW FAST HE CAN PEDAL.
HOW GROSS!
SO GROSS...
HE'S...

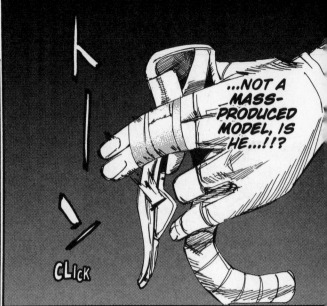

...NOT A MASS-PRODUCED MODEL, IS HE...!!?

CLICK

ZOOOOSH

HAH!

HEF!

AAH!

AAH!

HEF!

HEF!

HEF!

TESHIMA-SAN, AOYAGI-SAN... THANK YOU.

I'M SORRY, EVERYONE...

HFF!

IF I HAVE, THEN...

...TO, DO MY JOB?

HAVE I MADE IT BACK IN TIME...

WILL IT BE OKAY?

BAM!!

HANH! HANH!

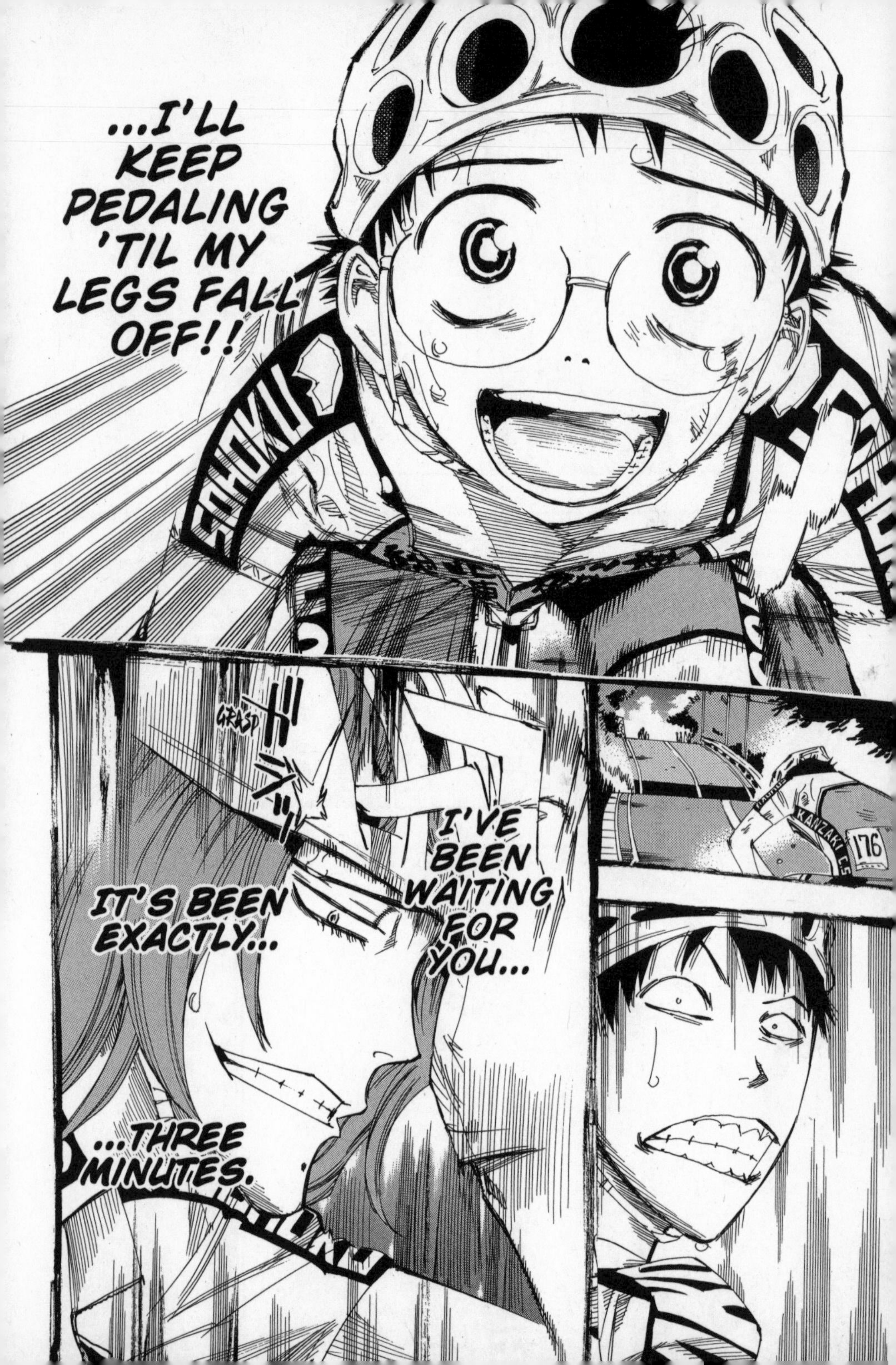
...I'LL KEEP PEDALING 'TIL MY LEGS FALL OFF!!
KANZAKI CS
176
GRASP
I'VE BEEN WAITING FOR YOU...
IT'S BEEN EXACTLY...
...THREE MINUTES.

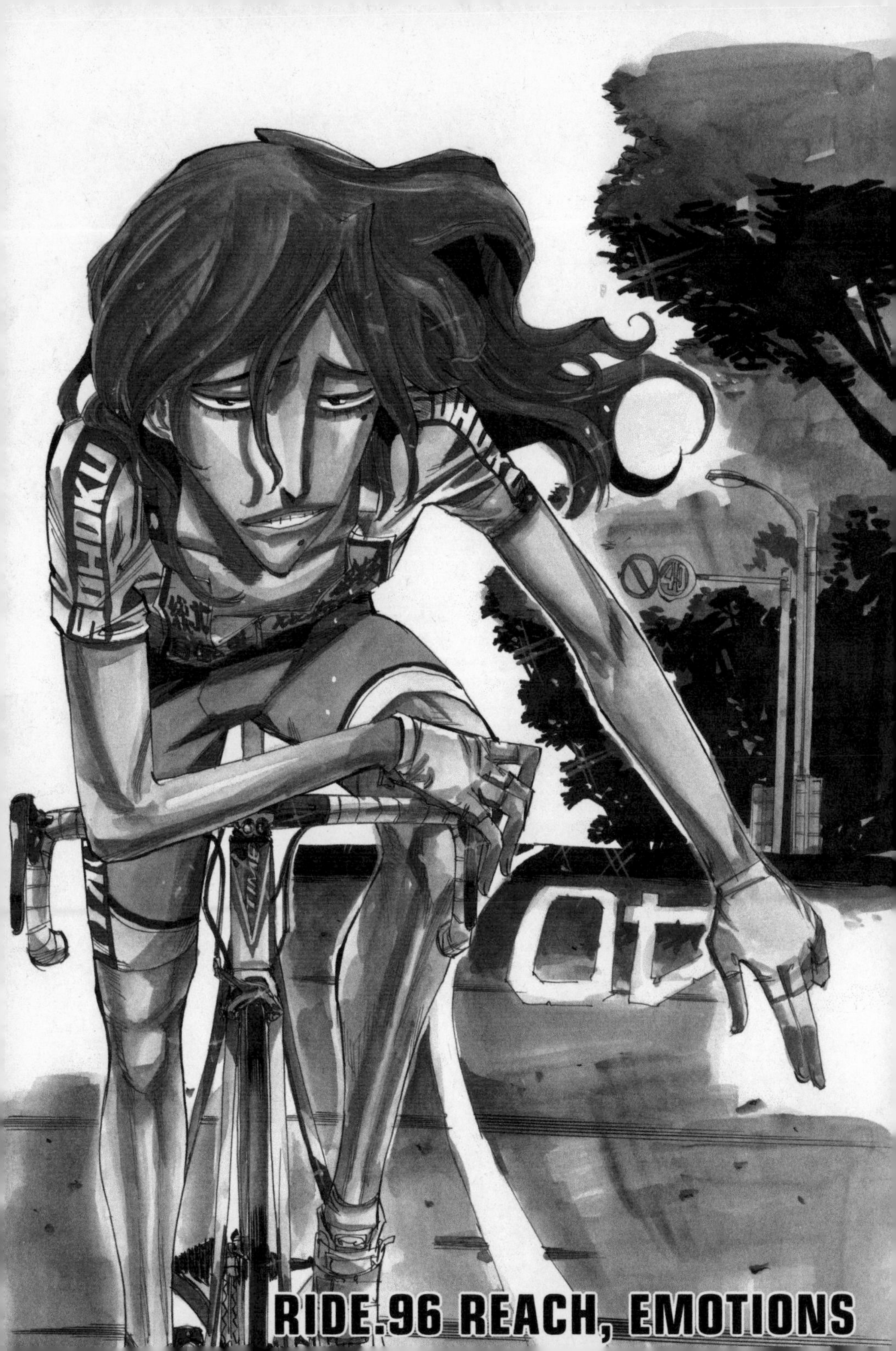

# RIDE.96 REACH, EMOTIONS

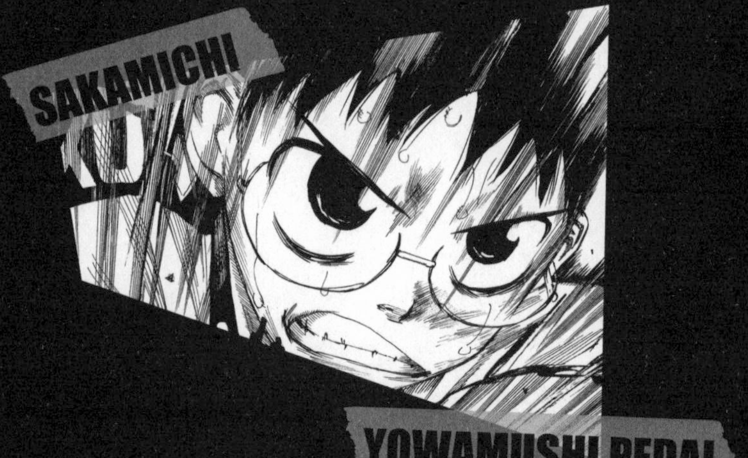
SAKAMICHI
YOWAMUSHI PEDAL

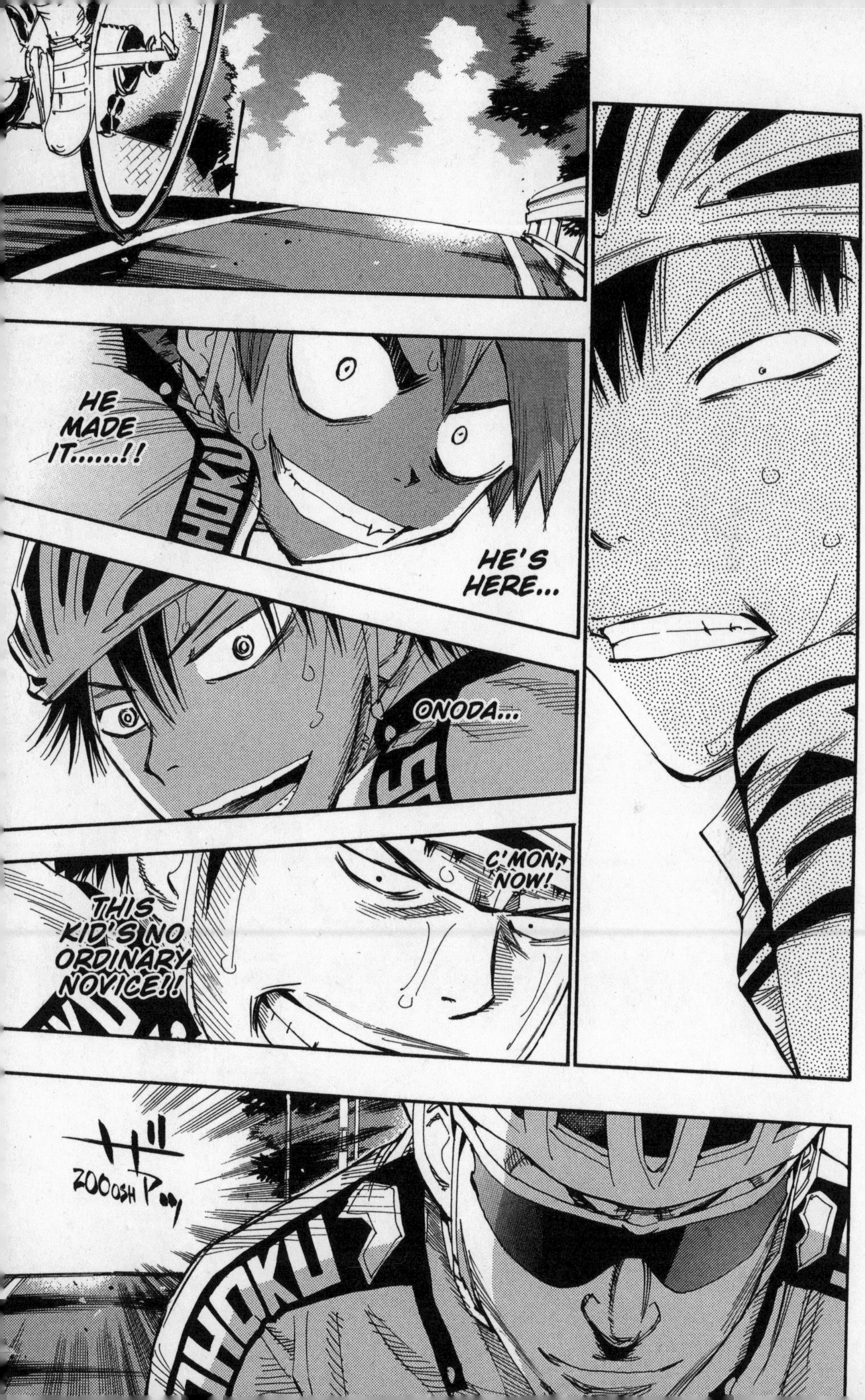
HE MADE IT......!!
HE'S HERE...
ONODA...
C'MON, NOW!
THIS KID'S NO ORDINARY NOVICE!!
ZOOOSH

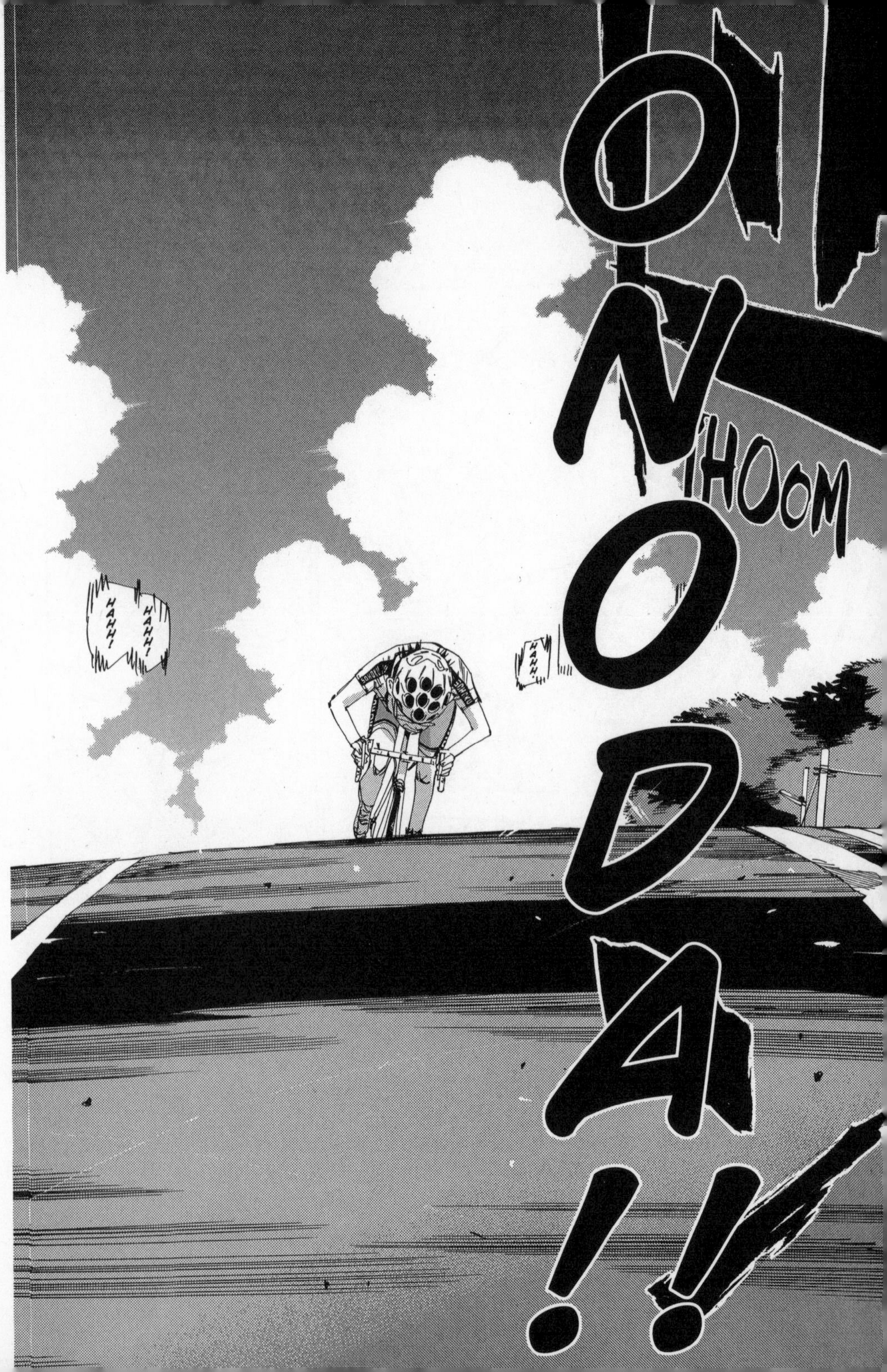
ONODA!!
HOOM
HAHH!
HAHH!
HAHH!

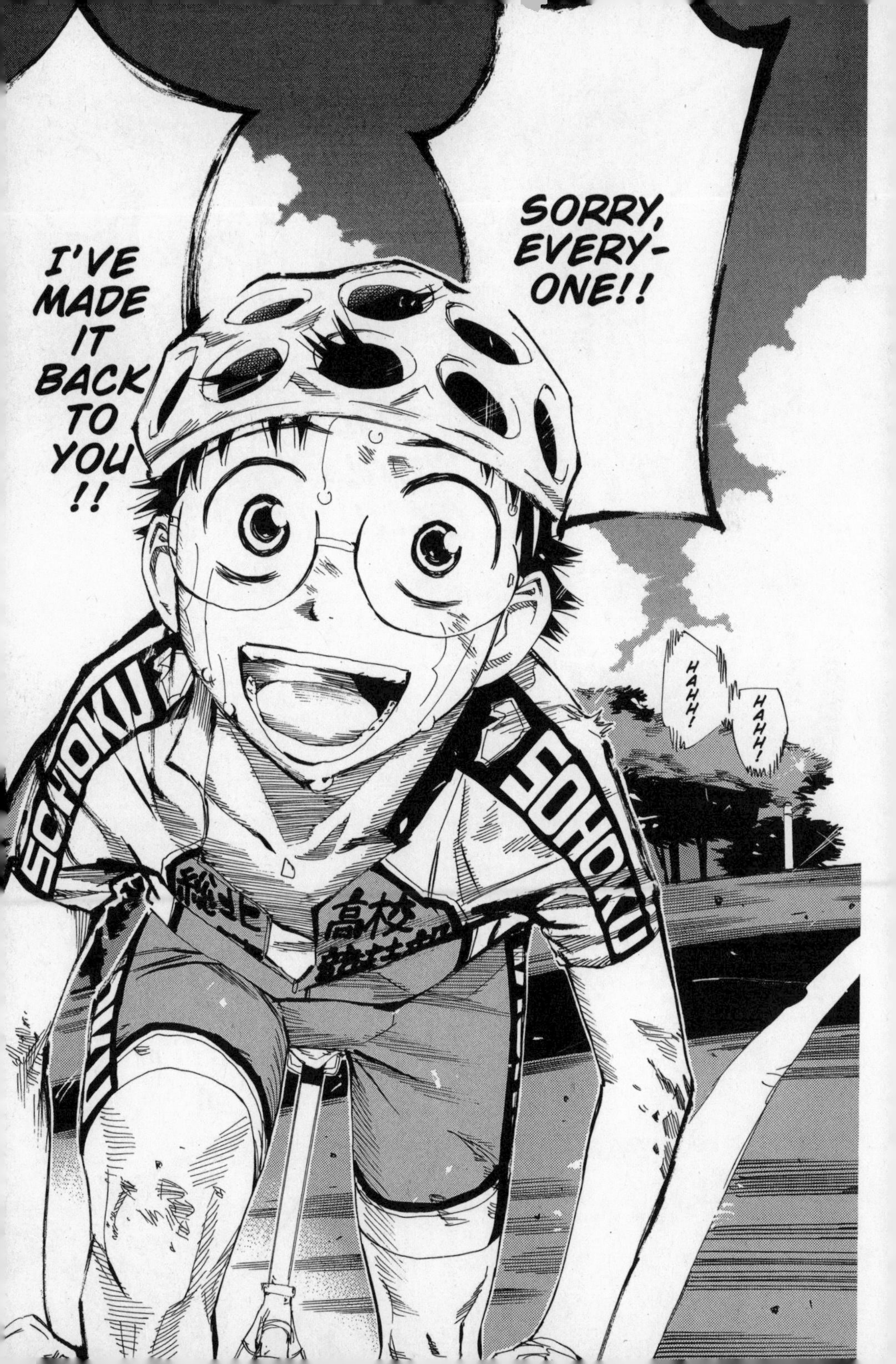
SORRY, EVERY-ONE!!
I'VE MADE IT BACK TO YOU!!
HAHH!
HAHH!
SOHOKU
SOHOKU
総北
高校

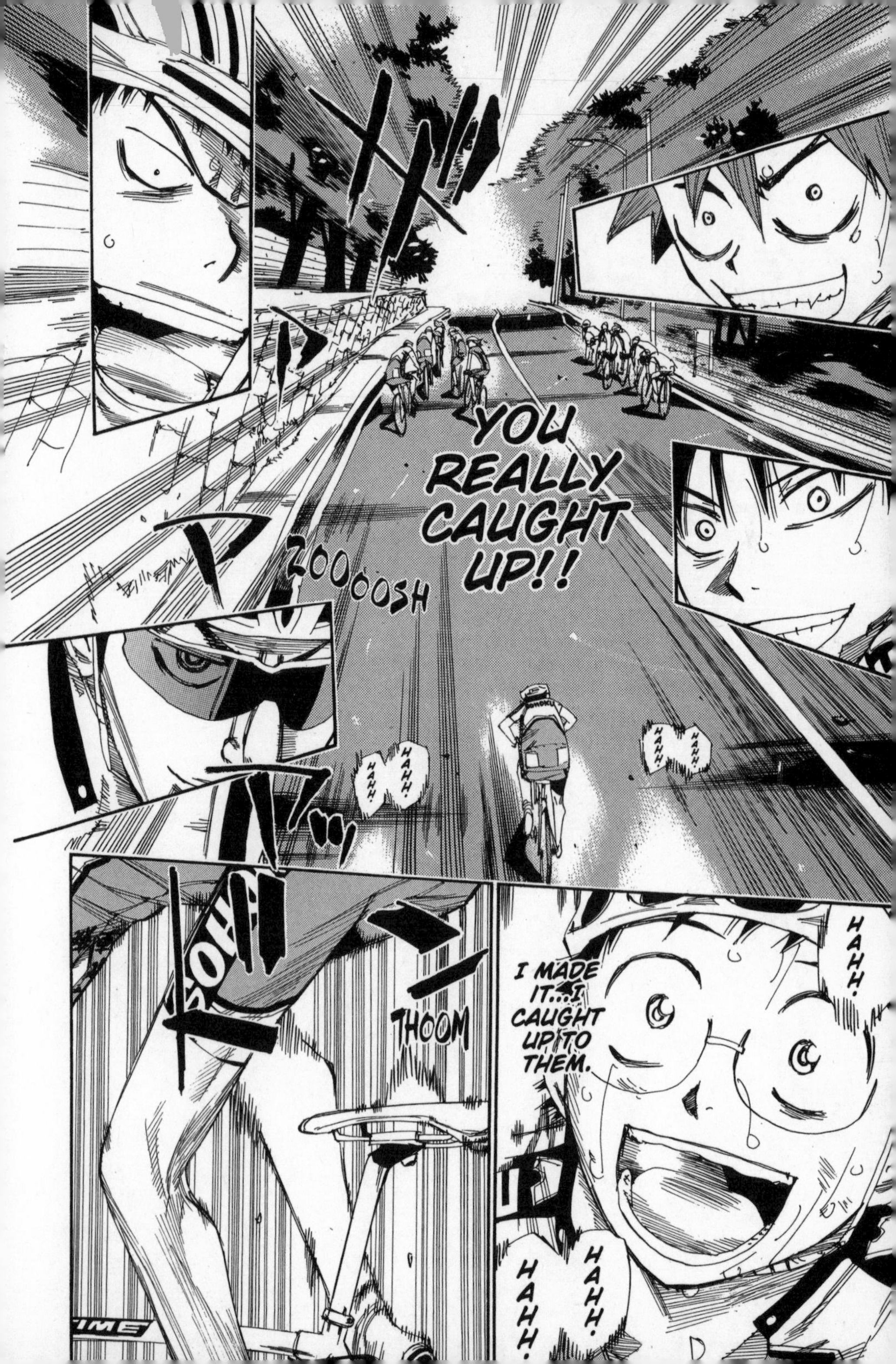
YOU REALLY CAUGHT UP!!
HAHH. HAHH.
ZOOOOSH
HAHH. HAHH.
HAHH.
I MADE IT...I CAUGHT UP TO THEM.
HAHH. HAHH.
THOOM

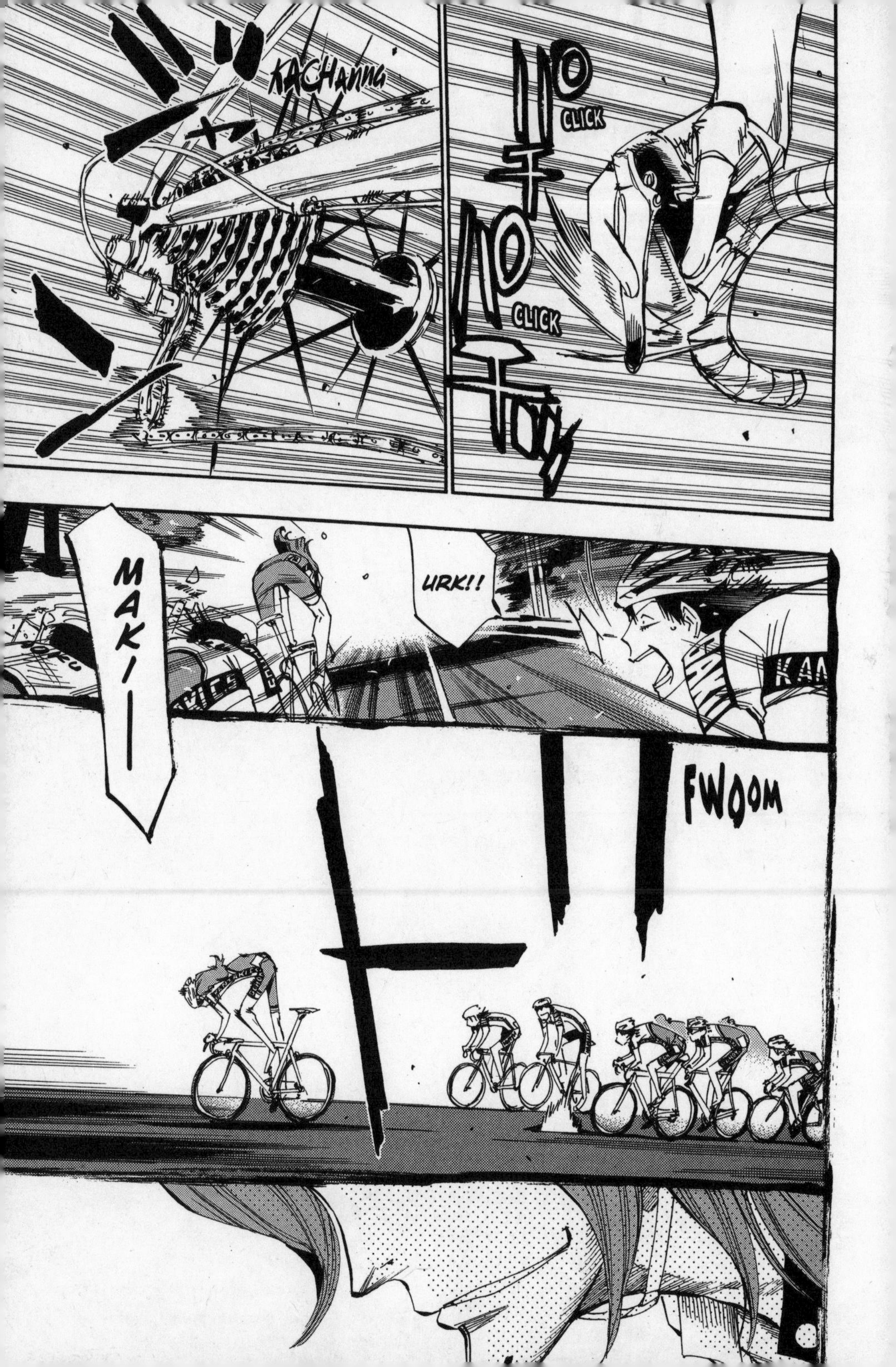
KACHANNG
CLICK
CLICK
URK!!
MAKI!!
FWOOM

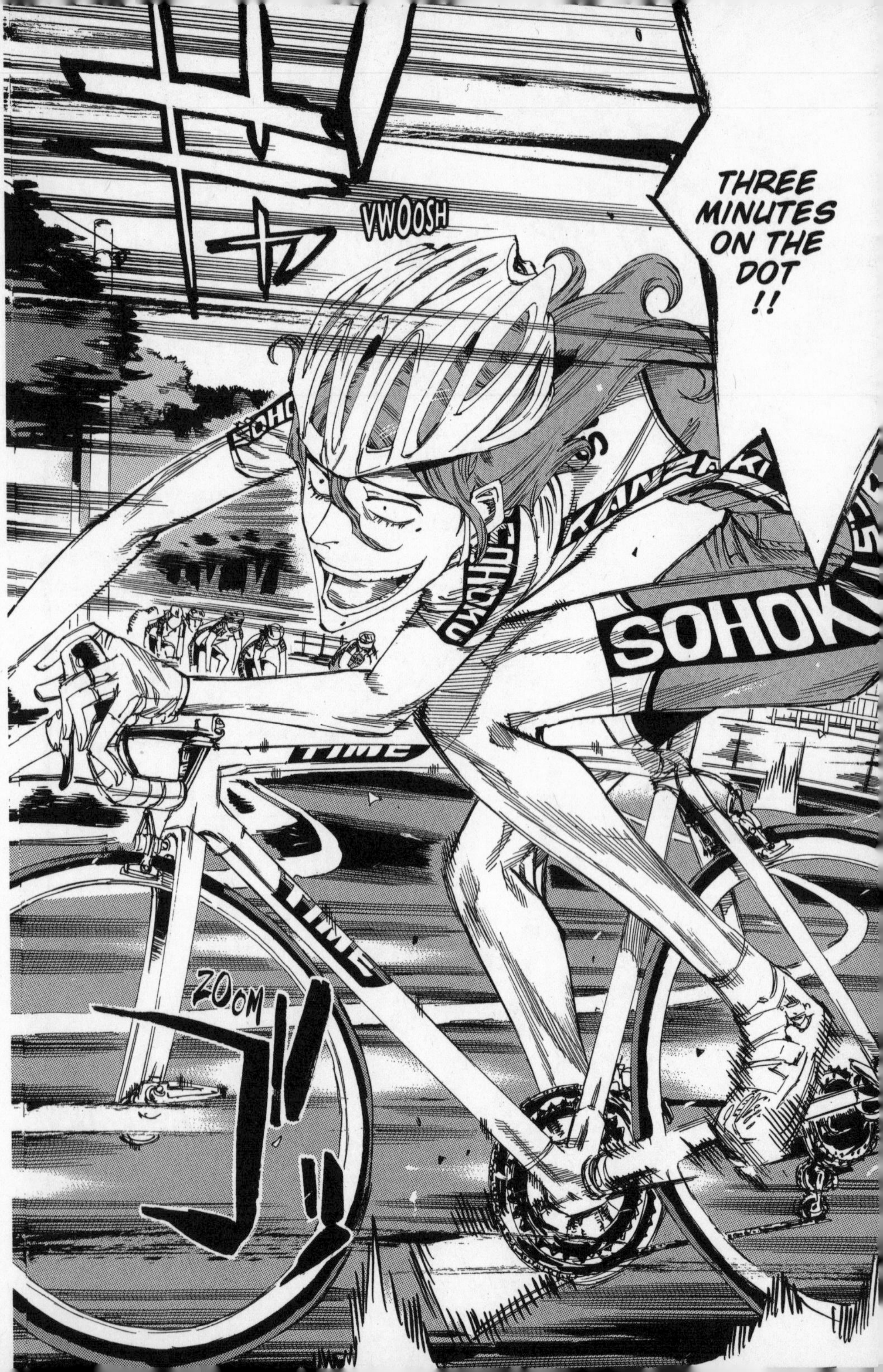
THREE MINUTES ON THE DOT !!
VWOOSH
TIME
ZOOM

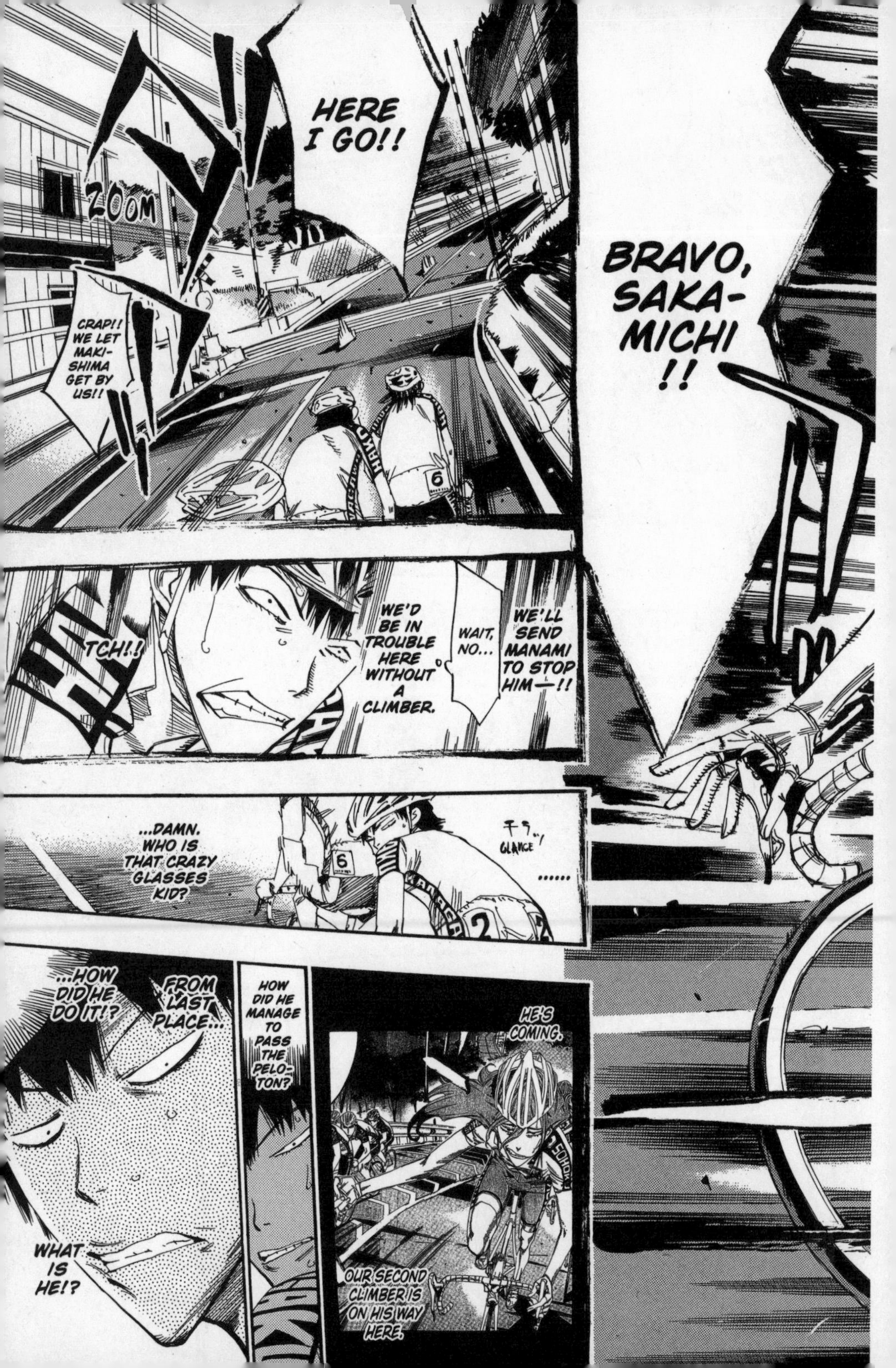
BRAVO, SAKA-MICHI!!
HERE I GO!!
ZOOM
CRAP!! WE LET MAKI-SHIMA GET BY US!!
WE'LL SEND MANAMI TO STOP HIM—!!
WAIT, NO...
WE'D BE IN TROUBLE HERE WITHOUT A CLIMBER.
TCH!!
GLANCE
......
...DAMN. WHO IS THAT CRAZY GLASSES KID?
HE'S COMING.
OUR SECOND CLIMBER IS ON HIS WAY HERE.
HOW DID HE MANAGE TO PASS THE PELO-TON?
FROM LAST PLACE...
...HOW DID HE DO IT!?
WHAT IS HE!?

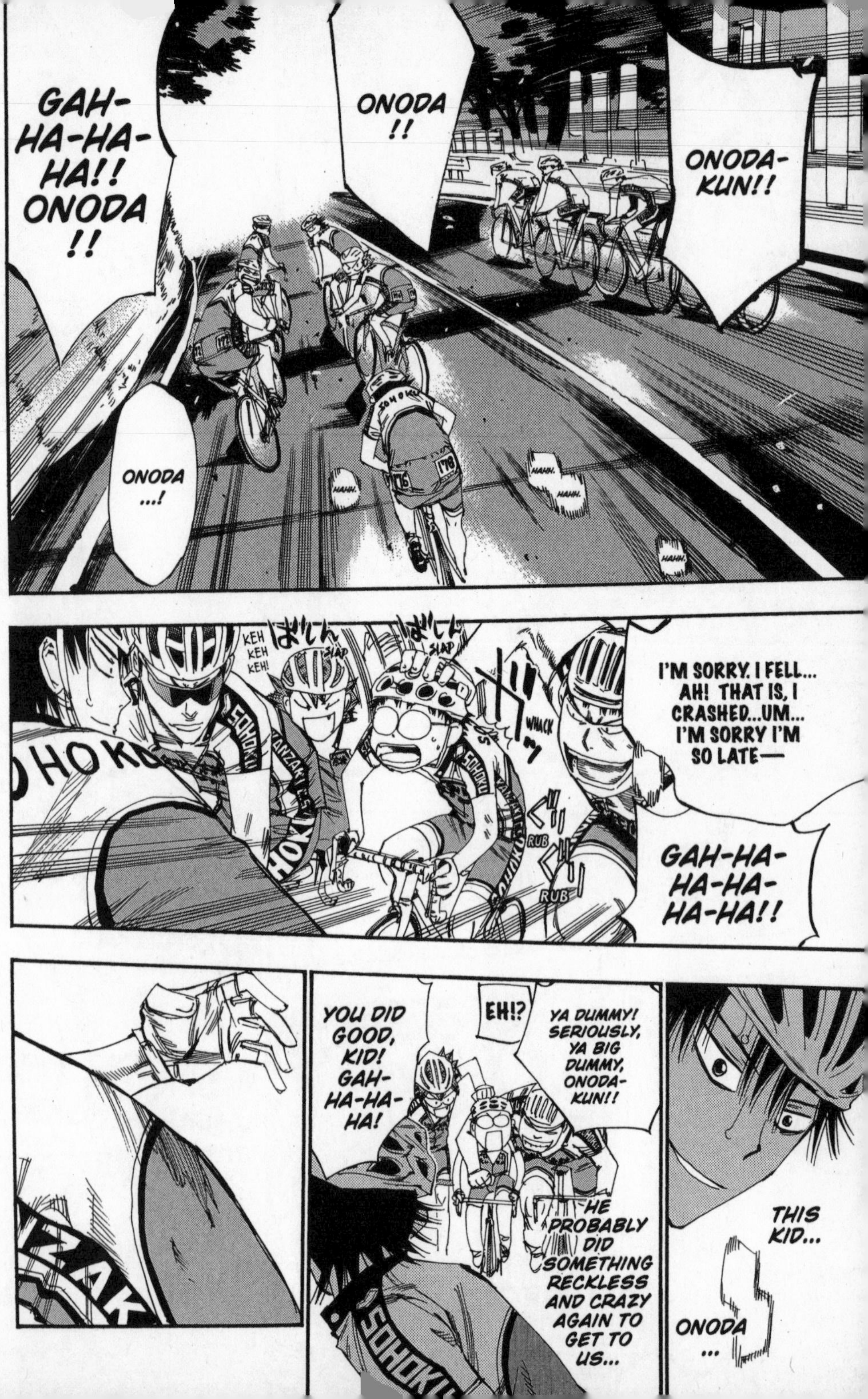
ONODA-KUN!!
ONODA !!
GAH-HA-HA-HA!! ONODA !!
ONODA ...!
HAHH.
HAHH.
HAHH.
HAHH.
I'M SORRY. I FELL... AH! THAT IS, I CRASHED...UM... I'M SORRY I'M SO LATE—
GAH-HA-HA-HA-HA-HA!!
WHACK
SLAP
SLAP
KEH KEH KEH!
RUB
RUB
THIS KID...
ONODA ...
YA DUMMY! SERIOUSLY, YA BIG DUMMY, ONODA-KUN!!
EH!?
YOU DID GOOD, KID! GAH-HA-HA-HA!
HE PROBABLY DID SOMETHING RECKLESS AND CRAZY AGAIN TO GET TO US...

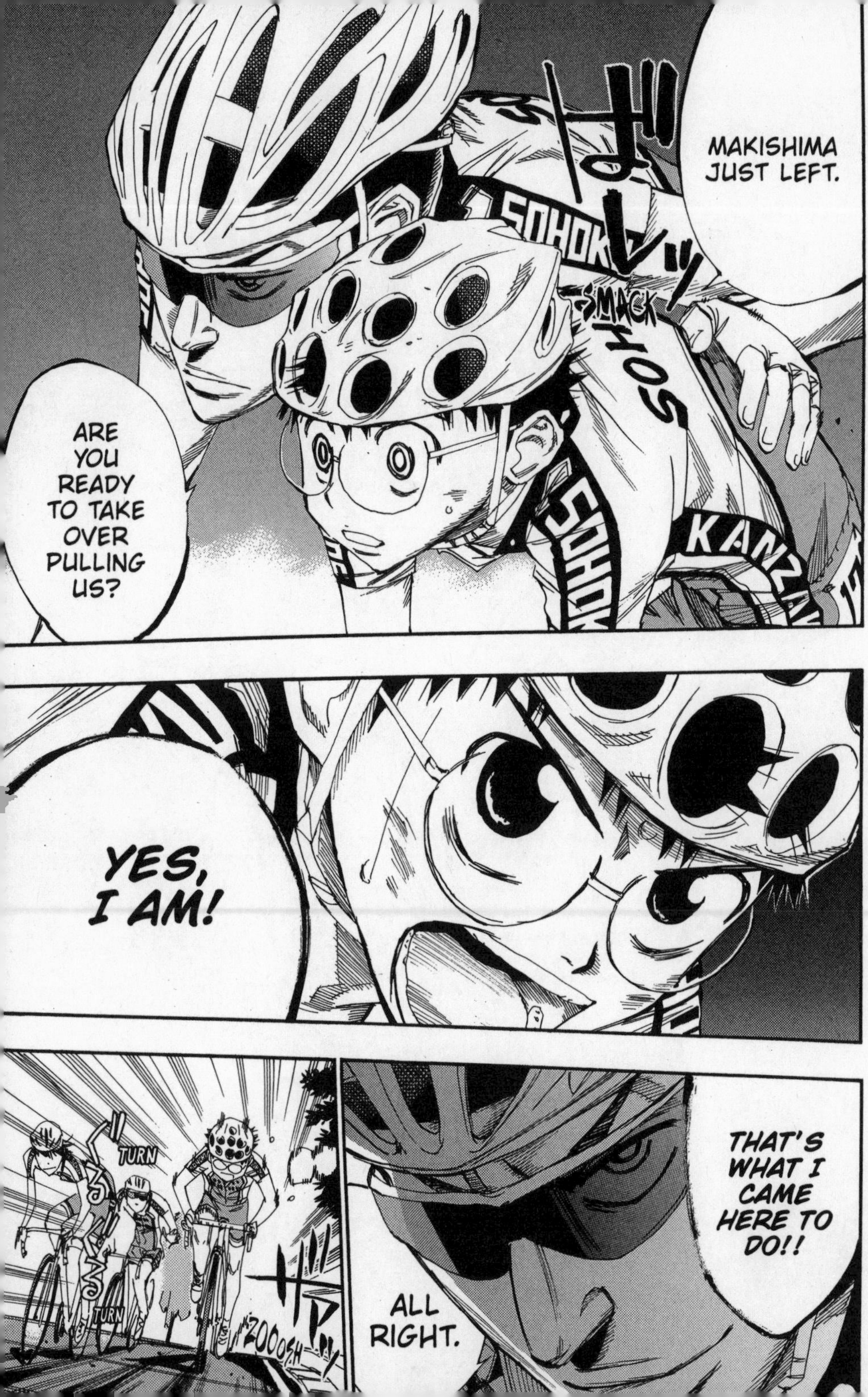
MAKISHIMA JUST LEFT.
SMACK
ARE YOU READY TO TAKE OVER PULLING US?
YES, I AM!
THAT'S WHAT I CAME HERE TO DO!!
ALL RIGHT.
TURN
TURN
ZOOOSH

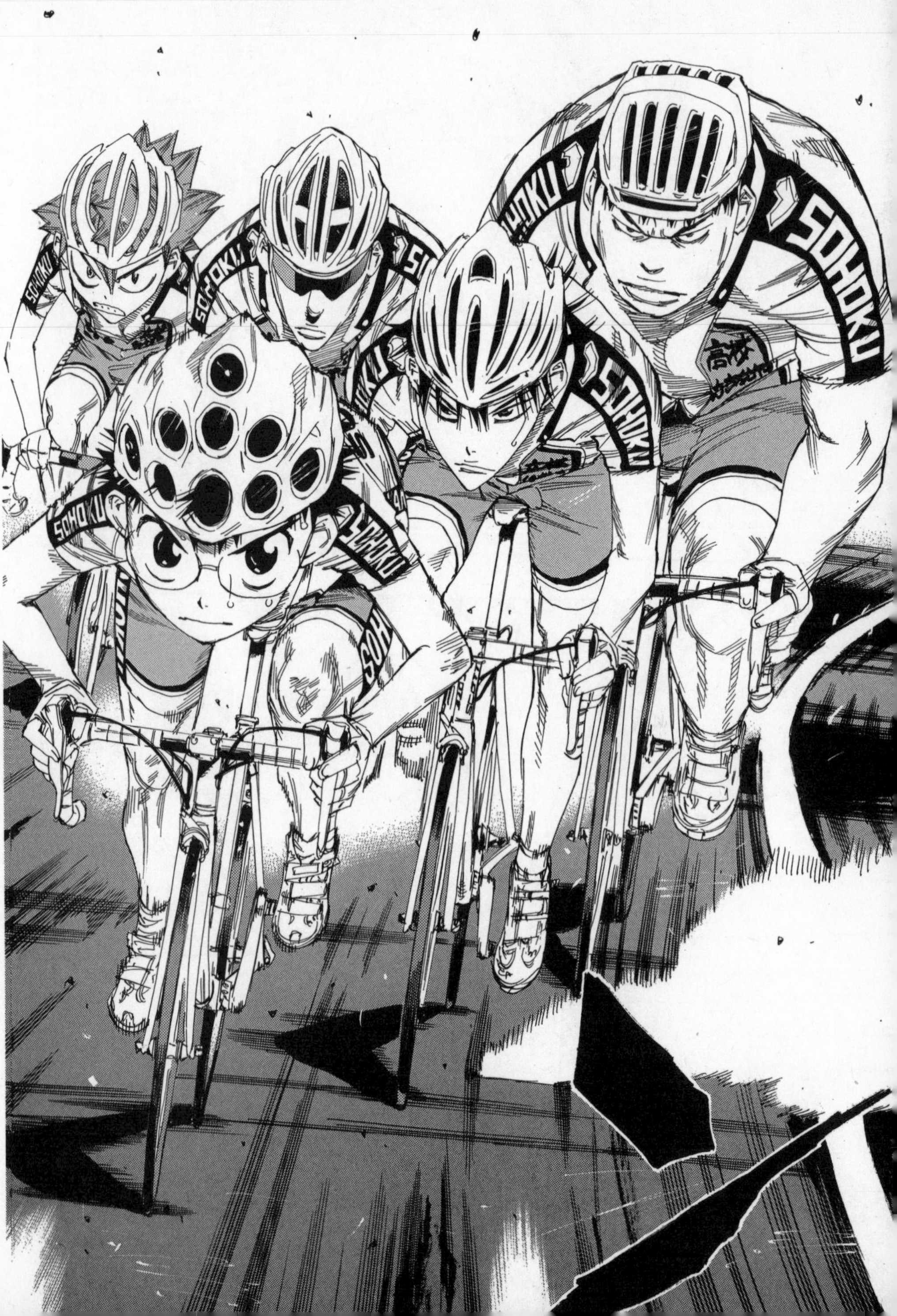
SOHOKU

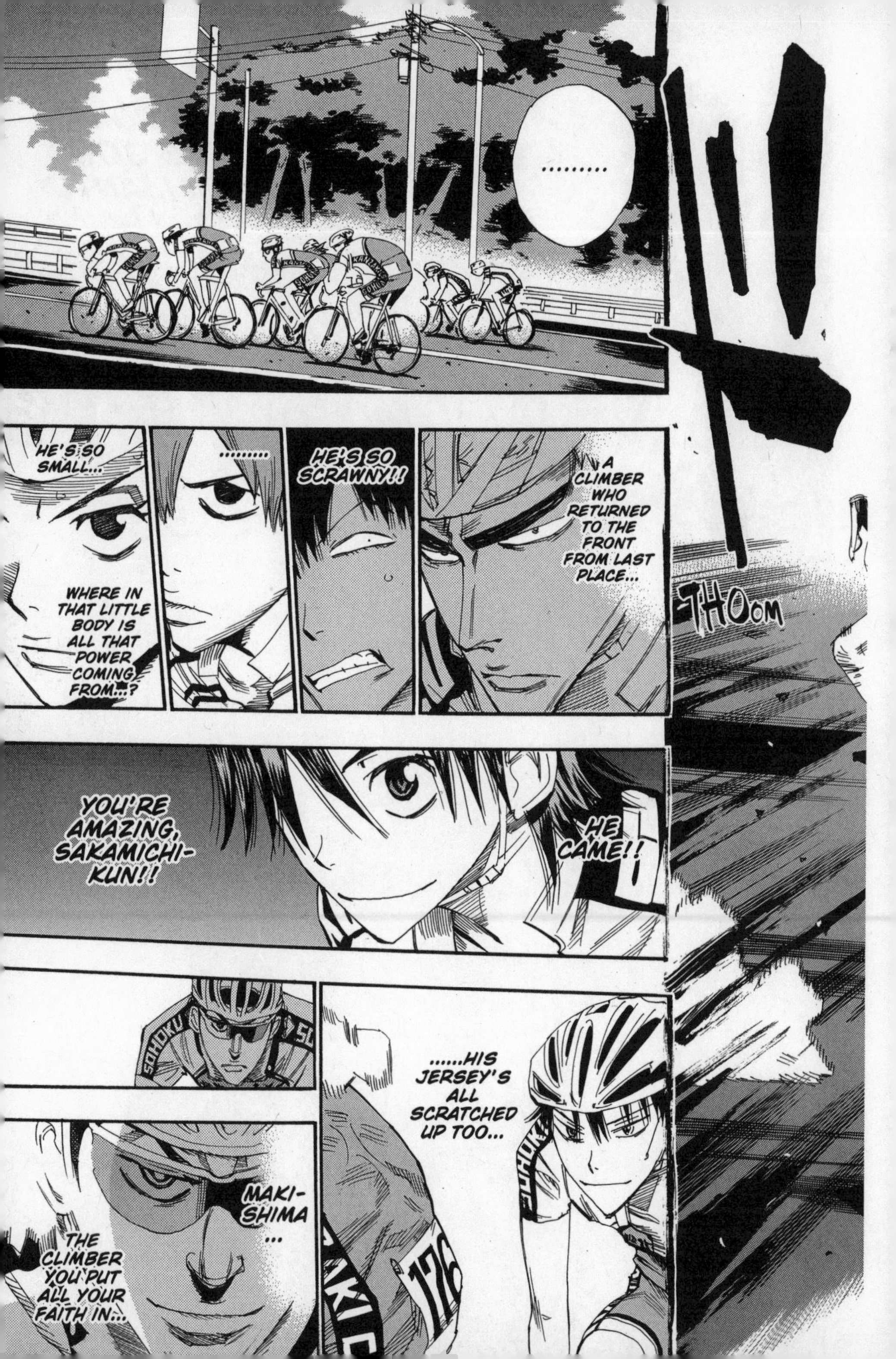
THOom
..........
A CLIMBER WHO RETURNED TO THE FRONT FROM LAST PLACE...
HE'S SO SCRAWNY!!
.........
HE'S SO SMALL...
WHERE IN THAT LITTLE BODY IS ALL THAT POWER COMING FROM...?
HE CAME!!
YOU'RE AMAZING, SAKAMICHI-KUN!!
......HIS JERSEY'S ALL SCRATCHED UP TOO...
MAKI-SHIMA ...
THE CLIMBER YOU PUT ALL YOUR FAITH IN...

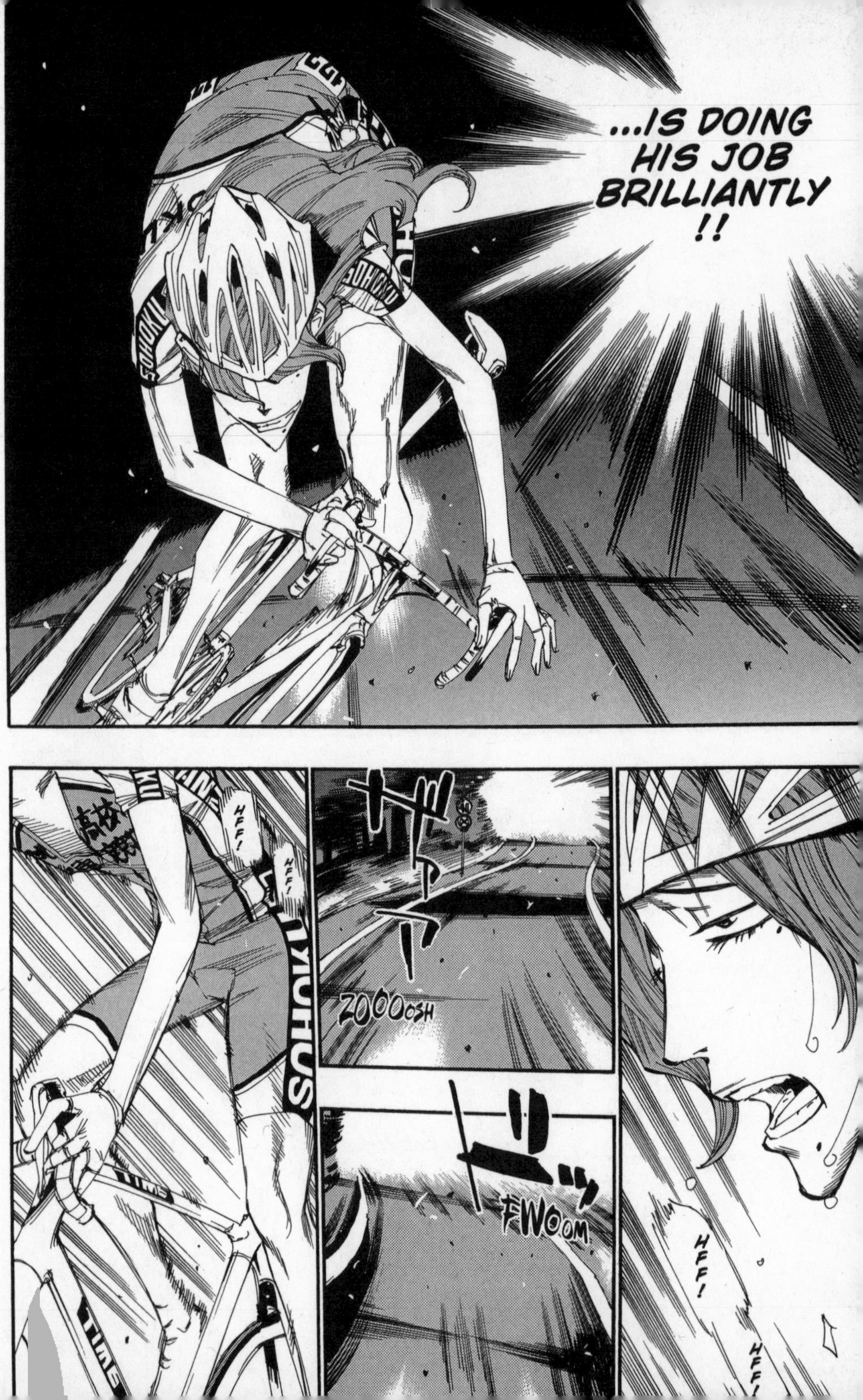
...IS DOING HIS JOB BRILLIANTLY !!
HFF!
HFF!
ZOOOOSH
FWOOM
HFF!
HFF!

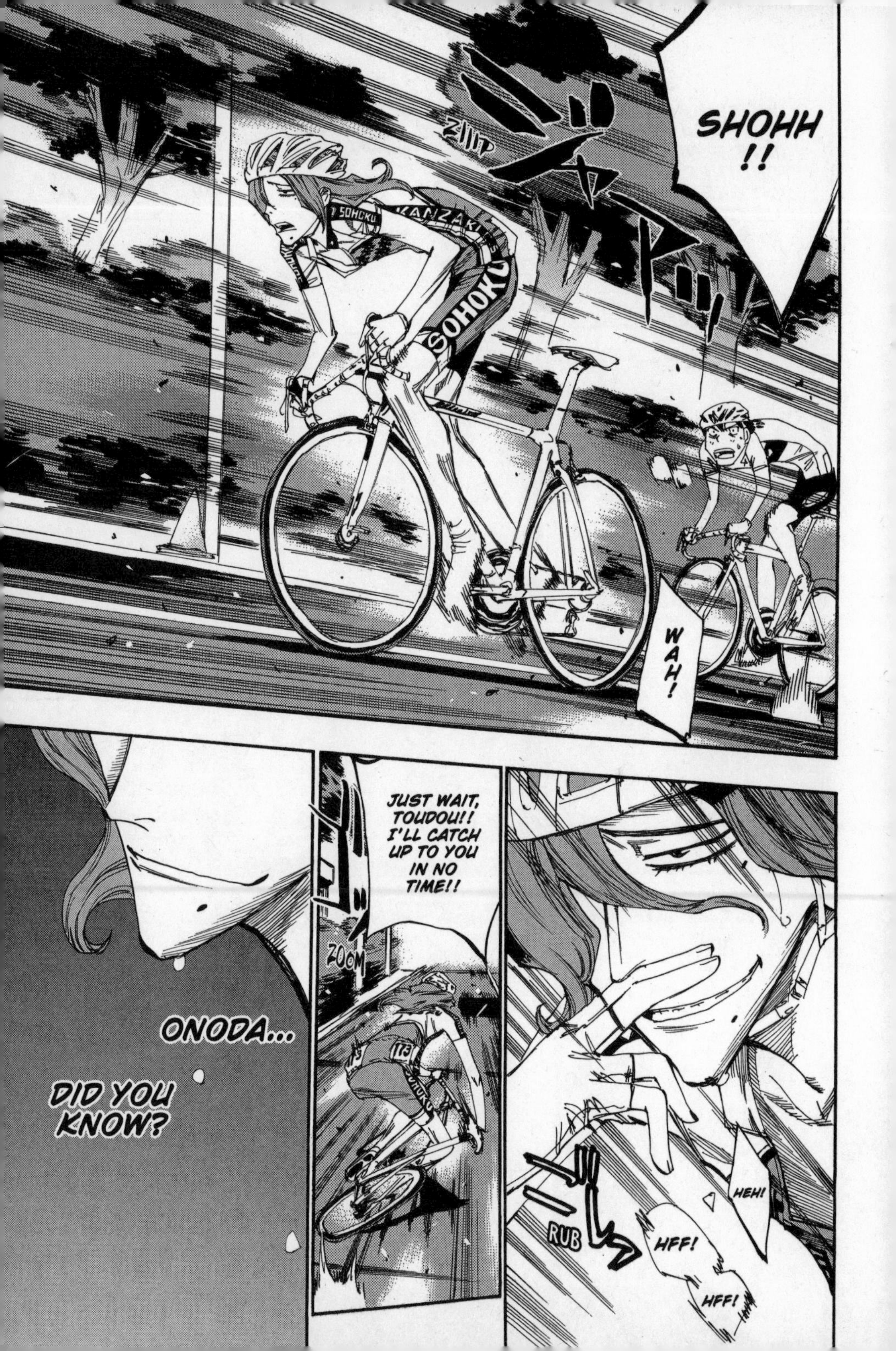
SHOHH !!
ZIIIP
WAH!
HEH!
RUB
HFF!
HFF!
JUST WAIT, TOUDOU!! I'LL CATCH UP TO YOU IN NO TIME!!
ZOOM
ONODA...
DID YOU KNOW?

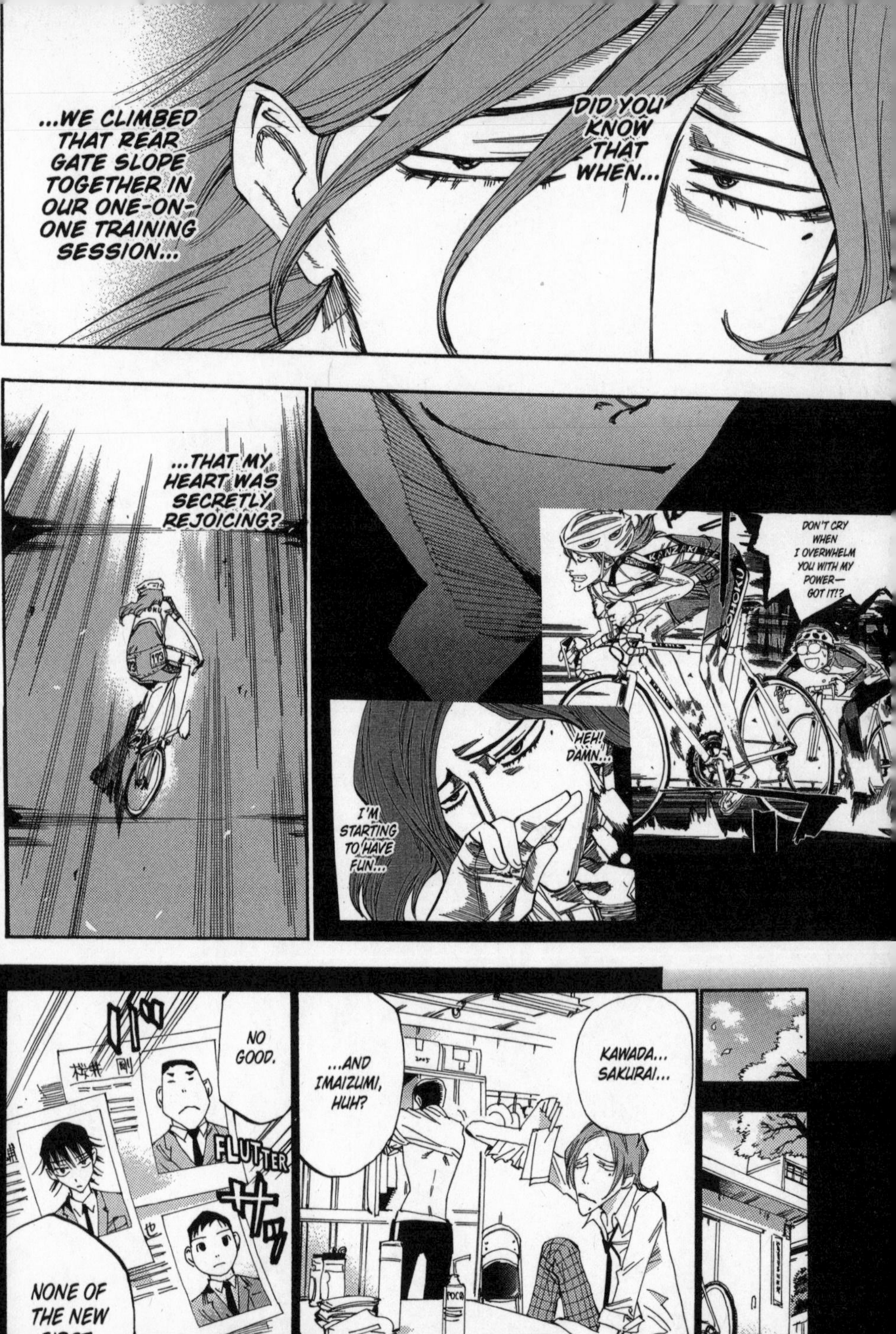
DID YOU KNOW THAT WHEN...
...WE CLIMBED THAT REAR GATE SLOPE TOGETHER IN OUR ONE-ON-ONE TRAINING SESSION...
DON'T CRY WHEN I OVERWHELM YOU WITH MY POWER—GOT IT!?
HEH! DAMN...
I'M STARTING TO HAVE FUN...
...THAT MY HEART WAS SECRETLY REJOICING?
KAWADA... SAKURAI...
...AND IMAIZUMI, HUH?
NO GOOD.
FLUTTER
NONE OF THE NEW FIRST-YEARS...

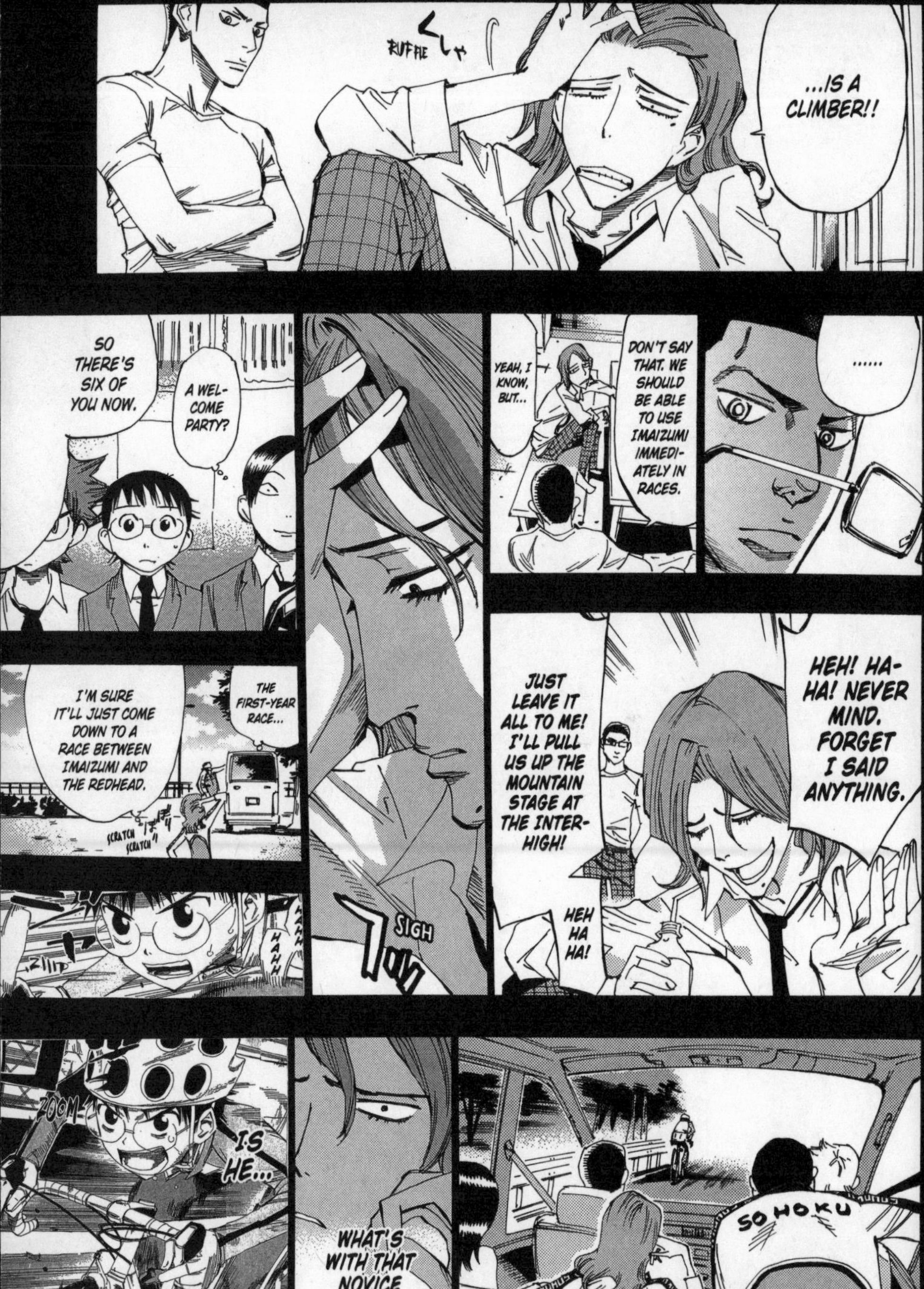

...IS A CLIMBER!!
RUFFLE
......
DON'T SAY THAT. WE SHOULD BE ABLE TO USE IMAIZUMI IMMEDIATELY IN RACES.
YEAH, I KNOW, BUT...
HEH! HA-HA! NEVER MIND. FORGET I SAID ANYTHING.
JUST LEAVE IT ALL TO ME! I'LL PULL US UP THE MOUNTAIN STAGE AT THE INTER-HIGH!
HEH HA HA!
SIGH
SO THERE'S SIX OF YOU NOW.
A WEL-COME PARTY?
THE FIRST-YEAR RACE...
I'M SURE IT'LL JUST COME DOWN TO A RACE BETWEEN IMAIZUMI AND THE REDHEAD.
SCRATCH SCRATCH
HAHH HAHH
WHAT'S WITH THAT NOVICE KID......?
IS HE...
ZOOM
SOHOKU

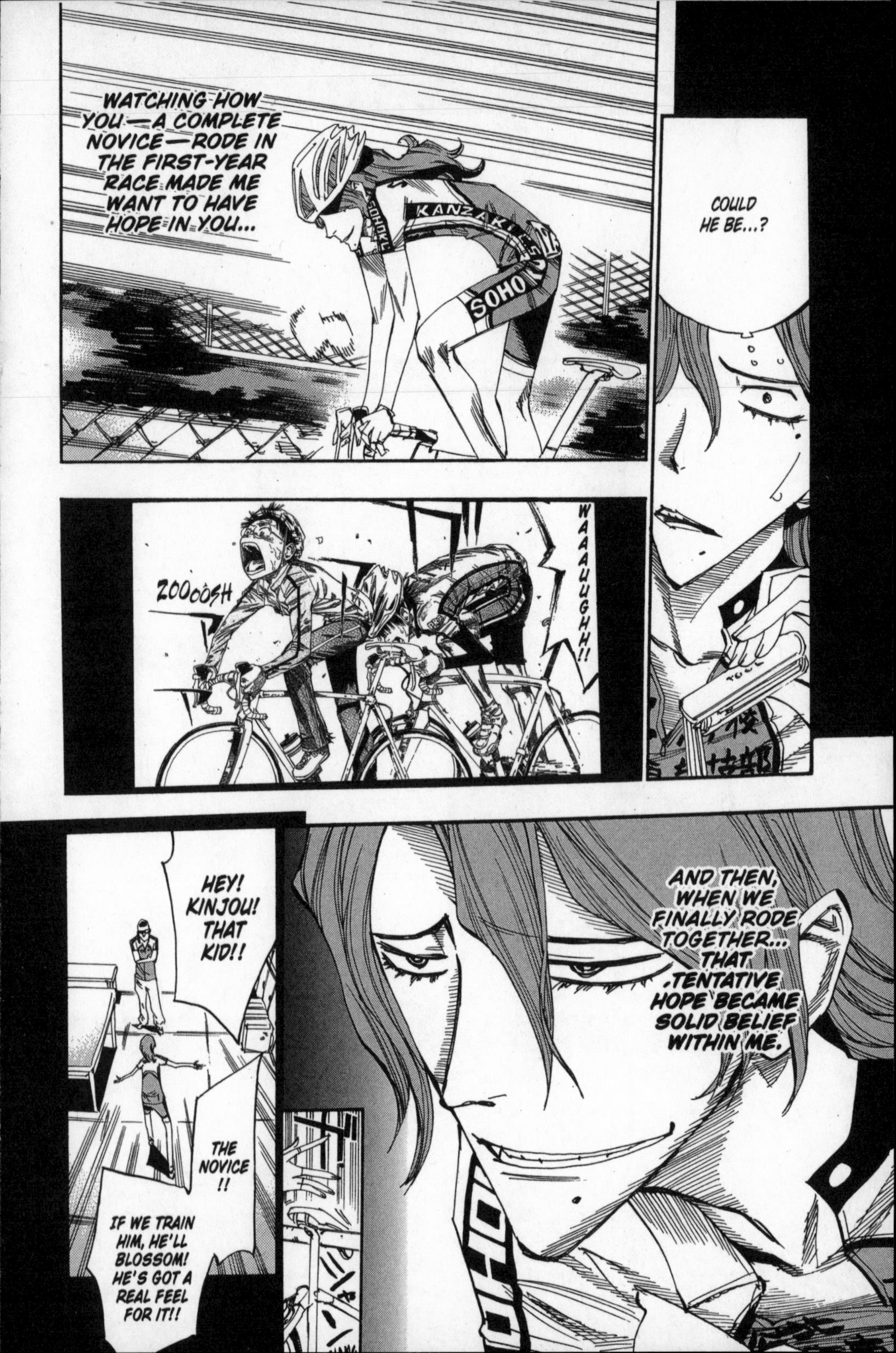
COULD HE BE...?
WATCHING HOW YOU—A COMPLETE NOVICE—RODE IN THE FIRST-YEAR RACE MADE ME WANT TO HAVE HOPE IN YOU...
WAAAAUGHH!!
ZOOOOSH
AND THEN, WHEN WE FINALLY RODE TOGETHER... THAT TENTATIVE HOPE BECAME SOLID BELIEF WITHIN ME.
HEY! KINJOU! THAT KID!!
THE NOVICE!!
IF WE TRAIN HIM, HE'LL BLOSSOM! HE'S GOT A REAL FEEL FOR IT!!

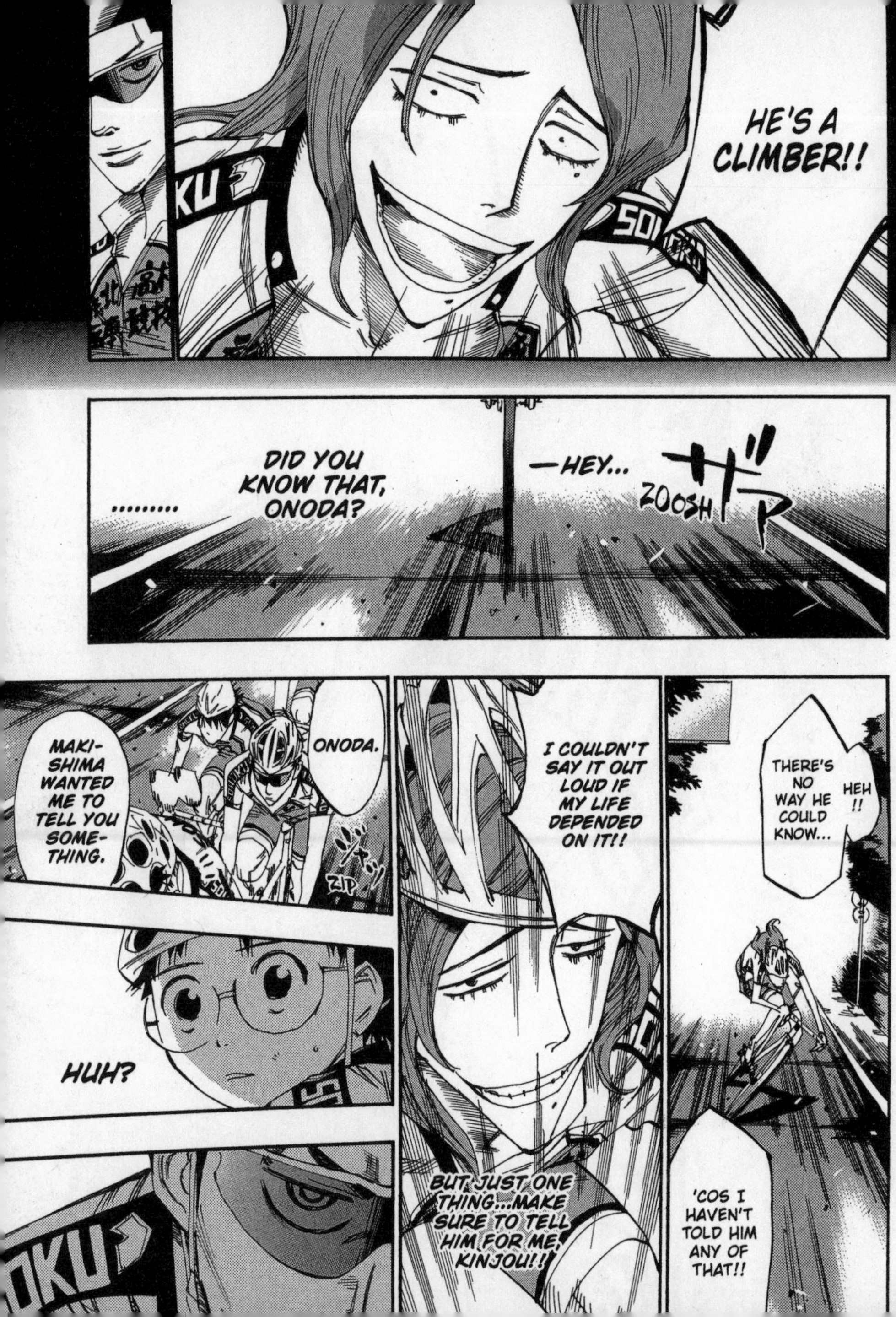
HE'S A CLIMBER!!
ZOOSH
—HEY...
DID YOU KNOW THAT, ONODA?
.........
HEH!!
THERE'S NO WAY HE COULD KNOW...
'COS I HAVEN'T TOLD HIM ANY OF THAT!!
I COULDN'T SAY IT OUT LOUD IF MY LIFE DEPENDED ON IT!!
BUT JUST ONE THING...MAKE SURE TO TELL HIM FOR ME, KINJOU!!
ONODA.
MAKI-SHIMA WANTED ME TO TELL YOU SOME-THING.
ZIP
HUH?

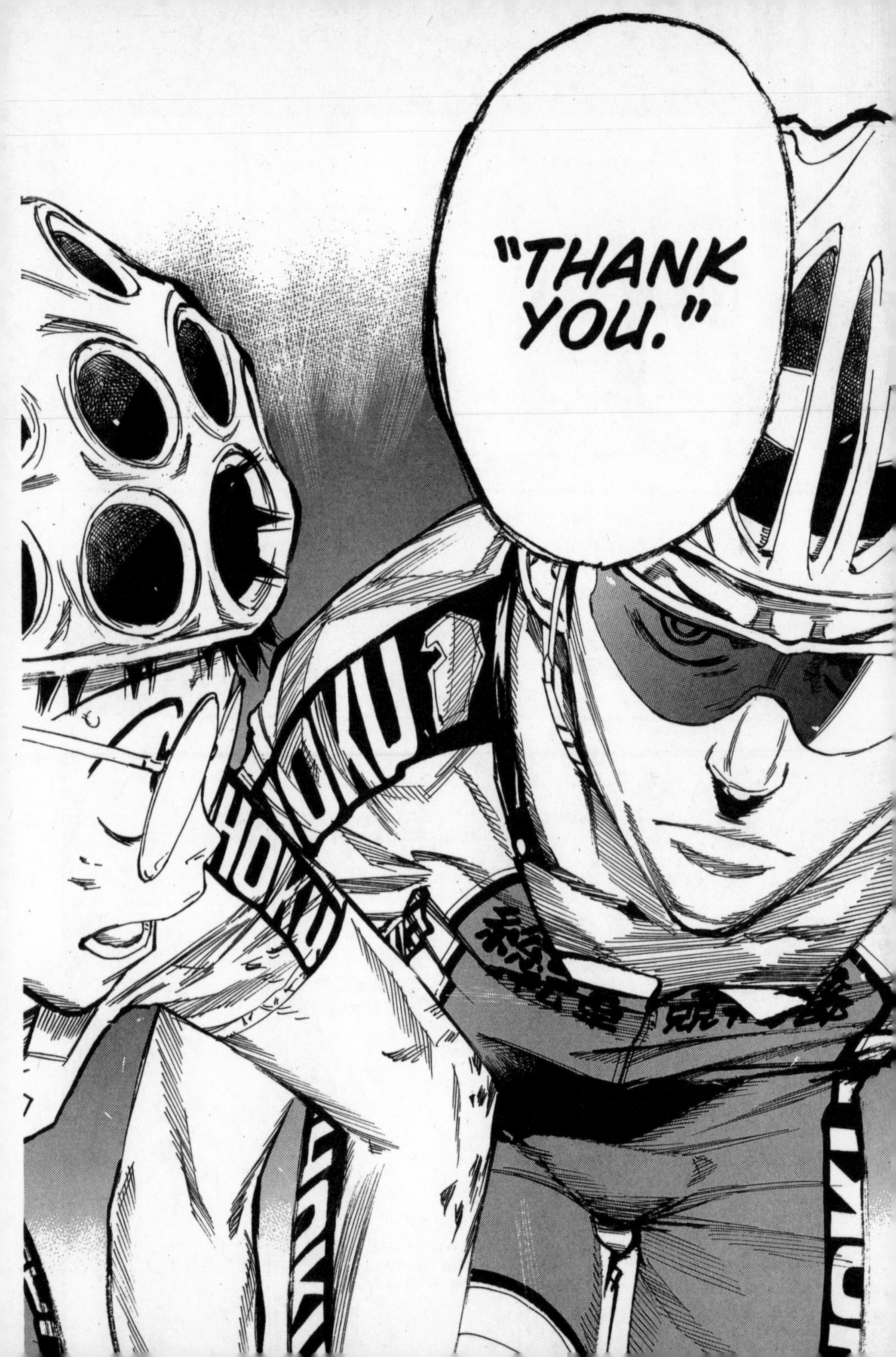
"THANK YOU."

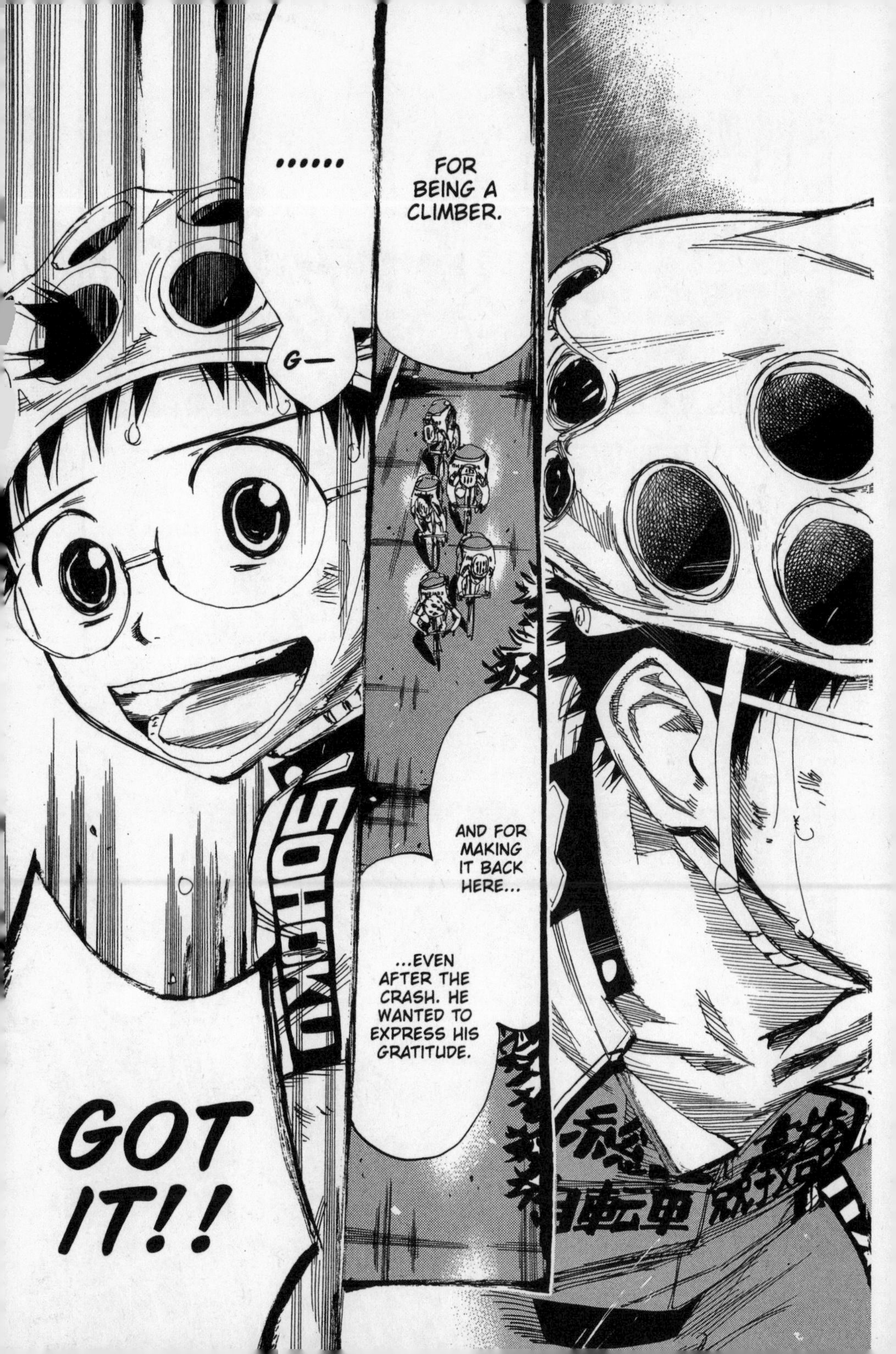
FOR BEING A CLIMBER.
AND FOR MAKING IT BACK HERE...
...EVEN AFTER THE CRASH. HE WANTED TO EXPRESS HIS GRATITUDE.
......
G—
GOT IT!!
SOHOKU

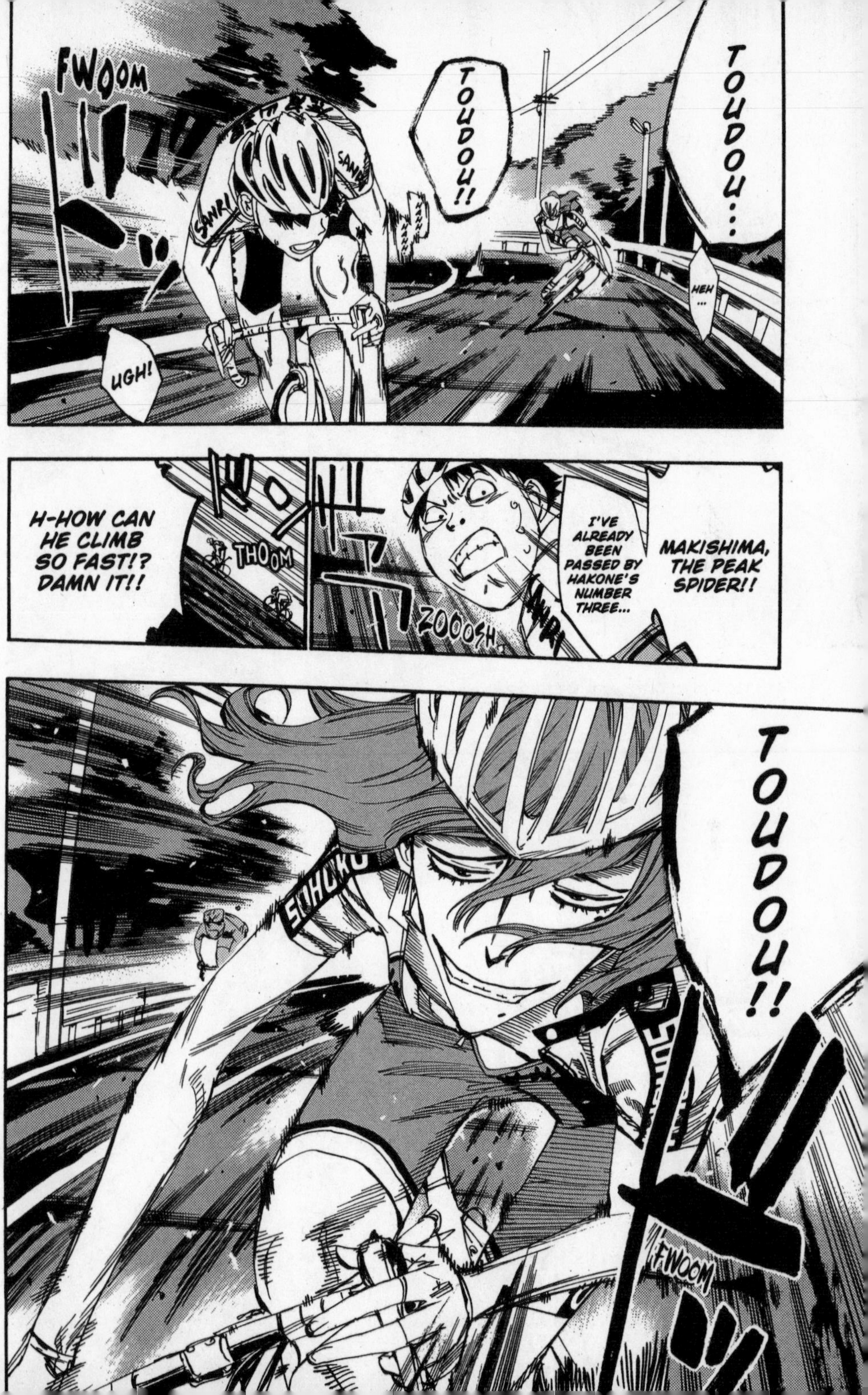
TOUDOU...
HEH...
TOUDOU!!
FWOOM
UGH!
MAKISHIMA, THE PEAK SPIDER!!
I'VE ALREADY BEEN PASSED BY HAKONE'S NUMBER THREE...
ZOOOSH
THOOM
H-HOW CAN HE CLIMB SO FAST!? DAMN IT!!
TOUDOU!!
FWOOM

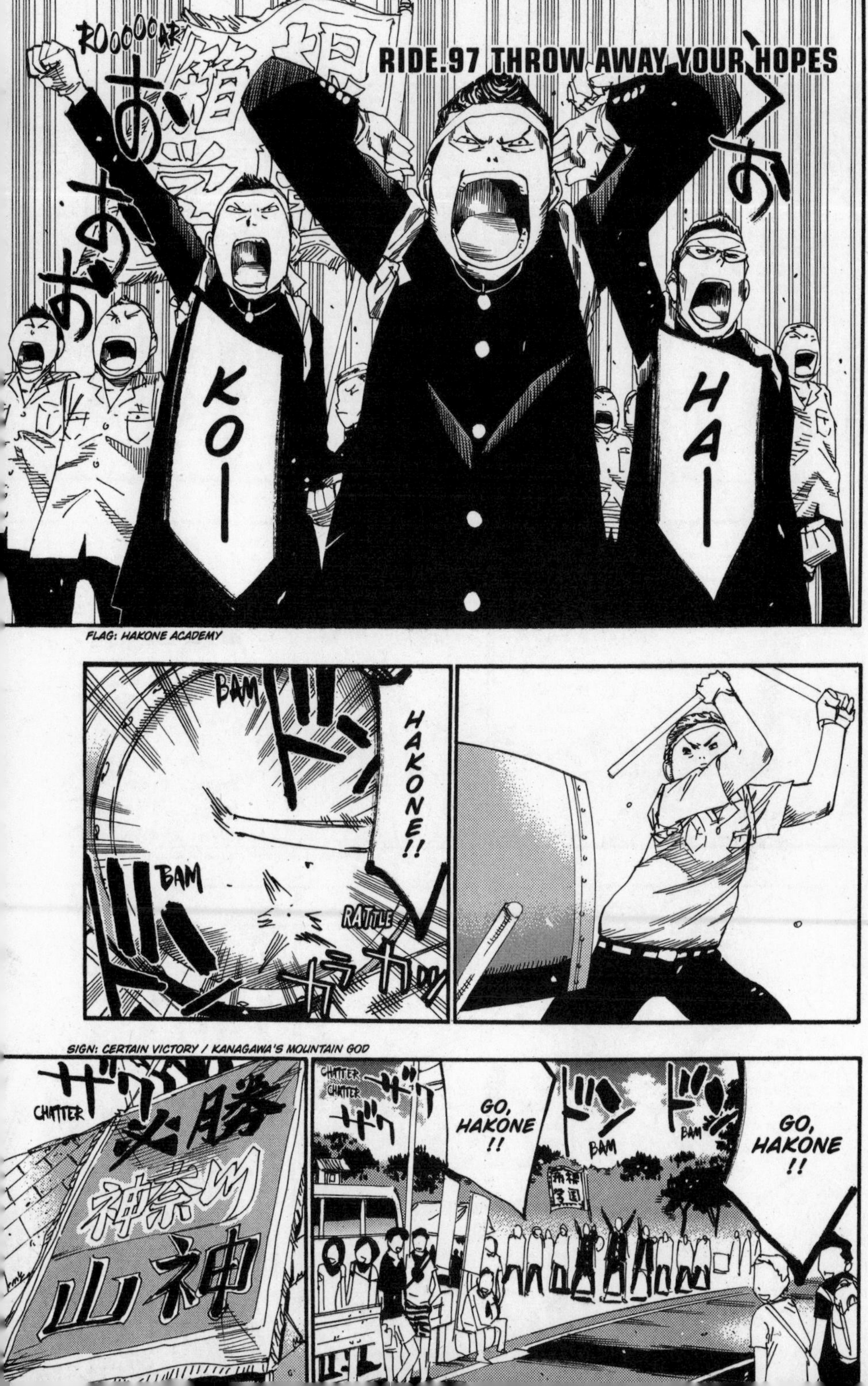
RIDE.97 THROW AWAY YOUR HOPES
ROOOOOAR
KO—
HA—
FLAG: HAKONE ACADEMY
HAKONE!!
BAM
BAM
RATTLE
SIGN: CERTAIN VICTORY / KANAGAWA'S MOUNTAIN GOD
GO, HAKONE!!
BAM
BAM
GO, HAKONE!!
CHATTER CHATTER
CHATTER

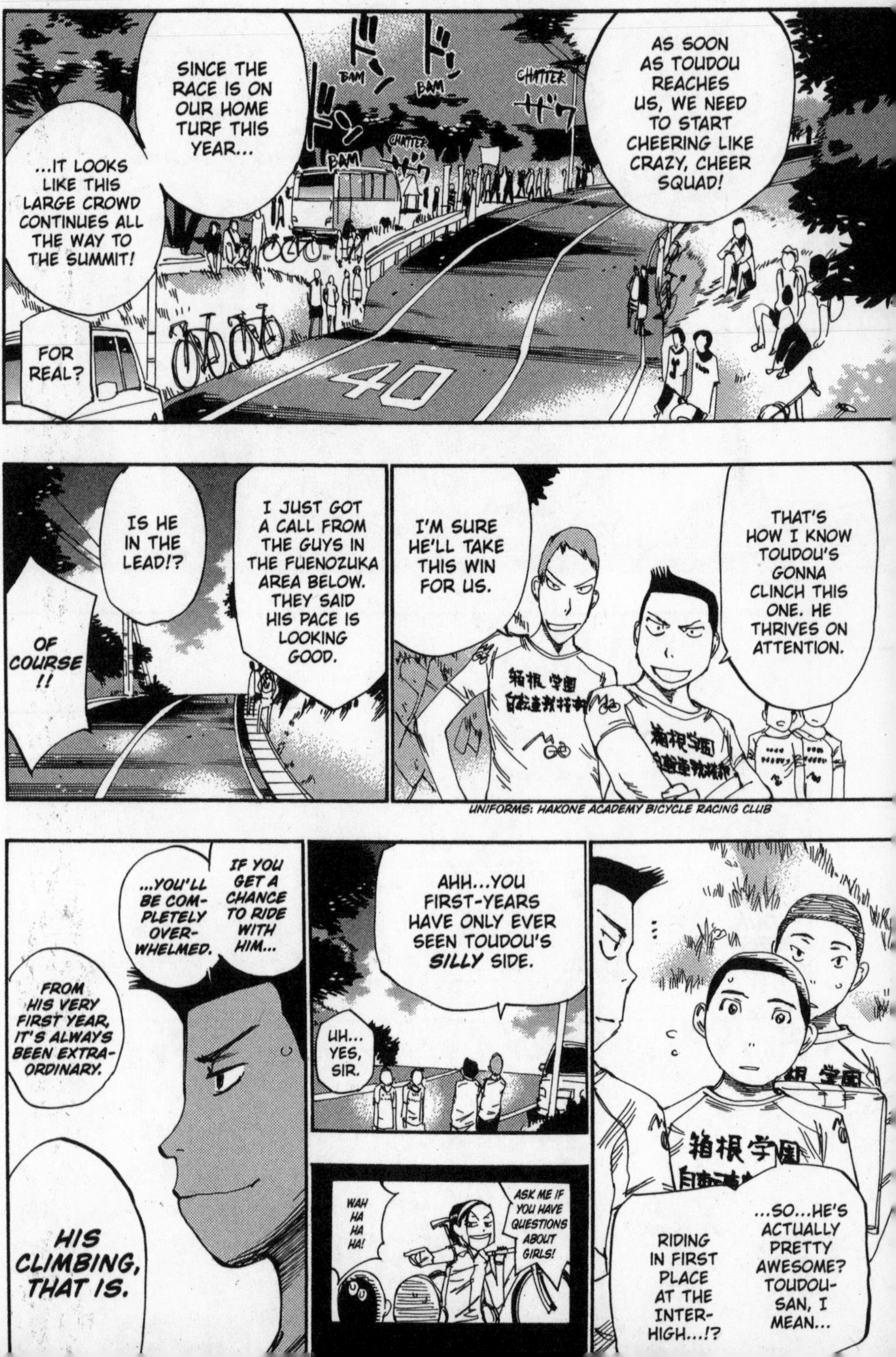
AS SOON AS TOUDOU REACHES US, WE NEED TO START CHEERING LIKE CRAZY, CHEER SQUAD!
CHATTER
BAM
BAM
CHATTER
BAM
SINCE THE RACE IS ON OUR HOME TURF THIS YEAR...
...IT LOOKS LIKE THIS LARGE CROWD CONTINUES ALL THE WAY TO THE SUMMIT!
FOR REAL?
THAT'S HOW I KNOW TOUDOU'S GONNA CLINCH THIS ONE. HE THRIVES ON ATTENTION.
I'M SURE HE'LL TAKE THIS WIN FOR US.
I JUST GOT A CALL FROM THE GUYS IN THE FUENOZUKA AREA BELOW. THEY SAID HIS PACE IS LOOKING GOOD.
IS HE IN THE LEAD!?
OF COURSE!!
UNIFORMS: HAKONE ACADEMY BICYCLE RACING CLUB
...SO...HE'S ACTUALLY PRETTY AWESOME? TOUDOU-SAN, I MEAN...
RIDING IN FIRST PLACE AT THE INTER-HIGH...!?
AHH...YOU FIRST-YEARS HAVE ONLY EVER SEEN TOUDOU'S SILLY SIDE.
UH... YES, SIR.
ASK ME IF YOU HAVE QUESTIONS ABOUT GIRLS!
WAH HA HA HA!
IF YOU GET A CHANCE TO RIDE WITH HIM...
...YOU'LL BE COM-PLETELY OVER-WHELMED.
FROM HIS VERY FIRST YEAR, IT'S ALWAYS BEEN EXTRA-ORDINARY.
HIS CLIMBING, THAT IS.

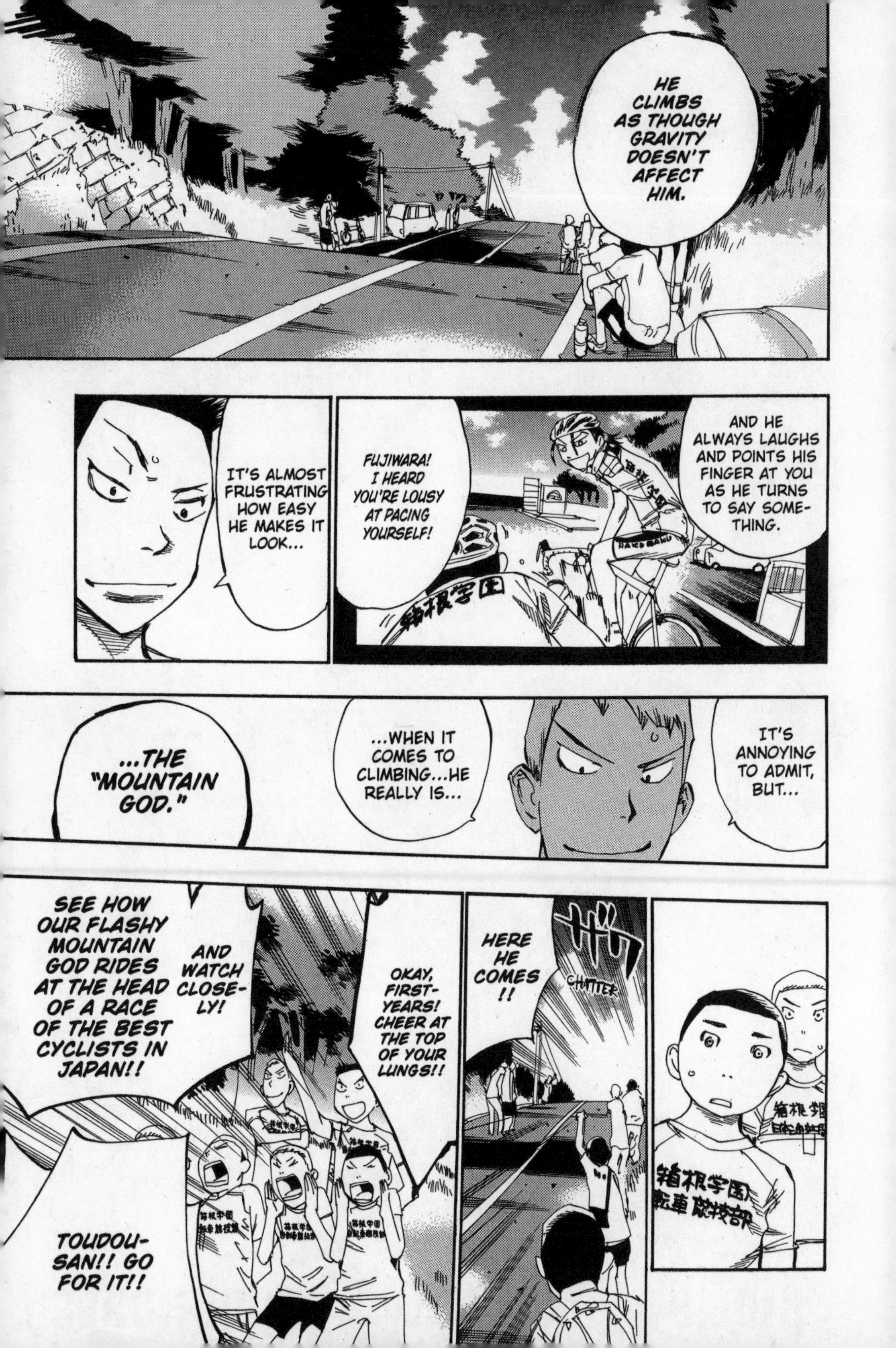
HE CLIMBS AS THOUGH GRAVITY DOESN'T AFFECT HIM.
AND HE ALWAYS LAUGHS AND POINTS HIS FINGER AT YOU AS HE TURNS TO SAY SOMETHING.
FUJIWARA! I HEARD YOU'RE LOUSY AT PACING YOURSELF!
IT'S ALMOST FRUSTRATING HOW EASY HE MAKES IT LOOK...
IT'S ANNOYING TO ADMIT, BUT...
...WHEN IT COMES TO CLIMBING...HE REALLY IS...
...THE "MOUNTAIN GOD."
HERE HE COMES!!
CHATTER
OKAY, FIRST-YEARS! CHEER AT THE TOP OF YOUR LUNGS!!
AND WATCH CLOSELY!
SEE HOW OUR FLASHY MOUNTAIN GOD RIDES AT THE HEAD OF A RACE OF THE BEST CYCLISTS IN JAPAN!!
TOUDOU-SAN!! GO FOR IT!!

# RIDE.97 THROW AWAY YOUR HOPES

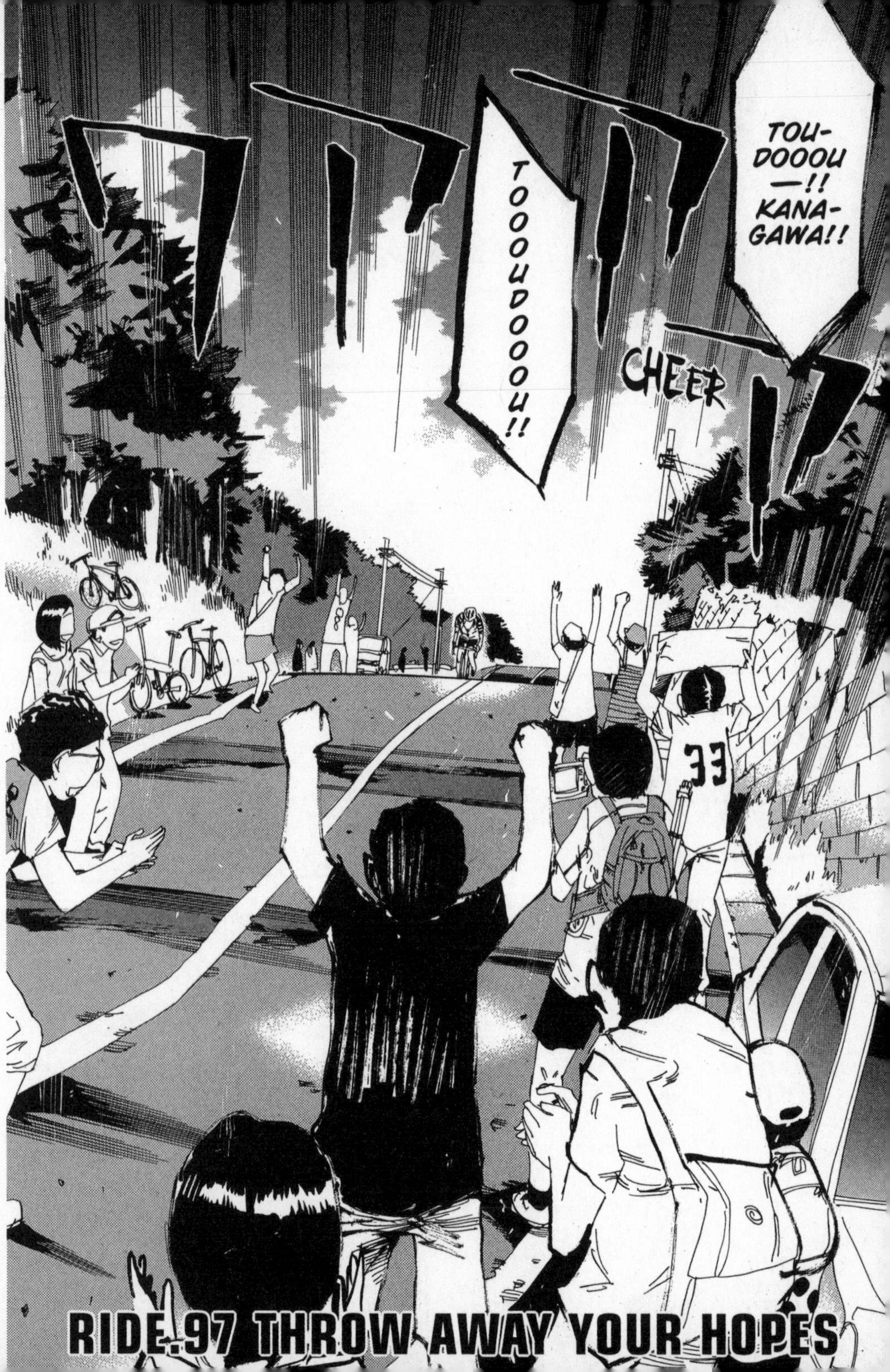
TOU-DOOOU—!! KANA-GAWA!!
TOOOOUDOOOOU!!
CHEER

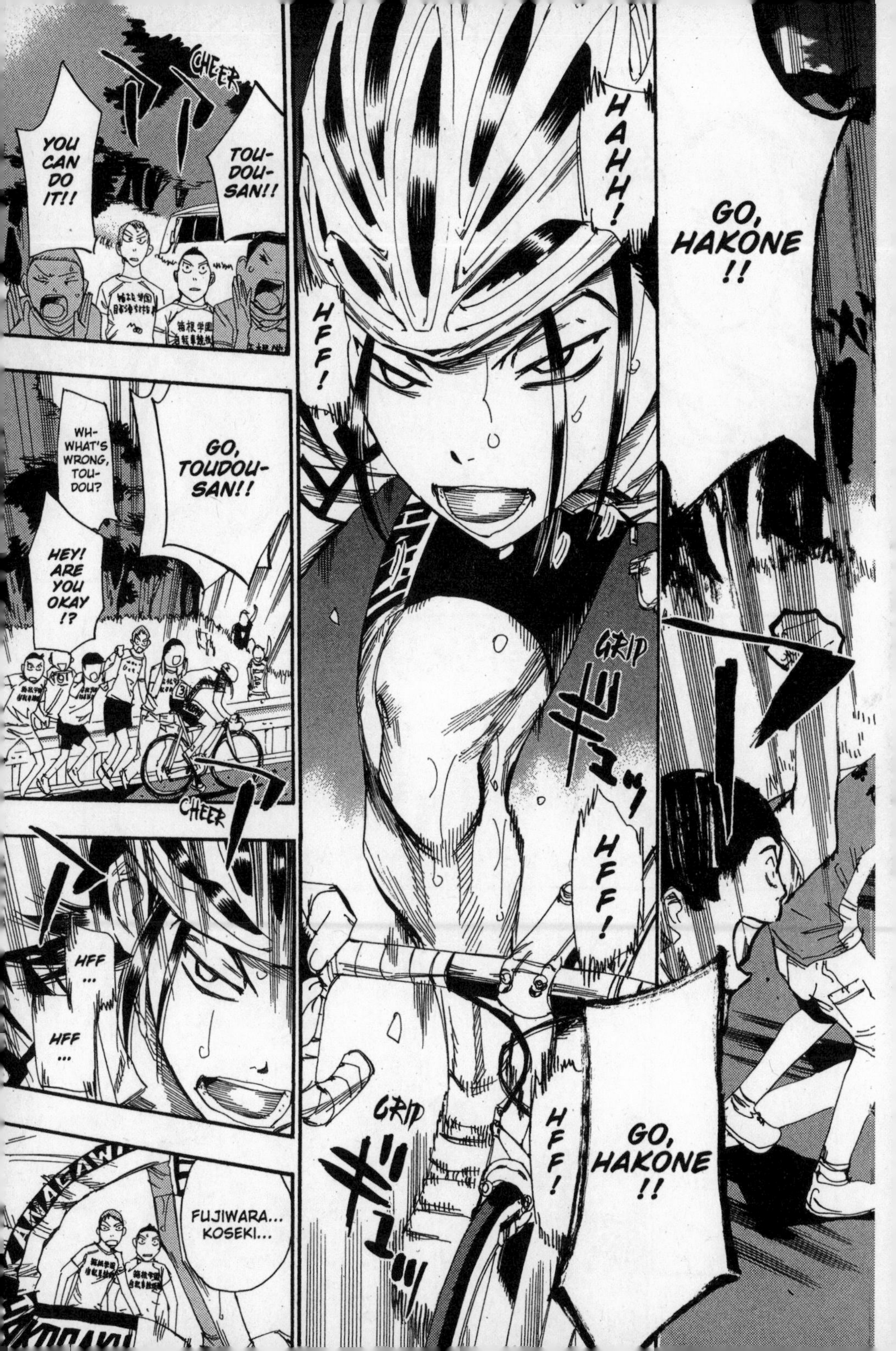
GO, HAKONE !!
GO, HAKONE !!
HAHH!
HFF!
GRIP
HFF!
GRIP
HFF!
CHEER
TOU-DOU-SAN!!
YOU CAN DO IT!!
GO, TOUDOU-SAN!!
WH-WHAT'S WRONG, TOU-DOU?
HEY! ARE YOU OKAY !?
CHEER
HFF ...
HFF ...
FUJIWARA... KOSEKI...

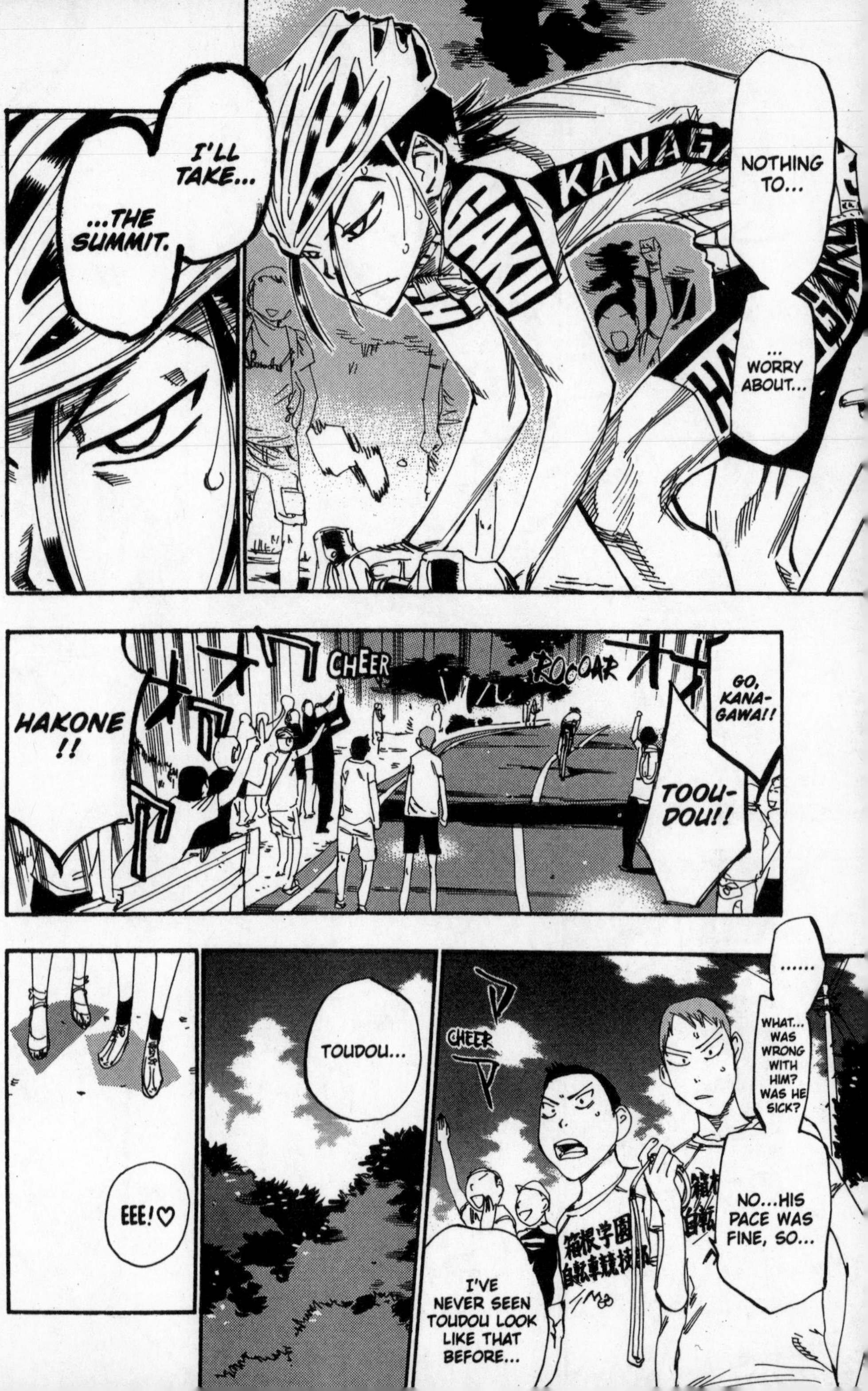
NOTHING TO...
...WORRY ABOUT...
I'LL TAKE...
...THE SUMMIT.
GO, KANA-GAWA!!
ROOOAR
CHEER
TOOU-DOU!!
HAKONE!!
......
WHAT... WAS WRONG WITH HIM? WAS HE SICK?
CHEER
NO...HIS PACE WAS FINE, SO...
箱根学園自転車競技部
I'VE NEVER SEEN TOUDOU LOOK LIKE THAT BEFORE...
TOUDOU...
EEE!♡

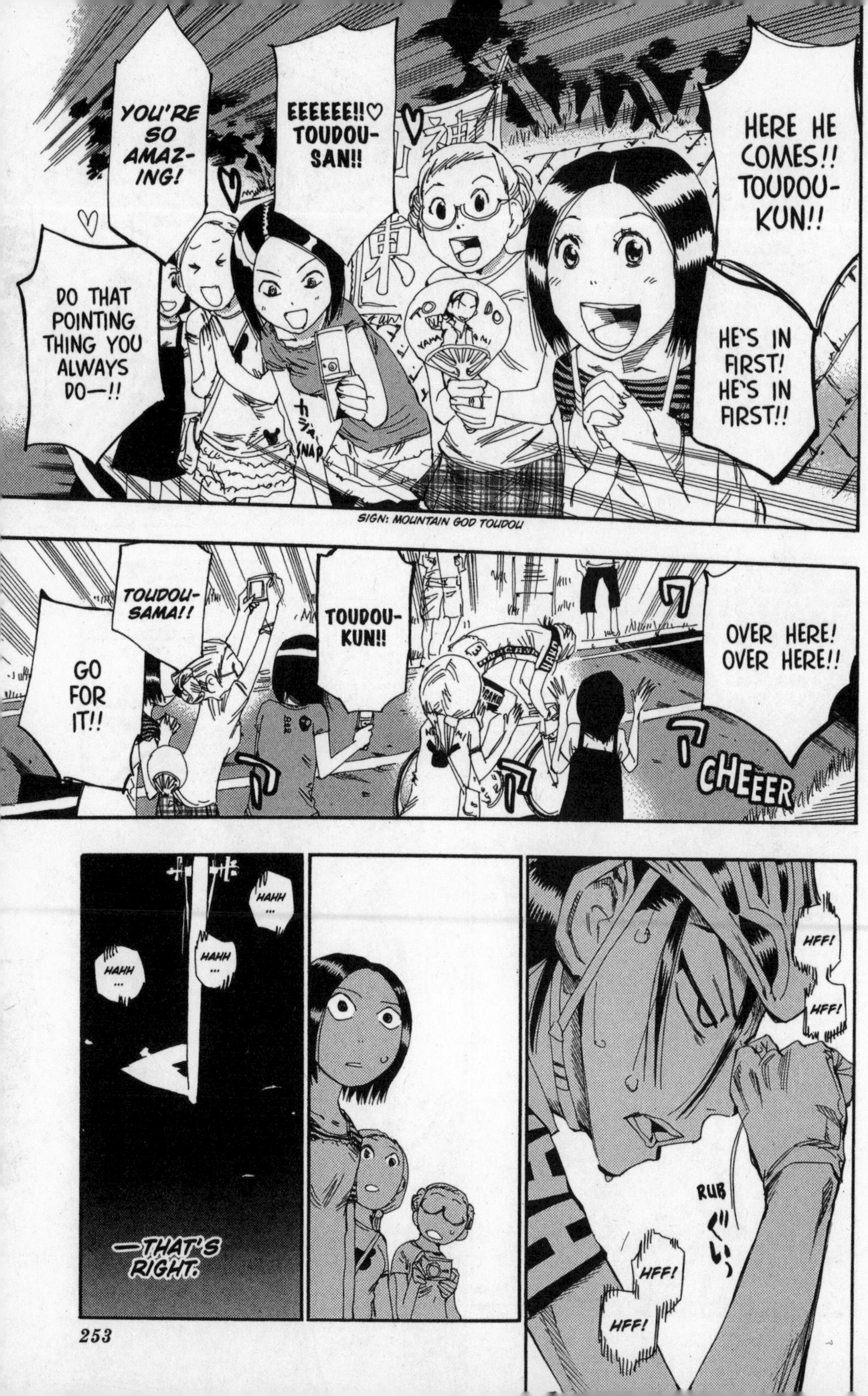
HERE HE COMES!! TOUDOU-KUN!!
HE'S IN FIRST! HE'S IN FIRST!!
EEEEEE!!♡ TOUDOU-SAN!!
YOU'RE SO AMAZ-ING!
DO THAT POINTING THING YOU ALWAYS DO—!!
SNAP
SIGN: MOUNTAIN GOD TOUDOU
OVER HERE! OVER HERE!!
TOUDOU-KUN!!
TOUDOU-SAMA!!
GO FOR IT!!
CHEEER
HFF!
HFF!
RUB
HFF!
HFF!
HAHH...
HAHH...
HAHH...
—THAT'S RIGHT.

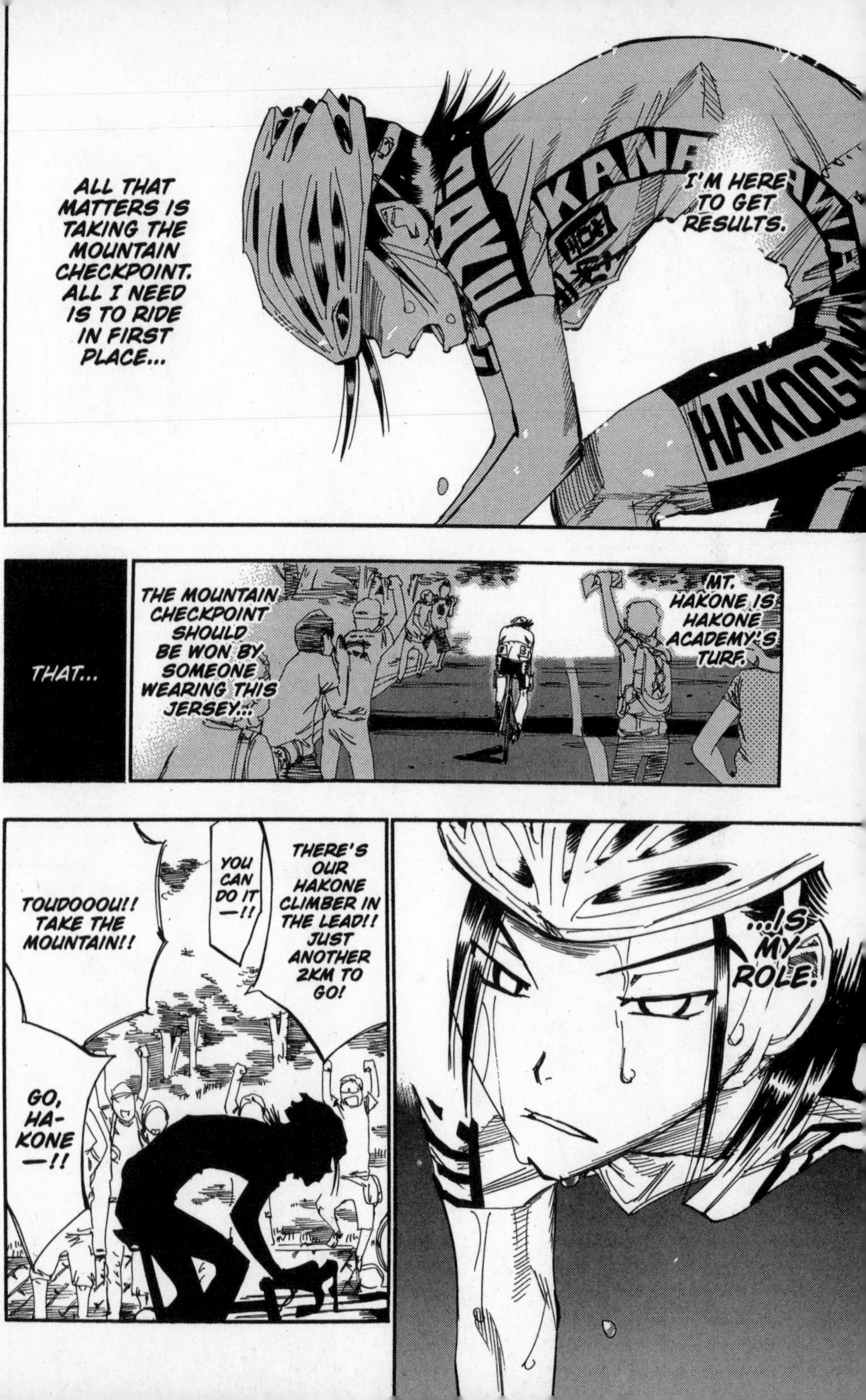
I'M HERE TO GET RESULTS.
ALL THAT MATTERS IS TAKING THE MOUNTAIN CHECKPOINT. ALL I NEED IS TO RIDE IN FIRST PLACE...
MT. HAKONE IS HAKONE ACADEMY'S TURF.
THE MOUNTAIN CHECKPOINT SHOULD BE WON BY SOMEONE WEARING THIS JERSEY...
THAT...
...IS MY ROLE.
THERE'S OUR HAKONE CLIMBER IN THE LEAD!! JUST ANOTHER 2KM TO GO!
YOU CAN DO IT—!!
TOUDOOOU!! TAKE THE MOUNTAIN!!
GO, HAKONE—!!

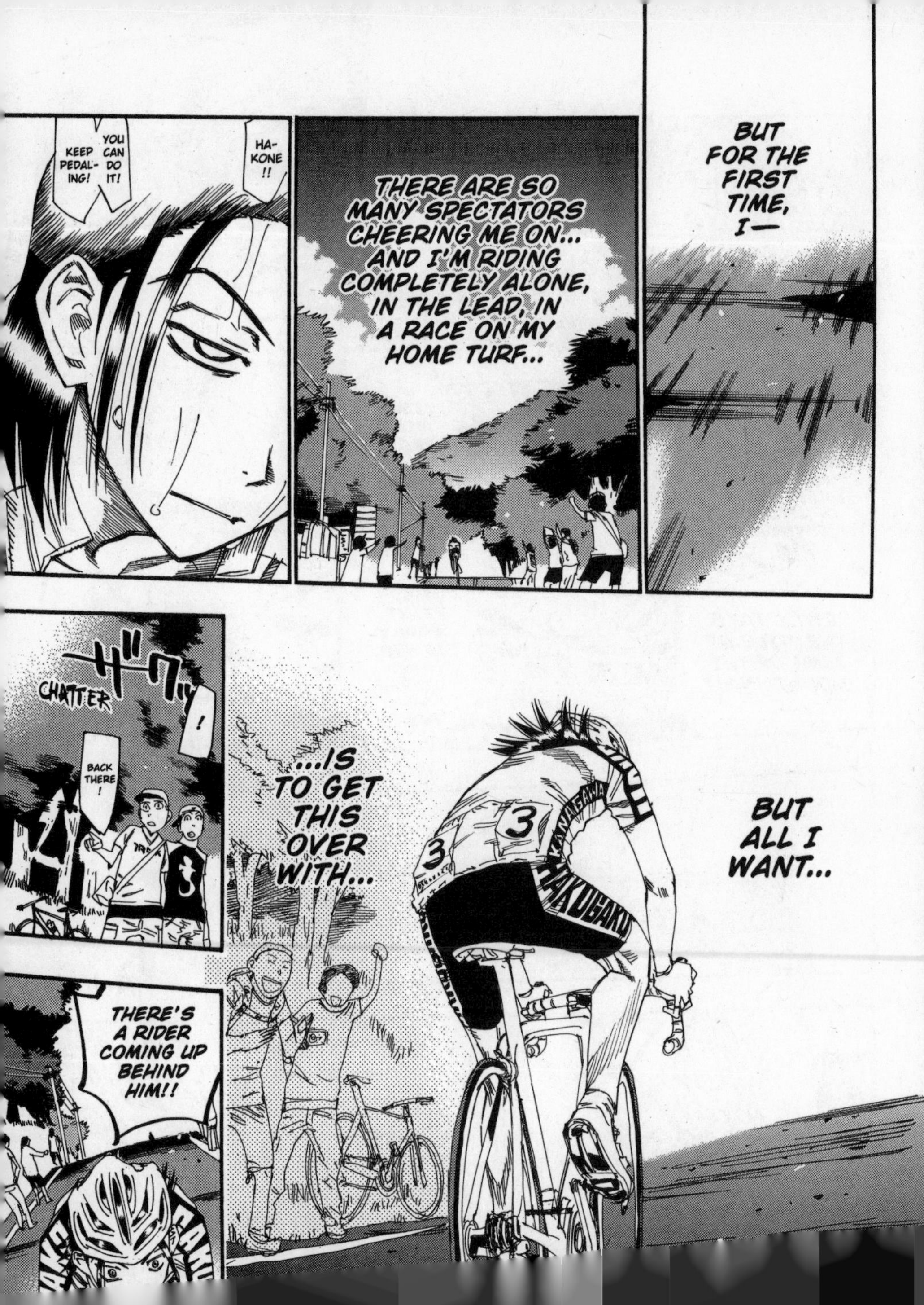

BUT FOR THE FIRST TIME, I—
THERE ARE SO MANY SPECTATORS CHEERING ME ON... AND I'M RIDING COMPLETELY ALONE, IN THE LEAD, IN A RACE ON MY HOME TURF...
HA-KONE!!
YOU CAN DO IT!
KEEP PEDAL-ING!
BUT ALL I WANT...
...IS TO GET THIS OVER WITH...
ザワッ
CHATTER
!
BACK THERE!
THERE'S A RIDER COMING UP BEHIND HIM!!

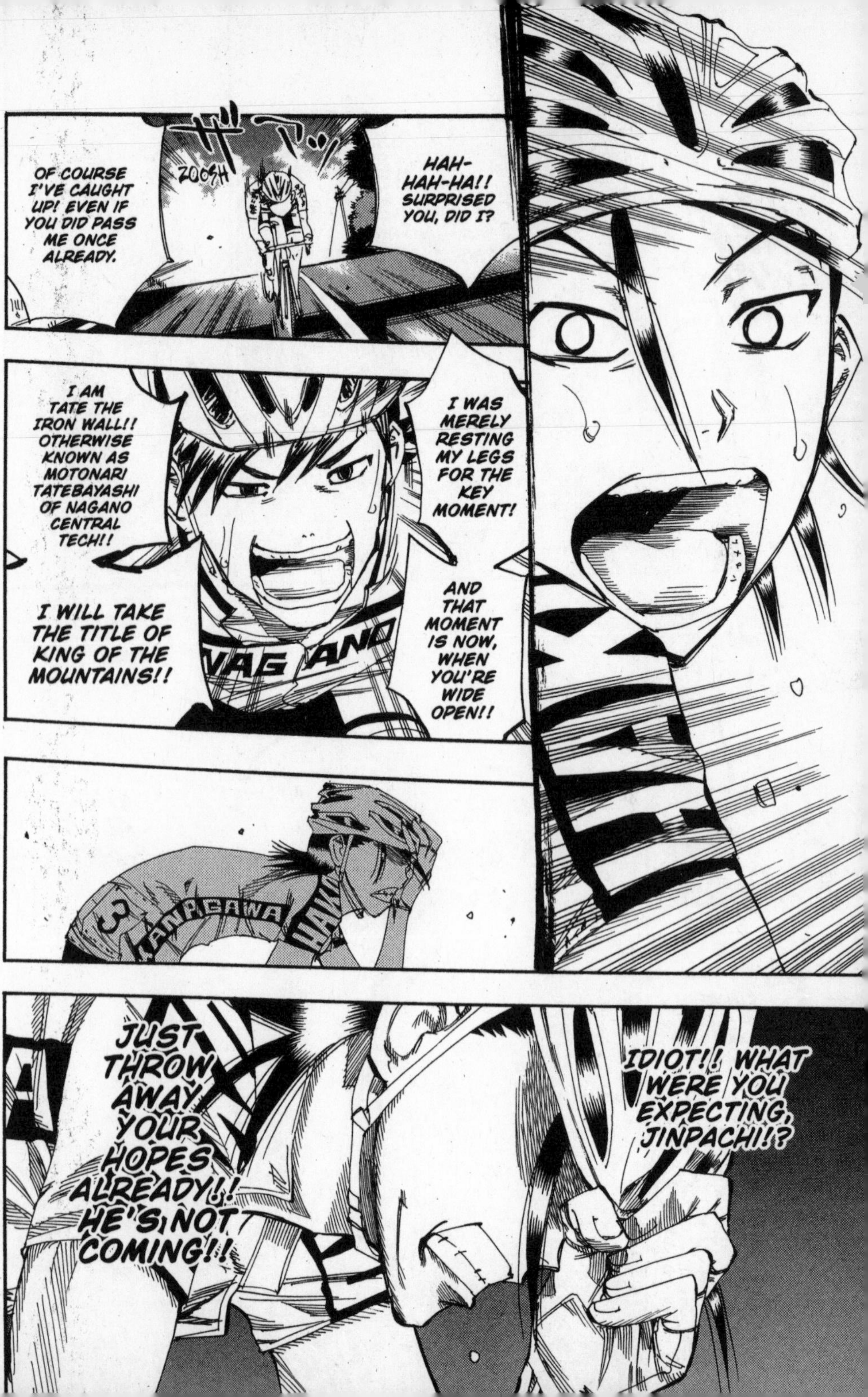
HAH-HAH-HA!! SURPRISED YOU, DID I?
ZOOSH
OF COURSE I'VE CAUGHT UP! EVEN IF YOU DID PASS ME ONCE ALREADY.
I WAS MERELY RESTING MY LEGS FOR THE KEY MOMENT!
AND THAT MOMENT IS NOW, WHEN YOU'RE WIDE OPEN!!
I AM TATE THE IRON WALL!! OTHERWISE KNOWN AS MOTONARI TATEBAYASHI OF NAGANO CENTRAL TECH!!
I WILL TAKE THE TITLE OF KING OF THE MOUNTAINS!!
IDIOT!! WHAT WERE YOU EXPECTING, JINPACHI!?
JUST THROW AWAY YOUR HOPES ALREADY!! HE'S NOT COMING!!

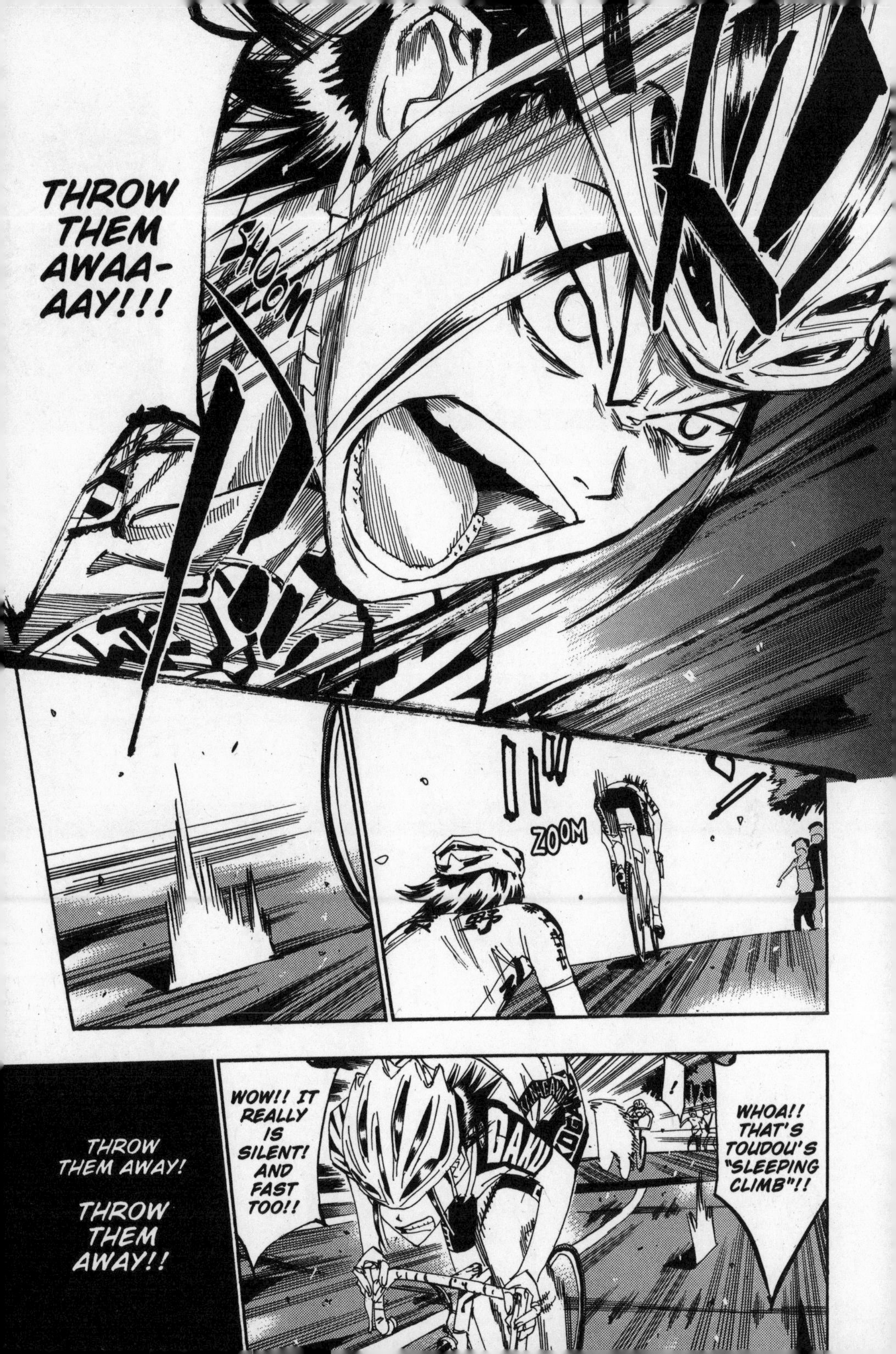
THROW THEM AWAAA-AAY!!!
SHOOM
ZOOM
WHOA!! THAT'S TOUDOU'S "SLEEPING CLIMB"!!
WOW!! IT REALLY IS SILENT! AND FAST TOO!!
THROW THEM AWAY!
THROW THEM AWAY!!

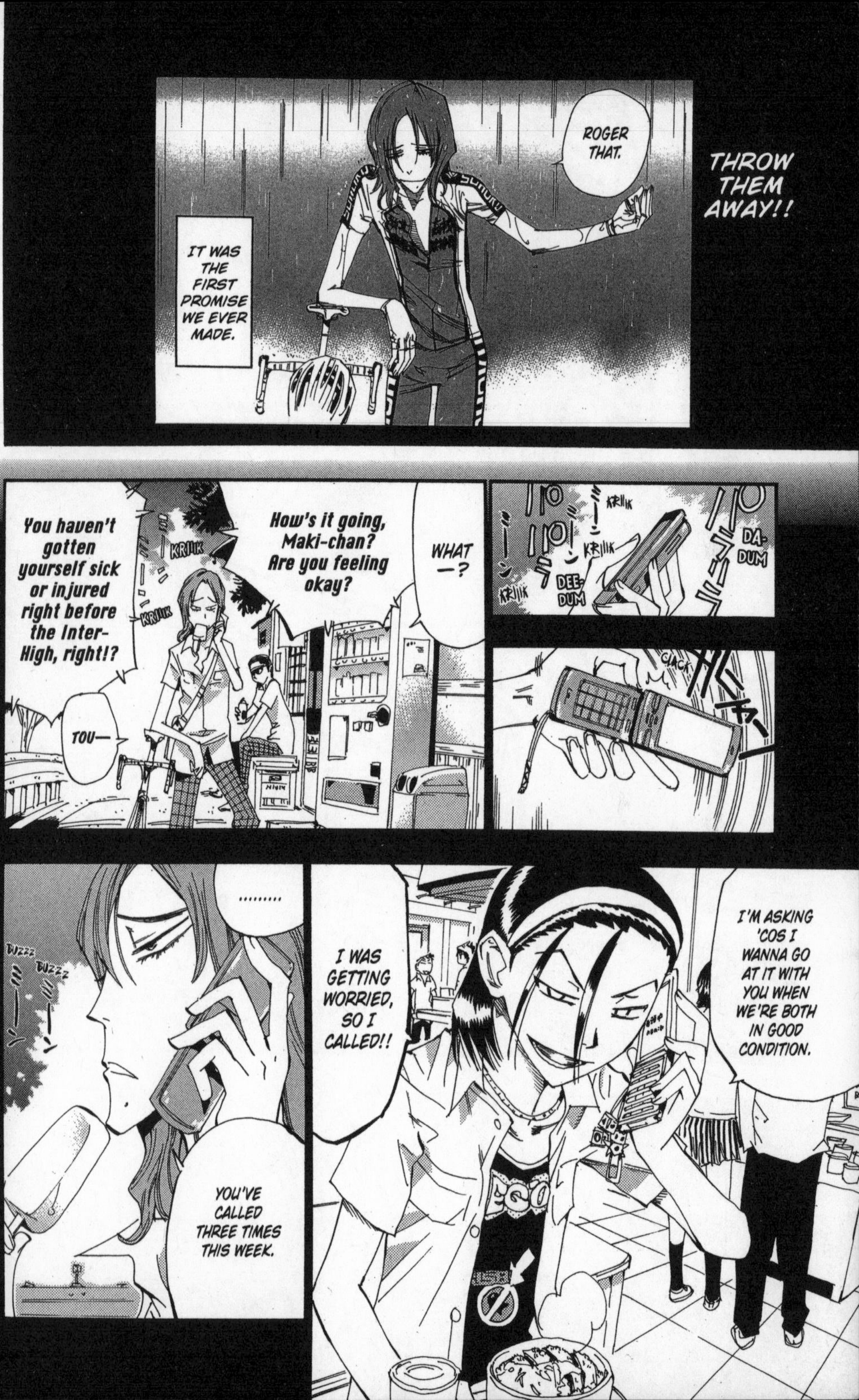

THROW THEM AWAY!!
ROGER THAT.
IT WAS THE FIRST PROMISE WE EVER MADE.
DA-DUM
KRIIIK
KRIIIK
DEE-DUM
KRIIIK
CLACK
WHAT—?
How's it going, Maki-chan? Are you feeling okay?
KRIIIK
KRIIIK
You haven't gotten yourself sick or injured right before the Inter-High, right!?
TOU—
I'M ASKING 'COS I WANNA GO AT IT WITH YOU WHEN WE'RE BOTH IN GOOD CONDITION.
I WAS GETTING WORRIED, SO I CALLED!!
.........
BUZZZ
BUZZZ
YOU'VE CALLED THREE TIMES THIS WEEK.

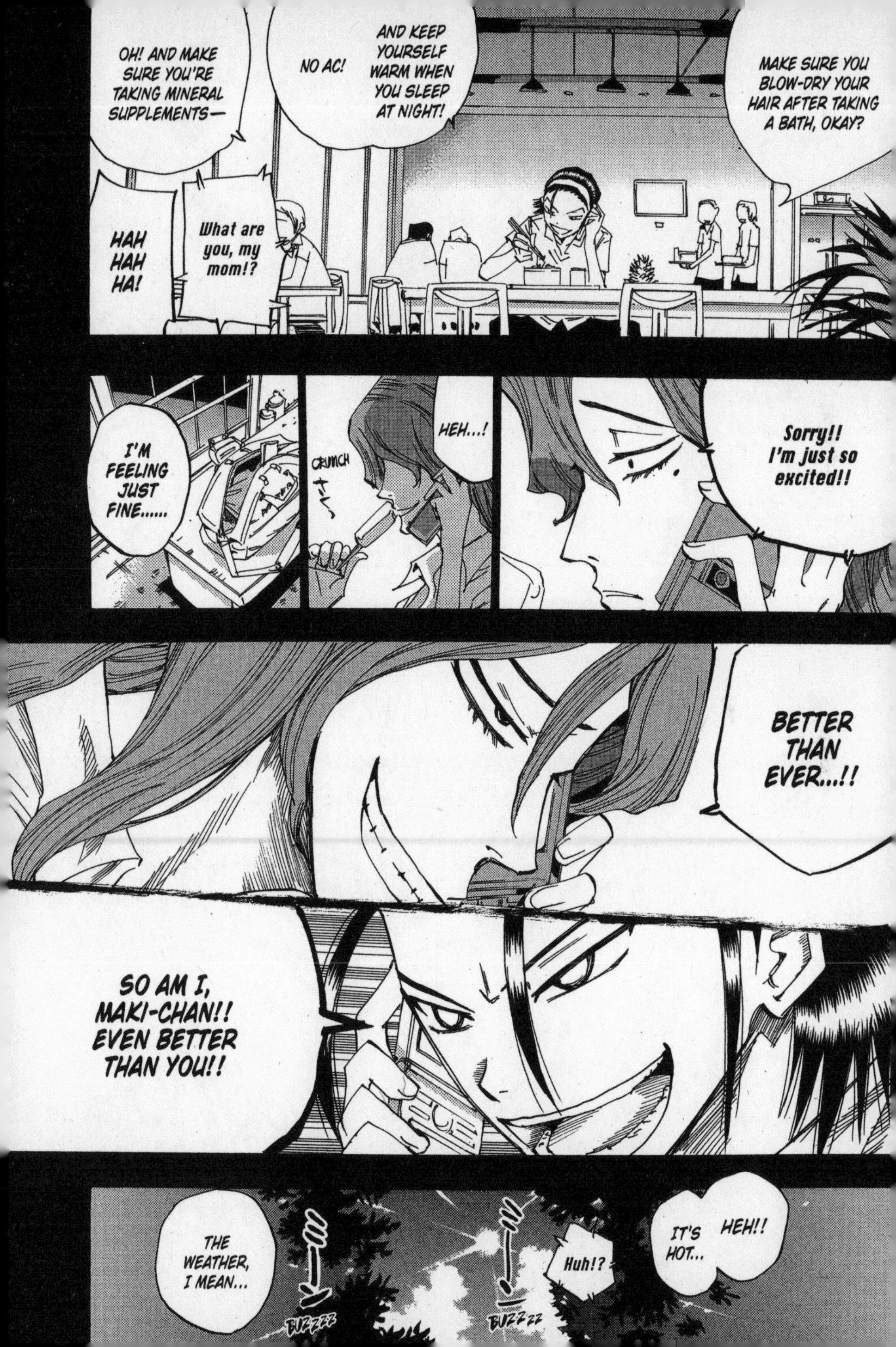
MAKE SURE YOU BLOW-DRY YOUR HAIR AFTER TAKING A BATH, OKAY?
AND KEEP YOURSELF WARM WHEN YOU SLEEP AT NIGHT!
NO AC!
OH! AND MAKE SURE YOU'RE TAKING MINERAL SUPPLEMENTS—
What are you, my mom!?
HAH HAH HA!
Sorry!! I'm just so excited!!
HEH...!
CRUNCH
I'M FEELING JUST FINE......
BETTER THAN EVER...!!
SO AM I, MAKI-CHAN!! EVEN BETTER THAN YOU!!
HEH!!
IT'S HOT...
Huh!?
BUZZzz
THE WEATHER, I MEAN...
BUZZZZ

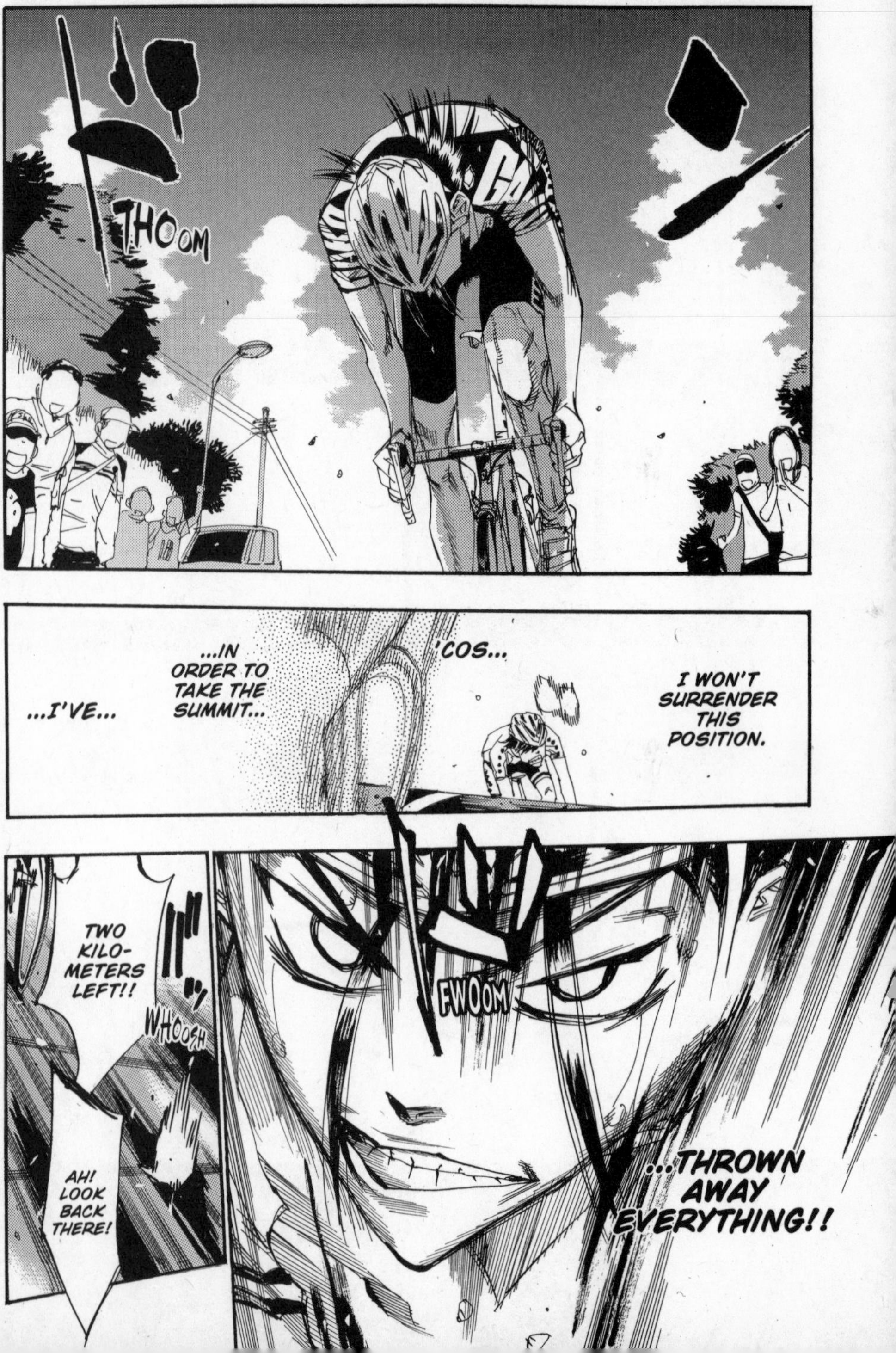
THOOM
I WON'T SURRENDER THIS POSITION.
'COS...
...IN ORDER TO TAKE THE SUMMIT...
...I'VE...
FWOOM
...THROWN AWAY EVERYTHING!!
TWO KILO-METERS LEFT!!
WHOOSH
AH! LOOK BACK THERE!

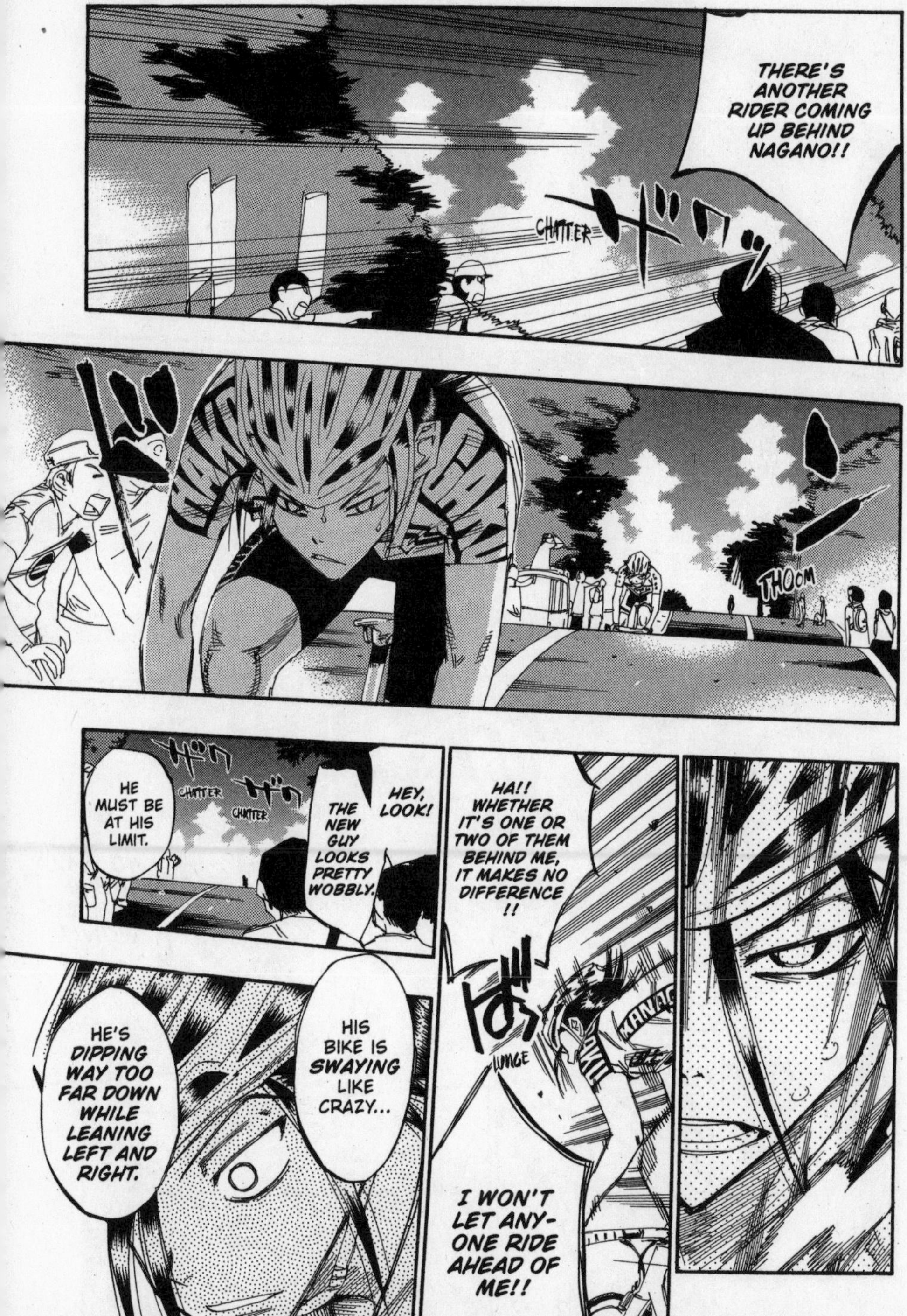
THERE'S ANOTHER RIDER COMING UP BEHIND NAGANO!!
CHATTER
THOOM
HA!! WHETHER IT'S ONE OR TWO OF THEM BEHIND ME, IT MAKES NO DIFFERENCE!!
LUNGE
I WON'T LET ANY-ONE RIDE AHEAD OF ME!!
HEY, LOOK!
THE NEW GUY LOOKS PRETTY WOBBLY.
HE MUST BE AT HIS LIMIT.
CHATTER
CHATTER
HIS BIKE IS SWAYING LIKE CRAZY...
HE'S DIPPING WAY TOO FAR DOWN WHILE LEANING LEFT AND RIGHT.

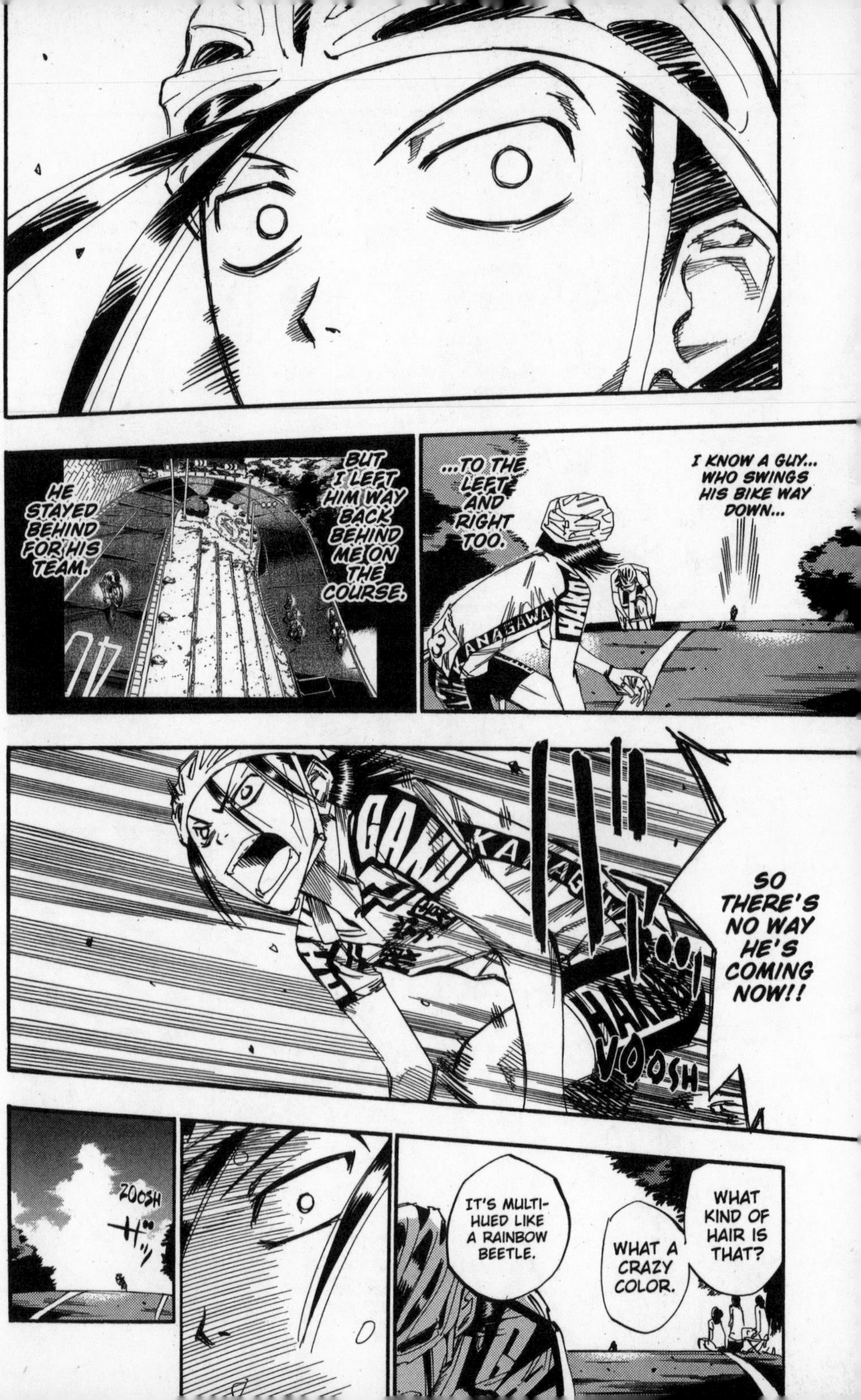
I KNOW A GUY... WHO SWINGS HIS BIKE WAY DOWN...
...TO THE LEFT AND RIGHT TOO.
BUT I LEFT HIM WAY BACK BEHIND ME ON THE COURSE.
HE STAYED BEHIND FOR HIS TEAM.
SO THERE'S NO WAY HE'S COMING NOW!!
VOOSH
WHAT KIND OF HAIR IS THAT?
WHAT A CRAZY COLOR.
IT'S MULTI-HUED LIKE A RAINBOW BEETLE.
ZOOSH

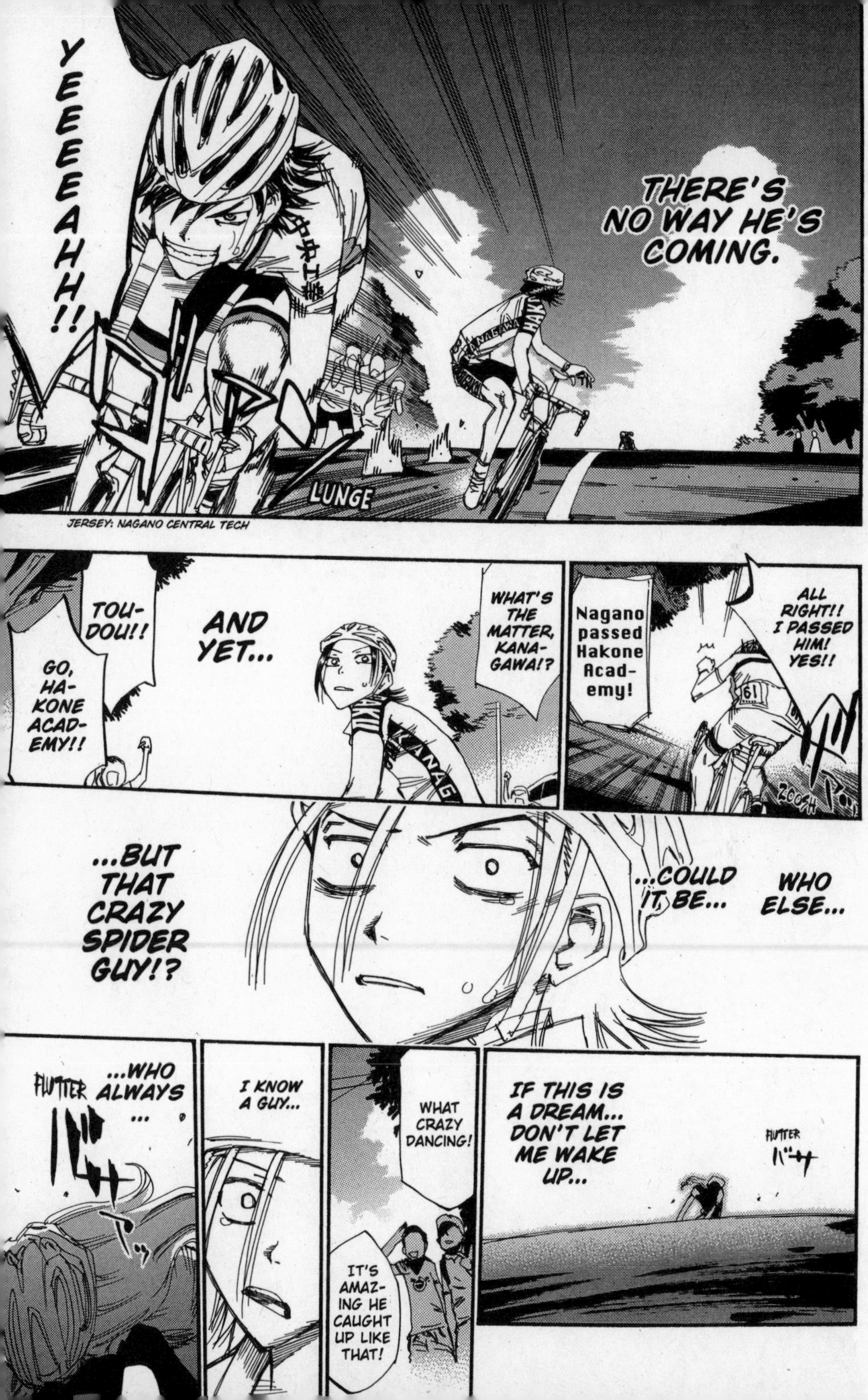
THERE'S NO WAY HE'S COMING.
YEEEEEAHH!!
LUNGE
JERSEY: NAGANO CENTRAL TECH
ALL RIGHT!! I PASSED HIM! YES!!
Nagano passed Hakone Academy!
ZOOSH
WHAT'S THE MATTER, KANAGAWA!?
AND YET...
TOUDOU!!
GO, HAKONE ACADEMY!!
WHO ELSE...
...COULD IT BE...
...BUT THAT CRAZY SPIDER GUY!?
IF THIS IS A DREAM... DON'T LET ME WAKE UP...
FLUTTER
WHAT CRAZY DANCING!
IT'S AMAZING HE CAUGHT UP LIKE THAT!
I KNOW A GUY...
...WHO ALWAYS ...
FLUTTER

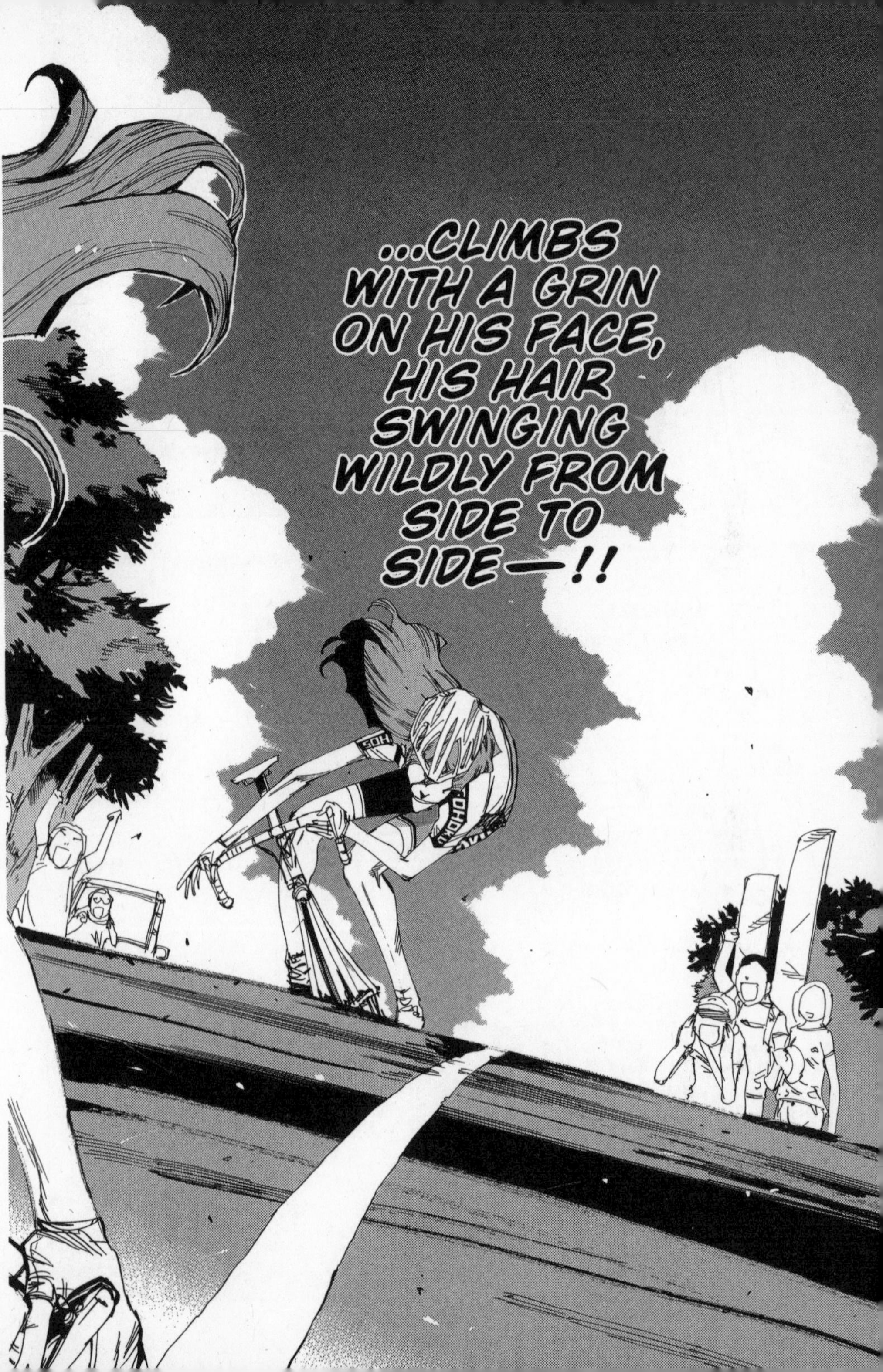
...CLIMBS WITH A GRIN ON HIS FACE, HIS HAIR SWINGING WILDLY FROM SIDE TO SIDE—!!

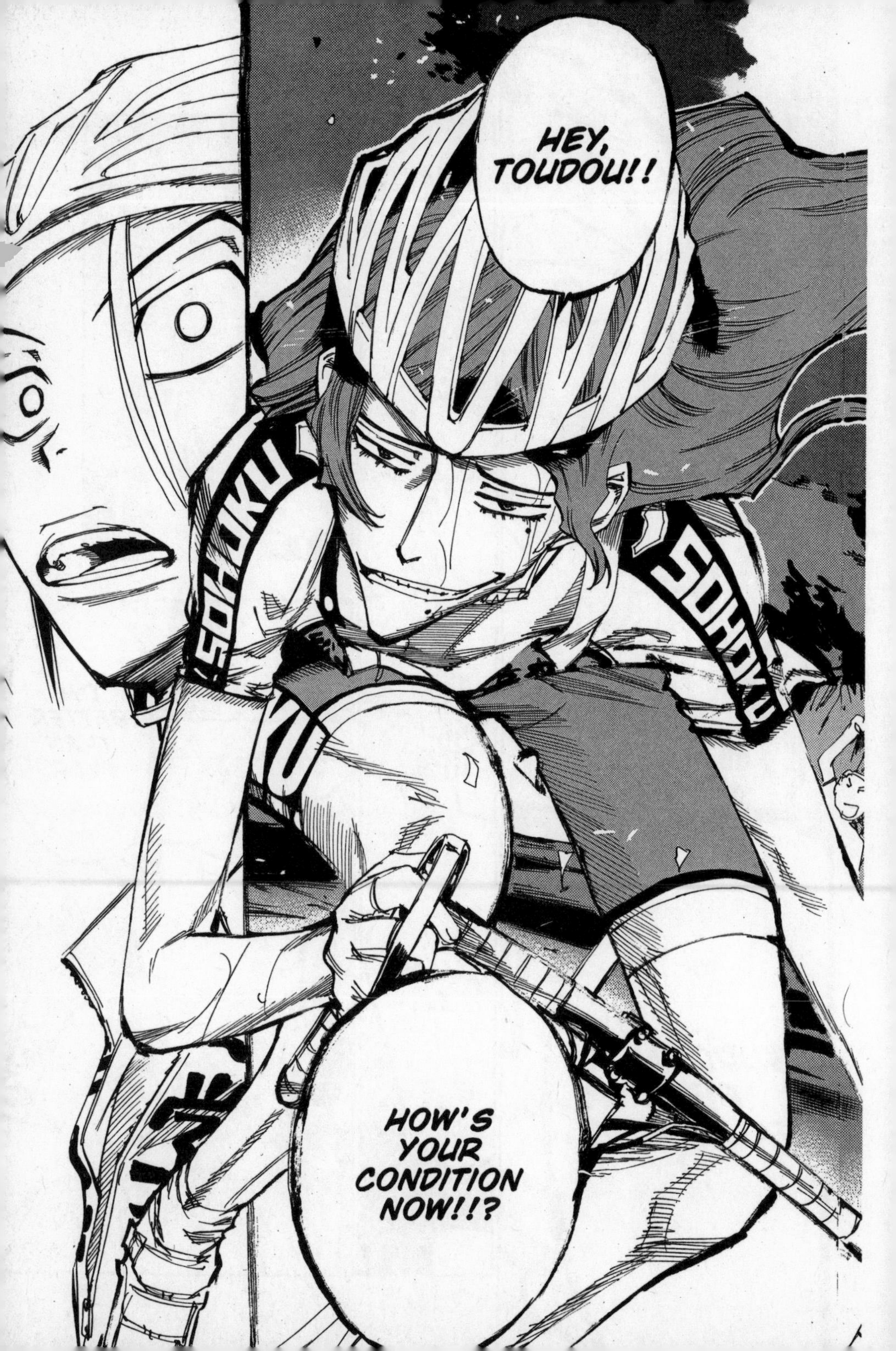
HEY, TOUDOU!!
HOW'S YOUR CONDITION NOW!!?
SOHOKU
SOHOKU

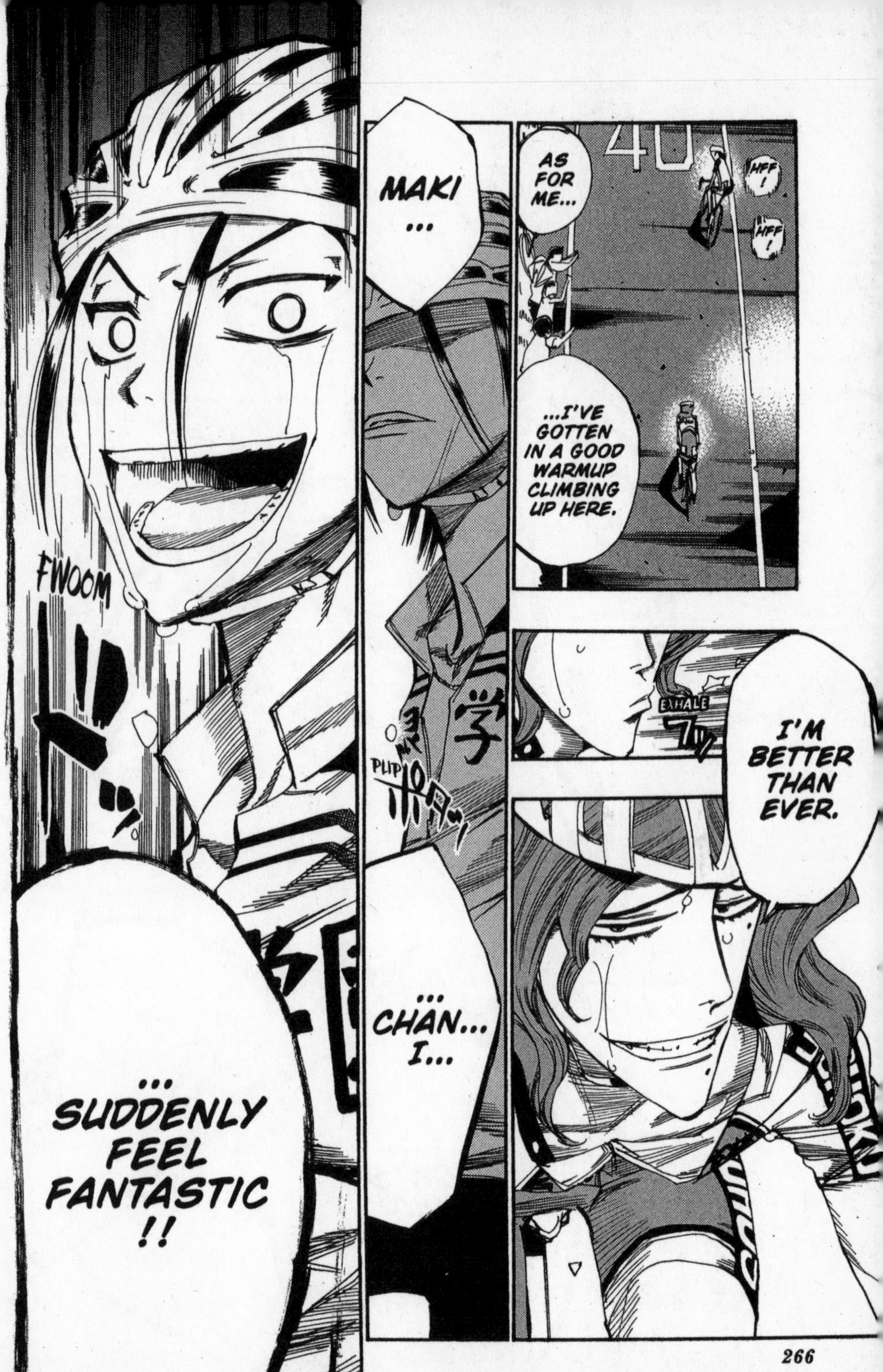

AS FOR ME...
HFF!
HFF!
...I'VE GOTTEN IN A GOOD WARMUP CLIMBING UP HERE.
EXHALE
I'M BETTER THAN EVER.
MAKI ...
PLIP
...CHAN... I...
FWOOM
...SUDDENLY FEEL FANTASTIC!!

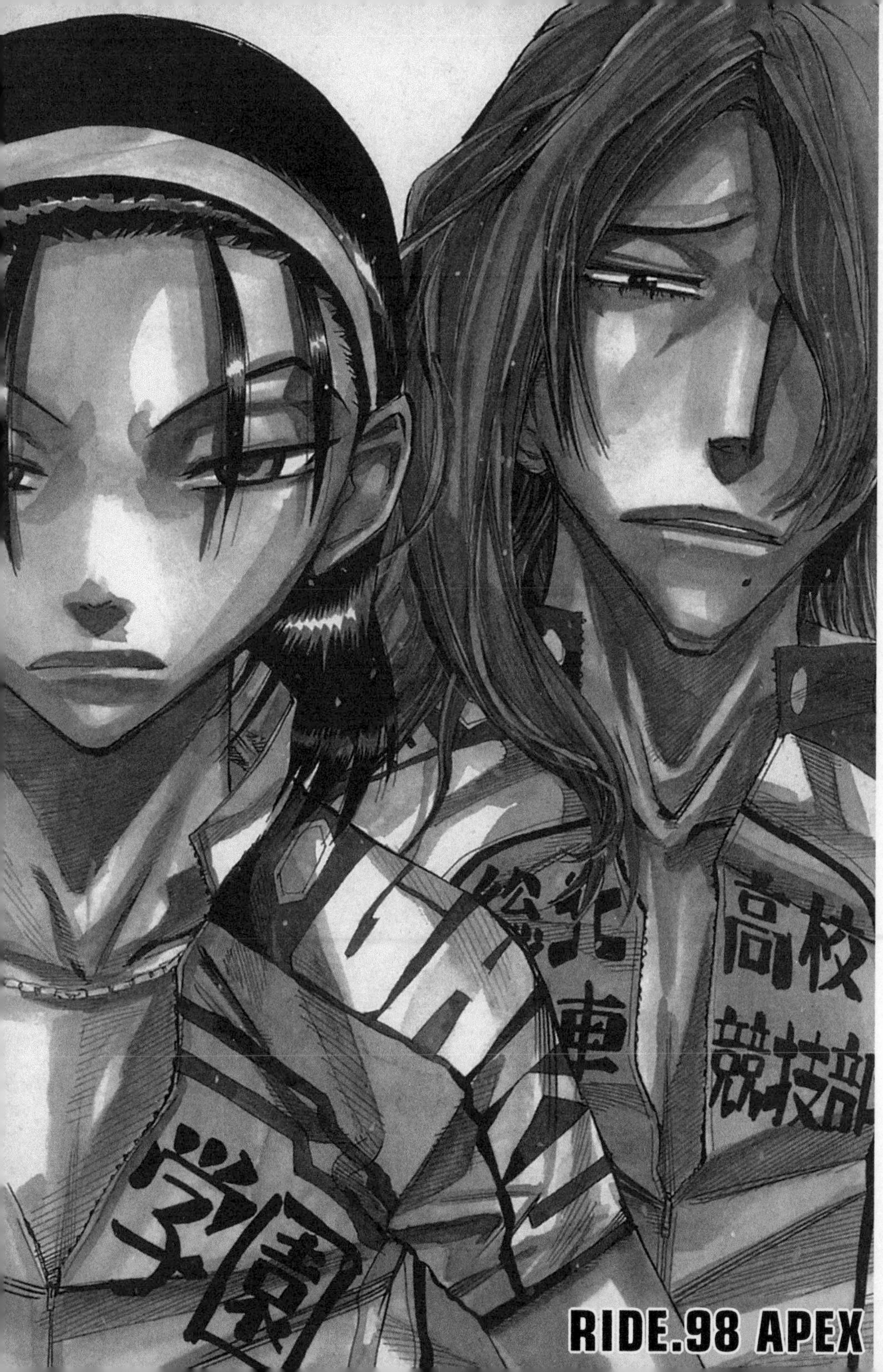
高校
競技部
学園

# RIDE.98 APEX

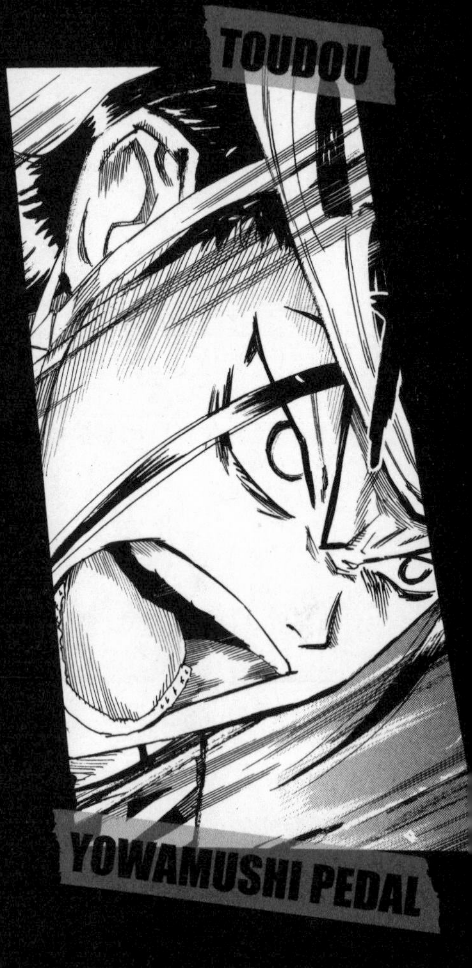
TOUDOU
YOWAMUSHI PEDAL

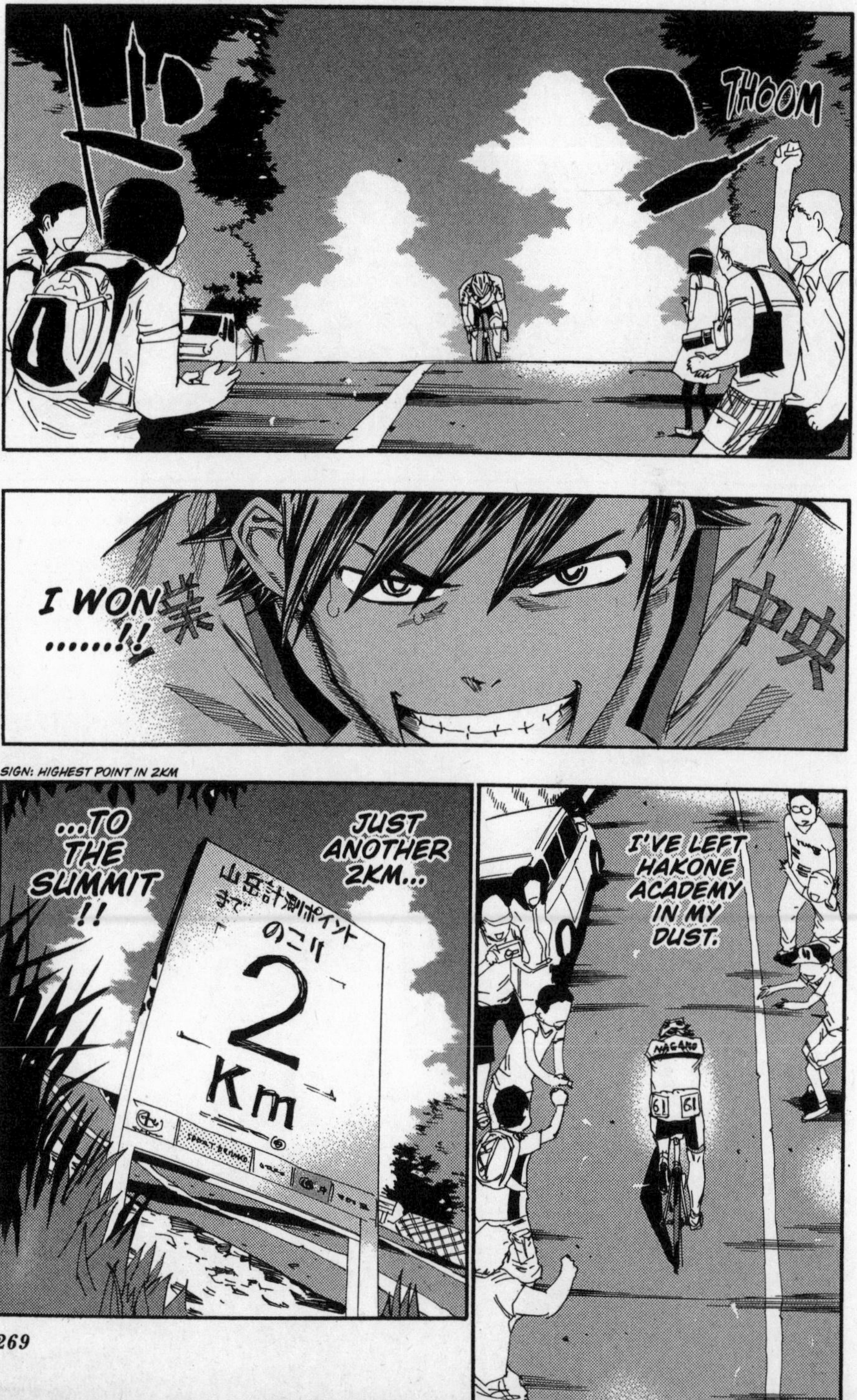
THOOM
I WON ......!!
I'VE LEFT HAKONE ACADEMY IN MY DUST.
SIGN: HIGHEST POINT IN 2KM
山岳計測ポイントまで のこり
2 Km
JUST ANOTHER 2KM...
...TO THE SUMMIT!!

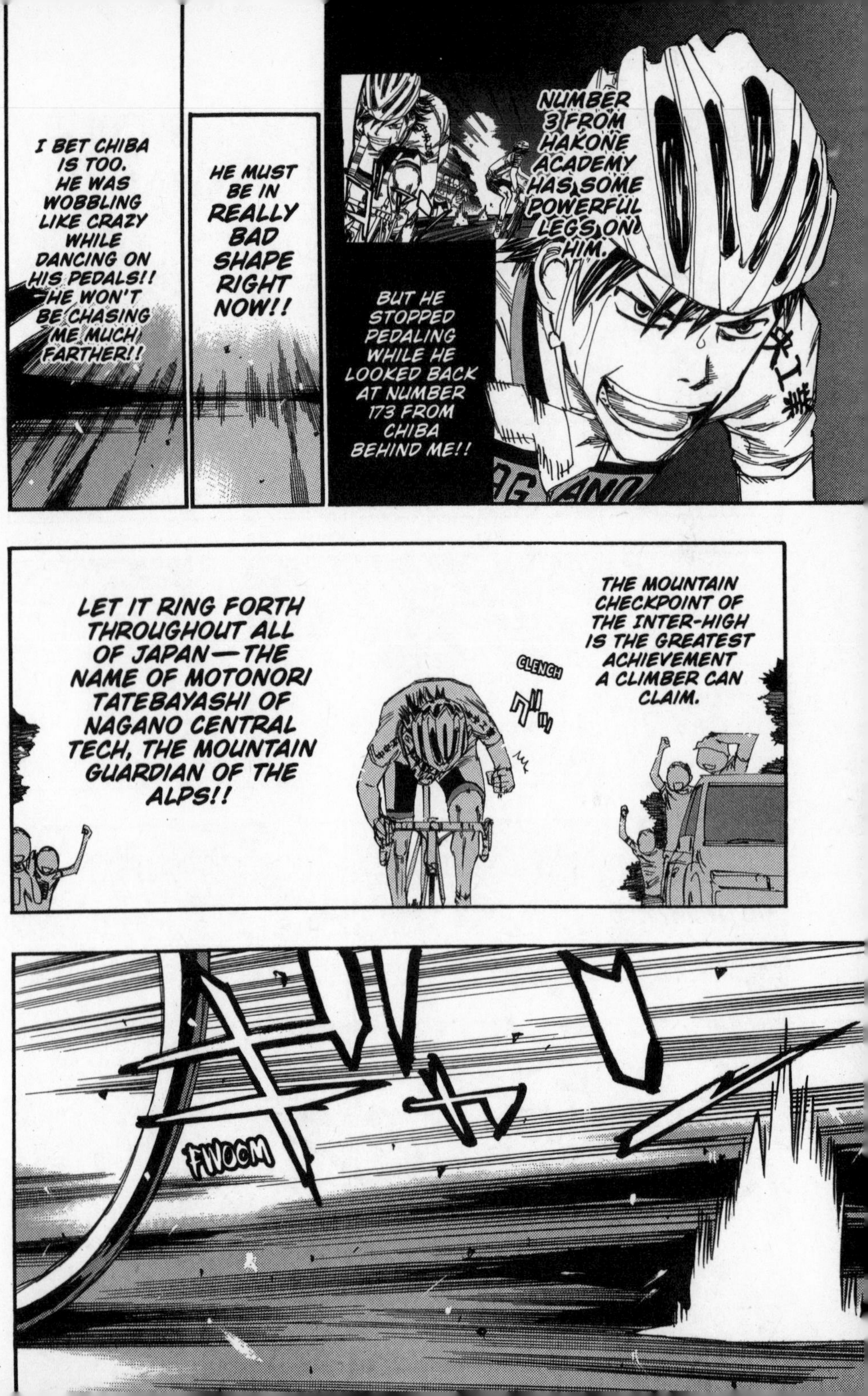
NUMBER 3 FROM HAKONE ACADEMY HAS SOME POWERFUL LEGS ON HIM.
BUT HE STOPPED PEDALING WHILE HE LOOKED BACK AT NUMBER 173 FROM CHIBA BEHIND ME!!
HE MUST BE IN REALLY BAD SHAPE RIGHT NOW!!
I BET CHIBA IS TOO. HE WAS WOBBLING LIKE CRAZY WHILE DANCING ON HIS PEDALS!! HE WON'T BE CHASING ME MUCH FARTHER!!
THE MOUNTAIN CHECKPOINT OF THE INTER-HIGH IS THE GREATEST ACHIEVEMENT A CLIMBER CAN CLAIM.
CLENCH
LET IT RING FORTH THROUGHOUT ALL OF JAPAN—THE NAME OF MOTONORI TATEBAYASHI OF NAGANO CENTRAL TECH, THE MOUNTAIN GUARDIAN OF THE ALPS!!
FWOOM

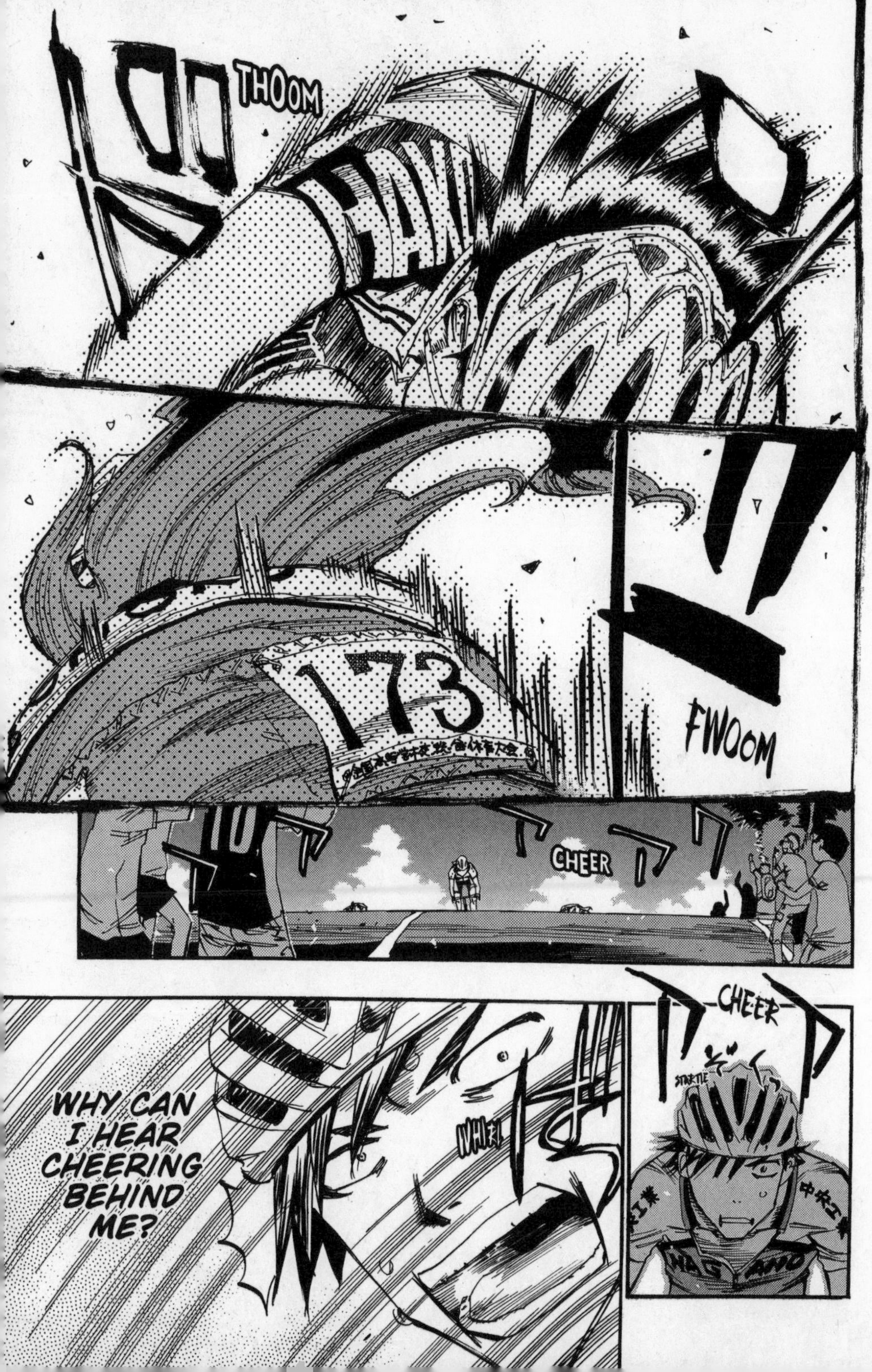

THOOM
173
FWOOM
CHEER
CHEER
STARTLE
WHIRL
WHY CAN I HEAR CHEERING BEHIND ME?

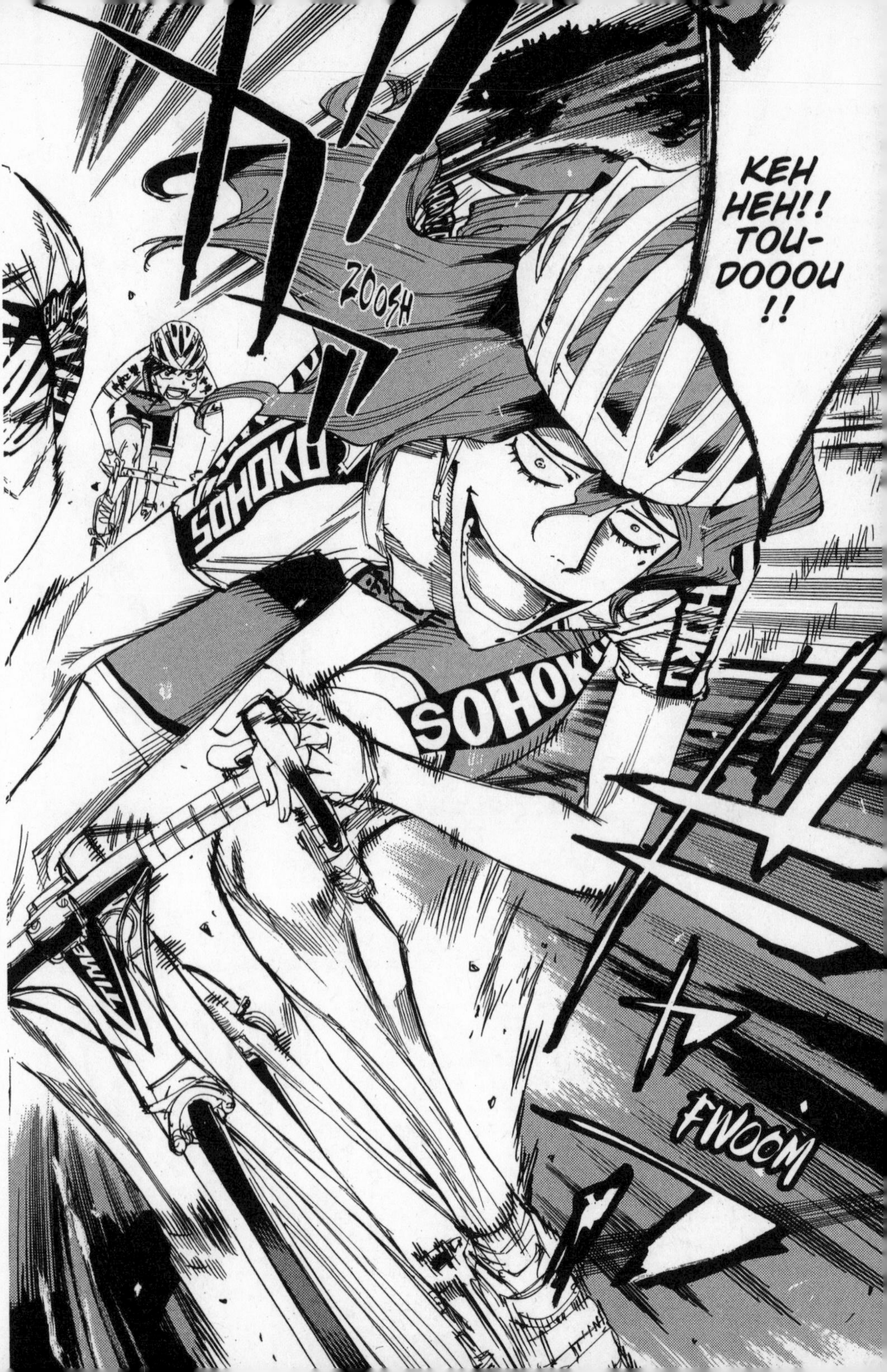
KEH HEH!! TOU-DOOOOU!!
ZOOSH
FWOOM

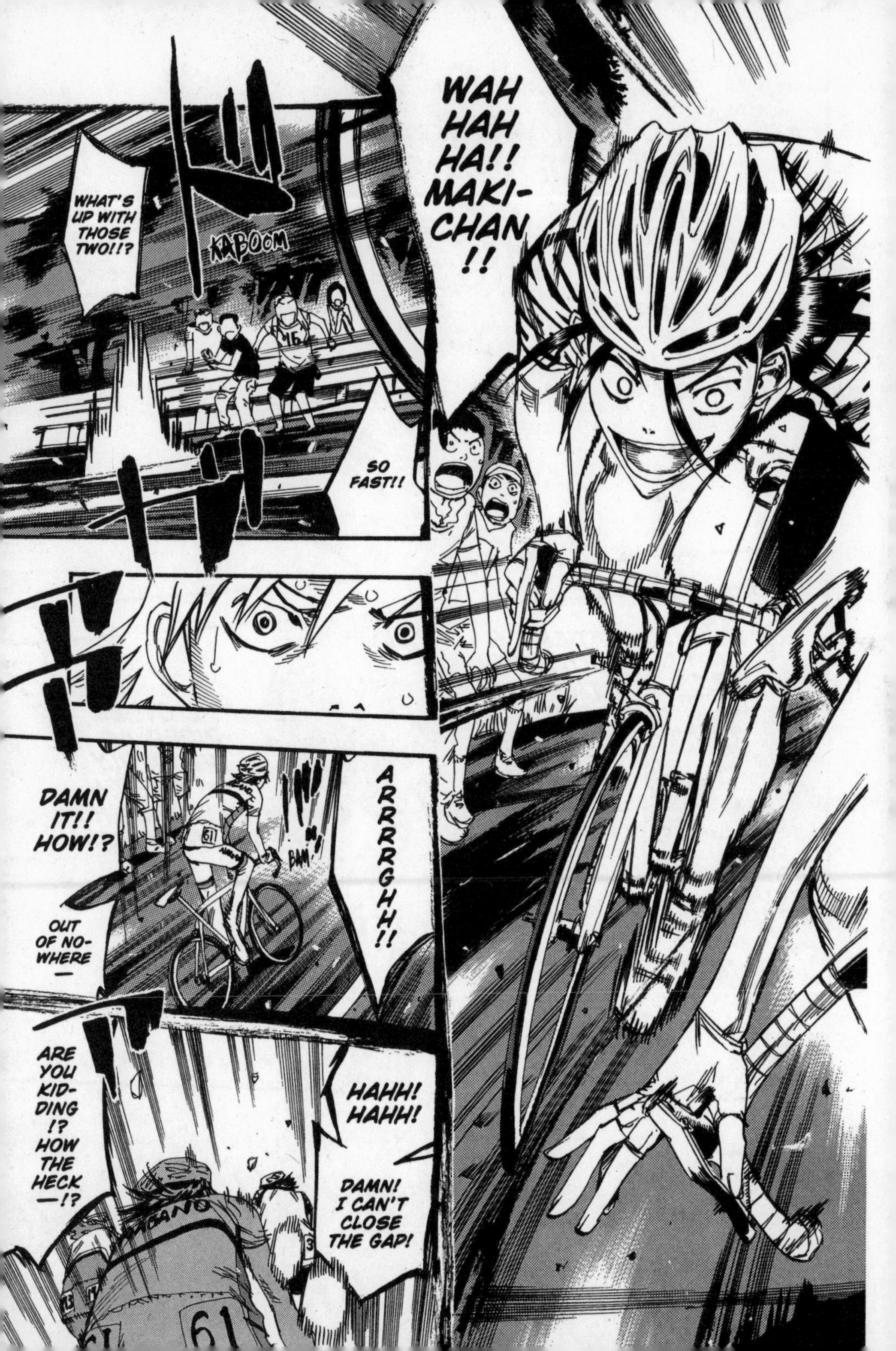
WAH HAH HA!! MAKI-CHAN!!
SO FAST!!
KABOOM
WHAT'S UP WITH THOSE TWO!!?
ARRRRGHH!!
BAM
DAMN IT!! HOW!?
OUT OF NO-WHERE—
HAHH! HAHH!
DAMN! I CAN'T CLOSE THE GAP!
ARE YOU KIDDING!? HOW THE HECK—!?

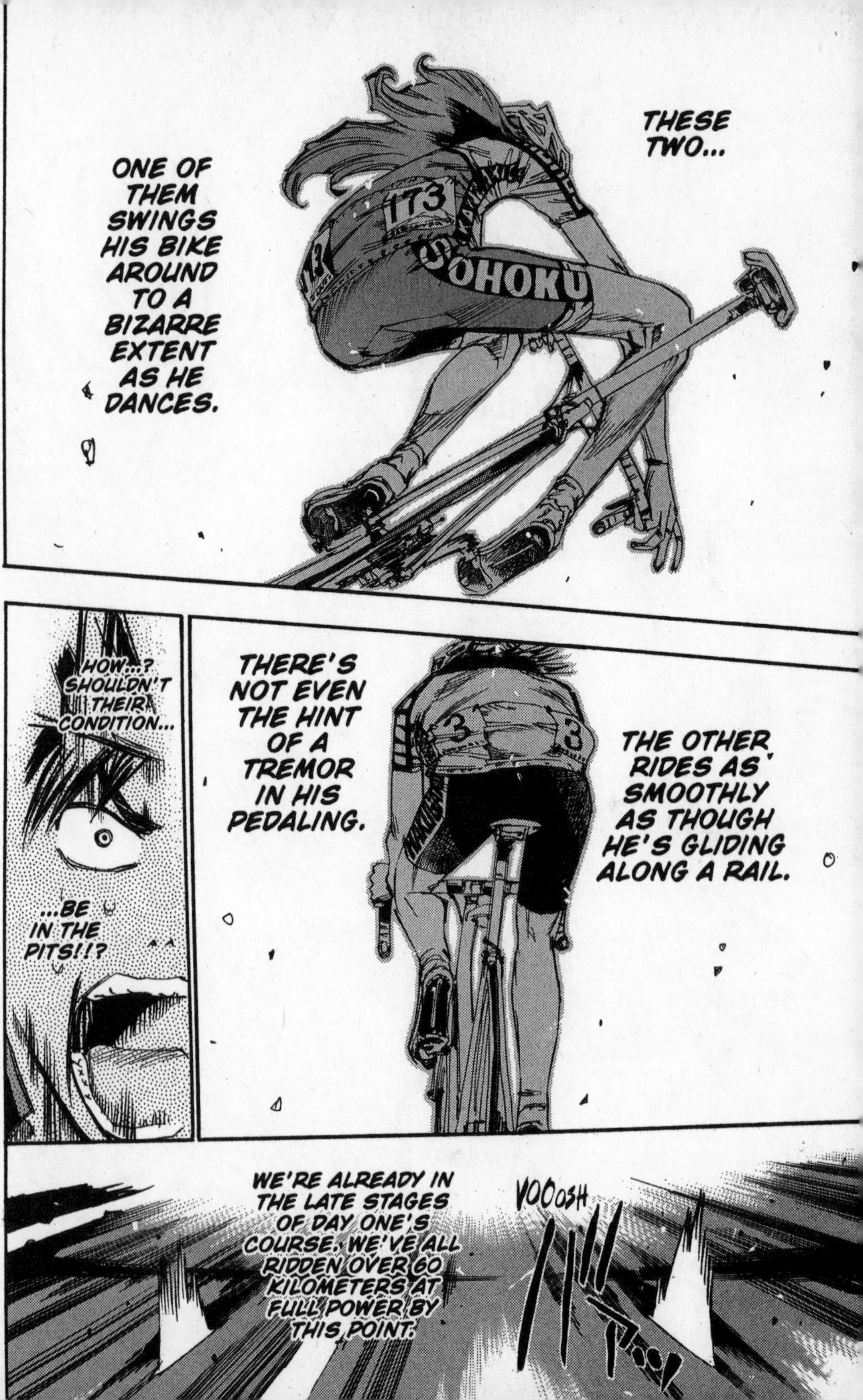
THESE TWO...
ONE OF THEM SWINGS HIS BIKE AROUND TO A BIZARRE EXTENT AS HE DANCES.
THE OTHER RIDES AS SMOOTHLY AS THOUGH HE'S GLIDING ALONG A RAIL.
THERE'S NOT EVEN THE HINT OF A TREMOR IN HIS PEDALING.
HOW...? SHOULDN'T THEIR CONDITION...
...BE IN THE PITS!!?
VOOosh
WE'RE ALREADY IN THE LATE STAGES OF DAY ONE'S COURSE. WE'VE ALL RIDDEN OVER 60 KILOMETERS AT FULL POWER BY THIS POINT.

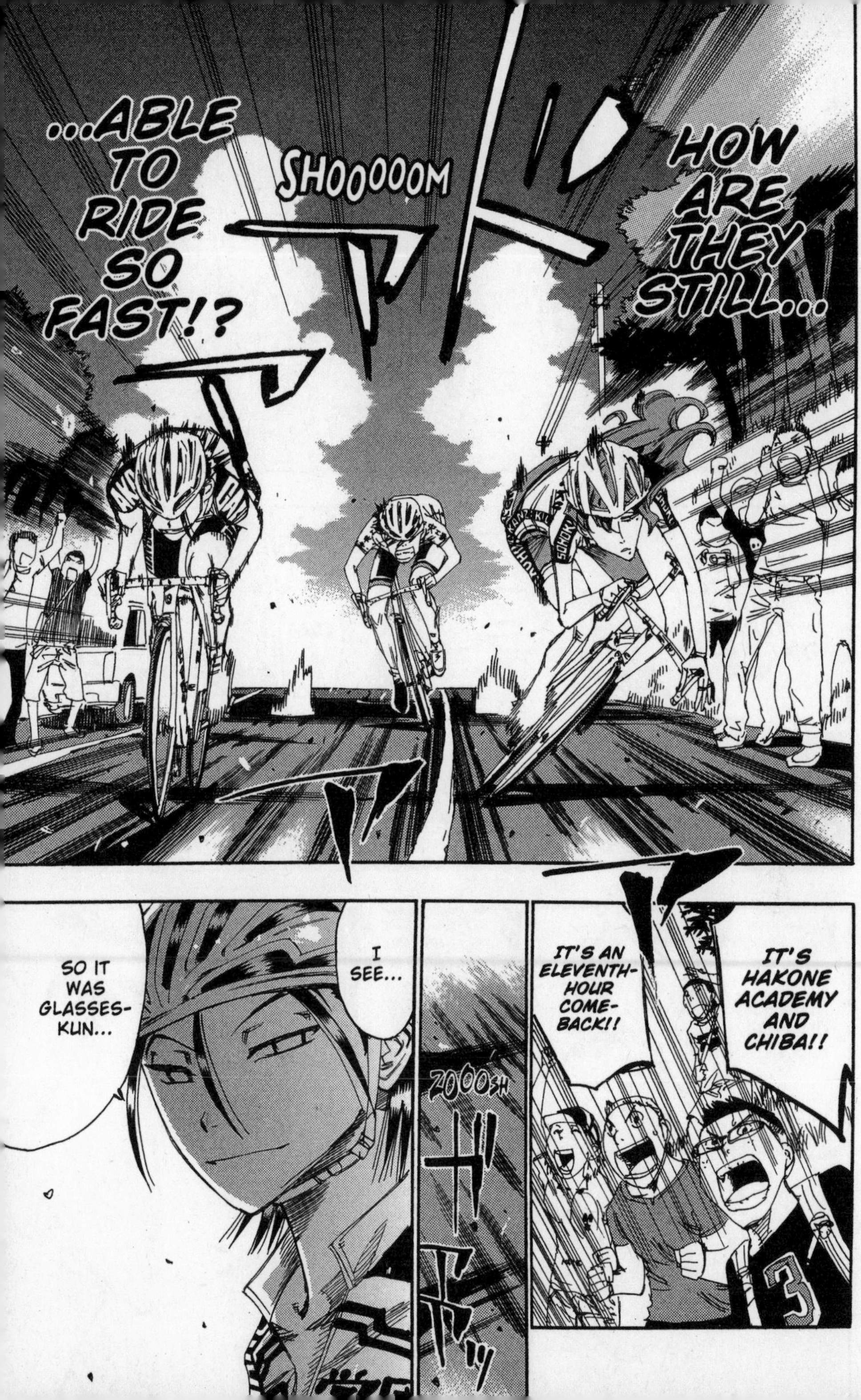
HOW ARE THEY STILL...!
SHOOOOOM
...ABLE TO RIDE SO FAST!?
IT'S HAKONE ACADEMY AND CHIBA!!
IT'S AN ELEVENTH-HOUR COME-BACK!!
ZOOOSH
I SEE...
SO IT WAS GLASSES-KUN...

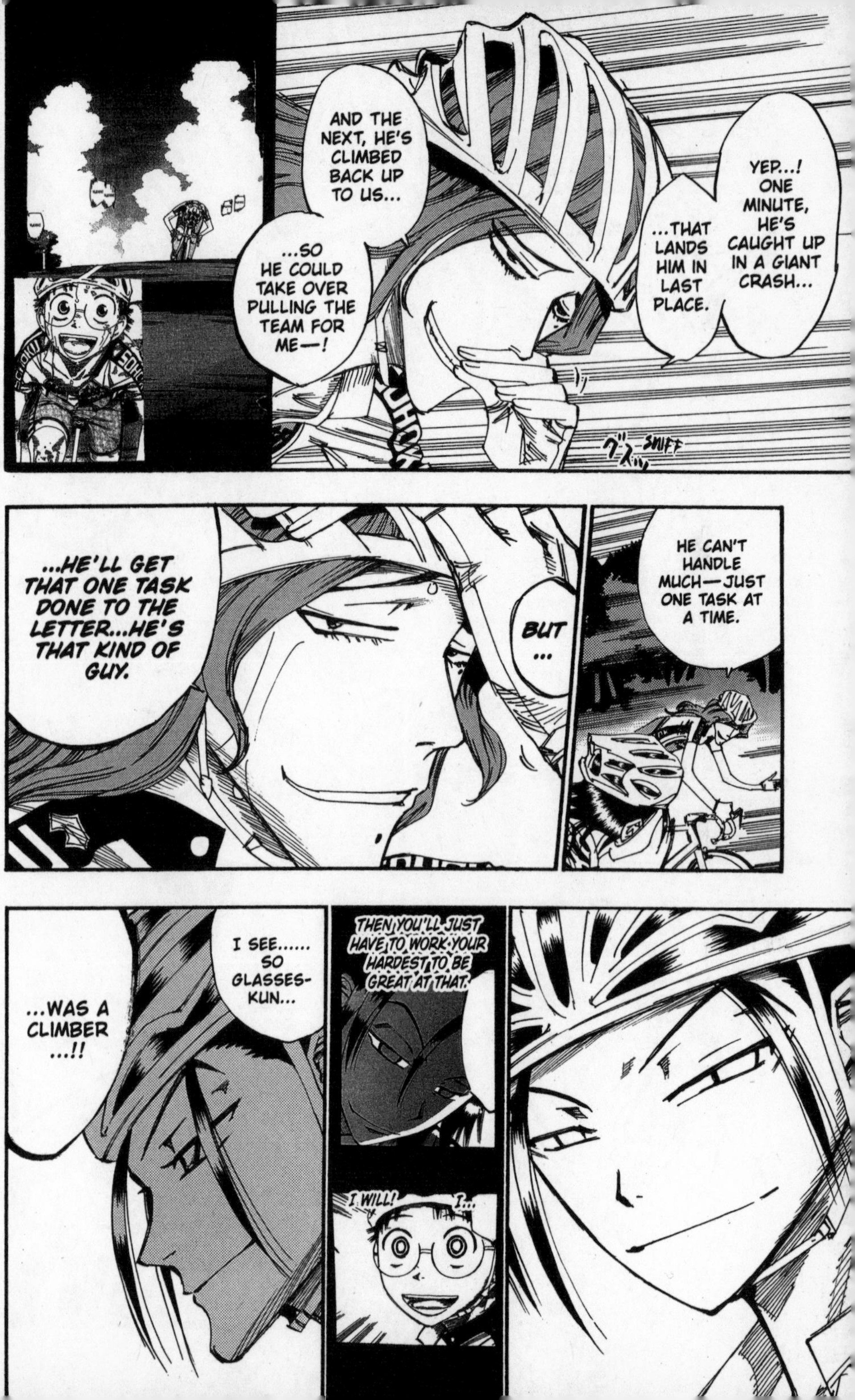
YEP...! ONE MINUTE, HE'S CAUGHT UP IN A GIANT CRASH...
...THAT LANDS HIM IN LAST PLACE.
AND THE NEXT, HE'S CLIMBED BACK UP TO US...
...SO HE COULD TAKE OVER PULLING THE TEAM FOR ME—!
SNIFF
HE CAN'T HANDLE MUCH—JUST ONE TASK AT A TIME.
BUT...
...HE'LL GET THAT ONE TASK DONE TO THE LETTER...HE'S THAT KIND OF GUY.
THEN YOU'LL JUST HAVE TO WORK YOUR HARDEST TO BE GREAT AT THAT.
I...
I WILL!
I SEE...... SO GLASSES-KUN...
...WAS A CLIMBER ...!!

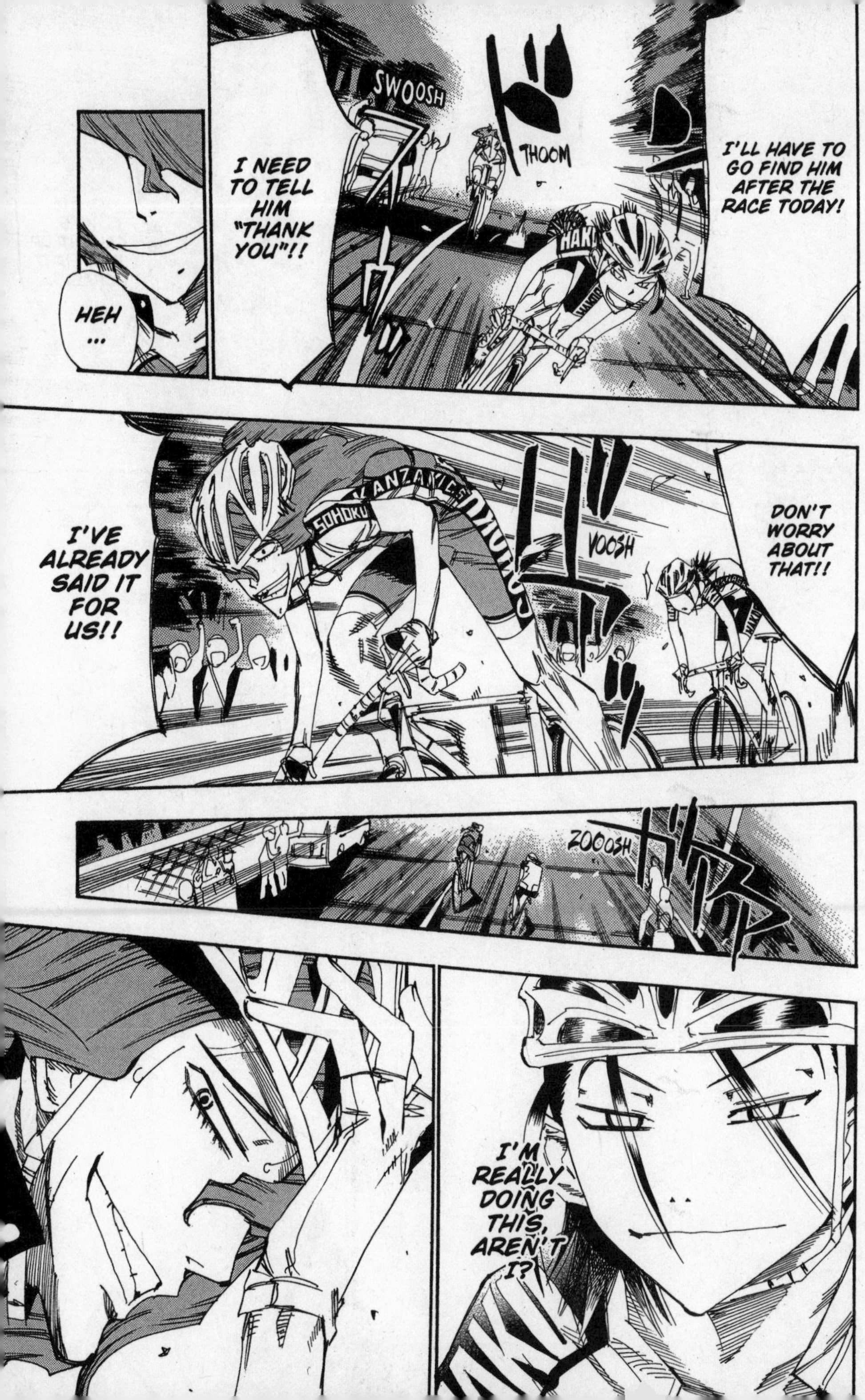

I'LL HAVE TO GO FIND HIM AFTER THE RACE TODAY!
SWOOSH
THOOM
I NEED TO TELL HIM "THANK YOU"!!
HEH ...
DON'T WORRY ABOUT THAT!!
VOOSH
I'VE ALREADY SAID IT FOR US!!
ZOOOSH
I'M REALLY DOING THIS, AREN'T I?

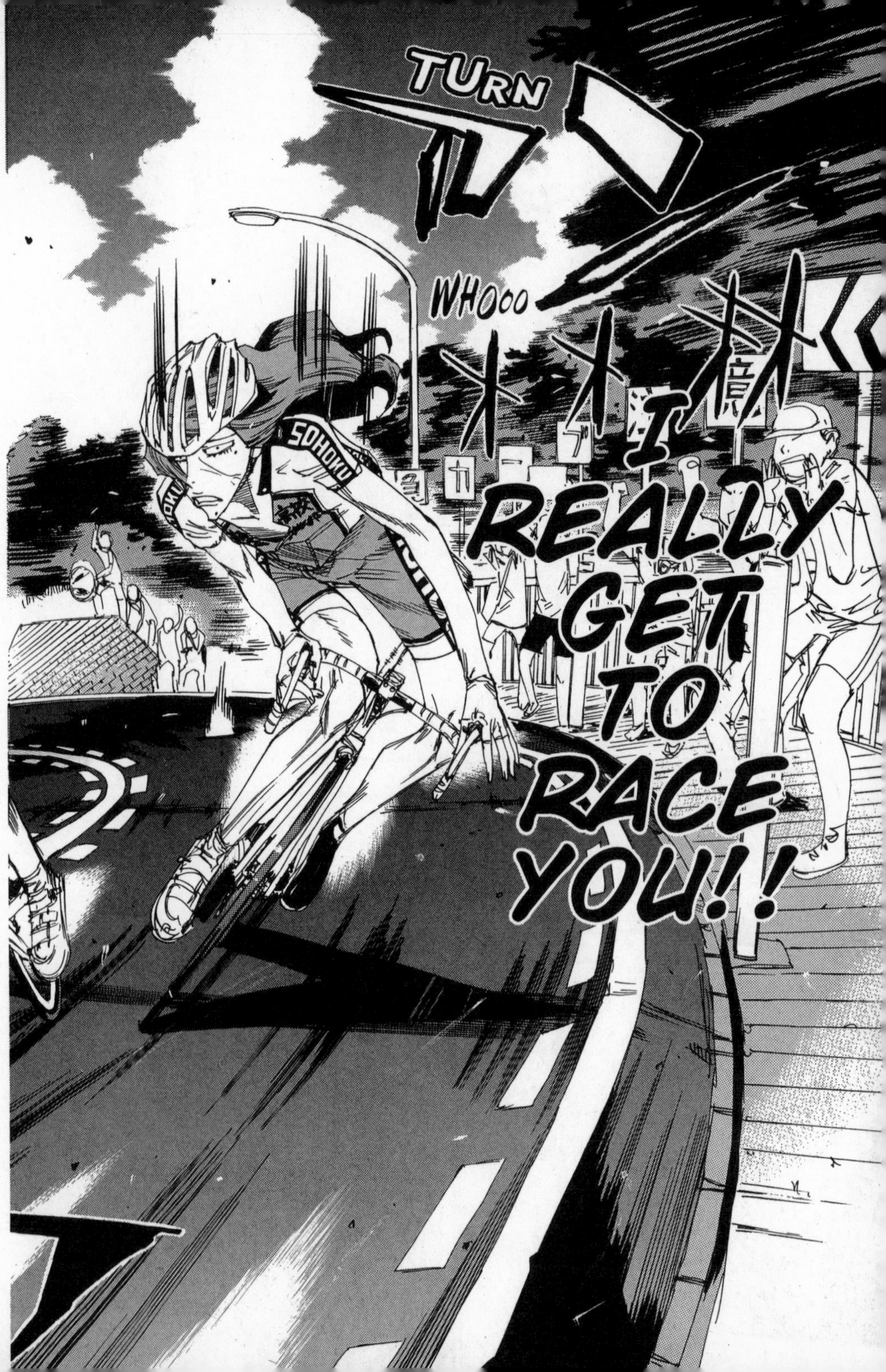
TURN
WHOOO
I REALLY GET TO RACE YOU!!

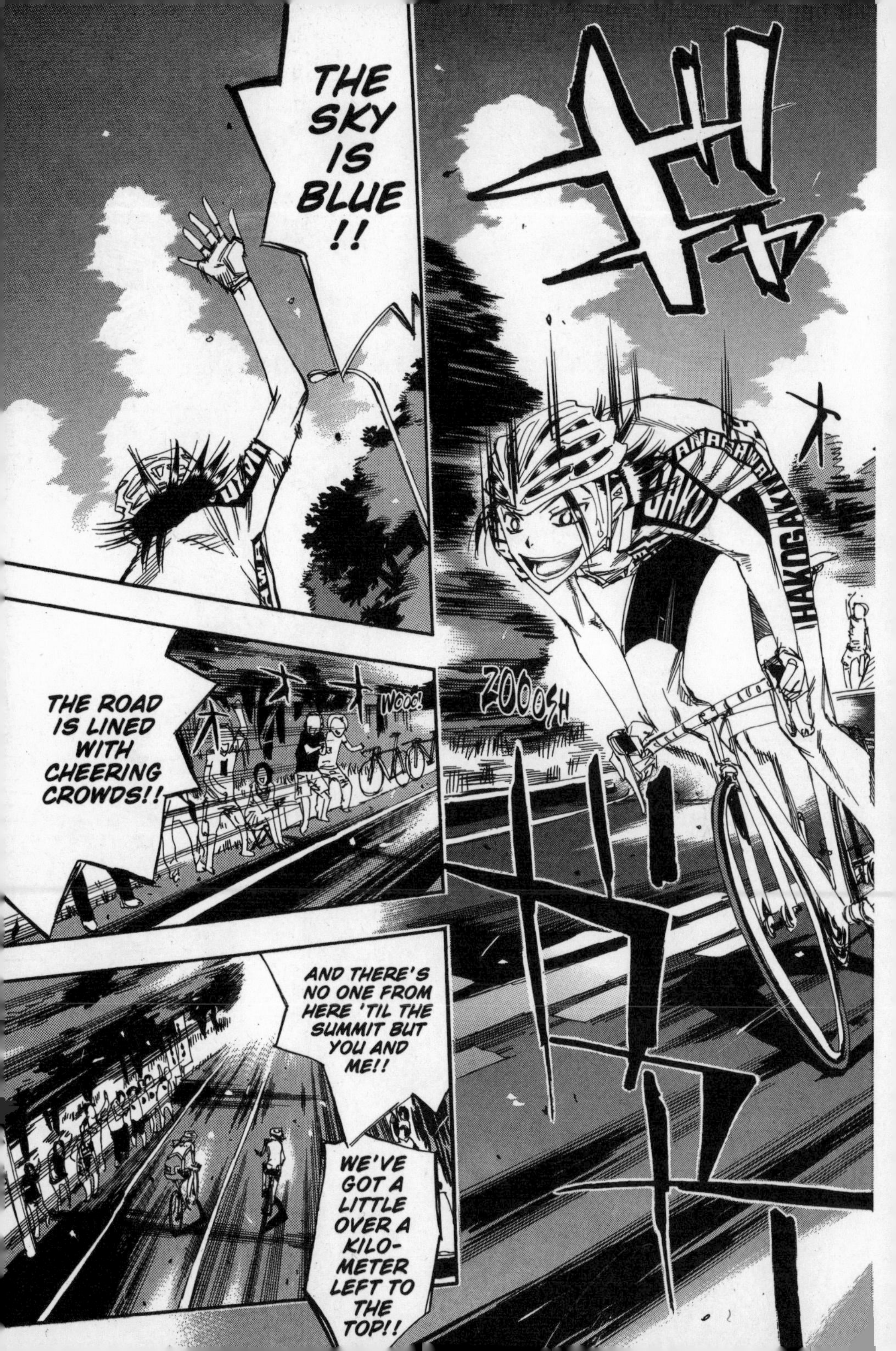
ZOOOSH
THE SKY IS BLUE!!
THE ROAD IS LINED WITH CHEERING CROWDS!!
WOOO!
AND THERE'S NO ONE FROM HERE 'TIL THE SUMMIT BUT YOU AND ME!!
WE'VE GOT A LITTLE OVER A KILOMETER LEFT TO THE TOP!!

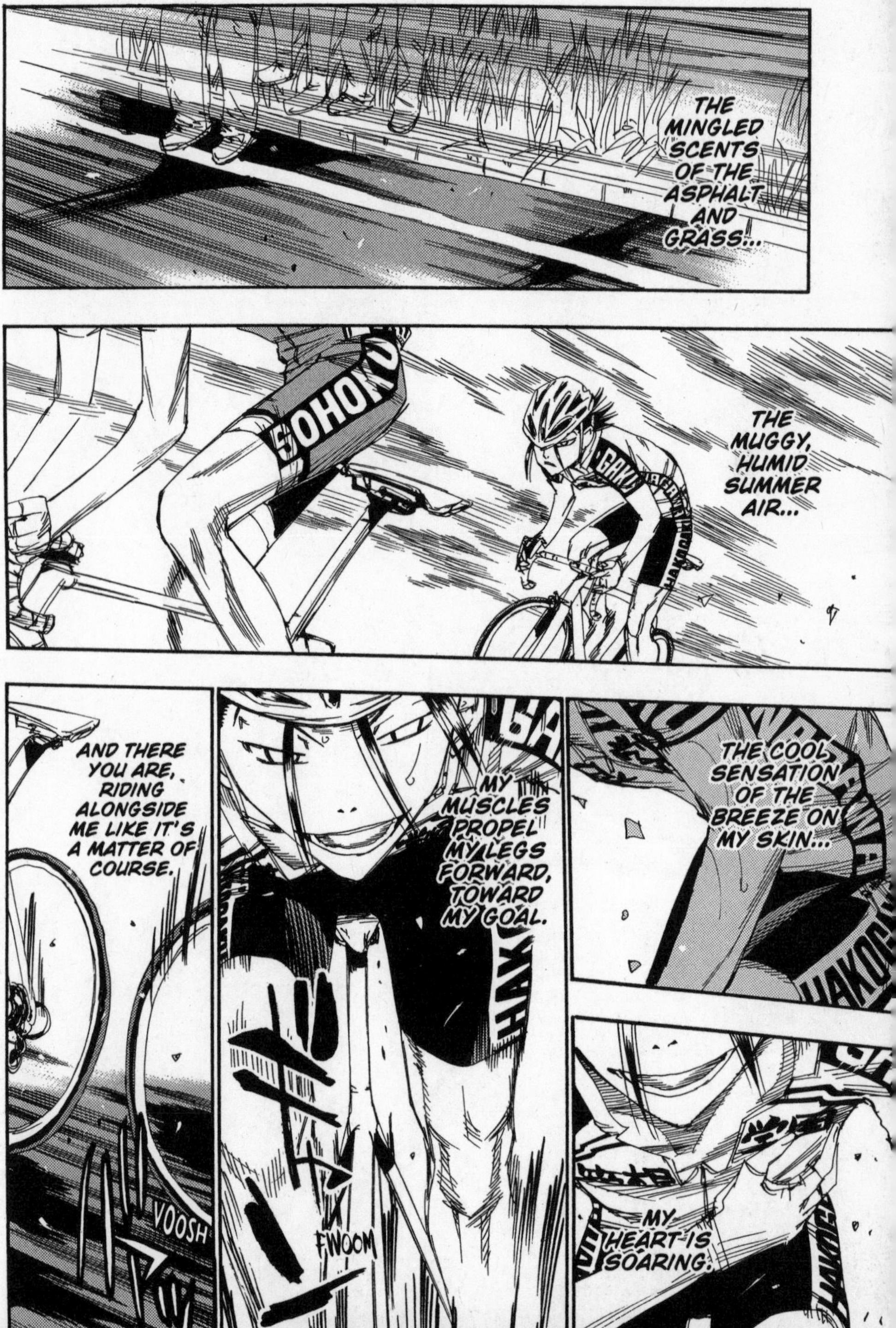
THE MINGLED SCENTS OF THE ASPHALT AND GRASS...
THE MUGGY, HUMID SUMMER AIR...
THE COOL SENSATION OF THE BREEZE ON MY SKIN...
MY HEART IS SOARING.
MY MUSCLES PROPEL MY LEGS FORWARD, TOWARD MY GOAL.
FWOOM
AND THERE YOU ARE, RIDING ALONGSIDE ME LIKE IT'S A MATTER OF COURSE.
VOOSH

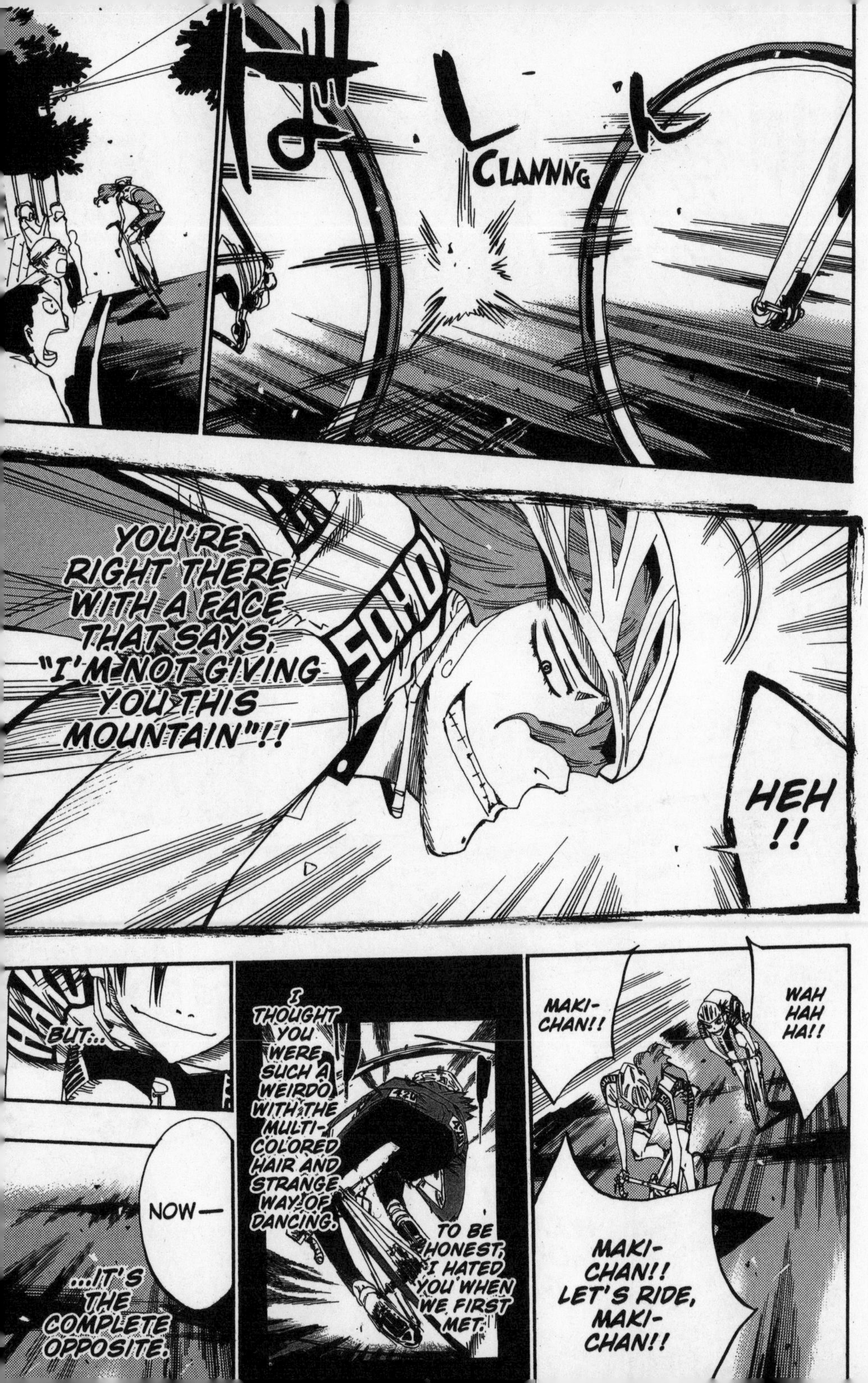
CLANNNG
HEH !!
YOU'RE RIGHT THERE WITH A FACE THAT SAYS, "I'M NOT GIVING YOU THIS MOUNTAIN"!!
WAH HAH HA!!
MAKI-CHAN!!
MAKI-CHAN!! LET'S RIDE, MAKI-CHAN!!
I THOUGHT YOU WERE SUCH A WEIRDO WITH THE MULTI-COLORED HAIR AND STRANGE WAY OF DANCING.
TO BE HONEST, I HATED YOU WHEN WE FIRST MET.
BUT...
NOW—
...IT'S THE COMPLETE OPPOSITE.

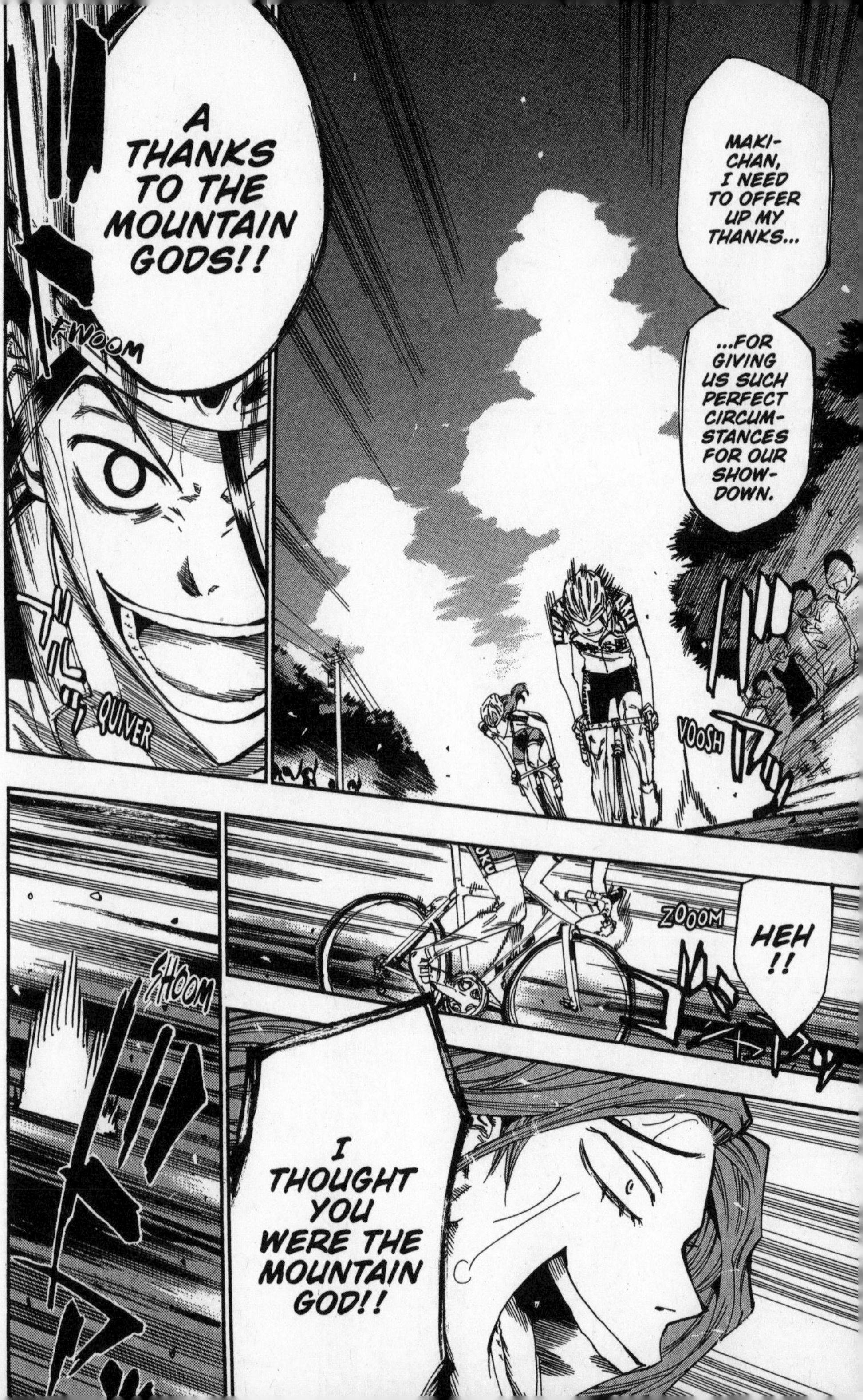
MAKI-CHAN, I NEED TO OFFER UP MY THANKS...
...FOR GIVING US SUCH PERFECT CIRCUM-STANCES FOR OUR SHOW-DOWN.
VOOSH
A THANKS TO THE MOUNTAIN GODS!!
FWOOM
QUIVER
ZOOOM
HEH!!
SHOOM
I THOUGHT YOU WERE THE MOUNTAIN GOD!!

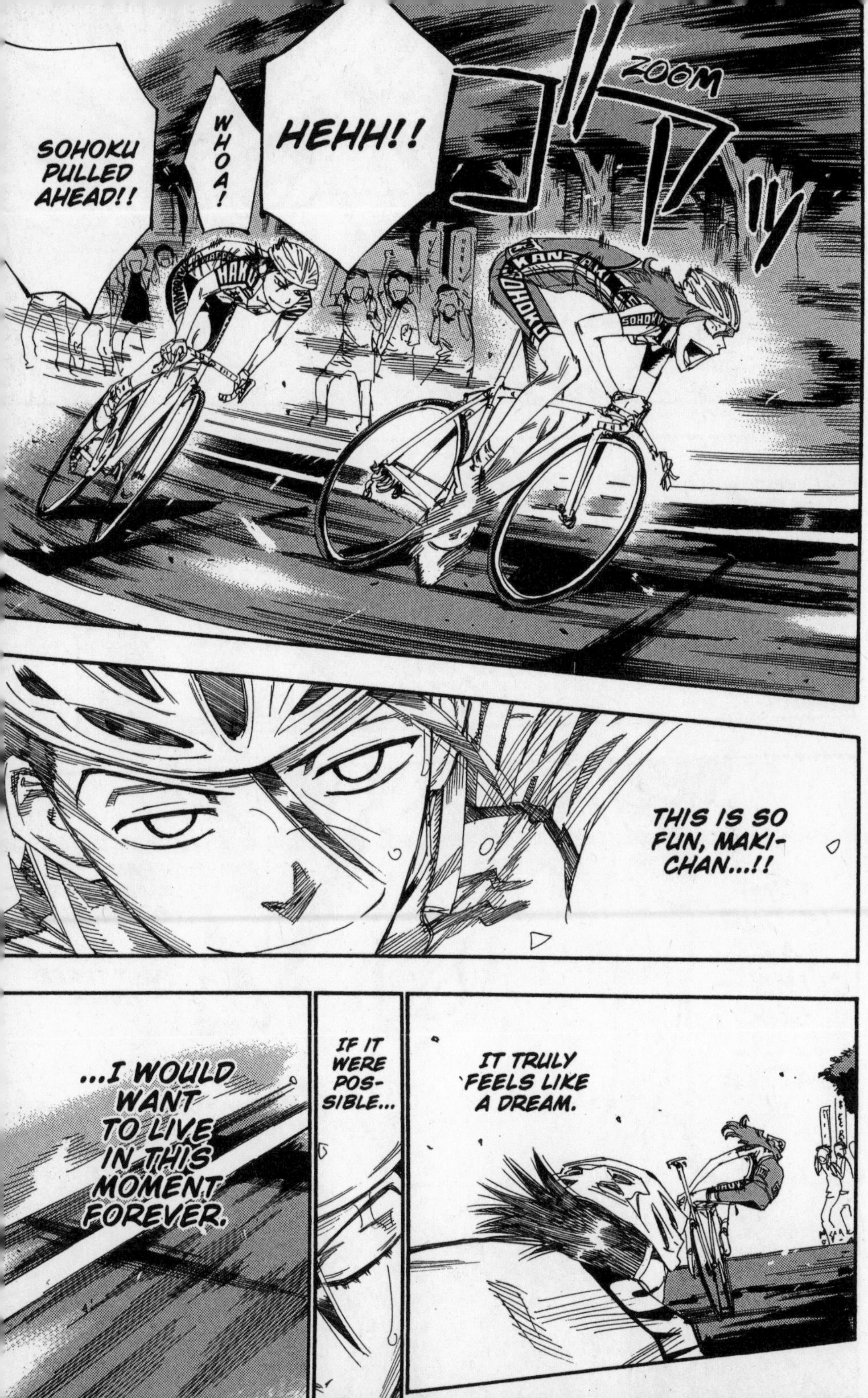
ZOOM
HEHH!!
WHOA!
SOHOKU PULLED AHEAD!!
THIS IS SO FUN, MAKI-CHAN...!!
IT TRULY FEELS LIKE A DREAM.
IF IT WERE POS-SIBLE...
...I WOULD WANT TO LIVE IN THIS MOMENT FOREVER.

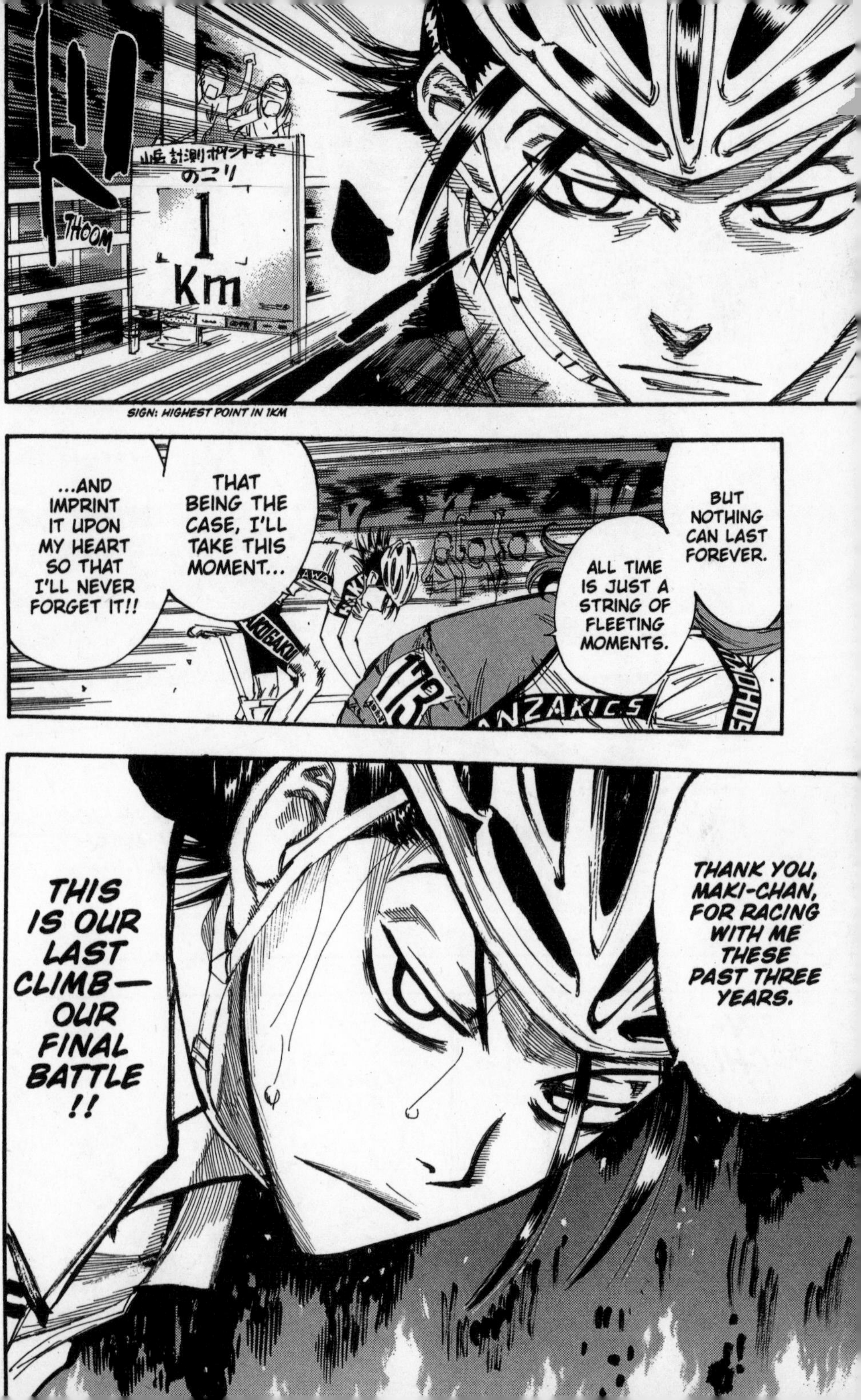
THOOM
山岳計測ポイントまで
のこり
1
Km
SIGN: HIGHEST POINT IN 1KM
BUT NOTHING CAN LAST FOREVER.
ALL TIME IS JUST A STRING OF FLEETING MOMENTS.
THAT BEING THE CASE, I'LL TAKE THIS MOMENT...
...AND IMPRINT IT UPON MY HEART SO THAT I'LL NEVER FORGET IT!!
THANK YOU, MAKI-CHAN, FOR RACING WITH ME THESE PAST THREE YEARS.
THIS IS OUR LAST CLIMB—OUR FINAL BATTLE!!

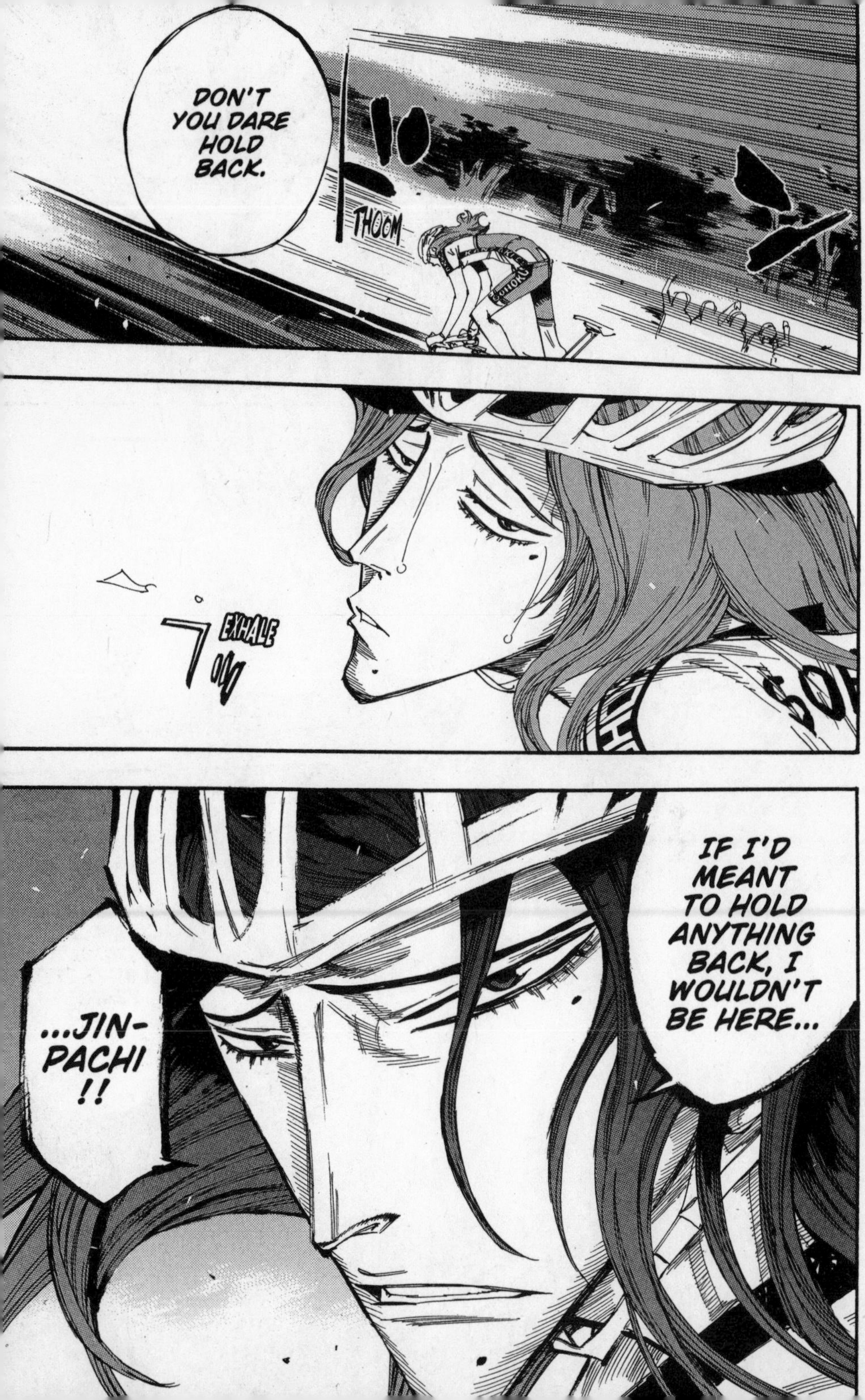
DON'T YOU DARE HOLD BACK.
THOOM
EXHALE
IF I'D MEANT TO HOLD ANYTHING BACK, I WOULDN'T BE HERE...
...JIN-PACHI!!

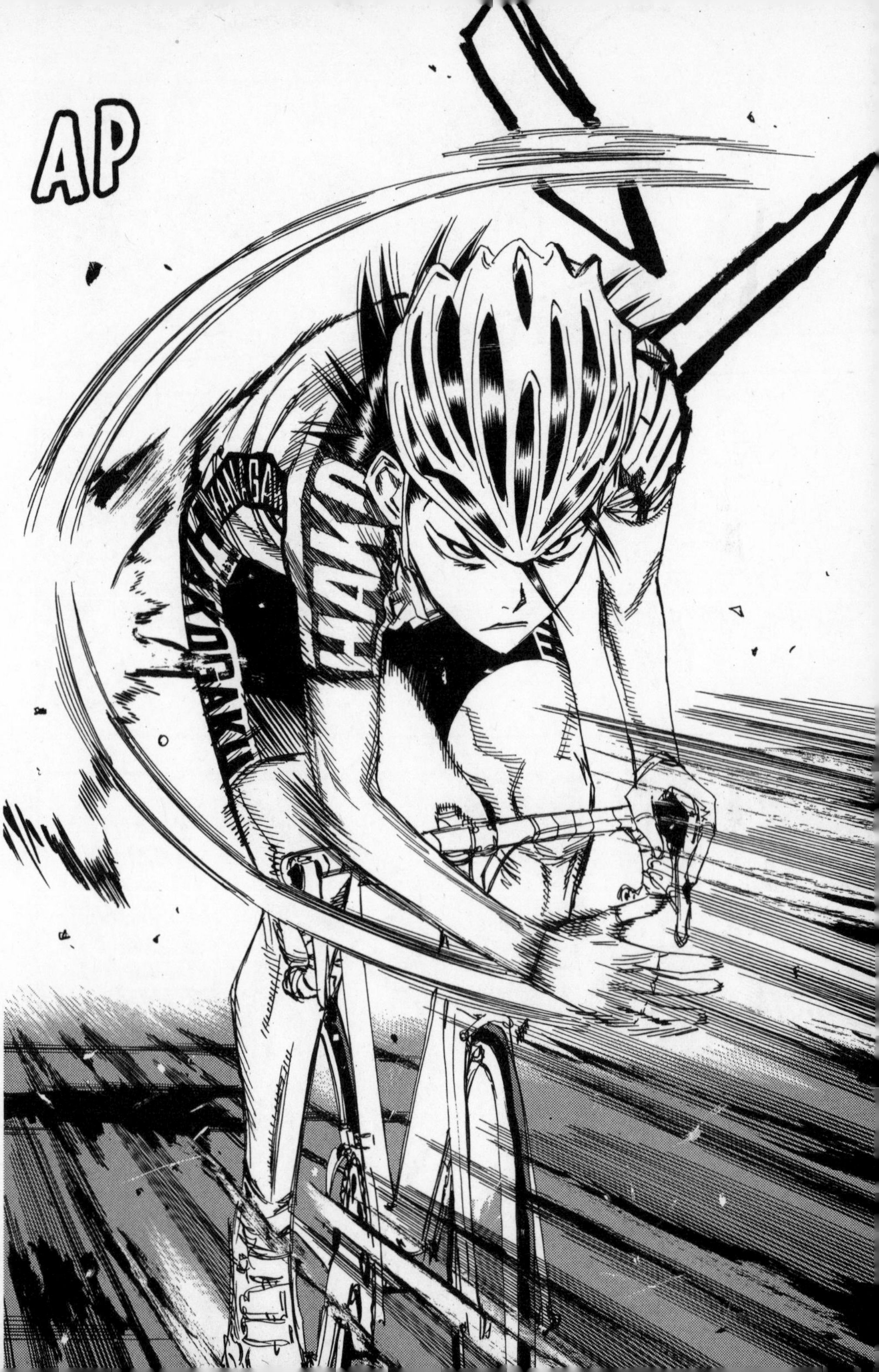
AP

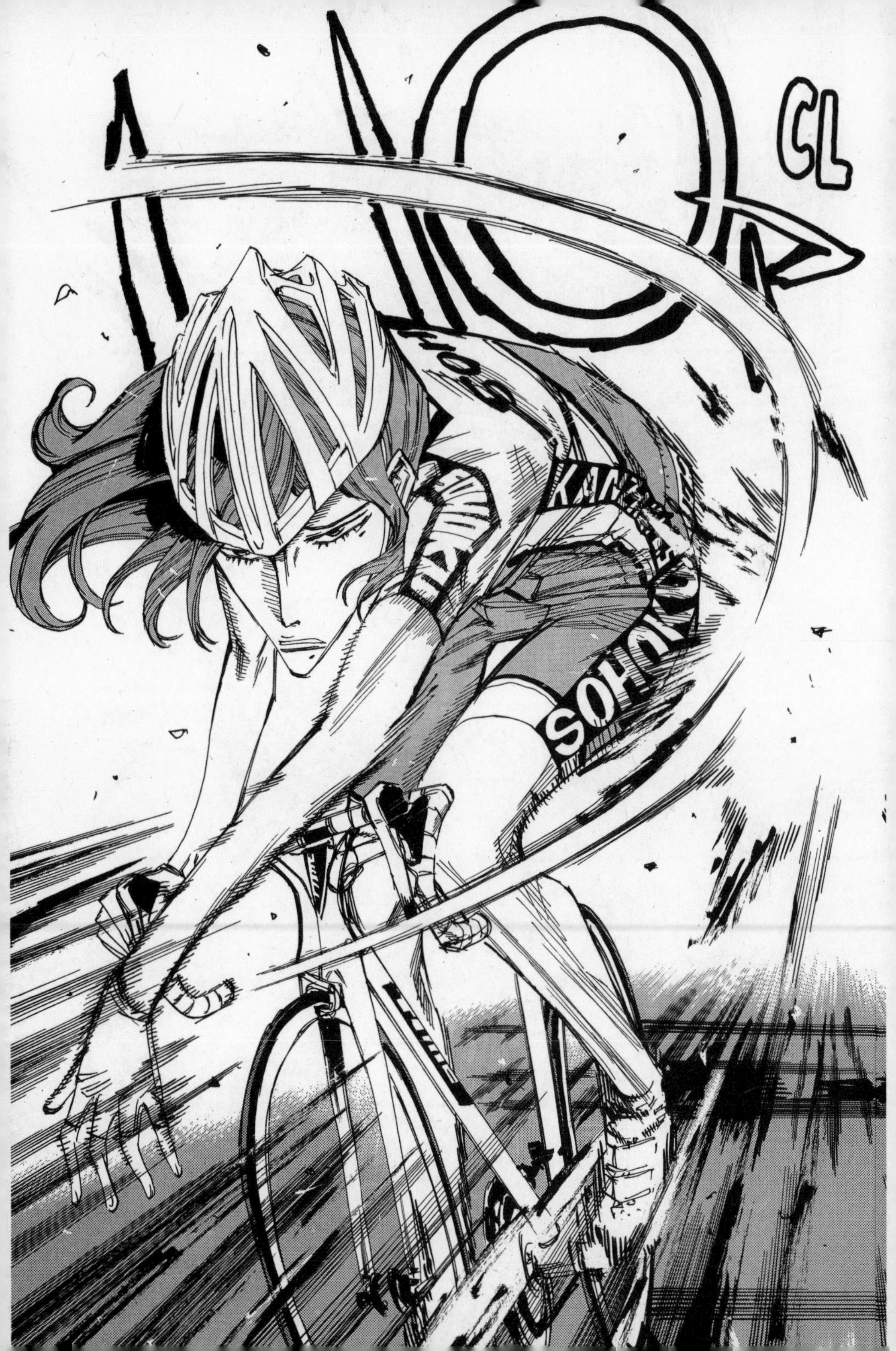
CL

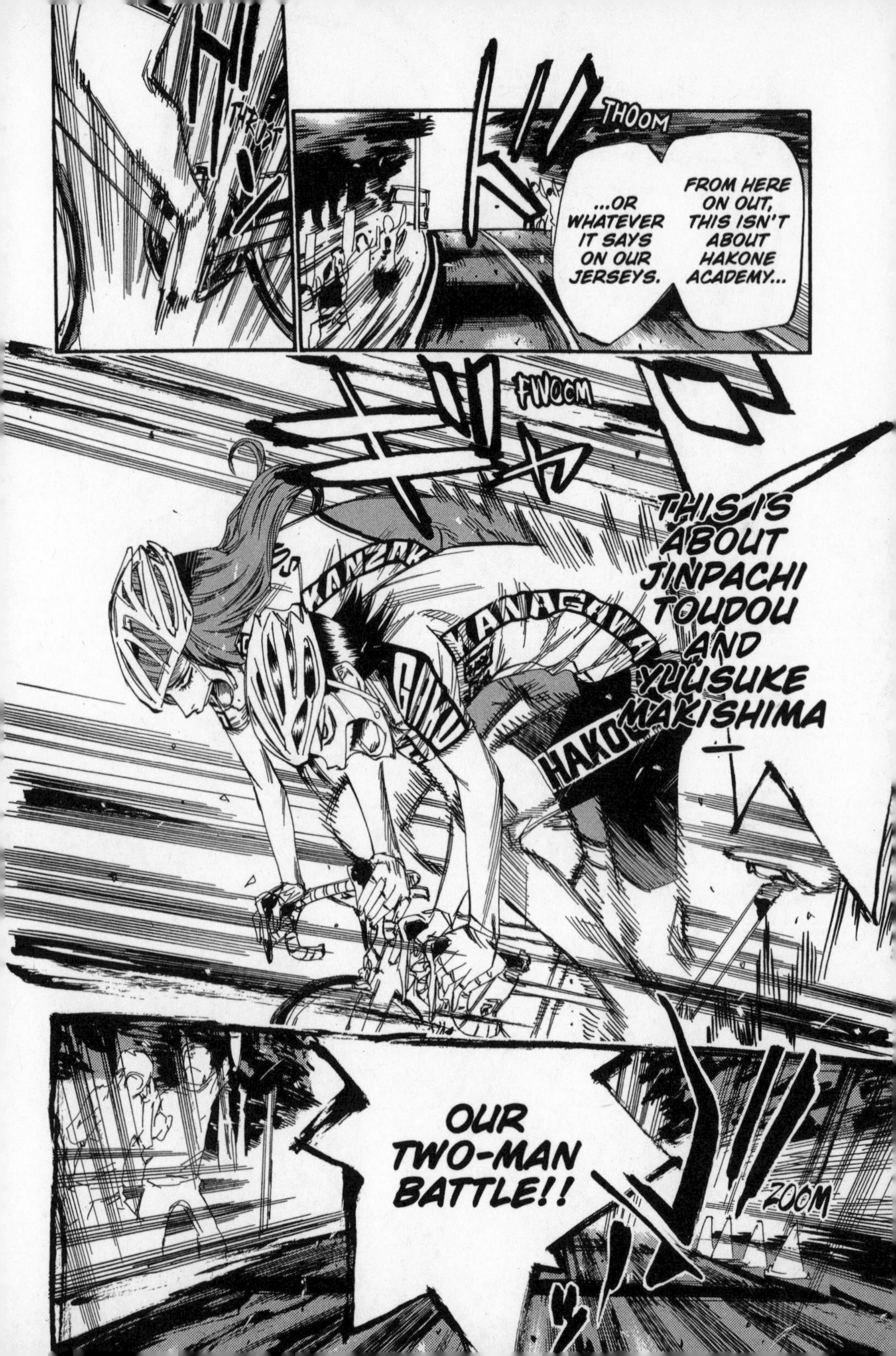
THOOM
FROM HERE ON OUT, THIS ISN'T ABOUT HAKONE ACADEMY...
...OR WHATEVER IT SAYS ON OUR JERSEYS.
THRUST
FWOOM
THIS IS ABOUT JINPACHI TOUDOU AND YUUSUKE MAKISHIMA—
ZOOM
OUR TWO-MAN BATTLE!!

# RIDE.99 THE LAST CLIMB

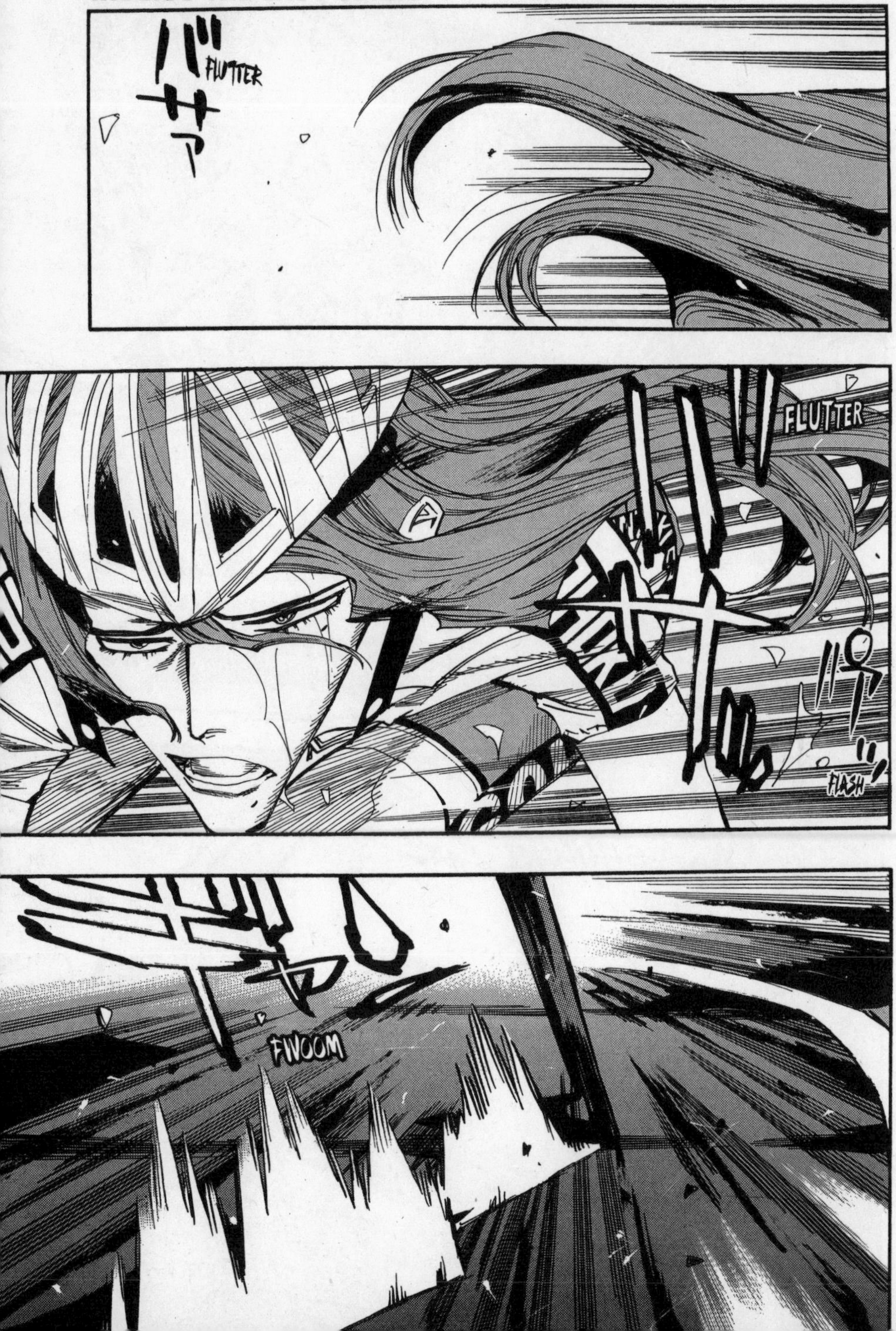
バサァ
FLUTTER
FLUTTER
FLASH
FWOOM

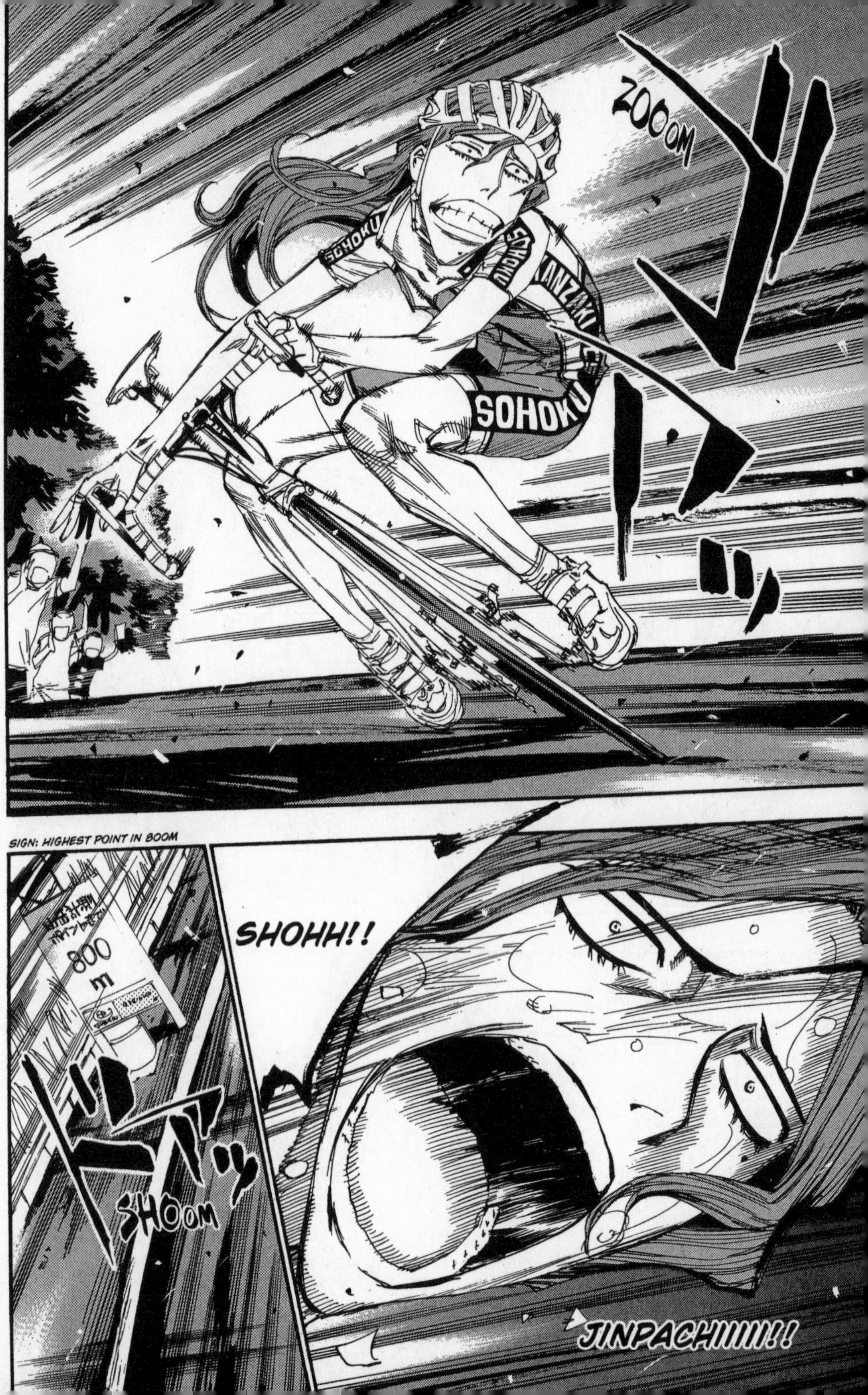
ZOOOM
SHOHH!!
JINPACHIIIIII!!
SIGN: HIGHEST POINT IN 800M
800 m
SHOOM

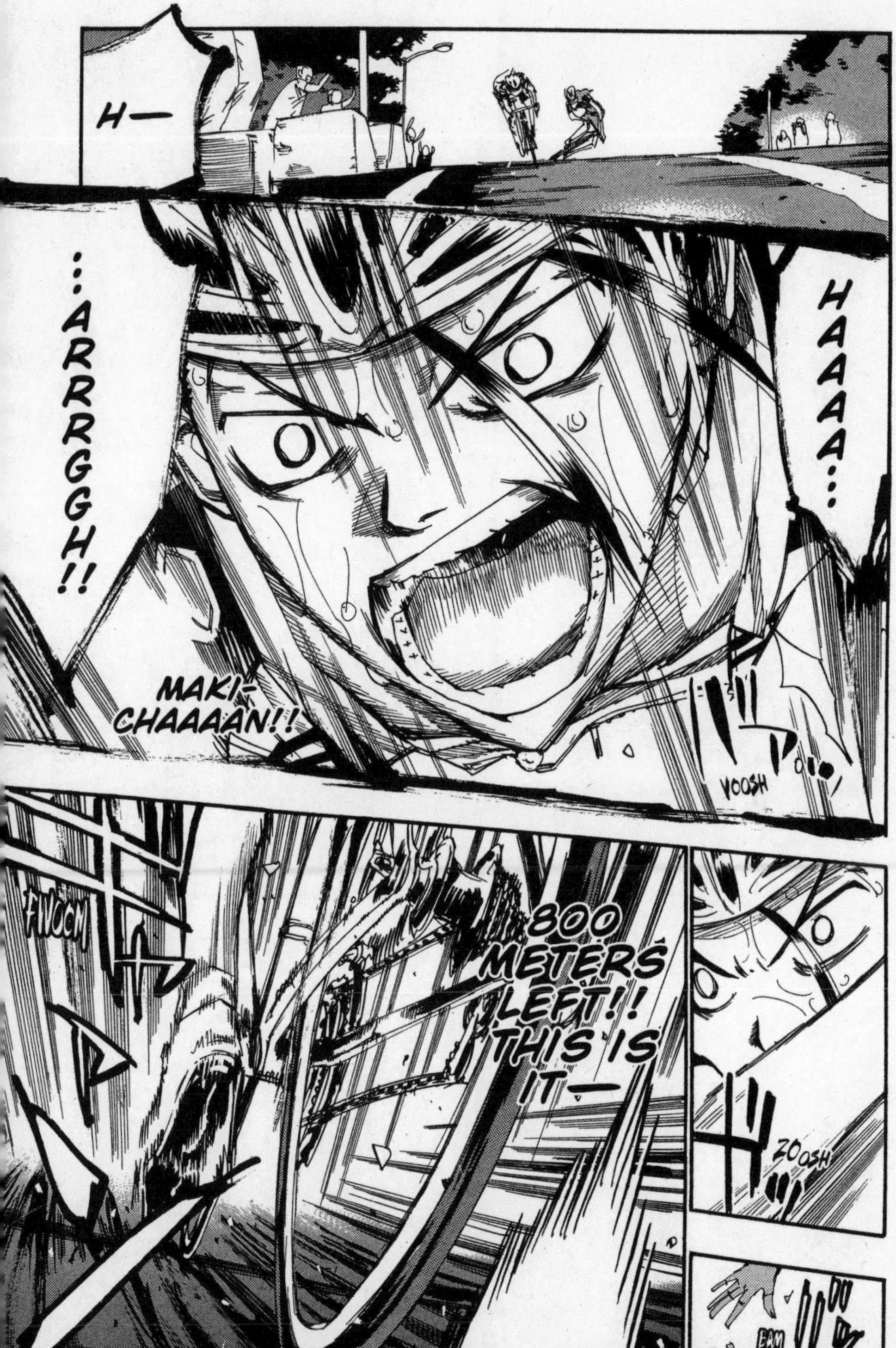
H—
HAAAAA...
...ARRRRGGH!!
MAKI-CHAAAAN!!
VOOSH
ZOOSH
800 METERS LEFT!! THIS IS IT—
FWOOM
BAM

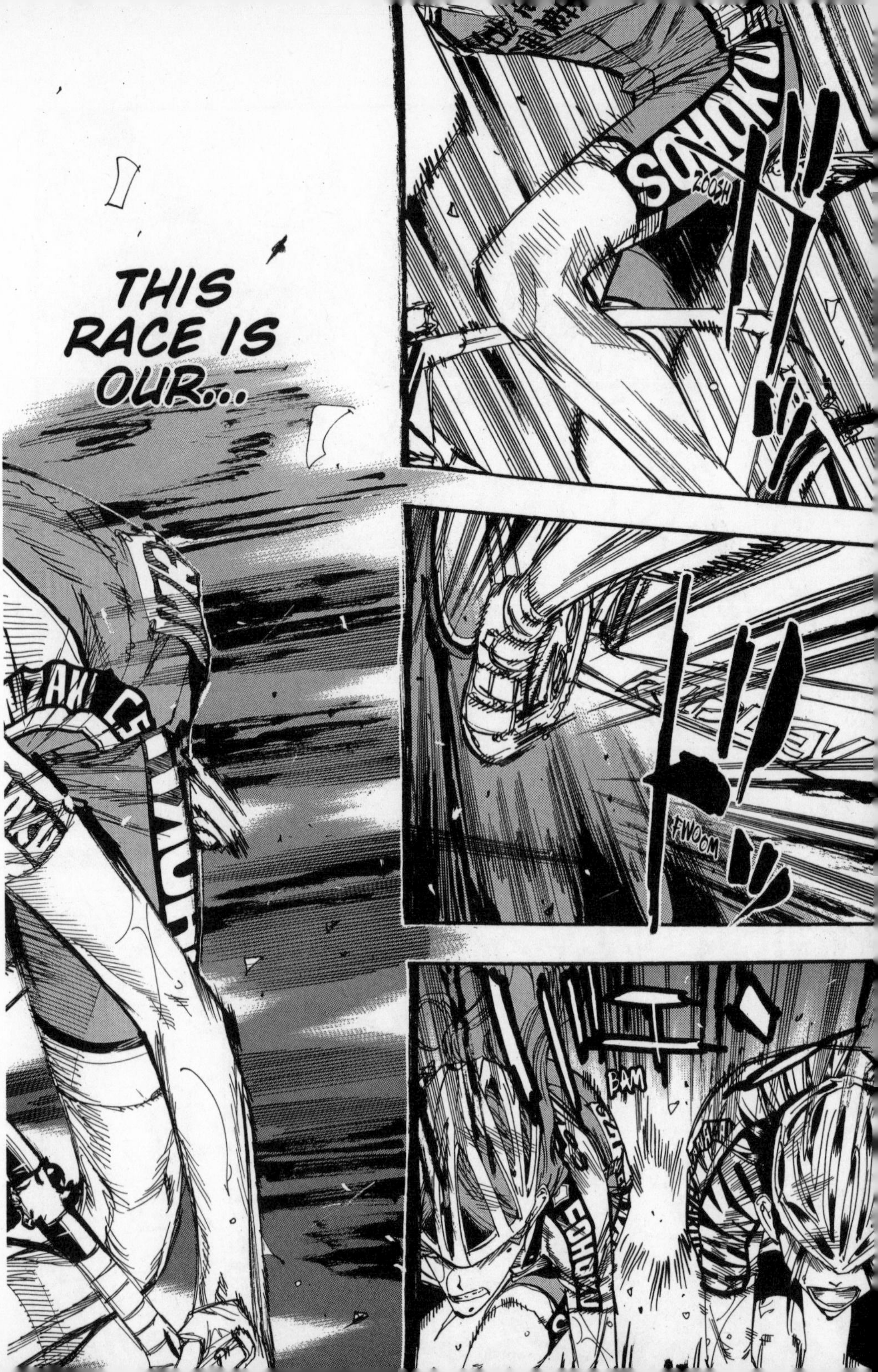

SOHOKU
ZOOSH
FWOOM
BAM
THIS RACE IS OUR...

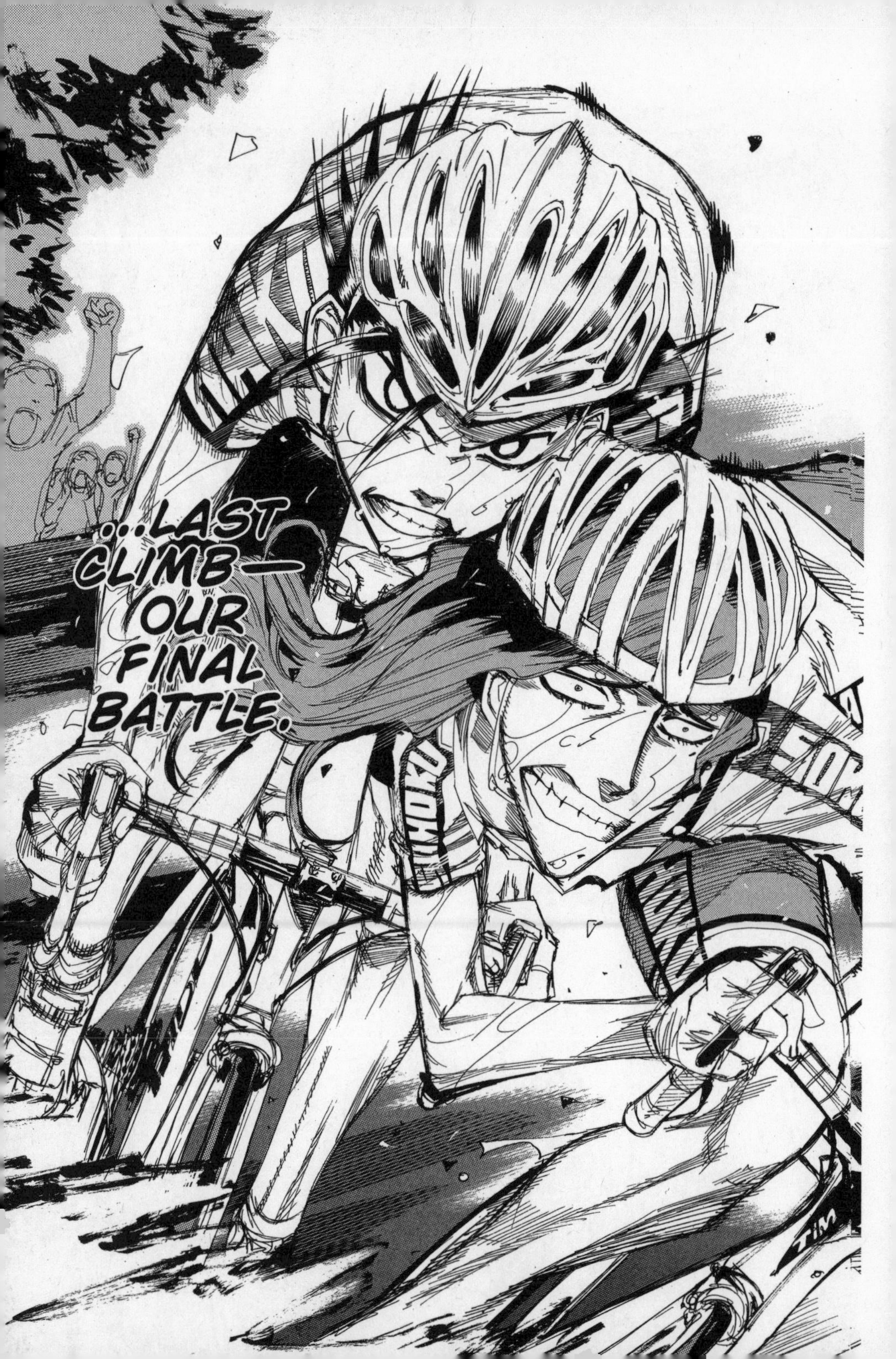
...LAST CLIMB—OUR FINAL BATTLE.

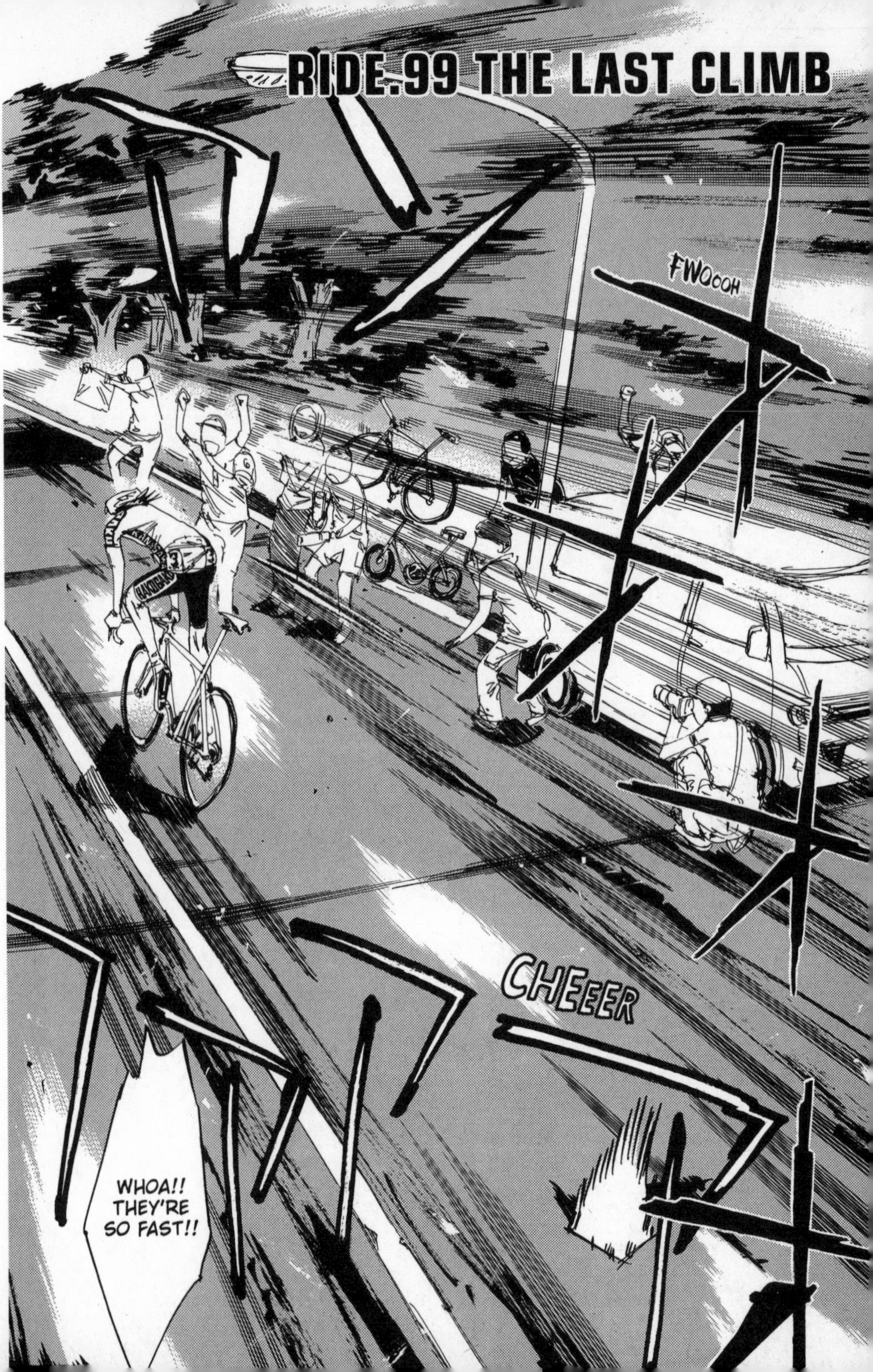
RIDE.99 THE LAST CLIMB
FWOOOH
CHEEER
WHOA!! THEY'RE SO FAST!!

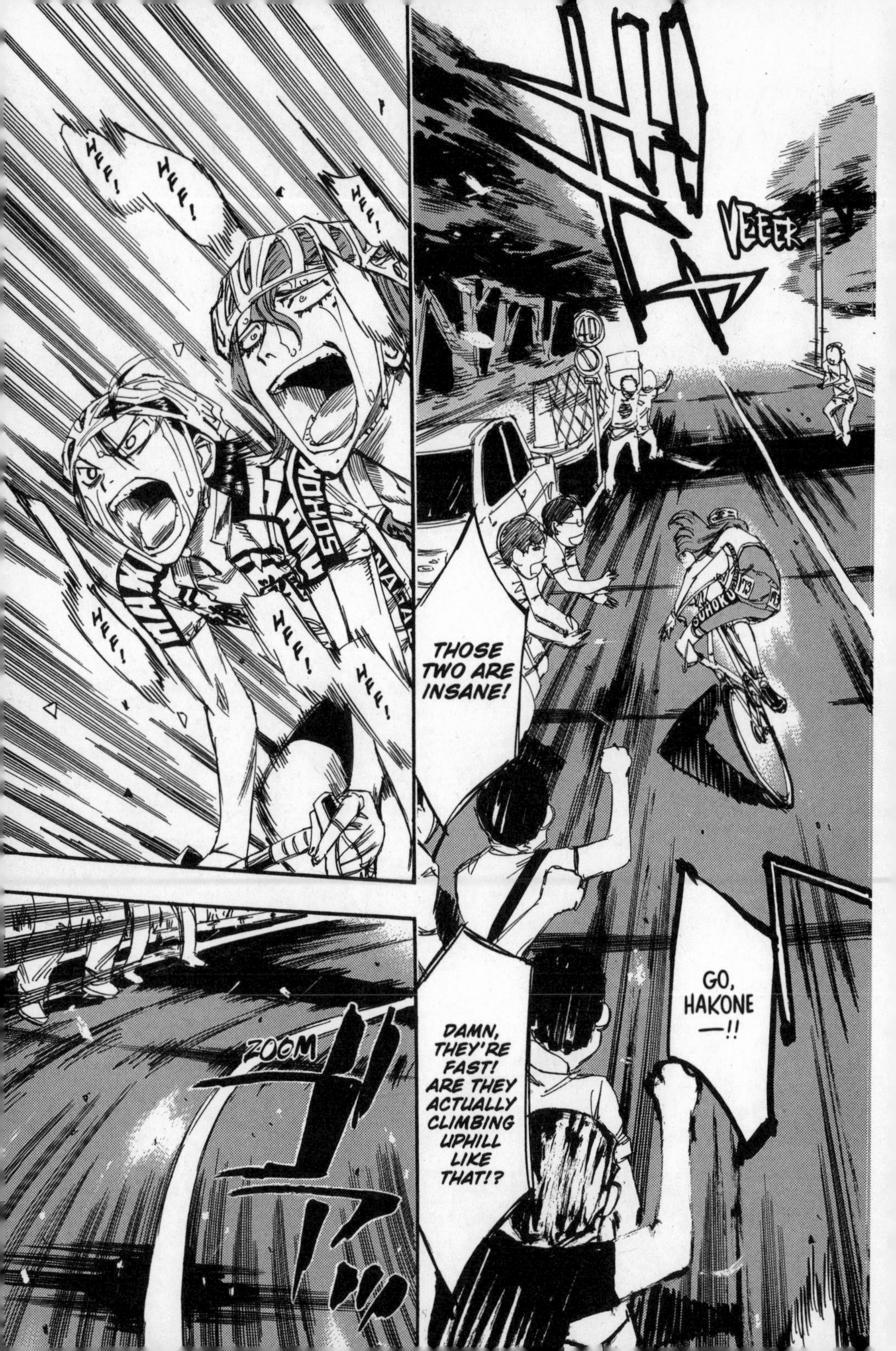
VEEER
THOSE TWO ARE INSANE!
GO, HAKONE—!!
DAMN, THEY'RE FAST! ARE THEY ACTUALLY CLIMBING UPHILL LIKE THAT!?
HFF! HFF!
HFF!
HFF!
HFF!
HFF!
ZOOM

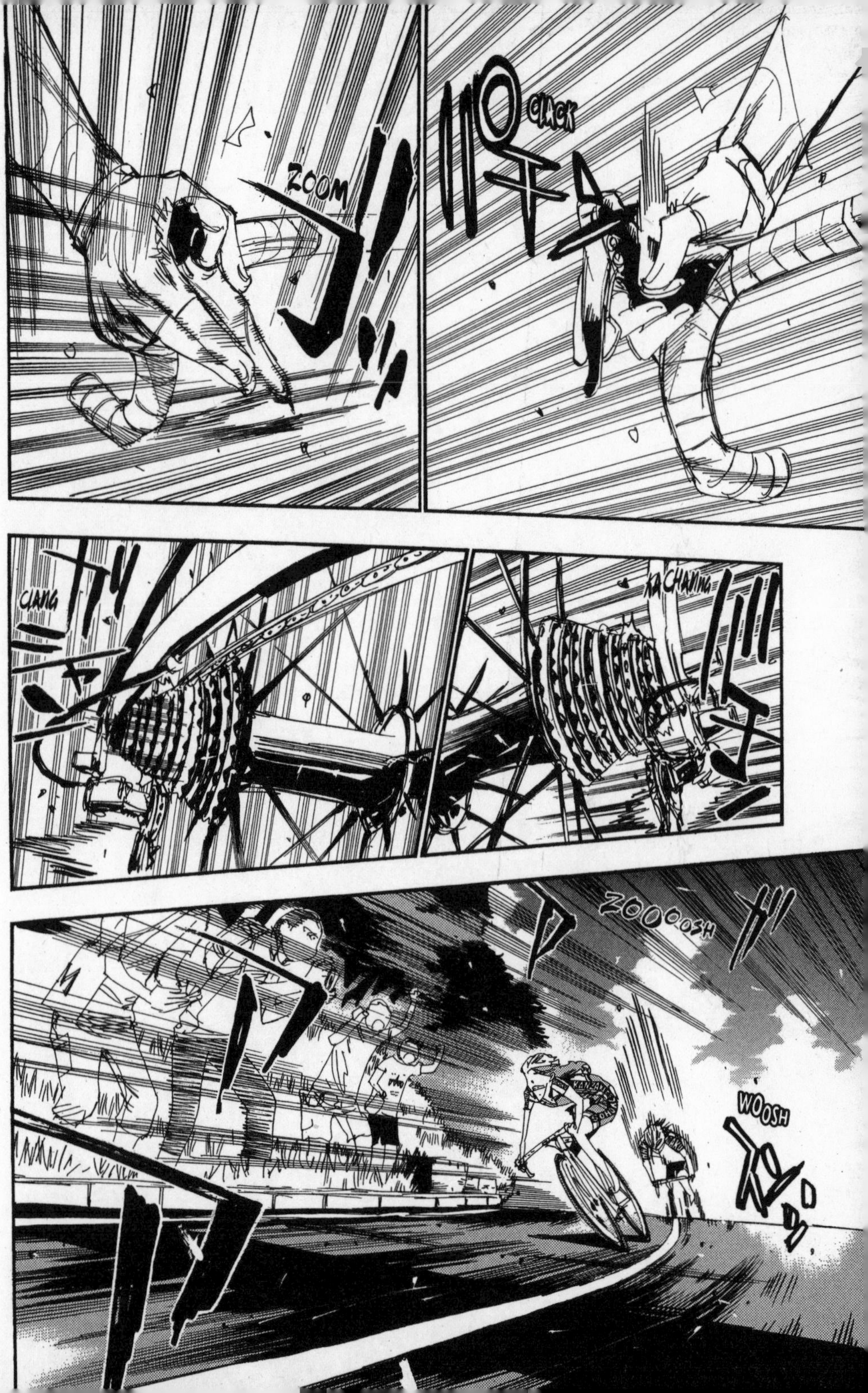
CLACK
ZOOM
KACHANG
CLANG
ZOOOOSH
WOOSH

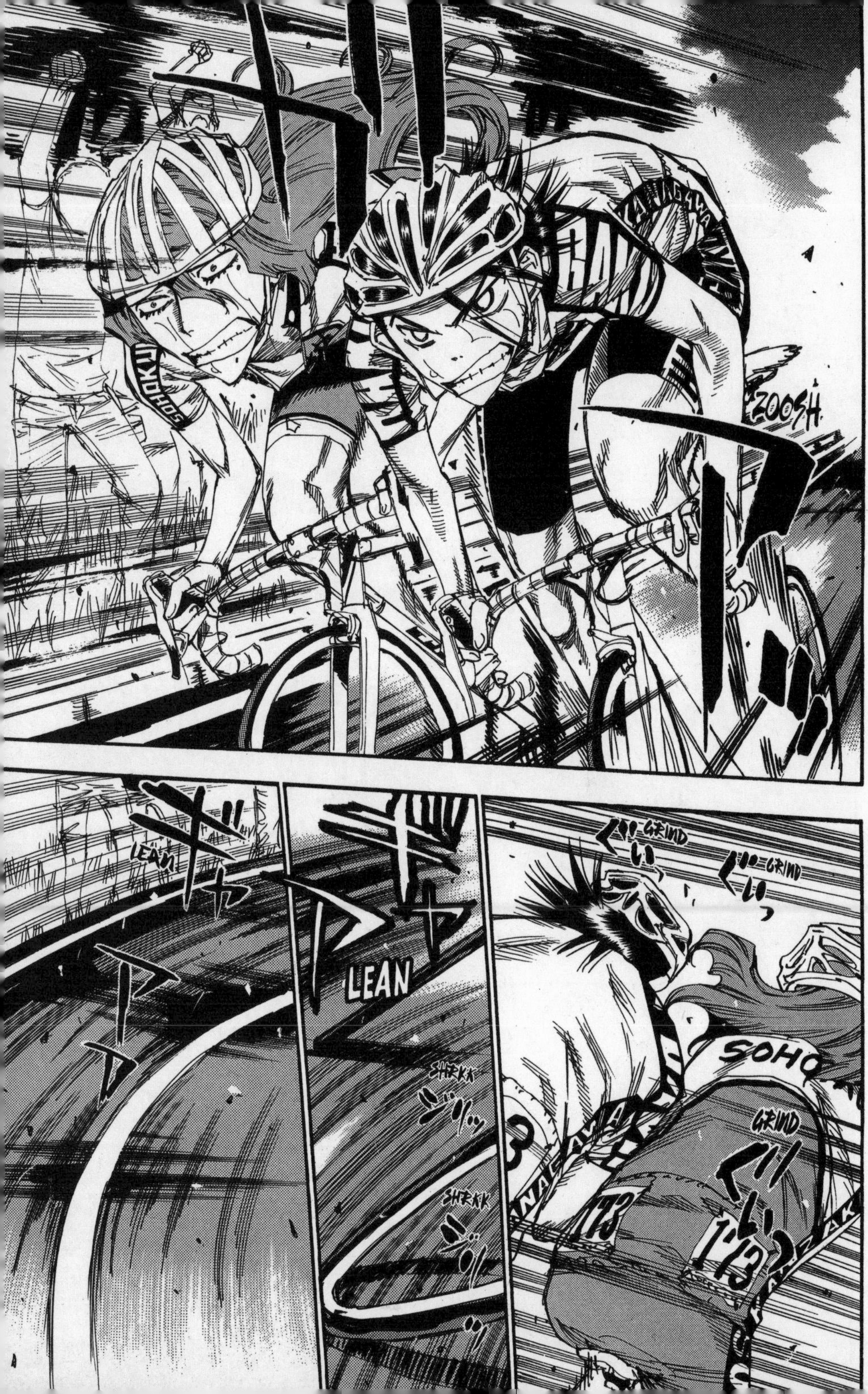
ZOOSH
GRIND
GRIND
GRIND
LEAN
SHRKK
SHRKK
LEAN

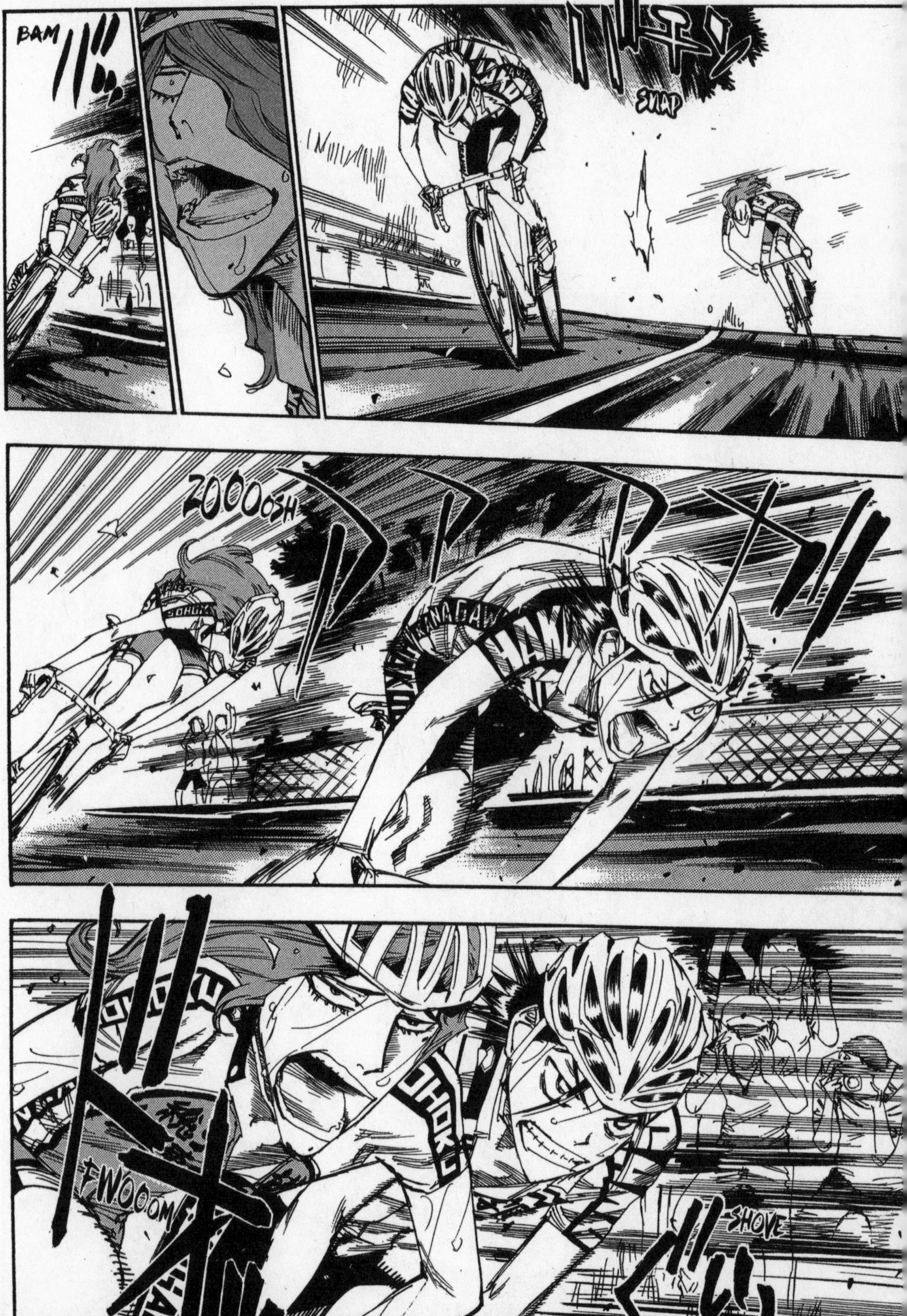
SNAP
BAM
ZOOOOSH
SHOVE
FWOOOM

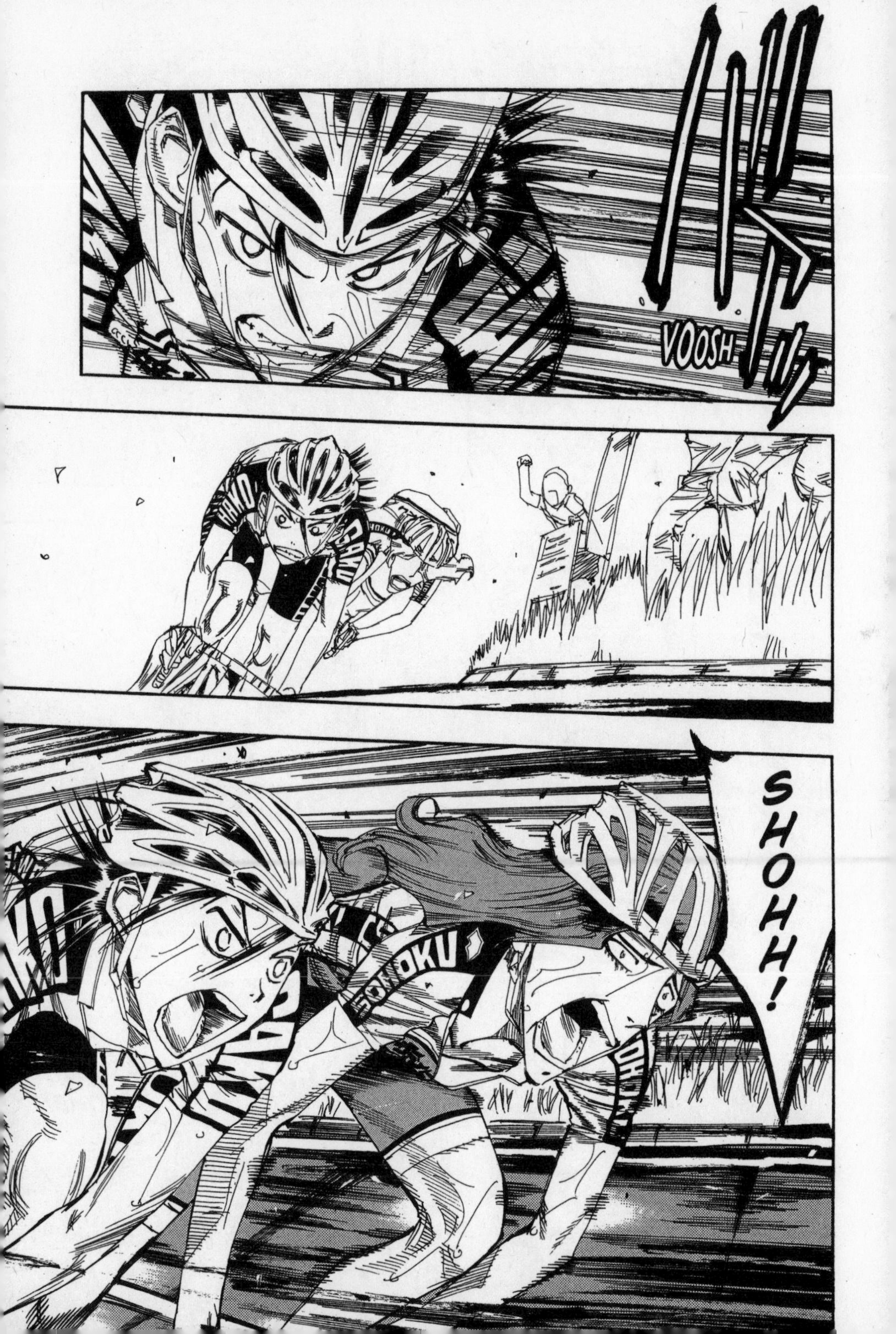
VOOSH
SHOHHH!

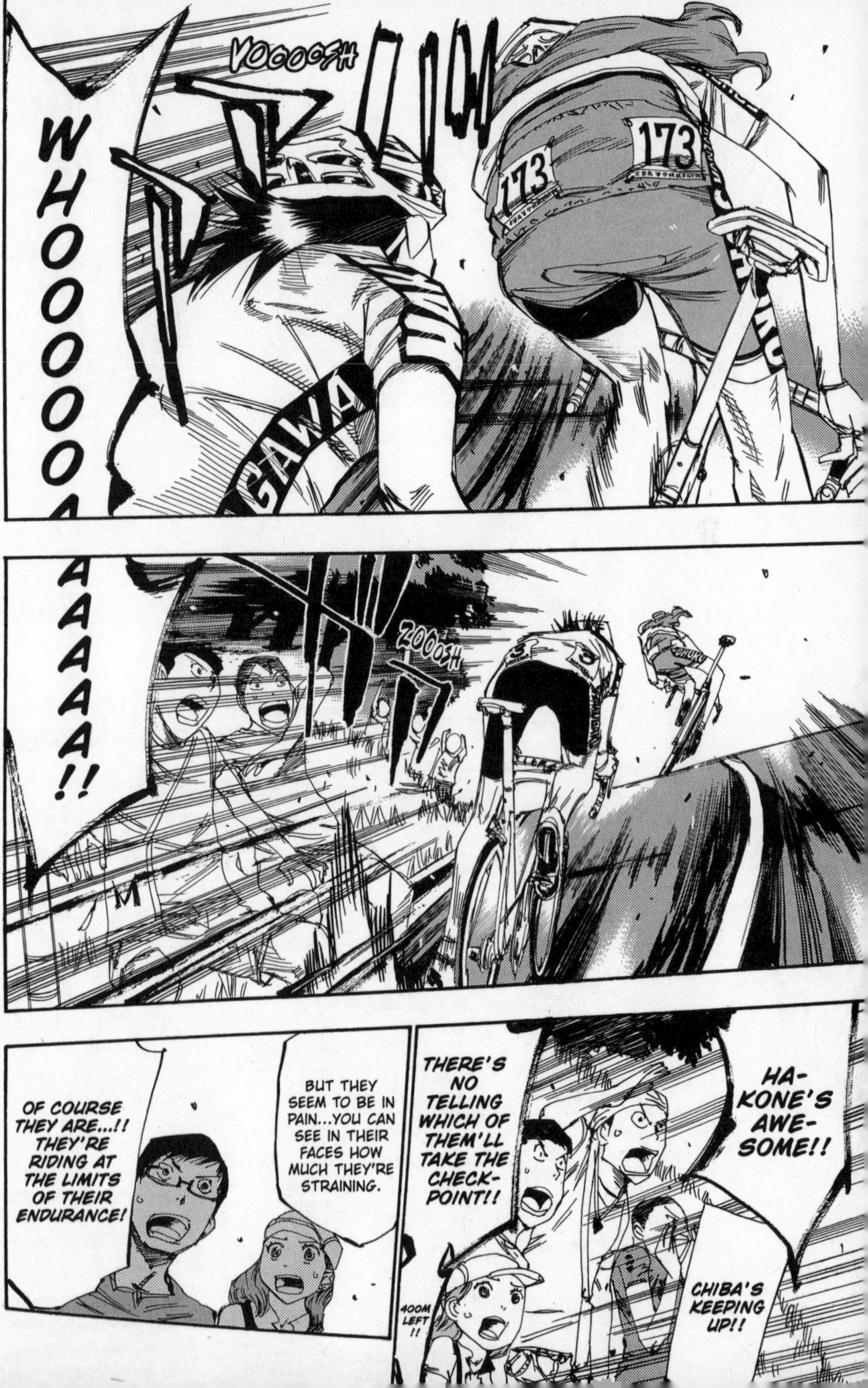
VOOOOOSH
WHOOOOOOAAAAAAA!!
ZOOOSH
HA-KONE'S AWE-SOME!!
THERE'S NO TELLING WHICH OF THEM'LL TAKE THE CHECK-POINT!!
CHIBA'S KEEPING UP!!
400M LEFT!!
BUT THEY SEEM TO BE IN PAIN...YOU CAN SEE IN THEIR FACES HOW MUCH THEY'RE STRAINING.
OF COURSE THEY ARE...!! THEY'RE RIDING AT THE LIMITS OF THEIR ENDURANCE!

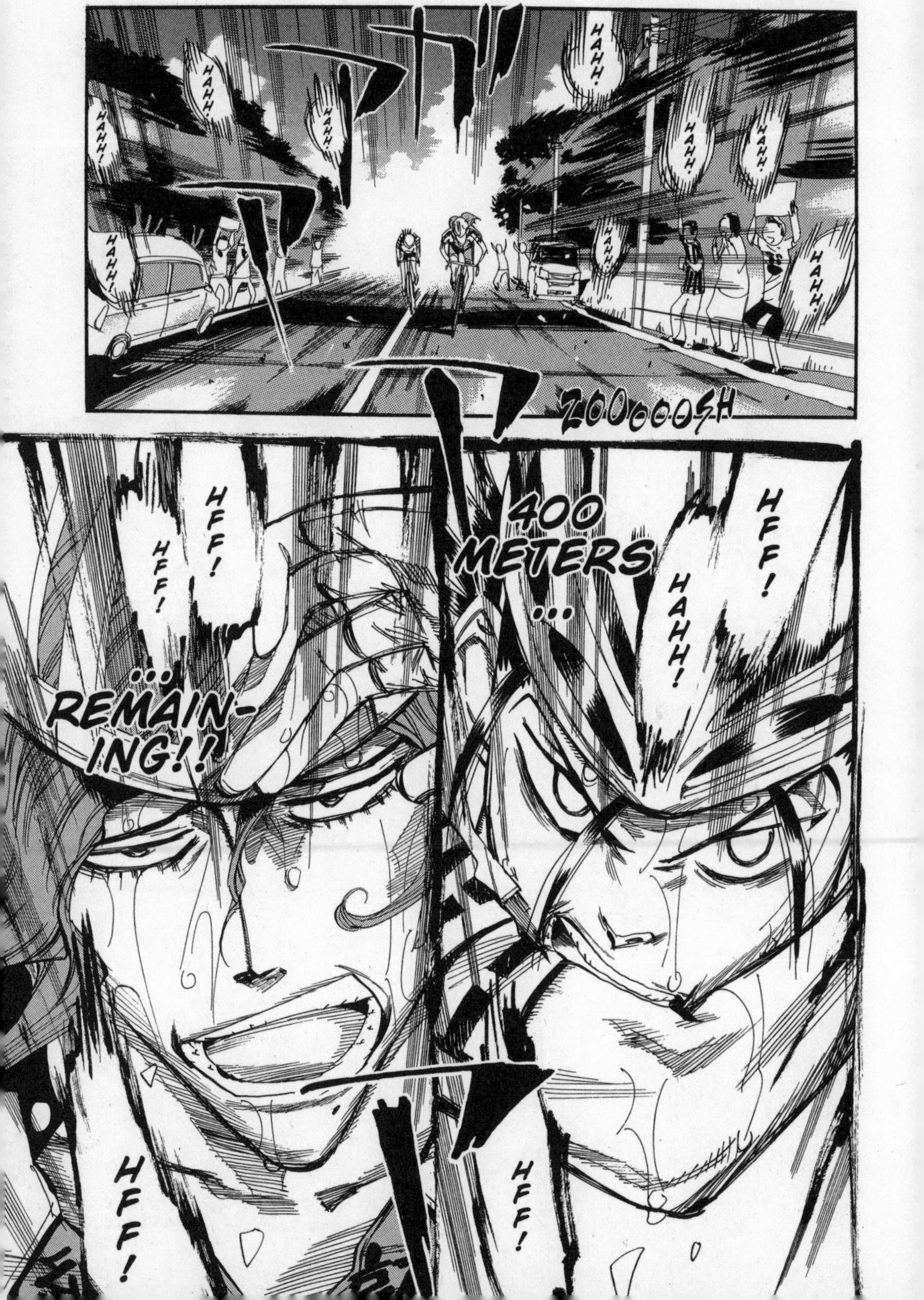
HAHH!
HAHH!
HAHH!
HAHH!
HAHH!
HAHH!
HAHH!
HAHH!
HAHH!
ZOOOOOOSH
HFF!
HAHH!
400 METERS ...
...REMAIN-ING!!
HFF!
HFF!
HFF!
HFF!

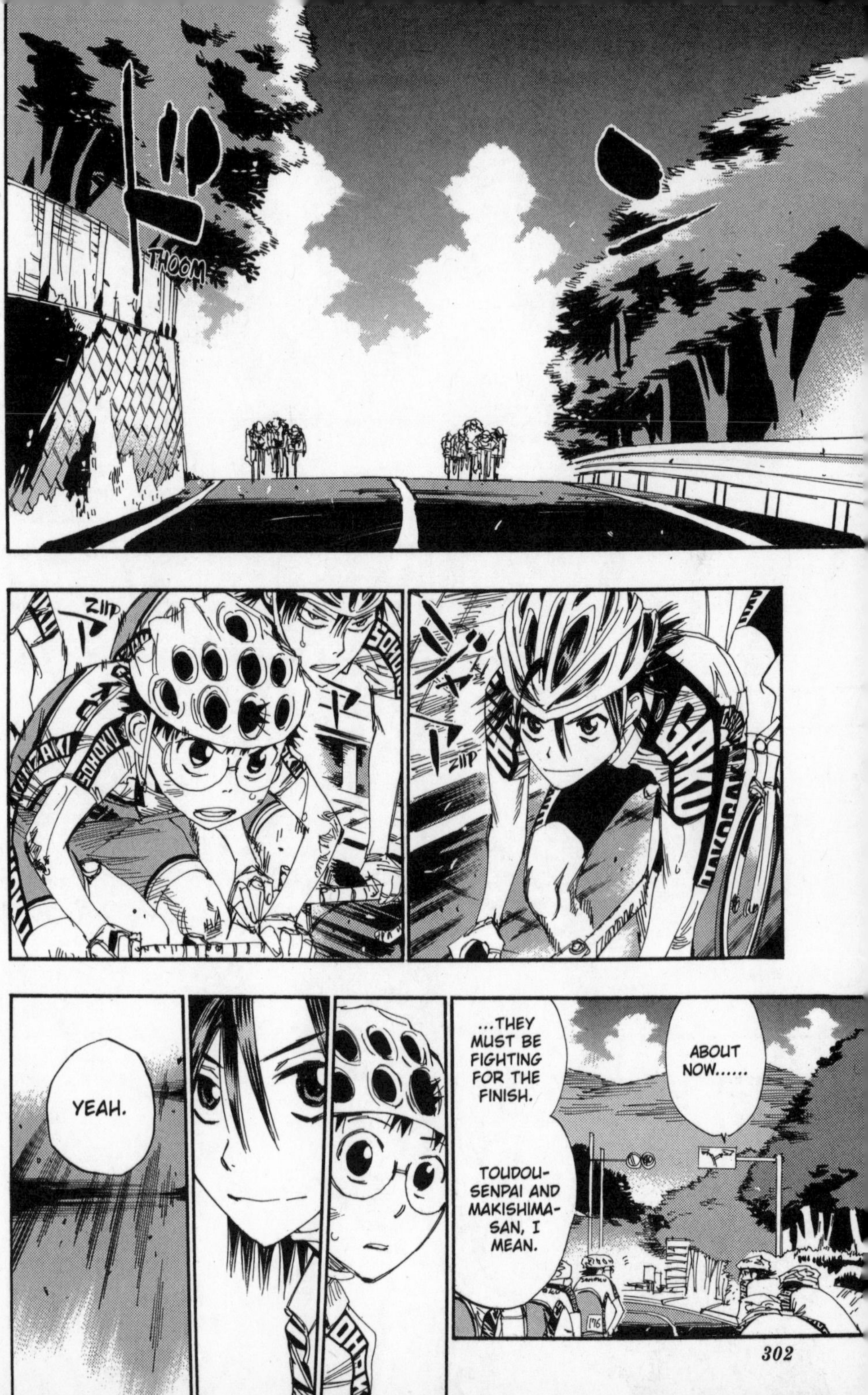
THOOM
ZIIP
ZIIP
ABOUT NOW......
...THEY MUST BE FIGHTING FOR THE FINISH.
TOUDOU-SENPAI AND MAKISHIMA-SAN, I MEAN.
YEAH.

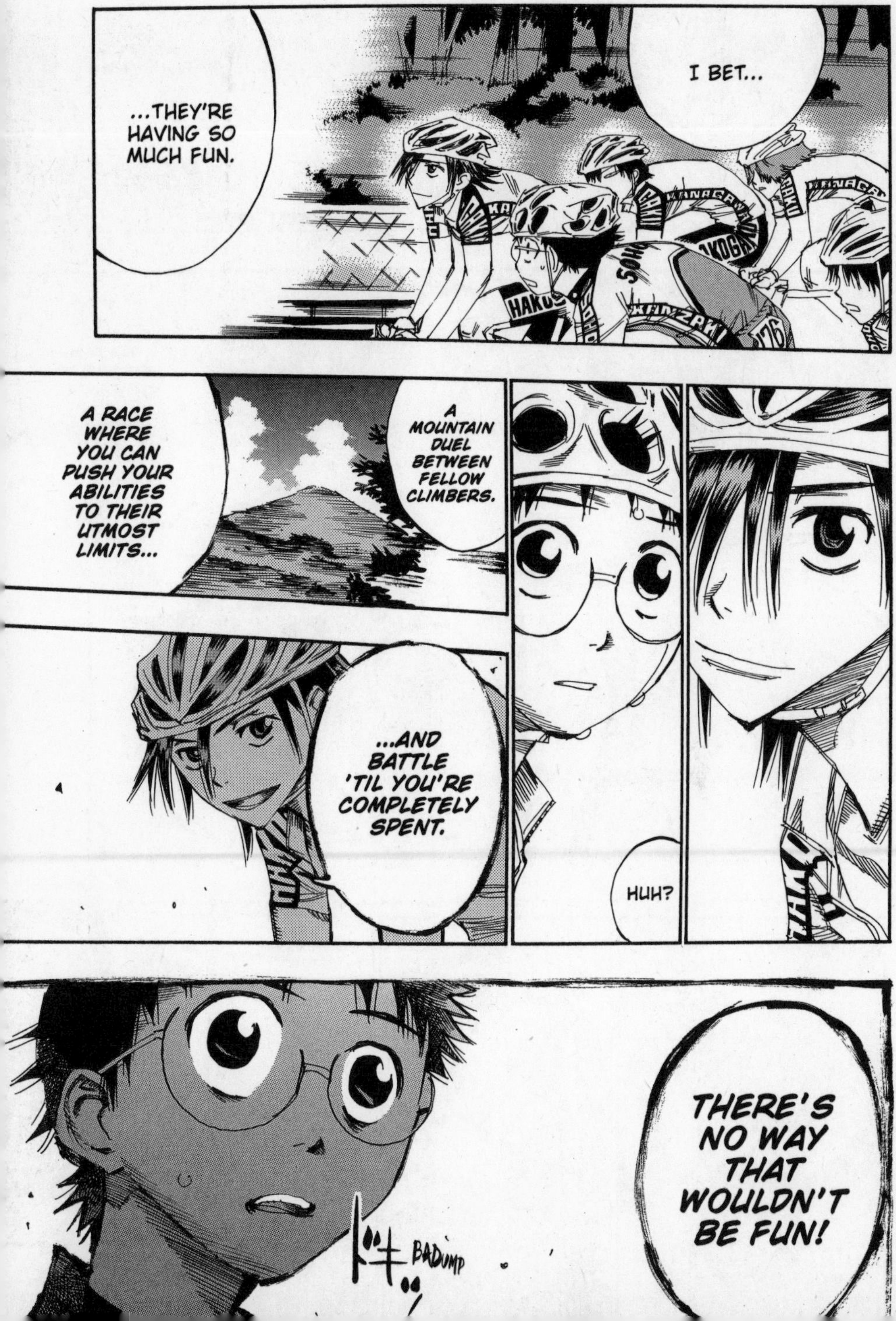
I BET...
...THEY'RE HAVING SO MUCH FUN.
HUH?
A MOUNTAIN DUEL BETWEEN FELLOW CLIMBERS.
A RACE WHERE YOU CAN PUSH YOUR ABILITIES TO THEIR UTMOST LIMITS...
...AND BATTLE 'TIL YOU'RE COMPLETELY SPENT.
THERE'S NO WAY THAT WOULDN'T BE FUN!
BADUMP

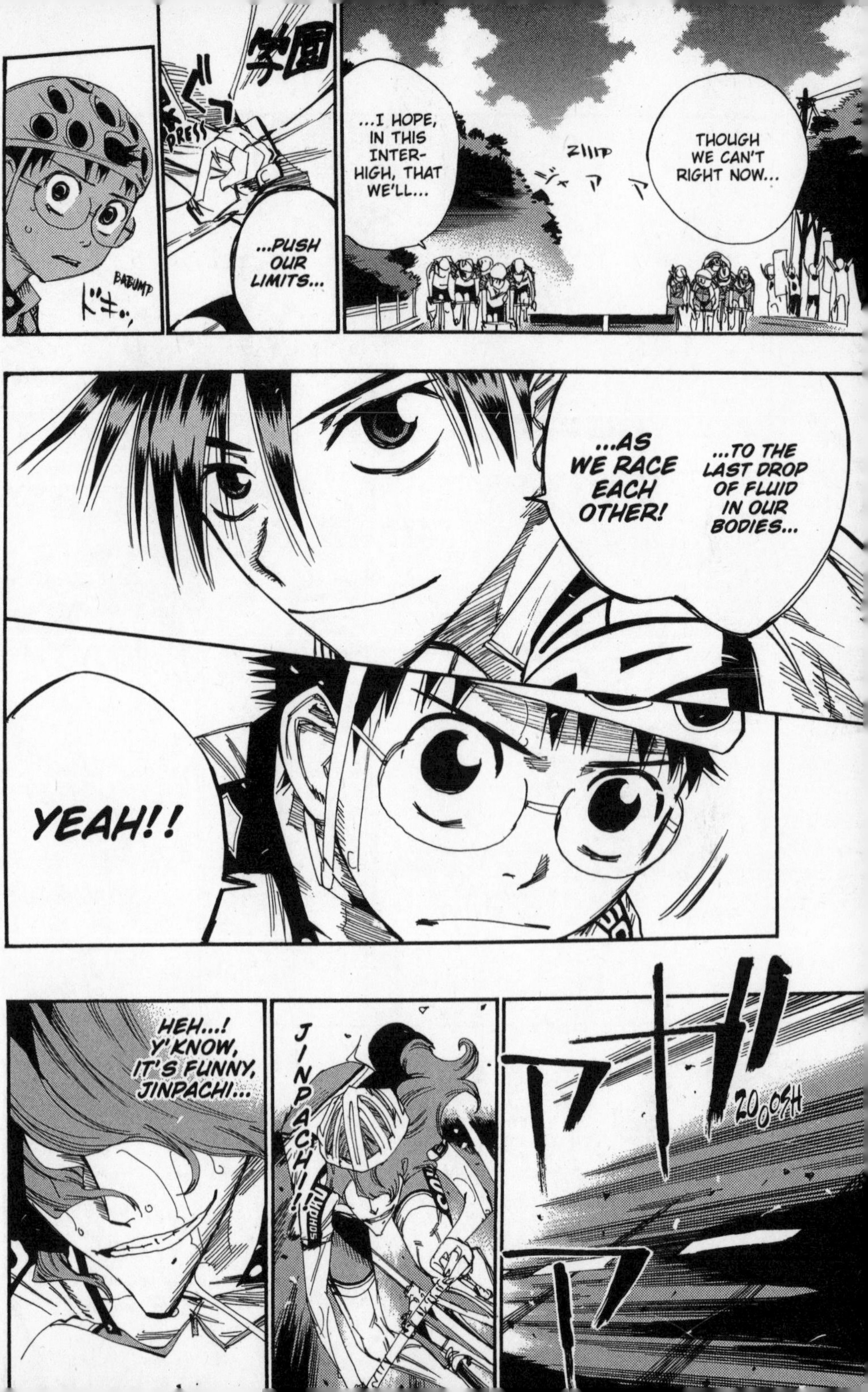
THOUGH WE CAN'T RIGHT NOW...
...I HOPE, IN THIS INTER-HIGH, THAT WE'LL...
...PUSH OUR LIMITS...
PRESS
BABUMP
...TO THE LAST DROP OF FLUID IN OUR BODIES...
...AS WE RACE EACH OTHER!
YEAH!!
ZOOOSH
JINPACHI!!
HEH...! Y'KNOW, IT'S FUNNY, JINPACHI...

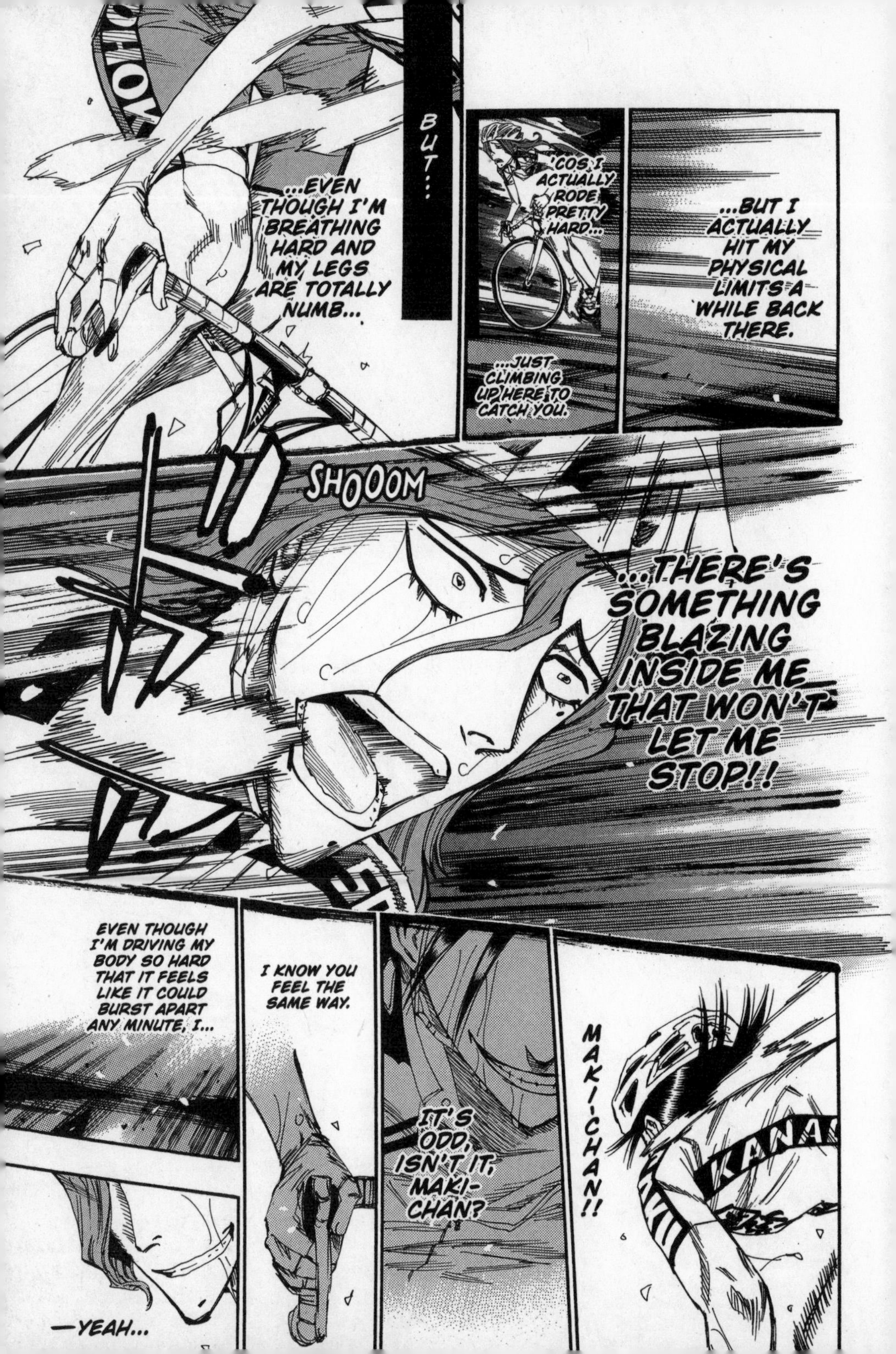
...BUT I ACTUALLY HIT MY PHYSICAL LIMITS A WHILE BACK THERE.
'COS I ACTUALLY RODE PRETTY HARD...
...JUST CLIMBING UP HERE TO CATCH YOU.
BUT...
...EVEN THOUGH I'M BREATHING HARD AND MY LEGS ARE TOTALLY NUMB...
SHOOOM
...THERE'S SOMETHING BLAZING INSIDE ME THAT WON'T LET ME STOP!!
MAKI-CHAN!!
IT'S ODD, ISN'T IT, MAKI-CHAN?
I KNOW YOU FEEL THE SAME WAY.
EVEN THOUGH I'M DRIVING MY BODY SO HARD THAT IT FEELS LIKE IT COULD BURST APART ANY MINUTE, I...
—YEAH...

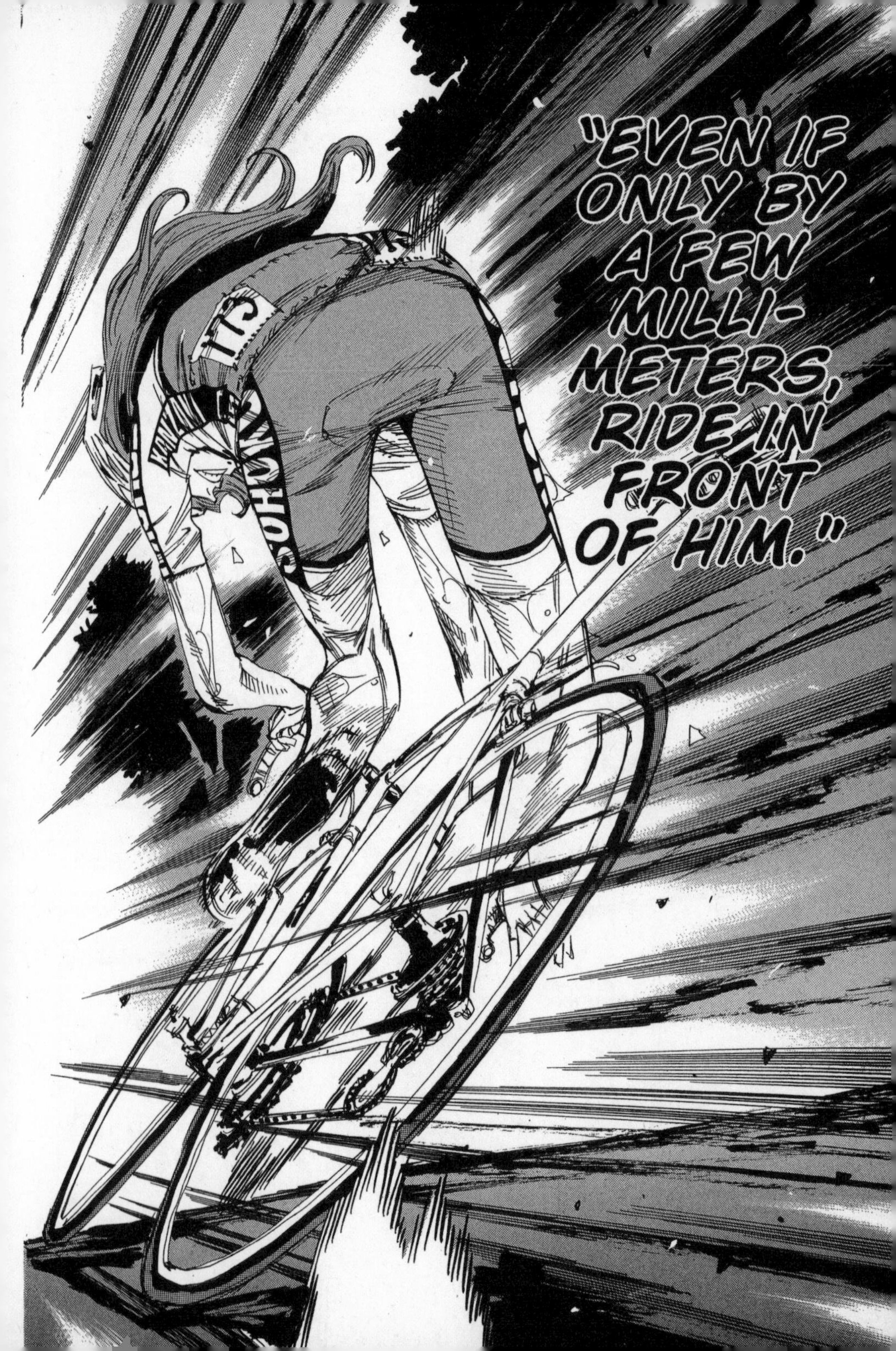
"EVEN IF ONLY BY A FEW MILLI-METERS, RIDE IN FRONT OF HIM."

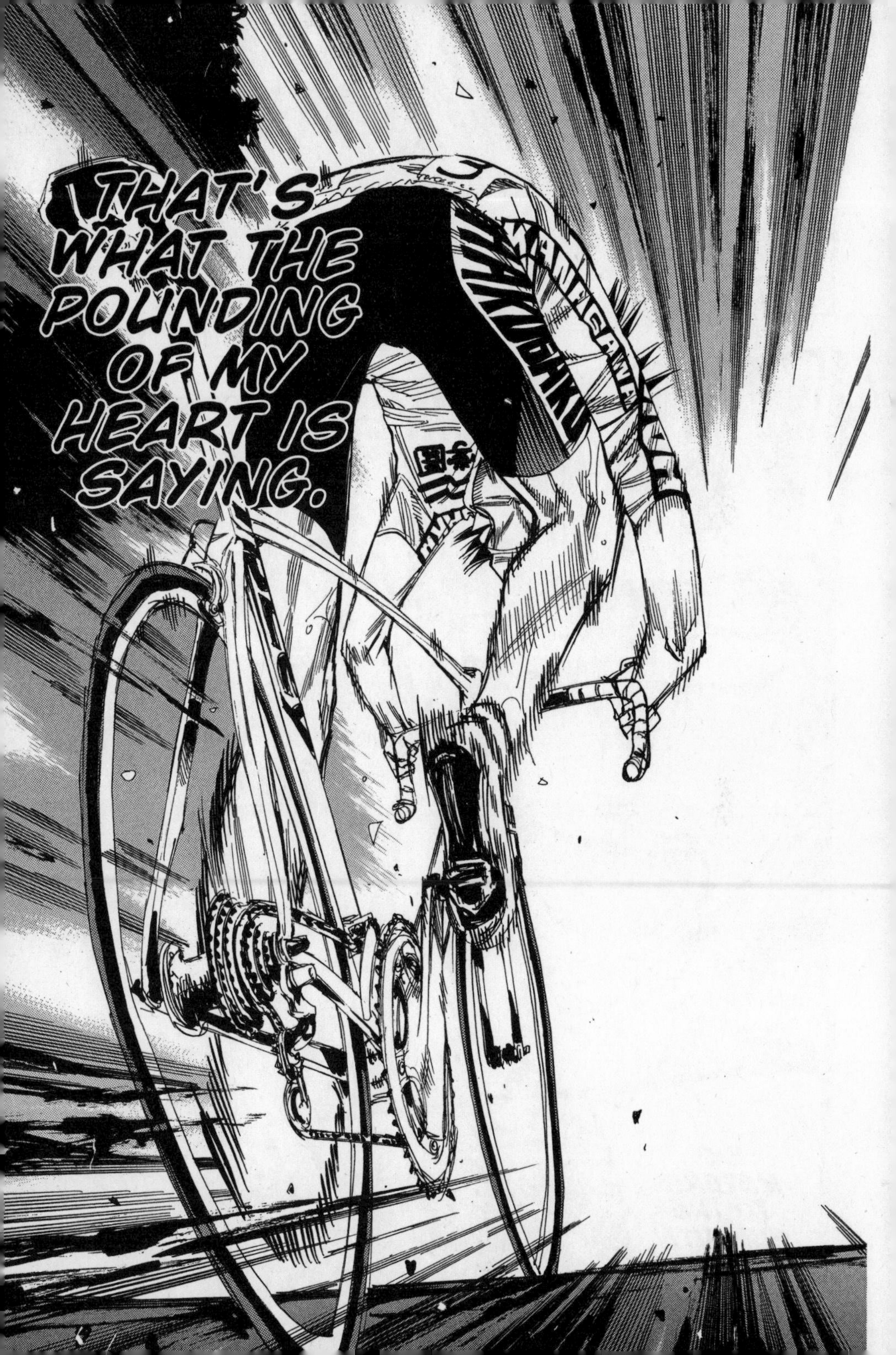
THAT'S WHAT THE POUNDING OF MY HEART IS SAYING.

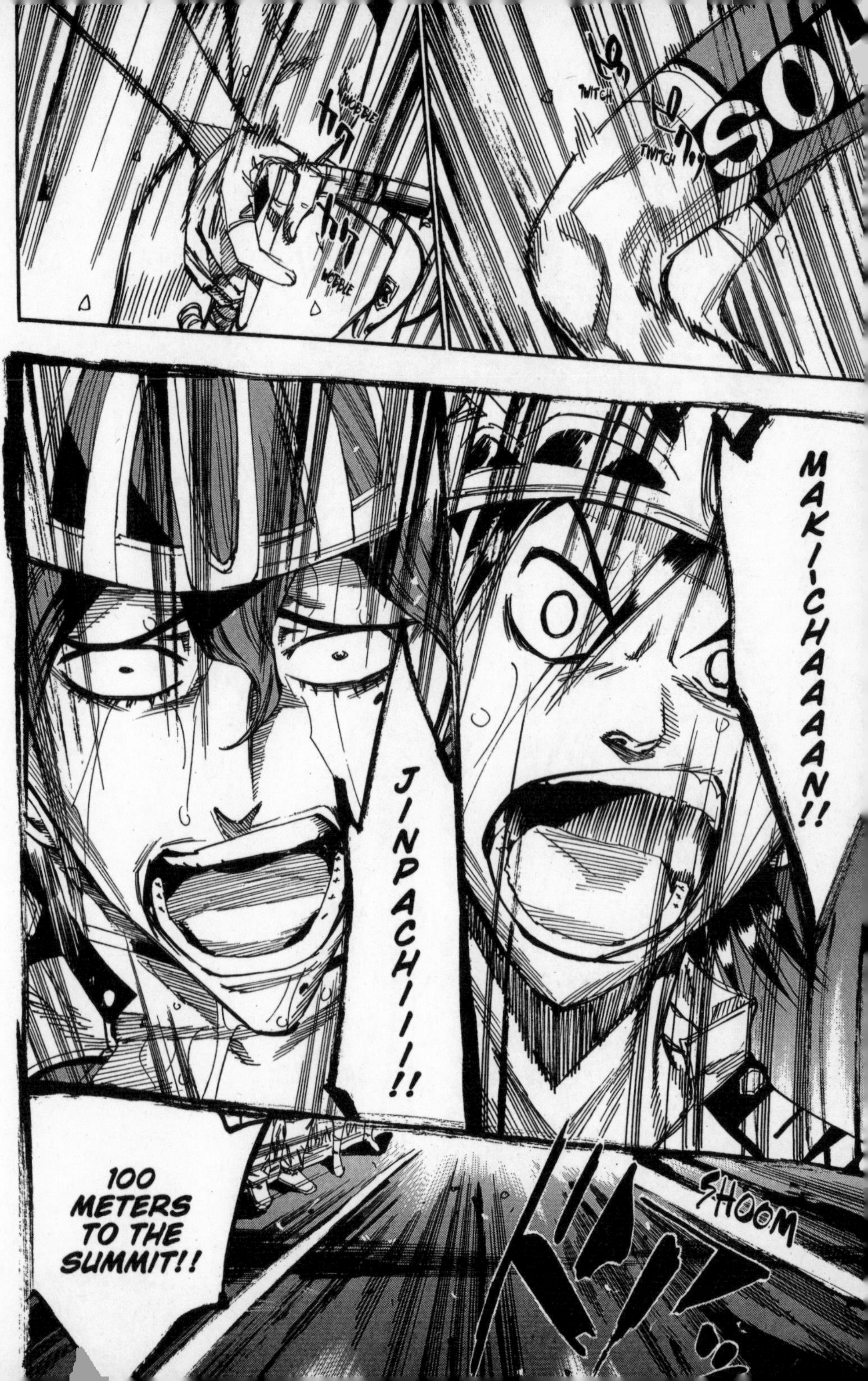
TWITCH
TWITCH
WOBBLE
WOBBLE
MAKI-CHAAAAAN!!
JINPACHIIIII!!
SHOOM
100 METERS TO THE SUMMIT!!

# RIDE.100 THE SUMMIT

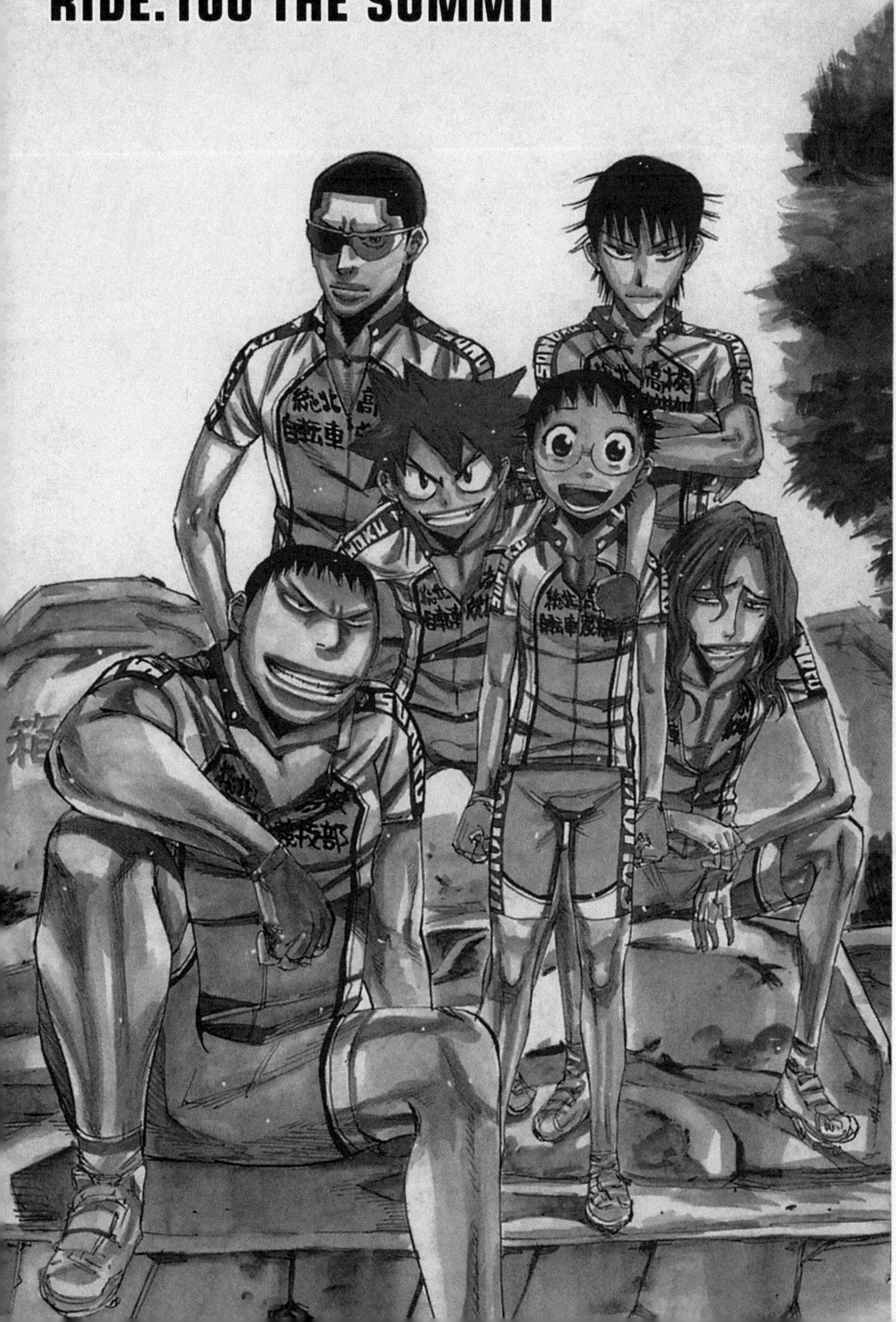

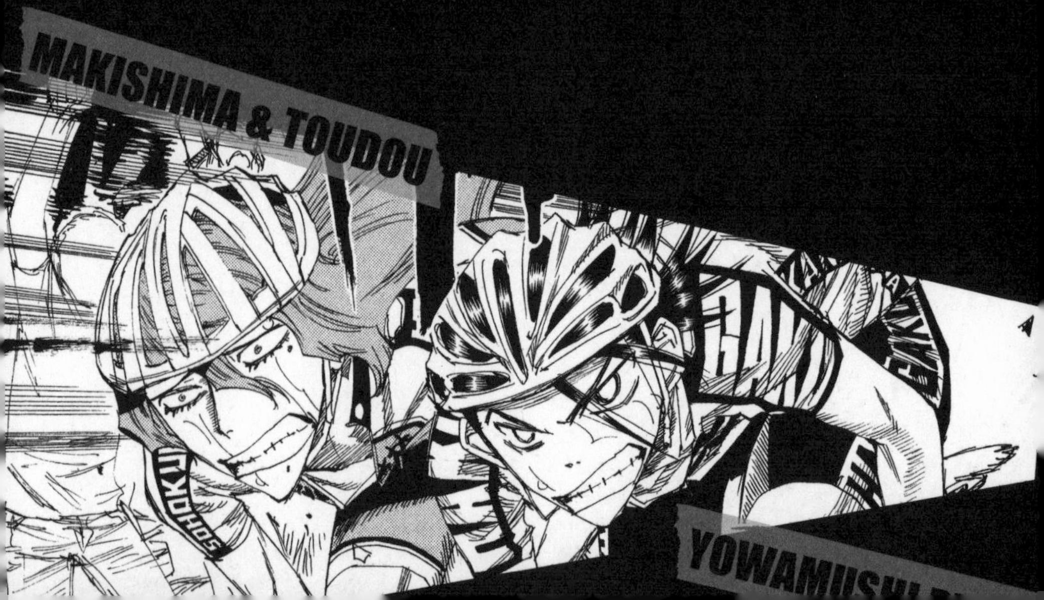
MAKISHIMA & TOUDOU
YOWAMUSHI

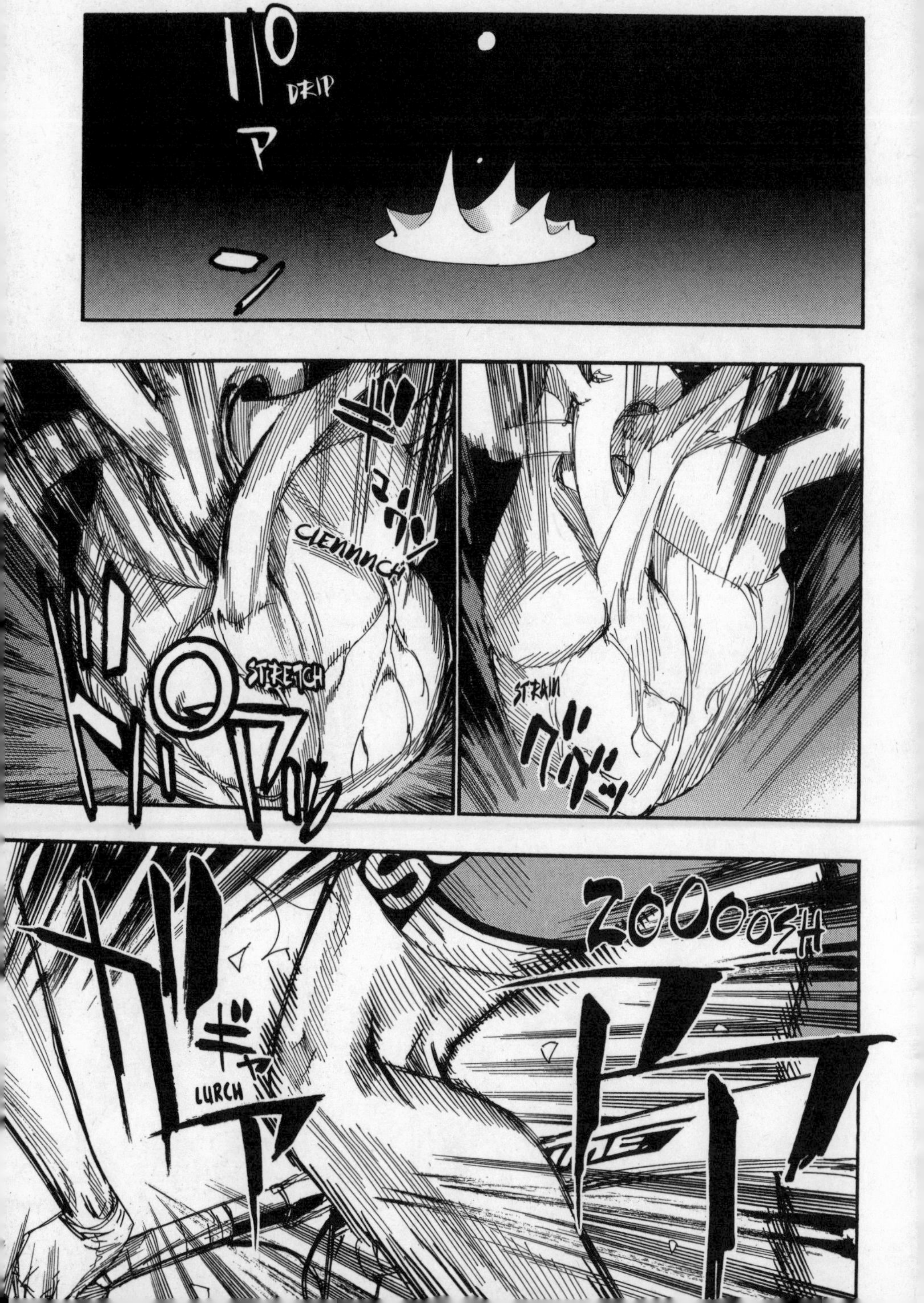
DRIP
STRAIN
CLENNNCH
STRETCH
ZOOOOSH
LURCH

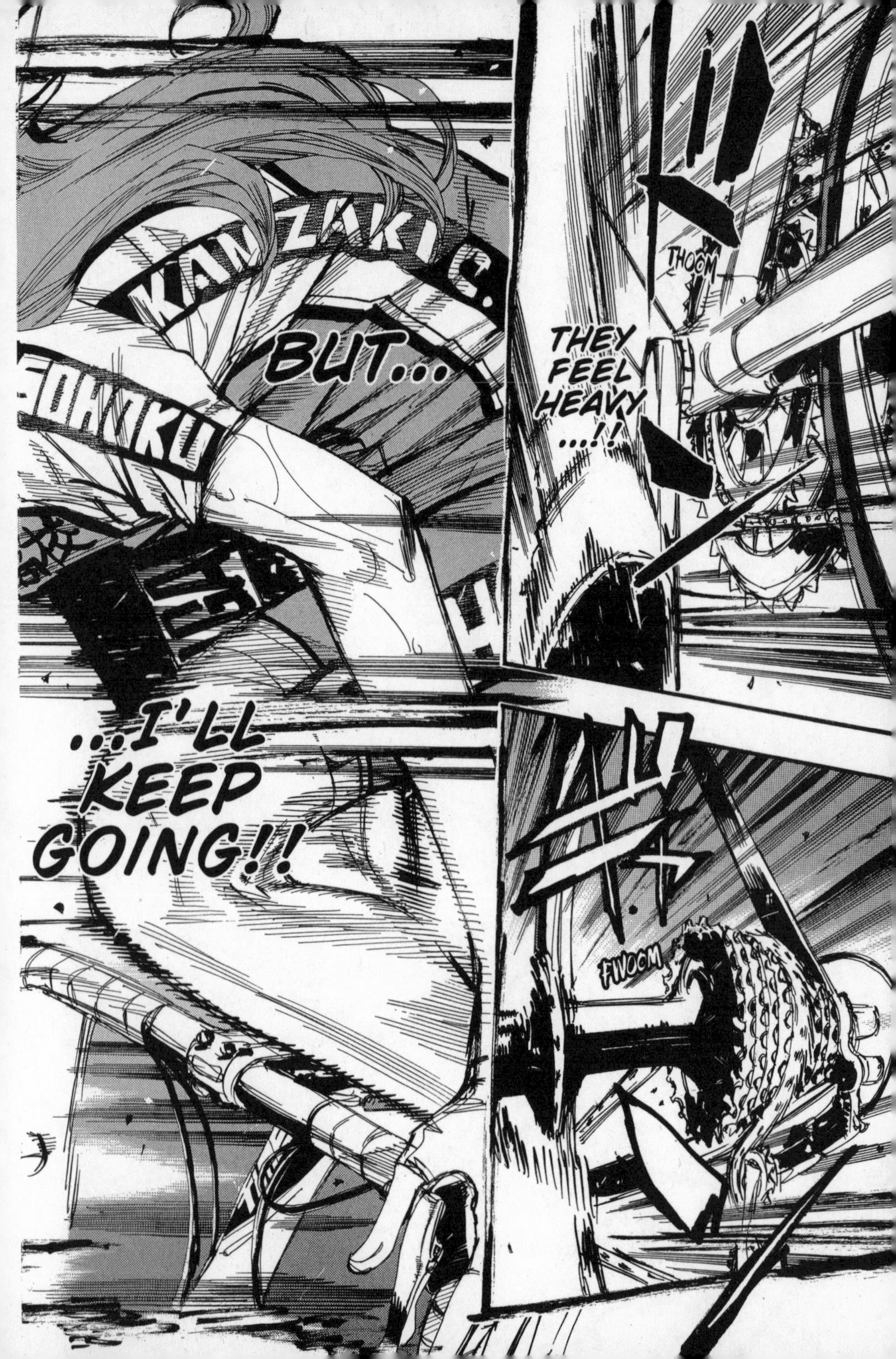
THOOM
THEY FEEL HEAVY ...!!
FWOOM
BUT...
...I'LL KEEP GOING!!

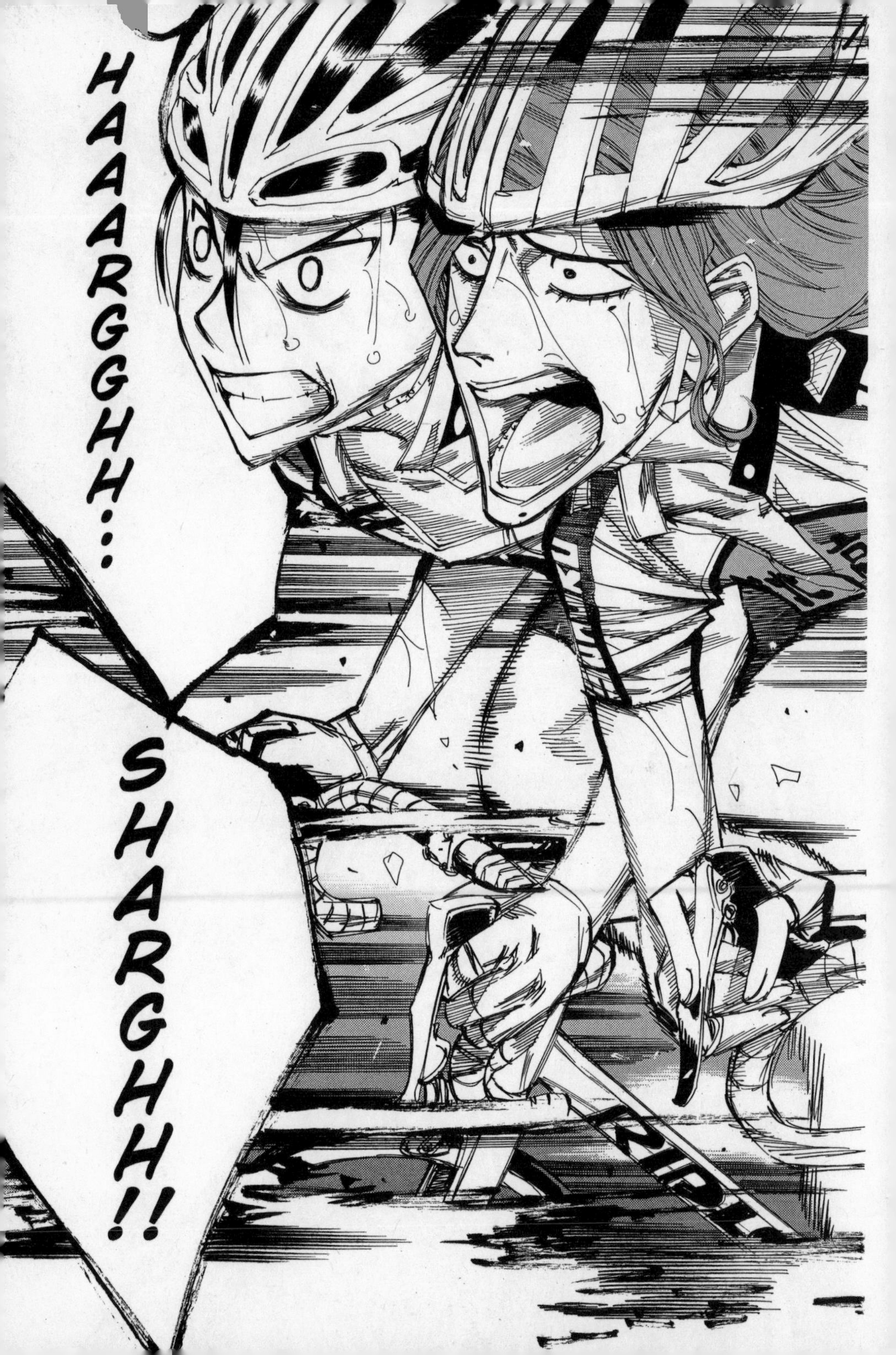
HAAARGGHHH...
SHARGHH!!

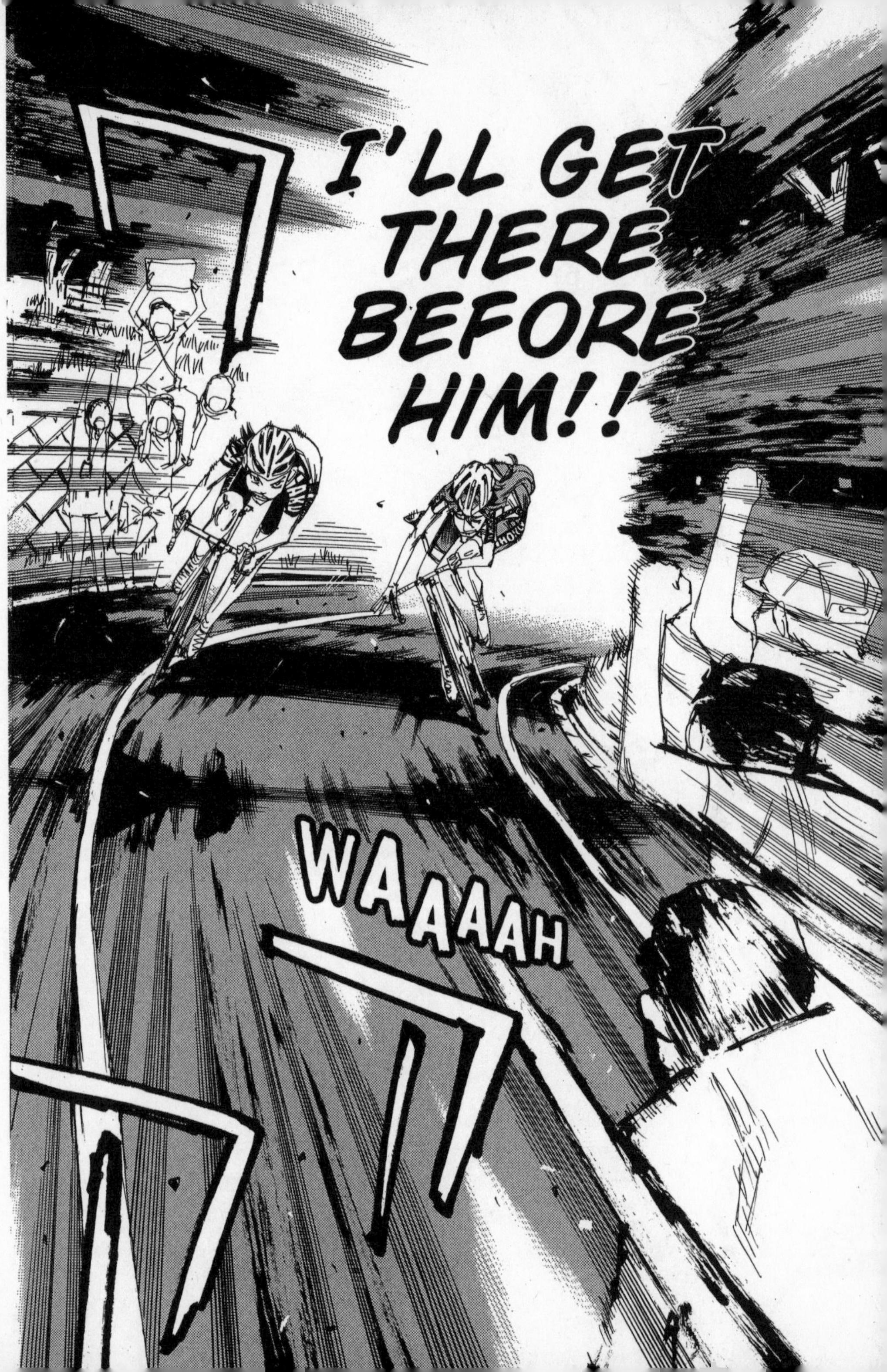
I'LL GET THERE BEFORE HIM!!
WAAAAH

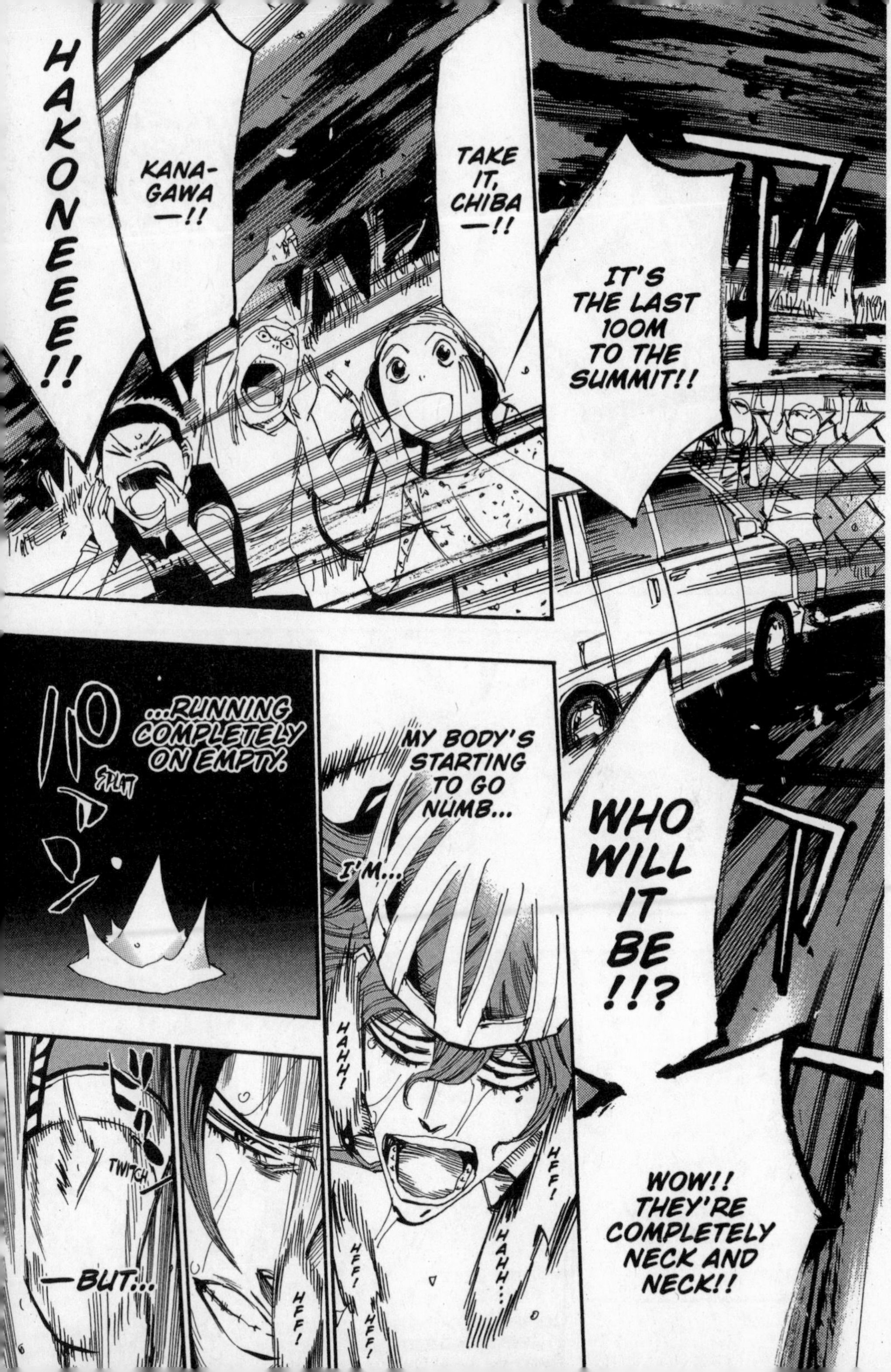
IT'S THE LAST 100M TO THE SUMMIT!!
WHO WILL IT BE!!?
WOW!! THEY'RE COMPLETELY NECK AND NECK!!
TAKE IT, CHIBA—!!
KANA-GAWA—!!
HAKONEEEE!!
MY BODY'S STARTING TO GO NUMB...
I'M...
...RUNNING COMPLETELY ON EMPTY.
SPLAT
HAHH!
HFF!
HAHH...
HFF!
HFF!
HFF!
TWITCH
—BUT...

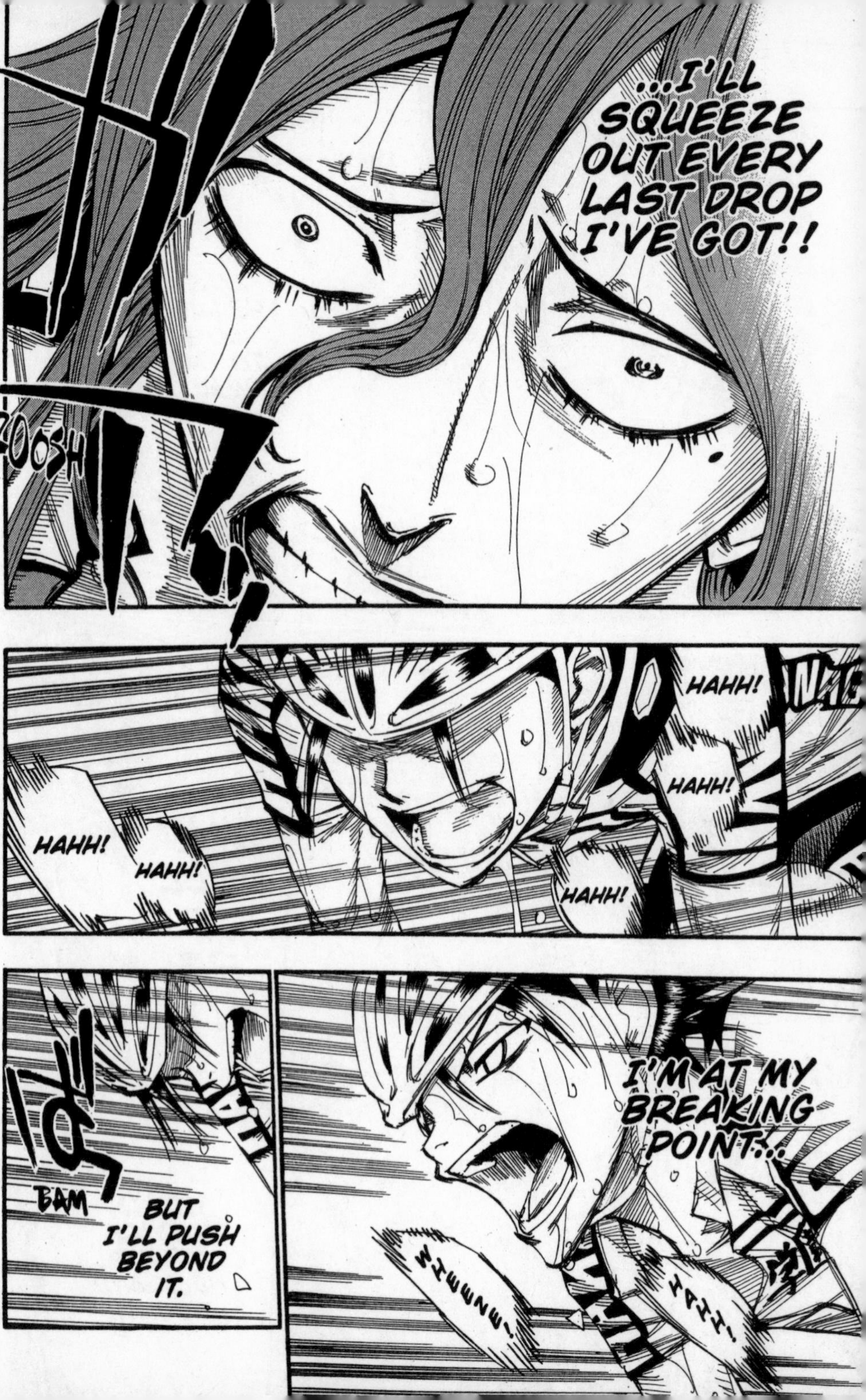
...I'LL SQUEEZE OUT EVERY LAST DROP I'VE GOT!!
ZOOSH
HAHH!
HAHH!
HAHH!
HAHH!
HAHH!
I'M AT MY BREAKING POINT...
BAM
BUT I'LL PUSH BEYOND IT.

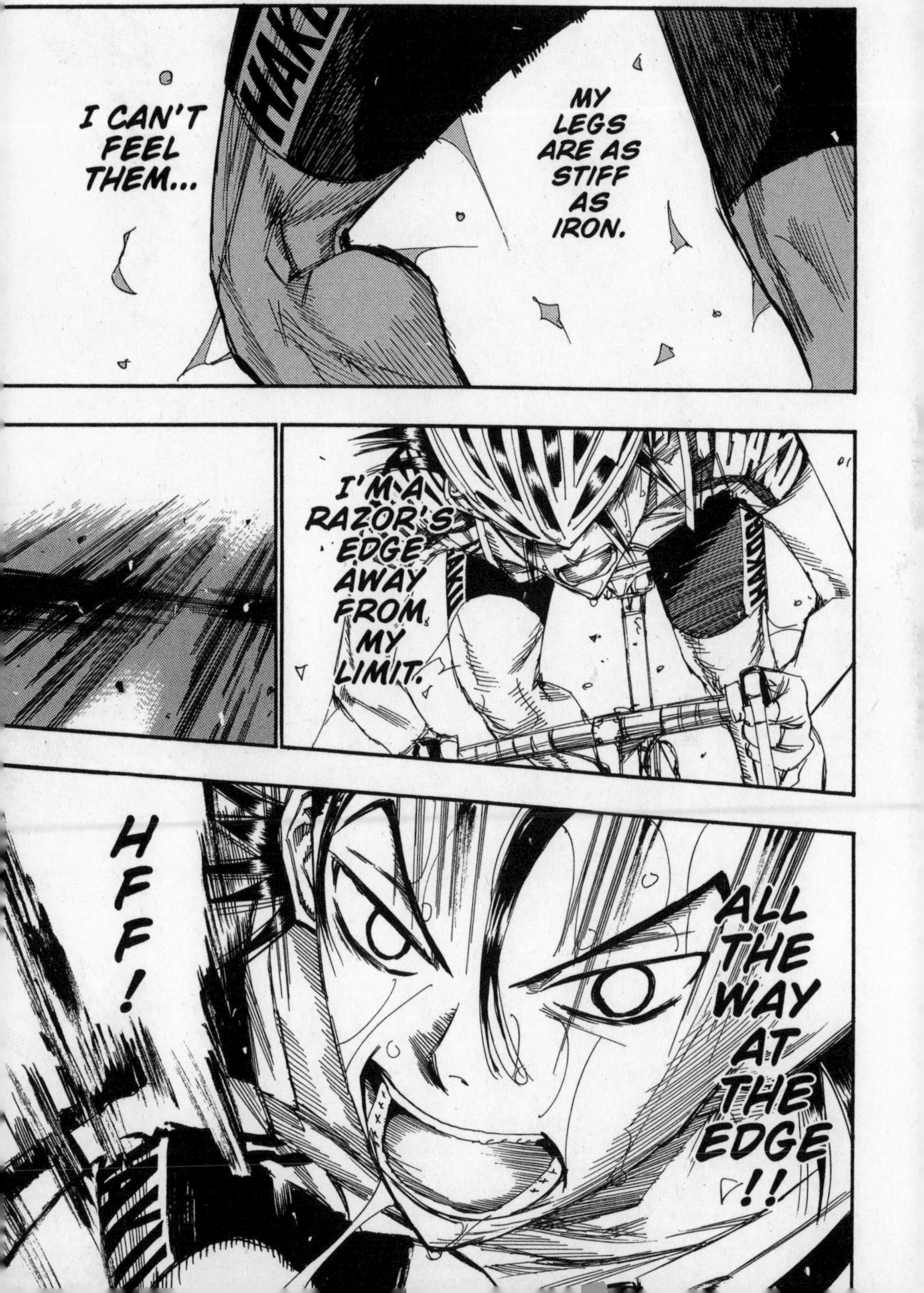
MY LEGS ARE AS STIFF AS IRON.
I CAN'T FEEL THEM...
I'M A RAZOR'S EDGE AWAY FROM MY LIMIT.
ALL THE WAY AT THE EDGE!!
HFF!

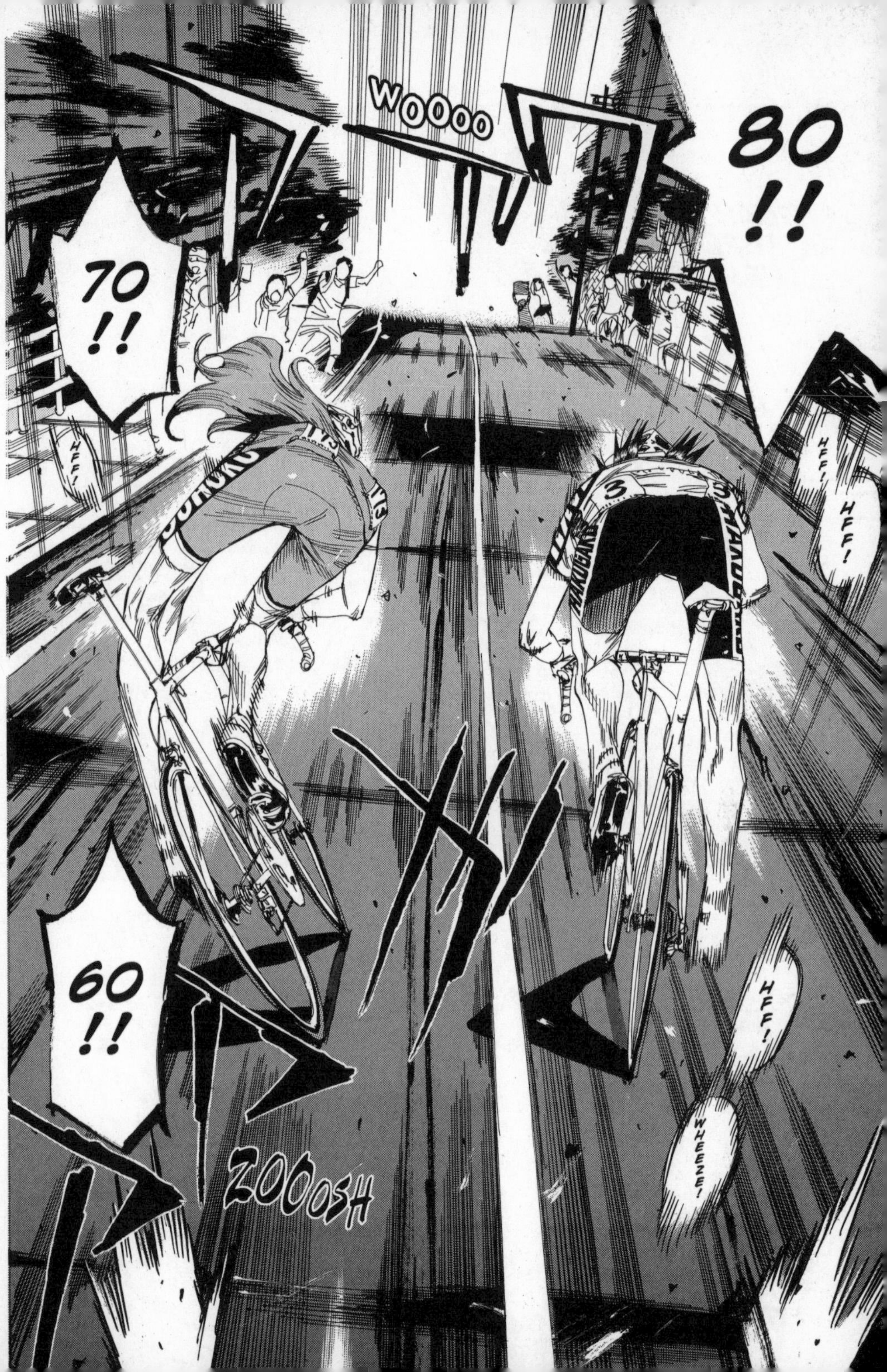
80!!
WOOOO
70!!
HFF!
HFF! HFF!
HFF!
WHEEZE!
60!!
ZOOOSH

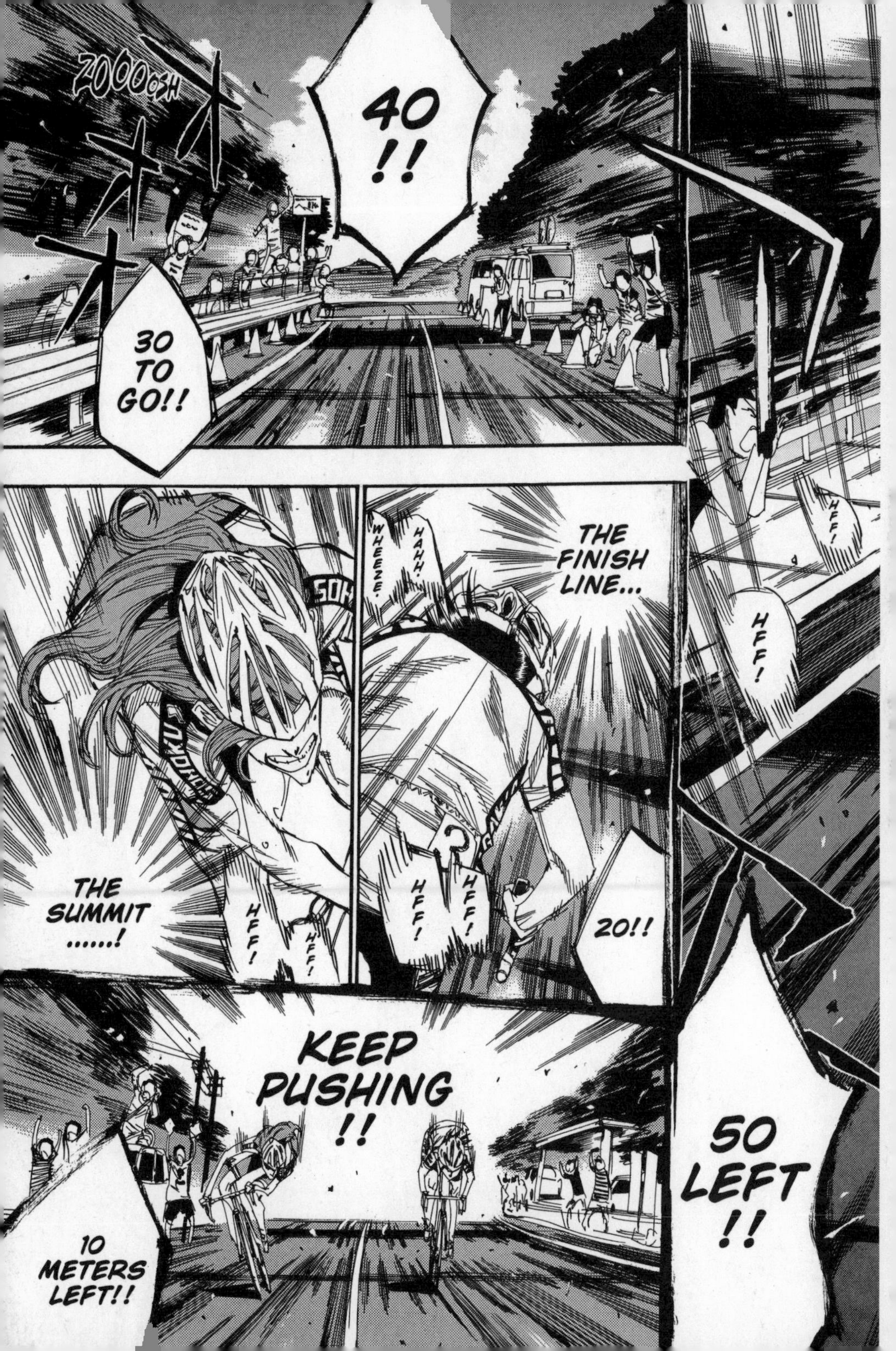

HFF!
HFF!
50 LEFT!!
40!!
ZOOOOSH
30 TO GO!!
THE FINISH LINE...
HAHH.
WHEEZE.
HFF!
HFF!
20!!
THE SUMMIT ......!
HFF!
HFF!
KEEP PUSHING!!
10 METERS LEFT!!

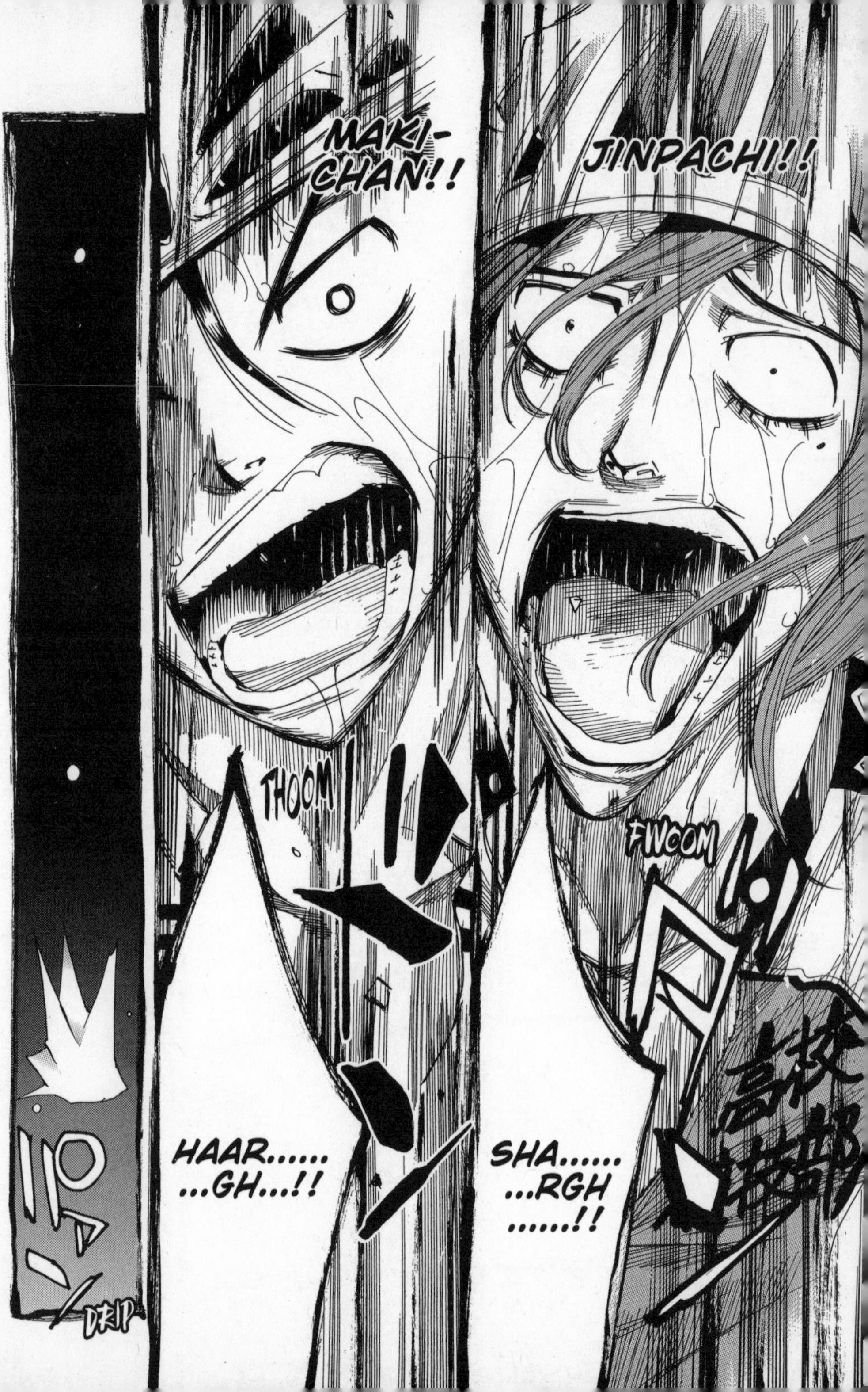
JINPACHI!!
FWOOM
SHA......
...RGH
......!!
MAKI-
CHAN!!
THOOM
HAAR......
...GH...!!
DRIP

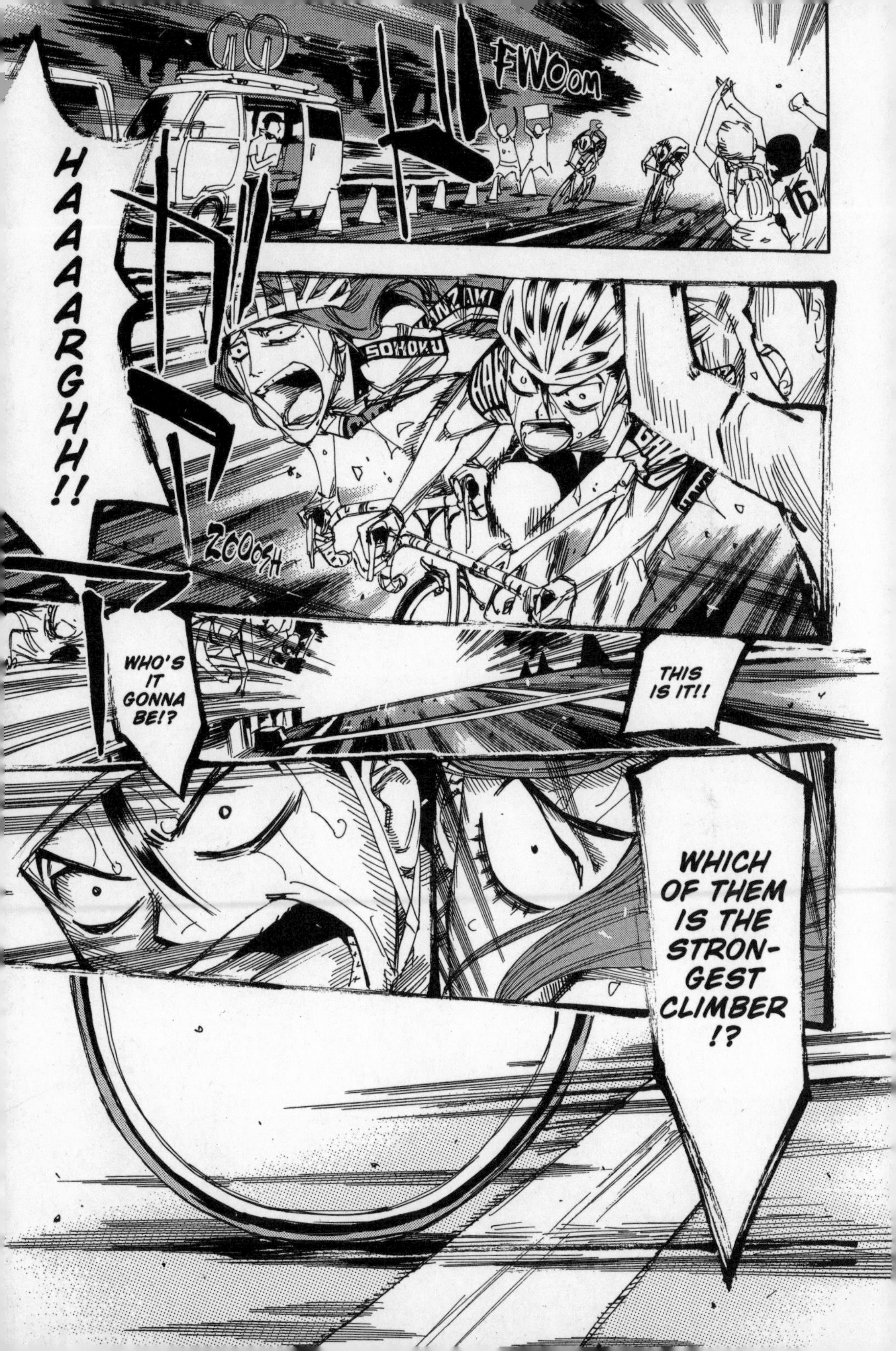
FWOOM
HAAAAARGHH!!
SOHOKU
ZOOOSH
THIS IS IT!!
WHO'S IT GONNA BE!?
WHICH OF THEM IS THE STRONGEST CLIMBER!?

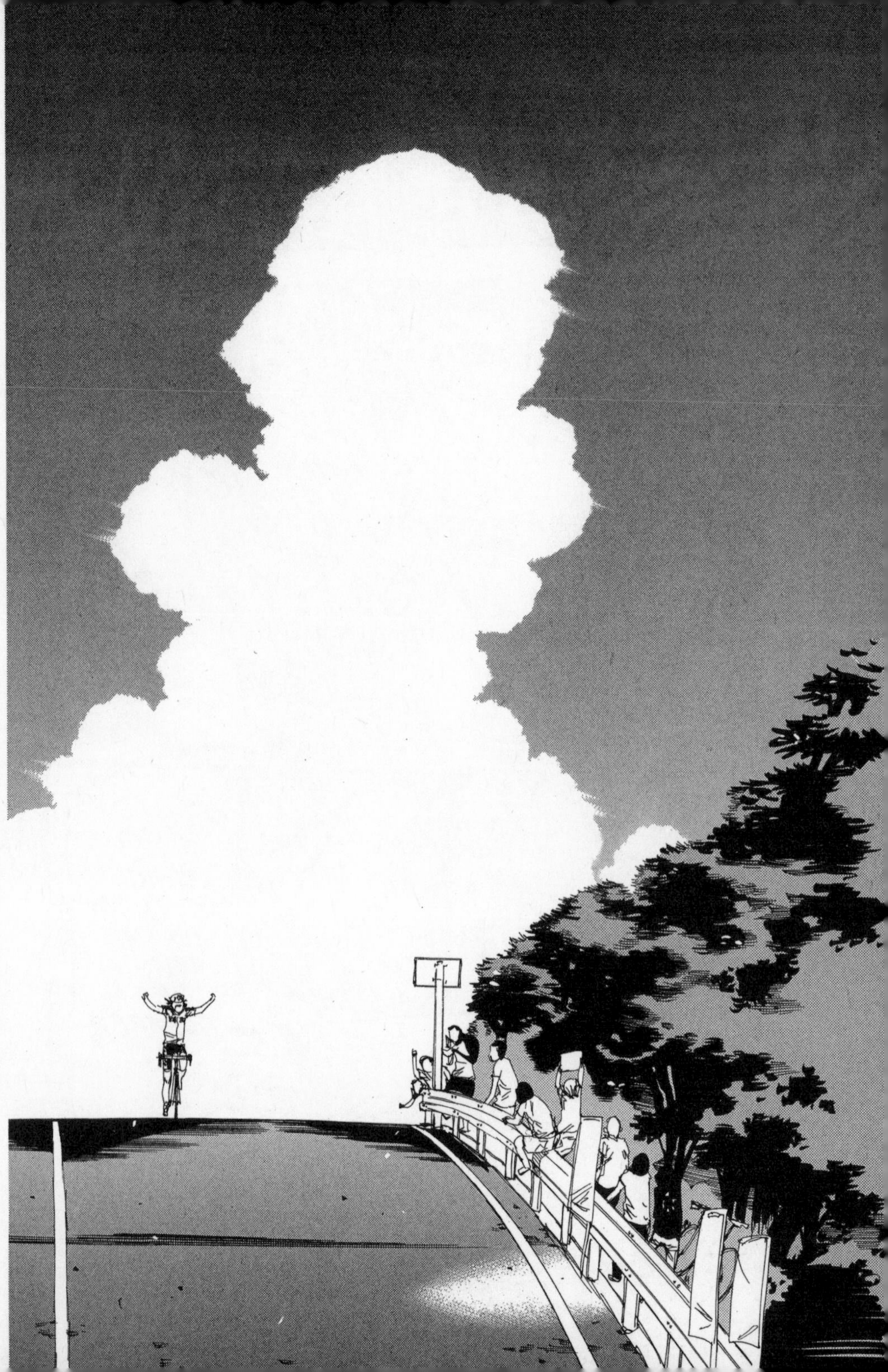

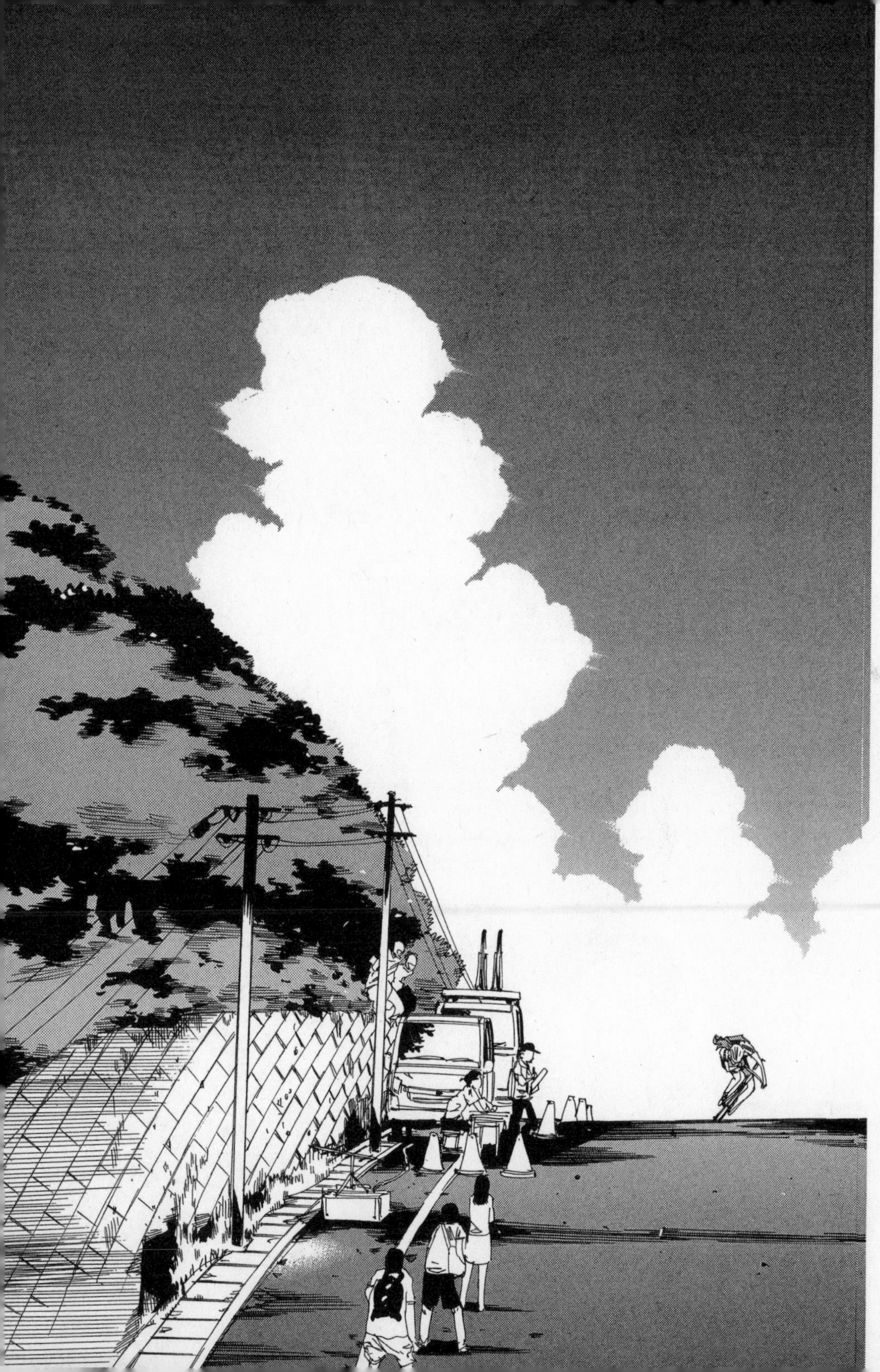

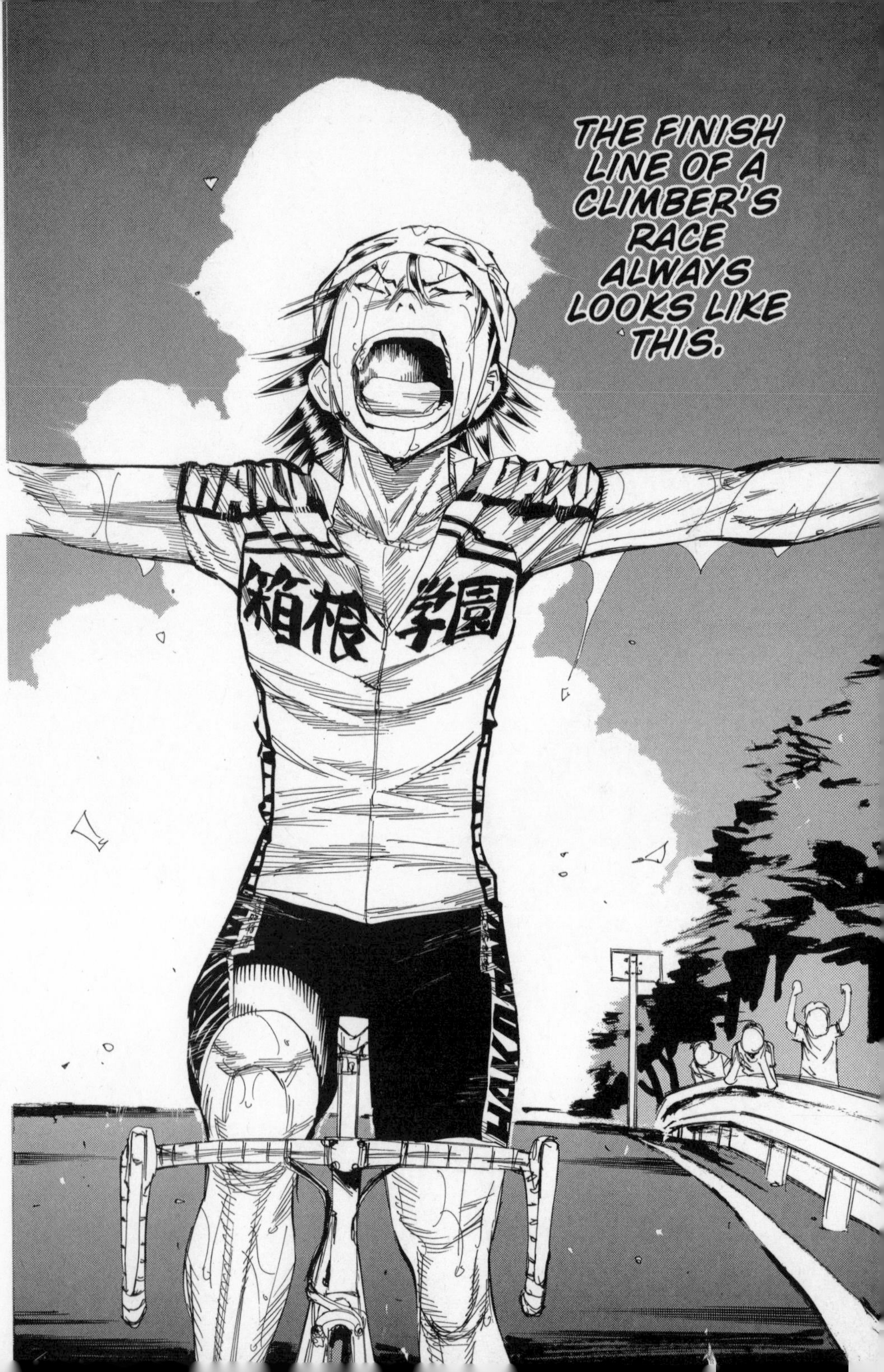
THE FINISH LINE OF A CLIMBER'S RACE ALWAYS LOOKS LIKE THIS.
箱根学園

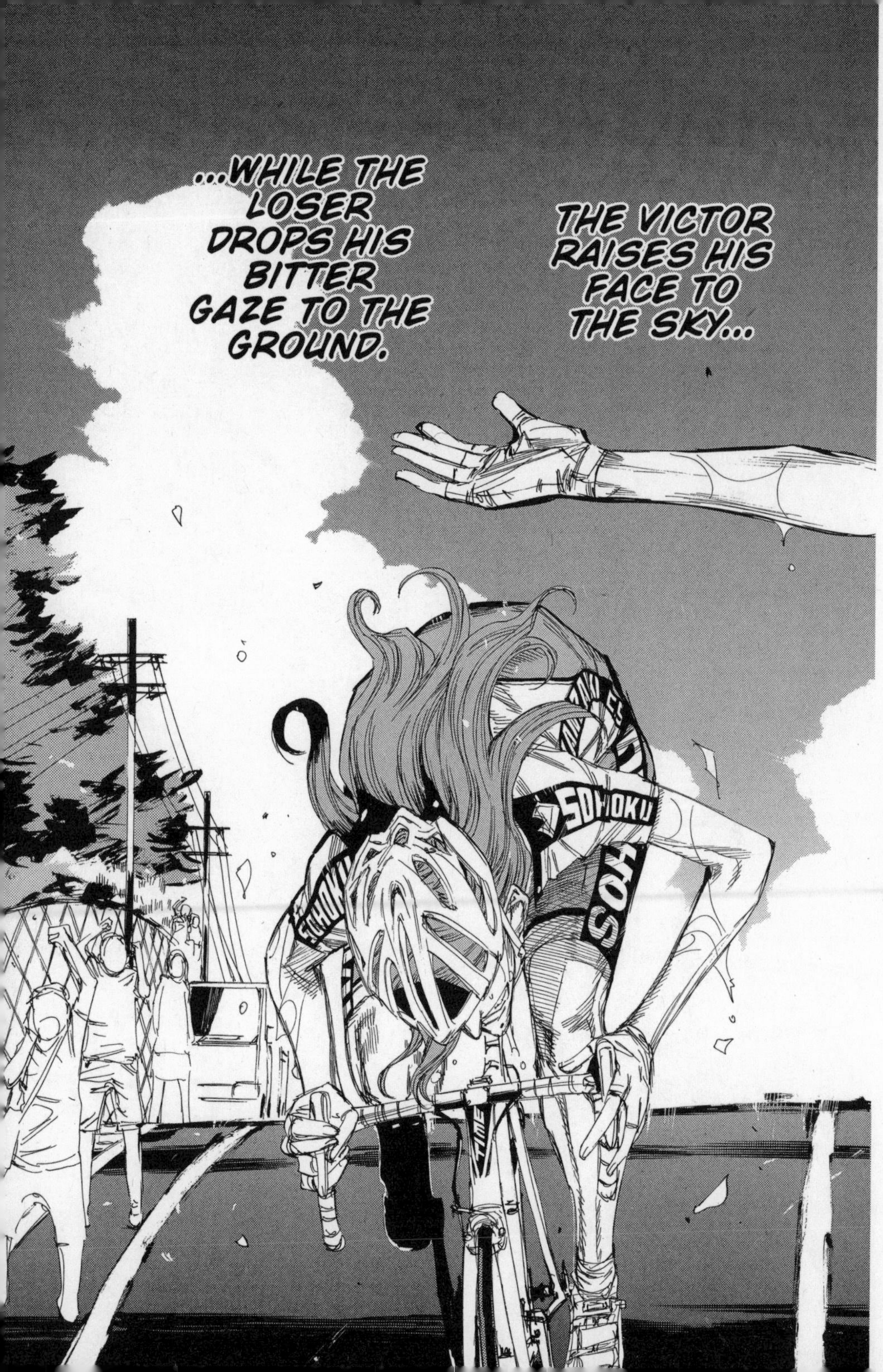
THE VICTOR RAISES HIS FACE TO THE SKY...
...WHILE THE LOSER DROPS HIS BITTER GAZE TO THE GROUND.

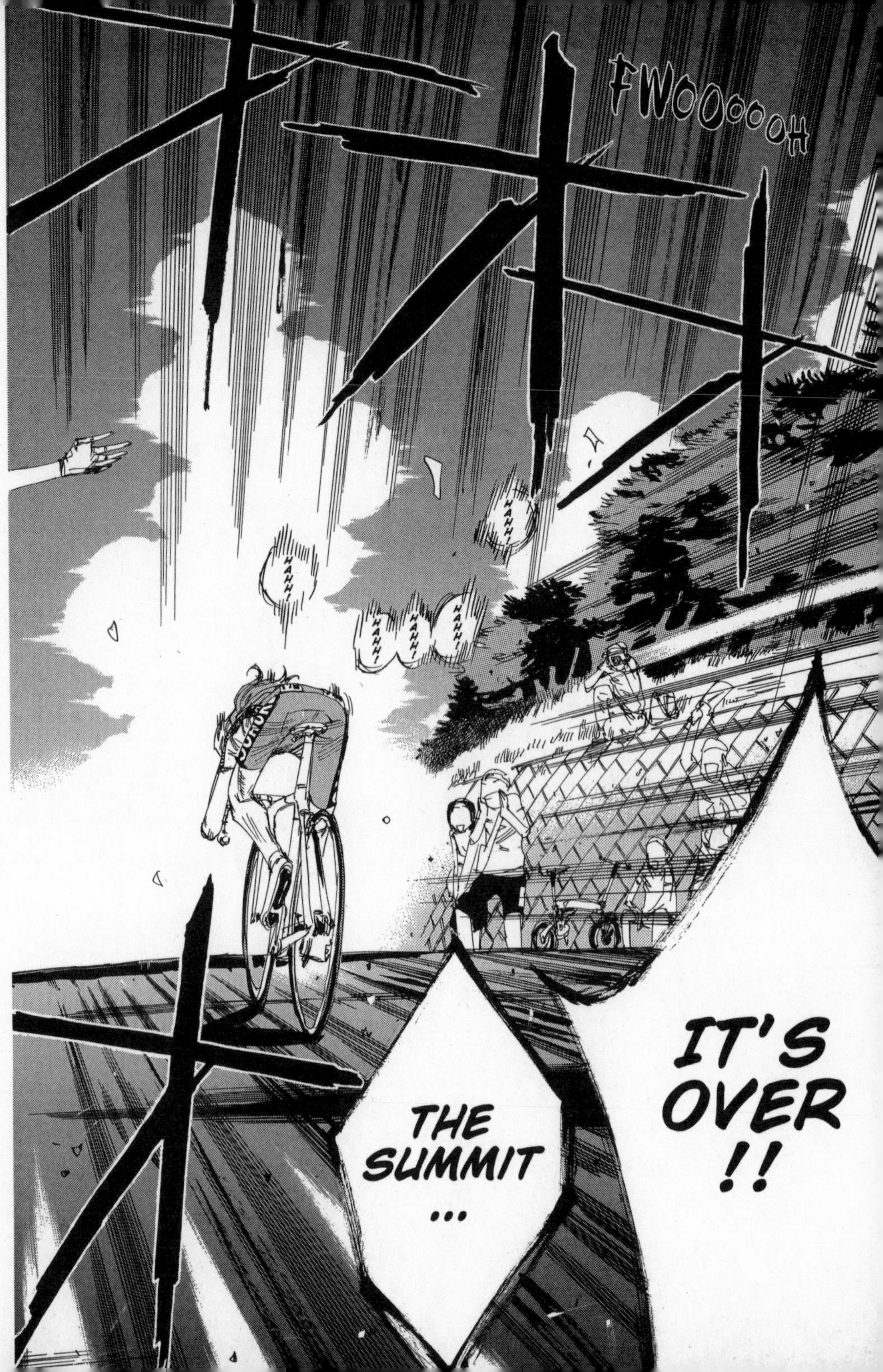
FWOOOOOH
HAHH!
HAHH!
HAHH!
HAHH!
HAHH!
IT'S OVER!!
THE SUMMIT...

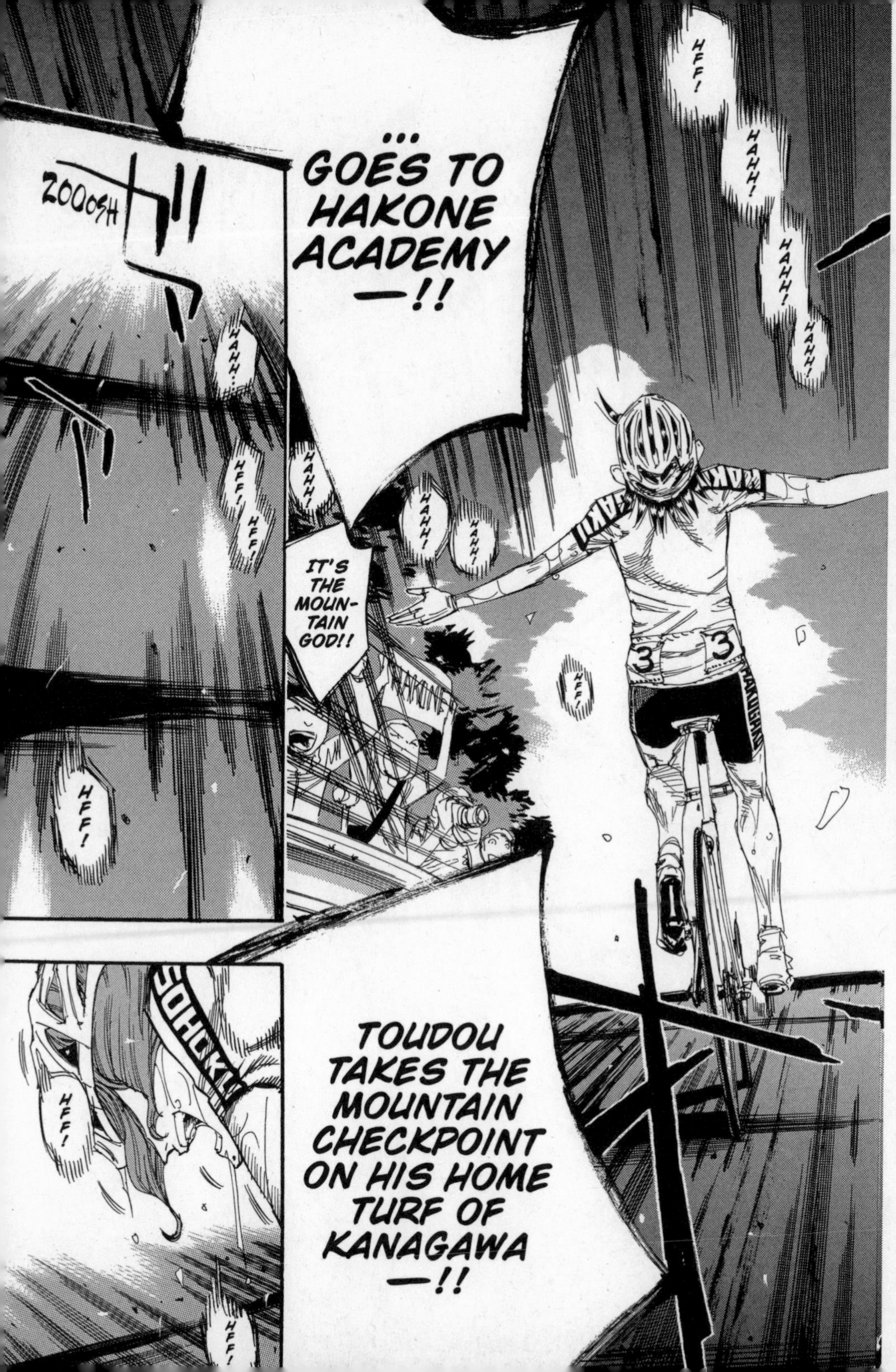
HFF!
HAHH!
HAHH!
HAHH!
...GOES TO HAKONE ACADEMY —!!
HAHH!
HAHH!
HAHH!
IT'S THE MOUN-TAIN GOD!!
HFF!
TOUDOU TAKES THE MOUNTAIN CHECKPOINT ON HIS HOME TURF OF KANAGAWA —!!
ZOOOSH
HAHH...
HFF!
HFF!
HFF!
HFF!
HFF!

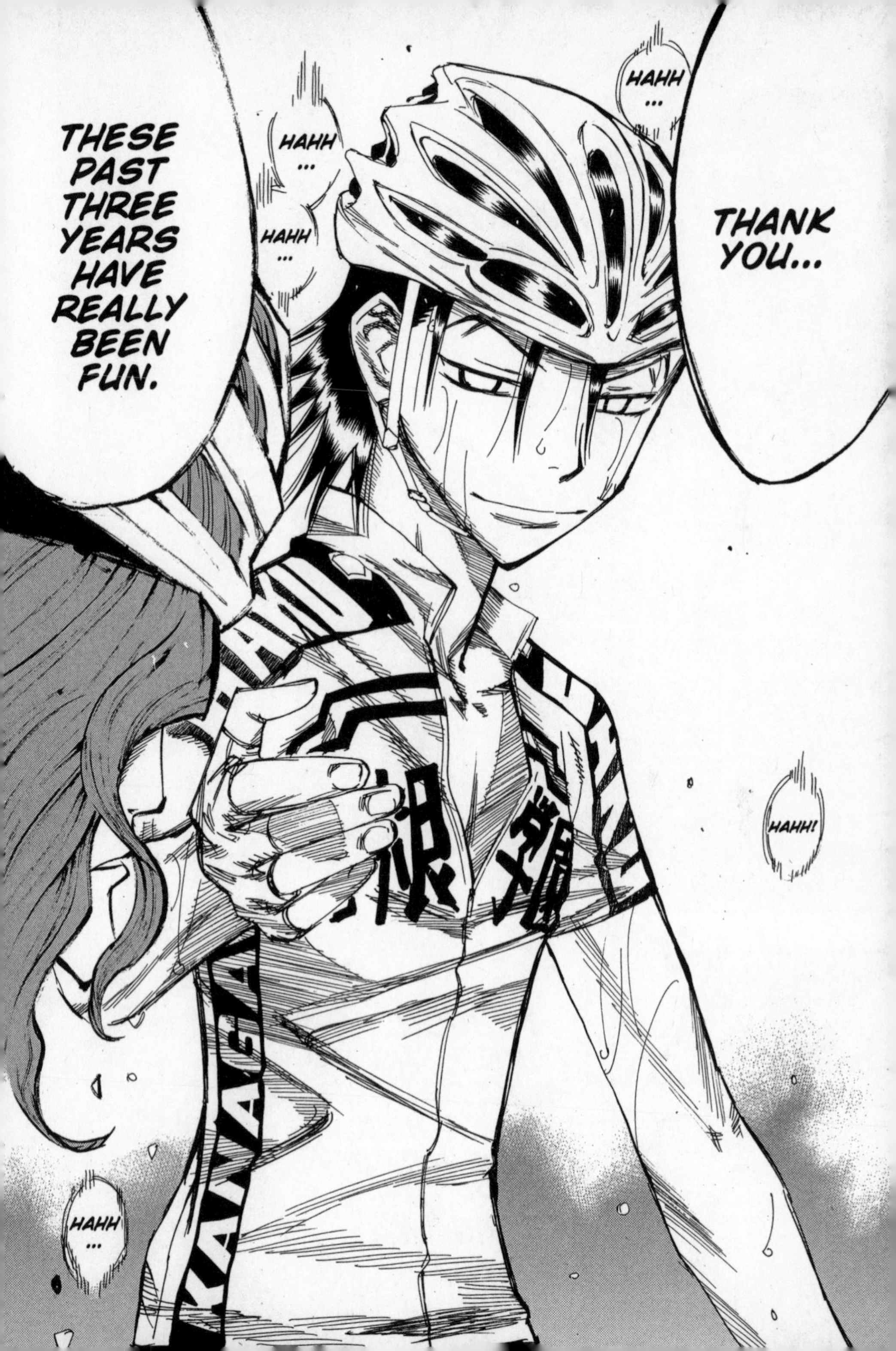
HAHH...
THANK YOU...
HAHH...
HAHH...
THESE PAST THREE YEARS HAVE REALLY BEEN FUN.
HAHH!
HAHH...

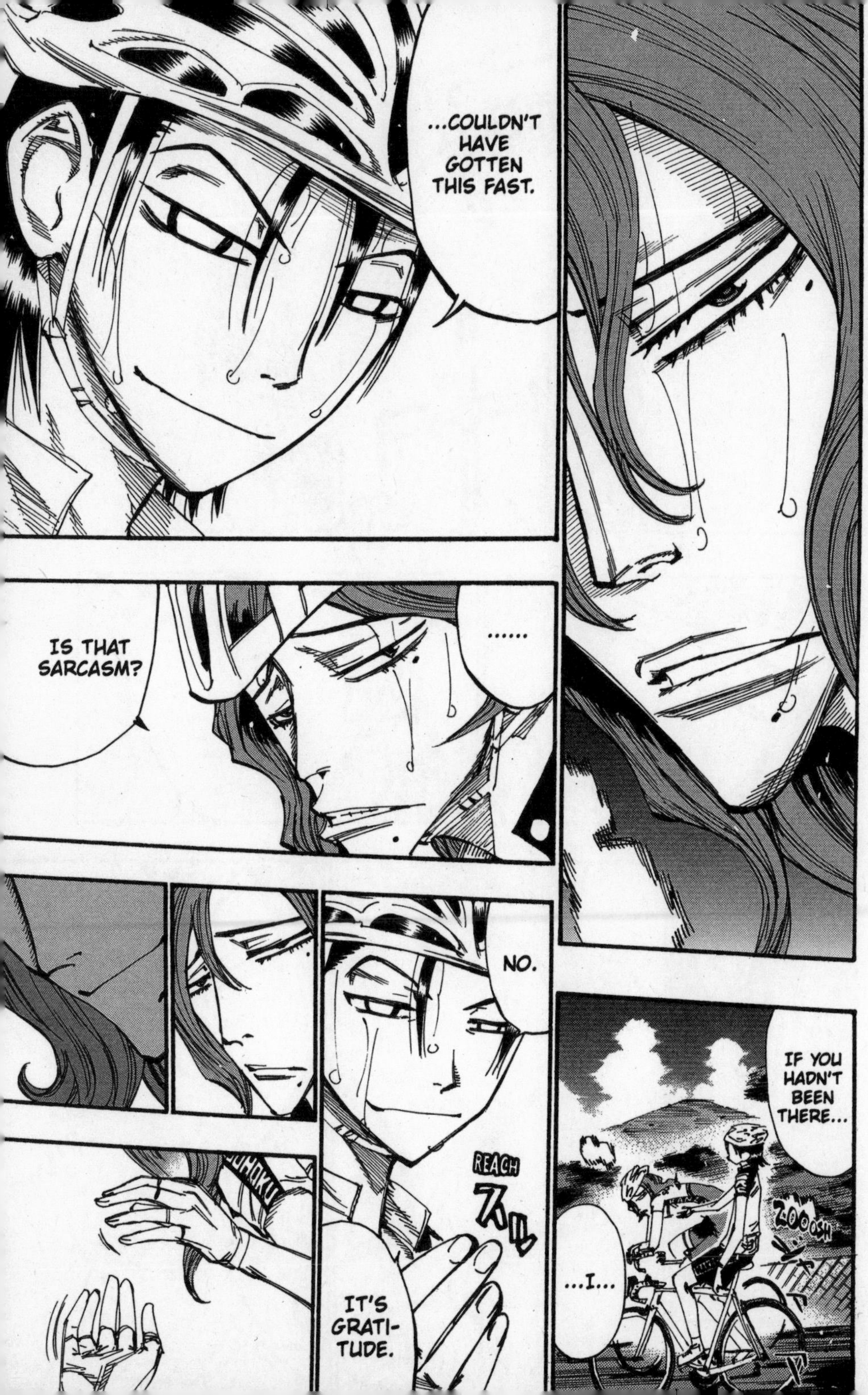
...COULDN'T HAVE GOTTEN THIS FAST.
......
IS THAT SARCASM?
IF YOU HADN'T BEEN THERE...
ZOOOSH
...I...
NO.
REACH
IT'S GRATI-TUDE.

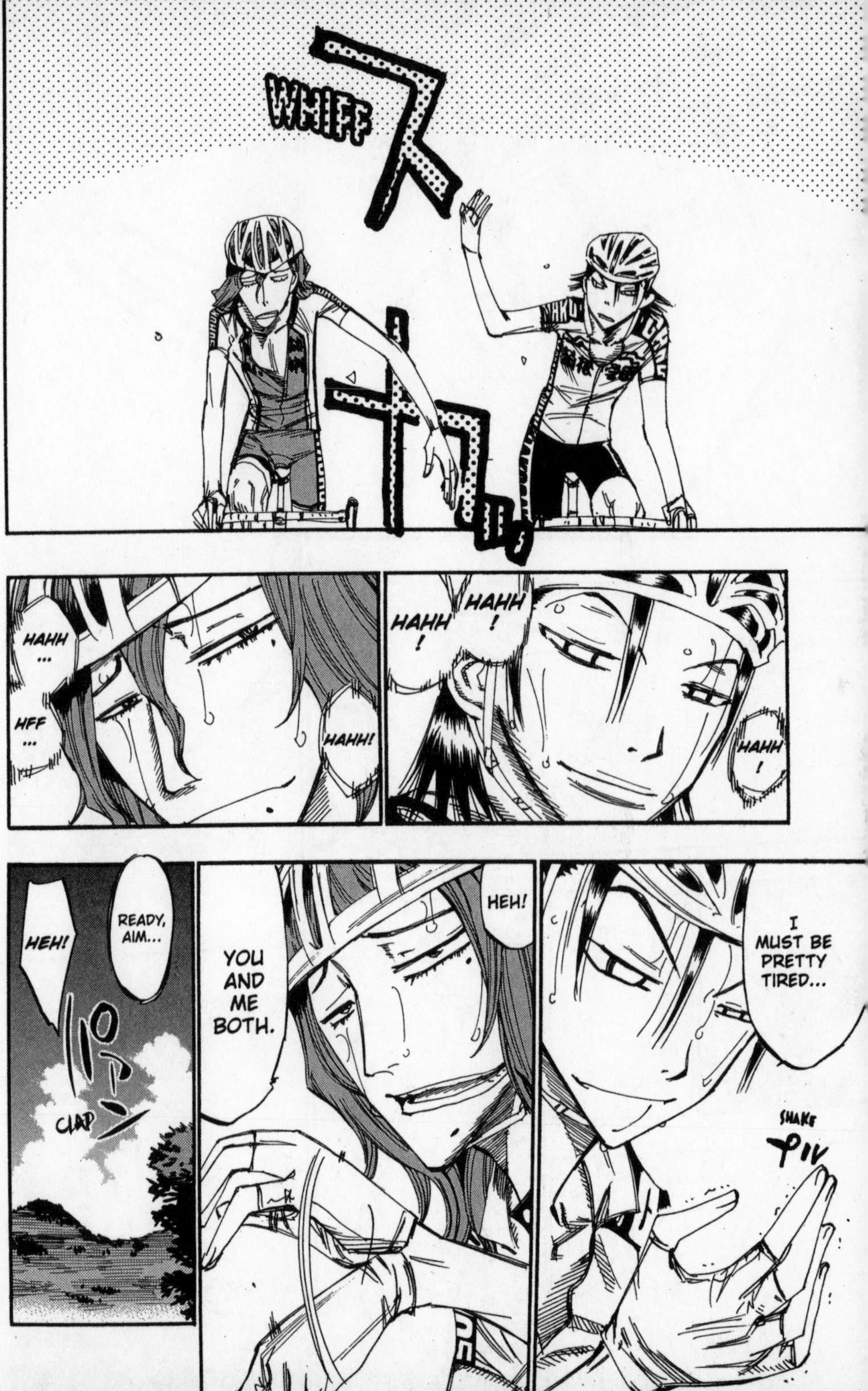
WHIFF
HAHH!
HAHH!
HAHH!
HAHH...
HFF...
HAHH!
I MUST BE PRETTY TIRED...
SHAKE
HEH!
YOU AND ME BOTH.
READY, AIM...
HEH!
CLAP

# RIDE.101
# THE ACES MAKE THEIR MOVES

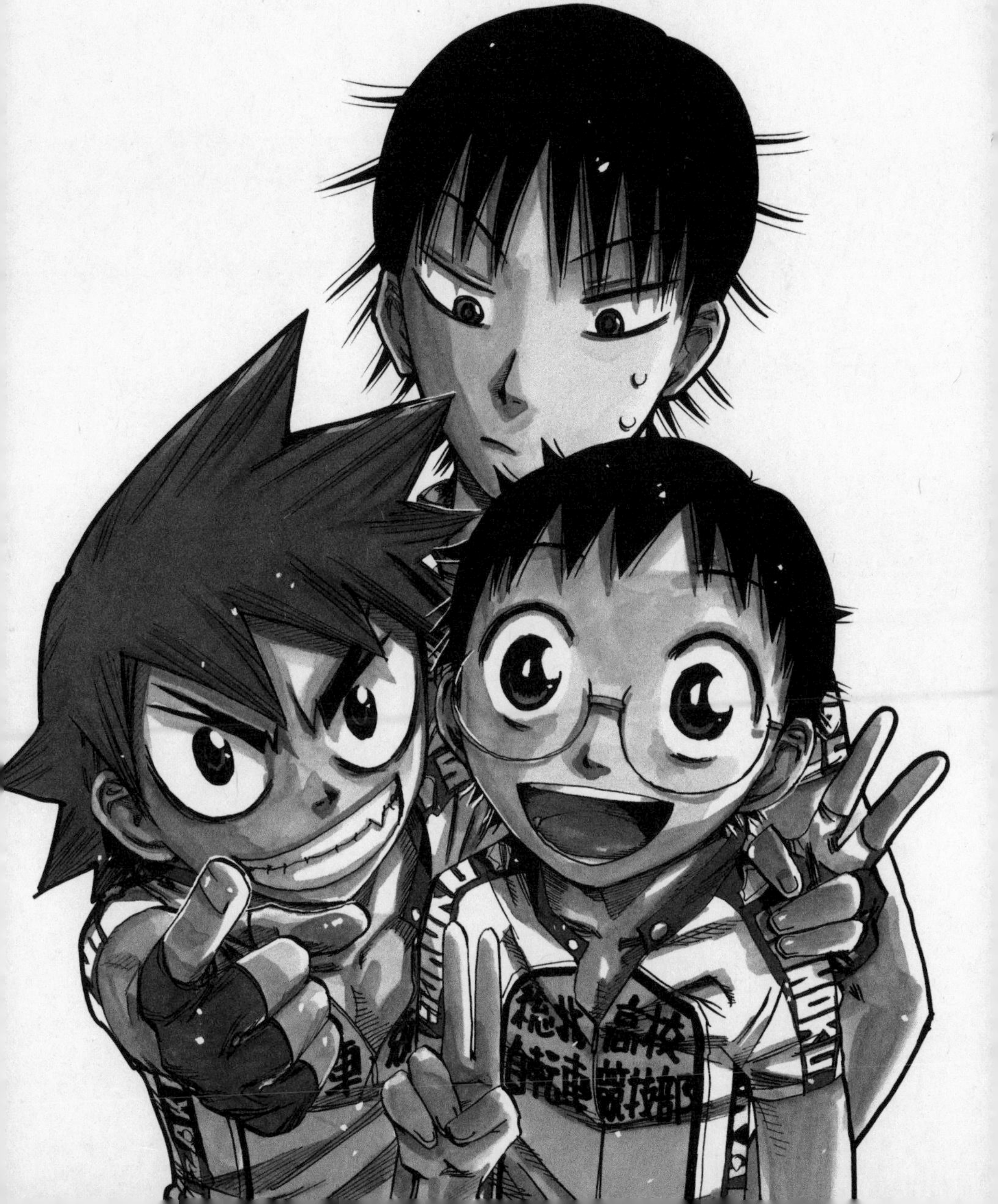
総北高校
自転車競技部

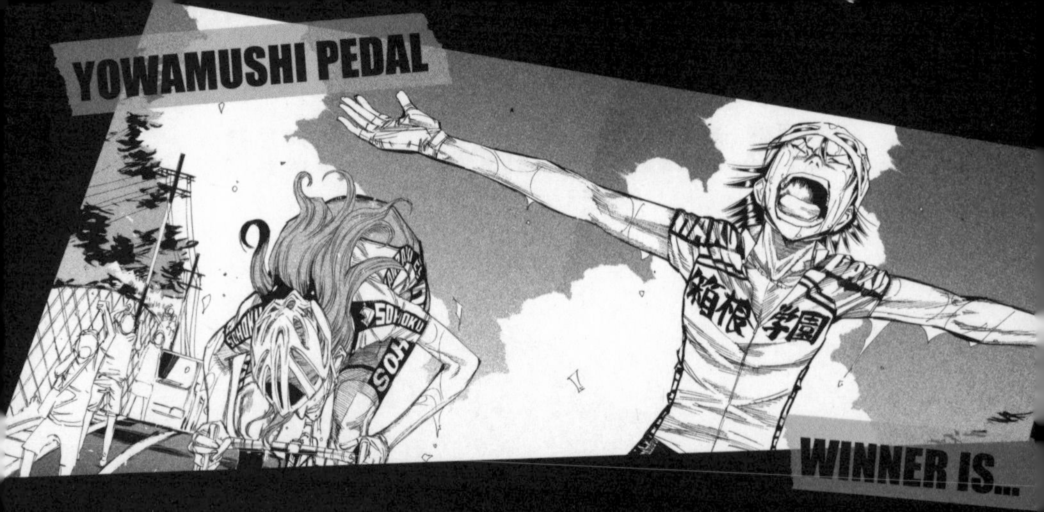
YOWAMUSHI PEDAL
箱根学園
SOHOKU
WINNER IS...

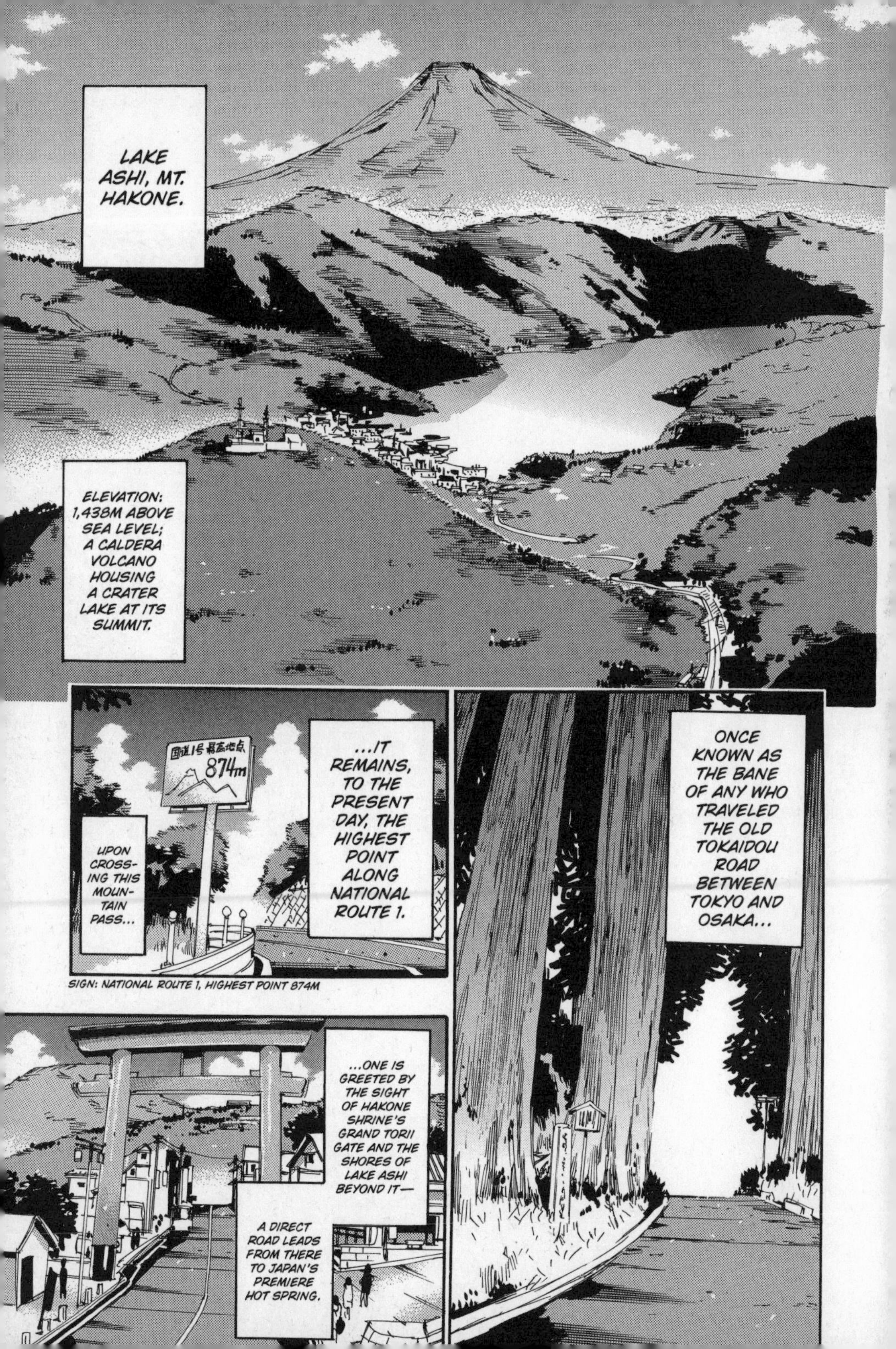
LAKE ASHI, MT. HAKONE.
ELEVATION: 1,438M ABOVE SEA LEVEL; A CALDERA VOLCANO HOUSING A CRATER LAKE AT ITS SUMMIT.
ONCE KNOWN AS THE BANE OF ANY WHO TRAVELED THE OLD TOKAIDOU ROAD BETWEEN TOKYO AND OSAKA...
...IT REMAINS, TO THE PRESENT DAY, THE HIGHEST POINT ALONG NATIONAL ROUTE 1.
国道1号 最高地点
874m
UPON CROSSING THIS MOUNTAIN PASS...
SIGN: NATIONAL ROUTE 1, HIGHEST POINT 874M
...ONE IS GREETED BY THE SIGHT OF HAKONE SHRINE'S GRAND TORII GATE AND THE SHORES OF LAKE ASHI BEYOND IT—
A DIRECT ROAD LEADS FROM THERE TO JAPAN'S PREMIERE HOT SPRING.

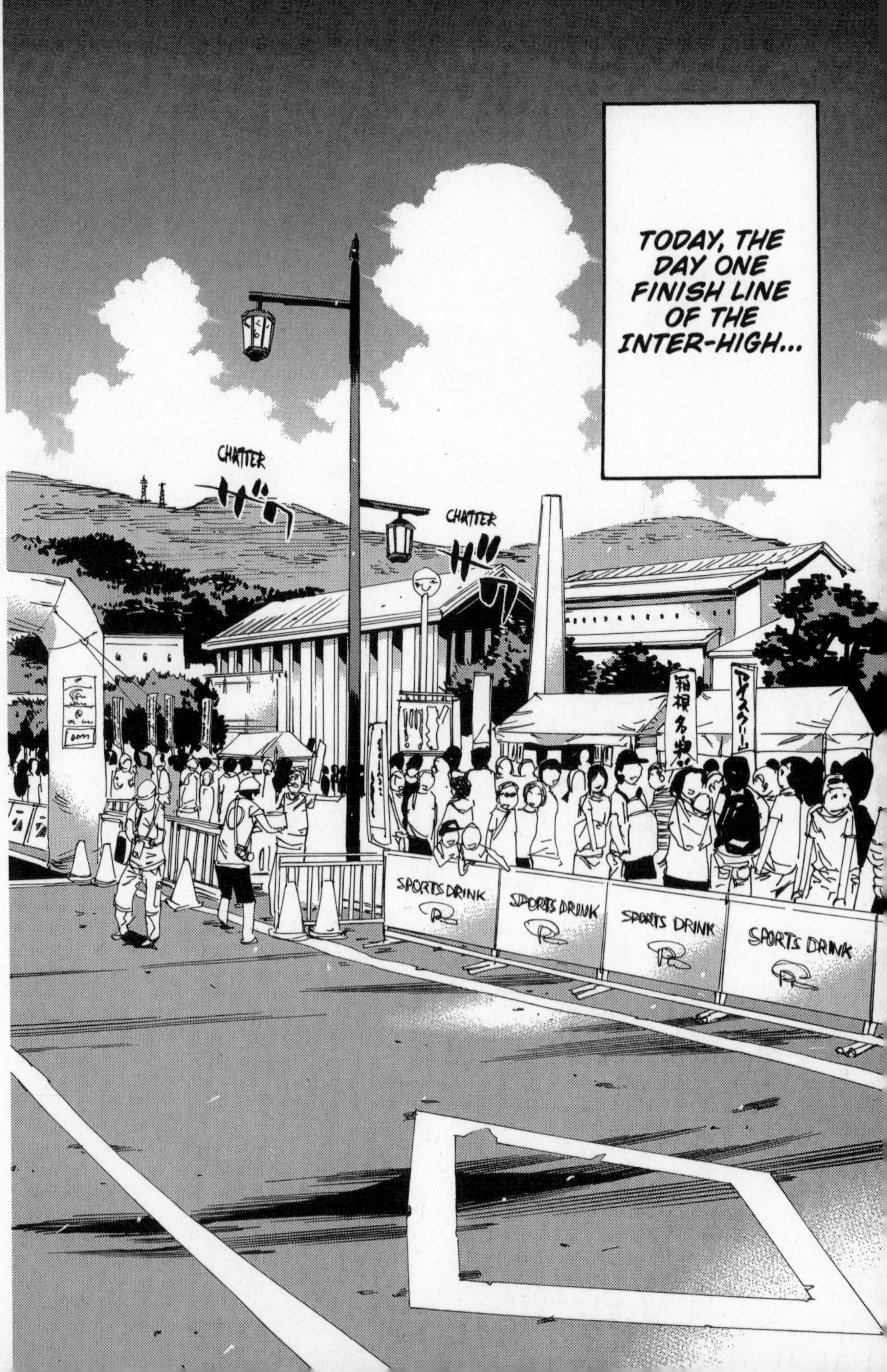
TODAY, THE DAY ONE FINISH LINE OF THE INTER-HIGH...
CHATTER
CHATTER
SPORTS DRINK
SPORTS DRINK
SPORTS DRINK
SPORTS DRINK

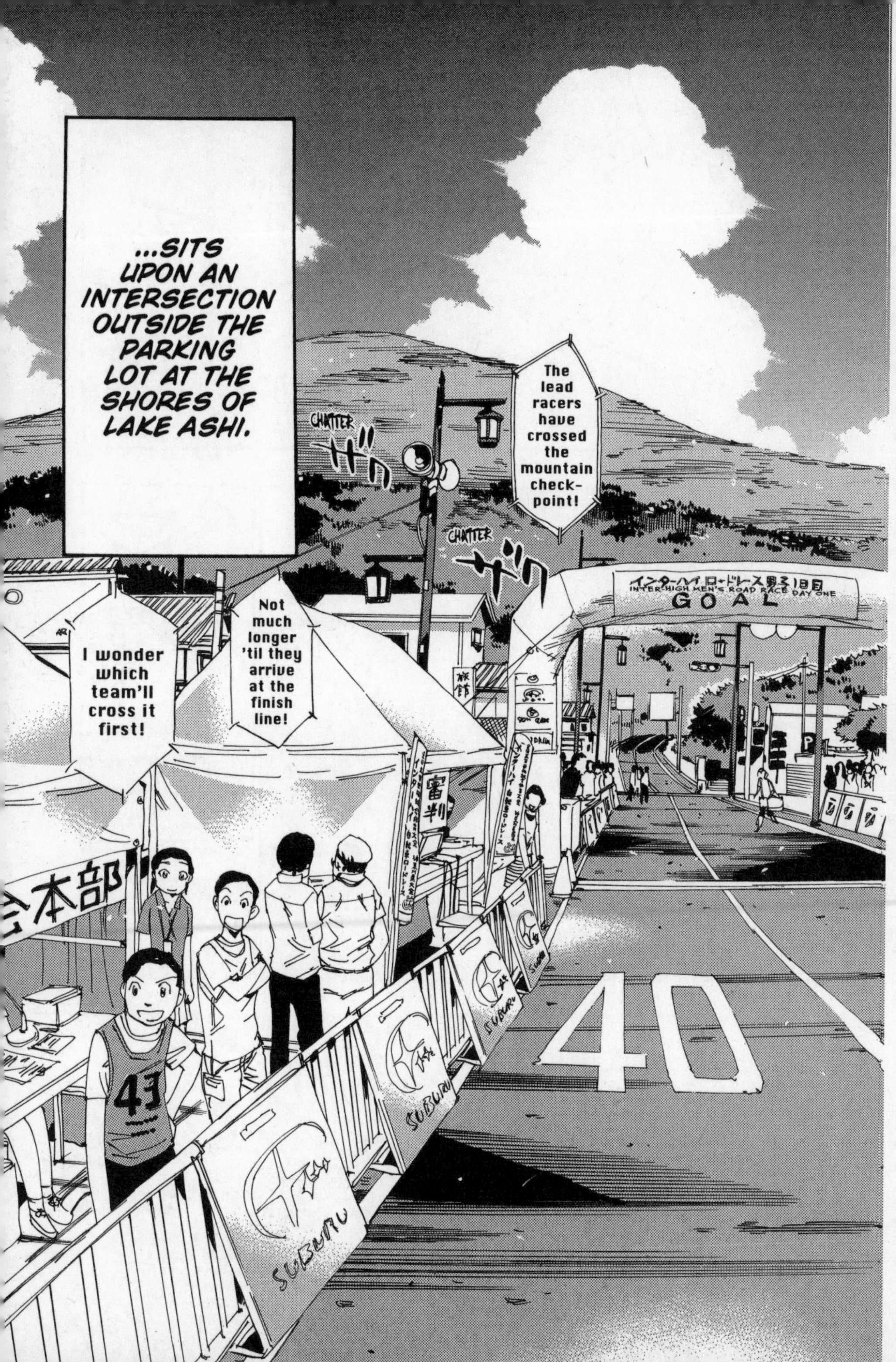
...SITS UPON AN INTERSECTION OUTSIDE THE PARKING LOT AT THE SHORES OF LAKE ASHI.
The lead racers have crossed the mountain check-point!
CHATTER
CHATTER
INTER-HIGH MEN'S ROAD RACE DAY ONE
GOAL
Not much longer 'til they arrive at the finish line!
I wonder which team'll cross it first!
40
SUBURU

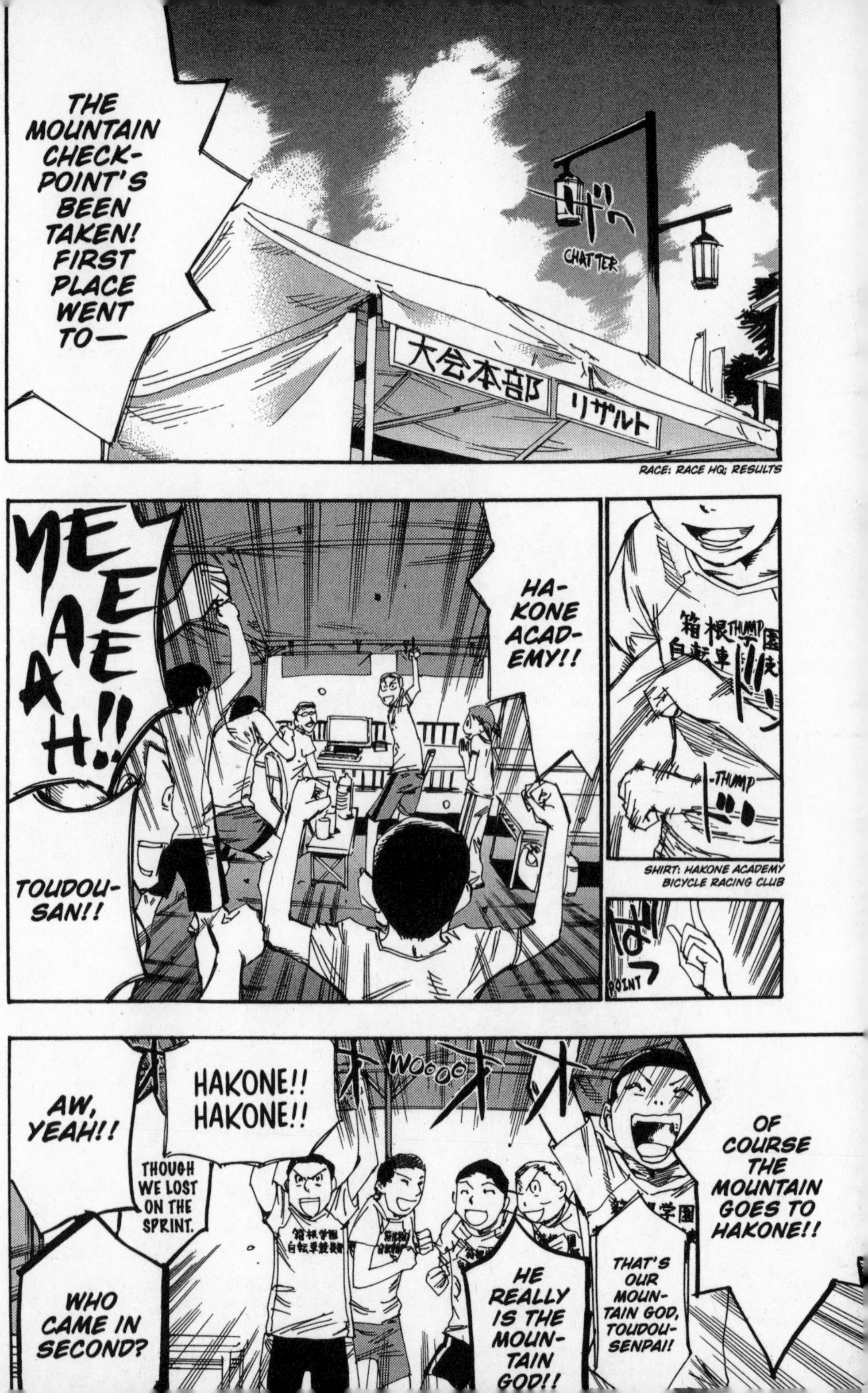
THE MOUNTAIN CHECKPOINT'S BEEN TAKEN! FIRST PLACE WENT TO—
CHATTER
大会本部
リザルト
RACE: RACE HQ; RESULTS
THUMP
THUMP
SHIRT: HAKONE ACADEMY BICYCLE RACING CLUB
POINT
HAKONE ACADEMY!!
YEEEEAAAH!!
TOUDOU-SAN!!
OF COURSE THE MOUNTAIN GOES TO HAKONE!!
WOOOO
HAKONE!! HAKONE!!
AW, YEAH!!
THOUGH WE LOST ON THE SPRINT.
THAT'S OUR MOUNTAIN GOD, TOUDOU-SENPAI!
HE REALLY IS THE MOUNTAIN GOD!!
WHO CAME IN SECOND?

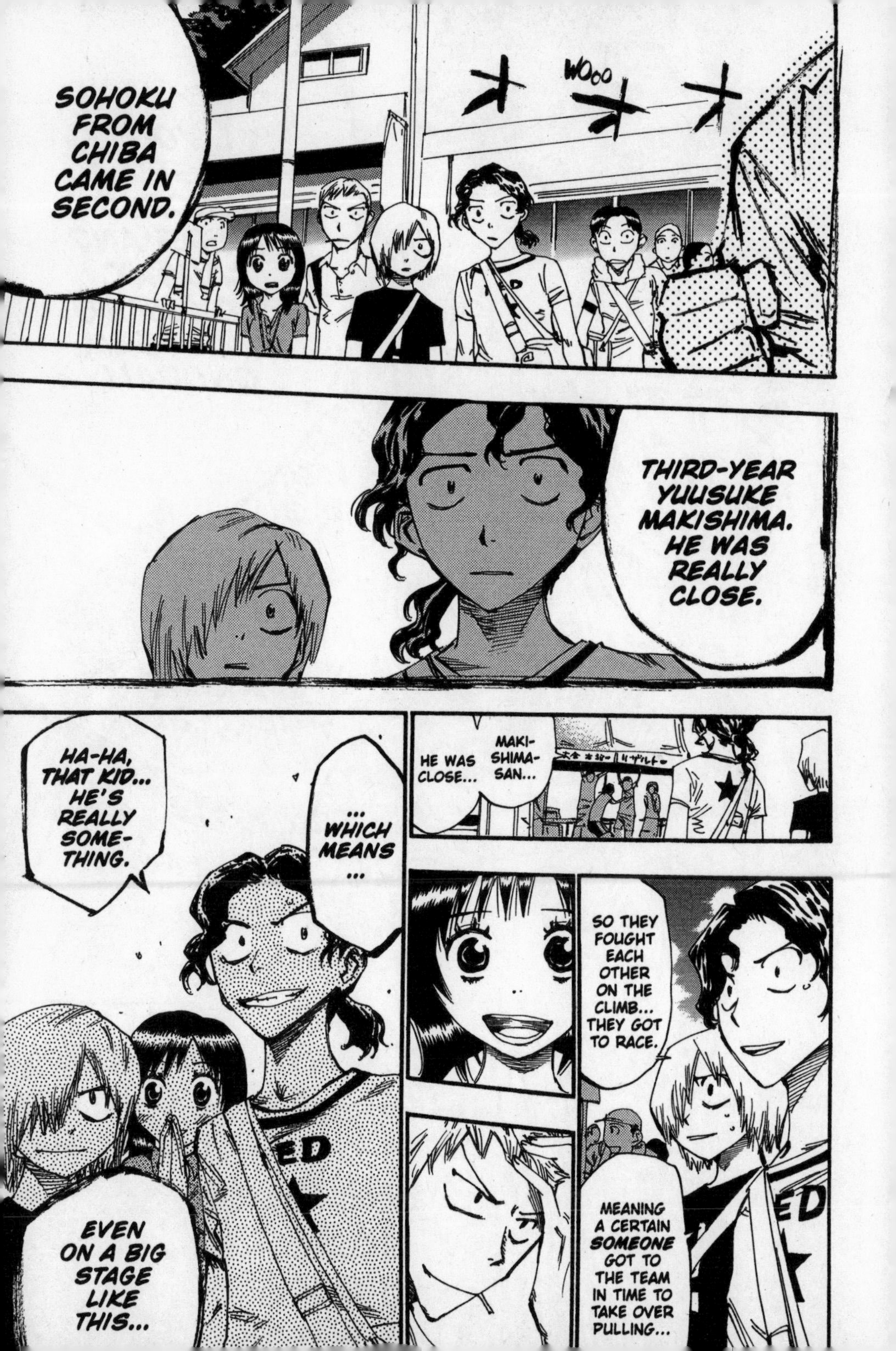
WOOO
SOHOKU FROM CHIBA CAME IN SECOND.
THIRD-YEAR YUUSUKE MAKISHIMA. HE WAS REALLY CLOSE.
MAKI-SHIMA-SAN...
HE WAS CLOSE...
SO THEY FOUGHT EACH OTHER ON THE CLIMB... THEY GOT TO RACE.
MEANING A CERTAIN SOMEONE GOT TO THE TEAM IN TIME TO TAKE OVER PULLING...
...WHICH MEANS...
HA-HA, THAT KID... HE'S REALLY SOME-THING.
EVEN ON A BIG STAGE LIKE THIS...

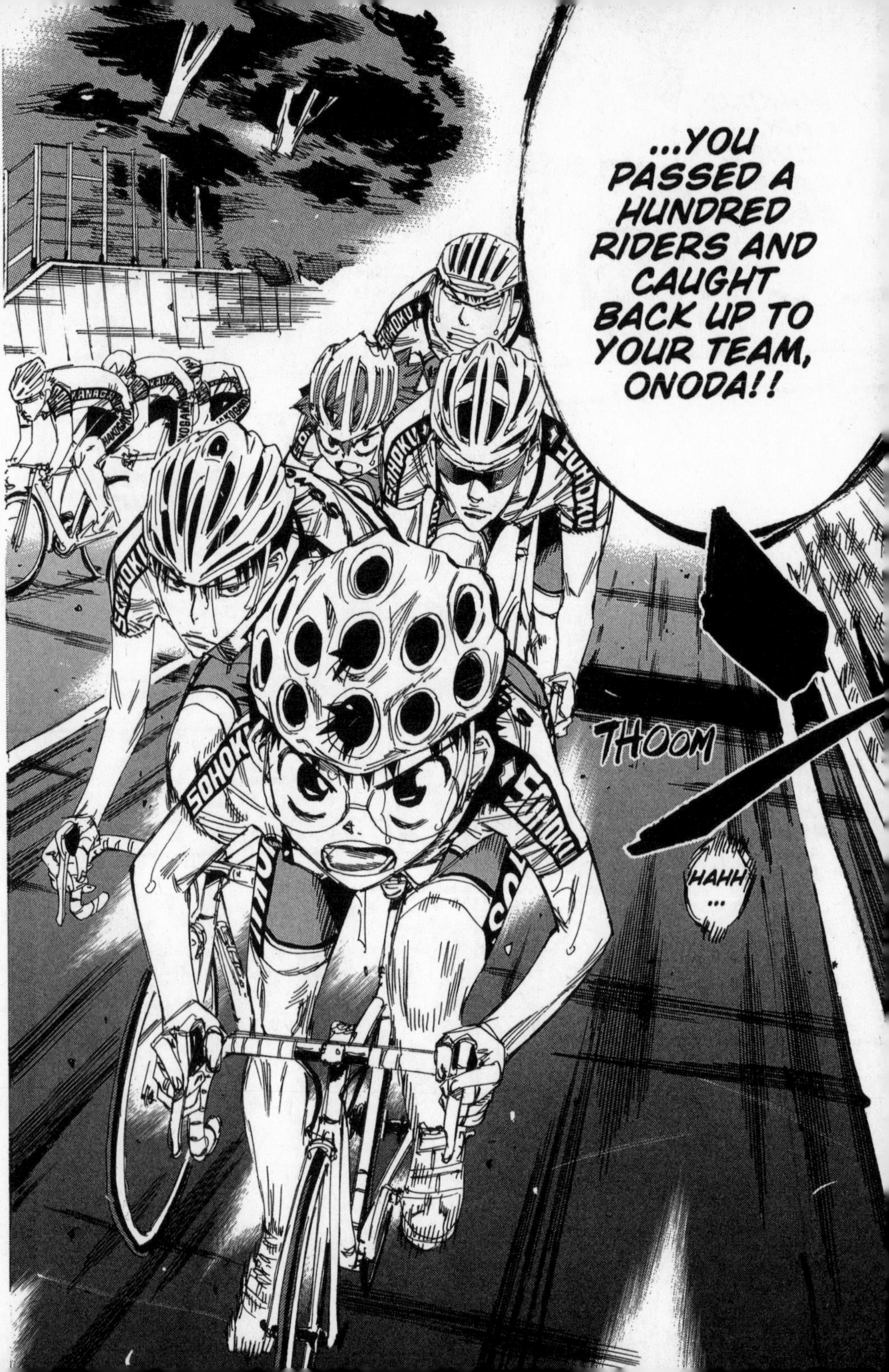
...YOU PASSED A HUNDRED RIDERS AND CAUGHT BACK UP TO YOUR TEAM, ONODA!!
THOOM
HAHH ...

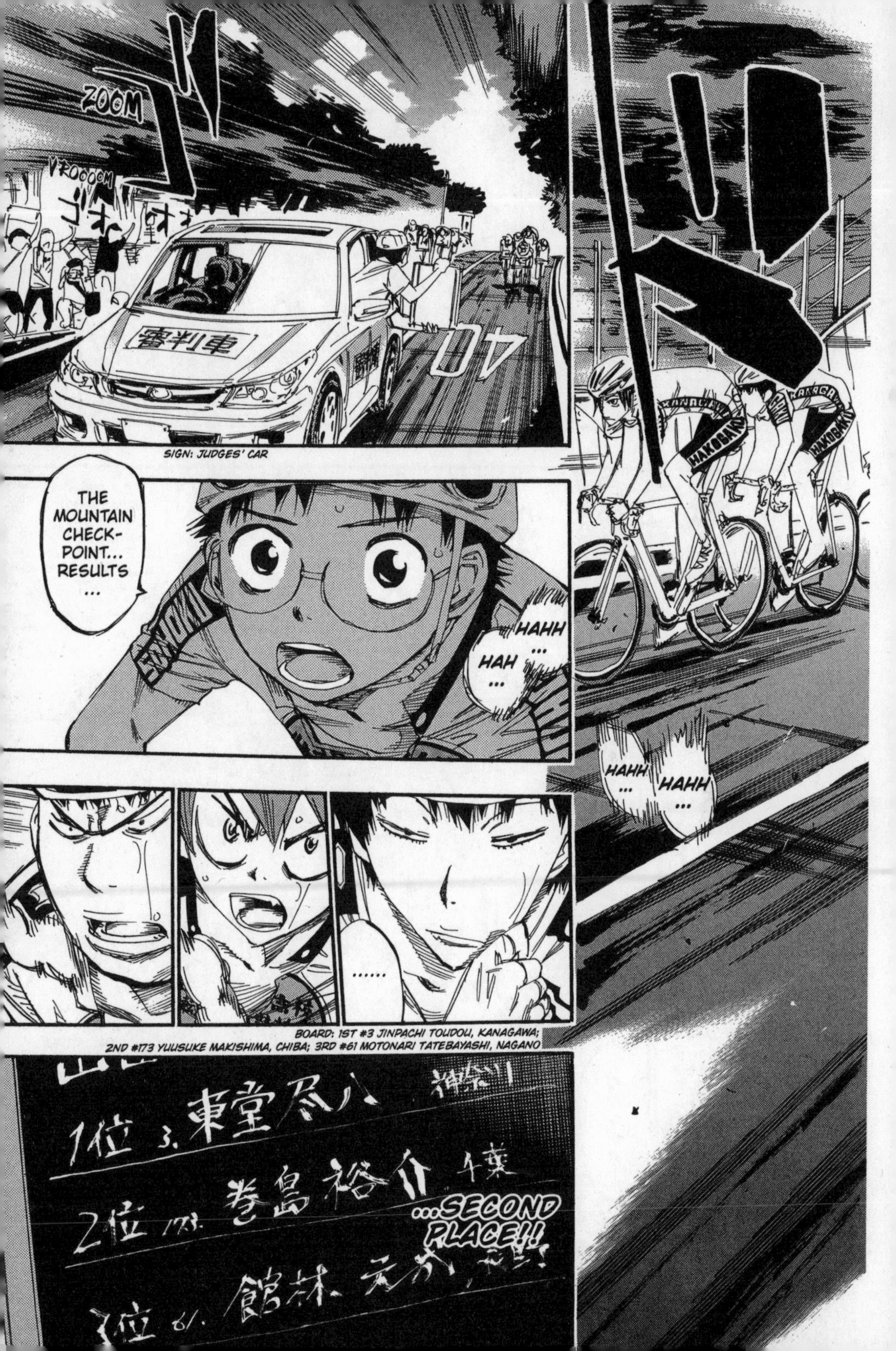
HAHH...
HAHH...
ZOOM
VROOOOM
審判車
SIGN: JUDGES' CAR
THE MOUNTAIN CHECK-POINT... RESULTS...
HAHH...
HAH...
......
BOARD: 1ST #3 JINPACHI TOUDOU, KANAGAWA; 2ND #173 YUUSUKE MAKISHIMA, CHIBA; 3RD #61 MOTONARI TATEBAYASHI, NAGANO
...SECOND PLACE!!

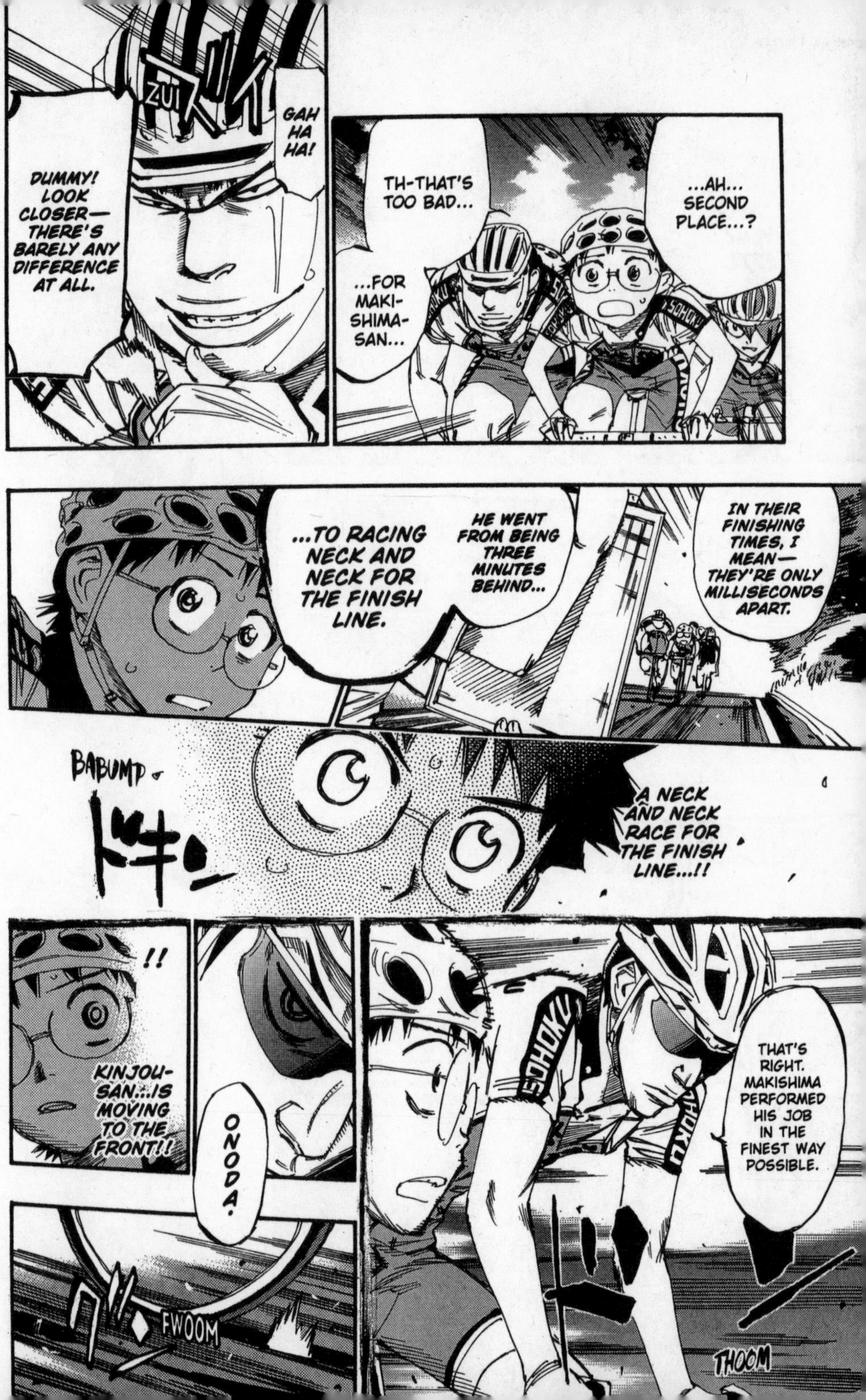
...AH... SECOND PLACE...?
TH-THAT'S TOO BAD...
...FOR MAKI-SHIMA-SAN...
ZUI
GAH HA HA!
DUMMY! LOOK CLOSER— THERE'S BARELY ANY DIFFERENCE AT ALL.
IN THEIR FINISHING TIMES, I MEAN— THEY'RE ONLY MILLISECONDS APART.
HE WENT FROM BEING THREE MINUTES BEHIND...
...TO RACING NECK AND NECK FOR THE FINISH LINE.
A NECK AND NECK RACE FOR THE FINISH LINE...!!
BABUMP
THAT'S RIGHT. MAKISHIMA PERFORMED HIS JOB IN THE FINEST WAY POSSIBLE.
ONODA.
THOOM
!!
KINJOU-SAN...IS MOVING TO THE FRONT!!
FWOOM

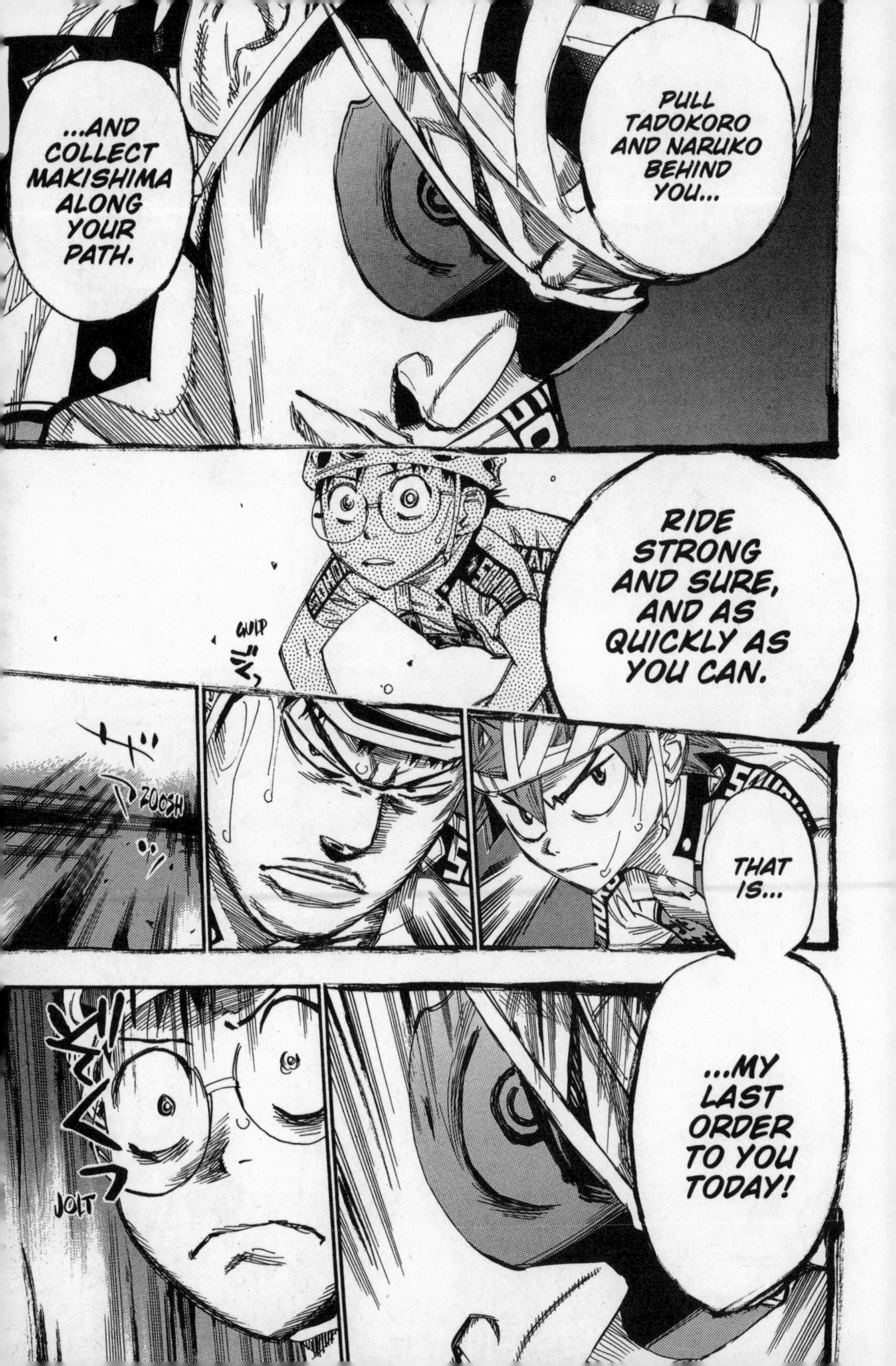
PULL TADOKORO AND NARUKO BEHIND YOU...
...AND COLLECT MAKISHIMA ALONG YOUR PATH.
RIDE STRONG AND SURE, AND AS QUICKLY AS YOU CAN.
GULP
THAT IS...
ZOOSH
...MY LAST ORDER TO YOU TODAY!
JOLT

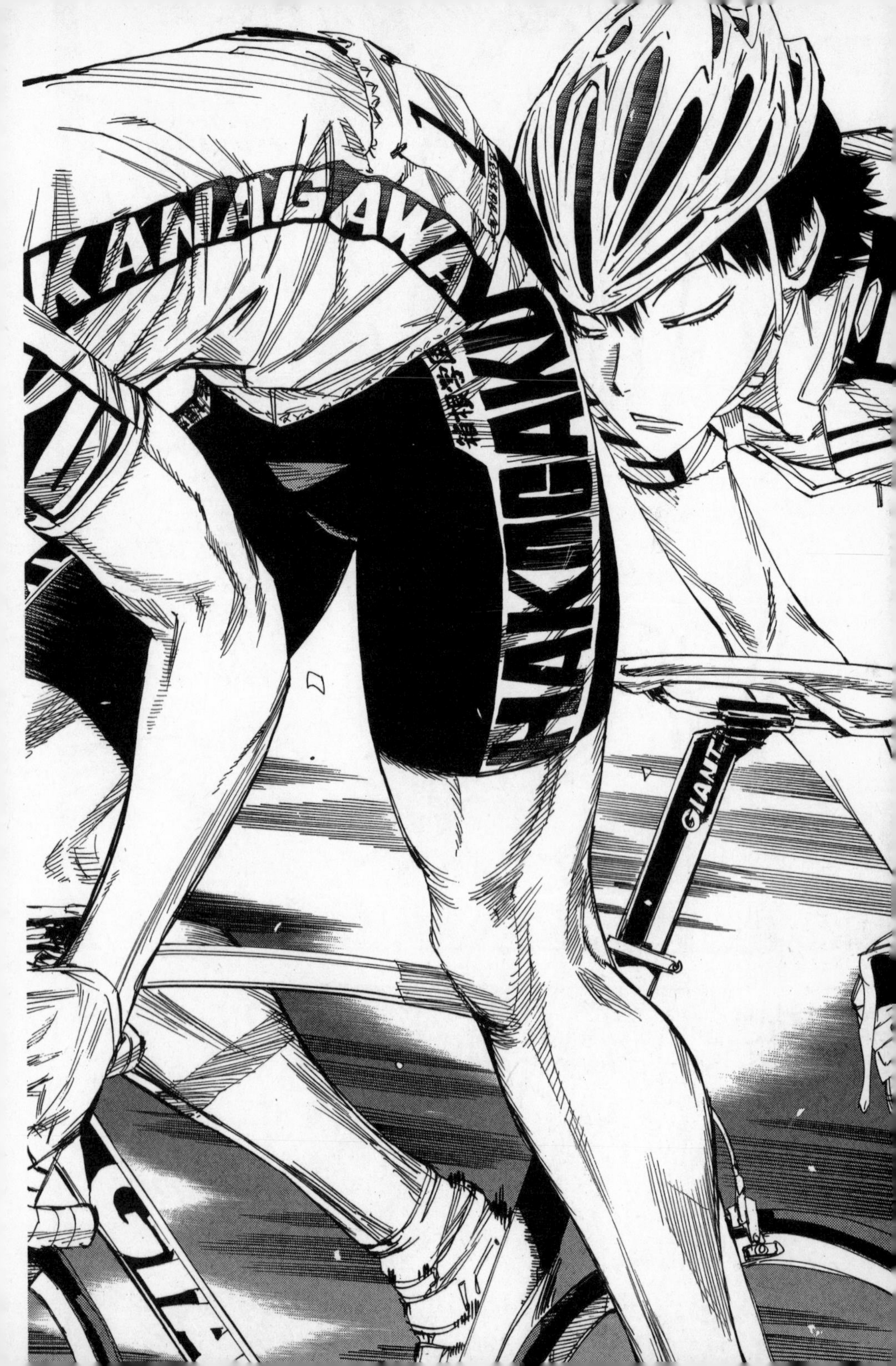
HAKOGAKU
GIANT

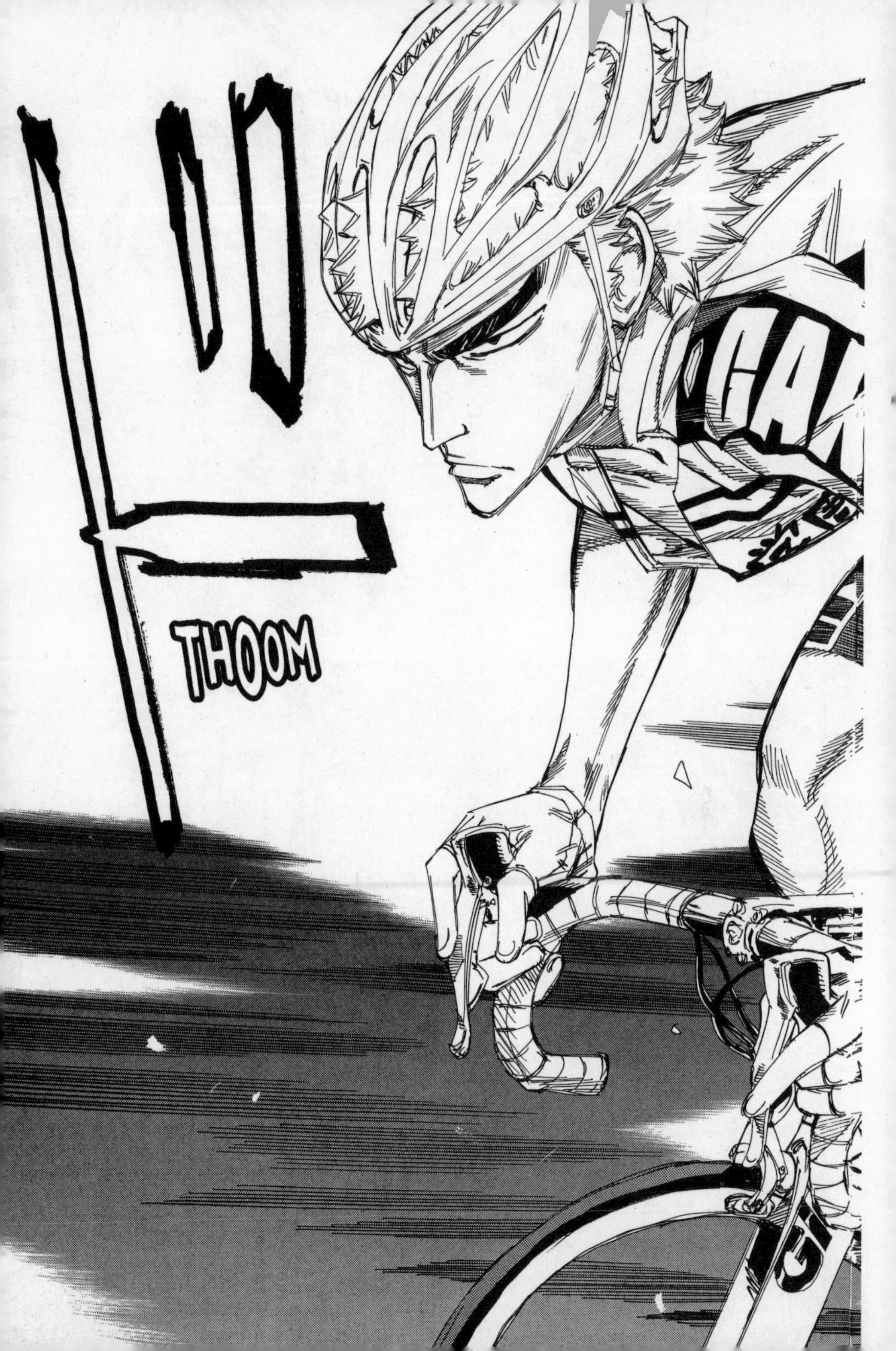
THOOM

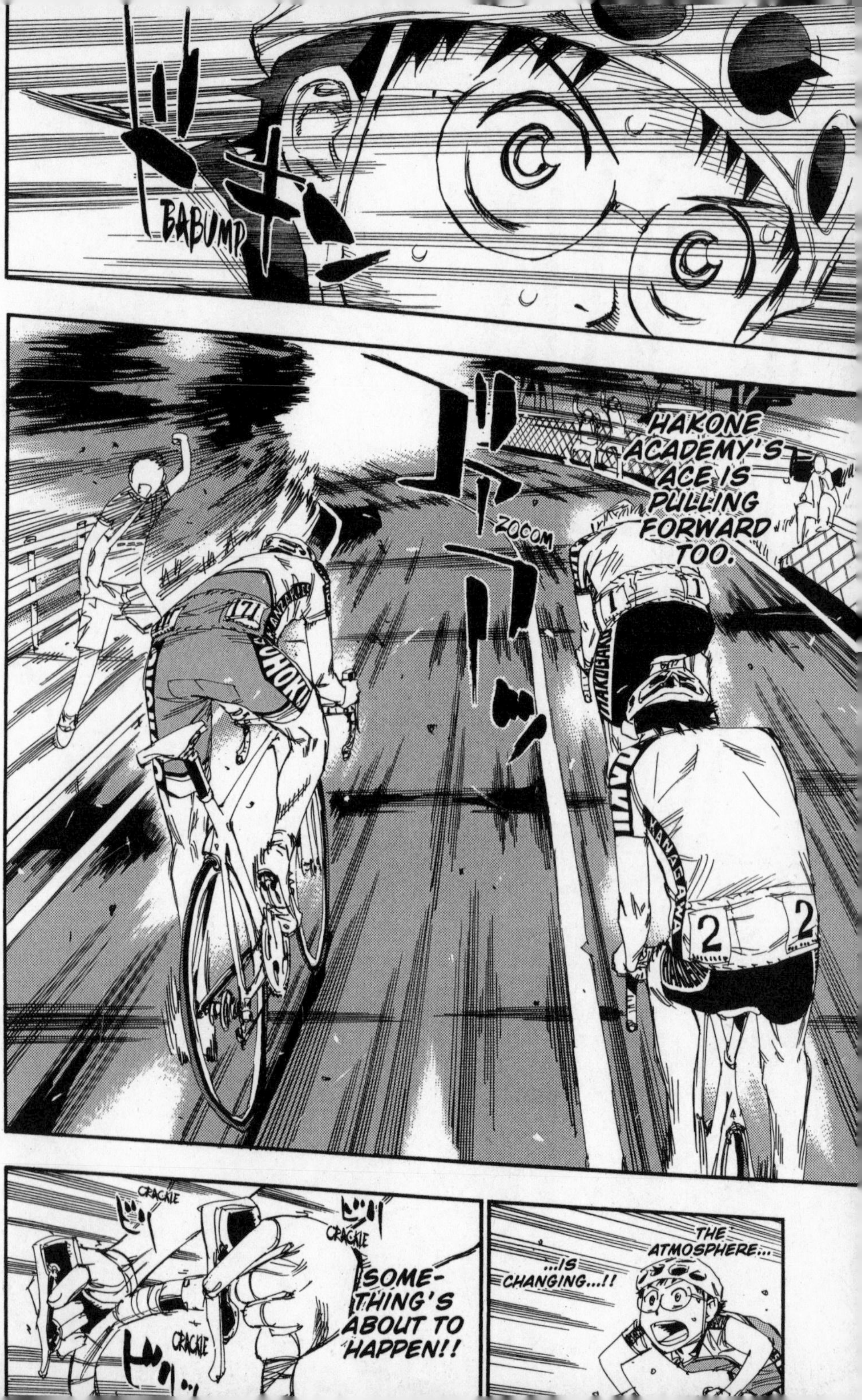
BABUMP
HAKONE ACADEMY'S ACE IS PULLING FORWARD TOO.
ZOCOM
THE ATMOSPHERE...
...IS CHANGING...!!
CRACKLE
CRACKLE
CRACKLE
SOME-THING'S ABOUT TO HAPPEN!!

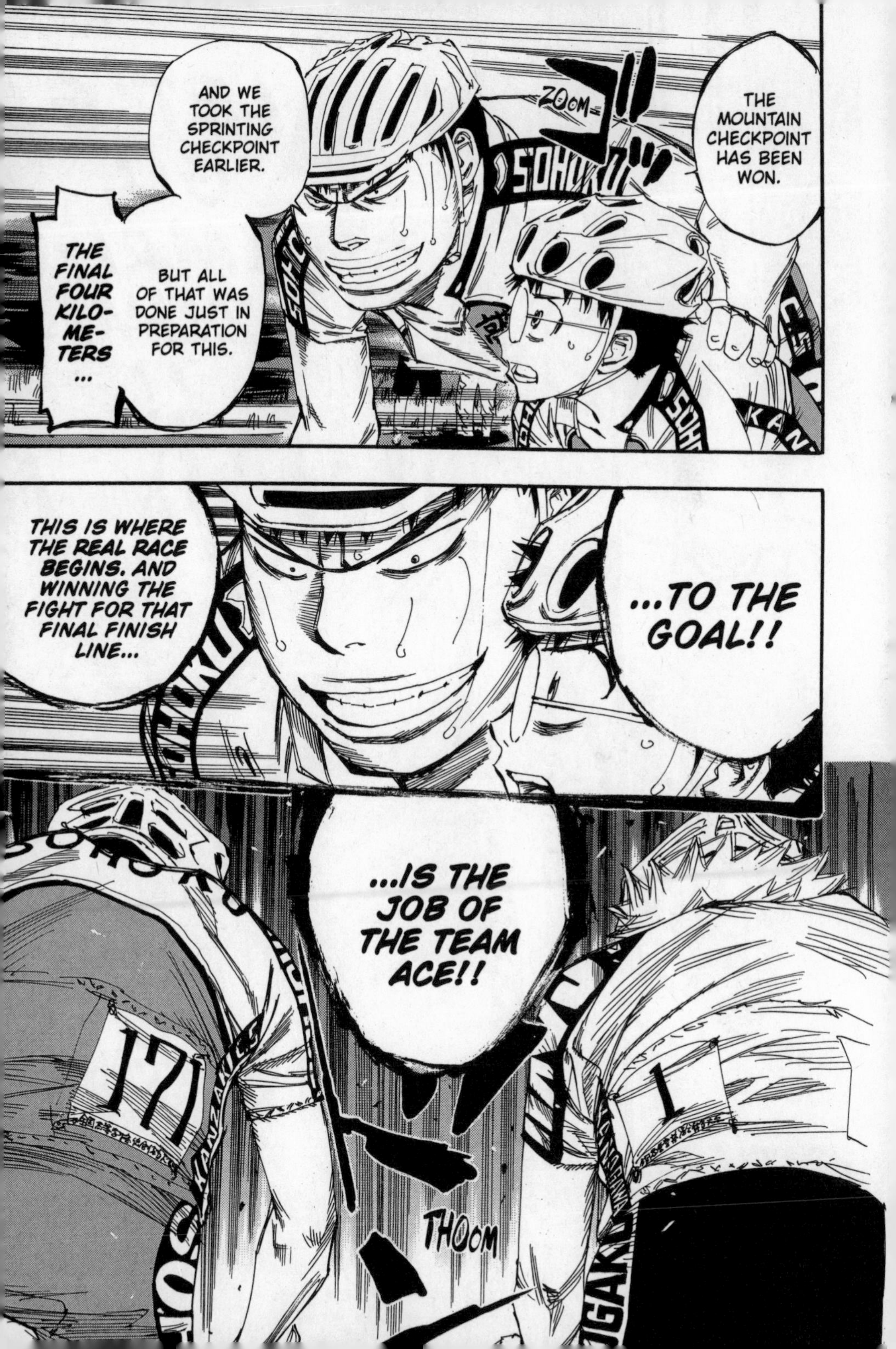
THE MOUNTAIN CHECKPOINT HAS BEEN WON.
ZOOM
AND WE TOOK THE SPRINTING CHECKPOINT EARLIER.
BUT ALL OF THAT WAS DONE JUST IN PREPARATION FOR THIS.
THE FINAL FOUR KILO-ME-TERS...
THIS IS WHERE THE REAL RACE BEGINS. AND WINNING THE FIGHT FOR THAT FINAL FINISH LINE...
...TO THE GOAL!!
...IS THE JOB OF THE TEAM ACE!!
THOOM

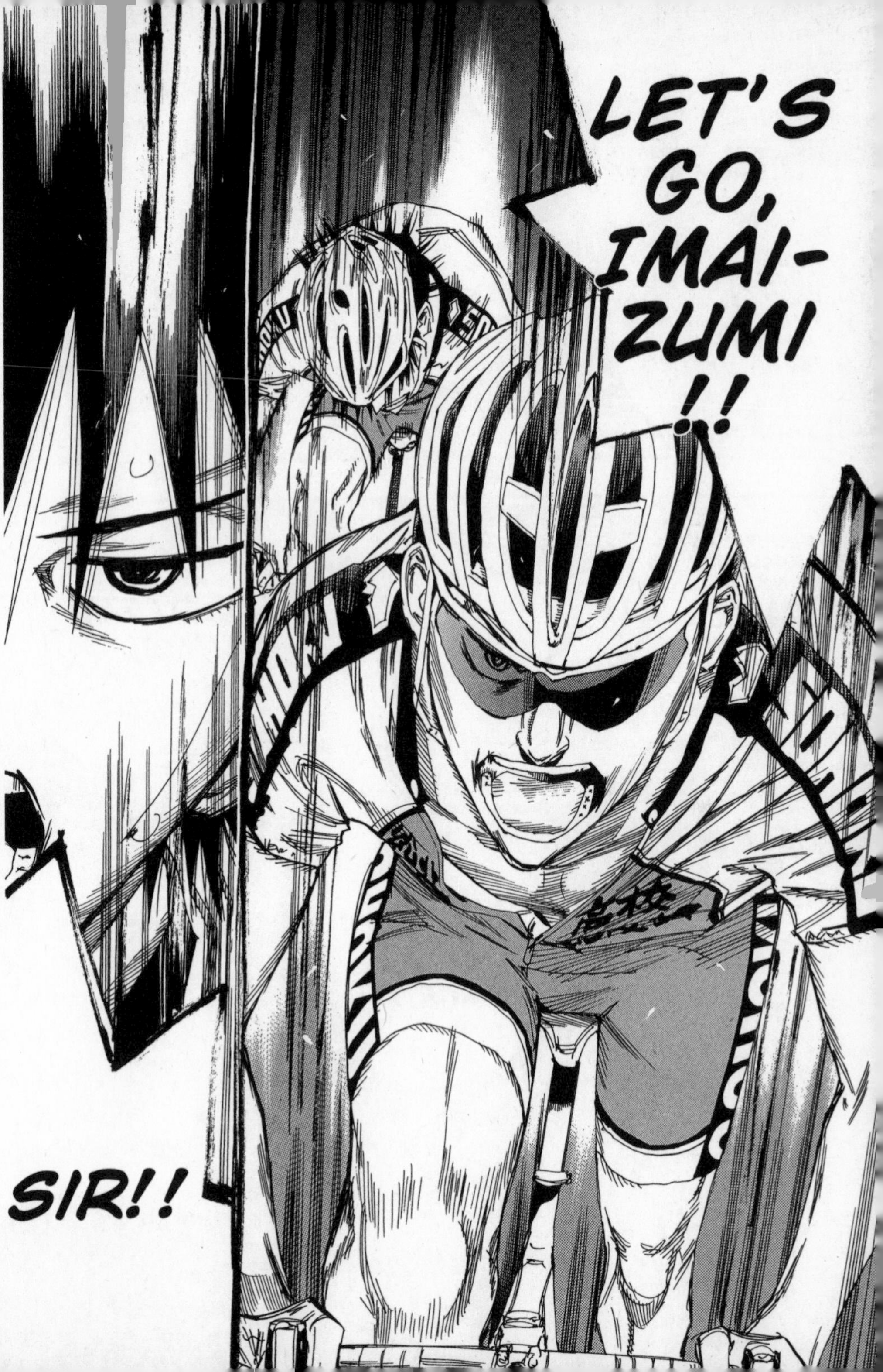
LET'S GO, IMAI-ZUMI!!
SIR!!

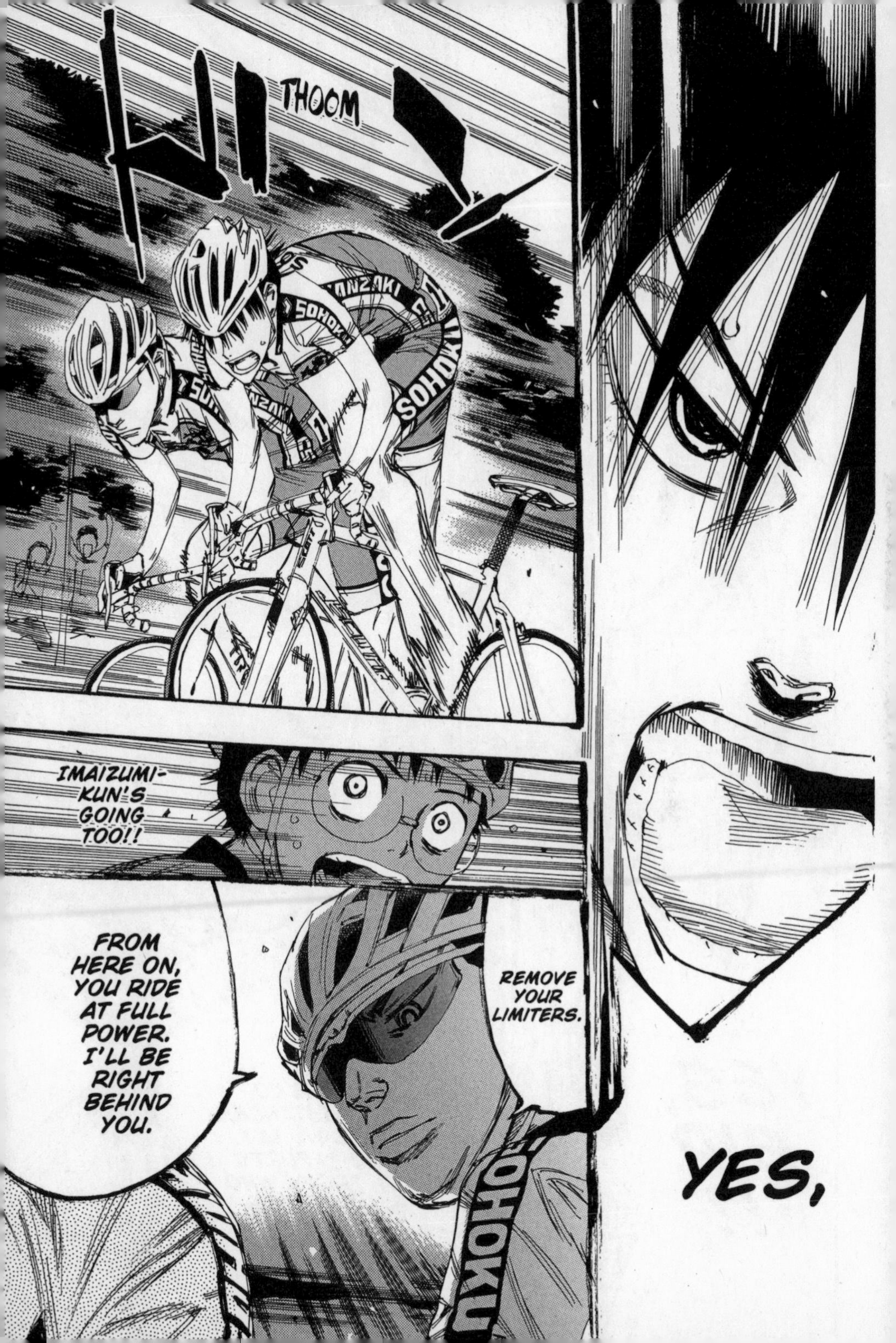
THOOM
IMAIZUMI-KUN'S GOING TOO!!
REMOVE YOUR LIMITERS.
FROM HERE ON, YOU RIDE AT FULL POWER. I'LL BE RIGHT BEHIND YOU.
YES,

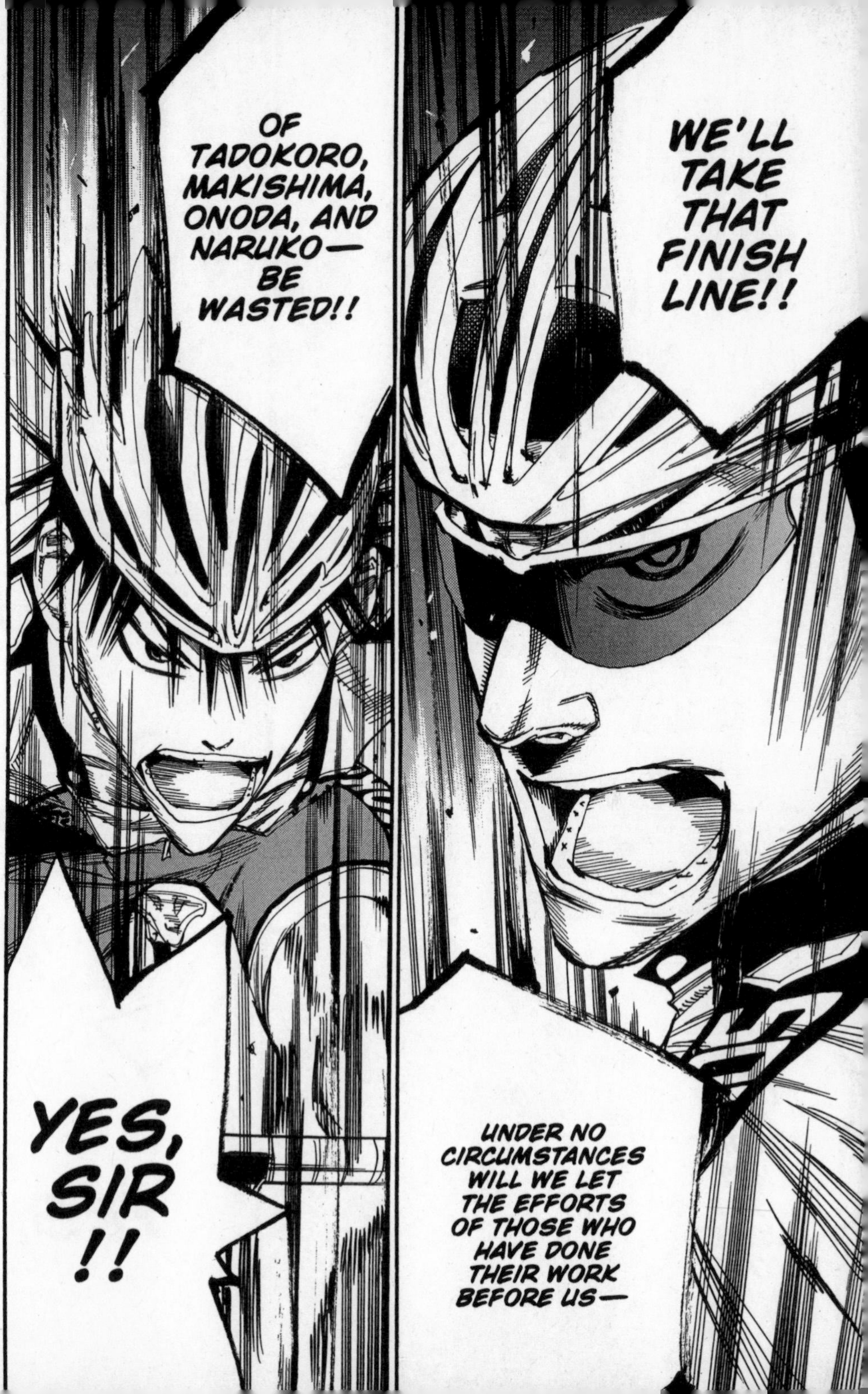
WE'LL TAKE THAT FINISH LINE!!
UNDER NO CIRCUMSTANCES WILL WE LET THE EFFORTS OF THOSE WHO HAVE DONE THEIR WORK BEFORE US—
OF TADOKORO, MAKISHIMA, ONODA, AND NARUKO— BE WASTED!!
YES, SIR!!

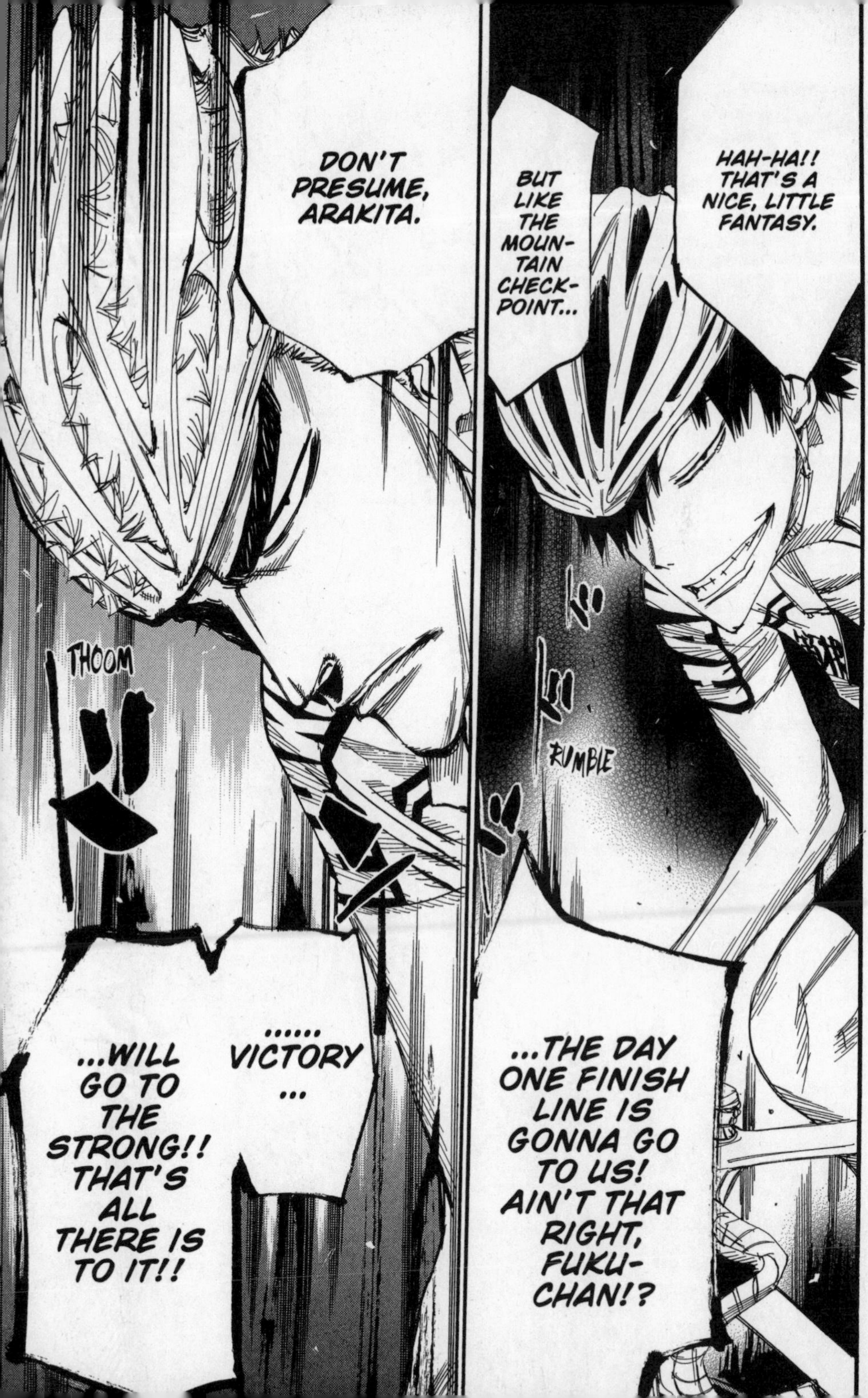
HAH-HA!! THAT'S A NICE, LITTLE FANTASY.
BUT LIKE THE MOUN-TAIN CHECK-POINT...
RUMBLE
...THE DAY ONE FINISH LINE IS GONNA GO TO US! AIN'T THAT RIGHT, FUKU-CHAN!?
DON'T PRESUME, ARAKITA.
THOOM
......VICTORY...
...WILL GO TO THE STRONG!! THAT'S ALL THERE IS TO IT!!

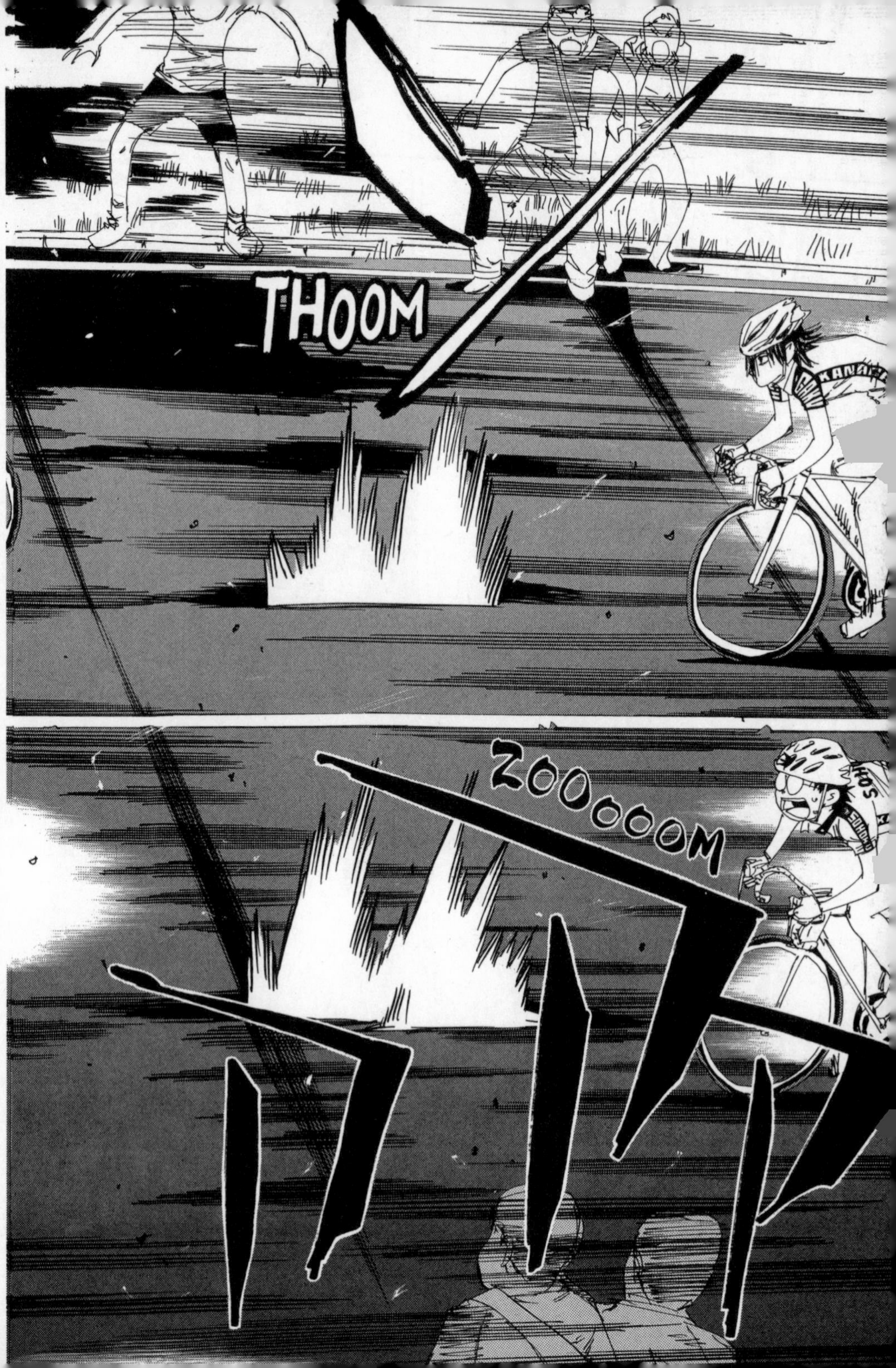
THOOM
ZOOOOOM

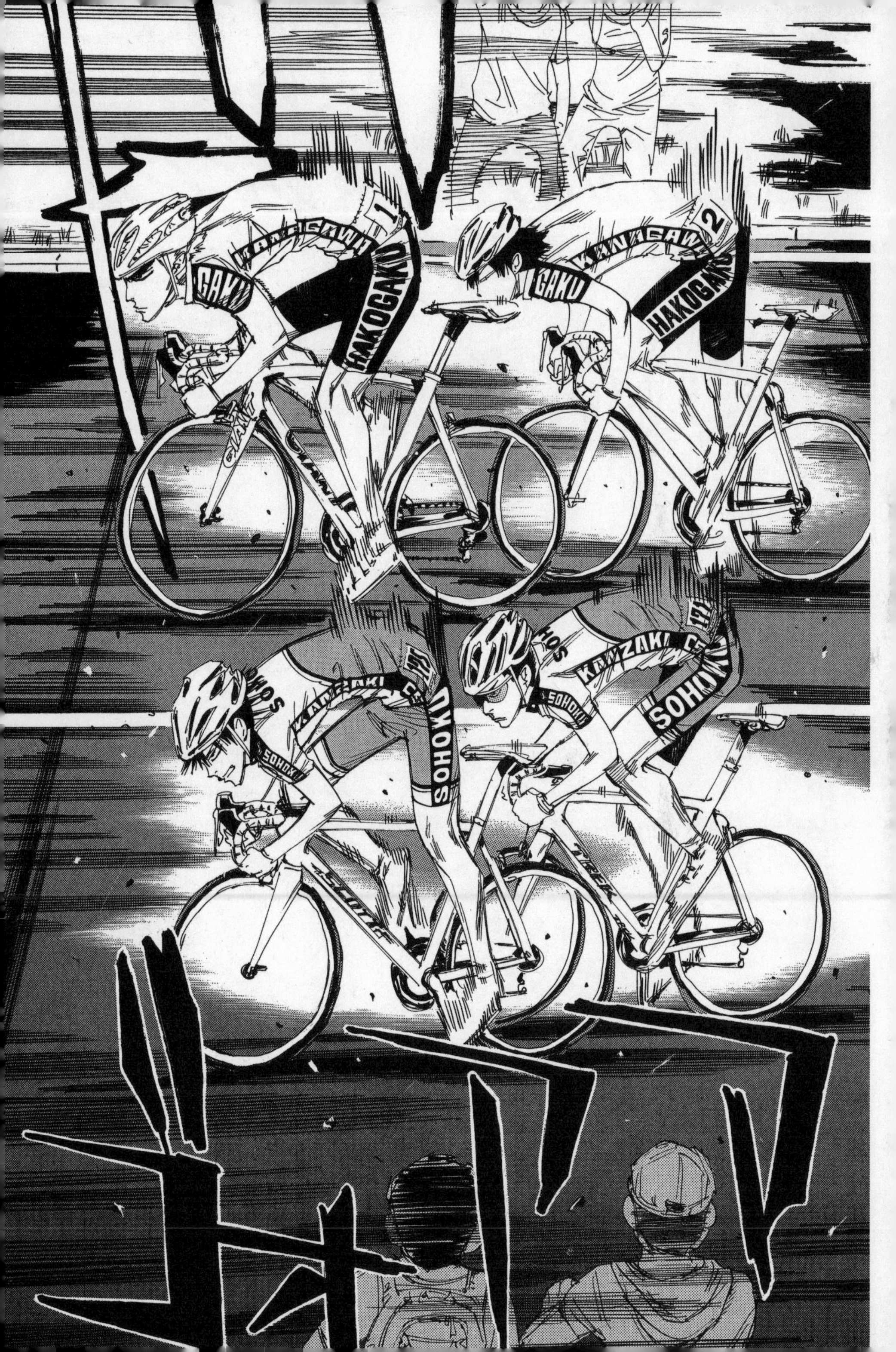
HAKOGAKU
HAKOGAKU
SOHOKU
SOHOKU

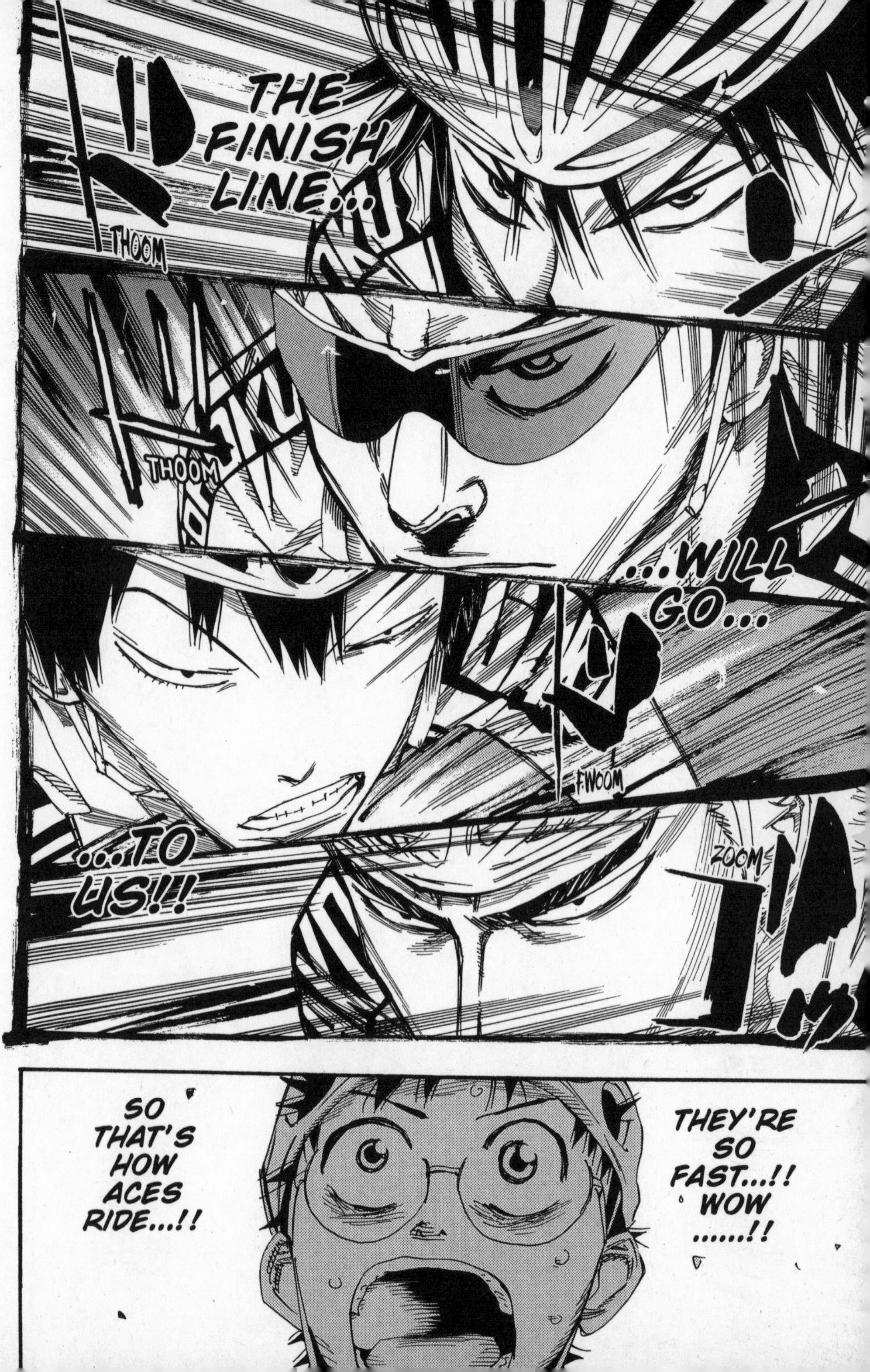
THE FINISH LINE...
THOOM
THOOM
...WILL GO...
F.WOOM
ZOOM
...TO US!!
THEY'RE SO FAST...!! WOW ......!!
SO THAT'S HOW ACES RIDE...!!

## RIDE.102 TAKING THE LEAD!!

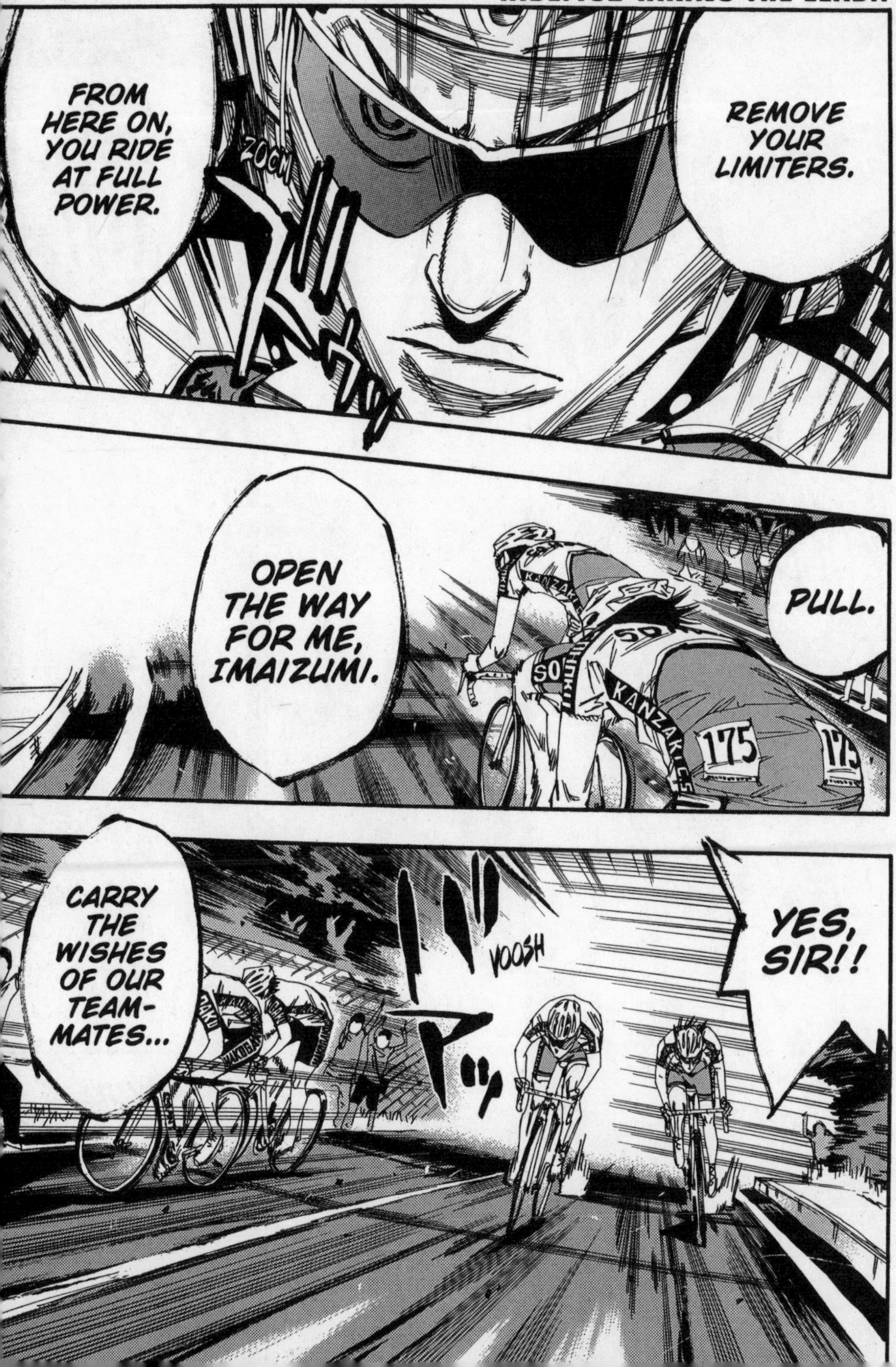
REMOVE YOUR LIMITERS.
FROM HERE ON, YOU RIDE AT FULL POWER.
ZOOM
PULL.
OPEN THE WAY FOR ME, IMAIZUMI.
YES, SIR!!
VOOSH
CARRY THE WISHES OF OUR TEAM-MATES...

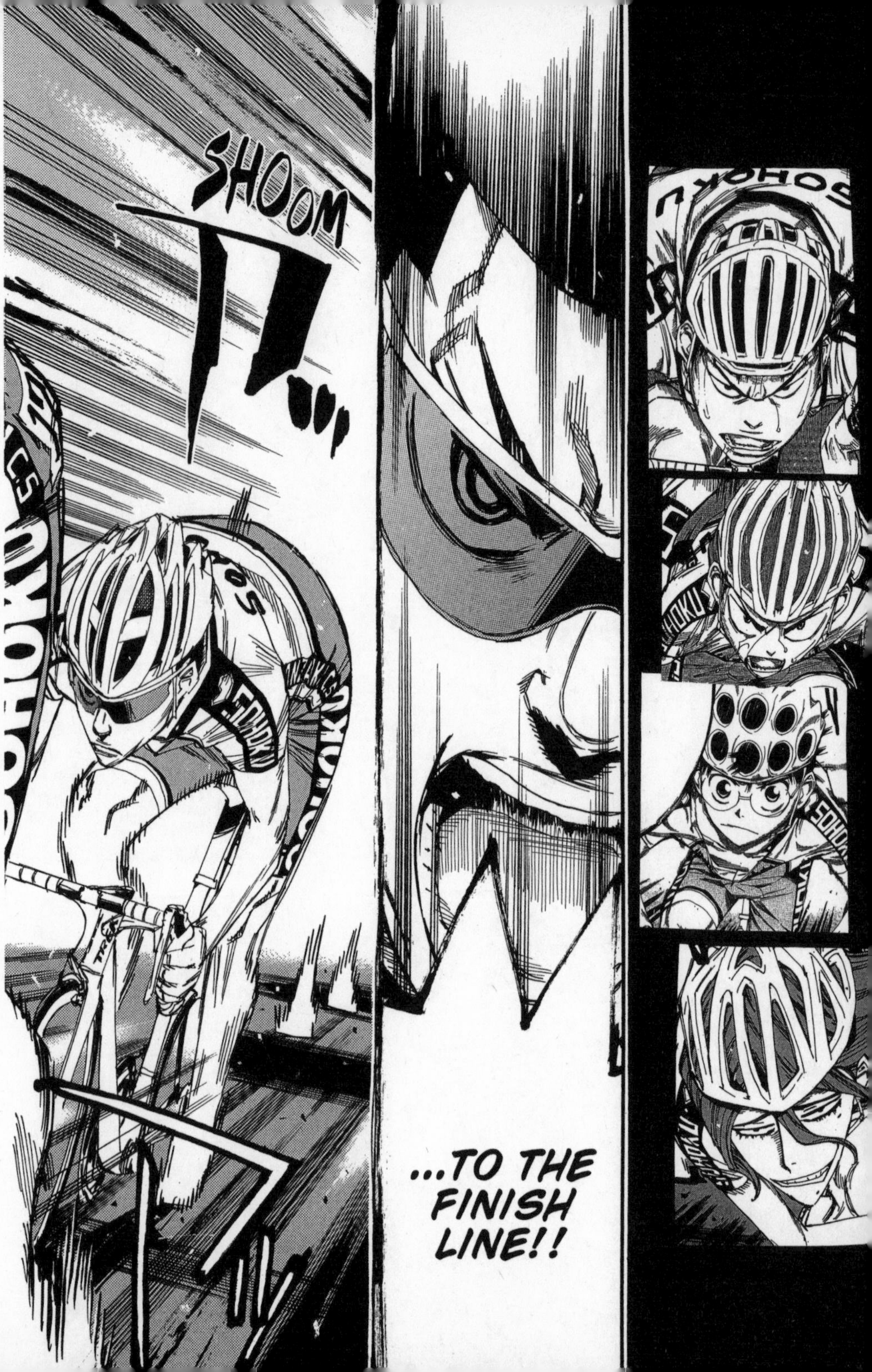
...TO THE FINISH LINE!!
SHOOM

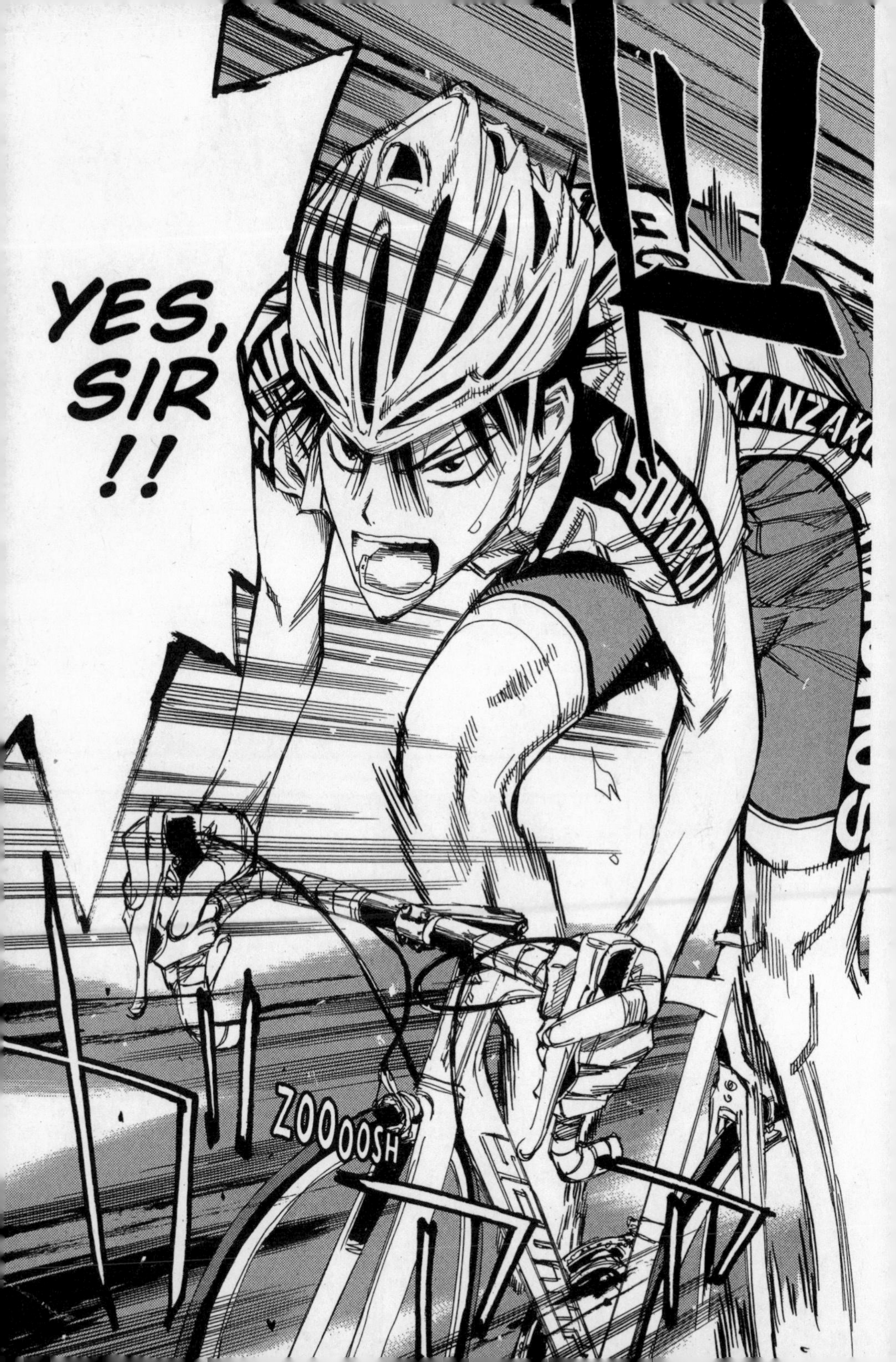
YES, SIR!!
ZOOOOSH

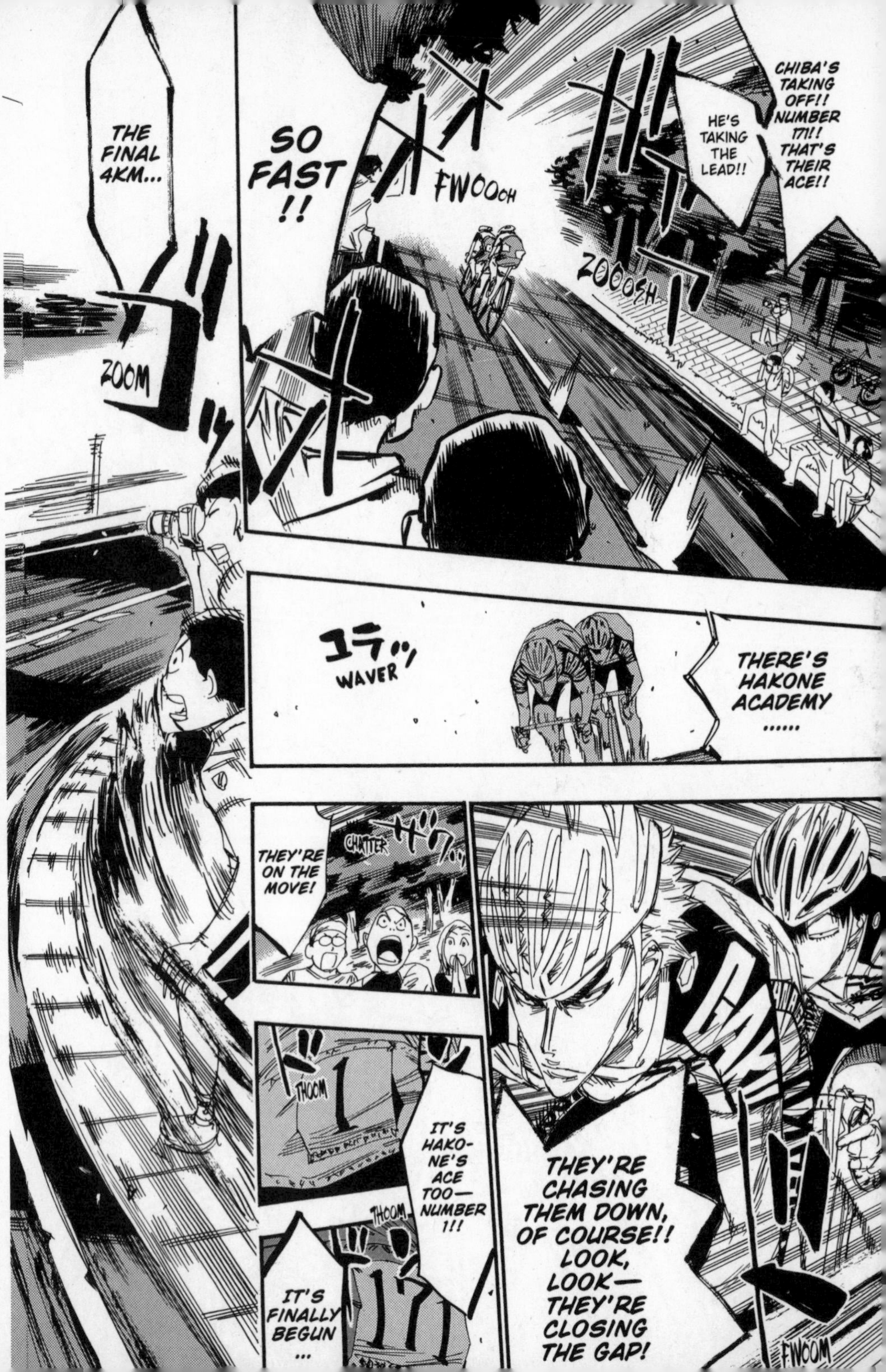
CHIBA'S TAKING OFF!! NUMBER 171!! THAT'S THEIR ACE!!
HE'S TAKING THE LEAD!!
ZOOOSH
FWOOoCH
SO FAST!!
THERE'S HAKONE ACADEMY ......
WAVER
THEY'RE CHASING THEM DOWN, OF COURSE!! LOOK, LOOK—THEY'RE CLOSING THE GAP!
FWOOM
CHATTER
THEY'RE ON THE MOVE!
THOOM
IT'S HAKONE'S ACE TOO—NUMBER 1!!
THOOM
IT'S FINALLY BEGUN ...
THE FINAL 4KM...
ZOOM

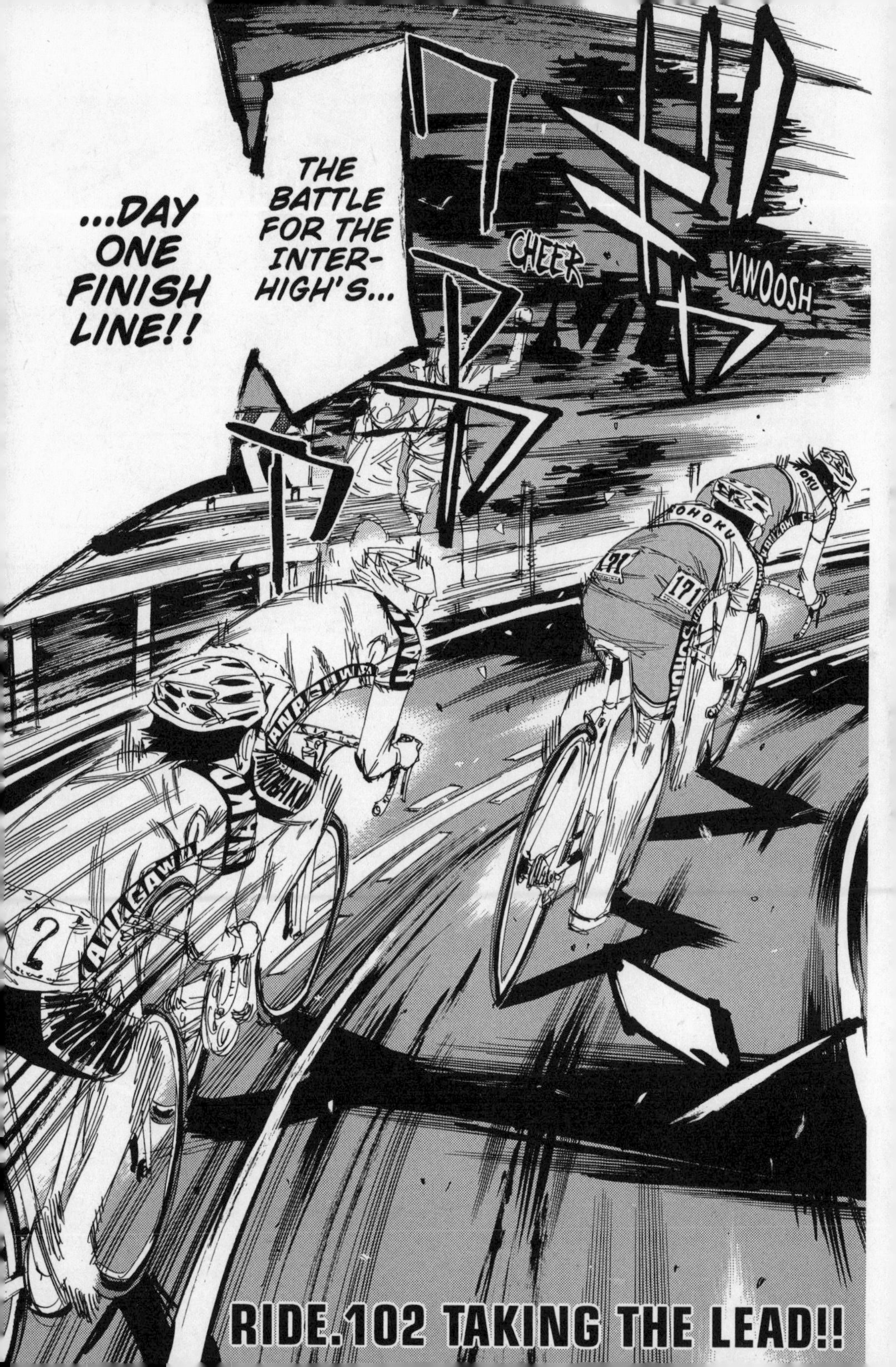
THE BATTLE FOR THE INTER-HIGH'S...
...DAY ONE FINISH LINE!!
VWOOSH
CHEER
RIDE.102 TAKING THE LEAD!!

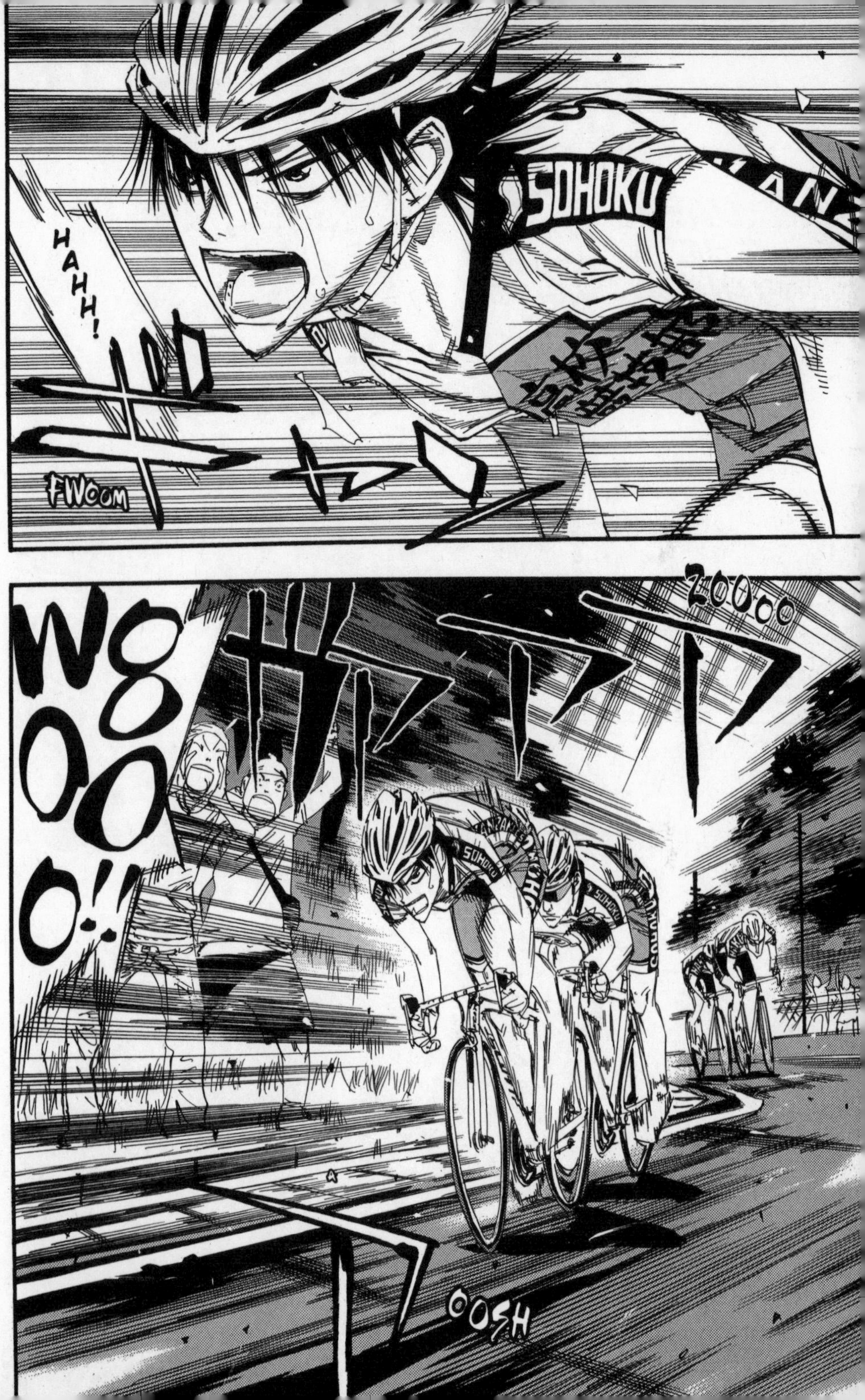

SOHOKU
HAHHH!
FWOOM
ZOOOO
WOOOOO!!
OOSH

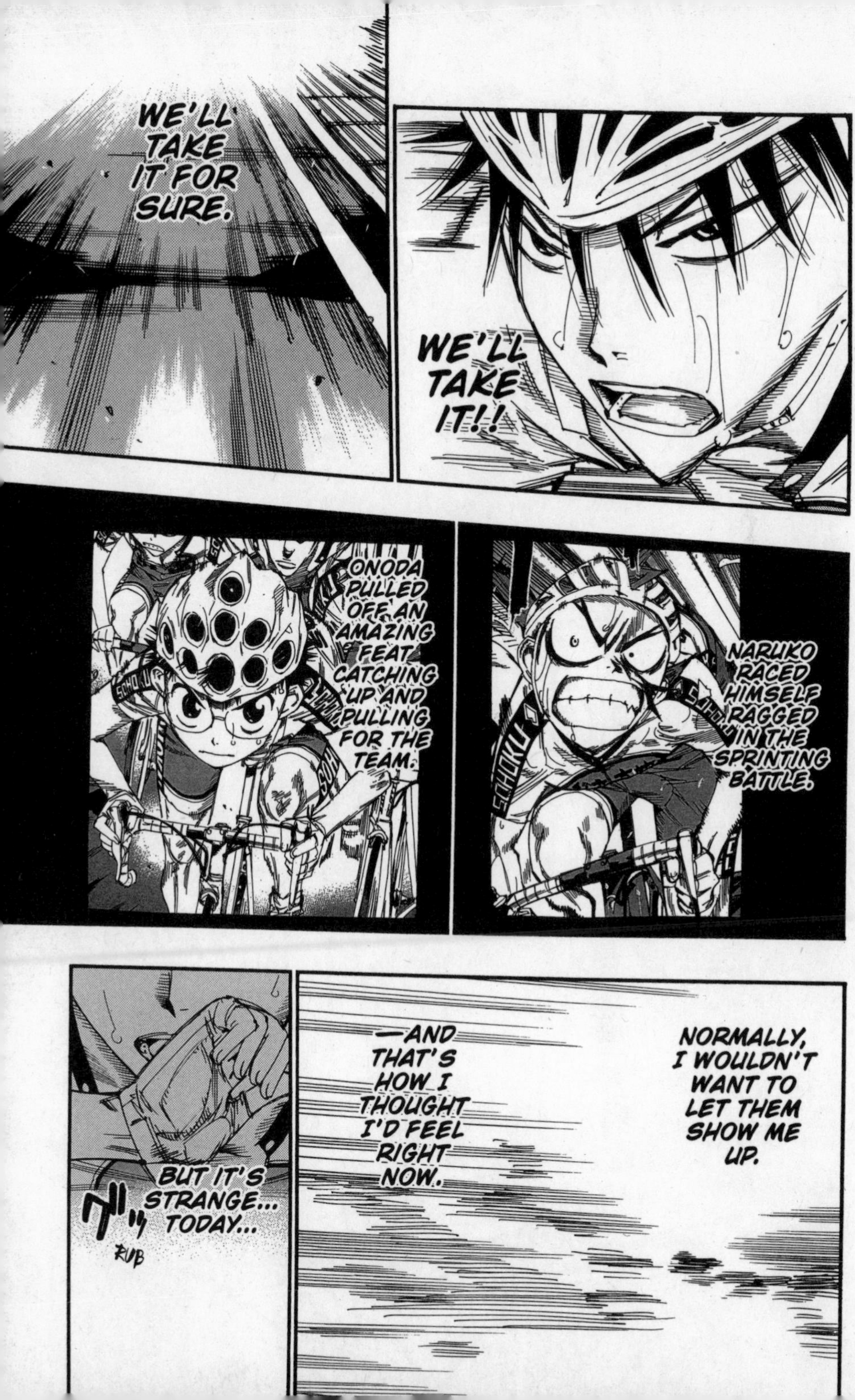
WE'LL TAKE IT!!
WE'LL TAKE IT FOR SURE.
NARUKO RACED HIMSELF RAGGED IN THE SPRINTING BATTLE.
ONODA PULLED OFF AN AMAZING FEAT CATCHING UP AND PULLING FOR THE TEAM.
NORMALLY, I WOULDN'T WANT TO LET THEM SHOW ME UP.
—AND THAT'S HOW I THOUGHT I'D FEEL RIGHT NOW.
BUT IT'S STRANGE... TODAY...
RUB

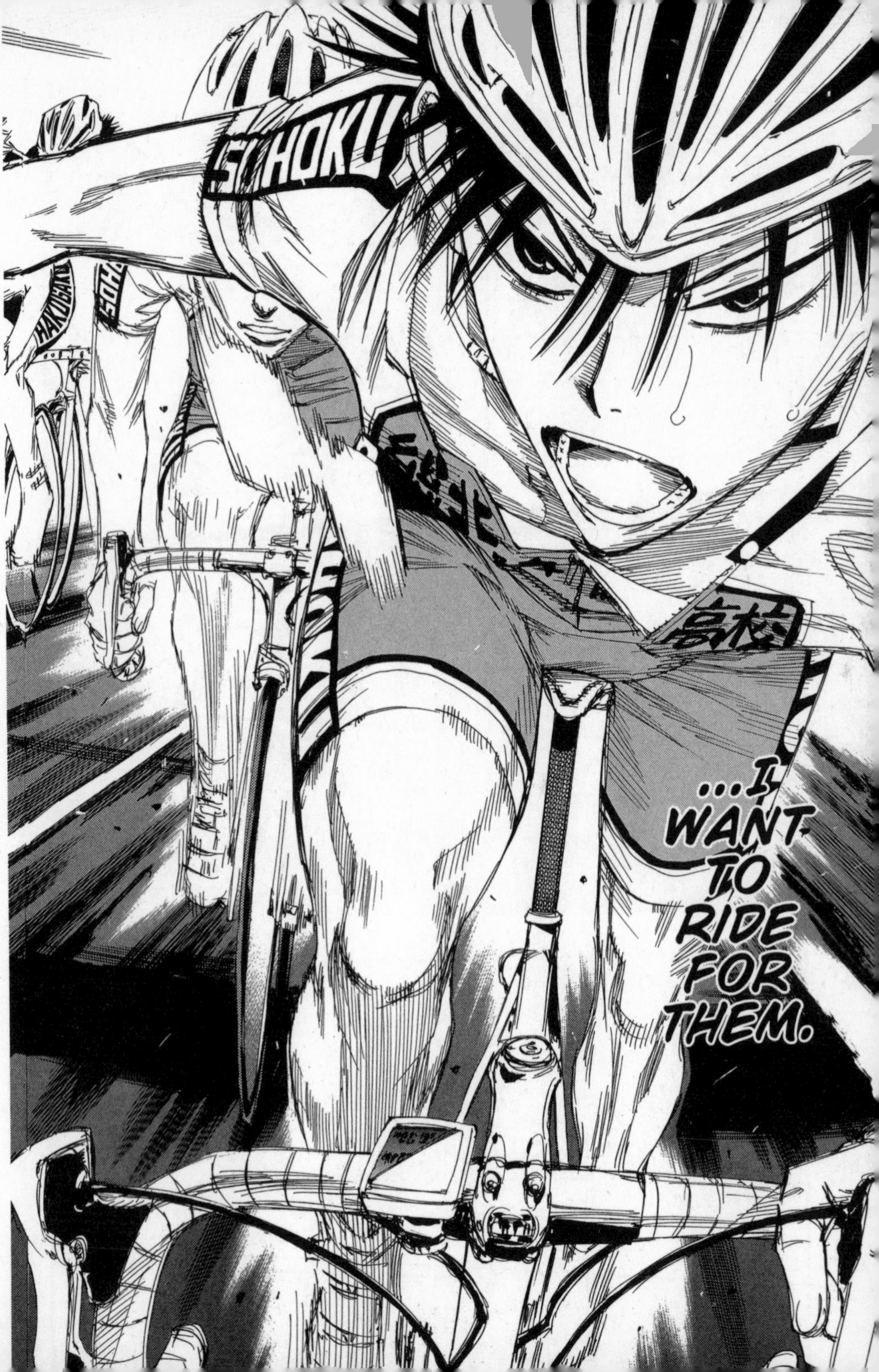
SOHOKU
HAKOGAKU
高校
...I WANT TO RIDE FOR THEM.

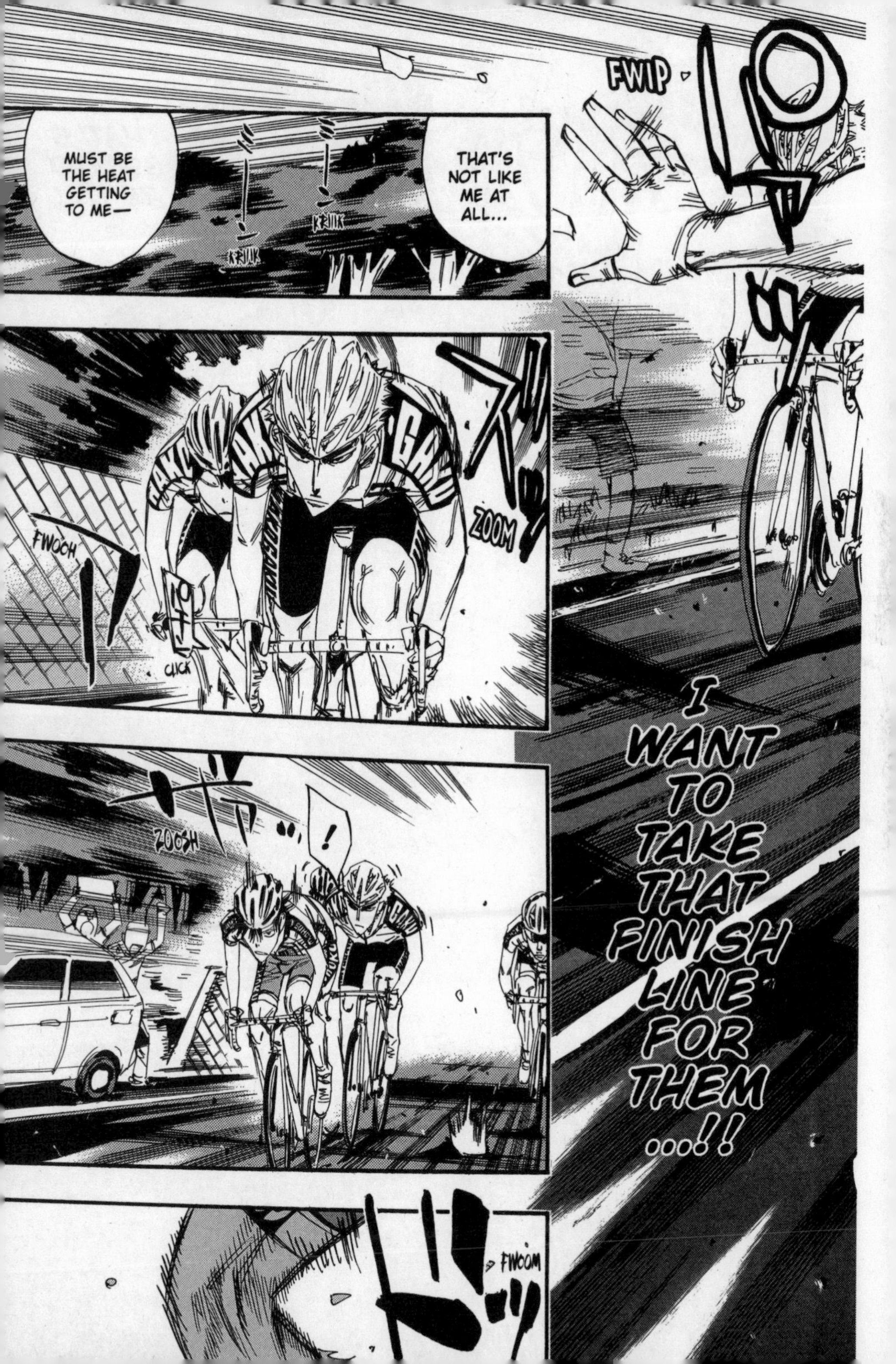
FWIP
I WANT TO TAKE THAT FINISH LINE FOR THEM ...!!
THAT'S NOT LIKE ME AT ALL...
KRIIK
KRIIK
MUST BE THE HEAT GETTING TO ME—
ZOOM
FWOOH
CLICK
ZOOSH
!
FWOOM

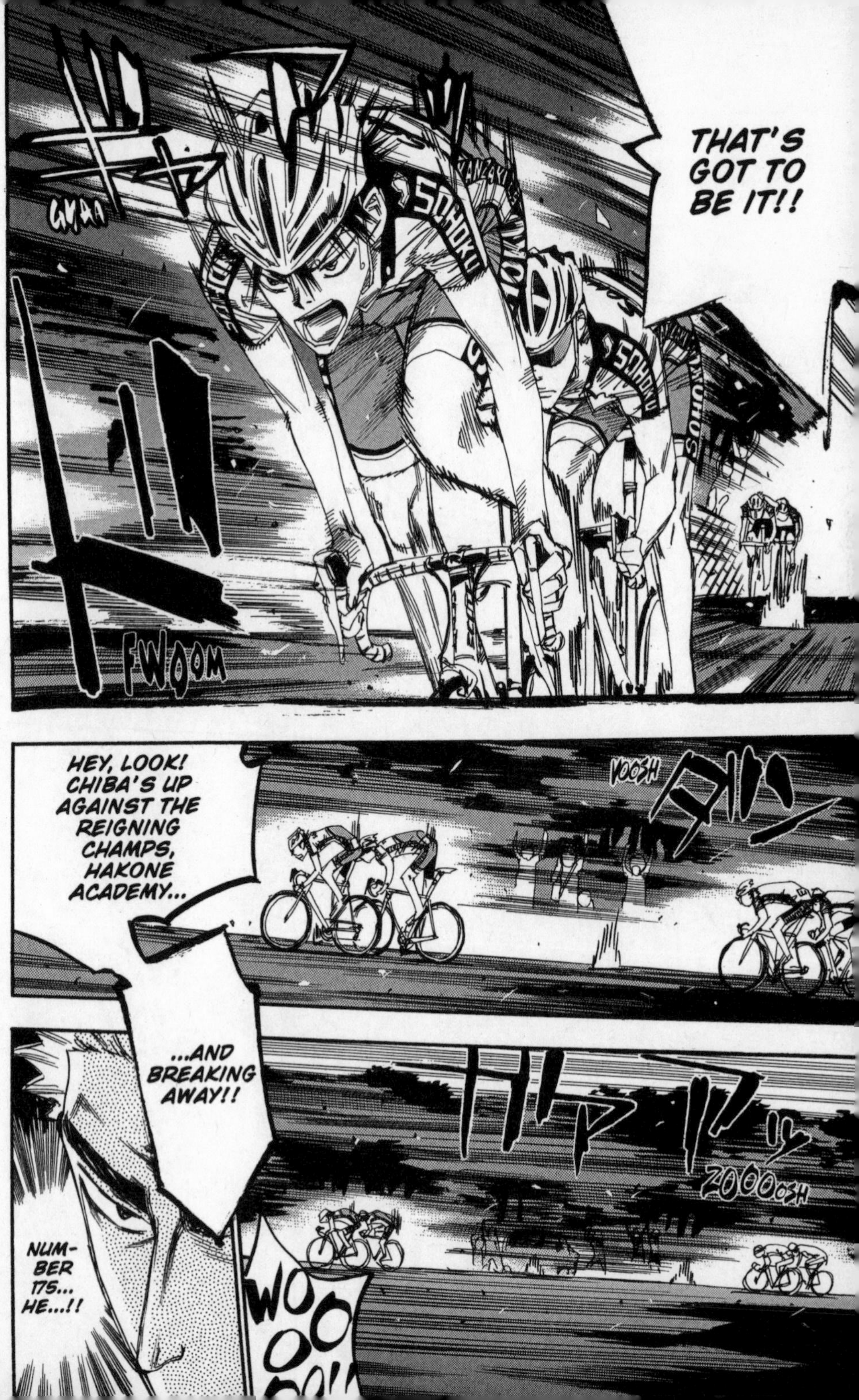
THAT'S GOT TO BE IT!!
GWAA
FWOOM
VOOSH
HEY, LOOK! CHIBA'S UP AGAINST THE REIGNING CHAMPS, HAKONE ACADEMY...
ZOOOOOSH
...AND BREAKING AWAY!!
NUMBER 175... HE...!!
WOOOO

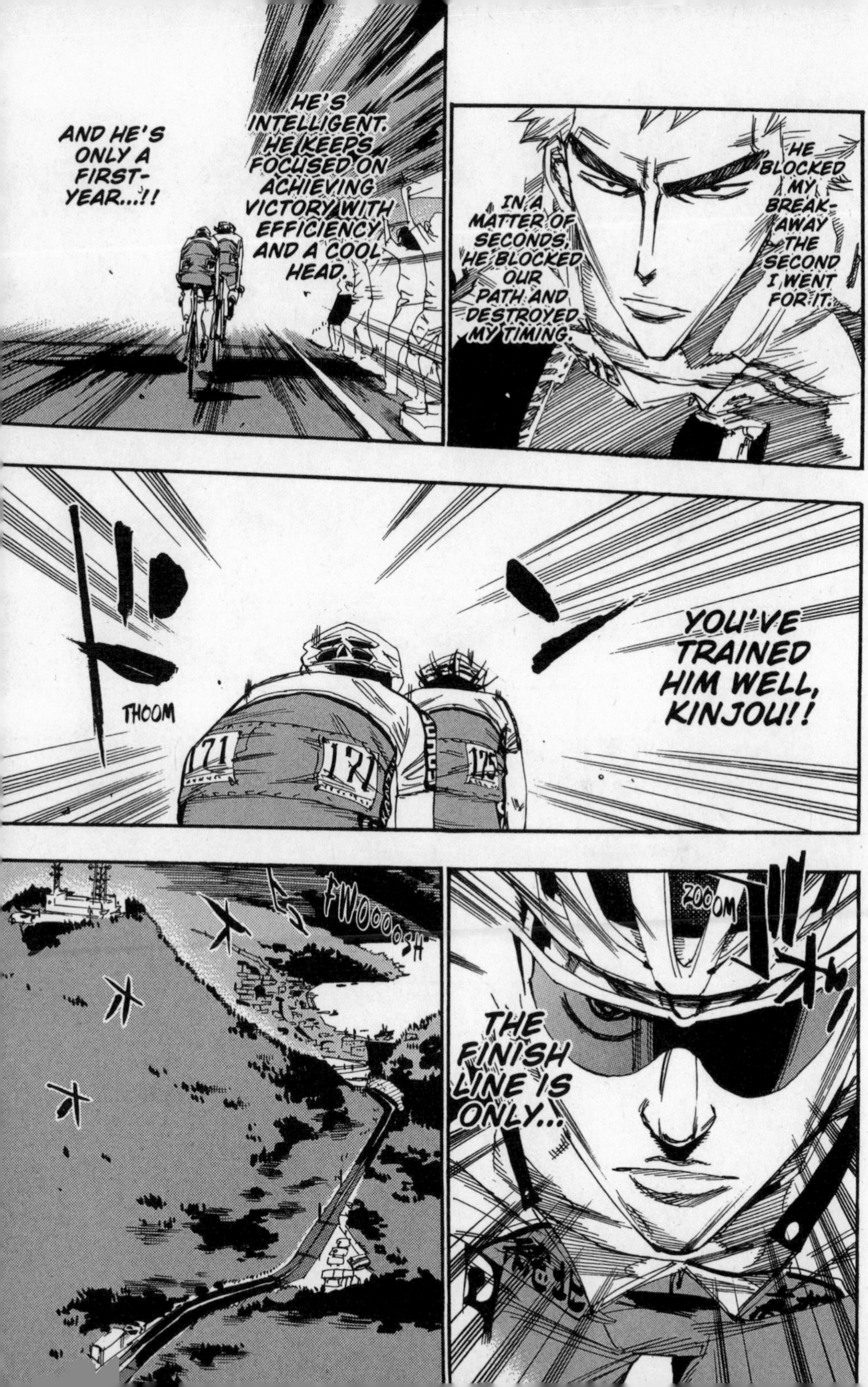
HE BLOCKED MY BREAK-AWAY THE SECOND I WENT FOR IT.
IN A MATTER OF SECONDS, HE BLOCKED OUR PATH AND DESTROYED MY TIMING.
HE'S INTELLIGENT. HE KEEPS FOCUSED ON ACHIEVING VICTORY WITH EFFICIENCY AND A COOL HEAD.
AND HE'S ONLY A FIRST-YEAR...!!
YOU'VE TRAINED HIM WELL, KINJOU!!
THOOM
171
171
175
ZOOOM
THE FINISH LINE IS ONLY...
FWOOOOOSH

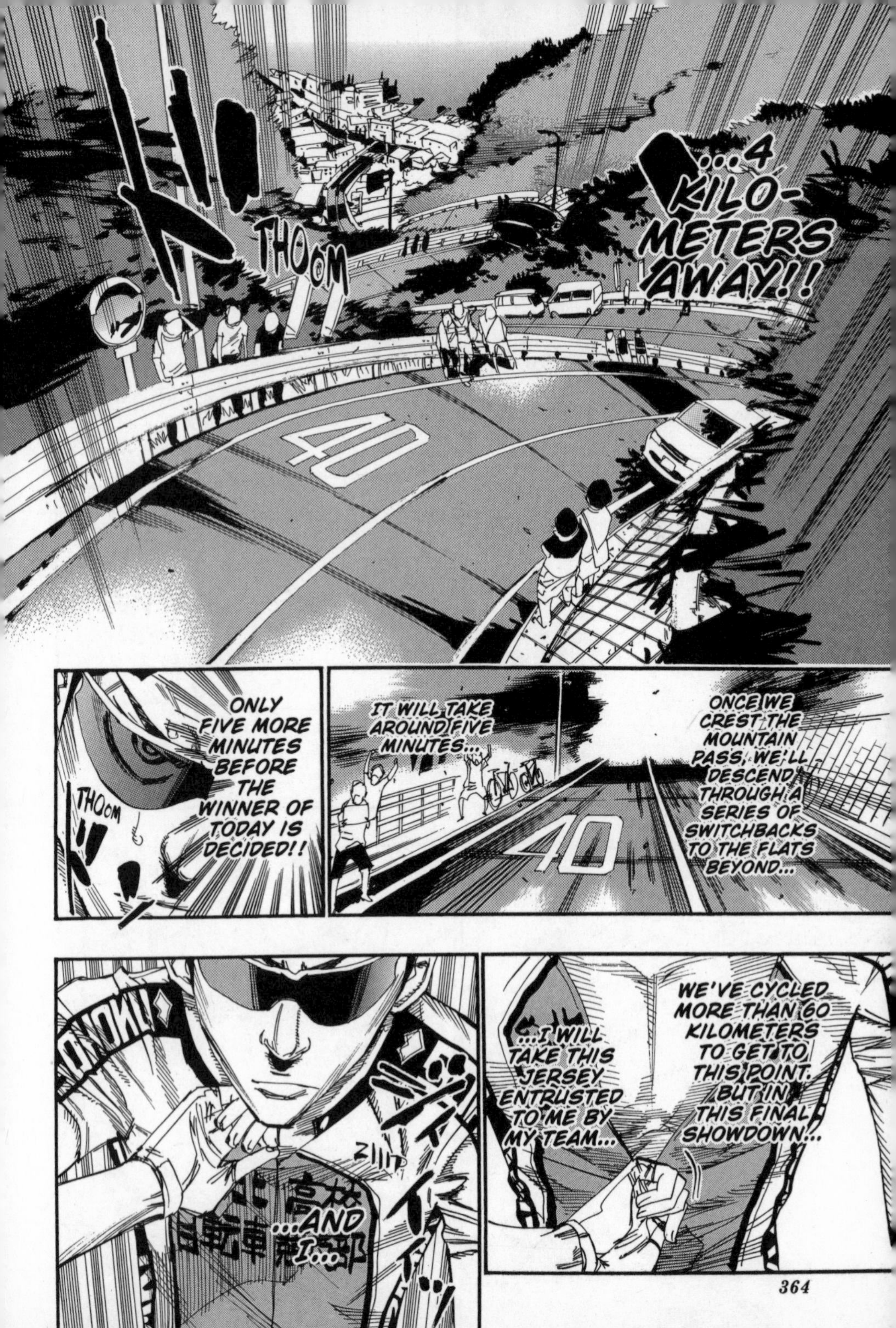
...4 KILO-METERS AWAY!!
THOOM
ONCE WE CREST THE MOUNTAIN PASS, WE'LL DESCEND THROUGH A SERIES OF SWITCHBACKS TO THE FLATS BEYOND...
IT WILL TAKE AROUND FIVE MINUTES...
ONLY FIVE MORE MINUTES BEFORE THE WINNER OF TODAY IS DECIDED!!
THOOM
WE'VE CYCLED MORE THAN 60 KILOMETERS TO GET TO THIS POINT. BUT IN THIS FINAL SHOWDOWN...
...I WILL TAKE THIS JERSEY ENTRUSTED TO ME BY MY TEAM...
ZIIIP
...AND I...

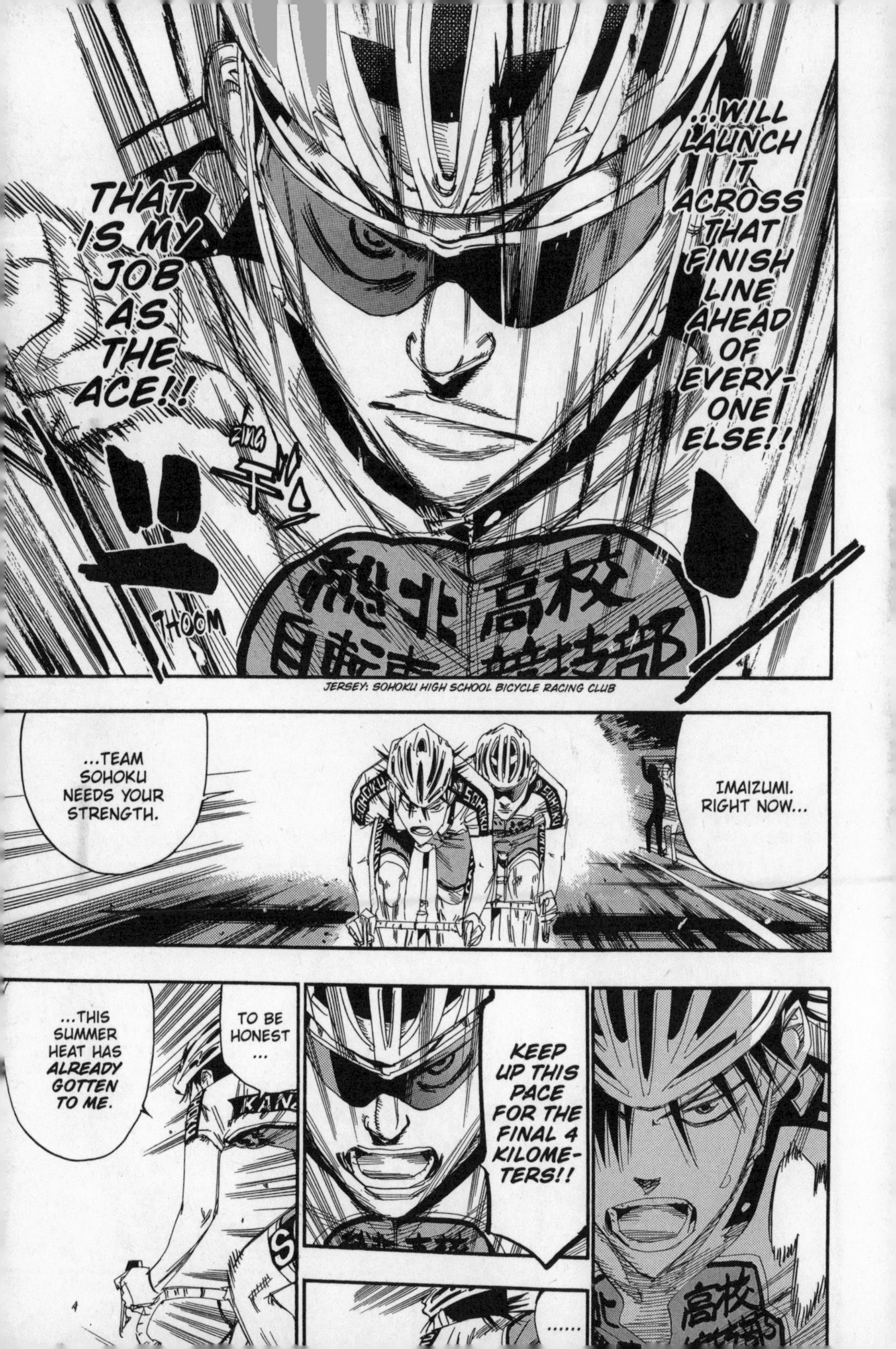
...WILL LAUNCH IT ACROSS THAT FINISH LINE AHEAD OF EVERY-ONE ELSE!!
THAT IS MY JOB AS THE ACE!!
ZING
THOOM
JERSEY: SOHOKU HIGH SCHOOL BICYCLE RACING CLUB
IMAIZUMI. RIGHT NOW...
...TEAM SOHOKU NEEDS YOUR STRENGTH.
KEEP UP THIS PACE FOR THE FINAL 4 KILOME-TERS!!
......
TO BE HONEST ...
...THIS SUMMER HEAT HAS ALREADY GOTTEN TO ME.

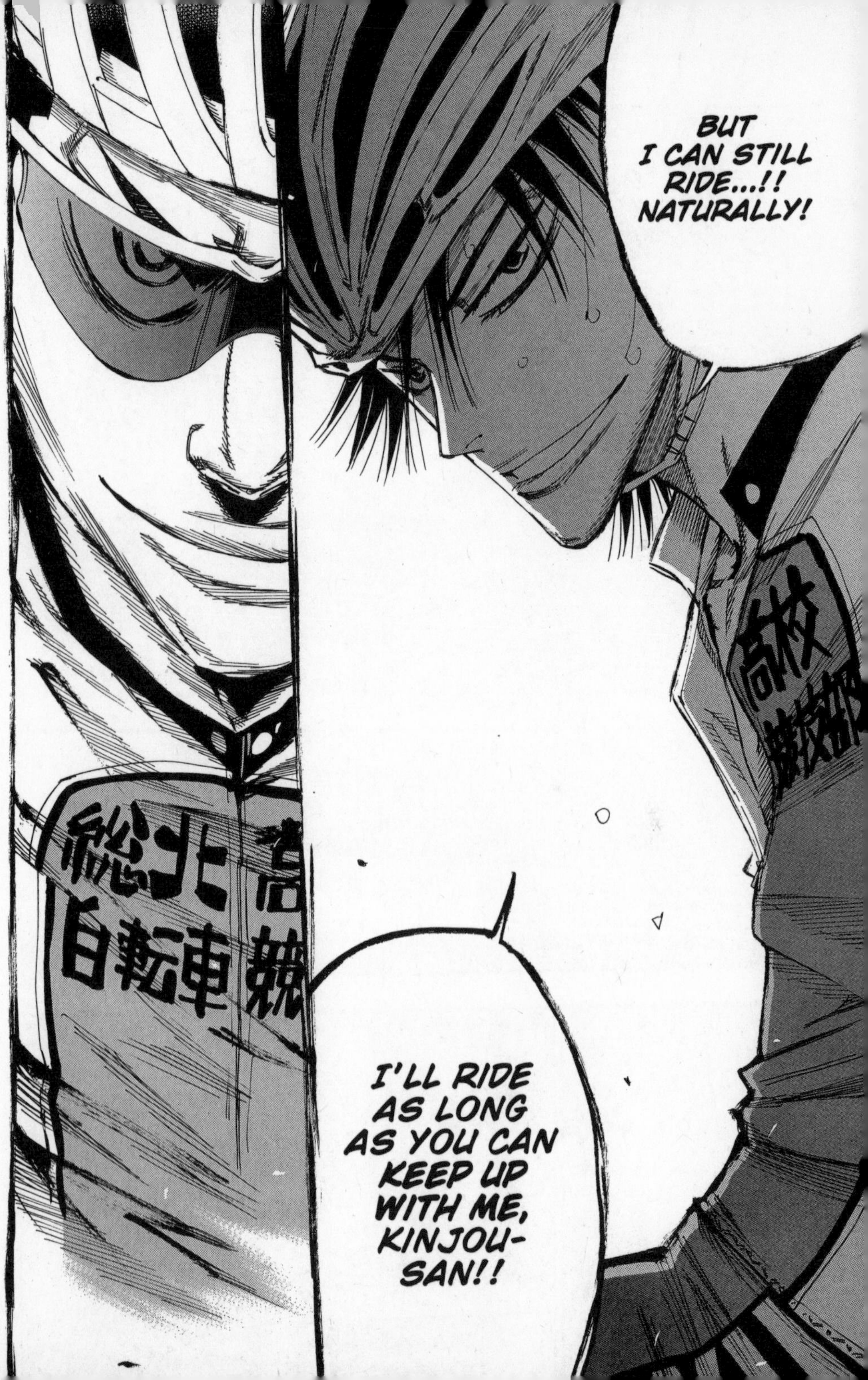
BUT I CAN STILL RIDE...!! NATURALLY!
I'LL RIDE AS LONG AS YOU CAN KEEP UP WITH ME, KINJOU-SAN!!

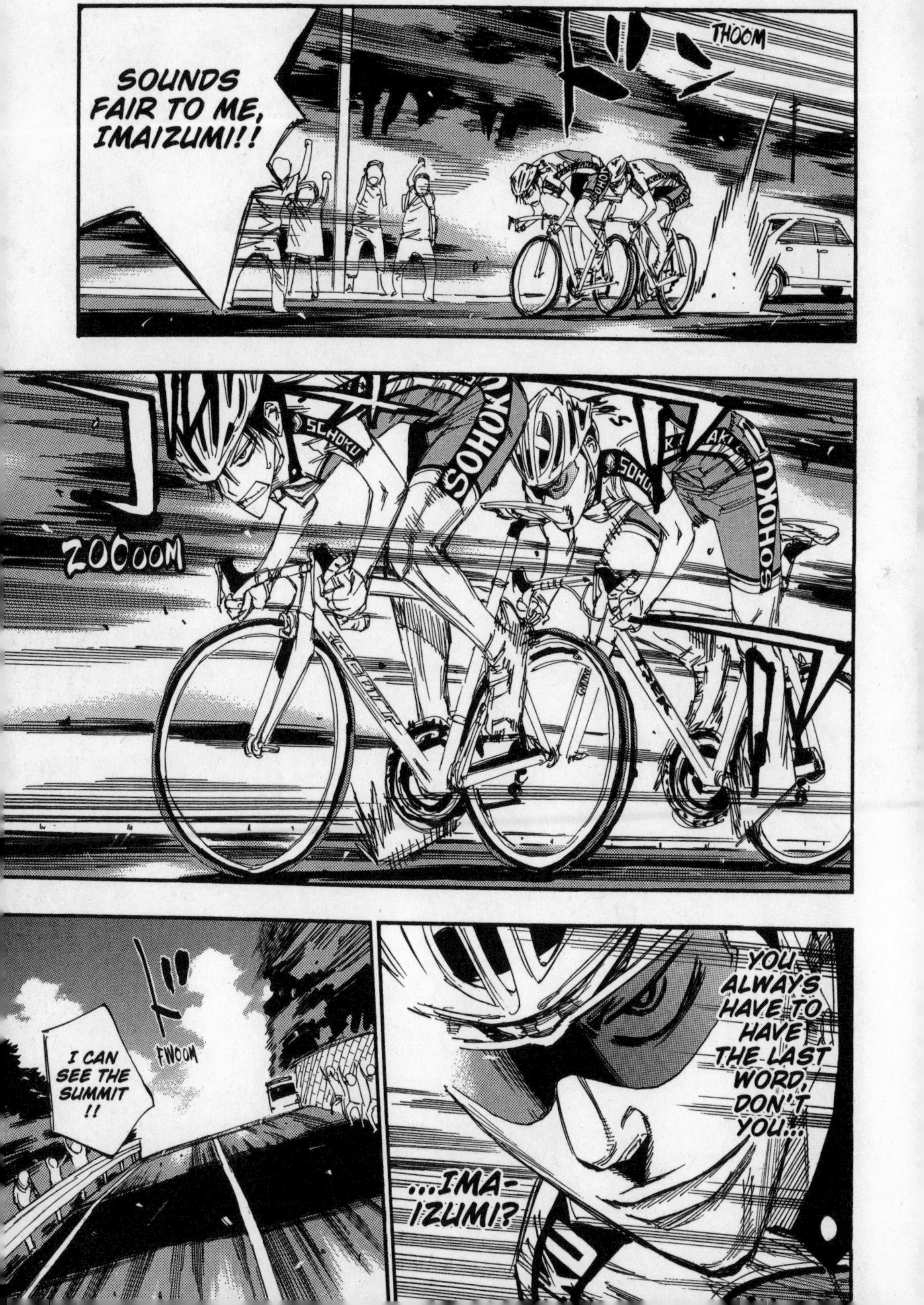
THOOM
SOUNDS FAIR TO ME, IMAIZUMI!!
ZOOOOM
YOU ALWAYS HAVE TO HAVE THE LAST WORD, DON'T YOU...
...IMA-IZUMI?
FWOOM
I CAN SEE THE SUMMIT!!

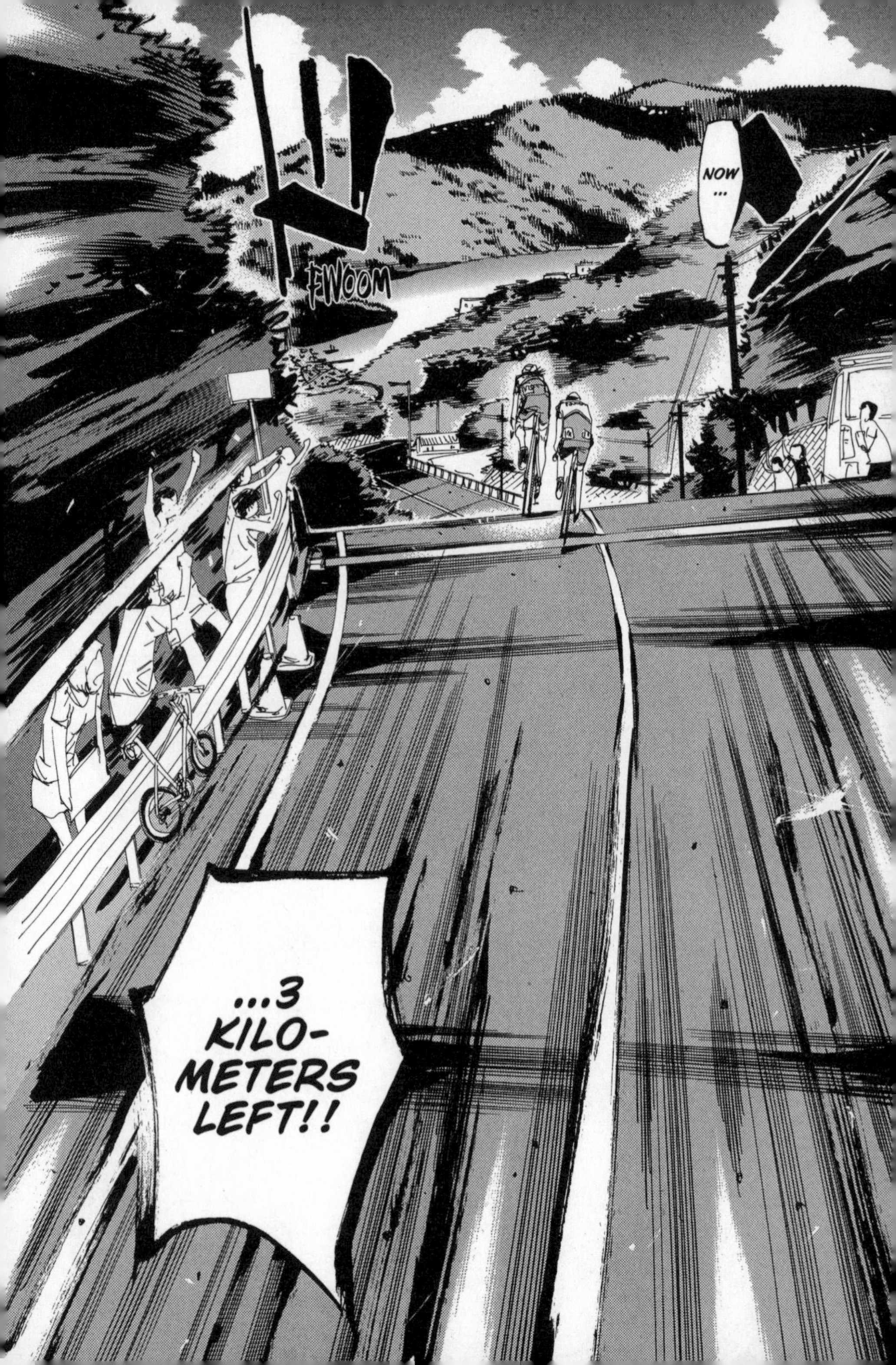
NOW ...
FWOOM
...3 KILO-METERS LEFT!!

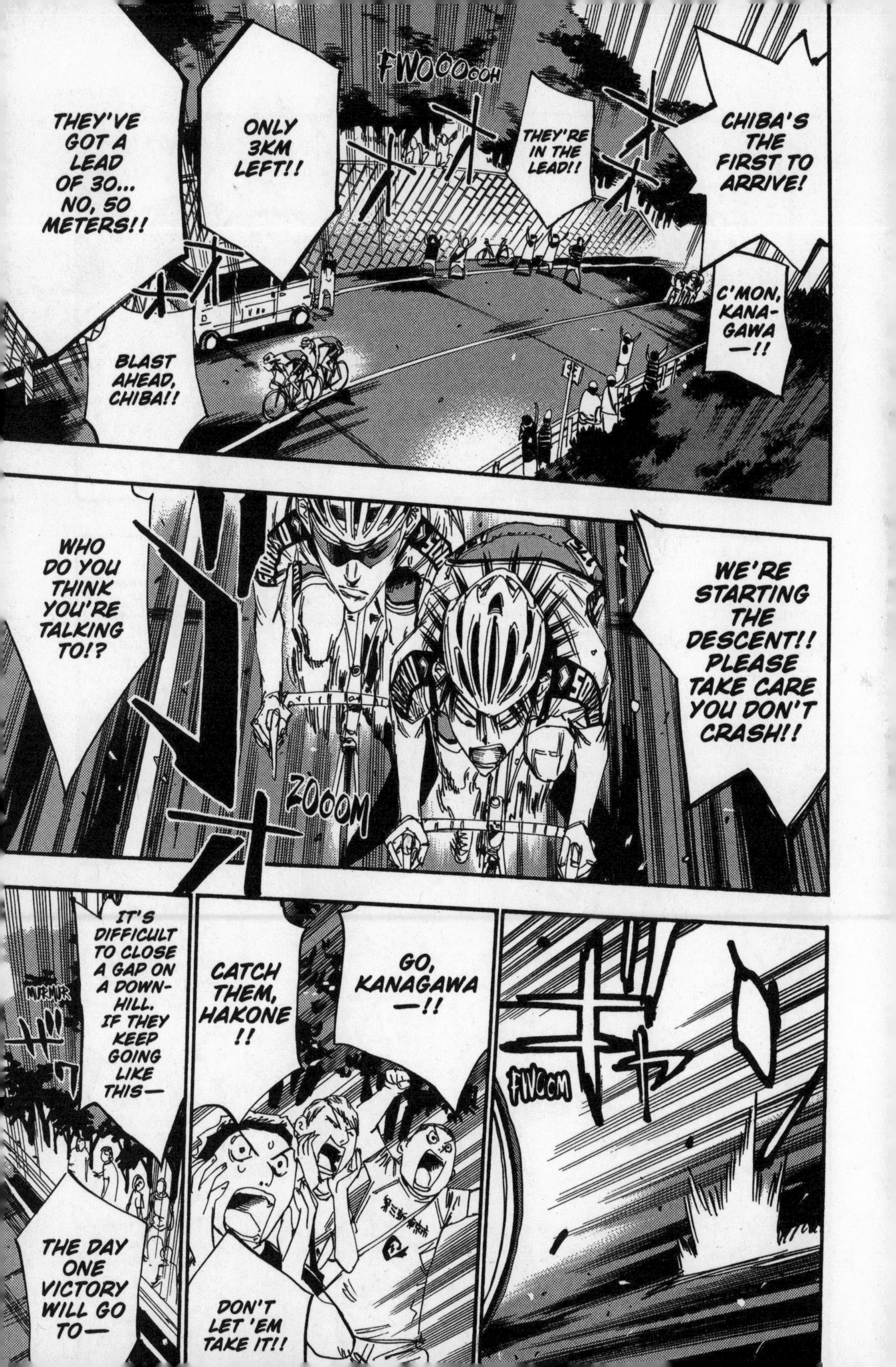
FWOOOoOH
CHIBA'S THE FIRST TO ARRIVE!
THEY'RE IN THE LEAD!!
ONLY 3KM LEFT!!
THEY'VE GOT A LEAD OF 30... NO, 50 METERS!!
C'MON, KANAGAWA—!!
BLAST AHEAD, CHIBA!!
WE'RE STARTING THE DESCENT!! PLEASE TAKE CARE YOU DON'T CRASH!!
ZOOOM
WHO DO YOU THINK YOU'RE TALKING TO!?
FWOOM
GO, KANAGAWA—!!
CATCH THEM, HAKONE!!
DON'T LET 'EM TAKE IT!!
MURMUR
IT'S DIFFICULT TO CLOSE A GAP ON A DOWNHILL. IF THEY KEEP GOING LIKE THIS—
THE DAY ONE VICTORY WILL GO TO—

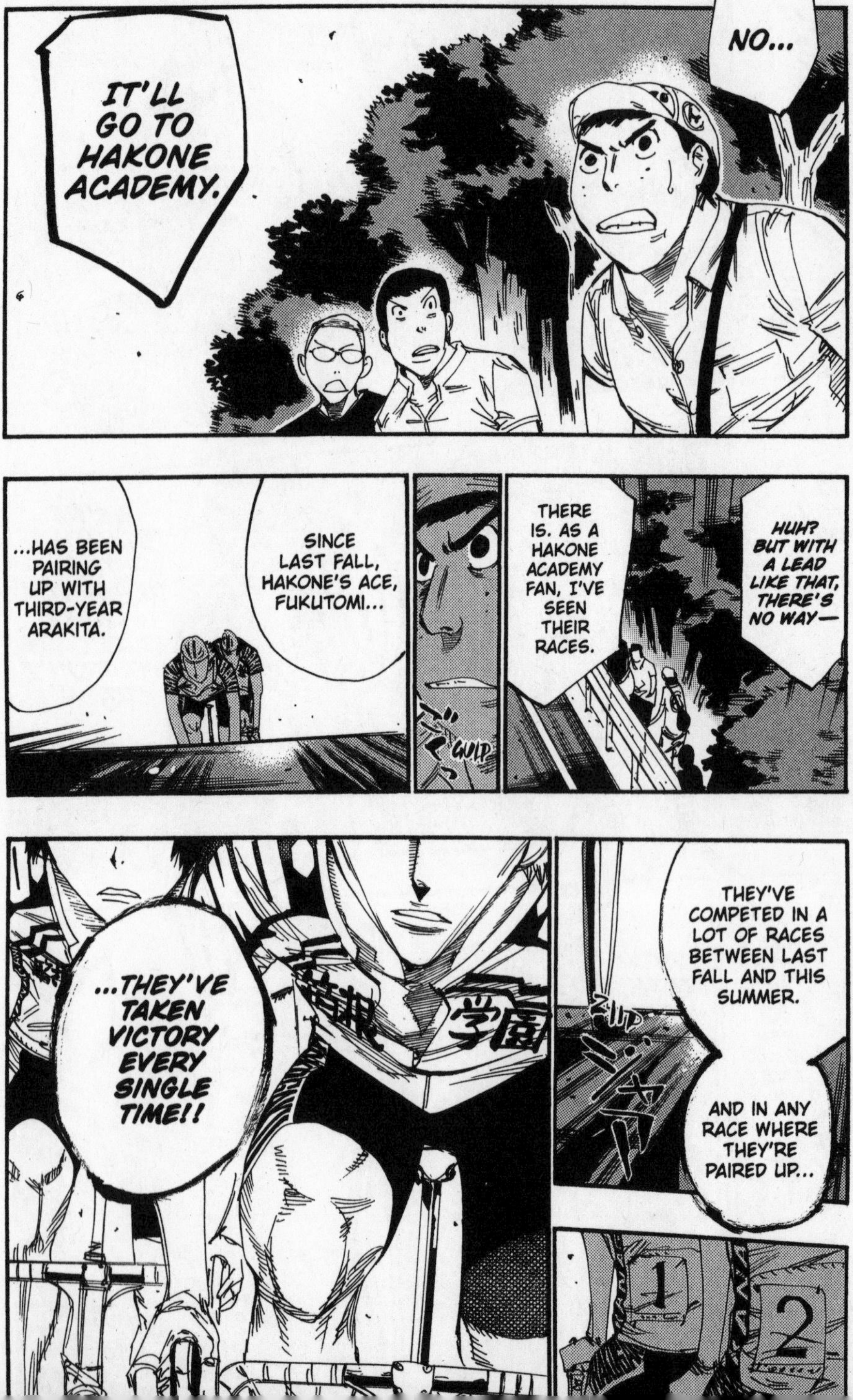
NO...
IT'LL GO TO HAKONE ACADEMY.
HUH? BUT WITH A LEAD LIKE THAT, THERE'S NO WAY—
THERE IS. AS A HAKONE ACADEMY FAN, I'VE SEEN THEIR RACES.
GULP
SINCE LAST FALL, HAKONE'S ACE, FUKUTOMI...
...HAS BEEN PAIRING UP WITH THIRD-YEAR ARAKITA.
THEY'VE COMPETED IN A LOT OF RACES BETWEEN LAST FALL AND THIS SUMMER.
AND IN ANY RACE WHERE THEY'RE PAIRED UP...
...THEY'VE TAKEN VICTORY EVERY SINGLE TIME!!
1
2

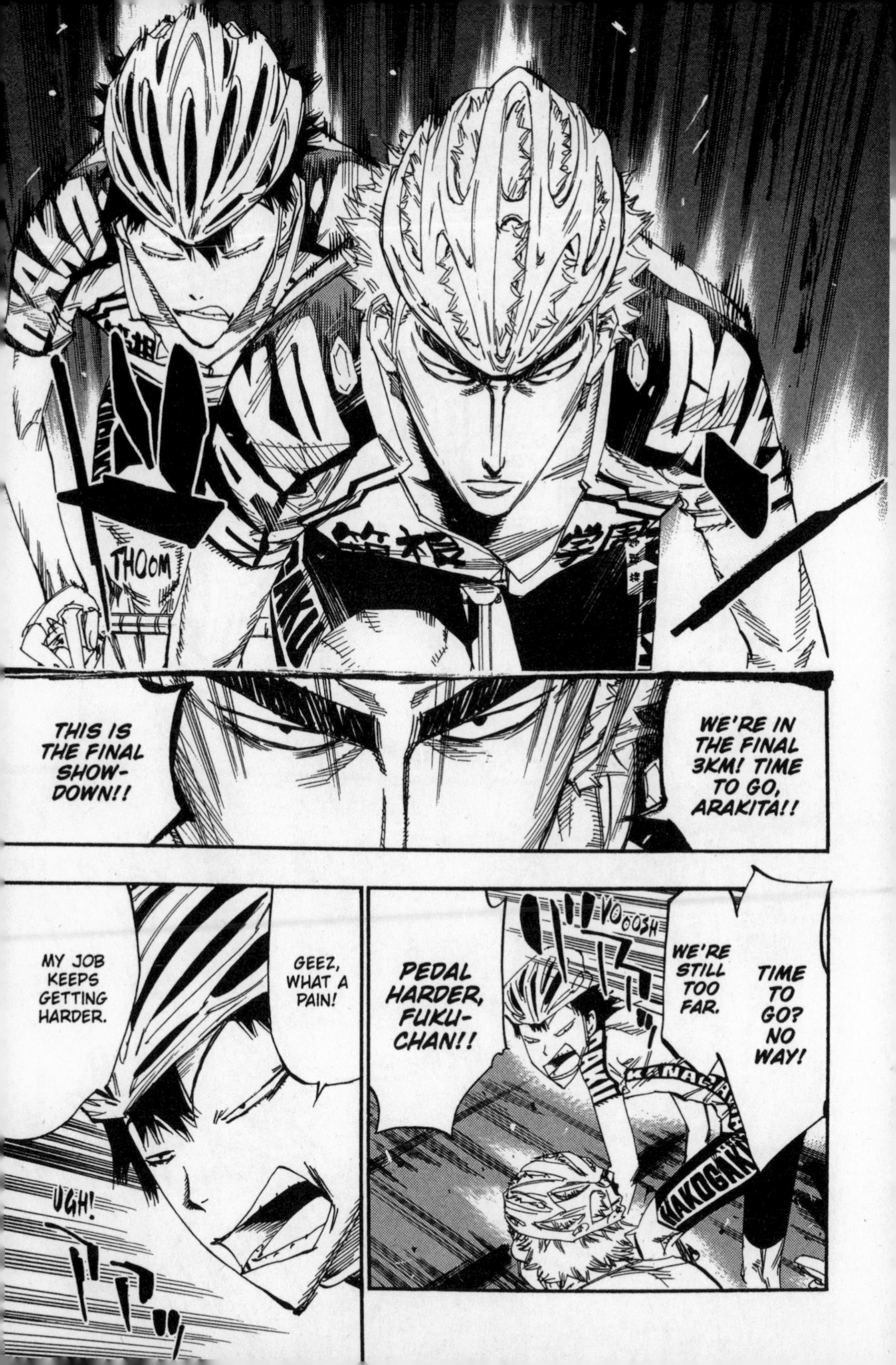
THOOM
WE'RE IN THE FINAL 3KM! TIME TO GO, ARAKITA!!
THIS IS THE FINAL SHOW-DOWN!!
TIME TO GO? NO WAY!
WE'RE STILL TOO FAR.
VOOOSH
PEDAL HARDER, FUKU-CHAN!!
GEEZ, WHAT A PAIN!
MY JOB KEEPS GETTING HARDER.
UGH!

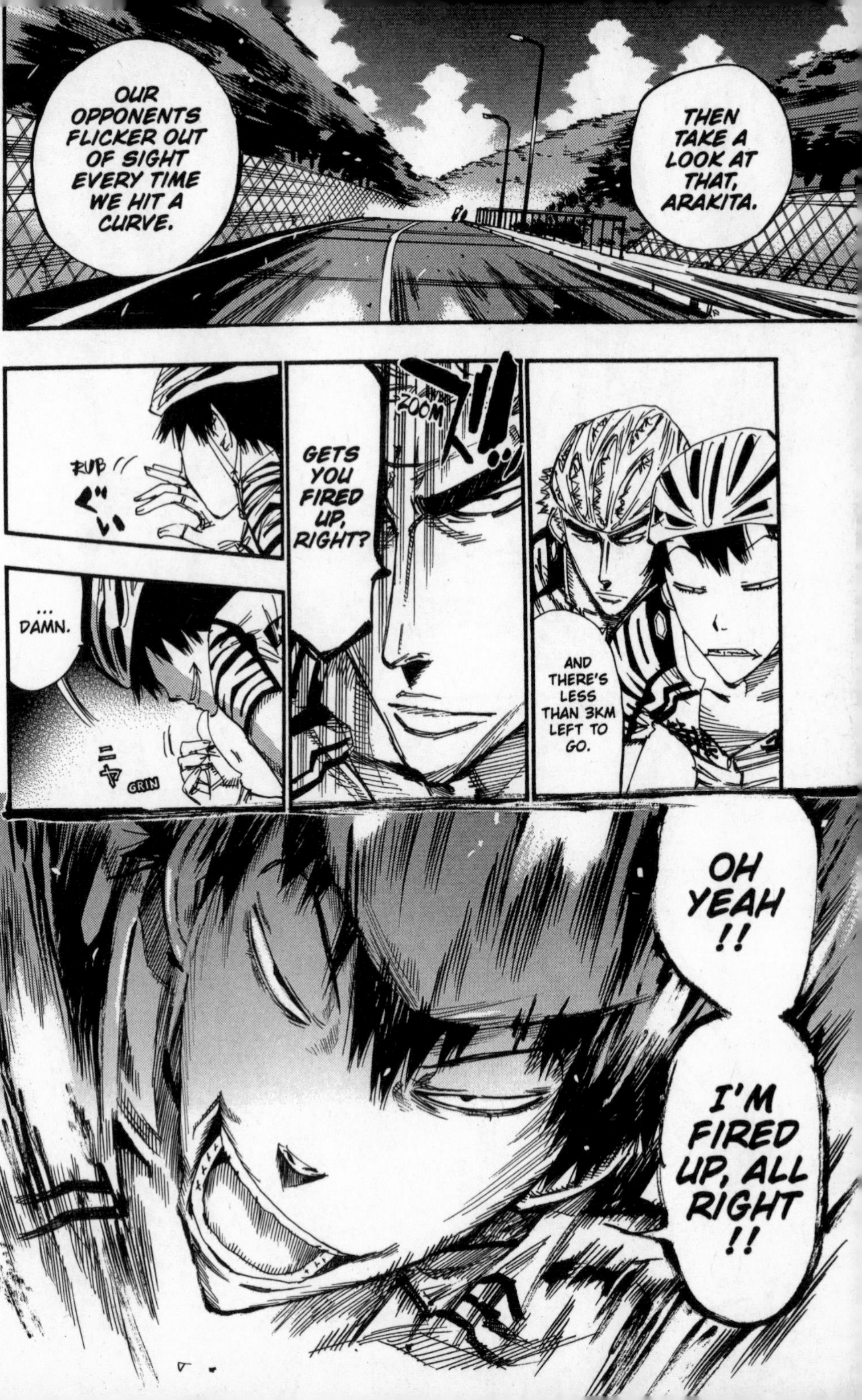
OUR OPPONENTS FLICKER OUT OF SIGHT EVERY TIME WE HIT A CURVE.
THEN TAKE A LOOK AT THAT, ARAKITA.
AND THERE'S LESS THAN 3KM LEFT TO GO.
ZOOM
GETS YOU FIRED UP, RIGHT?
RUB
ぐい
...DAMN.
ニヤ
GRIN
OH YEAH!!
I'M FIRED UP, ALL RIGHT!!

# RIDE.103 ARAKITA

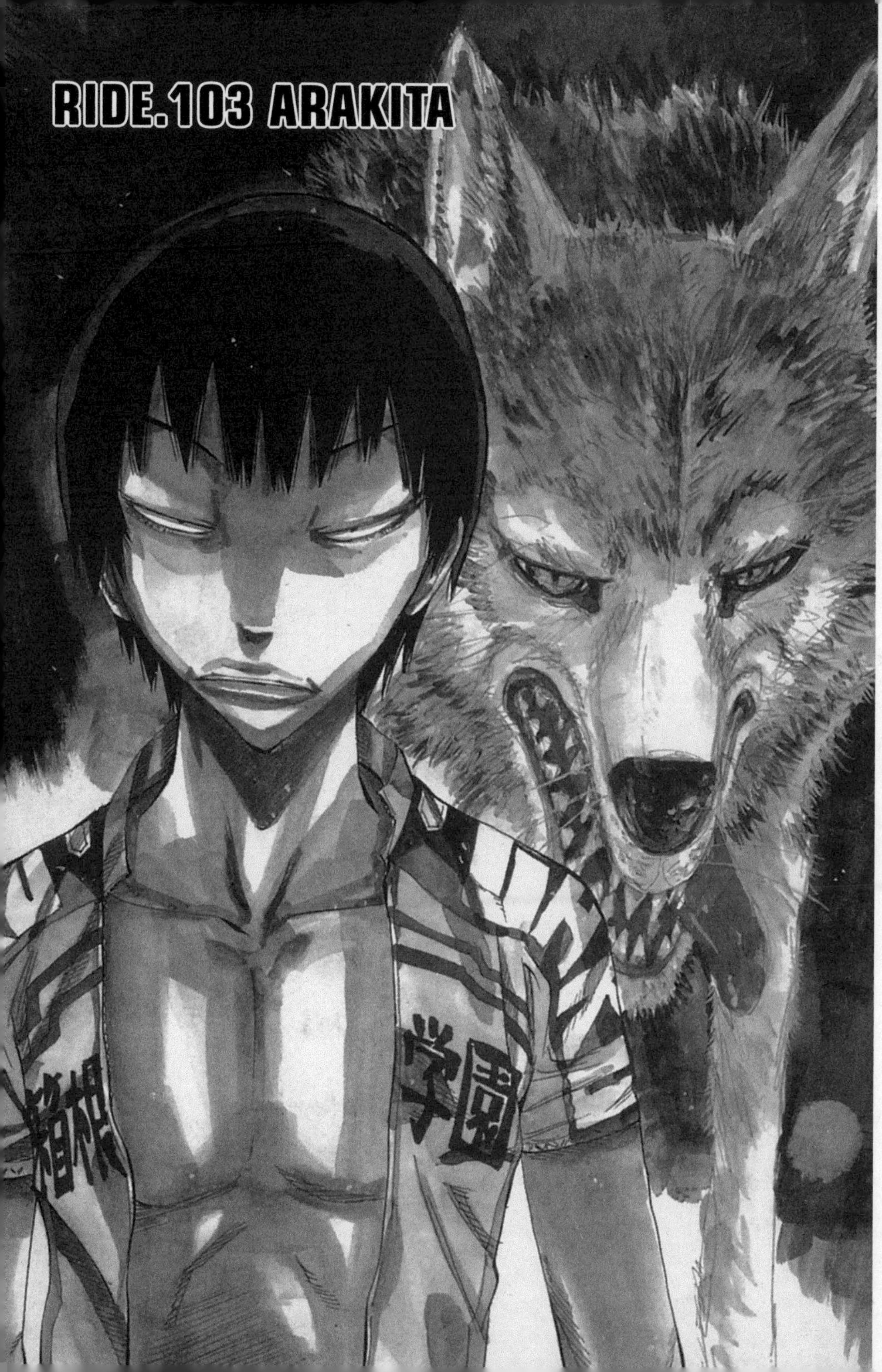
箱根
学園

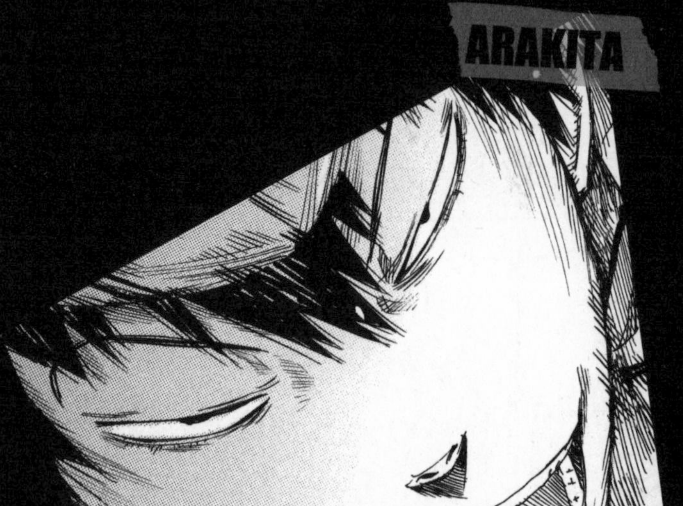
ARAKITA
YOWAMUSHI PEDAL

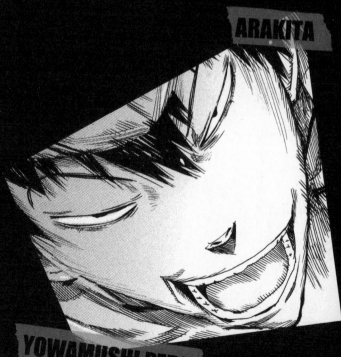

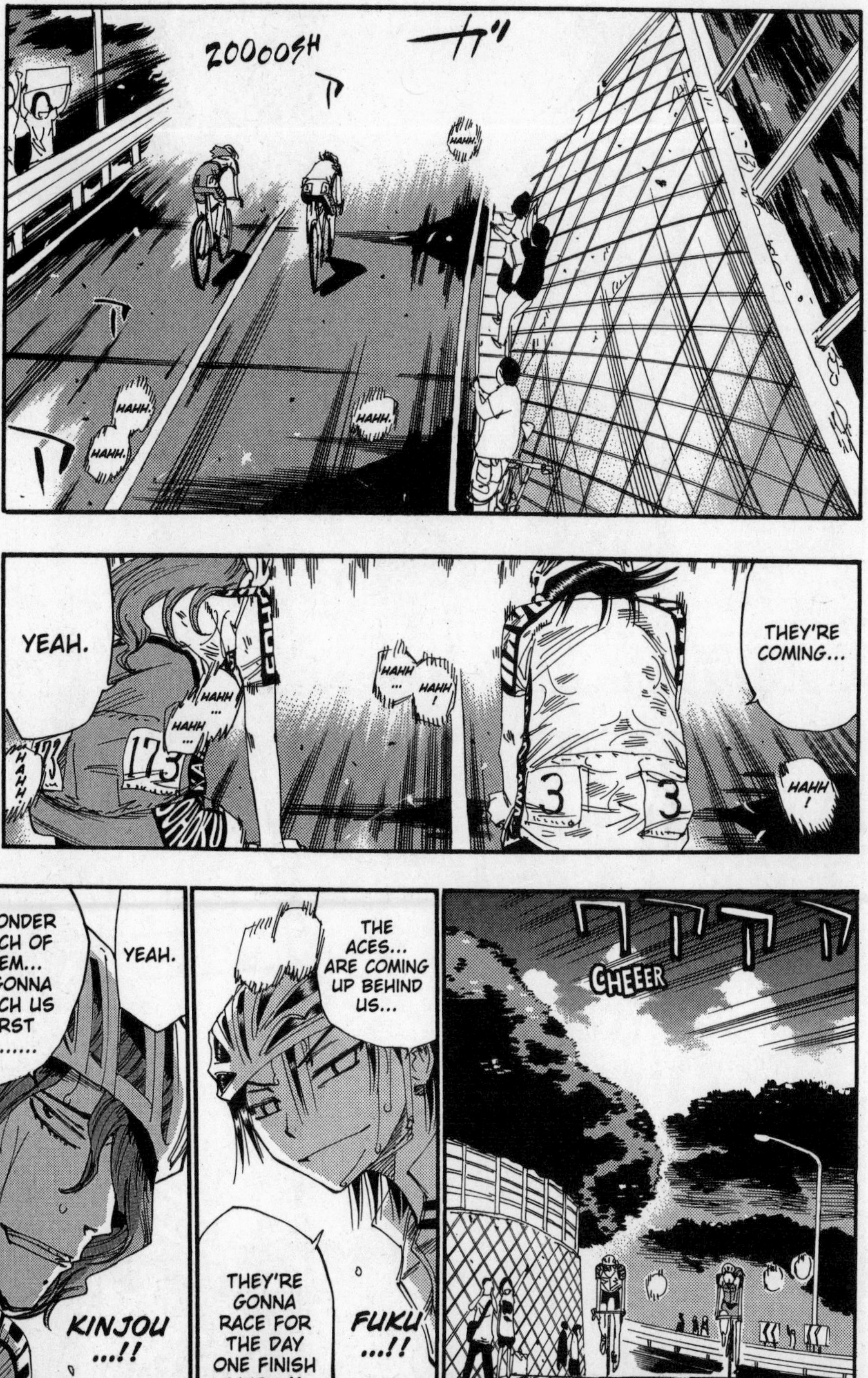
ZOOOOSH
HAHH.
HAHH.
HAHH.
HAHH.
THEY'RE COMING...
HAHH!
HAHH...
HAHH!
HAHH...
HAHH...
HAHH.
YEAH.
CHEEER
THE ACES... ARE COMING UP BEHIND US...
THEY'RE GONNA RACE FOR THE DAY ONE FINISH LINE...!!
FUKU...!!
YEAH.
I WONDER WHICH OF THEM... IS GONNA REACH US FIRST.........
KINJOU...!!

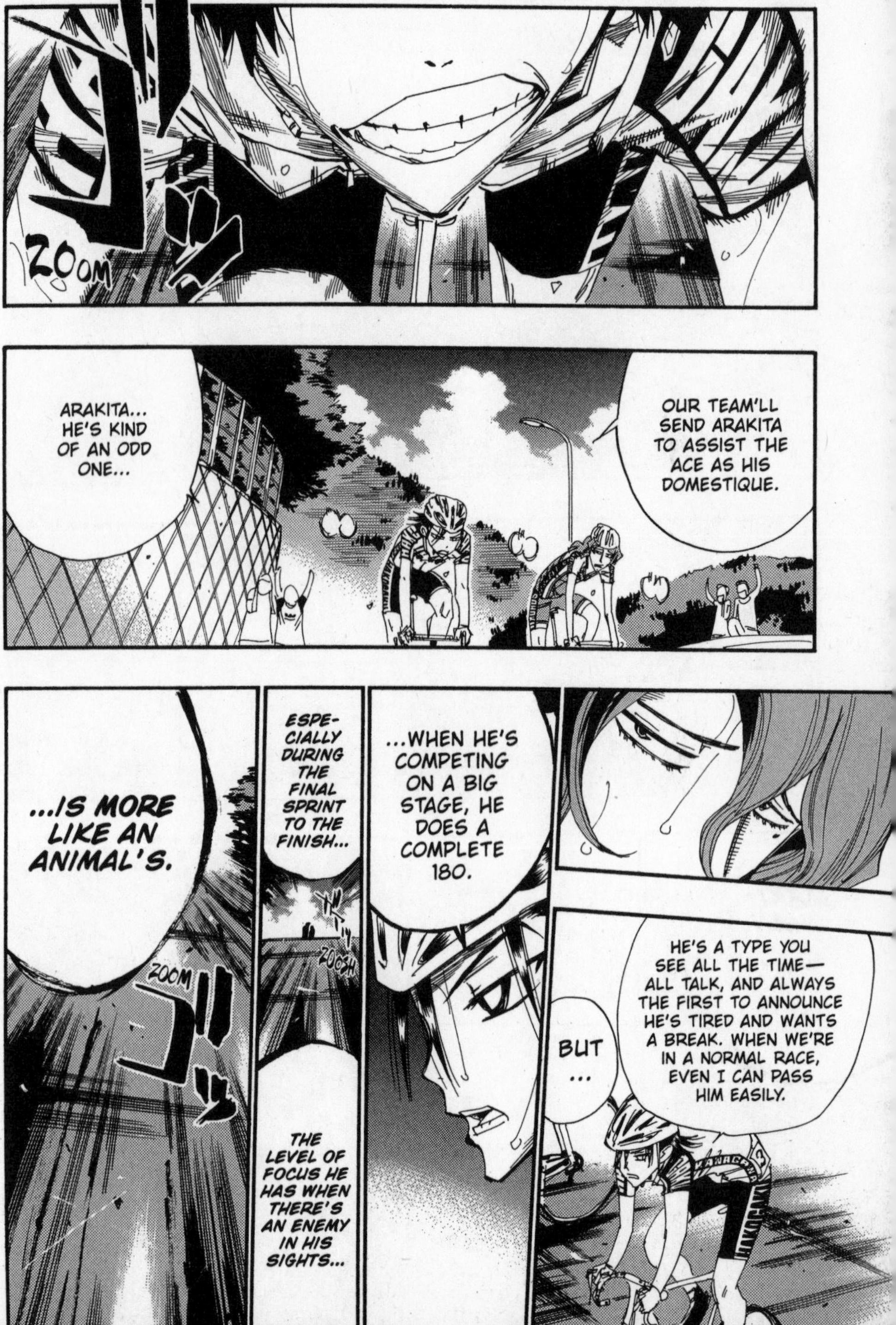

ZOOM
OUR TEAM'LL SEND ARAKITA TO ASSIST THE ACE AS HIS DOMESTIQUE.
ARAKITA... HE'S KIND OF AN ODD ONE...
HE'S A TYPE YOU SEE ALL THE TIME—ALL TALK, AND ALWAYS THE FIRST TO ANNOUNCE HE'S TIRED AND WANTS A BREAK. WHEN WE'RE IN A NORMAL RACE, EVEN I CAN PASS HIM EASILY.
BUT ...
...WHEN HE'S COMPETING ON A BIG STAGE, HE DOES A COMPLETE 180.
ESPE-CIALLY DURING THE FINAL SPRINT TO THE FINISH...
ZOOSH
THE LEVEL OF FOCUS HE HAS WHEN THERE'S AN ENEMY IN HIS SIGHTS...
...IS MORE LIKE AN ANIMAL'S.
ZOOM

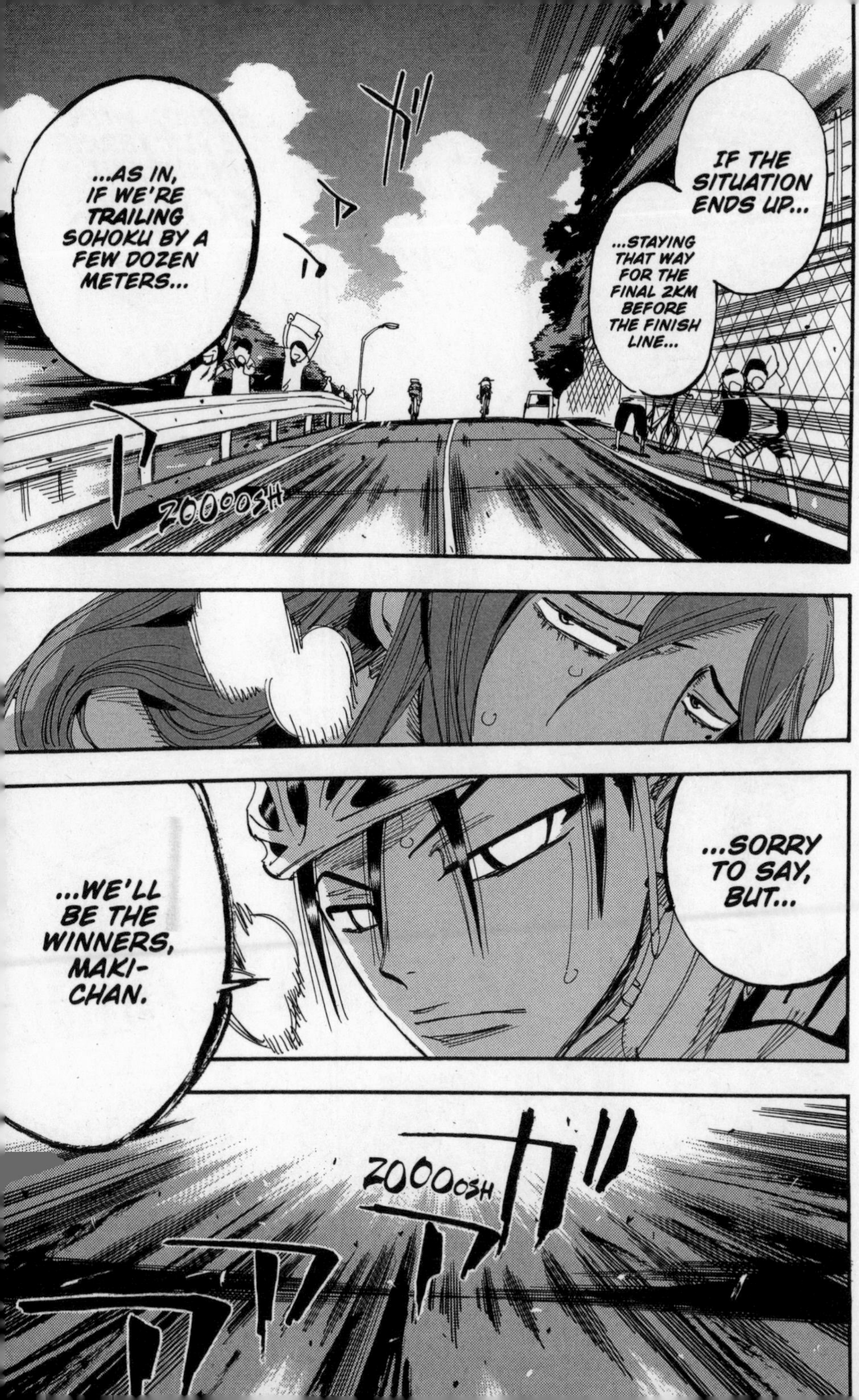
IF THE SITUATION ENDS UP...
...STAYING THAT WAY FOR THE FINAL 2KM BEFORE THE FINISH LINE...
...AS IN, IF WE'RE TRAILING SOHOKU BY A FEW DOZEN METERS...
ZOOOOSH
...SORRY TO SAY, BUT...
...WE'LL BE THE WINNERS, MAKI-CHAN.
ZOOOOSH

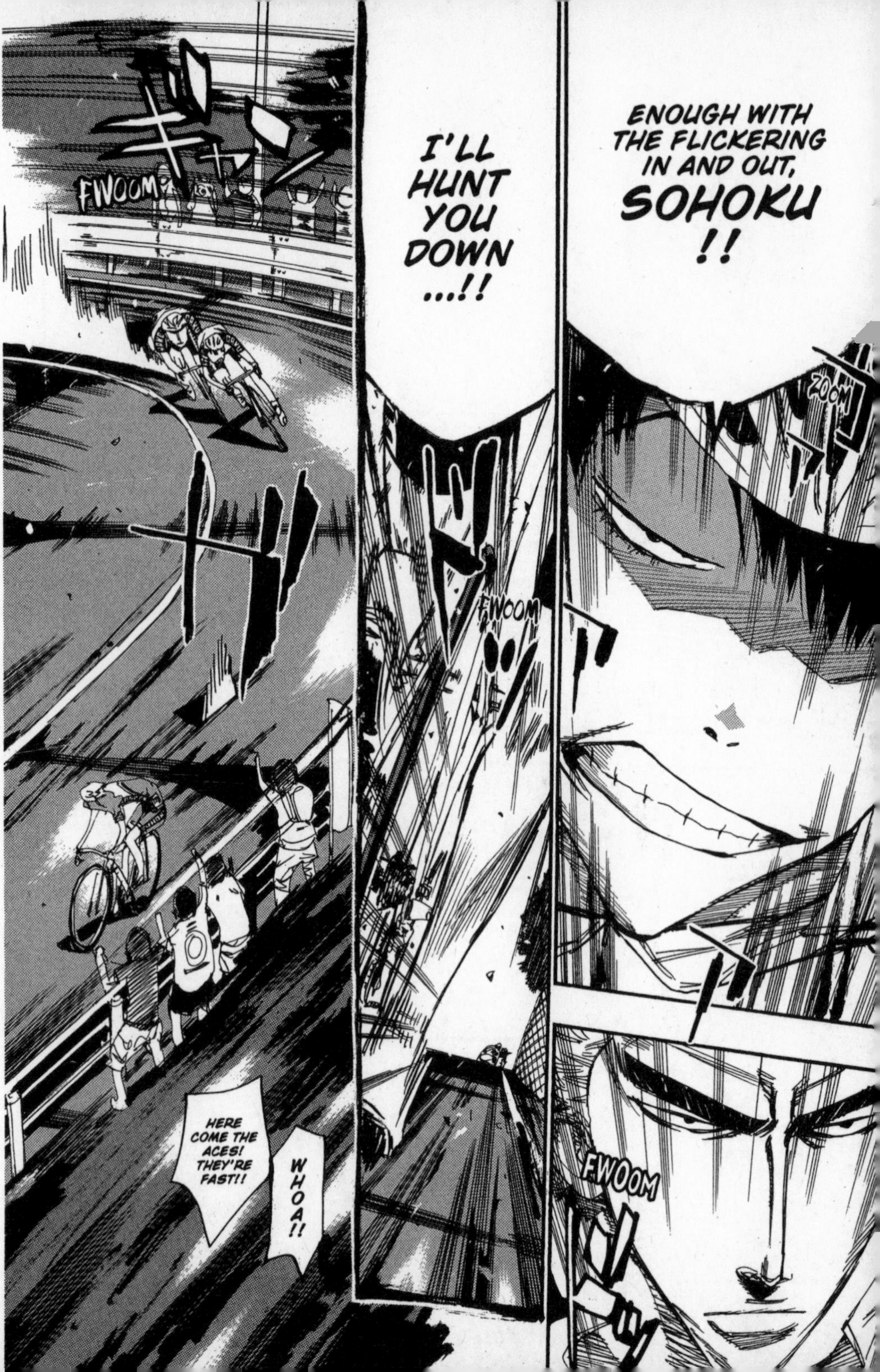

ENOUGH WITH THE FLICKERING IN AND OUT, SOHOKU!!
ZOOM
FWOOM
I'LL HUNT YOU DOWN...!!
FWOOM
FWOOM
WHOA!!
HERE COME THE ACES! THEY'RE FAST!!

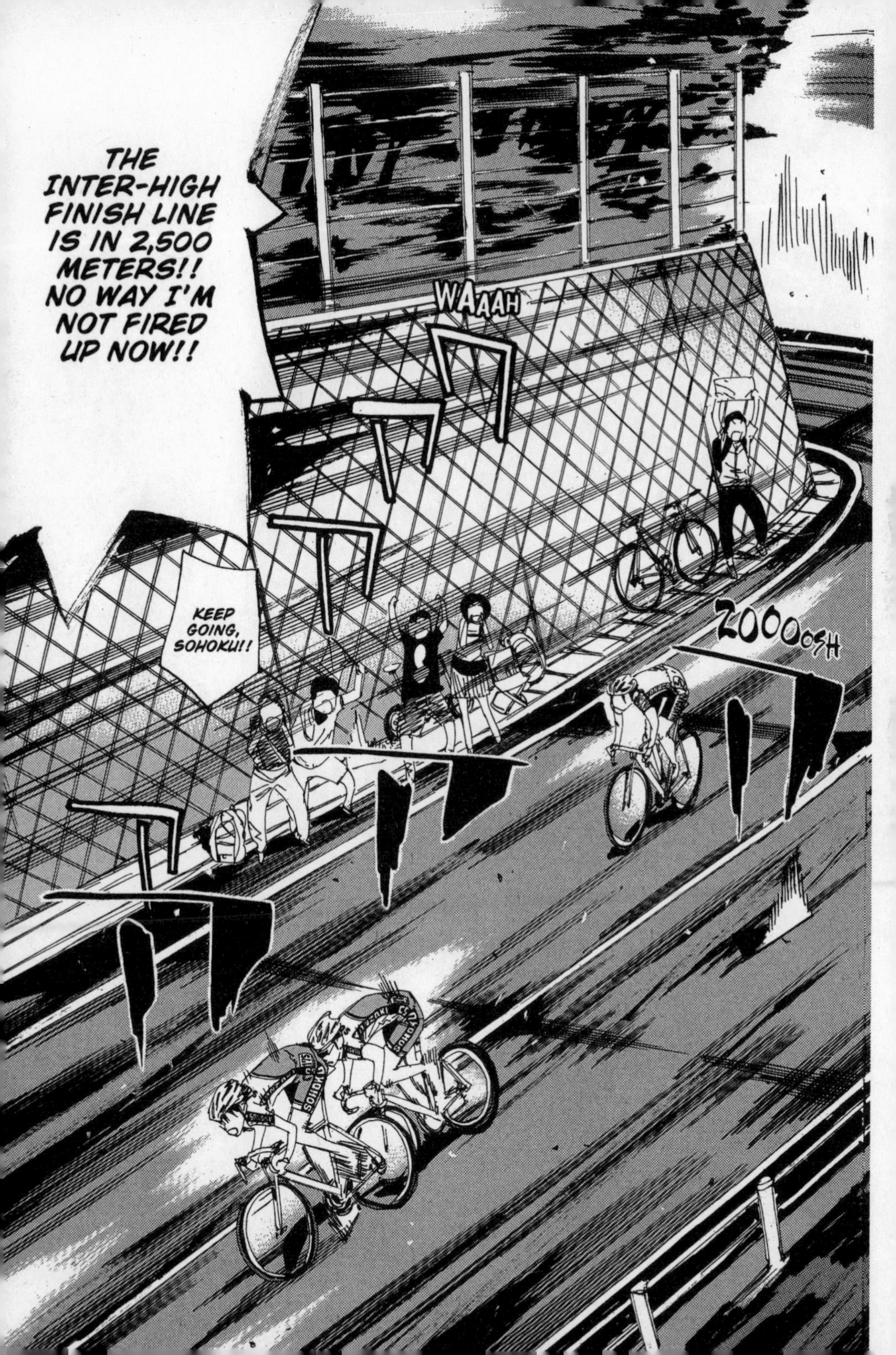
THE INTER-HIGH FINISH LINE IS IN 2,500 METERS!! NO WAY I'M NOT FIRED UP NOW!!
WAAAH
ZOOOOSH
KEEP GOING, SOHOKU!!

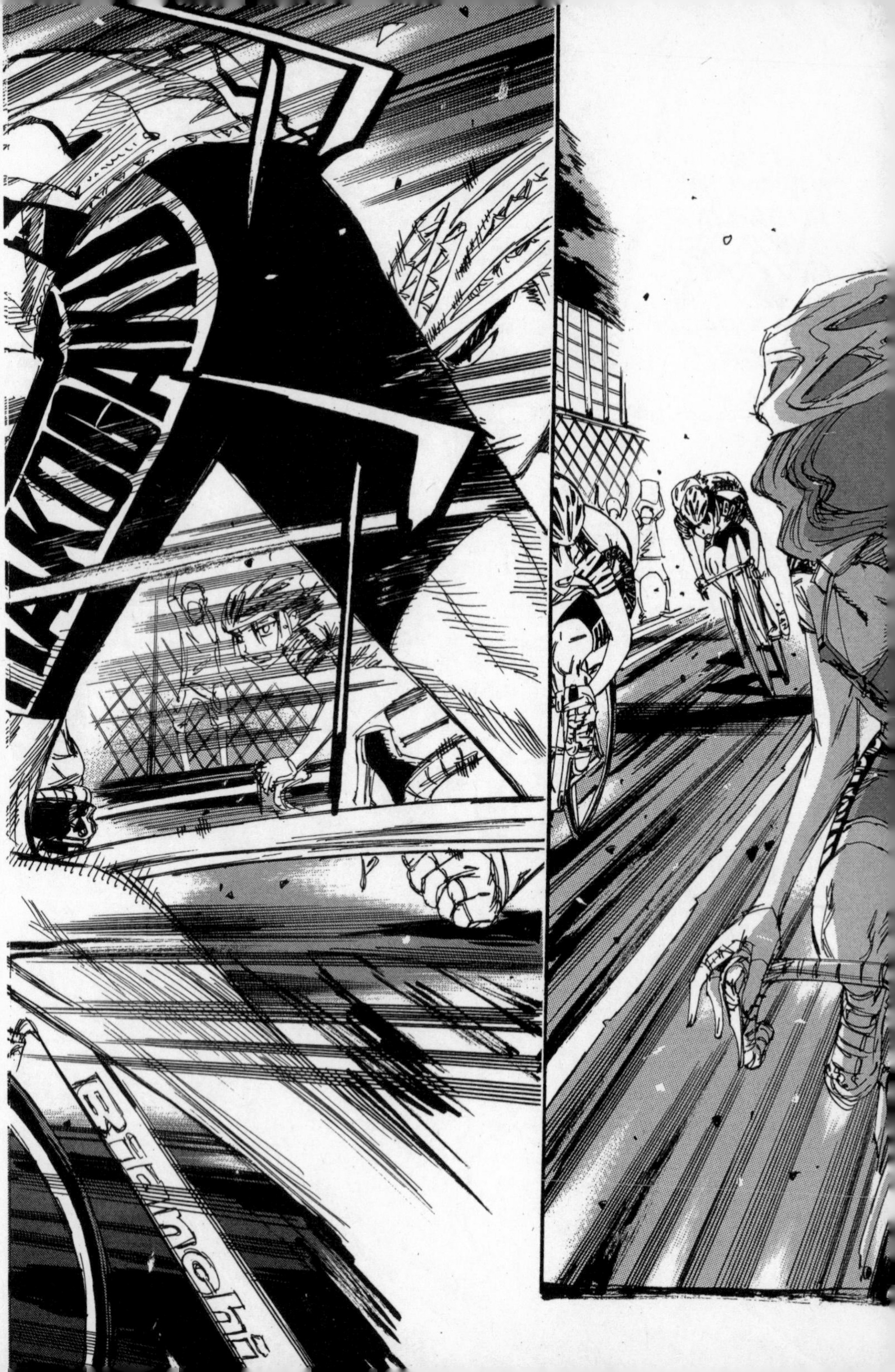
Bianchi

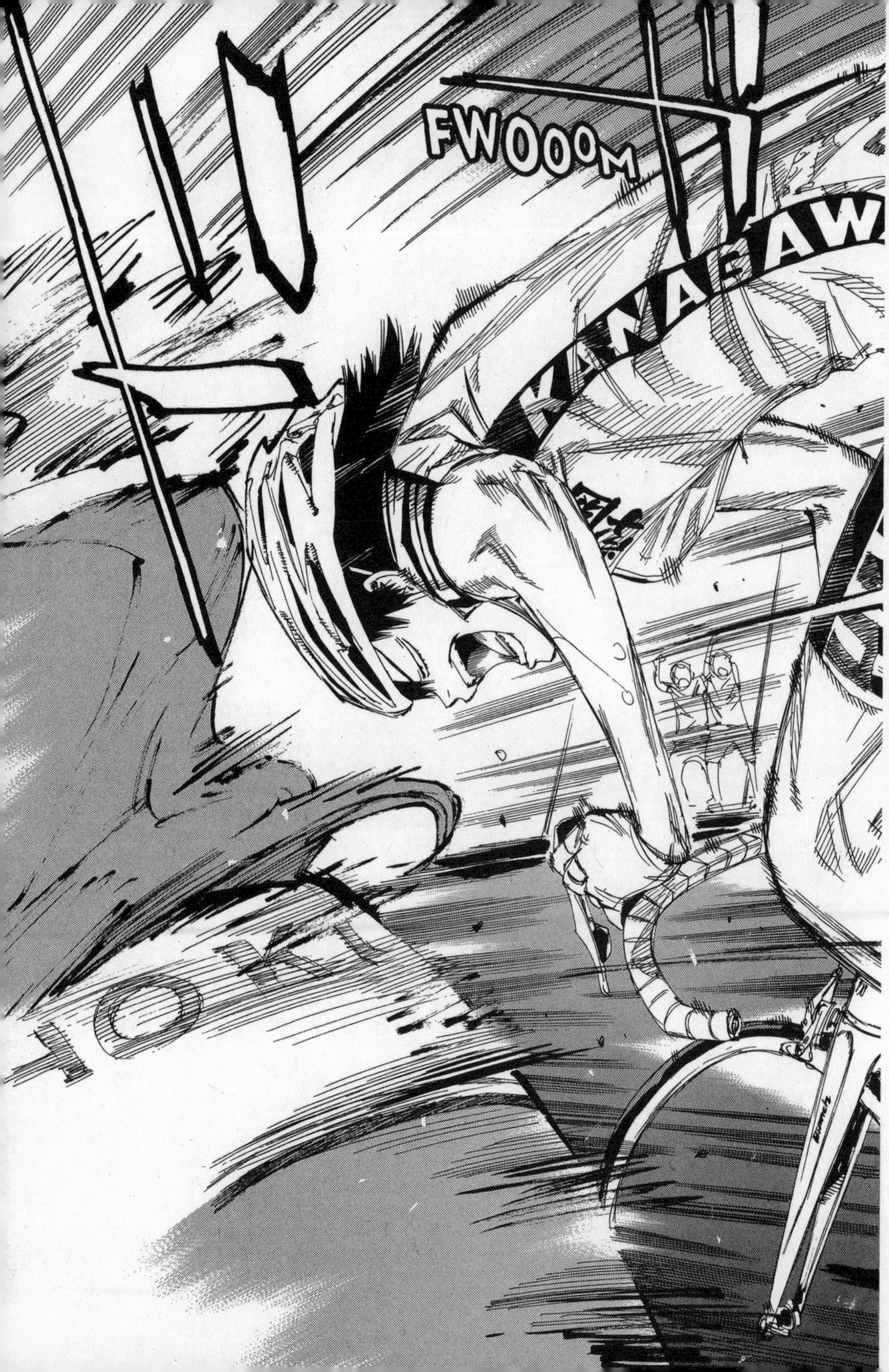
FWOOOM
KANAGAW

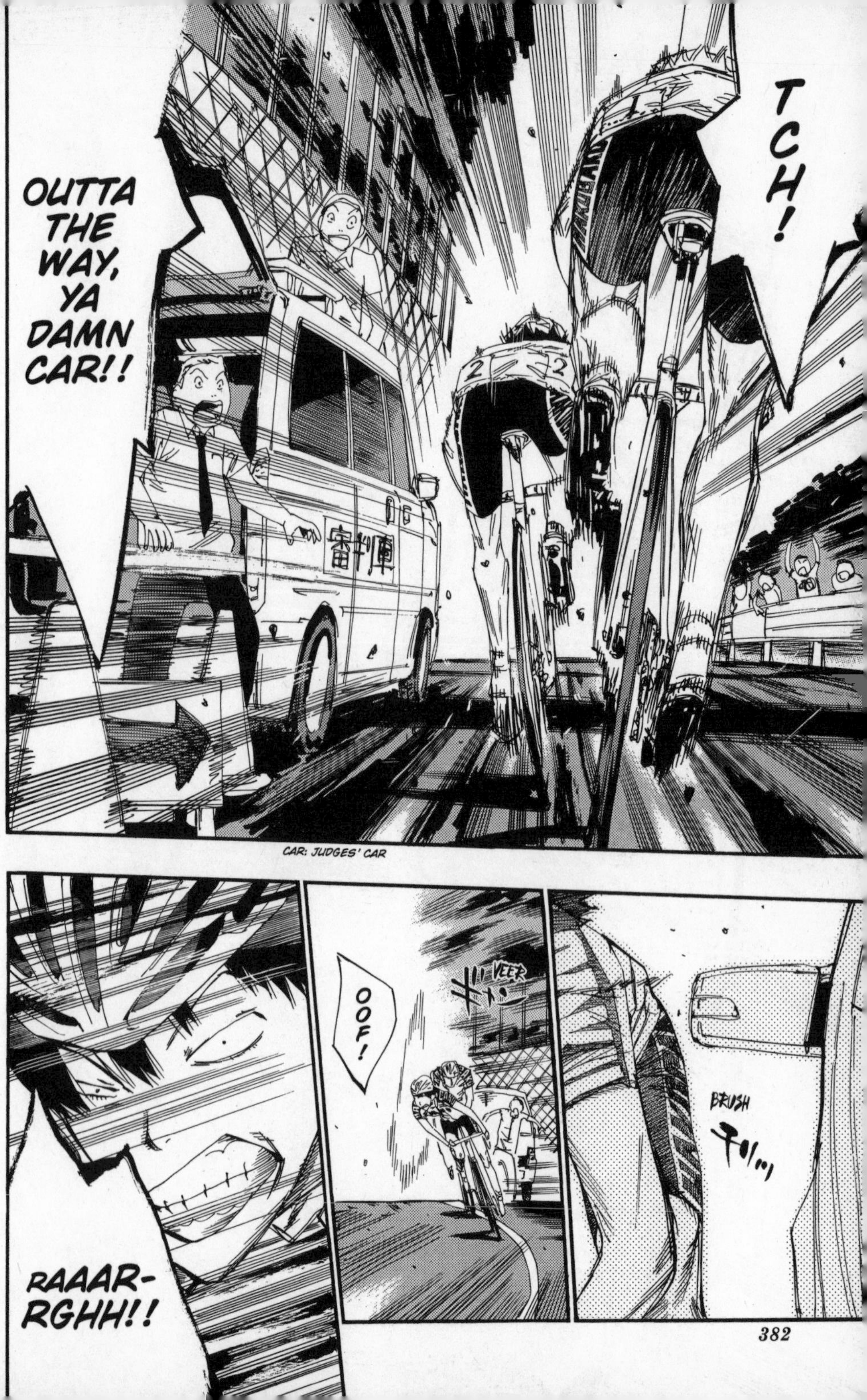
TCH!
OUTTA THE WAY, YA DAMN CAR!!
CAR: JUDGES' CAR
BRUSH
VEER
OOF!
RAAAR-RGHH!!

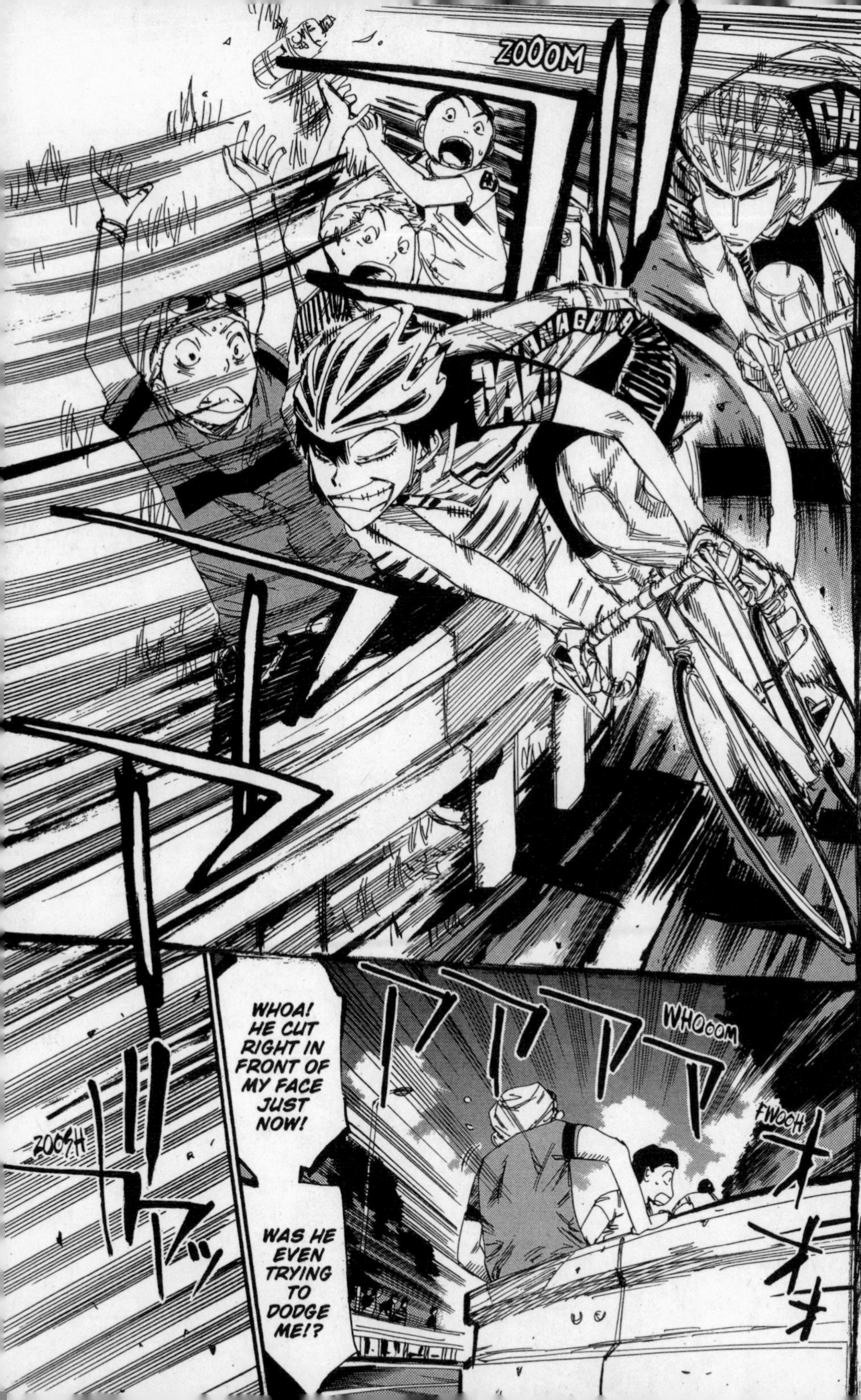
ZOOOM
FWOOH
WHOOOM
WHOA! HE CUT RIGHT IN FRONT OF MY FACE JUST NOW!
WAS HE EVEN TRYING TO DODGE ME!?
ZOOSH

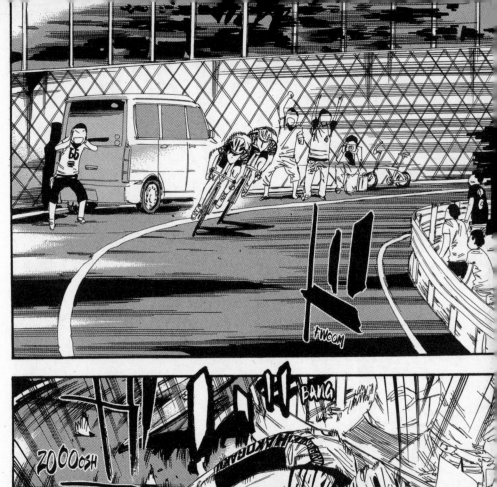

FWOOM

ZOOOOSH

BANG

WHOA,
HE'S
FALL-
ING—

THAT
WAS
CLOSE
!!

WAAAH!

HIS
HELMET HIT
THE GUARD-
RAIL JUST
NOW!

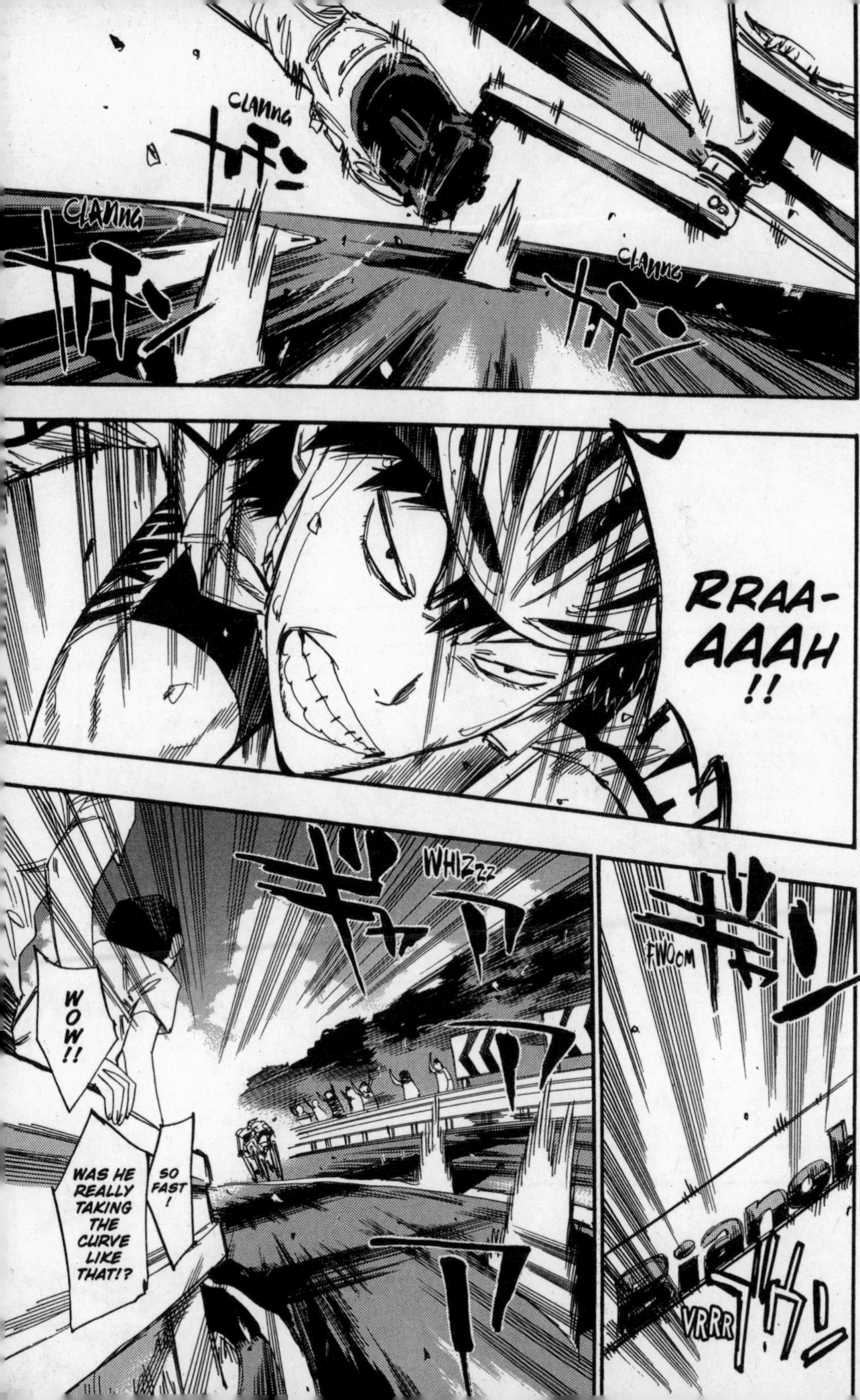
CLANNG
CLANNG
CLANNG
RRAA-AAAH!!
FWOOM
VRRR
WHIZZZ
WOW!!
SO FAST!
WAS HE REALLY TAKING THE CURVE LIKE THAT!?

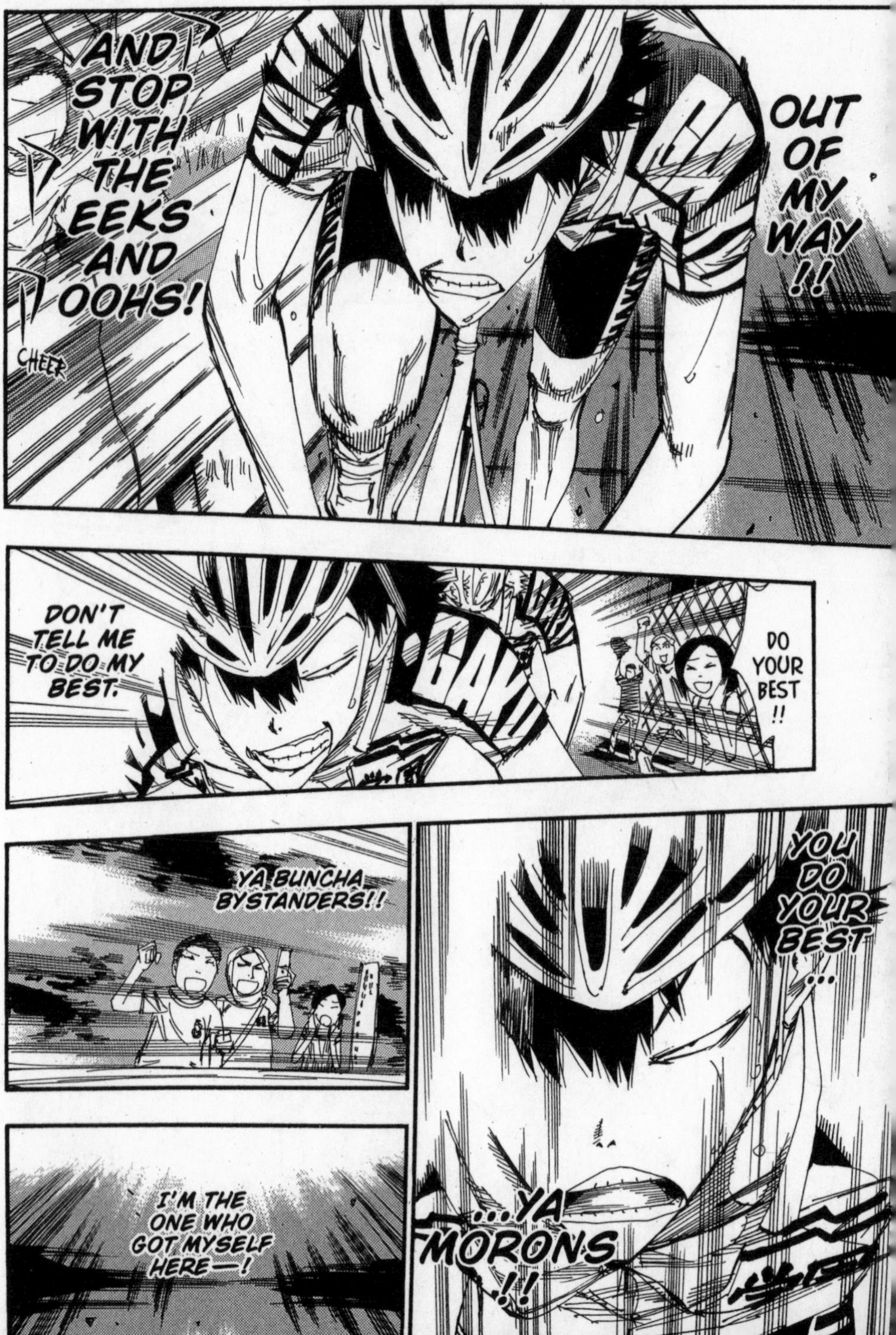
OUT OF MY WAY!!
AND STOP WITH THE EEKS AND OOHS!
CHEER
DO YOUR BEST!!
DON'T TELL ME TO DO MY BEST.
YOU DO YOUR BEST...
...YA MORONS!!
YA BUNCHA BYSTANDERS!!
I'M THE ONE WHO GOT MYSELF HERE—!

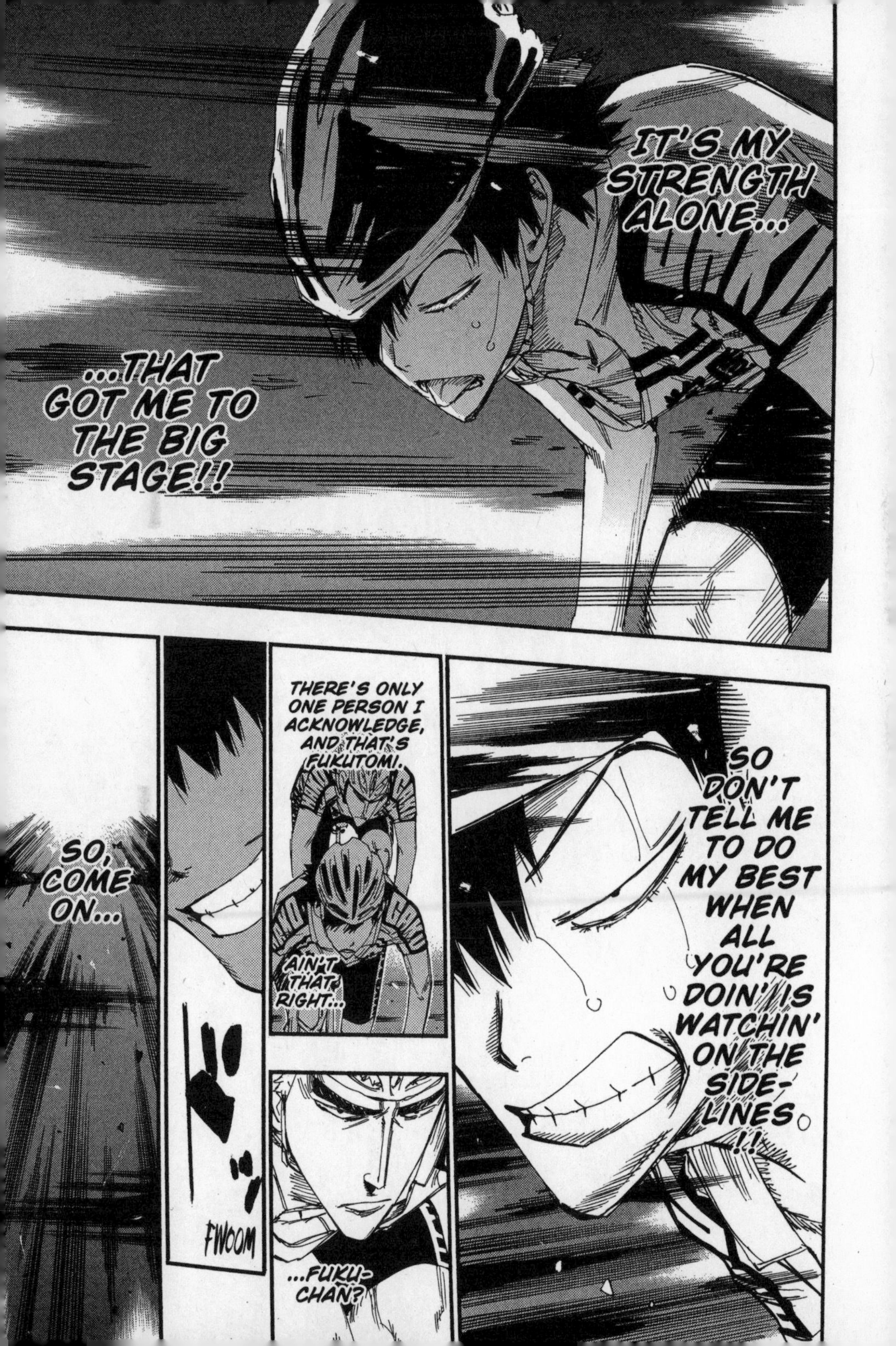
IT'S MY STRENGTH ALONE...
...THAT GOT ME TO THE BIG STAGE!!
SO DON'T TELL ME TO DO MY BEST WHEN ALL YOU'RE DOIN' IS WATCHIN' ON THE SIDE-LINES!!
THERE'S ONLY ONE PERSON I ACKNOWLEDGE, AND THAT'S FUKUTOMI.
AIN'T THAT RIGHT...
...FUKU-CHAN?
SO, COME ON...
FWOOM

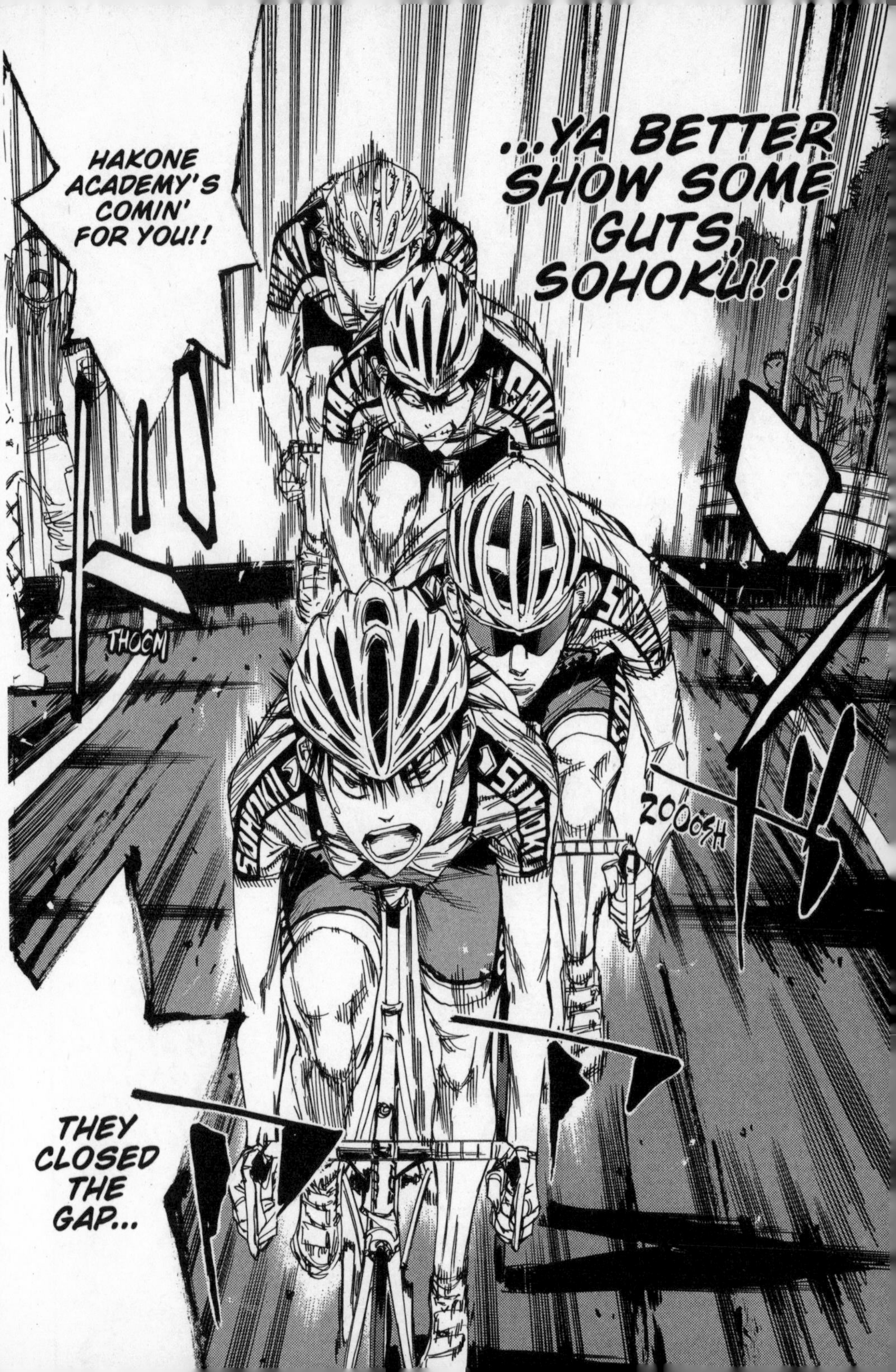
...YA BETTER SHOW SOME GUTS, SOHOKU!!
HAKONE ACADEMY'S COMIN' FOR YOU!!
ZOOOSH
THOOM
THEY CLOSED THE GAP...

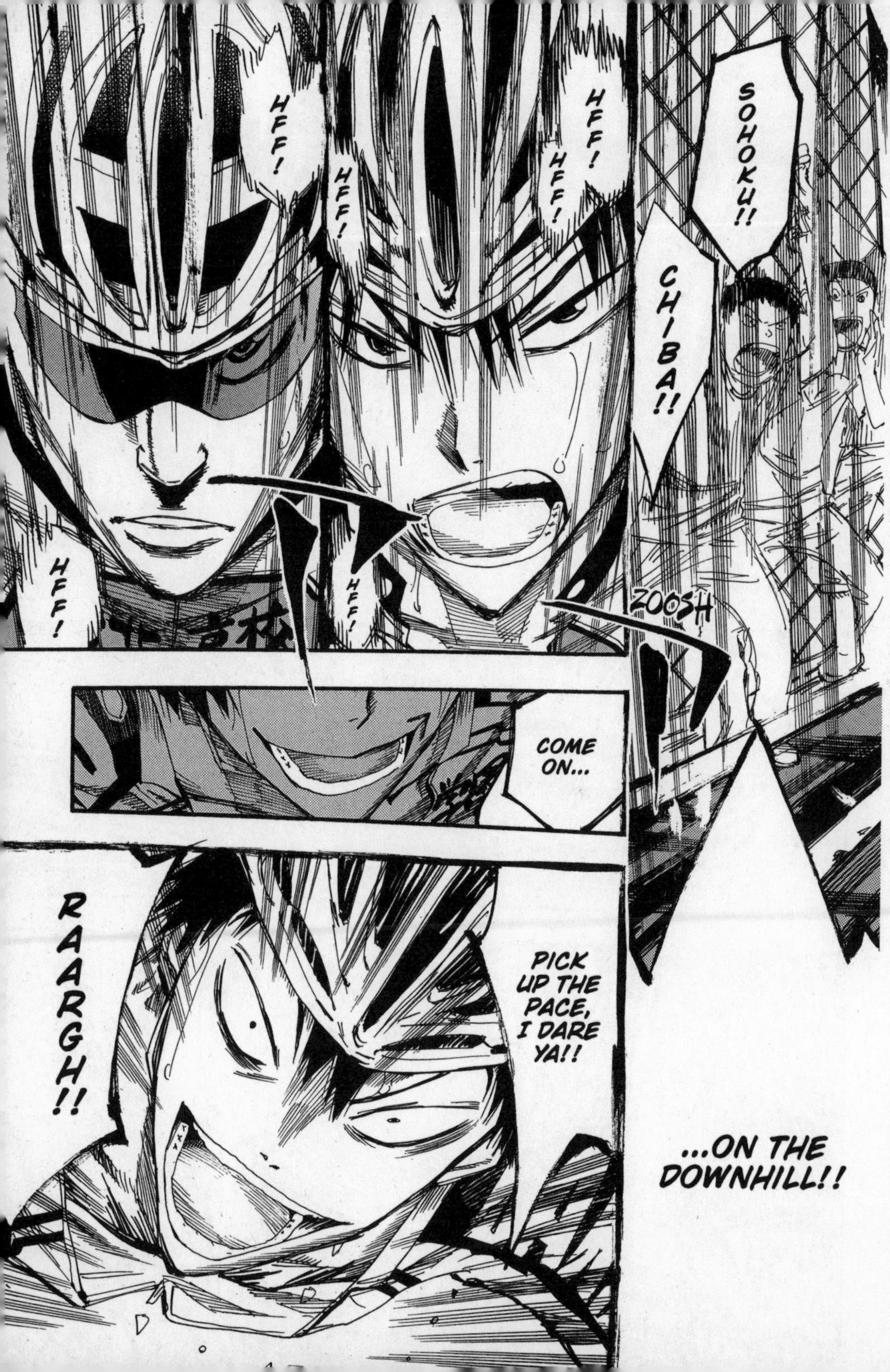
SOHOKU!!
CHIBA!!
HFF! HFF!
HFF!
HFF!
HFF!
HFF!
ZOOSH
COME ON...
PICK UP THE PACE, I DARE YA!!
...ON THE DOWNHILL!!
RAAARGH!!

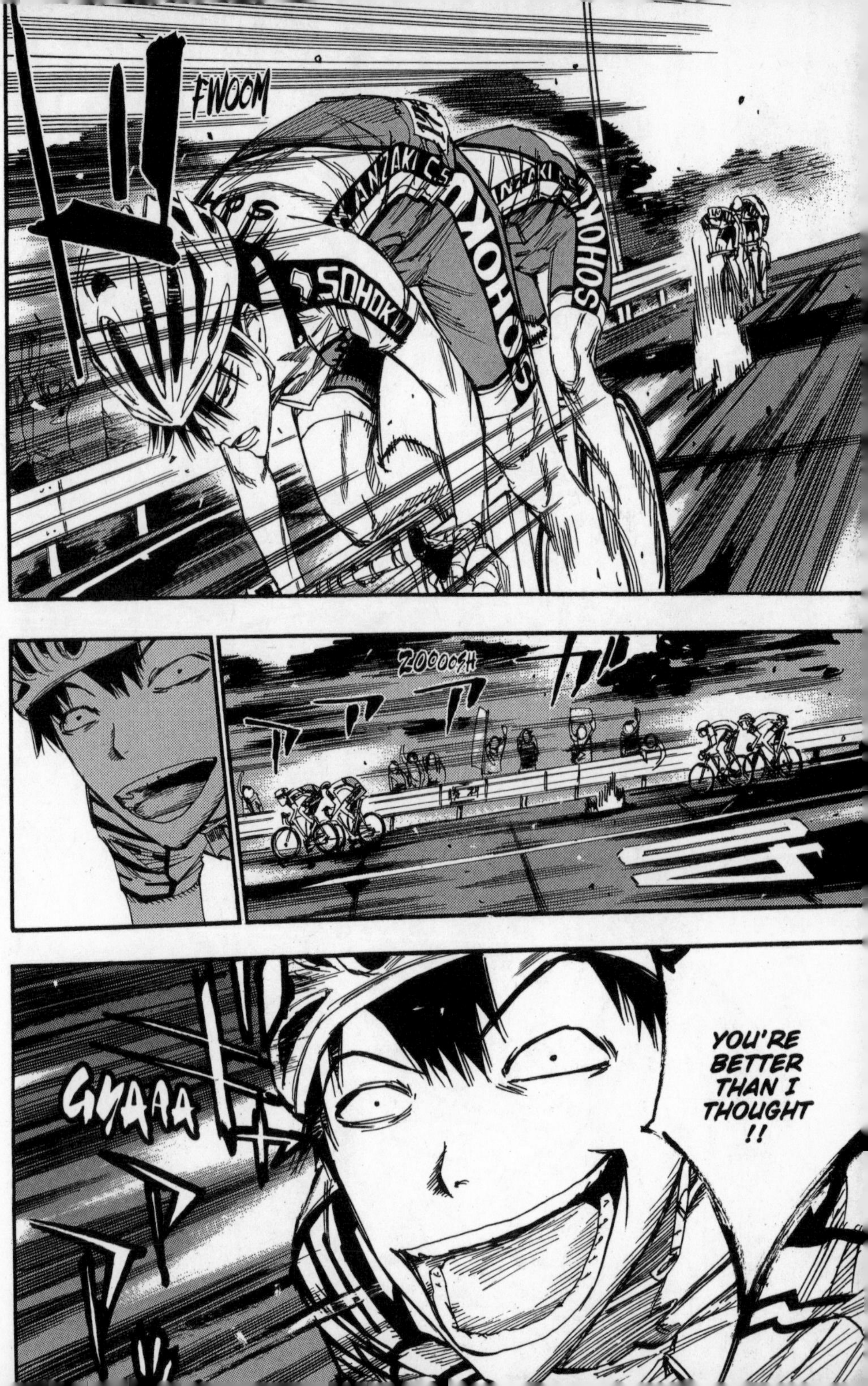
FWOOM
ZOOOOSH
YOU'RE BETTER THAN I THOUGHT!!
GYAAA

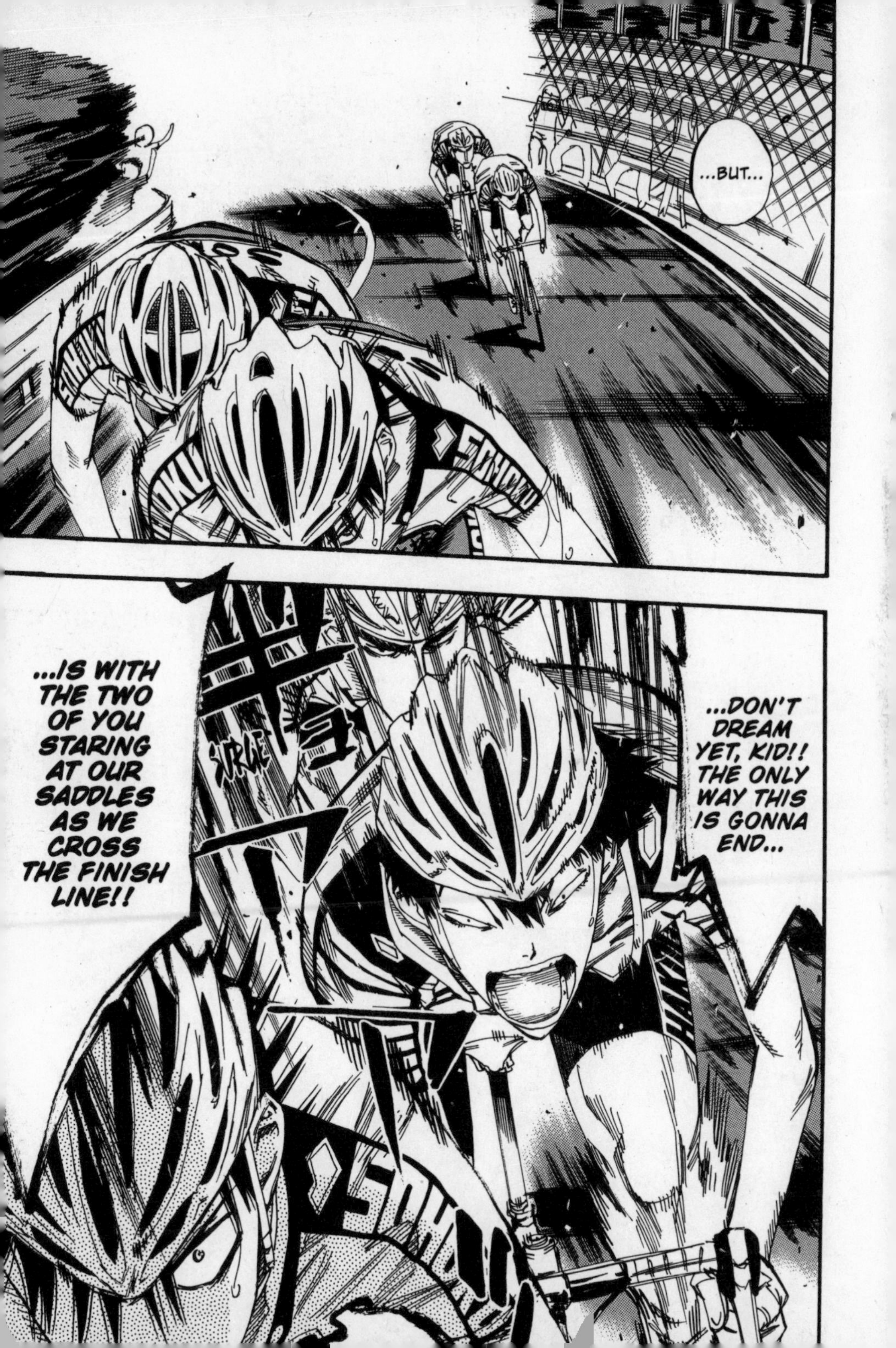
...BUT...
...DON'T DREAM YET, KID!! THE ONLY WAY THIS IS GONNA END...
...IS WITH THE TWO OF YOU STARING AT OUR SADDLES AS WE CROSS THE FINISH LINE!!

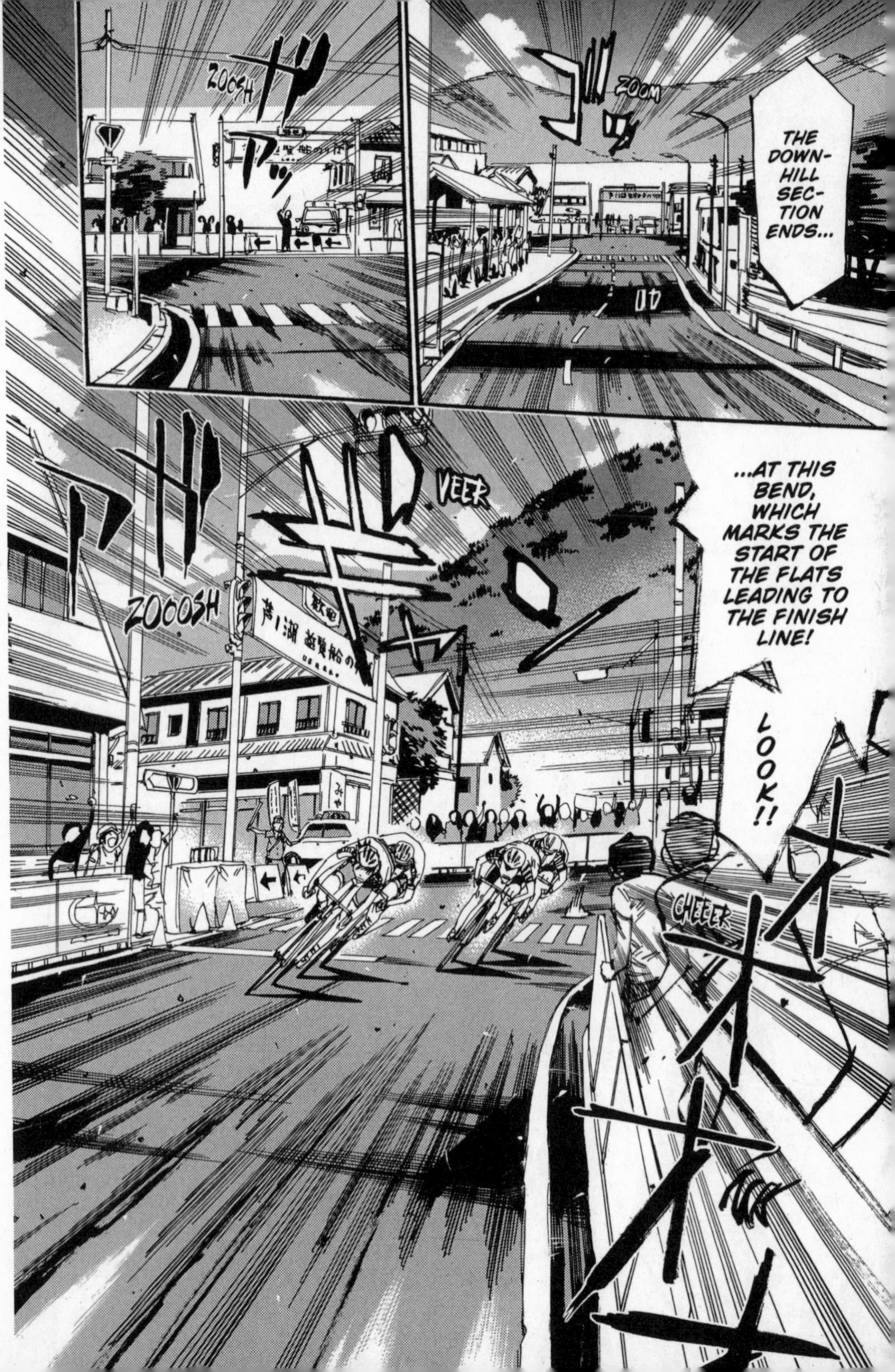
ZOOM
THE DOWN-HILL SEC-TION ENDS...
ZOOSH
...AT THIS BEND, WHICH MARKS THE START OF THE FLATS LEADING TO THE FINISH LINE!
VEER
ZOOOSH
LOOK!!
CHEEER

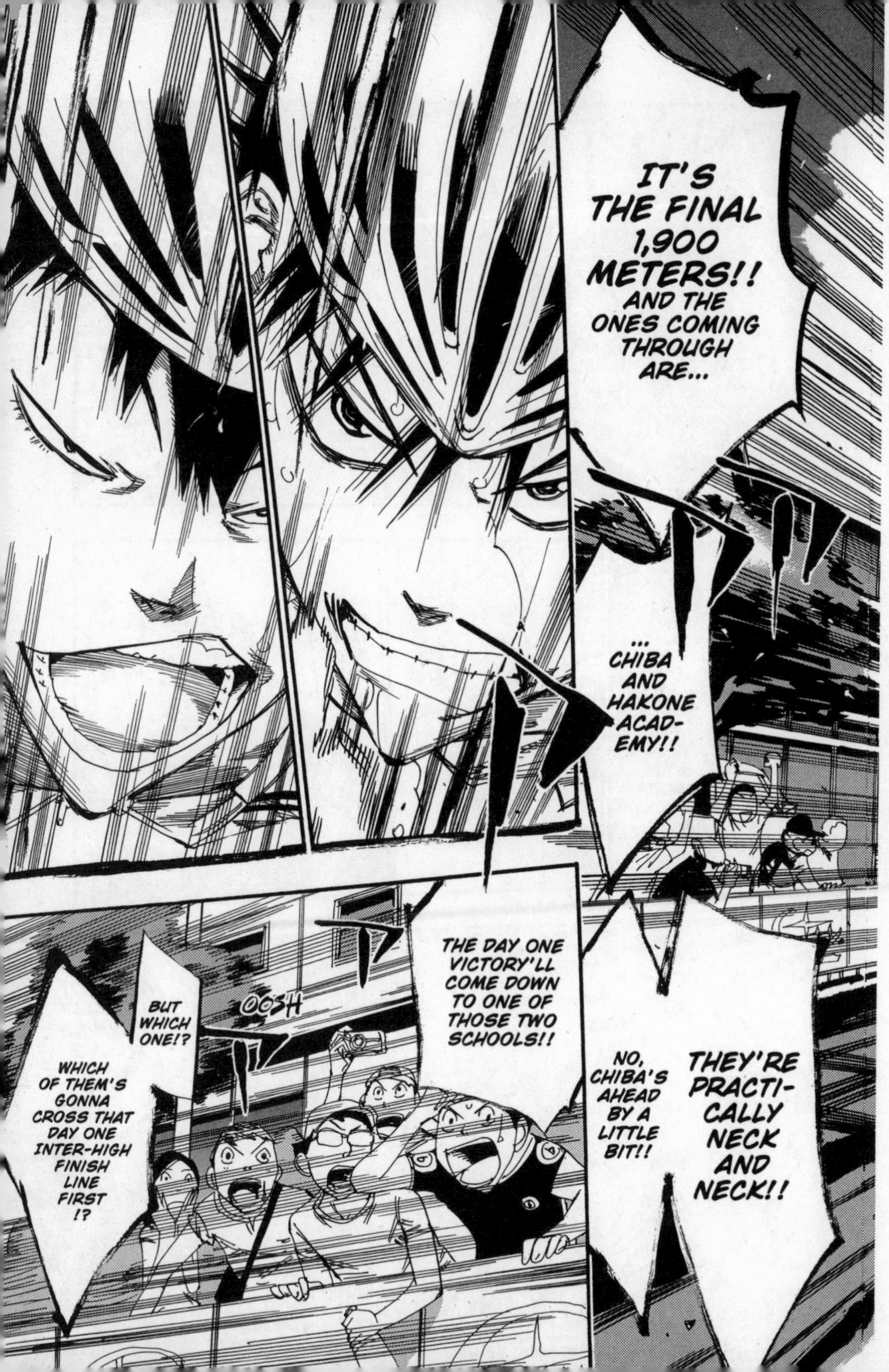
IT'S THE FINAL 1,900 METERS!! AND THE ONES COMING THROUGH ARE...
...CHIBA AND HAKONE ACAD-EMY!!
THEY'RE PRACTI-CALLY NECK AND NECK!!
NO, CHIBA'S AHEAD BY A LITTLE BIT!!
THE DAY ONE VICTORY'LL COME DOWN TO ONE OF THOSE TWO SCHOOLS!!
OOSH
BUT WHICH ONE!?
WHICH OF THEM'S GONNA CROSS THAT DAY ONE INTER-HIGH FINISH LINE FIRST!?

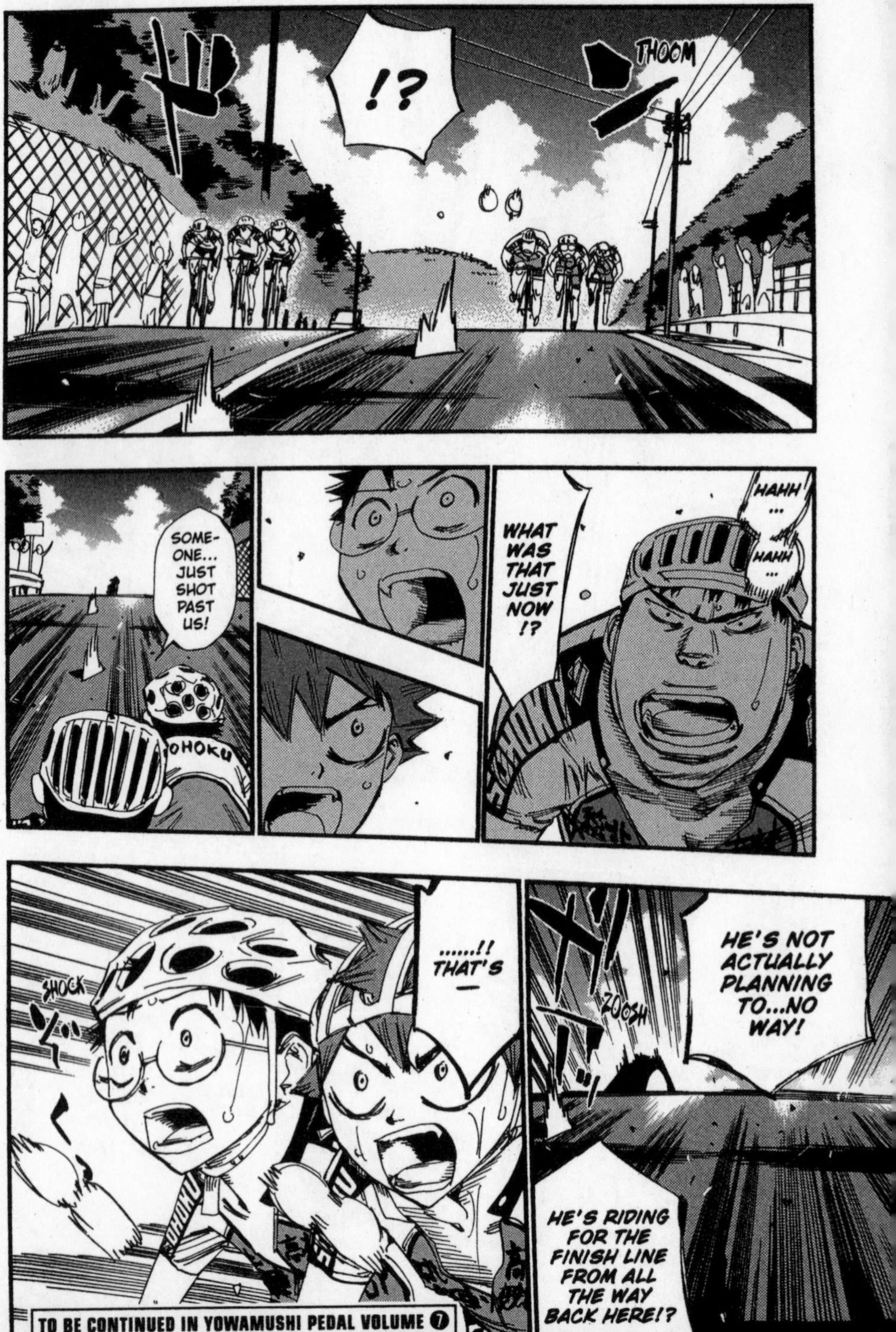
!?
THOOM
HAHH ...
HAHH ...
WHAT WAS THAT JUST NOW !?
SOME-ONE... JUST SHOT PAST US!
HE'S NOT ACTUALLY PLANNING TO...NO WAY!
ZOOSH
HE'S RIDING FOR THE FINISH LINE FROM ALL THE WAY BACK HERE!?
......!! THAT'S —
SHOCK
TO BE CONTINUED IN YOWAMUSHI PEDAL VOLUME 7

YOWAMUSHI PEDAL
BICYCLES ARE FUN
CORNER

# LET'S EXPLAIN SOME STUFF

I CAN'T.
I'VE BEEN RIDING ON MY RIMS FOR A WHILE NOW.
BUT MY FRONT WHEEL BLEW OUT TOO.
SO NOW BOTH OF THEM ARE FLAT...

IN THE FIRST HALF OF THIS VOLUME, THERE'S A PART WHERE MAKI-CHAN GETS A FLAT TIRE DURING A RACE. THIS ACTUALLY OCCURS FREQUENTLY ENOUGH IN REAL RACES THAT YOU COULD CALL IT THE NUMBER ONE ISSUE RACERS ENCOUNTER. BUT IT'S NOT SURPRISING CONSIDERING HOW DELICATE SOME OF THESE RACE-CALIBER BICYCLE PARTS ARE. THEY GIVE THE RIDER SUCH UNBELIEVABLE PERFORMANCE, BUT THE STRESS ON THOSE DELICATE PARTS DURING A RACE CAN RESULT IN A FLAT TIRE. IT DOESN'T REALLY HAPPEN DURING DAILY TRAINING THOUGH. WITH THAT SAID...

## LET'S TALK ABOUT BICYCLE WHEELS

A BICYCLE WHEEL'S BASIC CONFIGURATION IS THIS:

AS WITH MOMMY BIKES AND OTHER TYPES OF BICYCLES, A ROAD BIKE'S WHEELS CONTAIN A TIRE AND INNER TUBE (THOUGH THERE ARE WHEELS THAT DON'T USE THESE AS WELL).

VALVE
THE RIM, SPOKES, AND HUB TOGETHER ARE WHAT WE CALL THE BICYCLE "WHEEL"
RIM
SPOKE
HUB
TIRE
CROSS-SECTION VIEW:
TUBE
TIRE
RIM

SPOKES CAN LOOK QUITE DIFFERENT, DEPENDING ON CONSTRUCTION METHOD. MOMMY BIKES TEND TO HAVE MORE SPOKES, WHILE ROAD BIKES TEND TO HAVE FEWER.

THEY FIT A LOT OF AIR INSIDE!

(BETWEEN 59 P.S.I. AND 73 P.S.I. FOR A MOMMY BIKE)

INFLATE YOUR TIRE TO BETWEEN 118 P.S.I. - 132 P.S.I. IT SHOULD FEEL HARD TO THE TOUCH (ALLOWING LESS CONTACT WITH THE ROAD SURFACE CREATES LESS ROLLING RESISTANCE).

A FLAT TIRE IS...

UGH!
HISS

IN TERMS OF THE AUTHOR'S PERSONAL EXPERIENCE (AND REMEMBER, THIS IS JUST MY PERSONAL EXPERIENCE), YOU GET A FLAT TIRE ROUGHLY ONCE EVERY 1,000KM YOU RIDE. (AND I DON'T KNOW WHY, BUT IT TENDS TO HAPPEN DURING TRAINING RIDES FOR ME). WELL, TAKE THAT AS YOU WILL.

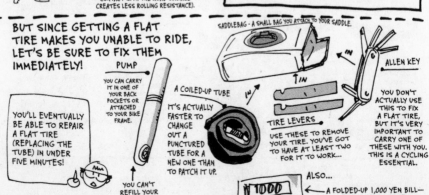

BUT SINCE GETTING A FLAT TIRE MAKES YOU UNABLE TO RIDE, LET'S BE SURE TO FIX THEM IMMEDIATELY!

SADDLEBAG - A SMALL BAG YOU ATTACH TO YOUR SADDLE.
PUMP
YOU CAN CARRY IT IN ONE OF YOUR BACK POCKETS OR ATTACHED TO YOUR BIKE FRAME.
YOU CAN'T REFILL YOUR TIRE WITHOUT THIS!!
A COILED-UP TUBE
IT'S ACTUALLY FASTER TO CHANGE OUT A PUNCTURED TUBE FOR A NEW ONE THAN TO PATCH IT UP.
IN
IN
IN
TIRE LEVERS
USE THESE TO REMOVE YOUR TIRE. YOU'VE GOT TO HAVE AT LEAST TWO FOR IT TO WORK...
ALLEN KEY
YOU DON'T ACTUALLY USE THIS TO FIX A FLAT TIRE, BUT IT'S VERY IMPORTANT TO CARRY ONE OF THESE WITH YOU. THIS IS A CYCLING ESSENTIAL.

YOU'LL EVENTUALLY BE ABLE TO REPAIR A FLAT TIRE (REPLACING THE TUBE) IN UNDER FIVE MINUTES!

ALSO...

1000

A FOLDED-UP 1,000 YEN BILL—IT'S BOUND TO COME IN HANDY SOMEHOW (LOL)!!

KEEP IT INSIDE A PLASTIC BAGGIE

# LET'S EXPLAIN EVEN MORE

## ABOUT THE VALVE

WHEN YOU GO TO FILL YOUR TIRE WITH AIR, THE PLACE YOU ATTACH YOUR PUMP IS CALLED THE "VALVE." →

THIS
TIRE
PROS

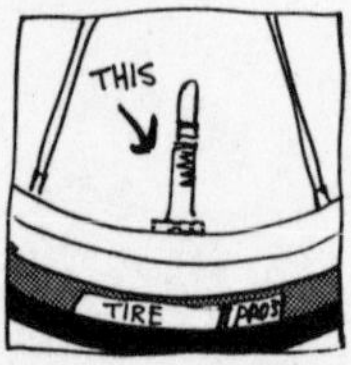

THE VALVES USED ON A MOMMY BIKE AND THOSE USED ON A ROAD BIKE OR MTB (OR A HIGHER-END HYBRID BICYCLE) **HAVE COMPLETELY DIFFERENT STRUCTURES, ACTUALLY.** (BASICALLY, THE LATTER USE VALVES THAT SEAL THEMSELVES BASED ON THE TIRE'S AIR PRESSURE.)

THAT'S WHY, IF YOU TRY TO FILL YOUR TIRE USING THE PUMP YOU HAVE AT HOME...
FSHH
FSHH
I CAN'T EVEN GET THE TINIEST BIT OF AIR TO GO IN THERE!
...THIS SORT OF THING OFTEN HAPPENS.

## YOU HAVE TO USE A SPECIALIZED PUMP

THOOM
APPEARANCE-WISE, IT DOESN'T LOOK SO DIFFERENT
STEEL FLOOR DRIVE
ON THE TAG, IT SHOULD SAY IT'S FOR USE WITH A PRESTA OR SCHRADER VALVE.
BE SURE TO BUY ONE OF THESE
THE CHUCK (END PIECE) OF THE HOSE IS USUALLY INTERCHANGEABLE FOR DIFFERENT VALVE TYPES.
AIR PRESSURE GAUGE

THERE ARE TWO TYPES OF VALVES: "PRESTA" (FRENCH STYLE) AND "SCHRADER" (AMERICAN STYLE). CURRENTLY, THE PRESTA STYLE OF VALVE IS MAINLY WHAT'S POPULAR, SO LET ME EXPLAIN A LITTLE FURTHER ABOUT IT.

ATTACH
VALVE CAP
LOOSEN THIS SCREW AND THEN ATTACH THE PUMP HOSE.
INCIDENTALLY, IF YOU PRESS DOWN ON THE VALVE, IT WILL RELEASE AIR FROM THE TIRE.
HISSSS

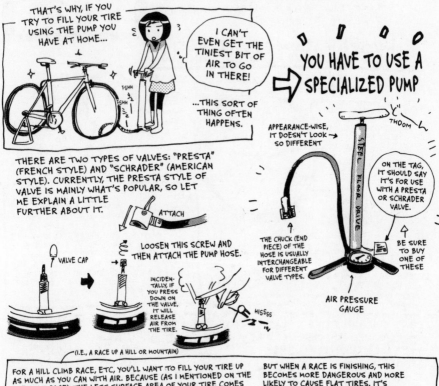

(I.E., A RACE UP A HILL OR MOUNTAIN)

FOR A HILL CLIMB RACE, ETC, YOU'LL WANT TO FILL YOUR TIRE UP AS MUCH AS YOU CAN WITH AIR. BECAUSE (AS I MENTIONED ON THE PREVIOUS PAGE), THE LESS SURFACE AREA OF YOUR TIRE COMES IN CONTACT WITH THE ROAD SURFACE, THE BETTER.

AIR PRESSURE AT 88 P.S.I.

STIFF
STIFF

AIR PRESSURE AT 147 P.S.I.

BUT WHEN A RACE IS FINISHING, THIS BECOMES MORE DANGEROUS AND MORE LIKELY TO CAUSE FLAT TIRES. IT'S BETTER TO LET SOME AIR OUT LIKE I'VE SHOWN ABOVE. WHEN RIDERS ARE COMING DOWN AFTER A HILL CLIMB, YOU CAN HEAR "HISS! HISS!" ALL OVER THE PLACE.

OF COURSE, THIS ONE PROVIDES THE MORE COMFORTABLE-FEELING RIDE.

THIS ONE WILL FEEL LIKE A BUMPIER RIDE.

# BICYCLE TIRES COME IN MANY DIFFERENT WIDTHS

A STANDARD ROAD BIKE'S TIRE HAS A DIAMETER OF 700C (29 INCHES), BUT YOU CAN CHOOSE ITS WIDTH FROM A VARIETY OF SIZES.

(WOMEN'S ROAD BIKES USE A SLIGHTLY SMALLER WHEEL DIAMETER OF 650C).

IN GENERAL, ROAD BIKES USE "23C" (2.3CM) WIDTH TIRES. THIS ONE:

20c
(2.0cm)
SLIMMER
23c
WIDER
25c
(2.5cm)
NO TREAD


(THERE ARE EVEN WIDER OPTIONS, LIKE 28C AND 32C.)

USED FOR HILL CLIMBS, WHEN YOU WANT TO MINIMIZE THE TIRE'S CONTACT WITH THE ROAD SURFACE. MANEUVERING IS MORE DIFFICULT.

APPROPRIATE FOR GENERAL RIDING, HIGHLY VERSATILE.

WIDER THAN THE 23C TIRE; ALLOWS VERY EASY MANEUVERING AND MAKES FOR A COMFORTABLE-FEELING RIDE. WHEN RACING ON COBBLESTONE ROADS, PRO CYCLISTS WILL GENERALLY CHOOSE THIS WIDTH OF TIRE.

---

FOR THOSE WHO ARE MAINLY RIDING ON PAVED ROADS AND WANT A MORE COMFORTABLE-FEELING RIDE, I'D RECOMMEND TRYING OUT SOMETHING BETWEEN A 25C AND 28C TIRE WIDTH.

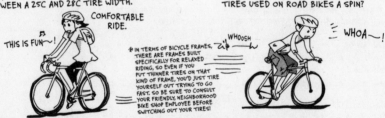

COMFORTABLE RIDE.
THIS IS FUN~!


ON THE OTHER HAND, FOR THOSE OF YOU ON CITY BIKES (OR HYBRID BIKES, ETC.) WHO WANT TO TRY RIDING A BIT MORE BRISKLY, HOW ABOUT GIVING THE 23C TIRES USED ON ROAD BIKES A SPIN?

WHOOSH
WHOA~!


*IN TERMS OF BICYCLE FRAMES, THERE ARE FRAMES BUILT SPECIFICALLY FOR RELAXED RIDING, SO EVEN IF YOU PUT THINNER TIRES ON THAT KIND OF FRAME, YOU'D JUST TIRE YOURSELF OUT TRYING TO GO FAST. SO BE SURE TO CONSULT YOUR FRIENDLY, NEIGHBORHOOD BIKE SHOP EMPLOYEE BEFORE SWITCHING OUT YOUR TIRES!

## EVEN MORE INFO

BICYCLE TIRES COME IN A VARIETY OF GRADES TOO. IN GENERAL, HIGHER QUALITY CORRELATES WITH A HIGHER PRICE TAG. MORE EXPENSIVE TIRES WILL BE LIGHTER AND RUN MORE NICELY (BRISKLY). YOUR TIRES MAKE A LOT OF NOTICEABLE DIFFERENCE IN YOUR RIDING EXPERIENCE. PLUS, THEY'RE A RELATIVELY CHEAP UPGRADE...!! TOTALLY REASONABLY PRICED!!

ONLY 5,000 YEN* PER WHEEL FOR THESE !?
COMPARED TO CAR AND MOTORCYCLE TIRES, THESE ARE SUPER AFFORDABLE!!


*APPROXIMATELY $48 USD.

RIDING WITH THE NEW TIRES:
WHOA!
MY BUTT FEELS SO MUCH COMFIER THAN USUAL DURING THIS CLIMB!


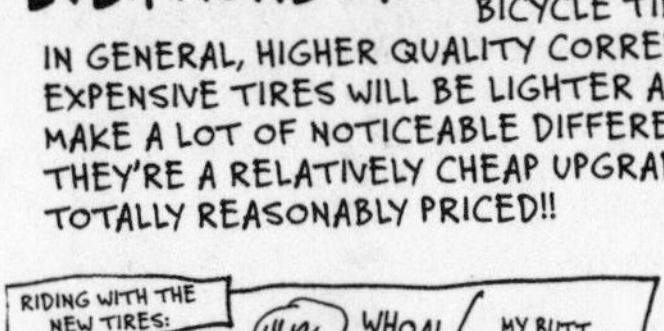

YOU CAN FEEL THE DIFFERENCE!!

AFTER SWITCHING BACK AGAIN...
I'M COVERING SUCH LITTLE GROUND...THE TIRES KEEP SLIPPING... SO HEAVY...


SO WHY NOT TRY SWITCHING THINGS UP A LITTLE?

JUST CHANGING MY TIRES RAMPED UP MY FUN WHILE RIDING SO MUCH!! BICYCLES REALLY ARE SUCH FUN... DON'T YOU THINK?

# Translation Notes

Common Honorifics
*-san*: The Japanese equivalent of Mr./Mrs./Miss. If a situation calls for politeness, this is the fail-safe honorific.
*-kun*: Used most often when referring to boys, this indicates affection or familiarity. Occasionally used by older men among their peers, but it may also be used by anyone referring to a person of lower standing.
*-chan*: An affectionate honorific indicating familiarity used mostly in reference to girls; also used in reference to cute persons or animals of either gender.
*-senpai*: A suffix used to address upperclassmen or more experienced co-workers
no honorific: Indicates familiarity or closeness; if used without permission or reason, addressing someone in this manner would constitute an insult.

A kilometer is approximately .6 of a mile.

**PAGE 6**
Hakone: A town located in a mountainous area of Kanagawa Prefecture, it's popular among tourists for its scenic views and hot springs.

**PAGE 7**
Kyoto: Former capital of Japan located in the Kansai region. It's known for its plethora of traditional Japanese architecture, having come out of World War II relatively unscathed.

**PAGE 19**
Peloton: A cycling term for the "pack," or the main group of riders in a race.

**PAGE 31**
Hakogaku: This phrase, present on all Hakone Academy uniforms, is a shortened version of the school's name in Japanese (*Hakone Gakuen*).

**PAGE 128**
Nagano: A prefecture in the Chubu region of Japan. It is known for a wide variety of beautiful nature sites, including snowy mountains for winter sports (such as the 1998 Winter Olympics) and hot springs.

**PAGE 147**
Chiba: A prefecture in the Kantou region of Japan. Chiba has both long stretches of mountains and large areas of flat plains, and is known for having mild summers and winters.

**PAGE 202**

Goofs: Midousuji uses the term *zaku* in the Japanese version, which means "assorted vegetables for *sukiyaki* hot pot," but is also the name of the common enemy robot in the anime *Mobile Suit Gundam*. The former meaning refers to the rest of Kyoto-Fushimi being there to serve Midousuji, while the latter refers to how Midousuji treats his teammates as generic and interchangeable.

**PAGE 211**

Wussyzumi: In the Japanese version, Midousuji calls Imaizumi "Yowaizumi," playing off of the Japanese word for weak (*yowai*).

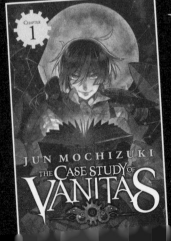

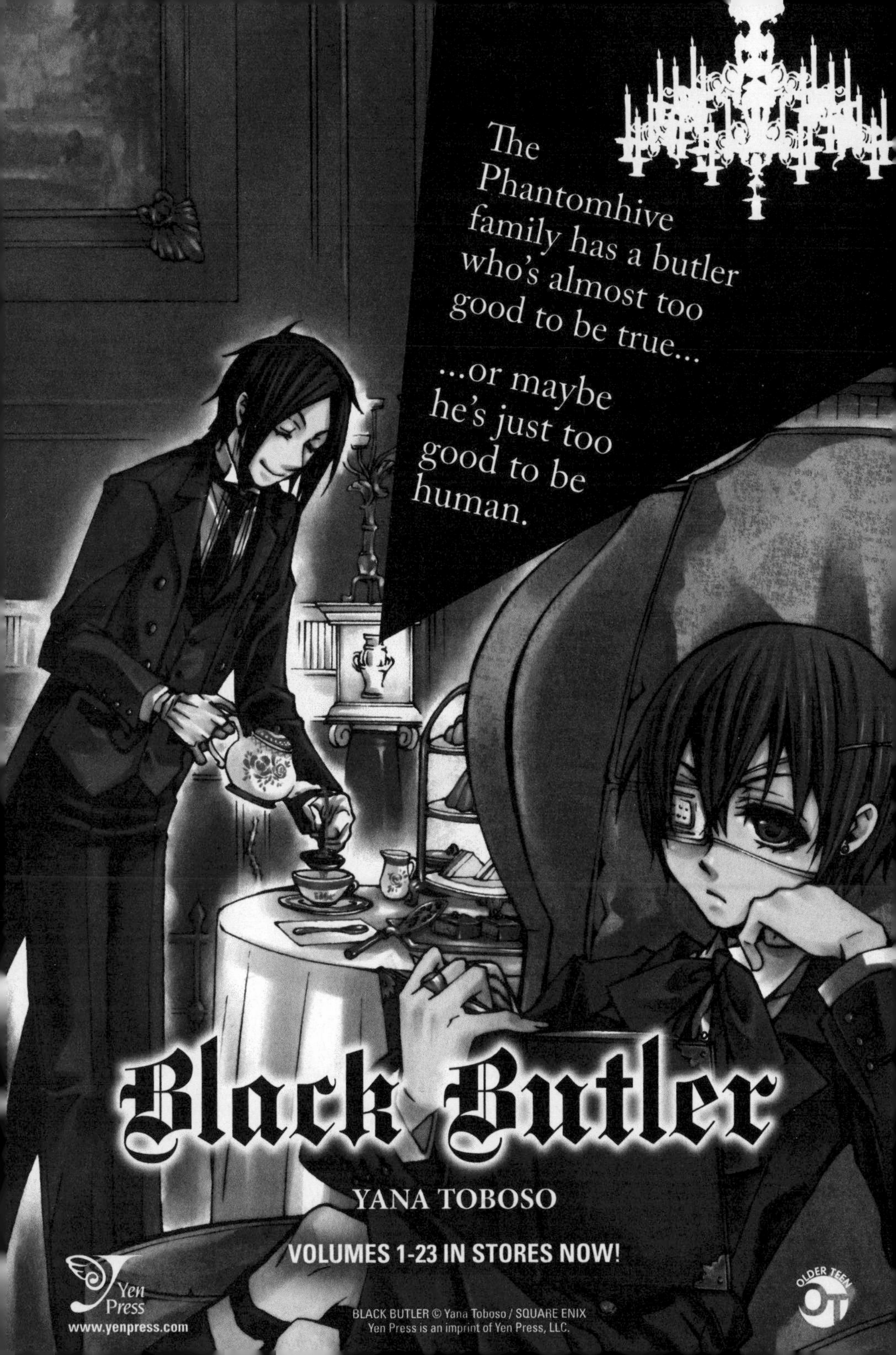
The Phantomhive family has a butler who's almost too good to be true...
...or maybe he's just too good to be human.
Black Butler
YANA TOBOSO
VOLUMES 1-23 IN STORES NOW!
Yen Press
www.yenpress.com
BLACK BUTLER © Yana Toboso / SQUARE ENIX
Yen Press is an imprint of Yen Press, LLC.
OLDER TEEN
OT

# YOWAMUSHI PEDAL ❻

## WATARU WATANABE

Translation: Su Mon Han

Lettering: Lys Blakeslee, Brndn Blakeslee

This book is a work of fiction. Names, characters, places, and incidents are the product of the author's imagination or are used fictitiously. Any resemblance to actual events, locales, or persons, living or dead, is coincidental.

YOWAMUSHI PEDAL Volume 11, 12
© 2010 Wataru Watanabe
All rights reserved.
First published in Japan in 2010 by Akita Publishing Co., Ltd., Tokyo.
English translation rights arranged with Akita Publishing CO., Ltd. through Tuttle-Mori Agency, Inc., Tokyo.

English translation © 2017 by Yen Press, LLC

Yen Press
1290 Avenue of the Americas
New York, NY 10104

Visit us at yenpress.com
facebook.com/yenpress
twitter.com/yenpress
yenpress.tumblr.com
instagram.com/yenpress

First Yen Press Edition: August 2017

Yen Press is an imprint of Yen Press, LLC.
The Yen Press name and logo are trademarks of Yen Press, LLC.

The publisher is not responsible for websites (or their content) that are not owned by the publisher.

Library of Congress Control Number: 2015960124

ISBNs: 978-0-316-39368-3 (paperback)
       978-0-316-47133-6 (ebook)

10  9  8  7  6  5  4  3  2  1

BVG

Printed in the United States of America